STUDENTS WITH

DISABILITIES AND

SPECIAL EDUCATION

TENTH EDITION

Published by
Data Research, Inc.
P.O. Box 490
Rosemount, Minnesota 55068

OTHER TITLES PUBLISHED
BY DATA RESEARCH, INC.:

Deskbook Encyclopedia of American School Law
Private School Law in America
U.S. Supreme Court Education Cases
Deskbook Encyclopedia of American Insurance Law
Deskbook Encyclopedia of Public Employment Law
U.S. Supreme Court Employment Cases
Deskbook Encyclopedia of Employment Law

Library of Congress Cataloging-in-Publication Data
Students with disabilities and special education. 10th ed.
p. cm.
Includes index.
ISBN 0-939675-34-x
1. Special education—Law and legislation—United States. 2. Handicapped children—Education—Law and legislation—United States. I. Data Research, Inc. (Rosemount, Minn.)

LC4031.5875 1993   93-13784
371.91'0973—dc20   CIP

PREFACE

Federal law requires that school districts provide each child with a disability with a free appropriate education. This volume has been published in response to the need of school administrators and others involved in providing special education services to have a reference available when confronted with any of the multitude of problems in the special education area. The Tenth Edition represents a completely reorganized treatment of special education cases which we believe will be even more useful and easier to use than previous editions. This volume contains the full text of the Individuals with Disabilities Education Act, as amended through 1992, as well as the full text of the major federal regulations governing the education of children with disabilities. The full legal citation is given for each case reported, and all cases have been indexed and placed in a Table of Cases following the Table of Contents. A Subject Matter Table of Recent Law Review Articles is also included.

The intent of this volume is to provide professional educators and lawyers with access to important case, statutory and regulatory law in the field of special education and disabled student rights.

EDITORIAL STAFF
DATA RESEARCH, INC.

INTRODUCTORY NOTE ON
THE JUDICIAL SYSTEM

In order to allow the reader to determine the relative importance of a judicial decision, the cases included in *Students With Disabilities and Special Education, Tenth Edition*, identify the particular court from which a decision has been issued. For example, a case decided by a state supreme court generally will be of greater significance than a state circuit court case. Hence a basic knowledge of the structure of our judicial system is important to an understanding of school law.

Almost all the reports in this volume are taken from appellate court decisions. Although most education law decisions occur at trial court and administrative levels, appellate court decisions have the effect of binding lower courts and administrators so that appellate court decisions have the effect of law within their court systems.

State and federal court systems generally function independently of each other. Each court system applies its own law according to statutes and the determinations of its highest court. However, judges at all levels often consider opinions from other court systems to settle issues which are new or arise under unique fact situations. Similarly, lawyers look at the opinions of many courts to locate authority which supports their clients' cases.

Once a lawsuit is filed in a particular court system, that system retains the matter until its conclusion. Unsuccessful parties at the administrative or trial court level generally have the right to appeal unfavorable determinations of law to appellate courts within the system. When federal law or constitutional issues are present, lawsuits may be appropriately filed in the federal court system. In those cases, the lawsuit is filed initially in the federal district court for that area.

On rare occasions, the U.S. Supreme Court considers appeals from the highest courts of the states if a distinct federal question exists and at least four justices agree on the question's importance. The federal courts occasionally send cases to state courts for application of state law. These situations are infrequent and in general, the state and federal court systems should be considered separate from each other.

The most common system, used by nearly all states and also the federal judiciary, is as follows: a legal action is commenced in district court (sometimes called trial court, county court, common pleas court or superior court) where a decision is initially reached. The case may then be appealed to the court of appeals (or appellate court), and in turn this decision may be appealed to the supreme court.

Several states, however, do not have a court of appeals; lower court decisions are appealed directly to the state's supreme court. Additionally, some states have labeled their courts in a nonstandard fashion.

In Maryland, the highest state court is called the Court of Appeals. In the state of New York, the trial court is called the Supreme Court. Decisions of this court may be appealed to the Supreme Court, Appellate Division. The highest court in New York is the Court of Appeals. Pennsylvania has perhaps the most complex court system. The lowest state court is the Court of Common Pleas. Depending on the circumstances of the case, appeals may be taken to either the Commonwealth Court or the Superior Court. In certain instances the Commonwealth Court functions as a trial court as well as an appellate court. The Superior Court, however, is strictly an intermediate appellate court. The highest court in Pennsylvania is the Supreme Court.

While supreme court decisions are generally regarded as the last word in legal matters, it is important to remember that trial and appeals court decisions also create important legal precedents. For the hierarchy of typical state and federal court systems, please see the diagram below.

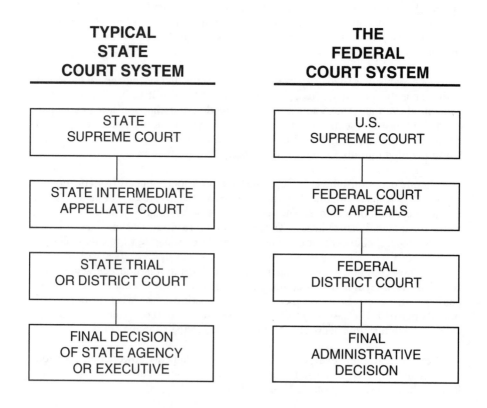

TYPICAL STATE COURT SYSTEM

| STATE SUPREME COURT |
| STATE INTERMEDIATE APPELLATE COURT |
| STATE TRIAL OR DISTRICT COURT |
| FINAL DECISION OF STATE AGENCY OR EXECUTIVE |

THE FEDERAL COURT SYSTEM

| U.S. SUPREME COURT |
| FEDERAL COURT OF APPEALS |
| FEDERAL DISTRICT COURT |
| FINAL ADMINISTRATIVE DECISION |

Federal courts of appeals hear appeals from the district courts which are located in their circuits. Below is a list of states and the federal circuits in which they are located.

First Circuit — Puerto Rico, Maine, New Hampshire, Massachusetts, Rhode Island

Second Circuit — New York, Vermont, Connecticut

Third Circuit — Pennsylvania, New Jersey, Delaware, Virgin Islands

Fourth Circuit — West Virginia, Maryland, Virginia, North Carolina, South Carolina

Fifth Circuit — Texas, Louisiana, Mississippi

Sixth Circuit — Ohio, Kentucky, Tennessee, Michigan

Seventh Circuit — Wisconsin, Indiana, Illinois

Eighth Circuit — North Dakota, South Dakota, Nebraska, Arkansas, Missouri, Iowa, Minnesota

Ninth Circuit — Alaska, Washington, Oregon, California, Hawaii, Arizona, Nevada, Idaho, Montana, Northern Mariana Islands, Guam

Tenth Circuit — Wyoming, Utah, Colorado, Kansas, Oklahoma, New Mexico

Eleventh Circuit — Alabama, Georgia, Florida

District of Columbia Circuit — Hears cases from the U.S. District Court for the District of Columbia.

Federal Circuit — Sitting in Washington, D.C., the U.S. Court of Appeals, Federal Circuit hears patent and trade appeals and certain appeals on claims brought against the federal government and its agencies.

TABLE OF CONTENTS

TABLE OF CONTENTS

TABLE OF CONTENTS

TABLE OF CASES

TABLE OF CASES

TABLE OF CASES

TABLE OF CASES

TABLE OF CASES

TABLE OF CASES

CHAPTER ONE

THE INDIVIDUALS WITH DISABILITIES EDUCATION ACT

I. THE INDIVIDUALS WITH DISABILITIES EDUCATION ACT

The Individuals with Disabilities Education Act (IDEA), originally enacted as the Education of the Handicapped Act (EHA)* was created by Congress to assist the states in providing children with disabilities with a free appropriate public education. Under the IDEA, local school districts and states may be sued by children with disabilities, or their parents or guardians, if the school fails to provide a free appropriate public education. The Handicapped Children's Protection Act of 1986 (HCPA), encourages disabled students to bring such lawsuits by requiring the losing defendants in IDEA cases to pay attorney's fees and/or money damages to children with disabilities. The 1986 amendments brought infants and preschool children with disabilities within IDEA coverage.

A. Background

The IDEA establishes minimum requirements which must be complied with in order for states to be eligible to receive financial assistance. First, each state must have "in effect a policy that assures all children with disabilities the right to a free appropriate public education" [20 U.S.C. § 1412(1)], and must develop a plan which details the policies and procedures which insure the provision of that right [§ 1412(2)]. Each state must also establish the requisite procedural safeguards [§ 1412(5)], and must insure that local educational agencies in the state will establish the individualized educational programs (IEPs) required by the act [§ 1412(4)]. Individual states are responsible for establishing and maintaining education standards for the disabled [§ 1412(6)]. The Act additionally requires that each state must formulate a plan for educating its children with disabilities which must be submitted to and approved by the Secretary of Education before the state is entitled to federal assistance.

---

* Also referred to as the EAHCA (Education for All Handicapped Children Act).

States receiving federal assistance under the IDEA must prepare an IEP for each student with a disability and review the program at least annually. Both the preparation and review processes must be conducted with participation by the child's parents or guardian and current teachers. The IDEA and its accompanying regulations, the full text of which are reprinted in the appendix, also require that a participating state provide specified administrative procedures by which the child's parents or guardians may challenge any change in evaluation and education of the child.

Even severely disabled students are entitled to IDEA protection. A New Hampshire student was multiply disabled and profoundly mentally retarded. His mother attempted to obtain appropriate education for him but the local school district refused. It stated that because of the student's severe disability she would not benefit from education and was therefore not entitled to receive it. The student filed a complaint with the New Hampshire Department of Education for immediate educational placement. The department ordered placement, but the district again refused. The district then appealed the department's order. Meanwhile, the local school board found that the student was not entitled to special education. The student then sued the district in a U.S. district court, seeking special education services and damages under the EHA. Two years later, the district court ruled that the student had not exhausted his administrative remedies. A hearing officer then found for the student, and the school district appealed to the district court, which ruled that the student was not capable of benefiting from special education services. Thus, the district was not obligated to provide educational services. The student then appealed to the U.S. Court of Appeals, First Circuit.

The court of appeals held that the EHA was intended to ensure that all children with disabilities receive a free appropriate education regardless of the severity of the disability. The court noted that severely disabled students had priority under the act. The student was mentally retarded and multiply disabled and unquestionably was entitled to a free appropriate public education. The appeals court reversed the district court's decision, and remanded it for a determination of a suitable IEP and damages. The student was entitled to an interim special education placement until a final IEP was developed. *Timothy W. v. Rochester, N.H., School Dist.*, 875 F.2d 954 (1st Cir.1989).

The IDEA was enacted in order to vindicate the rights of disabled students, not to provide a general forum for claims in federal court. A three-year-old Pennsylvania child suffered severe head injuries in a traffic accident. As a result, she required special education services for which her parents sued their insurance company. After making initial payments for educational services, the insurer refused to provide further benefits. The parents sued the insurance company in a federal district court. The insurer then filed a third-party complaint against the student's school district under the EHA. The insurer alleged that the school district was primarily responsible for providing special education services. The district court ruled that the EHA did not provide general jurisdiction for special education issues in federal courts. Only students seeking special education services could invoke the EHA. Federal regulations under the statute [34 CFR § 300.301(b)] stated that insurers were not relieved from paying for services to students with disabilities. Accordingly, the insurer had no standing to bring an EHA lawsuit against the school district. There was no connection between the insurance company's obligation to satisfy its claim and an appropriate education for the student under the EHA. The EHA provided a minimum educational opportunity level for students with disabilities, not a clearly defined entitlement or benefit. The court dismissed the insurance company's third-party complaint. *Gehman v. Prudential Property and Cas. Ins. Co.*, 702 F.Supp. 1192 (E.D.Pa.1989).

In order to invoke the IDEA, litigants must exhaust their administrative remedies. Several mentally impaired students at a Michigan school alleged that they received inappropriate discipline ranging from bodily humiliation and the withholding of food and medicine to repeated physical assault. The students sued the teachers, administrators, and the school district in a federal district court. The students asserted causes of action under the EHA, § 504 of the Rehabilitation Act, 42 U.S.C. § 1983, and Michigan tort law, seeking compensatory damages, costs and attorney's fees. The defendants moved to dismiss the case.

The court ruled on four matters. First, the court stated that a previous case, *Sanders by Sanders v. Marquette Public Schools*, 561 F.Supp. 1361 (W.D.Mich. 1983), held that a damage remedy is not available under the EHA unless there are exceptional circumstances. Since there were no exceptional circumstances in this case, the court determined that no damages could be awarded under the EHA. Second, the court determined that the plaintiffs had failed to exhaust their administrative remedies as required under the EHA. The plaintiffs contended that because they sought monetary relief, not available under the EHA, the lawsuit should be allowed to proceed. The court, however, determined that to allow the lawsuit to proceed would open up the courts to numerous lawsuits and allow other plaintiffs to circumvent the EHA procedural process. Therefore, it remanded the case to the Michigan Department of Education. Third, the court ruled that the school district and the Michigan Department of Education had concurrent EHA jurisdiction over child abuse cases which arose in the context of classroom discipline. And finally, the court ruled that the Department of Education afforded the appropriate remedy, to return for exhaustion of administrative remedies. The court remanded the case to the Department of Education. *Waterman v. Marquette-Alger Intermediate School Dist.*, 739 F.Supp. 361 (W.D.Mich.1990).

Georgia's local educational agencies (LEAs) sought a declaratory judgment in a federal district court that the Georgia Department of Education (DOE) and Georgia Department of Human Resources (DHR) were obligated under the EHA to provide all children with disabilities in Georgia with a free appropriate public education, including residential placement services. The two state educational agencies had originally entered into an interagency cooperative agreement which required the DHR to assist the DOE with the placement of severely disabled children in twenty-four-hour residential programs in Georgia state-operated facilities. The DOE and the DHR later amended their agreement and placed sole responsibility for providing residential services on the LEAs. The LEAs alleged that the state agencies had failed to uphold their duty. The LEAs claimed that without the assistance of the DOE and DHR they were unable to provide appropriate daycare programs for severely disabled children. The district court dismissed the LEAs' motion and they appealed to the U.S. Court of Appeals, Eleventh Circuit.

The court of appeals held that the LEAs did not have standing to sue under the EHA in order to force the state agencies to provide needed services. The court noted that nothing in the statute itself and no case authority construed the act to support the LEAs' authority to sue. Under the act, LEAs had the right to challenge disabled children's IEPs, including appealing state educational agencies' administrative hearing decisions regarding such provisions. However, there was no indication that Congress intended to grant LEAs standing to bring suit to compel a state agency to fulfill its statutory duty. The court of appeals affirmed the district court's decision. *Andrews v. Ledbetter*, 880 F.2d 1287 (11th Cir.1989).

B. Overview

"Special education" means specially designed instruction, at no cost to parents or guardians, to meet the unique needs of a child with a disability, including classroom instruction, instruction in physical education, home instruction, and instruction in hospitals and institutions § 1401(16). The term *children with disabilities* is defined in the IDEA as children "with mental retardation, hearing impairments including deafness, speech or language impairments, visual impairments including blindness, serious emotional disturbance, orthopedic impairments, autism, traumatic brain injury, other health impairments, or specific learning disabilities; and who, by reason thereof need special education and related services" § 1401(1). The public schools must provide all children with disabilities with a *free appropriate public education*, which means "special education and related services that— (A) have been provided at public expense, under public supervision and direction, and without charge, (B) meet the standards of the State educational agency, (C) include an appropriate preschool, elementary, or secondary school education in the State involved, and (D) are provided in conformity with the individualized education program required under section 1414(a)(5)." [§ 1401(18)].

Related services are defined as "transportation, and such developmental, corrective, and other supportive services (including speech pathology and audiology, psychological services, physical and occupational therapy, recreation, and medical and counseling services, except that such medical services shall be for diagnostic and evaluation purposes only) as may be required to assist a child with a disability to benefit from special education, and includes the early identification and assessment of disabling conditions in children." [§ 1401(17)]. While medical services are excluded from the definition of related services, insofar as they may be needed by a child for diagnostic and evaluative purposes, medical services must also be provided free of charge.

Section 1401(17) states that psychological services are related services and thus are to be provided free of charge by school districts to students with disabilities who require such services. While it is clear that not all services involving psychotherapy are related services, if the psychotherapy required by the child is of the type that could be provided by a social worker, school psychologist, nurse or counselor, it will be considered a related service. Where the required psychotherapy is of such a nature that it can only be competently administered by a licensed psychiatrist, then it will be considered a medical service and the school district will not be required to furnish it. Thus, a U.S. district court in New Jersey held that a school district was required to pay $25,200 for a child's stay at a day school which provided individualized psychotherapy, family therapy, group therapy, and individual and group counseling. The court held that the psychotherapy provided here was an integral part of the child's special education. See *T.G. v. Board of Education*, 576 F.Supp. 420 (D.N.J.1983).

It is important to remember that under § 1401(17), even medical and psychiatric services must be provided free of charge if such services are required for evaluative or diagnostic purposes. See *Darlene L. v. Illinois State Bd. of Educ.*, 568 F.Supp. 1340 (N.D. Ill. 1983).

Section 1415 of the IDEA contains mandatory procedures designed to safeguard the rights of students with disabilities. The safeguards emphasize, among other things, notice to parents and an opportunity for parental participation in the development of a child's special education program. Most important, the various subsections under § 1415 require that parents be informed of all available procedures and methods by which any grievances or dissatisfaction may be resolved. Written notice must be given to parents if a school proposes to change or refuses to initiate a change in a child's educational program, or if the school refuses to perform an initial evaluation and placement of the child [§ 1415(b)(1)(C)].

In case of any dispute over their child's IEP, IDEA § 1415 states that parents have the right to an impartial hearing before a hearing officer who is neither an employee of the school district nor of the state education department [§ 1415(b)(2)]. If either the parents or the school are unhappy with the hearing officer's decision, appeal may be taken to the state education department [§ 1415(c)]. During pendency of a dispute over any aspect of a special education program, the child must remain in his or her "then current" program [§ 1415(e)(3)]. The Supreme Court held that indefinite suspensions of students with disabilities is a violation of this provision. See *Honig v. Doe*, 484 U.S. 305, 108 S.Ct. 592 (1988), in Chapter Two. A lawsuit may be commenced in either state or federal court after a decision has been reached by the state education department [§ 1415(e)(2)]. If the parents or guardians are successful in a special education lawsuit, the defendant will be liable for their attorney's fees. However, parents or guardians who are unsuccessful will not be required to pay the school district's (or state's) attorney's fees [§ 1415(e)(4)(B)]. Money damages, under other laws, such as the Rehabilitation Act, may be awarded on behalf of a child with a disability [§ 1415(f)].

II.   STATE AND LOCAL RESPONSIBILITIES TO CHILDREN WITH DISABILITIES: *BOARD OF EDUCATION v. ROWLEY.*

The U.S. Supreme Court case of *Board of Education v. Rowley* established the following standard for evaluating the appropriateness of a disabled child's education: the child's program must be reasonably calculated to allow him or her to receive educational benefits. However, states may enact higher standards for educating disabled students.

Parents of an eight-year-old child, deaf since birth, claimed the child was entitled to have a sign language interpreter in her classroom to enable her to have the same educational opportunity as her classmates. The district court held that the child was entitled to have a sign language interpreter in her classroom (483 F.Supp. 528). The case was appealed to the U.S. Court of Appeals, Second Circuit, which affirmed the district court (632 F.2d 945). The school board then made a final appeal to the U.S. Supreme Court, which reversed the two lower courts. The Supreme Court held that the EHA is satisfied when a school provides personalized instruction with sufficient support services to permit the child with a disability to *benefit educationally* from that instruction. The court went on to state that the IEP should be reasonably calculated to enable the child to achieve passing marks and to advance from grade to grade. The EHA does not require a school to provide a sign language interpreter as requested by a child's parents. The court stated that the EHA was not meant to guarantee a child with a disability a certain level of education but merely to open the door of education to children with disabilities by means of special educational services. Under the EHA a school is not required to maximize the potential of each disabled child, nor is it required to provide equal educational opportunity commensurate with the opportunity provided to nondisabled children. However, several states have education laws which surpass EHA standards. In such cases the state standard is incorporated into the EHA and such states are required to meet the standard in educating students with disabilities. *Board of Education v. Rowley*, 458 U.S. 176, 102 S.Ct. 3034, 73 L.Ed.2d 690 (1982).

A Maryland 13-year-old boy suffered from dyslexia which prevented him from achieving the reading and writing skills that were expected from students his age. The placement team recommended an IEP which enabled the student to attend regular classes with 20 hours per week of special instruction. The parents rejected this placement and had their son evaluated by a private educational consultant. Based upon the consultant's recommendation the parents enrolled their son in a special full-time summer program and hired a private tutor during the school year. When the placement team again recommended the same placement for the next year, the parents unilaterally placed their son in a private school and sought administrative review. The State Board of Education determined that the recommended placement was appropriate. The parents then sought judicial review in a federal district court. The trial court ruled that the placement was appropriate but should be augmented by private tutoring sessions and awarded the parents the cost of the private tutor they had hired. The parents appealed to the U.S. Court of Appeals, Fourth Circuit. The appellate court performed a careful analysis of the EHA and its history and determined that Congress intended to provide America's neglected disabled children with some form of meaningful education. The EHA only provided a basic floor of educational opportunity. The parents argued that since their son was not advancing from grade to grade he was not receiving the basic floor of opportunity. The EHA states that the "achievement of passing marks and advancement from grade to grade ... will be one important factor in determining educational benefit." However, the court stated that a child with a disability who was not receiving passing marks and reasonably advancing from grade to grade was not necessarily being deprived of an appropriate education. Due to the severity of their disabilities, some children, even with "Herculean efforts" will never be able to receive passing marks and reasonably advance from grade to grade. Therefore, the court determined that the boy received a basic floor of opportunity and that the IEP provided him with a free appropriate education. However, the court noted that Maryland education laws did not conform to the federal laws and this divergence in the wording *might* indicate that Maryland intended to provide its disabled children with a level of educational services above the federal minimum. The appellate court then remanded the case to the trial court to determine what if any violations of state law had occurred. *In Re Conklin*, 946 F.2d 306 (4th Cir.1991).

A class action was brought by disabled Pennsylvania students seeking declaratory and injunctive relief under § 504 of the Rehabilitation Act and the EHA against the Secretary of Education of the Commonwealth of Pennsylvania. In Pennsylvania, disabled students who needed special education programs which could not be provided by the district were referred to the intermediate unit (IU) serving that district. The IUs did not own or operate regular schools. Instead, IUs obtained classroom space from member school districts or from other sources. The Carbon-Lehigh Intermediate Unit (CLIU) served the students instituting this class action. The secretary of education had admitted that a number of problems existed with the CLIU program. The problems stemmed from inadequate classroom space for students with disabilities enrolled in the program. Thus, the CLIU had to place students in facilities that were not comparable to those furnished to nondisabled students. It also had been required to shift students with disabilities from one district to another and from one school to another, had placed students in facilities that were excessively restrictive and separate from the facilities for nondisabled students, and was unable to open new classes needed by disabled students assigned to it. The students sued the secretary of education in a federal district court seeking summary judgment.

The court stated that the EHA and § 504 of the Rehabilitation Act both prohibit funding recipients from providing objectively inferior facilities and services to disabled individuals. Although the acts do not require that the classroom space afforded CLIU students be precisely equivalent to that of nondisabled students, the CLIU classrooms were unequal to those furnished nondisabled students in several important areas including size, sanitation, ventilation, noise level and furnishings. The court held that the secretary had violated the students' statutory rights by failing to ensure that their educational facilities were comparable to those of nondisabled students. It further held that inter school or interdistrict CLIU classroom relocations, resulting from the failure of the school district to provide adequate space for CLIU classes, constituted a violation of the secretary's duty to assure that students with disabilities were educated to the maximum extent appropriate in a regular educational environment. In addition, the court pointed out that the failure to open classes necessary for the appropriate special education of class members violated the state's duty under the EHA and § 504 to ensure that disabled students received a free appropriate education. The court granted the class members' motion for summary judgment and ordered the secretary to submit a plan as a remedial order to ensure that the violations were remedied. *Hendricks v. Gilhool*, 709 F.Supp. 1362 (E.D.Pa.1989).

A New York student's teacher noticed that he was experiencing problems with handwriting, organization, and following instructions. She recommended that he be referred to the child study team in an attempt to ascertain if he had any learning problems. The team determined that the child was not learning disabled but did suffer from some remedial problems which might be addressed with modifications in his current classroom programs. After receiving a letter from the parent's lawyers, the child study team agreed to label the child as disabled to avoid litigation and instituted an IEP. The mother rejected the IEP and requested an administrative hearing. The hearing officer found that the child was not disabled and the student was not entitled to receive special education services. The parents then instituted this action in a federal district court.

The court determined that a child who exhibited a weak attention span and handwriting difficulties was not disabled within the meaning of the EHA. Furthermore, the program instituted by the school was reasonably calculated to enable the child to receive educational benefit and thus complied with the EHA. Therefore, the court found for the school district. *Hiller v. Bd. of Educ. of Brunswick Central School Dist.*, 743 F.Supp. 958 (N.D.N.Y.1990).

In 1978, the state of New York agreed to pay the tuition costs of a schizophrenic boy who had been placed in a residential psychiatric hospital which operated an accredited academic high school. Behavioral problems prevented the boy from attending the high school, but he continued to reside at the hospital. His doctors hoped that the behavior problems could be overcome. The boy's parents, after petitioning state officials in vain, sought to compel the state to pay the cost of the boy's residential care at the hospital from the time of his placement, July 1978, through June 1983.

The state contended before a U.S. district court that as long as the child's behavioral problems prevented him from attending the high school at the institution, he was in effect uneducable and therefore the state had no responsibility for any of his expenses. The court ruled that once the state placed the boy at the psychiatric hospital, it became obligated to pay the entire expense of the placement. The state could not escape its responsibility for costs of the boy's residential care simply by stating that those costs did not directly address educational problems. As long as the boy could be educated (however little) through a residential placement, the state remained responsible for the cost of that placement. *Vander Malle v. Ambach*, 667 F.Supp. 1015 (S.D.N.Y.1987).

Three school districts in Pennsylvania brought suit against the state's Department of Education challenging a change in the special education plan of an "intermediate unit" which had been educating children with disabilities. The unit proposed to suspend operation of classes for the educable mentally retarded (EMR). The unit's decision placed responsibility for operation of all EMR classes on each individual school district, with the unit providing support services and supervision for the classes. The adopted changes affected four school districts, one of which acceded to the plan changes. The remaining three districts argued in the Commonwealth Court of Pennsylvania that the unit had an obligation to continue to operate EMR classes in their districts unless each district consented to the cessation of the classes.

The court disagreed stating "that the primary responsibility for identifying all exceptional children and developing appropriate educational programs to meet their needs is placed on the local school districts." Because the unit was not bound to continue EMR classes absent a showing that the districts could not "efficiently and effectively" provide appropriate educational programs for EMR children in the districts, the proposed changes were upheld. *Bermudian Springs School Dist. v. Dep't of Educ.*, 475 A.2d 943 (Pa.Cmwlth.1984).

A New York child with Down's Syndrome resided at a home certified by the State Department of Social Services to provide care. The child had resided at the home since he was two weeks old. His parents resided in a different county whose school district reimbursed the school district where the child attended school. The parents moved to another state and their former school district ceased tuition payments. The child's school district then informed the parents that tuition would have to be paid if the child was to continue attending school. The parents appealed to the commissioner of education who concluded that the school district where the child lived was not his "actual and only residence" and therefore he was not a resident of that school district. The parents sued the commissioner in a federal district court challenging the constitutionality of the residency requirement. After the district court found for the commissioner, the parents appealed to the U.S. Court of Appeals, Second Circuit. The U.S. Court of Appeals, Second Circuit, determined that the meaning of actual and only residence was a matter of state law. The parents then instituted this action in a New York trial court asking that the child be declared a resident. The trial court granted summary judgment to the parents, concluding that because the child had spent his entire life in the residence home, this satisfied a simple reading of the "actual and only residence" clause. The commissioner appealed to the Supreme Court, Appellate Division. The court noted that the child's residence was presumed to be the same as the parents, but that it could be rebutted by showing that the child had lived at a residence home for virtually all his life and had never visited the parents' home. The court affirmed the trial court's decision and determined that the child was a resident of the school district where the resident home was located and was thus entitled to a free education in that district. *Catlin by Catlin v. Sobol*, 553 N.Y.S.2d 501 (A.D.3d Dep't 1990).

A child born in Yuma, Arizona, to Mexican parents, was significantly hearing impaired. Her parents resided in Puerto Penasco, Mexico, where the child was raised until 1984, when she was sent to live with long-time family friends in Ajo, Arizona. The friends attempted to enroll her in Ajo public schools but were advised by school personnel that they did not have a suitable program for the student. The school recommended the Arizona State School for the Deaf and Blind (ASDB). The ASDB informed them that a guardianship would be necessary so that a responsible person living in the United States could make decisions for the child's welfare. The friends obtained the guardianship and the child was admitted to the ASDB. After obtaining guardianship of the child, the friends received no financial support from her natural parents. The guardians maintained health and dental insurance. Following an action by the attorney general's office, ASDB officials ordered the removal of six children from the school because they were allegedly not U.S. citizens. As a result of legal action initiated by their guardians, however, the removal was stopped due to the violation of their due process rights under the EHA. At an administrative hearing, the hearing officer determined that the child was entitled to the benefits of U.S. citizenship as a minor child of noncitizens. An appeals hearing officer determined that the child's residence was that of her parents. The guardians appealed to a federal district court.

On appeal, the ASDB contended that the guardianship was invalid because it was a sham and obtained only in order to evade tuition. The court, however, found that the guardianship was validly granted after a full hearing and full disclosure of the child's Mexican parentage. To qualify for federal assistance a state must submit a detailed plan which demonstrates a policy assuring all children with disabilities the right to a free appropriate public education. The state is obligated to identify, locate and evaluate all children residing in the state who are disabled. If states are to accept funding under the act, then they have an obligation to educate the disabled children within their borders. The only way that the child can claim the benefits of her U.S. citizenship before reaching adulthood is if a guardianship is established for her. The court found that the guardians had demonstrated that the child had been an Arizona resident entitled to free education services since she came to live there. *Sonja C. by and through Olivas v. ASDB*, 743 F.Supp. 700 (D.Ariz.1990).

III. DUTY TO PROVIDE A FREE APPROPRIATE EDUCATION

The IDEA does not define free appropriate education, and in practice, parents and schools do not always agree on what is appropriate to the education of a particular child with a disability. The *Rowley* case, above, provides the standard to which courts are to look in determining whether an education is appropriate.

The parents of a seven-year-old deaf Illinois student disagreed with the IEP proposed by their school district. The district proposed placement in its self-contained classroom for hearing-impaired students for at least half the school day. The parents wanted education in a regular classroom near their home with the assistance of a full-time speech instructor. The proposed IEP called for integration into regular classrooms where possible. The parents requested and received due process hearings at local and state levels at which hearing officers affirmed the placement. The parents then filed a lawsuit in a federal district court, alleging that the district failed to provide their son with a free appropriate public education under the EHA. The court applied the U.S. Supreme Court test for a school district's obligation to provide students with disabilities with a free appropriate education under *Board of Education v. Rowley*, 458 U.S. 176 (1982). The *Rowley* test determined whether the state complied with procedures under the EHA, and whether the IEP was reasonably calculated to enable a child to receive educational benefits. Finding that the school district had satisfied these requirements, the court dismissed the complaint. The parents then appealed to the U.S. Court of Appeals, Seventh Circuit.

The appeals court noted that the district court had properly applied the *Rowley* test. The EHA preference for mainstreaming must be balanced against the possibility that some students could be better educated in segregated facilities. The EHA granted school districts the primary responsibility for formulating IEPs. Although parents have an important role to play in proposed IEPs, this dispute was primarily over the appropriate methodology, which was within the school district's primary discretion. The appeals court affirmed the district court's dismissal of the lawsuit. *Lachman v. Illinois Bd. of Educ.*, 852 F.2d 290 (7th Cir.1988).

A group of children with disabilities and their parents brought a class action lawsuit against the Commonwealth of Pennsylvania, challenging its system of special education. Pennsylvania's system involves the use of both public and private schools for the placement of students with disabilities (public schools and mainstreaming are favored over private schools and more restrictive settings). Further, funding is only provided for placements in private schools which are approved by the Department of Education. As a result, children with disabilities whose districts lack the means to provide them with appropriate special education incur delays in placement, partly because of the limited access to private schools.

The students and parents first asserted, in federal court, that the state failed to insure that class members would have access to appropriate placements, in violation of the IDEA, because of the long delays in locating appropriate placements. The result was that students were forced to remain in unsuitable placements for long periods of time. Next, the class charged that the state system failed to make available a "continuum of alternative placements" to meet the needs of the disabled students.

The over-emphasis on private school placements (and underemphasis on publicly run programs and facilities) constituted an inadequate continuum of services.

Third, the class alleged that the system failed to place students in the least restrictive environment as required by the IDEA because some students were being assigned to private schools even where they could function in a public school setting with the proper support services. Finally, they maintained that the system failed to identify and correct violations of their rights because the state was aware of the problems which existed, but it did little to intervene and correct the situation.

In defending the motion for summary judgment, the state contended that the local school districts were primarily responsible for administering and maintaining the availability of special education services. It argued that its duties under the IDEA were essentially to provide funds, to promulgate regulations, and to review individual complaints, which it believed it had done. However, the court did not agree with the state's assessment of its level of responsibility under the IDEA. According to the court, it was the state's obligation to insure that the system it put in place was operating properly, and to correct problems that arose. Because there were numerous students with disabilities who were not receiving a free appropriate public education, the court determined that Pennsylvania's special education system needed to be reworked to make it more responsive and flexible. The court granted summary judgment to the plaintiff class and ordered injunctive relief in the form of an order to modify the system. *Cordero v. Pennsylvania Dep't of Education,* 795 F.Supp. 1352 (M.D.Pa.1992).

A moderately mentally retarded California student spent time in special education classes while her parents attempted to have her placed in fulltime regular classes. Although the district created an individualized education program (IEP) and eventually proposed parttime placement in regular classes for all academic subjects, her parents sought fulltime placement. After this was denied, they removed her from the school and enrolled her in a private school in regular classes. In the meantime, they proceeded to appeal the public school's parttime placement decision. A hearing officer found in favor of the student and ordered the school to place her in the regular classroom with appropriate support services. The school appealed to a federal district court.

On appeal to the U.S. District Court for the Eastern District of California, the court held that the student must be placed fulltime in the regular classroom with support services. The court emphasized that the requirements under the Individuals with Disabilities Education Act (IDEA) allowed a student with disabilities a "free appropriate education" and to be educated "to the maximum extent appropriate" with students without disabilities. Regarding the second requirement, the court applied four factors: educational benefits, nonacademic benefits, effect on the teacher and other children, and cost. The first factor, educational benefit, allows a student with disabilities to be in a regular classroom "if the child can receive a satisfactory education there even if it is not the best academic setting." The California student met this requirement through progress in her IEP goals and objectives and her increased motivation to learn. Second, the student can derive benefits from language and behavior models. Nonacademic benefits were evidenced in her improved self-confidence, excitement about school and development of friendships. Third, the California student did not present a discipline problem and did not distract the other students. Finally, the cost of fulltime regular class enrollment would not increase beyond the funding needed for special education. *Board of Education, Sacramento City Unified School District v. Holland*, 786 F.Supp. 874 (E.D.Cal.1992).

A Florida autistic child had been diagnosed as mentally retarded by the age of three. At five he showed a variety of behavioral problems, including a short attention span, repetitive speech patterns and difficulty establishing and maintaining eye contact. By ten his aggressive and maladaptive behavior at home and in school increased dramatically; he cursed, destroyed property, bit, pulled hair, struck others, and engaged in head-banging and window smashing. An outside evaluation found that he was autistic. The school district's IEP required the boy to be placed in a trainable mentally handicapped class (TMH). The Florida Department of Health and Rehabilitative Services evaluated the boy and issued a habilitation plan, which recommended an away-from-home residential facility. The school district continued his placement but added speech classes and parent counseling. The boy's parents rejected the placement and asked for a due process hearing requesting residential placement for their son. The hearing officer determined that the IEP was inadequate and ordered residential placement. The school district appealed to the Florida District Court of Appeal which concluded that the 1985 IEP was appropriate under the IDEA and remanded the case to the hearing officer to find accordingly unless there were other circumstances to consider. The parents then brought this action in a federal district court which found for the school district. The parents appealed to the U.S. Court of Appeals, Eleventh Circuit.

The parents claimed that the federal district court should not have relied on the state court's decision. The appellate court disagreed and determined that full faith and credit must be given the state court. The full faith and credit statute declares that "[t]he records and judicial proceedings of any [state] court ... shall have the same full faith and credit in every Court within the United States." However, the federal district court erred in concluding that it must also grant full faith and credit to the administrative hearing officer's final order. The district court must give full faith and credit to the ruling that the IEP was appropriate but could make its own determination as to whether the IEP *as applied* provided an appropriate education. The appellate court remanded the case to decide these issues. *JSK by and through JK v. Hendry County School Board*, 941 F.2d 1563 (11th Cir.1991).

A disabled Alabama student was manic-depressive. The illness caused the student substantial academic difficulty. His district provided the student with a three hour per week home tutoring program until he began attending special education and regular academic classes at a junior high school. The student again began to experience emotional disturbances and he was suspended at the end of the school year. The next year, after attending only one day of classes, the student refused to return to the high school. His parents then unilaterally decided to enroll him in a residential school. The student attended this residential school for two weeks and again refused to return to school there. Later that year, the parents and the school district developed an IEP which called for the student to attend classes five days a week for three hours a day and to receive counseling services to bolster his self-esteem. The student was unable to complete that school year. The following year the school proposed a schedule which called for several revisions during the year so that the student would gradually be required to spend more time in school until by the end of the year he would spend a full day.

The parents rejected the proposed IEP and obtained an independent evaluation by a clinical psychologist. The psychologist recommended residential school placement for the student. The parents then unilaterally placed the student at a private residential school in Georgia. The student did relatively well at the school, but was expelled in April for sharing his medication with a fellow student. After the student returned to the school district, the school officials and the parents met to discuss a new IEP for the student. However, an IEP was not agreed upon and the student did not begin school in the fall. At another IEP meeting in December, the school was to provide someone to coordinate the student's program of education. The parents sought and received a due process hearing to challenge the IEP proposed by the school. The hearing officer determined that the IEP was reasonably calculated to provide the student with a free appropriate education. The parents filed suit in a federal district court. After the district court upheld the hearing officer's determination, the parents appealed to the U.S. Court of Appeals, Eleventh Circuit.

The parents contended that the school district violated the student's substantive right to a free appropriate public education. In particular, they alleged that the only appropriate education for the student was in a residential setting. The court noted that the state must provide a child with a basic floor of opportunity, consisting of access to specialized instruction and related services. The court determined that the proposed schedule for the school year met the student's psychological needs; it provided for the student's school day to begin with a counseling session. Further, the court noted that the residential facility where the student spent part of his school year was an inappropriate placement for him because it did not provide the facilities necessary to deal with the student's psychological and emotional needs. The nearest residential school that even approached the full benefits sought by the parents was in Texas and experts testified that sending the student so far from his home would be counterproductive to his development. Therefore, the court affirmed the trial court's decision and determined that the IEP provided the student with a free appropriate education. *Doe v. Alabama State Dep't of Educ.*, 915 F.2d 651 (11th Cir.1990).

The parents of a Pennsylvania hearing impaired student objected to their son's IEP because they felt it provided insufficient speech and language therapy. The student lost his hearing at the age of ten months, but prior to this had a high level of language ability for his age. Because he retained this early language ability and a small percentage of his hearing, his parents argued that he would benefit from increased speech and language therapy. They requested a due process hearing. At the hearing, the parents requested that their son be given one-to-one speech therapy three times a week, that they be given sign language training, that he be enrolled in an extended school year program, that a signing aide be present on the school bus, and that a deaf adult visit his classroom once a week. The hearing officer granted the first three requests, but rejected the final two. Both the school district and the parents appealed to the Secretary of Education. The secretary reversed the decisions favorable to the parents, except for the provision regarding the extended school year program. Having exhausted their administrative remedies under the EHA, the parents then filed suit in federal court.

The trial court reviewed the transcript from the administrative proceedings. The parents argued that the secretary's decision should be vacated and the hearing officer's decision be reinstated, because the secretary was not an impartial agency as required by the EHA. The court agreed and vacated the secretary's decision;

however, it refused to reinstate the hearing officer's decision. The court next considered whether the student received an educational program sufficient for him to make meaningful educational progress. The student was taught using the "total communication" method which requires the development of both oral and manual communication. Although the student made excellent nonverbal progress, testimony showed that he lagged behind his peers in verbal communication. Also, the fact that he was not mainstreamed indicated that he was not making sufficient educational progress. The court concluded that the student's IEP was not sufficiently individualized, since his early language skills and residual hearing were not considered when determining the amount of speech therapy he would receive. Therefore, the student's IEP did not provide him with a free appropriate public education as required by the EHA. The court ordered the school district to provide him with four weekly thirty minute sessions of speech therapy, and to reimburse his parents for expenses for private speech therapy. *Johnson v. Lancaster-Lebanon Intermediate Unit 13*, 757 F.Supp. 606 (E.D.Pa.1991).

An Alabama student began experiencing behavioral problems when he entered first grade in 1983. He failed all his subjects and was required to repeat the first grade. He continued to receive failing grades, but was not evaluated to determine whether he had an educational disability until 1987. The evaluation committee determined that he was not entitled to special education. Because the student's disruptive behavior continued, his parents asked that he be reevaluated. The committee concluded that he was educable mentally retarded (EMR) and placed him in a class for EMR students. A few months later, the parents informed the school of their objections to their son's IEP. In response, the school reclassified him as emotionally conflicted, but did not change his IEP. In mid-1989, the parents retained a professor of special education to evaluate their son. He concluded that the boy was not mentally retarded and recommended that he be placed in a self-contained classroom. The school district placed him in a class for emotionally conflicted students. His teacher wrote a new IEP which included only broad objectives and vague methods for monitoring his progress. The parents also requested that the school board provide them with counseling and other services to enable them to help manage their son's behavior and contribute to his education.

In December 1989, the parents requested a due process hearing to determine whether the school district's treatment of their son violated the EHA. The hearing officer determined that the school district was not providing the student with a free appropriate education. The district failed to identify the student's disability in a timely manner and develop an adequate educational program for him. The hearing officer ordered an independent evaluation to be made to develop a new IEP, but did not rule on the parents' request for counseling. The parents brought suit in a federal trial court under the EHA, challenging the hearing officer's decision. On appeal, the court noted that disabled students have a right to personalized instruction with sufficient support services to permit them to benefit educationally from the instruction. The court held that the previous IEP's were inadequate because they were not individualized. Counseling and training for the parents were included in the broadly defined "related services" which the EHA requires school districts to provide. Noting that the student was reaching a critical age, the court ordered the school board to adopt the IEP formulated by the outside consultant and to provide counseling and training for the student's parents. *Chris D. v. Montgomery County Bd. of Educ.*, 753 F.Supp. 922 (M.D.Ala.1990).

The following cases demonstrate that states may establish higher standards for special education than the EHA's "appropriate" standard. In the first, a disabled student received special education through a California school district. Her parents were not satisfied with the child's individual education plan (IEP) and requested a due process hearing. The California hearing officer set forth the standard for review set out under the Education of the Handicapped Act (EHA). The parents, however, appealed the decision to a federal district court, moving for a higher standard.

To provide an appropriate education the school need only comply with the EHA. The school district must develop an IEP reasonably calculated to enable the child to receive educational benefits. Some states, however, have enacted a higher standard for the education of disabled students. California Code of Regulations § 3001(b) requires education programs for the disabled to "provide the equal opportunity for each individual with exceptional needs to achieve his or her full potential." California's standard for the education of disabled students is higher than that required under the EHA. The court adhered to the higher standard for education because the EHA sets out the minimum required under federal law but leaves the states at liberty to require a higher standard. The district court then remanded the case to the Department of Education for a new hearing. *Pink by Crinder v. Mt. Diablo Unif. School Dist.*, 738 F.Supp. 345 (N.D.Cal.1990).

In the second case, the parents of a seventeen-year-old child with Down's Syndrome became dissatisfied with their child's IEP because they felt it did not adequately address his sexual misbehavior. They believed that the child required a twenty-four-hour residential program. A U.S. district court found that the child was entitled to twenty-four-hour residential school placement to attempt to correct his sexual misbehavior. The court noted that under Massachusetts law a special educational program must "assure the maximum possible development of a child with special needs." Accordingly, the child was entitled to the more comprehensive behavior therapy available in a residential program, especially in light of the degree of his sexual maladjustment. On appeal by the school district, the U.S. Court of Appeals, First Circuit, upheld the district court's decision. The appellate court held that where state law sets a minimum educational standard for disabled children, those standards are incorporated by reference into the federal EHA. The U.S. Supreme Court declined to review the decision. *David D. v. Dartmouth School Comm.*, 775 F.2d 411 (1st Cir.1985), *U.S. cert. denied*, 106 S.Ct. 1790 (1986).

A hearing-impaired student was enrolled in a cued speech program at a Virginia high school. He was mainstreamed into regular classes and he excelled academically. However, his parents objected to the location of the program since it was five miles further away from home than the student's neighborhood school. They requested that the school district duplicate the program at the nearby high school. The board denied this request. The parents appealed the board's decision through the administrative process provided by the EHA. After a hearing, the local hearing officer ordered the school district to provide the student with cued speech services at his neighborhood school. The school district appealed to a state hearing officer, who concluded that the district was not required to provide cued speech services at both schools. The parents then filed an action in federal court seeking an injunction requiring the district to provide the requested services at the student's neighborhood school. The court concluded that the district was not obligated to duplicate its services and, in light of the shortage of qualified staff, a centralization of the cued speech program met the requirements of the EHA.

Following this ruling, the parents withdrew their son from the cued speech program and enrolled him in their neighborhood school, where he received private interpreter services. They then appealed to the U.S. Court of Appeals, Fourth Circuit. The parents argued on appeal that the school district had failed to provide their son with a free appropriate education as required by the EHA. They claimed that the district failed to consider their son's individual needs, as required by the EHA. The court agreed with the lower court's assessment of the district's reason for centralizing the cued speech program. Accordingly, it held that the district's program met the procedural requirements of the EHA.

The court's final consideration was whether the district had provided the student with an appropriate program as required by the EHA. The U.S. Supreme Court has defined an appropriate program as that which consists of "educational instructions specifically designed to meet the unique needs of the disabled child." The court held that the student's placement at the centralized program was appropriate. The student made excellent academic progress, participated in extracurricular activities and as a result of mainstreaming was able to interact with both disabled and nondisabled peers. The parents' argument that the EHA requires that a student be placed as close to home as possible was rejected. The court noted that this was only one of several factors which needed to be taken into account when determining the appropriate placement. It affirmed the lower court's decision in favor of the school district. *Barnett by Barnett v. Fairfax County School Bd.*, 927 F.2d 146 (4th Cir.1991).

IV. INDIVIDUALIZED EDUCATION PROGRAMS

An individualized education program (IEP) is a statement of a disabled child's present education level, future educational goals for the child, future educational services to be provided, and the extent to which he or she will be able to participate in regular educational programs [§ 1401(20)]. At the heart of the IDEA's "individualized educational program" provision is the idea that each disabled child's particular needs are unique and thus require an educational program specifically tailored to a child's particular disability. Courts have viewed the failure to provide a program specifically designed to meet the unique needs of a child as a failure to provide a free appropriate education.

A Montana student exhibited poor performance throughout his academic career. The school never diagnosed the student's learning disability. His parents obtained an independent evaluation which led to a determination that the student had a significant, specific learning disability. The Office of Public Instruction required that the determination be made by a child study team (CST). The parents transferred the student to a private school where a CST found him learning disabled. The public school did not attempt to institute a CST for the student until two years later. The public school accepted the private school's CST finding and organized a meeting to develop an individual education program (IEP). At the meeting, the private school personnel (such as the student's regular teacher) were not present. Moreover, the public school presented an already completed IEP. The parents rejected it, requesting additional factors they wanted included. The public school rejected the requests. Subsequently, the parents enrolled their son in a private tutoring program following the suggestion of the CST. They then proceeded to file a complaint with the Montana Office of Public Instruction and requested reimbursement for the private tutoring. The hearing examiner denied the request. As a result, the parents brought suit in a federal district court.

The United States District Court for the District of Montana, found against the public school and ordered tuition reimbursement and attorney's fees. It applied the standard articulated in the IDEA that the "IEP is to be developed through the participation of the child's public school, the regular teacher, and the parents." The school neglected to meet these requirements because the school did not receive input from the parents, the student's regular teacher, or any representative of the private school. The court held that "the failure to develop an IEP according to the requirements of the Act result[ed] in the denial of a free appropriate education." Additionally, it found that the interim tutoring was an appropriate alternative. Therefore, reimbursement for the private tutoring and attorney's fees was ordered. *W. G. and B. G. v. Board of Trustees of Target Range School District Number 23 Missoula, Montana*, 789 F.Supp. 1070 (D.Mont.1991).

On appeal to the U.S. Court of Appeals, Ninth Circuit, the court noted that procedural flaws do not *automatically* require a finding of denial of a free appropriate education. However, in this case the public school developed the student's IEP without the input and participation of the parents or any representative of the private school. Further, the IEP was developed prior to the CST meeting in violation of the procedures set forth in the IDEA. Because these procedural flaws denied the student a free appropriate education, the private educational expenses incurred by the parents had to be reimbursed by the public school. The court found that the parents were entitled to obtain a special education placement for their son until an IEP was properly prepared. Accordingly, it affirmed the district court's order, and required the school to reimburse the parents. *W. G. v. Bd. of Trustees of Target Range School Dist.*, 960 F.2d 1479 (9th Cir.1992).

A learning disabled Connecticut student made substantial progress at a private school. His parents requested a meeting with public school officials to develop an individualized education program (IEP) for the following school year. The public school board agreed to pay for an independent psychological and educational evaluation and permitted a delay of the IEP to allow time for the evaluation. A psychologist hired by the parents determined that the private school's small size, low teacher-student ratio and other factors indicated that placement should continue there. The IEP meeting was convened almost a year later due to communication problems and many delays. The school district's psychologist read the private evaluator's report to other IEP team members at the meeting but not all team members received copies of the evaluator's report. The hearing officer determined that the student should attend the district's high school and that the district should not have an obligation to pay the student's expenses at the private school if the parents chose to keep him there. The parents complained that they had been deprived of due process because they felt the board had failed to consider the independent evaluator's report. They filed an appeal with the U.S. District Court for the District of Connecticut.

In addition to the complaint of due process violations, the parents claimed that the school district had "orchestrated" the outcome of the IEP by predetermining its decision, and that it had "censored" the meeting. The court ruled that the school district had provided the parents and students with adequate due process. There is no IDEA provision requiring school boards to accept the recommendations of independent evaluators or requiring them to assign independent reports a specific value. It was sufficient that the school district's psychologist had read the evaluator's report in order to "consider" it under 34 C.F.R. § 503, and Connecticut laws and regulations. The court granted the school district's motion for summary judgment and dismissed the complaints that the school board had censored and orchestrated the IEP. *T.S. v. Ridgefield Bd. of Educ.*, 808 F.Supp. 926 (D.Conn.1992).

A fourteen-year-old Virginia public school student suffered from a severe learning disability in reading. The school developed an individualized education plan (IEP) for the student which provided for public school placement. The student's parents refused to keep him in a public school and enrolled him in a private residential school. The parents requested a due process hearing demanding that the public school pay for the student's private residential schooling. The hearing officer found that the proposed IEP did not provide the student a free appropriate education. The school board appealed the hearing officer's decision to a reviewing officer. The reviewing officer affirmed the hearing officer's decision. The school board then brought an action in a Virginia trial court challenging the reviewing officer's decision. The trial court reviewed the evidence presented to the hearing officer and found the public school the most appropriate placement for the student. Residential placement was not necessary. The trial court reversed the hearing officer's decision and the student appealed to the Court of Appeals. The court of appeals reversed the trial court's decision and the school board appealed to the Supreme Court of Virginia.

The supreme court held that the appellate court erred when it redetermined facts and then reversed the trial court's decision. The trial court's decision was not plainly wrong or without evidence. It had found that the evidence led to the inescapable conclusion that the IEP was reasonably calculated and designed to provide the student educational benefits. It offered the student a program appropriate to his needs. He had received benefits from the program and would continue to benefit in the future. The supreme court reversed the court of appeals' decision and found that the school board had offered the student a free appropriate public education. *School Bd. of Campbell County v. Beasley*, 380 S.W.2d 884 (Va.1989).

A Georgia student was diagnosed as a chronic schizophrenic with borderline intellectual functioning. He initially attended an elementary school and received special instruction. However, at the age of ten, his behavioral problems increased and he was consequently hospitalized for two years. He then returned to the school system where he received instruction in a day program for the severely emotionally disturbed. When this IEP was determined to be inadequate, he was sent to a residential program in Florida. During a visit to his parents' home it became apparent to his family that he was not receiving basic care. He had lost sixty-five pounds and had a temperature of 104. The family also suspected that he was being abused. Consequently, they refused to allow him to return to the Florida facility. The local education agency was unable to find an appropriate residential facility for the student in Georgia and he attended a day program until his aggressive behavior prohibited his continuing there.

His parents then requested a due process hearing regarding the implementation of his IEP. In their view, the local education agency was responsible for providing services for the student in his home community or at least his home state. After failing to obtain relief at the administrative level, the parents filed a complaint in district court. The court determined that because the student could receive sufficient educational benefits in a facility outside his home state, he was not deprived of his right to an appropriate education. The parents then appealed to the U.S. Court of Appeals, Eleventh Circuit. On appeal, the appellate court first looked to the goals indicated in the student's IEP because, generally, courts pay great deference to these goals. The IEP stated that the student would participate in an ongoing family therapy program working toward a transition to his home community. The district court had essentially concluded that Georgia's obligations under the EHA could be better met by altering the transition goals of the IEP than by altering the student's placement. Consequently, the appellate court determined that the student must be placed at a facility close enough to his home community to allow implementation of his transition goals. The case was remanded to ascertain a new facility. *Todd D. by Robert D. v. Andrews*, 933 F.2d 1576 (11th Cir.1991).

A learning disabled Ohio student who suffered from dyslexia attended public schools until sixth grade. The student was disabled according to the EHA definition. The IEP developed for the student's fifth grade education was never used and the school failed to comply with EHA requirements. The student's parents unilaterally removed him to a private school without requesting a due process hearing or complying with school district requests to discuss an IEP for seventh grade. The student returned to the public school for ninth grade, during which the parents requested a due process hearing to determine whether the school district was complying with the EHA and state law. They also requested reimbursement for private school tuition for seventh and eighth grades. An independent hearing officer ruled that the student had received a free appropriate public education during the sixth and ninth grades and that the school district had developed an appropriate IEP for tenth grade. The parents were not entitled to reimbursement for private school tuition. A state level review officer upheld the independent hearing officer's decision and the parents appealed to the U.S. District Court for the Southern District of Ohio.

The court applied the two-step inquiry developed by the U.S. Supreme Court in *Board of Education v. Rowley*, 458 U.S.176 (1982), and ruled that the school district had provided the student a free appropriate education in the sixth grade, despite its lack of complete compliance with the EHA. The student had advanced academically and the district had followed the significant provisions of the IEP. The parents had failed to request a due process hearing before the student's entry into seventh grade and had also failed to comply with requests by school officials to discuss the seventh grade IEP. The court denied reimbursement for private school tuition during the seventh and eighth grades.

The court noted that there had been delays in formulating the tenth grade IEP, but that EHA procedural requirements had been essentially satisfied. However, because experts who testified at the due process hearing had agreed that the student should be placed in regular classrooms and that mainstreaming would not have presented a great burden for the district, the court ruled that the IEP for the tenth grade was insufficient. Because the district had failed to provide the student a free appropriate education, and because the IEP was not presented to the parents until immediately before the student's tenth grade school year, the unilateral placement of the student in the private school was the only remaining alternative for obtaining an appropriate education. Because the student was now in twelfth grade, it was not feasible to develop an appropriate IEP for the remainder of the student's high school career, and the student could remain at the private school with tuition reimbursement for the eleventh and twelfth grades. *Gillette v. Fairland Bd. of Educ.*, 725 F.Supp. 343 (S.D.Ohio 1989).

In a second case involving a dyslexic student, a California federal district court determined that the IEP developed by a public school was reasonably calculated to benefit the student. A free appropriate public education did not mean that school districts need to find the best or potentially most maximizing education for a student or to select the placement preferred by the family. *Bertolucci v. San Carlos Elem. School Dist.*, 721 F.Supp. 1150 (N.D.Cal.1989).

An Ohio child was born with Pierre-Robin Syndrome. At the age of two, she suffered an anoxic onset which deprived her body of oxygen for thirty minutes. As a result she sustained severe brain damage. She was left with severe psychomotor retardation and functioned at no better than a one-month level developmentally. She was legally blind and had borderline hearing loss. An IEP placement meeting was held and the group unanimously decided that the appropriate and least restrictive educational placement for the child would be a sensory motor integration program (SMI). SMI consisted of a teacher and several aides who worked with a small number of children requiring intensive stimulation of their motor and sensory development. While preparing to implement the IEP, the Cincinnati public schools indicated that they were now able to provide the student with one hour of home instruction per day. The original recommendation was based upon the only two options available at the time: one hour of home instruction per week or the SMI program. However, had this new option been available it certainly would have been the most appropriate placement because it provided the student the benefit of additional services while avoiding the possibility of subjecting her to an intolerable level of stimulation. Seven months after the IEP was to have been implemented the IEP team conducted a review conference indicating that the student would remain at home rather than being placed in the SMI program. After the student's mother requested a hearing, an impartial hearing officer determined that the SMI program was more advantageous and therefore the appropriate educational placement.

A state level review officer reversed the decision, deciding that home instruction was the appropriate placement. The mother then instituted an action in federal court, which reversed the state level reviewing officer's decision. The school district appealed to the U.S. Court of Appeals, Sixth Circuit. The court of appeals determined that an IEP which provided one hour of home instruction per day to a disabled child was reasonably calculated to enable the child to receive educational benefits. The court reversed the decision of the trial court. *Thomas v. Cincinnati Bd. of Educ.*, 918 F.2d 618 (6th Cir.1990).

A U.S. court of appeals held that an IEP must be developed prior to placement. A severely retarded nineteen-year-old student possessing the functional skills of an eighteen-month-old child was placed at a Pennsylvania residential facility. The county public school paid the full cost of the student's education at the residential facility, where his individualized education program (IEP) concentrated on basic skills. The student went to school throughout the year and received after school training and care. County officials began focusing on a new placement for the student at a local public school. At the public school he would attend class five and a half hours per day during a nine month school year and four hours daily during a six week summer session. After a series of letters and meetings between school officials and the student's parents, a new IEP was drawn up for the student to attend the public school.

The student's parents appealed the placement decision to the local hearing officer. The hearing officer found that there were no procedural violations of the EHA and that the new IEP was appropriate, but that the student required placement at the residential facility. The state reviewing officer affirmed the procedural compliance, but found that the student should be placed in the public school. The student's parents appealed this decision to a federal district court. The district court found that the school system had complied procedurally but that it had the burden of proof to show that the student would receive educational benefits at the public school. The court ordered the continuation of the residential placement. The student's parents appealed the finding of procedural compliance and the school appealed the decision regarding placement. On appeal, the U.S. Court of Appeals, Fourth Circuit, upheld the district court's order to have the student remain in his placement at the residential facility. Under the EHA regulation, placement should be based on the IEP. Placing the student at the public school before developing an IEP violated the EHA, which emphasized parental involvement. Involvement after the fact was not sufficient. The county failed to provide the student the free appropriate public education to which he was entitled. The district court's order requiring the student to remain at the residential facility was affirmed. *Spielberg v. Henrico County Pub. School*, 853 F.2d 256 (4th Cir.1988).

For four years, a disabled Washington, D.C., child's IEP called for a public school placement. After her parents became dissatisfied with her progress, they placed her in a private school and instituted a due process hearing. The hearing officer determined that the public school placement was appropriate and the parents appealed to a federal district court. The court determined the public school placement to be inappropriate and the private school placement to be appropriate. The school district moved to amend the district court's decision.

The school district contended that the court erred when it gave consideration to the fact that the child had progressed at the private school. The school district felt that such a consideration was inappropriate and suggestive of potential-maximizing (which is a higher standard than that required under *Board of Education v. Rowley*, 458 U.S. 176, 102 S.Ct. 3034, 73 L.Ed.2d 690 (1982)). *Rowley* also stressed that courts should not impose their view of preferable educational methods upon the states. The court in the instant case noted that the student's advancement was not necessarily potential-maximizing. In fact, in order to recognize the unique needs of each child, the school system should have in mind the placement and the advancement of the child where possible. Since the student in this case made significant progress at the private school, the court determined this placement to be the appropriate placement. *Angevine v. Jenkins*, 752 F.Supp. 24 (D.D.C.1990).

The parents then asked for federal district court review. The court determined that the private school placement was appropriate and ordered reimbursement for the three years the student had attended the private school. The school district later asked the court to modify its decision, but the court refused. The school district then appealed to the U.S. Court of Appeals, District of Columbia Circuit. The court of appeals stated that there was never any question that the student was entitled to special education assistance. Rather, the real question was whether the public schools had the capacity during the 1985-86 school year to implement the student's revised IEP. The court of appeals found that the district court had failed to address this central question and also failed to adequately explain its basis for upsetting the hearing officer's determination that the public school was the appropriate placement. Instead, the district court engaged in irrelevant comparison of her experiences in the public and private schools. The retrospective approach not only failed to address the central issue of the public school's ability to implement the new IEP, but it also seemed to require the school district to provide the student with the best possible education, which is not required by the IDEA (then known as the EHA). The court of appeals remanded, directing the district court to consider only whether the public school had the capacity to implement the revised IEP. *Angevine v. Smith,* 959 F.2d 292 (D.C.Cir.1992).

During the 1983-84 school year the teacher of a first grade student referred him to a psychologist for testing in order to determine if the student was in need of special education. In January 1984, a psychologist for the Roanoke (Virginia) County Schools (RCS) tested the student and informed his mother that he did not require testing for a learning disability (LD). On March 1, 1984, RCS conducted an eligibility meeting to determine if the student was disabled and to discuss an appropriate educational placement for him. A private school psychologist, who had evaluated the student on the mother's behalf, testified that the student should be placed in an LD classroom. However, RCS placed him in a "behavioral adjustment" (BA) classroom. The student's mother then removed him to a private school for learning disabled children.

Prior to the student's second grade year (1984-85) RCS held another eligibility meeting. RCS recommended a dual placement IEP in which the student would spend a part of each day in a BA classroom, an LD classroom and a regular classroom. The mother sued RCS seeking tuition reimbursement for the student's private school placement. After a U.S. district court concluded that she was entitled to reimbursement for the last three months (beginning March 1) of the 1983-84 school year only, she appealed to the U.S. Court of Appeals, Fourth Circuit.

The court of appeals agreed with the district court that the mother was entitled to tuition reimbursement for the last three months of 1983-84 but not the 1984-85 year. It reasoned that the 1984-85 dual placement was a reasonable judgment by RCS. It agreed with the district court's conclusion that the 1984-85 IEP enabled the student to benefit from the IEP. The mother was also entitled to reimbursement for the costs of the evaluation by the private school's psychologist. *Hudson v. Wilson,* 828 F.2d 1059 (4th Cir.1987).

The U.S. Court of Appeals, Ninth Circuit, has held that a homebound program for a disabled child was not an appropriate IEP. A girl in Hawaii suffered from cystic fibrosis and tracheomalacia. After the child was certified by the Hawaii Department of Education as eligible for special education services under the EHA, the child's school district proposed a homebound program because of the unavailability in the public schools of medical services which the child required. The child's parents rejected this IEP and the child remained in the private school. The school district then proposed for the following year a public school program whereby it would train its staff to see to the child's medical needs. The parents also rejected this IEP, enrolled their child in the private school for the following year, and brought suit against the school district to compel it to pay for the child's private education. A U.S. district court in Hawaii held in favor of the parents, and the school district appealed.

The U.S. Court of Appeals, Ninth Circuit, held that the proposed homebound program was decidedly inappropriate for the child's needs. Because the school district was unable to offer an appropriate public school program, it was liable for the child's tuition expenses for the year the proposed IEP was to be implemented. However, the alternative program offered by the school district wherein it would train its staff to take care of the child's medical needs was appropriate. Thus, the parents were not entitled to tuition reimbursement for the following year. *Dep't of Educ. v. Katherine D.*, 727 F.2d 809 (9th Cir.1983).

A Wisconsin school district developed a proposed IEP for a sixteen-year-old student with Down's Syndrome. The IEP called for her to be placed in a trainable mentally handicapped (TMH) program at her neighborhood high school. The student's parents disputed the appropriateness of this placement and sought an administrative review of the school's proposed program. After a hearing, the hearing officer concluded that the proposed placement met the requirements of the IDEA. The state education agency appointed an independent review officer, who reversed the hearing officer's decision and ordered that the child be placed in the totally segregated facility favored by her parents. The school district appealed the decision to a federal district court.

On appeal, the parents did not dispute that the IEP proposed by the school was generally appropriate or that it offered a less restrictive environment than the segregated placement. They contended, however, that placement in an integrated school would not advance their daughter's social or cultural needs, since the majority of her friends attended the segregated school and an integrated school would be more hostile towards her and less sensitive to the needs of students with disabilities. The court found that the student's social needs could be met at the integrated school and that her social skills would be further enhanced by contact with nondisabled peers. It also found that the integrated school had taken significant steps to sensitize its staff and nondisabled students to the needs of the mentally disabled. The court held that the school district's proposed placement satisfied the requirements of the IDEA and also constituted the least restrictive environment. It entered summary judgment in favor of the school district. *School Dist. of Kettle Morraine v. Grover*, 755 F.Supp. 243 (E.D.Wis.1990).

When a school district wishes to conduct an evaluation of a child for the purpose of developing an IEP, under the IDEA the district must notify the parents of the child of its intention to conduct the evaluation and the type of evaluation to be administered.

A Rhode Island case dealt with the issue of whether parental consent is required for a re-evaluation of the child after formulation of an IEP. A mother of a child with a disability sought to prevent the child's school district from making a second educational assessment of her child. The school district had based the boy's IEP on an evaluation conducted by a private school formerly attended by the child. The mother maintained that the assessment sought by the school district would constitute an original evaluation and, therefore, the school was barred from conducting it without her cooperation. The school district contended that its assessment would be a re-evaluation and under the law, a parent's consent was unnecessary. It further stated that any change in placement resulting from the re-evaluation would be subject to challenge by the parent in a statutorily mandated hearing. A U.S. district court agreed with the school district's position, stating that the private school assessment on which the IEP was based did not legitimately constitute an original pre-placement evaluation. Thus, the court held in favor of the school district and the case was dismissed. *Carroll v. Capalbo*, 563 F.Supp. 1053 (D.R.I.1983).

A Texas child was profoundly mentally and physically disabled. When he was eleven years old his functional development was that of an infant between two to six months. Both his neurological capabilities and negative physical responses to prolonged stimulation limited his ability to receive educational programming. In 1984, he underwent surgery to implant a gastric tube. Upon his return, his school day was reduced to four hours. His grandmother then initiated administrative proceedings in which she claimed that the free appropriate education mandated by the EHA entitled her grandson to a full school day of seven hours. The hearing officer determined that the student's physical difficulties and limited ability to process sensory input indicated that a four hour school day would constitute an appropriate education. The grandmother then sought relief in a federal court. After that court found for the school district, the grandmother appealed to the U.S. Court of Appeals, Fifth Circuit.

On appeal, the grandmother contended that the limitation of her grandson's school day to four hours was presumptively inappropriate. The court noted that the EHA created a presumption in favor of the educational placement established by a child's IEP, and the party attacking its terms should bear the burden of showing why the educational setting established by the IEP was not appropriate. The grandmother, therefore, had to bear the burden of demonstrating that the four-hour school day would not provide her grandson with a meaningful educational benefit. The only evidence presented was that the longer programming might increase the benefit he received. However, the EHA does not obligate the school district to supply the student with the maximum benefit possible, but only to provide a meaningful education. Moreover, the court concluded, to presume that every child's school day should be of uniform length was at odds with the conception of the individually tailored education embodied in the EHA. Therefore, the court affirmed the trial court's decision. *Christopher M. v. Corpus Christi Indep. School Dist.*, 933 F.2d 1285 (5th Cir.1991).

CHAPTER TWO

PLACEMENT

I. MAINSTREAMING

An important requirement of an "appropriate" education is that each child with a disability be educated in the "least restrictive environment." Section 1412(5)(B) of the IDEA requires that states provide procedures to ensure that children with disabilities are educated "to the maximum extent appropriate" with nondisabled children in regular classes. This is known as mainstreaming.

A learning disabled Massachusetts student attended public schools through the third grade. As he entered fourth grade, his parents enrolled him in a private school for children with learning disabilities. Although the parents later stated that school district employees had recommended private school attendance, they never obtained any formal school district approval of the transfer. They also failed to request a hearing to address the IEP, which recommended a public school placement. After two years of attending the private school, the student's parents became interested in obtaining funding for the private school placement and requested a new IEP. They also requested tuition payments for the student's past private school placement. The district refused to pay the private school tuition, but responded to the request for a new IEP. The parents had the student evaluated at a children's hospital. The proposed IEP included regular education instruction in all classes except language arts and mathematics instruction and a daily academic support class. The parents rejected the proposed IEP and requested a hearing before the Massachusetts Bureau of Special Education Appeals. The hearing officer determined that the school district's proposed IEP was appropriate and that the school district had no obligation to pay private school tuition. Two further hearings were held which substantially upheld the school district's position. The parents' attorney then withdrew from the proceedings.

The student's father requested a reopening of the proceedings and attempted to add a complaint for lead contamination in the district's public schools. A state hearing officer refused to reopen the case and the father appealed to the U.S. District Court for the District of Massachusetts. The district court ruled for the school district on all counts, and the father appealed to the U.S. Court of Appeals, First Circuit. The appeals court noted that Massachusetts statutes provide a standard of law which exceeds the IDEA's minimal requirement that school districts provide educational benefits reasonably calculated to enable students to receive a free appropriate education. The Massachusetts standard required "maximum possible development" by students. The court stated that both state and federal laws dictate a policy of mainstreaming. The court ruled that the hearing officer could have reasonably concluded that the IEP was appropriate, and it was unquestionably a less restrictive environment for the student than the private school. Accordingly, the proposed IEP "struck a suitable balance between the goals of mainstreaming and maximum possible development." The school district had not violated any IDEA procedures and it had no obligation to fund the private school placement. *Amann v. Stow School System*, 982 F.2d 644 (1st Cir.1992).

Parents of a Georgia child with Down's Syndrome attempted to enroll their daughter in a regular kindergarten class. The school district refused to allow enrollment without an evaluation. The parents enrolled their daughter in the regular kindergarten class the next year and a due process hearing was initiated. The hearing officer determined that the child should be evaluated. After the child was evaluated, a placement meeting was held where the placement team recommended a self-contained classroom. The parents rejected this placement and requested that their daughter be placed in the regular kindergarten class with speech therapy. The school board rejected the parents' proposal. The parents then instituted this suit in a federal district court alleging that the individualized education program (IEP) had violated the Individuals with Disabilities Education Act (IDEA) by failing to provide for mainstreaming. The trial court determined that the proposed IEP did not sufficiently provide for mainstreaming and the school district appealed to the U.S. Court of Appeals, Eleventh Circuit. The appellate court noted that the IDEA mandates that a child with a disability be educated in the regular classroom unless such education cannot be achieved satisfactorily with the use of supplemental aids and services. The school district, in this instance, did not consider an IEP which would allow the child to remain in the regular kindergarten with supplemental aids and services. Further, the court determined that such a consideration should be made prior to and during the development of the IEP, not afterward. Thus, the court held that the school district failed to comply with the mainstreaming requirement of the IDEA and ordered a new IEP developed. *Greer v. Rome City School Dist.*, 950 F.2d 688 (11th Cir.1991).

A New Jersey child was severely impaired in his intellectual functioning and his ability to verbally communicate as a result of a developmental disability associated with Down's Syndrome. The school district's child study team recommended a number of segregated, self-contained special education programs outside of the school district for the student's kindergarten year. The child's parents wanted a less restrictive placement. Eventually, a compromise was reached in which the student attended a developmental kindergarten class in the morning and a special education class in the afternoon. Even though the student made some progress, he exhibited certain inappropriate behaviors in the developmental kindergarten class. Thus, for the following school year, the school district proposed to place the student in an out-of-district, self-contained special education class. Again a compromise was reached in which the student was placed outside the district. However, seeking to place their son in a regular class in his neighborhood school, the student's parents then requested a due process hearing. A decision in favor of the school district was rendered. The parents then brought suit in a federal district court.

The court determined that the student's behavioral problems in the developmental kindergarten resulted from the school district's failure to provide him with adequate supplementary aids and services and an appropriate individualized education plan (IEP) for his placement. The court noted that while the student was in his out-of-district placement his behavioral problems had diminished as a result of the provision of those services. Here, the school district could justify its exclusion of the student from a regular classroom only if it could show that despite the assistance of supplementary aids and services, and after taking all reasonable steps to reduce the burden to the teacher, the other children in the class would still be deprived of their share of the teacher's attention. Here, the school district had failed to justify the exclusion of the student. By failing to consider less restrictive placements for the student, and by failing to provide adequate supplementary aids and services, the school district violated the Individuals with Disabilities Education Act. Further, the school district violated the Rehabilitation Act because the student was an individual with handicaps who was otherwise qualified for the benefits of education in his local school district and the school district had not shown that placement of the student in a self-contained special education class was educationally necessary. Accordingly, the court ordered a new IEP to be designed for the student in the upcoming school year. *Oberti v. Board of Educ. of Clementon School Dist.*, 801 F.Supp. 1392 (D.N.J.1992).

A thirteen-year-old Pennsylvania boy suffered from spinal muscular atrophy and was confined to a wheelchair. He was considered a disabled person within the meaning of § 504 of the Rehabilitation Act, the Pennsylvania Human Relations Act, and the Individuals with Disabilities Education Act (IDEA). He attended a special education program in another school district. During this time he obtained the services of a support/service dog which he hoped to bring to school with him. However, the school program's supervisor recommended against the use of the dog in school. He did state that the student and his dog would be welcome to attend school in the district where he resided — this would mean mainstreaming the student. The parents then kept their son home because the dog was not permitted in the special education classroom. In the individualized education program meeting set up for the following year, it was recommended that the student be mainstreamed at his local school. The parents requested a due process hearing, maintaining that the change in placement was recommended only because their son wanted to have his dog with him, and not because of his educational needs. The hearing officer called for the student to be mainstreamed, and the parents, rather than appealing that decision, filed suit in a federal district court under § 504 of the Rehabilitation Act.

The school defendants moved for summary judgment, asserting that § 504 did not provide the parents with a cause of action. The court agreed with the defendants, finding that the IDEA was the exclusive avenue through which the parents could assert a claim. The IDEA sets forth a comprehensive administrative plan which provides for a series of due process hearings to guarantee parents an opportunity for meaningful input into all decisions affecting their child's education. It further allows for review of decisions they think are inappropriate. This was a mainstreaming case under the IDEA (which favors mainstreaming to the maximum extent appropriate), and accordingly a § 504 action was not an available remedy. The court granted summary judgment to the school defendants. *Gaudiello v. Delaware County Intermediate Unit,* 796 F.Supp. 849 (E.D.Pa.1992).

An Alabama student with disabilities was placed in a variety of facilities throughout his academic career. The school district determined that residential placement was the most appropriate placement. The parents and school district disagreed on the facility. The parents refused to release their son's records for evaluation for admission to a public residential program. In addition, his parents enrolled their son in a private residential facility. The parents proceeded to request a due process hearing. Subsequently, the parents released their son's records, which led to his acceptance at the public school. At the hearing, the hearing officer held that the public school provided the least restrictive environment under the IDEA. The parents appealed.

Before the U.S. District Court for the Northern District of Alabama, the court held that the public school placement was appropriate. The public and private schools offered substantially similar programs and services. Moreover, the court found that under the IDEA continuum of less to more restrictive, the public school was less restrictive than the private school and thus was the more appropriate placement for the student. Overall, the public school placement met the requirement of being reasonably calculated to allow the student to receive educational benefits. *Mark Z. v. Mountain Brook Board of Ed.*, 792 F.Supp. 1228 (N.D.Ala.1992).

A mentally retarded Pennsylvania student's educational placement was in a classroom with an educable mentally retarded classification and a socially and emotionally disturbed classification (EMR/SED). During the 1987-88 school year, the school district officials recommended that the student continue his fulltime educational placement in the EMR/SED at the public school. The mother objected to this recommendation because it did not provide for any interaction between the student and his nondisabled peers. The student already had extracurricular activities with nondisabled peers including Cub Scouts, football and ballet classes, in which he functioned well and enjoyed the interaction with the other children. Therefore, the mother requested that her son be placed in an EMR classroom in a regular district school to enable him to be mainstreamed with his nondisabled peers. The school district refused and the mother invoked a due process hearing. During the prehearing conference, the district offered to integrate the student into an EMR class for one period per week. Under this proposal, integration would be increased gradually. The mother rejected this proposal and again requested a due process hearing pursuant to the EHA.

The hearing officer determined that the student's appropriate placement would be in the less restrictive environment of the EMR class. A transition from the EMR/SED to the EMR class would begin with two periods per day and lunch. Eventually, the hearing officer hoped the student would be placed in the EMR classroom on a full-time basis. The mother filed exceptions to the hearing officer's decision with the Secretary of Education. She specifically objected to the recommendation that the student be required to attend classes at both schools during the transition period. The secretary issued a decision ordering the district to place the student in the EMR class on a full-time basis. The school district appealed to a federal district court.

Pending the ruling of the district court, the mother and the school district agreed to an interim placement. The student was placed in an EMR class and mainstreamed to other nondisabled classes where he appeared to behave satisfactorily. The student made no progress, however, in the EMR class. He had difficulty completing assignments and did not interact socially with the other students in the EMR class. The school officials recommended that it was in the student's best interests that he be returned on a full-time basis to the more structured EMR/SED. The court noted that under the EHA the district court must make an independent determination based on the evidence presented. Applying this standard to the present case, the court concluded that a free appropriate public education required the placement of the student in the EMR/SED for academic subjects and the mainstreaming of the student in nonacademic subjects to the maximum extent possible. *Liscio v. Woodland Hills School Dist.*, 734 F.Supp. 689 (W.D.Pa.1989).

A sixteen-year-old profoundly deaf student was eligible for special education. He had been enrolled in Virginia public school special education programs since the age of two. From first grade on, the student had participated in the school system's cued speech programs and advanced in school with the aid of a cued speech interpreter and other support services. The district increasingly mainstreamed him into regular classes so that by high school he was taking academic classes with nondisabled students with the assistance of a cued speech interpreter. He also played on the high school baseball and basketball teams. The student's public school support services included one period per day in a special resource class taught by a fulltime staff teacher for the hearing impaired and several weekly speech and language therapy sessions taught by a therapist. The cued speech program was one of three different educational methods used by the school system in serving its three hundred hearing-impaired students and the district was one of only a few in the nation which offered a cued speech program.

The district established its hearing-impaired programs at centrally-located schools close to major arterials. Many participating students came from across the county and from other Virginia counties. Participating schools were located close together to allow program interpreters to easily travel to different schools. The high school which the student attended was located 5.1 miles farther from his home than the neighborhood high school he would have attended in the absence of his hearing impairment. Despite the success of the school district's mainstreaming efforts, the student's parents felt that the program should be offered at the closer school and they requested an administrative hearing. The local hearing officer required the school system to provide the cued speech service at the neighborhood high school. The district appealed to a state administrative hearing officer who determined that the student's placement constituted a free appropriate education in the least restrictive environment. The district was not required to duplicate its cued speech services at the neighborhood high school. The parents sued the district in a federal district court on a number of grounds, and the court issued two separate opinions.

In the first opinion, the court considered the student's request for $100,000 for alleged mental and emotional distress from his inability to attend the neighborhood school. The court granted the school district's motion for summary judgment. Apart from tuition reimbursement, the EHA did not authorize compensatory damage awards. To allow damages such as these would create a cause of action for educational malpractice, which was not the EHA's intent. The court also rejected the student's Rehabilitation Act § 504 complaint as another impermissible educational malpractice complaint. *Barnett v. Fairfax County School Bd.*, 721 F.Supp. 755 (E.D.Va.1989).

In the second opinion, the court considered the student's request for an order to provide cued speech services at his neighboring high school. The district had provided the student an appropriate public education as he had advanced academically and maintained a B average in regular classes while participating in two interscholastic sports. The school system had lived up to the EHA mainstreaming requirement. The cued speech program was offered at a regular public high school and constituted the least restrictive environment for disabled students under the EHA. The EHA did not create an absolute duty to place a student in the neighborhood school, and the district was free to locate its special education programs at a central site. While the EHA provided the minimal requirement for school districts, they were free to determine the particular method of providing services. The school district had employed a successful method for providing interpreters in hearing-impaired special education programs and had provided a free appropriate public education under the EHA. The district had also complied with § 504 of the Rehabilitation Act. The court granted the district's motion for summary judgment. *Barnett v. Fairfax County School Bd.*, 721 F.Supp. 757 (E.D.Va.1989).

A fourteen-year-old Nebraska child was born with Kniest Syndrome. It is a form of dwarfism, with a profound bilateral hearing loss. He also suffered from visual impairment and physical disabilities which affected his ambulation and impaired his ability to use his hands for sign language. He was adopted at the age of five, before which he had no language therapy and could only sign four words. He had made progress over the next few years and eventually reached a five to seven language development age. His placement then, due to his severe language delay, was at a school for the deaf. His father wished to place his son at a regular school, in a self-contained classroom, similar to his previous Minnesota placement. The school district denied this request and a due process hearing was held. The hearing officer concluded that the current placement was not inappropriate but a new IEP should be developed which included parental input and unambiguous goals and objectives for the boy. His father then instituted this suit in a federal trial court.

The trial court noted that the boy presented a unique set of problems and presented the school system with a very difficult language barrier. If the boy were to be educated at a regular school in a self-contained hearing-impaired classroom, he would only be exposed to nonhearing-impaired students at lunch, in the hallway, etc. The level of interaction would be minimal as the boy had a history of only "speaking" with adults and not initiating conversation with his peers. The father insisted that the boy's progress at the Minnesota placement was substantial due to the mainstream atmosphere of the school. The court disagreed and determined that his progress was likely due to the excellent teaching skills, and also noted that other evidence indicated that the boy did not interact with nonhearing-impaired or hearing-impaired students to any sufficient degree at the Minnesota school either. The court, therefore, entered judgment against the father and for the school district. *French v. Omaha Public Schools*, 766 F.Supp. 765 (D.Neb.1991).

A multiply-disabled Idaho student was classified as trainable mentally retarded. He was placed in a public school's disabled contained classroom, taught by special education teachers. The student's parents then decided to place him in a private school, but all the schools contacted required a full-time aide as a prerequisite. The parents enrolled him in a parochial school for the following school year. They then commenced an administrative proceeding to obtain reimbursement for the aide. The district's child study team met to determine financial responsibility for the full-time aide. The team was advised by its counsel that it had no financial responsibility and it then informed the parents about the public education system's educational opportunities. The district offered placement in a segregated special education program. The parents argued that the student was entitled to mainstreaming under the EHA. The district then offered to fund educational services in a private school, but refused to pay for the aide. The parents kept their son in the parochial school and began an administrative appeal for the cost of the aide and tuition. The hearing officer ruled in favor of the school district, and the parents appealed to an Idaho county court. The court overturned the hearing officer's determination and ruled in favor of the parents. The district then appealed to the Idaho Supreme Court.

The supreme court noted that the district had failed to rebut the parents' argument that mainstreaming was appropriate. Free appropriate education must be provided in the least restrictive environment and there was a strong preference for mainstreaming in conformity with the EHA. The court noted that school district documents did not qualify as an IEP, because they set forth no goals or other evaluation procedures for determining whether EHA educational objectives were being met. Because there was no appropriate IEP, the district was not in compliance with the EHA and the hearing officer's determination was erroneous. The court ordered the school district to reimburse the parents for their son's tuition and for his aide. *Thornock v. Boise Indep. School Dist. 1*, 767 P.2d 1241 (Idaho 1988).

The parents of a Down's Syndrome student enrolled him in a Texas public school system's half-day special education program. The following school year, the parents requested mainstreaming for their son in a half-day regular prekindergarten class. The school district's admissions committee met and agreed to combine a regular and special education program for the student. The student was unable to participate in classroom activities without individual supervision from the teacher or her aide. The school's committee met again and changed the student's placement to special education only. However, the committee made arrangements for the student to have contact with nondisabled students during lunch and recess. The student's parents appealed the committee's decision to a hearing officer under the EHA. The hearing officer determined that regular education was not appropriate since the student could not participate in a class without constant supervision and the curriculum was beyond his ability. The parents appealed the hearing officer's decision to a federal district court. The court ruled in favor of the school district, and the parents appealed to the U.S. Court of Appeals, Fifth Circuit.

The court of appeals held that because the prekindergarten curriculum was not within the student's reach, the school district was not required to mainstream him. It noted that the primary purpose of the EHA was to provide disabled students with meaningful access to education, sufficient to confer some educational benefit to the student. The district had taken creative steps to provide regular education access to the student and had mainstreamed him to the maximum extent appropriate. The appeals court affirmed the district court's decision in favor of the school district. *Daniel R.R. v. State Bd. of Educ.*, 874 F.2d 1036 (5th Cir.1989).

In May 1980, the parents of a Missouri boy with Down's Syndrome attempted to enroll him in a public elementary school. The public school recommended that he be placed at a private institution and referred him to the Missouri Department of Elementary and Secondary Education for evaluation and services. The department concluded that the boy was "severely handicapped" and was eligible for placement in State School No. 2, a school exclusively attended by and designed for disabled children. Questioning his "severely handicapped" classification, the parents requested a due process hearing. The hearing panel concluded that it was inappropriate to place the boy in State School No. 2, and ruled that an appropriate educational program would include interaction with nondisabled peers. The parents appealed to the state board of education which agreed with the department's "severely handicapped" label. It ruled that the boy should be placed in State School No. 2 and the parents appealed to a U.S. district court, which decided against them. The parents then appealed to the U.S. Court of Appeals, Eighth Circuit.

The parents took issue with the district court's interpretation of EHA mainstreaming provisions. They argued that the court was wrong in considering the cost of a mainstreaming placement to the school district. The court of appeals observed that EHA § 1412(5) provides that "to the maximum extent appropriate, disabled children are to be educated with children who are not disabled, and that . . . removal of disabled children from the regular educational program should occur only when the nature of the disability is such that education in regular classes cannot be achieved satisfactorily." The court noted that the EHA preference for mainstreaming is not absolute because regular classrooms are not suitable for many disabled students. It held that the district court was correct in concluding that the marginal benefit of the boy's mainstreaming was outweighed by the deprivation of benefits to other disabled children. The boy's placement at the public elementary school would have required the hiring of at least one special education teacher, thus diminishing funds available to other students. The district court decision was affirmed and the school district was not required to mainstream the boy. *A.W. v. Northwest R-1 School Dist.*, 813 F.2d 158 (8th Cir.1987).

A disabled child was placed in a private nonprofit daycare center for children ages one through six. The daycare center's educational program was designed to promote relationships between disabled and nondisabled children. The child's school district recommended that she be placed in a preschool development class in a public elementary school. The child's parents objected, believing that the child's placement at the private daycare center was more appropriate due to its commitment to the integration of disabled and nondisabled children. A hearing officer of the Iowa Department of Public Instruction affirmed the placement decision and the parents appealed to a U.S. district court. The district court upheld the decision and the parents appealed to the U.S. Court of Appeals, Eighth Circuit.

The issue before the court was whether the decision to place the child in a public educational program teaching disabled children only, rather than in a private program serving both nondisabled and disabled children, violated the EHA's mainstreaming requirement. The EHA requires that states are to educationally integrate disabled and nondisabled children "to the maximum extent appropriate." The child's parents alleged that the mainstreaming requirement was violated when she was placed in a program for disabled students only. The district court, however, rejected the idea that mainstreaming requirements are met only when the disabled child is educated in the same classroom as nondisabled children. It observed that the child could be educated in the same school as other disabled children, and that this did not necessarily violate the "maximum extent appropriate" requirement. The court further observed that while the private facility may have offered the best educational opportunity for the child, the EHA does not require states to provide parents with the best possible option. *Mark A. v. Grant Wood Area Educ. Agency*, 795 F.2d 52 (8th Cir.1986).

A Florida high school student who was disabled by a special learning disability brought suit against a local school district under the EHA and the Rehabilitation Act, alleging that her involuntary transfer from high school to an alternative learning center violated her right to a publicly financed appropriate special education. The student requested a preliminary injunction to allow her to attend high school during pendency of the proceedings. A U.S. district court denied the student's request and she appealed to the U.S. Court of Appeals, Eleventh Circuit. She argued that the hearing officer who upheld the decision to transfer her denied her the right to lay representation in the administrative proceedings. The student also contended that the record of the administrative proceedings contained uncontested evidence that the school district violated her procedural right to remain in the high school during the pendency of the action as guaranteed by the EHA. Finally, she claimed that neither the hearing officer nor the district judge determined whether the alternative learning center was the least restrictive environment in which she could be educated.

The court of appeals held that the Rehabilitation Act was not the appropriate provision under which to bring suit since the EHA provides the exclusive avenue for asserting rights to a publicly financed special education. Further, the student had no right under the EHA to lay representation in the administrative proceedings. The hearing officer's examination of the student's chosen representative revealed his almost complete ignorance of state administrative procedure. Thus, the hearing officer did not violate the EHA in limiting his role to offering advice. The uncontradicted evidence left no doubt that the student's behavior at the high school posed a threat to both students and school officials. Thus, the court found that the school district properly exercised its authority to transfer the student to the alternative learning center and the district did not violate her right to remain in the high school during the pendency of the action. Finally, the court held that because the student introduced no evidence that the proposed placement was inappropriate or that a less restrictive environment existed in which she could receive the special education she needed, the proposed placement was appropriate. *Victoria L. By Carol A. v. Dist. School Bd. of Lee County, Florida*, 741 F.2d 369 (11th Cir.1984).

The parents of a disabled child in Arizona brought suit against their local school district because of the district's proposed plan to relocate the child at a school which could provide assistance from an instructor specially qualified to train her. The child suffered from cerebral palsy and physical disabilities but possessed normal intelligence. However, because of her disabilities she had difficulty in learning to read and write. For this reason the child's school believed the child could best be served in a school which had teachers certified in physical disabilities. The parents objected to the move because they feared that moving the child from her neighborhood and friends would create emotional problems and would stigmatize her as "handicapped." The U.S. Court of Appeals, Ninth Circuit, held that the school district's decision was reasonable under the circumstances. In affirming a U.S. district court decision, the Court of Appeals stated that the importance of mainstreaming a disabled child must be balanced with the primary objective of providing disabled children with an "appropriate education." The court found that the objective of mainstreaming would not be "thwarted" by requiring the child to be instructed for a period of time by a physical disabilities teacher at another school. At issue here, said the court, is a school district's ability, after determining that a disabled student is not making satisfactory progress, to transfer that student to a school which can provide assistance from an instructor especially qualified to train a student with that particular disability. The court found that the school district's proposal complemented state and federal law by "providing the child with a teacher particularly suited to deal with her learning problems," and held that the transfer should be allowed. *Wilson v. Marana Unified School Dist. No. 6 of Pima County*, 735 F.2d 1178 (9th Cir.1984).

II. PLACEMENT IN SPECIAL EDUCATION PROGRAMS

Placements of children with disabilities in special education programs provided by public schools are generally upheld if the educational program offered by the school is appropriate and responsive to the particular child's needs. However, parents often challenge the school district's proposed IEP and seek an alternative placement.

A. Disputes in Placements

A New York student had dyslexia, compounded by attention deficit disorder which manifested itself in impulsivity and poor concentration. The student was classified as learning disabled and was entitled to receive special education under the Individuals with Disabilities Education Act (IDEA). By the time the student reached the tenth grade, he could only read at a third grade level because the individualized education programs which had been set up for him (including time in a special resource room, mainstreaming into regular classes, remedial reading, and counseling) were not very effective. The student's parents placed their son in a private residential school which had a high degree of success in teaching dyslexic children to read. They requested a due process hearing to challenge the IEP proposed for the student's sophomore year in high school, and the school district agreed at the meeting to place the student there. However, the parents were later told that the district could not authorize the private school placement because the school was not approved by the New York State Education Department. The parents enrolled their son at the school anyway. The following year, lacking the necessary tuition for the private school, the student was reenrolled in the public high school. The IEP for the year was the same as the ones that had not worked in the past. The parents then brought suit in a federal district court against the school district and the state education department challenging the placement of their son.

The lawsuit sought conditional approval of the private residential school. However, the court noted that the state maintained a list of preapproved schools and that one of them might be an appropriate placement for the student. Here, the state had offered a continuum of placement options for the student which satisfied the requirements of the IDEA. Further, it was not a violation of the IDEA for the state to require that placement of the student be made from the preapproved list of private schools. However, the court then noted that the school district had failed to provide the student with an appropriate IEP, and thus it had violated the IDEA. The court ordered the school district to provide the student with one year of remedial educational services after his high school graduation. However, it decided that the parents could not be reimbursed for the one year's tuition resulting from the unilateral placement of their son in the unapproved private school. *Straube v. Florida Union Free School District*, 801 F.Supp. 1164 (S.D.N.Y.1992).

The Georgia Department of Education Regulations and Procedures defines "mildly mentally handicapped" as intellectual functioning ranging between an upper limit of approximately 70 IQ to a lower limit of approximately 55 together with "deficits in adaptive behavior which significantly limit an individual's effectiveness in meeting the standards of maturation, learning, personal independence of social responsibility, and especially school performance that is expected of the individual's age level and cultural group, as determined by clinical judgment." The state regulations then define "moderately mentally handicapped" similarly, but with intellectual functioning in the 55 to 40 IQ range. A student with Down's Syndrome consistently tested to approximately a 51 IQ. When he first attended school in his district, he was placed in a self-contained class for the mildly mentally handicapped. The mild program stressed academic achievement and everyday survival skills, such as renting an apartment and comparison price shopping. The moderate program provided only basic "survival academics." This included telling time, counting money, and other such skills. The moderate program also included a work-study program for those students who had mastered the basic survival tasks. After a time in the mild program, the school district desired to change the student's placement to the moderate program. The school district claimed that the student functioned at a level far below that of the other students in the mild program, and that he was not benefitting from it. The student's mother refused the change in placement. She argued that the student would gain more social skills and be more academically stimulated in the mild program. Both a regional hearing officer and a state hearing officer concluded that the proper placement of the student was in the moderate program. The mother then brought suit in the U.S. District Court for the Northern District of Georgia.

The court noted that the student must be provided with a free appropriate education which confers some educational benefit upon him. Although the mother argued that the student was receiving "some educational benefit," the court took exception to her use of the term. In order to further the purposes of the idea, "some educational benefit" must mean some *appreciable* educational benefit. Since the student had made little progress in the mild program, the moderate program would be a better placement. Expert testimony also tended to establish that the appropriate placement was in the moderate program. The court also noted that the student had been isolated from his classmates during the pendency of the lawsuit because of the necessity that he receive individual classroom instruction due to his inability to perform tasks performed by the rest of the class. The court allowed the school district to place the student in the moderate program. *Chris C. v. Gwinnett County School Dist.*, 780 F.Supp. 804 (N.D.Ga.1991).

A Mississippi woman believed her daughter to be learning disabled and sought, unsuccessfully, to obtain special education for her. All the local school district's petitions to the state department of education for special education eligibility were rejected. The student was withdrawn from the school district and sent to live with her father in Long Beach, where she was ruled eligible for special education classes. Her mother then sued the local school district for violations of the IDEA and the Rehabilitation Act. A federal district dismissed the claims for declaratory and injunctive relief as moot, and an appeal to the U.S. Court of Appeals, Sixth Circuit, followed. The court of appeals noted that even though the student had been removed from the local school system, the IDEA claim was not necessarily moot. The student's entitlement under the IDEA survived; thus, the controversy could be repeated if the student returned to live with her mother. However, the state had since authorized special education eligibility for the student with the same special education placement as was available in Long Beach. Accordingly, in this instance, the case was moot and the district court's decision was affirmed. *Lee by and through MacMillan v. Biloxi School Dist.*, 963 F.2d 837 (5th Cir.1992).

Two moderately retarded Missouri brothers, ages twenty and eighteen, functioned between a kindergarten and third grade level. At a hearing before the Missouri State Board of Education, the school district and the students' parents could not agree on an educational program for the brothers. The parents filed a lawsuit in a Missouri trial court contesting the students' placement. Meanwhile, in response to the parents' request for vocational services, the school district held a meeting in which a vocational school representative was present. Educational plans for each student were drafted at the meeting. The vocational school rejected the plans, which would have required the vocational school to enroll the students for part of their education. The parents wanted their sons trained at the vocational school. The vocational school was not a party to the ongoing lawsuit. The school district filed a motion to add the vocational school as a party. It also filed a motion to require the state board to order the vocational school to accept the plans which had been discussed at the meeting. Approximately one month later an order was issued that added the vocational school as a party and ordered the board to direct the vocational school to accept the students based on the educational plans drafted at the meeting. The vocational school sought relief in the Missouri Court of Appeals, Western District.

The court of appeals held that the trial court lacked authority to add the vocational school to the litigation between the parents and the school district. It also lacked the authority to order the vocational school to provide part of the students' education without first remanding the case to the state board of education. The vocational school should have been provided proper notice and a hearing at the administrative level in order to be properly joined. Once the vocational school's ability to provide training became apparent, it should have been brought into the case. The vocational school could not be joined in the lawsuit. *Clinton Area Vocational School v. Dandurand*, 766 S.W.2d 169 (Mo.App.1989).

A Minnesota girl born with spina bifida required physical therapy, catheterization and bowel care. She lived five blocks from a nearby school and her parents requested that she attend there. However, the school district notified the parents that the school could not accommodate her physical limitations. It further notified the parents that it would not modify the school but would instead transport the girl to a disabled-accessible school four miles away. The parents then requested a due process hearing challenging their daughter's placement. The administrative law judge ruled that the district's placement did not constitute the least restrictive environment as required under the EHA. The district appealed this decision to the commissioner of education who found that the school district had provided the student with a free, appropriate education in the least restrictive environment. After a federal district court upheld the commissioner's decision, the parents appealed to the U.S. Court of Appeals, Eighth Circuit.

The parents claimed that the nearby school was the only school to which the district could assign their daughter and still be in compliance with the EHA. They argued that the school district erred when considering the cost of the modification. The appellate court noted that the record did not suggest that the district court had relied on a cost benefit analysis. It then determined that the EHA does not mandate that school districts must modify all their school buildings to accommodate physically disabled children when those children are already receiving an appropriate education. The parents further argued that the EHA required the school to place students near their home. The act specifically states that the school district must place students "as close as possible," and still provide a free appropriate education. The court determined that even if the modifications were made to the nearby school it still would not be the least restrictive environment due to the extensive physical limitations of the girl. Therefore, the court upheld the decision of the district court. *Schuldt v. Mankato School Dist. No. 77*, 937 F.2d 1357 (8th Cir.1991).

A disabled Oklahoma child suffered from autism with moderate mental retardation and seizures. She had received special education services since the age of eighteen months. Her IEP called for nine months of regular classroom instruction. Her parents sent her to a recreational day camp for children with disabilities for six weeks during the summer. After a few years of providing the student with summer studies themselves, the parents requested that the school district provide the student with a structured summer educational program. This request was denied and the parents invoked a due process hearing before an administrative hearing officer. At the hearing, the parents presented evidence in the form of testimony from the child's social worker, pediatrician, neurologist, and a psychologist who evaluated her. All agreed that she needed to continue her experience in a structured educational setting during the summer months to prevent regression. However, two teachers testified that the student had not regressed during the summer in which she had not participated in an extended school year program. The hearing officer determined that the student did not require an extended school year program. This decision was based on the premise that predictions of future regression are insufficient to compel the schools to provide an extended school year to children with disabilities. The hearing officer also determined that the student's parents failed to demonstrate that the student had regressed. The parents appealed this decision to the appeals officer who affirmed the hearing officer's decision. The parents then filed this action in a federal district court which granted summary judgment to the school district. The parents appealed to the U.S. Court of Appeals, Tenth Circuit.

The appellate court noted that the regression-recoupment analysis was not the only measure used to determine the necessity of a structured summer program. In addition to a degree of regression and the time necessary for recoupment, courts have considered many factors important in their discussions of what constitutes an appropriate educational program. These include: the degree of impairment, the resources of the child's parents to provide the educational structure at home, whether the service is extraordinary to the child's condition, the ability of the child to interact with nondisabled children, and the child's rate of progress. The analysis should consider retrospective data such as past regression and rate of recoupment but should also include predictive data based on the opinion of professionals in consultation with the child's parents. Since the factual record was inconclusive concerning many aspects of the student's progress and intended progress, the court remanded the case to the trial court. The court stated that "those who conducted the administrative review, the administrative appeal, and the federal district court review of that administrative process erred by converting what should have been a multifaceted inquiry into application of a single, inflexible criterion." *Johnson v. Indep. School Dist. No. 4 of Bixby*, 921 F.2d 1022 (10th Cir.1990).

An Oklahoma student who was learning disabled in math also experienced problems with peer interaction, impulse control, and excessive anxiety. She was suspended from school for theft, smoking, disruption of class, fighting, tardiness, and use of inappropriate language. She was then admitted to a psychiatric unit and diagnosed as having a conduct disorder related to emotional problems. Her psychologist recommended that she be placed in a class for seriously emotionally disturbed children. The parents requested the school district to develop an IEP that classified her as seriously disabled. The IEP committee met and determined that her behavioral problems did not relate to her learning disability and that she was therefore not entitled to classification as severely emotionally disturbed under the EHA. The parents then requested a due process hearing, at which the hearing officer determined that she was properly labeled as learning disabled. After the appellate level officer agreed and determined that she was not seriously emotionally disturbed, the parents filed suit in a federal district court. The district court affirmed and the parents appealed to the U.S. Court of Appeals, Tenth Circuit. The issue was whether an emotionally disturbed child who was diagnosed as having a conduct disorder was excluded from coverage under the EHA. Seriously emotionally disturbed children are clearly included within the EHA. However, the language of the statute excludes children who are merely socially maladjusted. The court noted that just because a child is socially maladjusted is not by itself conclusive evidence that she is seriously emotionally disturbed. It further found that the testimony supported the finding that she suffered from a conduct disorder, but was not seriously emotionally disturbed within the definition of the EHA. Therefore, the court upheld the decision of the trial court and found for the school district. *A.E. by and through Evans v. Indep. School Dist. No. 25*, 936 F.2d 472 (10th Cir.1991).

An Illinois child with a behavioral disorder was placed in a student support center at a public school. He did moderately well but at times his behavior was disruptive and violent. The school district became concerned that he would not receive adequate support services at the junior high school the following year and suggested an alternative public school for children with severe behavioral disorders. The parents objected and the school district deferred and placed the student in the junior high school. His behavior worsened rapidly. The parents still objected to the proposed placement with the alternative school and the school district initiated a due process hearing. The hearing officer determined that the school district's placement at the alternative school was appropriate. The state hearing officer reversed and determined that the parents' negative state of mind made the school district's placement inappropriate and ordered the district to find an acceptable private school placement. After a federal district court affirmed, the school district appealed to the U.S. Court of Appeals, Seventh Circuit.

The school district contended that the court erred in considering the parents' hostility to the proposed placement. The court had made a factual finding that the parents' attitudes were severe enough to doom any attempt to educate the student at the alternative school. The school district expressed a concern that this ruling would enable parents to feign opposition in order to obtain their preferred placement.

However, the court disagreed and determined that it would not alter the ability of hearing officers to make credibility determinations in the first instance. Therefore, the court concluded that it was permissible to consider parental hostility toward an IEP as part of an evaluation of the placement's expected educational benefits and affirmed the trial court's decision. *Bd. of Educ. of Cmty. Consol. School Dist. No. 21 v. Illinois State Bd. of Educ.*, 938 F.2d 712 (7th Cir.1991).

A New Hampshire boy suffered from intense emotional problems. He was labeled emotionally disabled and received special education. While in grade school, he tried to commit suicide several times. In September of the 1988-89 school year, the placement team recommended that the boy be placed in a day program for the emotionally disabled. The boy's mother rejected the placement and requested that the child be placed in a residential school. A due process hearing was held, one month after the school year had ended, and the hearing officer concluded that the team's placement was appropriate. The following year, the parents again sought a residential placement. The hearing officer ruled that a day school placement was appropriate. That decision was not appealed. However, the 1988-89 placement was appealed by the parents to a federal district court.

The school board argued that the issue was moot. The court noted that it could rule on a dispute only if it were clear that a controversy was still in effect or if the court determined that the dispute could arise again. The court noted that there were several factors that led it to the conclusion that it would not arise again. For instance, the child was now thirteen years old and had completed the fifth grade. Since the emotionally disabled day school only enrolled students in grades two through five, there was no reasonable likelihood that the school board could again offer such a placement. Further, the boy's condition had improved significantly and he was no longer a suicide risk. The court noted that although it was conceivable that the parents and the school board would again clash over the needs of the student, the child would never again be offered the same placement. Therefore, the court determined that the issue was moot and dismissed the case. *Greene by Greene v. Harrisville School Dist.*, 771 F.Supp. 1 (D.N.H.1990).

B. Public vs. Private School Placement

Private school placements are made when public schools are unable or unwilling to offer a program responsive and appropriate to a disabled child's unique needs.

A Virginia child was rendered profoundly learning disabled as a result of the surgical removal of a malignant brain tumor and subsequent chemotherapy and radiation therapy. Her school system and her parents agreed on an individualized education program (IEP) which provided that the student would attend a local elementary school with special education resource room support and occupational therapy for her first grade year. Before the start of the year, the parents changed their minds and placed the student at a private school in Washington D.C. Four years later, the parents requested that the school system place and fund the student at the Washington school. However, the school proposed an IEP which called for placement at a local classroom for learning disabled students. The parents objected to the IEP and requested an administrative hearing. The local hearing officer decided in favor of the parents. The board appealed to a state level review officer who found that the board's proposed IEP met the mandates of the Individuals with Disabilities

Education Act (IDEA). The parents then filed suit in a federal district court which affirmed the review officer's decision. The parents then appealed to the U.S. Court of Appeals, Fourth Circuit.

On appeal, the parents argued that the district court did not give proper deference to the factual findings of the local hearing officer. Specifically, they argued that the district court should not have given any weight to the state review officer's decision to discredit a witness whom the hearing officer had relied upon. The court of appeals agreed. The court noted that generally, in reviewing state administrative decisions in IDEA cases, courts are required to make an independent decision based on a preponderance of the evidence, while giving due weight to state administrative proceedings. In order to give due weight to these proceedings, a local hearing officer's findings of fact are entitled to be considered *prima facie* correct, or presumptively valid. If a court chooses not to accept the factual findings it must explain why. In this case, the district court did not do so when it followed the state review officer's decision to discredit the parents' witness. The court remanded the case for further proceedings. *Doyle v. Arlington County School Bd.*, 953 F.2d 100 (4th Cir.1991).

On remand, the district court summarized the many erroneous findings of the local hearing officer. The record reflected that the parents had fully participated in the IEP process and that there had been no procedural defects requiring reversal. There was substantial agreement by the parties about the student's educational goals and objectives. The only disagreement was in regard to placement and the local hearing officer had determined that the private school was superior without a substantial factual basis. The programs offered by both schools were substantially similar in twelve major areas including teacher credentials, student to teacher ratio, one-on-one instruction and instructional resources. The public school placement had the additional advantage of bringing the student into contact with non-disabled students whereas the private school was strictly for disabled students. In this respect, the public school placement was the least restrictive environment under the IDEA. The court entered judgment for the school district. *Doyle v. Arlington County School Bd.*, 806 F.Supp. 1253 (E.D.Va.1992).

A learning disabled student attended school in Mississippi in both public and private institutions. He had extreme difficulty in school and was held back several times. Eventually, he was advanced to the 9th grade to participate in a prevocational program. This meant he was in a certificate track, rather than a diploma track. The student spent three years in the prevocational program. At the end of that time, the school district convened an IEP conference, at which it recommended continuation of the certificate program. The student's mother refused to accept this placement and asked that her son be placed at a private day school instead. The school refused, but did not inform her of her right to a due process hearing under the IDEA. The student's mother then placed her son in the private school. A psychoeducational evaluation of the student was performed. The student was diagnosed as having average cognitive ability but with developmental language disorder and developmental dyslexia, both in the severe range. The private school developed an IEP based on this diagnosis and the mother submitted it to the school district for reconsideration of the private school as an alternative placement. The school district indicated that it was willing to reconvene an IEP conference, and informed the parents of their right to a due process hearing which they immediately sought.

The hearing officer concluded that the appropriate placement was the public schools and, therefore, the parents should not be reimbursed for tuition or related expenses incurred by the private school placement. The parents then appealed to the U.S. District Court, Northern District of Mississippi. The district court noted that in order for the parents to be entitled to reimbursement for the costs of the student's education they must show that the IEP developed by the school district was inappropriate and that the private school placement was appropriate. To determine whether the IEP was appropriate, however, the court needed to discover whether the district complied with the IDEA. The court noted that although the school district had committed procedural errors, including its failure to inform the parents of their due process rights, these shortcomings did not amount to a denial of a free appropriate public education. The decision to place the student in the certificate track was appropriate at the time. The school district provided the student with meaningful educational benefits. Therefore, the school district placement was appropriate, and the parents were not entitled to reimbursement. *Livingston v. DeSoto County School Dist.*, 782 F.Supp. 1173 (N.D.Miss.1992).

An autistic Virginia student attended a private special education school. The local school district paid his tuition. Public school officials developed an IEP which provided for the student's continued attendance at the private school. The student's mother requested that her son be transferred to a neighborhood public school where he could be mainstreamed with nondisabled students. When the district denied the request, the mother initiated an administrative hearing. A hearing officer affirmed the private school placement. The mother appealed the decision to a state reviewing officer who affirmed the placement. She then filed a lawsuit in a federal district court. The court dismissed the lawsuit because, in the interim, another IEP had been developed. The student's mother also contested the second IEP but the placement was affirmed by a local hearing officer and a state reviewing officer. The U.S. Court of Appeals, Fourth Circuit, then remanded the case to the district court to consider the second IEP. In the meantime, the student's mother filed another action in the district court contesting the second IEP. The district court consolidated the cases and held that the student had been properly placed in the private school. The mother appealed the district court's decision to the U.S. Court of Appeals, Fourth Circuit.

The court of appeals held that the IEP complied with EHA requirements. The court noted that the district court had fully considered the EHA's mainstreaming requirements and correctly concluded that the student could not be satisfactorily educated in regular classes even with the use of supplementary aids and services. The IEP which placed the student in the private school provided an appropriate education in the least restrictive environment. The court of appeals affirmed the district court's decision. *Devries by DeBlaay v. Fairfax County School Bd.*, 882 F.2d 876 (4th Cir.1989).

The parents of a learning disabled District of Columbia student requested that he be evaluated for special education services. An IEP meeting was held and the District of Columbia Public Schools (DCPS) assigned the student to a public school program designed for learning disabled students. The student's parents requested a hearing, arguing that a private school was the appropriate placement. The student's parents then enrolled the student at a private school for the 1985-86 school year. Because the hearing officer found that the DCPS had committed procedural violations, and in light of the student's attendance at the private school, the hearing officer ordered the student to remain in the private school for the academic year. All costs incurred were to be paid by the DCPS. The DCPS was to begin to plan for the student's return to a public school for the following school year. In June, the DCPS erroneously sent a letter to the student's parents which stated that the DCPS intended to continue to pay the student's tuition at the private school for the following school year. However, approximately one month later, the DCPS sent a correction letter which stated that the student would be placed at the public school for the following school year. The student's parents then requested a due process hearing to determine whether the DCPS could legally place the student at the public school after issuing the June letter and whether the public school was an appropriate placement for the student. The hearing officer found no procedural violations and found the public school appropriate. The student continued to attend the private school throughout the 1986-87 school year. During this time the student's parents challenged the hearing officer's determination in a federal district court. The district court affirmed the hearing officer's decision and the parents appealed to the U.S. Court of Appeals, District of Columbia Circuit.

The appeals court held that the public school placement was appropriate. There was no prejudice to the parents where they were inadvertently notified that the private school tuition would be paid. The corrective notice was mailed well in advance of the school year. The hearing officer had initially found the public school appropriate and allowed the student to complete the year at the private school only because of the procedural violations committed by the DCPS. The parents were on notice that the private school would cease to be the student's "current educational placement" after the 1985-86 school year. The DCPS was not required to pay for the student's private school tuition while the placement decision was being challenged. The court of appeals affirmed the lower court's decision. *Leonard by Leonard v. McKenzie*, 869 F.2d 1558 (D.C.Cir.1989).

A five-year-old District of Columbia multiply-disabled student was eligible for special education services under the EHA. Her parents requested private special education from the District of Columbia Public Schools (DCPS). They unilaterally placed her in a private daycare center. Each week the student received speech and occupational therapy from an outside source. The DCPS completed an IEP for the student, identifying her as multiply-disabled with motor and speech communication problems. The DCPS placed the student in a public school program for disabled children. The student's parents challenged the public school placement and re-quested two due process hearings. The hearing officer refused to award tuition expenses to the parents, and later determined that the school district's placement was appropriate. The hearing officer also stated that the student's placement at her private daycare program was inappropriate and did not provide the services described in her IEP. The hearing officer held that the DCPS should pay for the student's outside occupational and speech therapy because they were appropriate and because the DCPS had failed to timely place the student.

The parents appealed the decision to the U.S. District Court, District of Columbia, claiming that the DCPS placement was inappropriate. The district court ruled in the parents' favor because the DCPS program was inadequate and the district was completely incapable of providing occupational therapy. The district lacked adequate funding and had a lengthy waiting list for occupational therapy. The court approved the educational alternative proposed by the parents, which was a private special education school in Maryland specializing in educating children with severe sensory integration deficiencies and occupational therapy. The court also awarded attorney's fees to the parents under the EHA. *Kattan by Thomas v. Dist. of Columbia,* 691 F.Supp. 1539 (D.D.C.1988).

A Virginia student was of average to above-average intelligence. Because of a reading disability, however, he was deemed disabled and was eligible for special education services. For five years the student participated in special education programs. The student's progress in improving his reading skills was minimal. In the seventh grade the student was identified as being a nonreader. The county school board recommended the student continue in the same public school special education program for the following school year. The student's parents, however, placed the student at a private school. The student made significant progress in reading during his first year at the private school. A hearing was then conducted by the school board to consider the student's appropriate educational placement for the following school year. The hearing officer concluded that because of the student's lack of progress in reading at the public school, only "exceptional" circumstances would justify a change in placement. The school board appealed to a reviewing officer who upheld the hearing officer's decision. The reviewing officer found the student required residential placement at the private school. The school board challenged the decision of the reviewing officer in a Virginia circuit court. The circuit court reversed the decision of the administrative hearing officer and the student appealed to the Court of Appeals of Virginia.

The appeals court held that the public school had not provided the student with a free and appropriate public education. The student had remained a nonreader after nearly five years in the public school program. The proposed education plan by the public school was a continuation of that which had not benefited the student. The student had demonstrated an ability to learn to read while attending private school which offered a program not available within the public school system or a state facility. The court of appeals reversed the circuit court's decision. *Beasley v. School Bd. of Campbell County,* 367 S.E.2d 738 (Va.App.1988).

Two hearing-impaired Pennsylvania students attended DePaul Institute, a private school that specialized in educating the hearing-impaired. The school district evaluated the students and formulated an IEP for each student. Based on each student's IEP, the school district recommended that one be placed in a special program for the hearing-impaired at a public school and the other placed in a different program for the hearing-impaired at another public school. The students' mother rejected both proposals and requested an administrative hearing regarding the placement of both students. A hearing was held at which the hearing officer agreed with the school district's decision to transfer the students from DePaul. The hearing officer's decision was appealed by the students' mother and affirmed by the secretary of education. The mother rejected the secretary's decision and sued the school district in a federal district court.

The court held that the students were entitled to remain at DePaul. In determining a "free appropriate education" under the EHA, it was necessary to consider the individual requirements of each student along with the potential harm a program change might present. The court found that a change in schools for either student would mean a change in the educational method used to teach them. Both students were making satisfactory progress in their present educational environment and the risks of a program change outweighed the possible benefits. The court ordered the students to continue their education at DePaul. The district was required to continue to fund the students' education at DePaul. *Visco by Visco v. School Dist. of Pittsburgh*, 684 F.Supp. 1310 (W.D.Pa.1988).

An Alabama student was injured in an automobile accident which resulted in physical and emotional problems. She was placed in several public and private schools with marginal success. Her mother requested that the board of education suggest an appropriate placement for the student. The board recommended that she be enrolled at a public high school. While at the school, she attempted suicide by drug overdose. The student's doctor then recommended placement at a private facility where she could receive twenty-four-hour therapeutic and educational services. Her mother again asked the school board to propose an appropriate placement for the student. The mother rejected the board's proposal of public school placement and requested a hearing to determine whether the board was obligated to pay for the student's care at the private facility. The hearing officer upheld the student's current placement. Its decision was affirmed by a state administrative review officer. While the administrative proceedings were pending, the student had returned home. Thereafter, the board filed a lawsuit against the student under the Education of the Handicapped Act in a federal district court, seeking to place the student in a state mental hospital. The district court found for the student and the board appealed to the U.S. Court of Appeals, Eleventh Circuit.

The court of appeals held that the state mental hospital lacked the facilities to provide the student with an appropriate education. The private facility, however, provided the student with the educational and support services she needed. The board was required to reimburse the mother for the private facility expenses. The court also found that the student was entitled to two additional years of compensatory education to preserve the student's right to a free education. This was necessary because the board had failed to provide an appropriate education prior to the court's order. The court of appeals affirmed the trial court's decision. *Jefferson County Bd. of Educ. v. Breen*, 853 F.2d 853 (11th Cir.1988).

The U.S. Court of Appeals, Fourth Circuit, held that a Maryland school district was under no duty to consider private school placement where an appropriate public education could be provided. In this case, a student with disabilities and her parents brought suit seeking tuition reimbursement when the parents placed their child in a private school, which they deemed a more appropriate placement than that offered by their county board of education. They contended that the county board improperly failed to consider placing their child in a private school when formulating a special education program for her.

The court noted that, while state law permits placement of students with disabilities in an appropriate nonpublic educational program, such a placement is limited to those instances in which public educational services appropriate for the disabled child are not available. Thus, under EHA regulations, the duty of a state to pay for nonpublic schooling does not attach "if the [disabled] child has available a free appropriate public education and the parents choose to place the child in a private school or facility. . . ." Of course, parents retain the right to challenge the placement. In this case such a challenge resulted in the state board of education upholding the public school placement. *Hessler v. State Bd. of Educ. of Maryland*, 700 F.2d 134 (4th Cir.1983).

In a Rhode Island case, a U.S. district court found that a proposed public school placement of two learning disabled children violated the children's right to a free appropriate education. The proposed placement involved pupil/teacher ratios possibly as high as ten to one and provided for some mainstreaming. The children's father brought suit against the school district which had made the placement decision seeking a permanent injunction compelling the district to fund the children's placement at a private residential school.

The district court, persuaded by evidence that the children were severely learning disabled and that both children had significant accompanying emotional problems, found that the district's proposal to educate the children in a "self-contained" classroom for learning disabled children would not serve the children's needs and that only a residential placement would provide the children with the type of education anticipated by the EHA. The school district appealed the case to the U.S. Court of Appeals, First Circuit, which upheld the district court ruling. *Colin K. by John K. v. Schmidt*, 715 F.2d 1 (1st Cir.1983).

C. Residential vs. Day School Placement

Missouri parents of a student with personality disorders and mental impairment sought placement of their son in a residential education program to be funded by the school district. During a bench trial, the school district and parents agreed on an educational plan. Litigation did not continue, although the court proceeded to monitor the program. Additionally, the court rejected the parents' claim under the IDEA and the Rehabilitation Act that their son was not receiving a free, appropriate education to which he was entitled. Two years later, the court lifted the duty to provide educational services from the school district as a result of the student reaching the age of twenty-one. Additionally, the court affirmed its earlier ruling against claims under the IDEA and Rehabilitation Act. The parents appealed to the U.S. Court of Appeals, Eighth Circuit, arguing that the district court did not have jurisdiction in the second set of rulings because the agreement by the parties on an educational plan divested the court of jurisdiction over the legal issues of the case. The appellate court affirmed the lower court, holding that the "court continues to have jurisdiction over those controversies which remain alive." The trial court had properly retained jurisdiction over the issues and issued decisions to provide closure to the litigation. *Koester v. Wellsville-Middletown R-1 School Dist.*, 960 F.2d 69 (8th Cir.1992).

A Nebraska child with a developmental age of six months attended a residential school and the school district of the parents' residence paid for the educational services. When the child was six years old, the school district changed her IEP to an at-home placement with a nine-month school year. The child's mother contested the IEP and the hearing officer found that the child required a year-round educational placement but did not require residential care. A Nebraska trial court agreed and both parties appealed to the Supreme Court of Nebraska. On appeal, the supreme court affirmed the decision of the trial court noting that the child would certainly regress during the three months that educational services were not offered. The court also noted that since residential placement was not required to allow the child to benefit educationally, it was not required under the EHA. The court affirmed the decision of the trial court. *Williams v. Gering Public Schools*, 463 N.W.2d 799 (Neb.1990).

A Massachusetts school proposed an IEP which called for a disabled student to attend a day school program. The parents consented to the IEP. The school prepared a new IEP for the following school year which provided that the student continue his education at the day school. The student's parents rejected the proposed IEP and requested that the student be placed in a residential program. The parents then requested the state bureau of special education appeals to determine whether the recommended IEP was the least restrictive adequate and appropriate placement for the student. Meanwhile, the parents enrolled their son in an unapproved Arizona residential program. The bureau found that the school's proposed IEP provided an appropriate educational placement. The bureau denied the parents' request for reimbursement for the prior unapproved residential placement costs as the facility was not an "approved school."

The parents sued the Commissioner of Education in a Massachusetts trial court. The parents then moved for summary judgment, seeking reimbursement for the student's educational costs. The court denied the motion and found that reimbursement was unauthorized because the placement was not at an approved school. The parents appealed the decision and were granted direct review by the Supreme Judicial Court of Massachusetts. The court found that the bureau could order reimbursement when a student was placed in an unapproved school while contesting his IEP. The Arizona school was an appropriate school, although it was not a state approved school. The bureau had only specified the type of program for the student. The case was reversed and remanded to the bureau for further proceedings to determine if equity required reimbursement. *Carrington v. Comm'r of Educ.*, 535 N.E.2d 212 (Mass.1989).

An autistic and severely mentally retarded student attended a special education program in a Georgia school. The student's parents withdrew him from the school and placed him in a residential center for the severely mentally retarded. While at the center the student was evaluated and it was determined that he should be placed in a residential center with facilities for autistic children. The school district refused to pay for the student's placement. The student's parents requested an administrative hearing. A regional hearing officer found that the student did not require residential placement in a facility for autistic children and denied reimbursement for the center's costs. The parents appealed to a state hearing officer who affirmed the regional officer's decision. The student's parents then sued the school district in a federal district court. In the meantime, the student was placed in a residential center for autistic children in Tokyo, Japan. Thereafter he was transferred to a Boston sister school. The district court held that the student's educational needs had not been met by the Georgia school district. The court ordered the district to provide the student with residential treatment in a facility for autistic children until the age of twenty-one, and reimbursement for past educational expenses and attorney's fees. The district appealed to the U.S. Court of Appeals, Eleventh Circuit.

The court held that the student needed placement in a residential treatment facility for autistic children in order to provide him with a setting in which he could receive an educational benefit. The court further held that the student's parents should be reimbursed for past private school placement expenses in the Tokyo and Boston facilities and for their attorney's fees. The court noted that reimbursement was proper under the EHA if the court determined that the student's placement was proper. The student's parents were justified in placing him in the residential facilities for autistic children. The court further noted that if at the yearly IEP meeting the school district demonstrated that the student no longer needed residential placement, a new IEP reflecting this decision would control. The court of appeals affirmed the district court's decision. *Drew P. v. Clarke County School Dist.*, 877 F.2d 927 (11th Cir.1989).

A Virginia student suffered serious emotional disabilities such as lack of self-esteem and an inability to check his aggressive impulses or accept responsibility for his actions. His performance on various tests placed him in the low-average range of intelligence. School reports and tests indicated that the boy performed well in reading but was learning disabled in math. After a circuit court reversed an administrative decision which suggested residential placement for him, his parents appealed to the state court of appeals. In December 1983, the boy's parents had requested that the local school board place the boy in a residential setting with special education services. In March 1984, the local school proposed an IEP of segregated emotionally disturbed instruction in one of the local schools. The boy's parents rejected the proposal and requested a due process hearing. The hearing officer ruled that the local school's proposed placement was deficient and suggested that the boy be placed in a residential setting. On appeal, the court of appeals ruled that the hearing officer's concern, well-intended as it was, improperly focused on the total social and behavioral needs of the boy. The local school was not required to address social and psychological problems. By offering the boy a placement in a self-contained classroom for emotionally disturbed students, the school district had met its obligations under both the EHA and Virginia law. The court of appeals affirmed the circuit court decision. *Martin v. School Bd. of Prince George County*, 348 S.E.2d 857 (Va.App.1986).

A Washington, D.C., student who was severely retarded attended a private residential facility in Pennsylvania. The parents then moved to Washington, D.C. Before their move, they informed the new school district of their plans to seek special education for their son. As required by the EHA, the school officials formulated an IEP for the boy. They determined that a day placement at a public school would be appropriate. The parents disagreed and they presented evidence to a hearing officer who concluded that the student did not require a residential program. She found that his IEP required revision to incorporate certain specific services and to provide him with an extended day program. Both parties opposed the new program and a second hearing was held. Although the hearing officer recognized that the student could benefit from residential placement, she determined that the IEP proposed by the school would meet the requirements of the EHA. The parents sued in a federal district court. After a bench trial, the district court agreed that the student required a residential facility. The school district appealed and the court of appeals reversed and remanded. On remand, the district court concluded that a residential placement was necessary. Again the school district appealed to the U.S. Court of Appeals, District of Columbia Circuit.

On appeal, the court determined that the trial court had given insufficient weight to the findings of the hearing officer. Further, the court concluded that a residential placement far from home was more restrictive than a local extended day program. Therefore, the court concluded that the local extended day program offered by the school district met the standards of the EHA, even if the student may have made increased educational progress at the residential facility. The appellate court reversed the decision of the trial court. *Kerkham v. Supt., D.C. Public Schools*, 931 F.2d 84 (D.C.Cir.1991).

An emotionally disabled Alabama twelve-year-old boy received educational placements designed to address his behavioral difficulties. He was placed in the Davis Learning Center, a public school offering only special education programs. He made substantial progress during the year and had no major behavioral incidents. He was then mainstreamed into a public school with some behavioral classes. He had a number of behavioral incidents including a few in which the police were called to restrain him. He was then returned to the Davis Learning Center. He again had many behavioral incidents in which the police were called. His mother requested that the school place the boy in a residential school. The school refused, instead offering either homebound instruction or a return to the learning disabled school. The mother sued the board in a federal district court. All parties agreed that the placement of the child in the Davis Learning Center was inappropriate. The child had behavioral problems only in the classroom. Therefore, the intervention must take place in these settings in order to be effective. The court ruled that the homebound instruction would be ineffective since there would be no students around and the behavioral problems would not occur. It then determined that the residential school would meet the requirements of the EHA. The court ordered the school to place the student in a residential school. *Chris D. v. Montgomery County Bd. of Educ.*, 743 F.Supp. 1524 (M.D.Ala.1990).

A Tennessee student suffered from brain damage since birth and was afflicted with a serious emotional disturbance and mental retardation. Her condition was aggravated by a severe behavioral disorder which caused bizarre and uncontrollable outbursts endangering both herself and others. Since an effective residential program could not be found, the student's IEP consisted of homebound instruction. The student's parents learned of a residential rehabilitation facility in Tennessee for brain injury victims. After placement in the program, the student's behavior improved significantly.

After the parents were denied reimbursement, they instituted this action in a federal trial court. The court determined that the IEP offered by the district did not provide educational benefit to the student. The student had deteriorated rather than benefitted under the IEP which consisted of three hours per week of homebound instruction. The issue in determining the appropriateness of the residential placement was whether it was educational or medical in nature. The occupational therapy, psychological services, recreational therapy, physical therapy and medical evaluations provided were all specifically listed as special education and related services in the EHA. Therefore, the residential placement was educational and not medical in nature. Finally, the court determined that the school district was not required to provide compensatory education. *Brown v. Wilson County School Bd.*, 747 F.Supp. 436 (E.D.Tenn.1990).

In Massachusetts, the parents of a seventeen-year-old child with Down's Syndrome became dissatisfied with their child's IEP because they felt it did not adequately address his sexual misbehavior. The child, who had been receiving special educational services from his public school system in a highly structured day school program, exhibited no significant behavioral problems during the school day. However, after school he appeared preoccupied with sex, touching young girls in an inappropriate manner and attempting to sexually abuse animals. The boy's parents believed that in order to correct this misbehavior and instill in the child proper attitudes toward sex, thus enabling him to enter into private employment as an adult, the child required a twenty-four-hour residential program. School officials rejected this proposal, stating that the child was progressing satisfactorily at school and that his sexual misbehavior after school did not mandate his placement in a residential facility. They agreed to address the parents' concerns only by adding individual therapy and family counseling to the child's IEP. After a hearing officer ruled in favor of the school district the parents brought suit in U.S. district court. Reversing the hearing officer's decision, the court found that under the EHA, the child was entitled to twenty-four-hour residential school placement to attempt to correct his sexual misbehavior. The court noted that under Massachusetts law a special educational program must "assure the maximum possible development of a child with special needs." Accordingly, the child was entitled to the more comprehensive behavior therapy available in a residential program, especially in light of the degree of his sexual maladjustment.

The school district appealed to the U.S. Court of Appeals, First Circuit, contending that the district court had erroneously applied the requirements of Massachusetts state law to the case. This argument was rejected by the court of appeals. Where state law sets a minimum educational standard for children with disabilities, those standards are incorporated by reference into the EHA. Thus a Massachusetts child suing a school district will be able to hold it to the same educational standards regardless of whether the suit is brought in state or federal court. The court of appeals approved the federal district court's application of Massachusetts law, and the residential placement was upheld. *David D. v. Dartmouth School Comm.*, 775 F.2d 411 (1st Cir.1985), *U.S. cert. denied*, 106 S.Ct.1790 (1986).

The parents of a child with a disability challenged a local school district's decision denying tuition funding for residential placement of their child. The parents argued that a free appropriate education would not meet their child's needs unless it were a twenty-four-hour residential program. A U.S. district court in Delaware disagreed with the parents and held that the educational program offered by the public school system could provide an adequate free appropriate public education. The court found that although the child was better off emotionally because of her attendance at a private facility, the school district offered a free appropriate program which could confer educational benefits. The court also held that delays in the administrative and due process hearings did not violate the parents' right to due process and that there was no due process violation in the school district's unilateral appointment of a hearing officer and the seating of educators as hearing officers. The court held in favor of the school district. *Ahren v. Keene*, 593 F.Supp. 902 (D.Del.1984).

An Oregon child was diagnosed with infantile autism. The child's parents had received notices from the school board notifying them of their rights. The child's behavior deteriorated and he began to have tantrums every day. His psychiatrist and parents then decided to place him in a residential facility for autistic children in Japan. He was later transferred to a companion school in Boston where he remained at the time of this case. After four years, the parents contacted the school district about the possibility of reimbursement of the expenses incurred in sending their son to the Boston school. The school district maintained that it had no liability until it could complete an evaluation of the boy. The parents allowed an evaluation which resulted in an IEP recommending a special self-contained classroom at a nearby school. The parents instituted a due process hearing asking for tuition reimbursement and residential placement. The hearing officer determined that the IEP was appropriate, and further stated that although the boy could better maintain harmony with his family through a residential placement, he did not require residential placement in order to gain meaningful benefit from his education. The parents then instituted this action in a federal trial court. The trial court ordered reimbursement for the costs of providing the child with a residential placement when the school district's duty arose. That duty arose in September 1989, when the school district had been asked to provide educational services to the student and had been given a reasonable opportunity to complete the process of evaluating him. The court further determined that the parties must reach a mutually acceptable arrangement that would provide a residential placement for the student at a reasonable cost to the school district. *Ash v. Lake Oswego School Dist. No. 7J*, 766 F.Supp. 852 (D.Or.1991).

The school district appealed to the U.S. Court of Appeals, Ninth Circuit, arguing that the district court had failed to give adequate consideration to the state administrative hearing officer's findings, which stated that the student did not require residential placement. The district argued that the court's factual findings were in error because its expert determined that the student's learning deficiencies reflected nonconventional classroom skills such as toileting, eating and dressing. The parents cross-appealed, arguing that they were entitled to reimbursement for the period prior to September 1989, when they had first requested services from the school district. The court of appeals found no error in the district court's decision. The court had applied the appropriate legal and evidentiary standards in ruling that the district's IEP denied the student a free appropriate education. The court of appeals affirmed the district court's determination that the student was incapable of deriving educational benefits outside a residential placement. However, the parents had no right to reimbursement prior to their first request to the school district for services in September 1989, because any procedural deficiencies by the district to that point had not denied the student a free appropriate public education. The court also awarded the parents their requested attorney's fees. *Ash v. Lake Oswego School Dist.*, 980 F.2d 585 (9th Cir.1992).

The U.S. Court of Appeals, First Circuit, has affirmed a U.S. district court decision which upheld the right to a residential education program where an alternative public school program failed to meet a disabled child's particular needs. The parents of a severely retarded child in Massachusetts brought suit under the EHA, challenging the school district's placement of their child in a day school training program. The parents sought residential placement as well as a day educational program. When the parents' proposal was rejected, they appealed to the Massachusetts Bureau of Special Education Appeals. It found that the day school training would provide an appropriate education and that, while the child required residential care, such needs were not "educational" under the EHA, and thus not the responsibility of the school board.

The court of appeals disagreed, saying that the only way this child would make any educational progress would be through a combined day school and residential program. The court noted that under EHA regulations, if a public or private residential program (including nonmedical care and room and board) is necessary in order to provide services to a child with a disability, such services must be provided at no cost to the parents of the child. Here, the lower court properly concluded that not only would the child fail to make educational progress without a residential program, he would very likely regress without one. The combined day school-residential placement was upheld. *Abrahamson v. Hershman*, 701 F.2d 223 (1st Cir.1983).

The allegedly inordinate cost of residential placement, according to a U.S. district court in Illinois, did not preclude it from being the appropriate placement. This case arose after a hearing officer exonerated an Illinois school district from liability for all but "purely educational" expenses of a severely multiply disabled child and determined that residential expenses should be borne by another agency. The child's mother responded to this determination by placing the child in a residential school in Kansas. She then brought suit against state educational officials seeking an injunction to prohibit the district from adhering to its policy of distinguishing between "educational" and "noneducational" components of "related services" needed to enable children with disabilities to perform adequately in school. The court, finding that the child could be best served by placement in a residential facility, ordered the school district to fund the child's placement at the school in Kansas. *William S. v. Gill*, 572 F.Supp. 509 (E.D.Ill.1983).

Where a state elects to provide state-subsidized residential care for disabled children, the U.S. Court of Appeals, Second Circuit, has held that the state may require the parents of the children to transfer temporary custody of the children to the state. The parents in this case claimed that the temporary custody transfer requirement violated their right to privacy and family integrity without sufficient justification and that it discriminated against children with disabilities solely on the basis of their disabilities. The court of appeals, in upholding New York's custody transfer requirement, placed great emphasis on the voluntary nature of New York's benefits program and stressed that the state, while under no constitutional obligation to provide residential treatment for disabled children, elected to do so. Consequently when the state provided voluntary social services, it could administer the program without having to consult and satisfy the individual concerns of each of the recipients.

The court dealt with the disability discrimination issue by saying that "*all* parents whose children need state-subsidized home substitutes must transfer custody to the state, regardless of whether the child is or is not disabled." Therefore, New York's foster care scheme discriminated between children only as to the type of assistance needed and not solely on the basis of their disabilities. The court upheld the constitutionality of the New York law. *Joyner By Lowry v. Dumpson*, 712 F.2d 770 (2d Cir.1983).

Residential placement was held to be inappropriate for a profoundly disabled child in the following Virginia case. The child's parents asked the U.S. Court of Appeals, Fourth Circuit, to reverse certain administrative decisions made by a local school district and to issue both a preliminary and permanent injunction requiring the state of Virginia and county school officials to provide a twenty-four-hour residential placement for their son. The child had been placed in a residential program but local school officials later recommended that the child be placed in a day education program and live at home. The parents rejected this decision and applied for tuition assistance for the residential school. Tuition assistance was denied by a county special education committee on the ground that the day program could meet the child's needs.

The parents appealed to the Superintendent of Public Education of the Commonwealth of Virginia, who concurred in the committee's decision. After exhausting their administrative remedies, the parents brought suit in a U.S. district court, which released the school district from its obligation to provide twenty-four-hour residential care and education for the child.

The child and his parents appealed to the U.S. Court of Appeals, which upheld the district court ruling. The court of appeals was persuaded by testimony which indicated that the child had reached the point in his education at which a continuation of the residential program would at best yield only marginal results and probably none at all. Testimony by the school district's witnesses also indicated that basic living skills could easily be taught at home by teaching the child's family the cues the child had developed for implementing such skills. *Matthews v. Davis*, 742 F.2d 825 (4th Cir.1984).

III. CONTAGIOUS DISEASES AND PLACEMENT

In *School Board of Nassau County v. Arline*, 107 S.Ct. 1123 (1987), the U.S. Supreme Court ruled that tuberculosis (and any other contagious disease, such as AIDS) is a "disability" under § 504 of the Rehabilitation Act so long as the individual suffers some physical impairment from the disease. The Court refused to accept the school board's argument that the teacher was not protected by § 504 because her tuberculosis was contagious and therefore dangerous to her students. The Court remanded the case to the U.S. district court to determine if the teacher was "otherwise qualified" for her job. In light of *Arline*, students with AIDS should be considered disabled under § 504 and cannot "solely by reason of their disability, be excluded from participation in any program receiving federal financial assistance."

Courts have generally held that students with AIDS are disabled and must be admitted to public school programs if their enrollment is not a health threat to the school community. A federal district court held that three brothers who were hemophiliacs and who had tested positive for the HIV virus could not be excluded from public school classes. The school district contended that although no actual physical harm had been done to their classmates or teachers due to the brothers' class attendance, there was the possibility of future harm. This future harm allegedly included transmission of the HIV virus in the classroom setting and liability of the school district for allowing the brothers to attend the classes.

The court also cited the Supreme Court's decision in *School Board of Nassau County v. Arline*, 480 U.S. 273, 107 S.Ct. 1123, 94 L.Ed.2d 307 (1987). In *Arline*, the Supreme Court held that tuberculosis was a disability under § 504 of the Rehabilitation Act of 1973. The district court in the present case held that the HIV virus was also a disability within the meaning of § 504. Because § 504 prohibits recipients of federal funds from discriminating against the disabled solely because of their disability, the school district could not exclude the three brothers from class. *Ray v. School Dist. of Desoto County*, 666 F.Supp. 1524 (N.D.Fla.1987).

A girl born with respiratory distress received 39 blood transfusions during the first four months of her life and was diagnosed as having AIDS-Related Complex

(ARC) at the age of three. The girl was evaluated as having significant neurological impairment. It was not known how much damage was due to ARC, an AIDS precursor. The girl had attended schools for the disabled prior to the ARC diagnosis and spent parts of two years in healthcare facilities. She was classified as trainable mentally handicapped (TMH). At the age of six the girl had a mental age of between one and one-half years in expressive language and three and one-half years in perceptual motor skills. The girl was incontinent and was observed by doctors to drool and suck her thumb continually. In the past the girl had developed skin lesions. When these occurred, her mother kept her home. When the girl approached school age her mother attempted to enroll her in a Florida public school. The school district operated two schools which each maintained classes for TMH children. However, the school district excluded the girl from public schools based upon her incontinence. The school district recommended that the girl be educated in its homebound program.

The girl appealed to the Florida State Division of Administrative Hearings. The school district prevailed after an evidentiary hearing. The administrative decision was appealed to a federal district court which held in favor of the school district. The court stated that to grant an order to enroll the girl in public school it would have to find that she was likely to prevail on the merits of her claim, that her claimed injuries were irreparable and that others attending the school would not be harmed. *Martinez v. School Bd. of Hillsborough County, Florida*, 675 F.Supp. 1574 (M.D.Fla.1987).

In 1988, the U.S. District Court for the Middle District of Florida held a full trial on the matter of placing the student. The court allowed the student to join the school's TMH classroom with heavy restrictions. The court noted that the student was still incontinent and sucked her thumb and fingers continuously. Because there was a remote theoretical possibility of transmitting AIDS through bodily secretions the court again ruled that the student could not be mainstreamed. The court ordered the school district to construct a separate room within the TMH classroom conforming to the court's order. The separate room was to be no less than six by eight feet and secure from intrusions. It was also required to provide a clear view of the main classroom through a large picture window, with an adequate sound system so that the occupant could hear everything occurring in the main classroom. The room was also to be equipped with toilet facilities, an appropriate work area, and necessary furniture. The school board was also required to provide a full-time aide to remain with the student in her room at all times. Other children in the TMH class who had written parental waivers could be allowed into the separate room during class time. *Martinez v. School Bd. of Hillsboro County, Fla.*, 692 F.Supp. 1293 (M.D.Fla.1988).

The student's mother then appealed to the U.S. Court of Appeals, Eleventh Circuit. The court first determined that the student in this case was entitled to a free appropriate education under the EHA. She suffered from two disabilities under § 504 as she was both mentally retarded and had AIDS. The appropriate educational placement was the regular TMH classroom. The district court's finding of a "remote theoretical possibility" of transmission of AIDS was insufficient to exclude her from the TMH classroom. Because the district court had failed to make findings concerning the overall risk of transmitting AIDS through bodily secretions, it had failed to determine whether the student was "otherwise qualified" to attend the TMH classroom. If the court found on remand that the student was not "otherwise qualified" to attend the TMH classroom, it was bound to consider whether reasonable accommodations would qualify her. The lower court would also be required to hear evidence concerning the stigmatizing effect of segregating the student in a separate room. The appeals court vacated the district court's decision and remanded the case for rehearing. *Martinez v. School Bd. of Hillsboro County, Fla.*, 861 F.2d 1502 (11th Cir.1988).

On remand, the court noted that the American Academy of Pediatrics had eliminated its recommendation that students who could not control their bodily secretions be placed in more restrictive environments. It also noted that the Center for Disease Control had stated that the risk of transmission of HIV and HBV from feces, nasal secretion, saliva, sweat, tears, urine and vomit was extremely low or nonexistent unless visible blood was actually present. The student's behavior had changed since the initial consideration of the case. She sucked her fingers less often and was becoming toilet trained. The court ruled that the student could join the TMH classroom. The student was otherwise qualified to attend the TMH classroom which was therefore the most appropriate placement under the EHA. The court also required the school board to provide an educational program for parents whose children would be in the classroom. *Martinez v. School Bd. of Hillsborough County, Fla.*, 711 F.Supp. 1066 (M.D.Fla.1989). In 1989, Eliana Martinez died at the age of six from complications attributable to her affliction with AIDS.

A twelve-year-old student contracted the AIDS virus through blood transfusions when he had undergone open-heart surgery as a child. When the board of education of an Illinois school district learned that the student was infected with the AIDS virus, it excluded him from attending the school's regular education classes and extracurricular activities. The student filed a complaint in a federal district court, seeking an order to allow him to return to his regular classes as a full-time student. The student's claim was primarily based on § 504 of the Rehabilitation Act of 1973. In order for the student to prevail under this section, he had to be a "handicapped individual" and "otherwise qualified" to attend school.

The court found that the student would likely be considered an individual with a disability. As an AIDS victim, he was regarded as being impaired and this impairment substantially limited one or more of the student's major life activities. The court also deemed the student "otherwise qualified" to attend school. Medical authorities found no significant risk of transmission of AIDS in the classroom setting. The court found that the student had been harmed by loss of self-esteem which could be partially alleviated by returning him to the normal classroom environment. Any injury that might occur by issuing the order was insufficient to outweigh the harm to the student. In addition, the public interest would not be disserved by allowing the student to return to school since the threat of the student transmitting the AIDS virus to others was minimal. The court held that the student was entitled to return to school. The court also required carefully-drawn procedures to ensure that any potential risk of harm to the student's classmates and teachers was eliminated. *Doe v. Dolton Elementary School Dist. No. 148*, 694 F.Supp. 440 (N.D.Ill.1988).

A California school district learned that an eleven-year-old hemophilic student in the district had been exposed to the AIDS virus. The district instructed the student not to enroll in school and required him to study at home until the district formulated an AIDS policy. The student's guardian was unhappy with the home tutor program and repeatedly requested to have the student returned to regular classes. On each occasion the district told her that the student could not attend school until an AIDS policy had been formulated. The guardian filed a complaint in a California trial court, seeking both a preliminary and permanent order to allow the student to return to school. The guardian also sought attorney's fees. The school district stated that it was developing an AIDS policy and requested verification from the student's doctor and county health officials that his attendance at school would pose no health risk to students or staff members. Meanwhile, the guardian filed a motion for a temporary order and a permanent order for the student's admittance to school. The court ordered the school district to allow the student to attend a regular school within its district, subject to its evaluation of his medical condition every six months. Shortly after the court's order, the district's policy on AIDS and infectious diseases became effective. The matter then proceeded to trial where the court found for the guardian. An order was granted which required the school district to allow the student to attend a regular school, subject to periodic medical examinations. The guardian was also awarded attorney's fees. The school district appealed the decision to the California Court of Appeal, Fourth District.

On appeal, the school district argued that the trial court abused its discretion in issuing a permanent order. It insisted that a permanent order was not necessary because the student had been attending school. Alternatively it contended that even if the order was proper, attorney's fees were not warranted. The court of appeal ruled that the district had unreasonably delayed the formulation of its AIDS policy for more than five months. The permanent order was proper even though the school district had decided to allow the student to attend class. The record suggested that the student was allowed to attend solely because it was mandated by the court order. The court also found that attorney's fees were appropriately awarded as the lawsuit was instrumental in motivating the school district to address the issue of AIDS and to effectuate an appropriate policy without impairing the rights of students. *Phipps v. Saddleback Valley Unified School Dist.*, 251 Cal.Rptr. 720 (App.4th Dist.1988).

A seven-year-old hemophilic student was diagnosed as having AIDS-related complex (ARC). Prior to enrollment in public kindergarten his mother requested home instruction, as she believed mainstreaming would be inappropriate. After conducting a home instruction evaluation, the school district agreed. It developed an individualized educational program (IEP) for the student in compliance with the EHA and Illinois education statutes. After the school year began, the mother requested mainstreaming for her son. The school district placed the student in a separate "modular" classroom where he was the only student. It refused to mainstream the student even after an Illinois federal district court ordered mainstreaming of another AIDS-afflicted child.

The mother filed a lawsuit against the school district in a federal district court. She sought an order to declare the district in violation of the Rehabilitation Act and the Equal Protection Clause. The district argued that the student had failed to exhaust his EHA administrative remedies. The court noted that the EHA applied to ARC victims only if the condition affected their classroom performance and ability to learn. The district's IEP stated that the student's learning and behavioral problems were not the result of ARC. Because his learning and behavioral problems did not result from his condition, he was not "disabled" under the EHA. The court noted the considerable harm done to the student by placing him in a separate classroom. He did not pose any significant health threat to others at the school. A trial would commence on the issue of the Rehabilitation Act violation. In the meantime, the court ordered the district to mainstream the student. *Robertson v. Granite City Comm. School Dist. No. 9*, 684 F.Supp. 1002 (S.D.Ill.1988).

An Oklahoma hemophilic child tested positive for the HIV virus (AIDS) and was disabled within the meaning of the EHA due to his emotional disorders. A placement team determined that a placement within the emotionally disturbed class of his local public school was the least restrictive environment for him. A group of parents whose children attended the child's school sought a temporary restraining order from a state court to prevent his class attendance. They sought to bar the child from school on the basis of a state law regarding contagious diseases. The child's parents then asked a U.S. district court to disallow the temporary restraining order. The court held for the child's parents. When states accept federal funding as in this case, they accept limitations or restrictions on state statutes or regulations which conflict with federal statutes. Because the child was disabled under the EHA due to his emotional disability, the court did not need to address the issue of whether AIDS was a disability. Procedures were conducted under the EHA between the local school district and the child's parents, resulting in an unappealed placement decision. That decision was enforced by the court. The child could attend class. *Parents of Child, Code No. 870901W v. Coker*, 676 F.Supp. 1072 (E.D.Okl.1987).

After a kindergarten boy, who was infected with the AIDS virus, bit a fellow student's pant leg, his California school district instructed the boy's parents to keep him at home until the school district considered "whether his potential for again biting another student posed any danger to the health of others in the class." Following an examination a psychologist determined that the boy would behave aggressively in a kindergarten setting. The school district then recommended that the boy be kept out of class and in home tutoring for the rest of the academic year. The boy's parents sued the school district in a U.S. district court seeking an order allowing the boy to attend his kindergarten class.

The court observed that the boy was "disabled" within the meaning of § 504 of the Rehabilitation Act of 1973. It also noted that the school district had failed to demonstrate that he was not "otherwise qualified" to attend kindergarten. Specifically, the school district had failed to prove that the AIDS virus could be transmitted in the classroom setting through biting or otherwise. Therefore, it could not exclude the boy from his kindergarten class on the ground that he posed a risk of transmission of the AIDS virus to his classmates or teachers. The court also observed that the boy had been subjected to discrimination and had been excluded from class solely because of his disability. Section 504 triggered statutory protection for the boy. The court ordered the school district to allow him to attend his regular kindergarten class once again. *Thomas v. Atascadero Unified School Dist.*, 662 F.Supp. 376 (C.D.Cal.1987).

The Appellate Court of Illinois considered the question of what is the appropriate educational placement of a trainable mentally disabled child with Down's Syndrome who was also a carrier of an infectious disease, Hepatitis Type B. Local school officials contended that because of the risk of the child transmitting the disease to other children, the appropriate placement for her was in a "homebound" setting. The child maintained that the risk of transmission of the disease was remote and therefore not a sufficient reason to exclude her from classroom participation. A hearing officer, the State Superintendent of Education and a lower court agreed with the child. So did the Appellate Court of Illinois. The question on appeal was whether the child's homebound placement was mandated by the school district's health and safety obligations to its students so that she was being educated in the least restrictive environment as required by Illinois law and the EHA. The court held it was not. Using the *Rowley* case as its guide, the court first noted that the trial court gave due deference to the state agency's determination of educational policy under the present circumstances. Next, the court noted that there is a strong congressional preference in favor of mainstreaming wherever possible. A major goal of the educational process is the socialization process that takes place in the regular classroom, with the resulting capacity to interact in a social way with one's peers. The superintendent of education recognized this and determined that the risk of transmission of the disease did not outweigh the injury to the child if she remained isolated from her peers. After a thorough examination of the testimony of expert witnesses, the court concluded that the trial court's decision was not against the manifest weight of the evidence and thus the child could be integrated into the classroom if appropriate sanitary procedures were followed. *Comm. High School Dist. 155 v. Denz*, 463 N.E.2d 998 (Ill.App.1984).

IV. CHANGES IN PLACEMENT

Recognizing that a school district's unfettered discretion to change a disabled child's placement could result in a denial of a free appropriate education to the child, IDEA § 1415(b)(1)(C) requires that prior written notice of any proposed change in the educational placement of a child be afforded to the parents or guardians of the child. A hearing must be granted to parents wishing to contest a change in placement of their child. Under the IDEA "stay-put" provision, school officials are prevented from removing a child from his or her current placement over the parents' objection pending completion of review proceedings.

A severely mentally retarded Louisiana child was transferred from one school to another. Her parents were dissatisfied with the quality of education at the new school and with their daughter's progress. They placed her at a private residential facility and initiated an administrative hearing. The hearing officer ordered payment of the child's expenses for the year but ruled in favor of the school district as to future placement. Both parties appealed to the Louisiana Board of Elementary and Secondary Education (LBESE) which reversed that portion of the decision in favor of the parents and affirmed the ruling in favor of the school district. After a federal district court affirmed the LBESE's decision, the parents appealed to the U.S. Court of Appeals, Fifth Circuit.

The court noted that there was not an adequate record of why the child was transferred. The court was informed only that the transfer was for reasons beyond the control of the school. The parents were first informed when they heard the news report on television. Upon calling the school they were informed of the transfer. Also, there was no prior written notice. The EHA provides that the school district must notify the parents of a proposed change in educational placement of their child. However, the court noted that both schools were under the district's control and provided similar classes. Further, they both implemented the same IEP for the child. Therefore, the court concluded that the transfer was not a change in placement and the school did not have to comply with the notice requirements to the parents. The court further disallowed reimbursement expenses to the parents for the private residential placement. The decision of the trial court was affirmed. *Weil v. Bd. of Elementary and Secondary Educ.*, 931 F.2d 1069 (5th Cir.1991).

A Texas girl suffered from deafness, blindness, and mental retardation. She functioned cognitively at the level of a small child (less than two years old). In 1978, her local public school district decided to place her at the Texas School for the Blind and Visually Impaired, the only residential institution in Texas established for the specific purpose of educating blind and visually impaired people at public expense until they reached age twenty-two. In 1985, the school and the Texas Education Agency developed new eligibility criteria for students at the school, and a committee determined that the student did not meet the criteria. The committee recommended that the student be returned to a community placement and educated by her local school district. However, the school district found that the school for the blind was the least restrictive placement available to accommodate the student's needs. The student's grandmother appealed to a special education hearing officer who held that the student's placement at the school for the blind was appropriate, but who nevertheless recommended that she be transferred to a community placement because the school for the blind was not the least restrictive environment from which she could benefit educationally. However, the hearing officer also determined that if the school for the blind was the least restrictive placement, the school could not erect a barrier to the student's placement there by altering its eligibility criteria.

The student's grandmother filed suit in federal court, seeking to keep her granddaughter in the school for the blind. A magistrate judge ordered the student moved to a community residence with educational services to be provided by the local school district. Appeal was taken to the U.S. Court of Appeals, Fifth Circuit. The court of appeals noted that the magistrate judge had not altered the student's individualized educational program (IEP) by ordering her transferred from the school for the blind. This was a change in housing only; the student's IEP could remain the same. And if the IEP was the same, then the stay-put provision of the IDEA could not be violated. Even though the school for the blind might be able to provide better services than the local school district, the IDEA does not require that every child receive optimal services. The appellate court affirmed the lower court decision in relevant part and remanded the case. *Sherri A.D. v. Kirby,* 975 F.2d 193 (5th Cir.1992).

A profoundly retarded teenager was admitted to the District of Columbia's mentally retarded facility. In accordance with his IEP, the student was bused to instruction programs at the district's hospital for sick children. The student was suffering from foot injuries which his doctor stated were aggravated by the long daily bus trips. Without notifying the student's surrogate parent, the school district bused the student to his program only eleven days during a two month period. At an IEP conference district officials notified the parent about the student's sporadic attendance. The parent approved the IEP, but the district refused to bus the student for the following three months due to his injuries. The parent then filed a lawsuit in the U.S. District Court for the District of Columbia complaining that the student had been deprived of a free appropriate education under the EHA. She also complained that she had been deprived of an opportunity to contest a change in his educational program. She sought an order to continue his instruction at the hospital. The district court dismissed the complaint. Despite signing a consent form approving the student's IEP for the following year, the parent appealed the court's decision to the U.S. Court of Appeals, District of Columbia Circuit.

The appeals court ruled that the EHA required prior written notice for any change in educational placement, a description of available procedural safeguards, and explanation for the proposed change. The parental right to a hearing was preserved by the notice requirement and the district had failed to comply with it. By failing to implement the student's IEP during his confinement, the district also failed to provide free public education as required by the EHA. The fact that the student could not be safely bused did not excuse the district from its duty to notify the parent in writing of the discontinuance of his educational benefits. However, the parent had consented to the child's new IEP and could not complain about the change in his instruction after the three month interruption. The student was entitled to a declaration that the district had violated the EHA and the case was remanded to the district court to determine whether the parent was entitled to attorney's fees. *Abney by Kantor v. Dist. of Columbia*, 849 F.2d 1491 (D.C.Cir.1988).

Before a five-year-old child with Down's Syndrome matriculated into kindergarten, her parents met with school officials to discuss her placement. The school district recommended that she be placed in a special class with occupational, physical, speech and language therapies. Her parents opposed the placement and requested a due process hearing. They instituted this action in a federal district court seeking an injunction compelling the school district to enroll the student in a regular kindergarten class pending the hearing officer's decision.

The parents contended that pursuant to the stay-put provision of the EHA the student was entitled to be placed in a regular kindergarten class pending the outcome of the administrative appeals. The stay-put provision states that "during the pendency of any proceedings ... the child shall remain in the then current educational placement." The parents argued that because the child was applying for initial admission to the public school she should be placed in the public school program, i.e., a regular kindergarten class. However, the court determined that the purpose underlying the stay-put provision was to ensure that students with disabilities were not forced to wait outside an educational setting for the final outcome of the pending action. The court further determined that the school district's recommended placement was properly arrived at and provided an appropriate free public education. Therefore, the placement clearly met the policy goals of the EHA. The court denied the parents an injunction. *Logsdon v. Bd. of Educ. of Pavilion*, 765 F.Supp. 66 (W.D.N.Y.1991).

In January 1976, a Washington state boy was found to be eligible for special educational service having scored 70 on an I.Q. test. The district developed an IEP for him which recommended placement in an "educable disabled classroom." After further testing the school district recommended continued placement in a special education class, but his parents chose to have him repeat first grade in a regular class during the 1976-77 school year. In May 1979, another assessment by the district found the boy's I.Q. to be 69 and his academic performance less than half the expected grade level. The parents again refused the district's placement in an "educable disabled classroom" for mildly retarded students and placed him in a private school.

In the summer of 1981, a school district employee began tutoring the boy. When the parents placed the boy in a public school in the fall of 1981 they asked that the tutoring continue. After the tutor resigned, the district told the parents that a new tutor would instruct the boy. The parents alleged that this constituted a change of placement in violation of the EHA's "status quo" provision. The parents chose to remove the boy from school three hours daily to be tutored by the original tutor at their own expense. Another test was then performed by the school district which revealed that the boy's I.Q. was 66 and that he was "mildly mentally retarded." After two hearings favored the school district's position the parents appealed to a U.S. district court which ruled in their favor. The school district appealed to the U.S. Court of Appeals, Ninth Circuit.

The school district challenged the district court's ruling that the boy had a learning disability and was not mentally retarded. In 1982, a neurologist had concluded that the boy was dyslexic, not mildly retarded. The court of appeals agreed with the school district noting that the trial record provided no support for the district court's conclusion that the boy had a learning disability, not mild retardation, according to state regulations. It refused to accept the neurologist's subjective conclusion that the boy could not benefit from placement in the school district's special education classes. State regulations required placement to be based upon objective criteria such as the I.Q. test. The boy's eligibility for special education was correctly based on "mild mental retardation." The district court decision was reversed. *Gregory K. v. Longview School Dist.*, 811 F.2d 1307 (9th Cir.1987).

A thirteen-year-old student residing in the District of Columbia suffered from learning disabilities. He was injured in an automobile accident which resulted in multiple physical disabilities. The student was of above-average intelligence, but also suffered from gender-identity disorder and other emotional difficulties. The District of Columbia Public Schools (DCPS) placed the student in a private facility near the student's home pursuant to the EHA. A social worker at the school advised the DCPS that the school would not be an appropriate educational placement for the student during the following school year. His teachers, therapists and parents developed an IEP for the following school year and the DCPS recommended placement in a public day school.

The parents disagreed with the proposed IEP. They suggested placing the student at a private special education school for learning disabled students of average to above-average intelligence. They then asked for a hearing to challenge the student's placement under the EHA. The hearing officer upheld the DCPS's public school placement. Shortly thereafter, the student was enrolled in a private school. The parents then filed a lawsuit in the U.S. District Court, District of Columbia. The court ruled that the DCPS did not comply with the EHA. School districts are restricted from taking students from a private facility by the act's "stay-put" provision, "which directs that a disabled child shall remain in (his or her) then current educational placement, pending completion of any administrative or judicial review proceedings, unless the parents and state or local educational agencies otherwise agree." This required the DCPS to maintain the student at his current private placement until the resolution of the lawsuit. The parents were entitled to retroactive reimbursement for the student's private placement by the school district. *Knight v. Dist. of Columbia*, 691 F.Supp. 1567 (D.D.C.1988).

An emotionally disabled New York student attended a vocational school as a part of his mainstreaming. His parents were notified that the school district intended to graduate him at the end of the school year. When the vocational school notified the parents that the student should continue in its program for another year, the parents requested an impartial hearing. They objected to their son being graduated because he had not attained targets established by the vocational school. Following the hearing but prior to the hearing officer's decision, the student was graduated. The hearing officer agreed that graduation was appropriate and the parents appealed to the Commissioner of Education. They requested that their son be allowed to continue the vocational program until a final decision was reached. The commissioner denied the request and determined that the student had been properly graduated.

The parents sued the school district in a New York federal district court. They asserted that the school district violated the EHA's stay-put provision by graduating their son. They sought to have their son reinstated to the vocational program pending a final decision. The court noted that one of the purposes of the stay-put provision was to prevent school officials from removing a child from the classroom over the parents' objection pending completion of review proceedings. It then noted that what had to be determined was whether graduation constituted a change in placement. The court equated graduation to a long-term suspension because it resulted in the total exclusion of the student from his educational placement. Therefore, EHA procedural safeguards should be enforced. The court ordered the school district to reinstate the student to the vocational program during the pendency of the proceedings. *Cronan v. Bd. of Educ. of East Ramapo Cent. School Dist.*, 689 F.Supp. 197 (S.D.N.Y.1988).

School officials conducted an assessment of a Minnesota child. They found that the child was excessively active, did not conform well to rules, was argumentative and did not actively interact with adults. An individualized education program (IEP) team, which included the child's mother, met to discuss the assessment. Although the mother was reluctant to classify the child as disabled, she consented to special education in May 1985. In January 1986, the mother approved an annual IEP that placed the child in Level IV special education which included mainstreaming and separate special education classes. In March 1986, the school district modified the child's IEP to allow him to attend regular classes as a special education student. In May 1986, the school district recommended full mainstreaming as a special education student on a trial basis in the fall. However, the child went to live with his father and enrolled in another school system where he was placed in regular education classes. After one month the child returned to his mother's custody. In December 1986, she attempted to reenroll the child in the original school district as a regular education student. The school district asserted its right to continue the child's Level IV special education program.

In January 1987, the mother sued the school district in a federal district court. She claimed that the school district changed the child's educational status without affording her a hearing. This violated due process and the EHA's stay-put provision. The court denied the mother's motion and she appealed to the U.S. Court of Appeals, Eighth Circuit. The mother argued that the district court wrongly concluded that a § 1983 claim (under the Civil Rights Act) was not available to correct violations of the EHA or the Due Process Clause of the U.S. Constitution. She also contended that the child should be in regular classes because he transferred as a regular education student. The school district claimed that the child was a continuing student at the original school district in Level IV special education. Although the child was mainstreamed as a special education student, his permanent placement in regular education was contingent on an IEP assessment.

The court of appeals held for the mother on her § 1983 claim. The Handicapped Children's Protection Act of 1986 (HCPA) permits due process challenges to procedures employed by school districts under § 1983 in the EHA context. The HCPA provides that nothing in the EHA limits the rights of students with disabilities under other federal statutes. However, the court of appeals held for the school district on the stay-put issue. The child's one-month enrollment in regular classes at the second school system did not negate his history as a special education student. Although the Level IV program involved mainstreaming, the original school district had not taken the child out of the special education program. Furthermore, placing him in a special education program pending a determination of his proper educational program would not irreparably harm the child. The district court decision was affirmed. *Digre v. Roseville Schools Indep. Dist. No. 623*, 841 F.2d 245 (8th Cir.1988).

The U.S. Court of Appeals, Third Circuit, held that a change in the method of transportation of a severely disabled child to and from school did not constitute a "change in educational placement." A Pennsylvania school district changed the method of transportation from a system whereby the child's parents were reimbursed for their expenses in driving the child to school to a "combined run" involving other children and a small increase in travel time. The parents objected to the combined run on the ground that the increase in transportation time would be detrimental to the child's education. The school district denied the parents a due process hearing because it did not consider the change in transportation to be a "change in educational placement." The Court of Appeals agreed, finding that the change in the method of transporting the child did not constitute a "change in educational placement" under the EHA and thus could be implemented without a prior due process hearing. It is clear, said the court, that the "stay put" provision under the EHA does not entitle parents to demand a hearing when minor administrative decisions alter the school day of their children. The question is whether the school district's decision is likely to affect in some significant way a child's learning experience. Here, the parents' objections were merely speculative. *DeLeon v. Susquehanna Comm. School Dist.*, 747 F.2d 149 (3d Cir.1984).

In a similar case, the U.S. Court of Appeals, District of Columbia Circuit, held that a change in the feeding program that a profoundly disabled child would receive as a result of a transfer from a private hospital to a government-run institution did not constitute a "change in educational placement" within the meaning of the EHA. Here, although the child's transfer from one facility to another was decidedly a "change in placement," it was not alone sufficient to constitute a change in educational placement requiring the board of education to keep the child at the private hospital or a comparable facility until the hearings were completed. A move from a "mainstream" program to one consisting only of students with disabilities, said the court, would constitute a change in educational placement; a move from one mainstream program to another, with the elimination, for instance, of a theater arts class, would not be such a change. Here, the board of education, using the residential services of the public institution and the out-patient education program of the private hospital, had fulfilled its obligation under the EHA to maintain the child's educational placement pending the resolution of any complaint proceedings brought on the child's behalf. Thus, the court of appeals held that the child could be discharged from the private hospital prior to his guardian's consent and prior to a hearing. *Lunceford v. Dist. of Columbia Bd. of Educ.*, 745 F.2d 1577 (D.C.Cir.1984).

In Massachusetts, parents of an eleven-year-old boy who suffered from acquired encephalopathy challenged in U.S. district court a proposed change in their son's educational placement. For seven years the child had attended a special education center for brain-injured children. This center offered special teaching techniques which would not be available to the child at the new location. The parents argued that the transfer of their child from the center to the new program would halt his progress and cause him to regress. In deciding whether the placement change was appropriate, the court relied on language set forth by the U.S. Supreme Court in *Board of Education v. Rowley*. That case held that children with disabilities are to be provided a "basic floor of opportunity" and that educational services must be sufficient to confer some educational benefit upon them. Here, the court stated that the relative validity of the differing techniques used by the two institutes was a matter of dispute among special education experts. In light of the court's unwillingness to make educational policy and insufficient evidence that the child would regress at the new institute, the court refused to hold that the change of placement would be inappropriate. Judgment was rendered in favor of the school district. *Doe v. Lawson*, 579 F.Supp. 1314 (D.Mass.1984).

The Supreme Judicial Court of Massachusetts held that the decision to graduate a child with special education needs is a "change in placement," triggering mandatory EHA procedural safeguards. In this case a twenty-one-year-old student suffering from multiple cognitive and motor disabilities, emotional and behavioral difficulties, and also confined to a wheelchair, brought suit against a Massachusetts school district alleging that his graduation, which terminated his right to special education services, violated EHA procedural provisions. In the fall of 1980, the student's teachers had met to formulate his IEP for the 1980-81 school year. The teachers agreed that the student was to graduate at the end of the school year, although his IEP did not state this. Neither the student nor his parents were invited to the meeting at which this decision was made. The student signed the IEP but the parents did not. At no time were the parents provided formal, written notice of their right to challenge the IEP or of the procedural avenues open to them to make that challenge. Neither were they told that graduation would terminate their son's eligibility for special education services. In June 1981, the student was presented with a high school diploma; his eligibility for special education services was thereby terminated. In the time between the student's graduation and the commencement of this lawsuit, no special education services were offered to the student. The Massachusetts Supreme Judicial Court reversed a lower court decision in favor of the school district, holding that the failure to provide to the parents a formal, written notice concerning the decision to graduate the student, the failure to provide notice regarding the rights of the parents to involvement in that decision and the failure to notify them of their rights to a hearing and administrative review violated state and federal statutory law. This was true even though the parents had actual notice of the student's graduation and had participated to a limited extent in the transitional planning surrounding the graduation, and even though the student signed the IEP. *Stock v. Massachusetts Hospital School*, 467 N.E.2d 448 (Mass.1984).

A Texas student who was classified as emotionally disturbed, learning disabled and speech disabled advanced from an elementary school to junior high. The junior high IEP called for a behavior modification plan to be implemented in the least restrictive environment, namely the resource and mainstream setting rather than the self-contained behavioral modification classroom (BMC). Also, an individual aide was provided to assist the student with his studies and behavior. The school year began with some promise but deteriorated significantly. The school district sought to change his placement to a BMC. The parents then asked for an administrative hearing and also sought to enjoin the district from making a change in placement during the pendency of the hearing. The principal, several teachers, aides and psychologists testified that the student had been disruptive on numerous occasions. He had been physically aggressive, struck other students and had run away from his individual aide. He had tried to jump out of a second floor window and on one occasion had successfully exited the window. He had darted onto the roadway taunting a car to strike him. All those who testified considered the student to be severely dangerous to himself and to others. The student's psychologist was the only person to testify that he would not benefit from placement in a BMC. She felt the student would regress in his social skills if such a placement were implemented.

The court noted that under the EHA, during the pendency of administrative proceedings, the student is to remain in his current educational placement. The court also noted that under limited circumstances, school officials can change the educational placement of the child when maintaining the "current placement is substantially likely to result in injury either to the child or to others." The court must balance the potential harm between the parties. The court concluded that the student would not suffer any realistic harm by being placed in a BMC pending completion of the administrative review process. Therefore, since the potential harm to the student and others was substantial and the student would not suffer any real harm, the court balanced the decision in favor of the school district, allowing the school district to change his placement. *Texas City Indep. School Dist. v. Jorstad*, 752 F.Supp. 231 (S.D.Tex.1990).

V. SUSPENSION AND EXPULSION OF STUDENTS WITH DISABILITIES

Whether suspension or expulsion of students with disabilities from school constitutes a "change in placement" for purposes of the IDEA is an issue which has been presented before the U.S. Supreme Court in *Honig v. Doe*, 108 S.Ct. 592 (1988). Indefinite suspensions violate the IDEA's "stay put" provisions. Suspensions up to ten days do not constitute a change in placement. The Court seemed to leave intact the principle that where a student's misbehavior is caused by his or her disability, any attempt to expel the student from school will be turned aside.

Honig v. Doe involved two emotionally disturbed children in California who were given five day suspensions from school for misbehavior which included destroying school property and assaulting and making sexual comments to other students. Pursuant to state law, the suspensions were continued indefinitely during the pendency of expulsion proceedings. The students sued the school district in U.S. district court contesting the extended suspensions on the ground that they violated the EHA's stay put provision, which provides that a student must be kept in his or her "then current" educational placement during the pendency of proceedings which contemplate a change in placement. The district court issued an injunction preventing the expulsion of any disabled student for misbehavior which arises from the student's disability and the school district appealed.

The U.S. Court of Appeals, Ninth Circuit, determined that the indefinite suspensions constituted a prohibited change in placement under the EHA and that no "dangerousness" exception existed in the EHA's "stay put" provision. It ruled that indefinite suspensions or expulsions of disabled children for misconduct arising out of their disabilities violated the EHA. The court of appeals also ruled, however, that fixed suspensions of up to 30 school days did not constitute a "change in placement." It determined that a state must provide services directly to a disabled child when a local school district fails to do so. The California Superintendent of Public Instruction filed for a review by the U.S. Supreme Court on the issues of whether a dangerousness exception existed to the "stay put" provision and whether the state had to provide services directly when a local school district failed to do so.

The Supreme Court declared that the intended purpose of the stay put provision was to prevent schools from changing a child's educational placement over his or her parents' objection until all review proceedings were completed. While the EHA provided for interim placements where parents and school officials were able to agree on one, no emergency exception for dangerous students was included. The Court concluded that it was "not at liberty to engraft onto the EHA an exception Congress chose not to create." The Court went on to say that where a disabled student poses an immediate threat to the safety of others, school officials may temporarily suspend him or her for up to ten school days. The court held that this authority insured 1) that school officials can protect the safety of others by removing dangerous students, 2) that school officials can seek a review of the student's placement and try to persuade the student's parents to agree to an interim placement, and 3) that school officials can seek court rulings to exclude students whose parents "adamantly refuse to permit any change in placement." School officials could seek such a court order without exhausting EHA administrative remedies "only by showing that maintaining the child in his or her current placement is substantially likely to result in injury either to himself or herself, or to others."

The Court therefore affirmed the court of appeals' decision that indefinite suspensions violated the EHA's stay put provision. It modified that court's decision on fixed suspensions by holding that suspensions up to ten rather than up to 30 days did not constitute a change in placement. The Court also upheld the court of appeals' decision that states could be required to provide services directly to disabled students where a local school district fails to do so. *Honig v. Doe*, 484 U.S. 305, 108 S.Ct. 592, 98 L.Ed.2d 686 (1988).

A seventh grade student in southern California had a somewhat troubled educational background, including having been held back in the first grade. His parents were concerned about his behavior and school performance, and requested a school evaluation for special education services. After testing, the school concluded that the student did not qualify for special education. His parents then obtained an independent evaluation which they presented to the school. A week later, the student was suspended for frightening another student with a stolen starter pistol. The school district extended the suspension and eventually expelled the student. The Los Angeles Board of Education affirmed this decision. The parents' attorney then requested an administrative hearing to determine the student's eligibility for special education and related services, and to ascertain whether he had been expelled for acts which were a manifestation of his disability. After two days of hearings, a hearing officer determined that the student was disabled by a serious emotional disturbance, and that the actions for which he was expelled were a manifestation of his disability. She also found that the school district had wrongly denied the protection afforded by the Individuals with Disabilities Education Act by expelling the student. The school district then sued, challenging the hearing officer's jurisdiction. In response, the parents sought attorney's fees for the representation during the administrative hearing. A federal district court dismissed the school district's complaints and awarded attorney's fees to the parents. The school district appealed to the U.S. Court of Appeals, Ninth Circuit.

The court of appeals determined that it was not necessary for a school district or similar agency to identify a child as disabled before the procedural safeguards mandated by the IDEA could be invoked. Even though a student had not previously been identified as disabled by a school district, his or her alleged disability could be raised in an IDEA administrative due process hearing. Accordingly, it had been proper for the hearing officer to make a determination on the student's disability and to find that the school district had violated the IDEA. The court affirmed the district court's decision dismissing the school district's complaint, and awarding the attorney's fees to the parents. *Hacienda La Puente School District of Los Angeles v. Honig*, 976 F.2d 487 (9th Cir.1992).

A director of special education for the Ohio Department of Education sought clarification of the school district's obligation to students with disabilities who were expelled for reasons unrelated to their disability. The Office of Special Education and Rehabilitative Services of the United States Department of Education (OSERS) responded with a letter written by the Assistant Secretary for Special Education and Rehabilitation Services. The letter indicated that under the IDEA, schools would continue to be responsible for services for expelled students. The school district filed suit alleging that the letter was a legislative ruling subject to the notice and comment requirements of the Administrative Procedure Act (APA). The district court held in favor of the school district, deeming the rule to be legislative. The United States Department of Education appealed.

On appeal to the U.S. Court of Appeals, Seventh Circuit, the court reversed the district court's decision. The appellate court held that the OSERS' letter was interpretive, rather than legislative; therefore, the letter was exempt from the notice and comment requirements of the APA. The court found that the OSERS' letter was merely an interpretation of the requirements under the IDEA. Through reliance on legislative history and the language of the statute, the court found that the letter simply stated OSERS' understanding of the rule, as opposed to creating new law. The court also noted that the result of the rule did not impact the determination of whether it was legislative or interpretive. *Metropolitan School District of Wayne Township, Marion County, Indiana v. Davila*, 969 F.2d 45 (7th Cir.1992).

On January 9, 1986, after a severe temper tantrum at school, an eight-year-old boy was suspended for 35 days until a February 13, school board meeting. The boy was readmitted on January 13, but was suspended again after another disruptive incident on January 15. A January 20, examination by a psychologist found that the boy suffered from a learning disability. The school board was notified of the child's learning disability and the school psychologist began testing him on February 3. His parents requested on two occasions that in light of his learning disability he be readmitted to school. The school board suggested both times that they allow their child to receive homebound instruction and refused to lift the suspension until February 13. On February 4, the parents sued the school board seeking a temporary restraining order ordering the boy's readmission and a hearing. A U.S. district court ordered the school board to provide the boy with an appropriate educational program after which the board began devising an appropriate IEP for him. The school board then moved to dismiss the parents' lawsuit.

The parents argued that leaving the boy under disciplinary suspensions for 29 days with no educational services caused irreparable harm. The court observed that the facts of the case required a two-part examination: first, the child's due process rights had to be considered as those of a nondisabled child facing a 29 day disciplinary suspension since the school officials did not at first perceive him to be disabled. Second, once school officials were notified of the child's learning disability, his due process rights had to be considered in light of the EHA. The court ruled that both examinations revealed that the boy had due process rights. The U.S. Supreme Court held in *Goss v. Lopez* that a disciplinary suspension for even a nondisabled child gives rise to due process rights. *Goss* stated that notice of suspension proceedings must be sent to a student's parents and a hearing held with the student present "as soon as practicable." The district court ruled that under *Goss* a due process hearing 29 days after an incident would not be adequate. Such a time lapse would result in irreparable harm to the boy which justified the initiation of the civil lawsuit before February 13. Since his civil rights were violated he was entitled to relief under § 1983 including an award of attorney fees. Because the school board was in the process of devising a proper IEP, other measures of relief requested by the boy were denied. The boy was entitled to summary judgment in his favor. *Doe v. Rockingham County School Bd.*, 658 F.Supp. 403 (W.D.Va.1987).

A fourteen-year-old Virginia boy who had been identified by his school district as having a serious learning disability was suspended from school in March 1983. The boy had acted as a middleman for two nondisabled girls who desired to buy "speed" from another student. He made no money doing this and took no drugs himself. The boy was suspended, but during his suspension the school district's committee on the handicapped held proceedings which culminated in the determination that the boy's disability was not the cause of his involvement with drugs. The school board then voted to expel the boy for the remainder of the school year. One month later the parents requested and received a due process hearing at which the hearing examiner ordered the expulsion reversed because he found that the boy's misbehavior was related to his learning disability. A state reviewing officer affirmed this decision.

The school board then filed suit in U.S. district court contending that in situations like this, the EHA allows expulsions without review. The district court dismissed the school board's complaint and the U.S. Court of Appeals, Fourth Circuit, affirmed. The appeals court noted that it is settled law that any expulsion of a student with a disability is a change in placement for EHA purposes, triggering the Act's procedural safeguards. Also, the district court's determination that the boy's involvement in drug sales was caused by his disability would not be overturned on appeal unless it was "clearly erroneous." The dismissal of the school board's complaint was therefore affirmed. *School Bd. of Prince County v. Malone*, 762 F.2d 1210 (4th Cir.1985).

A Maine student suffered from severe emotional problems that necessitated his admission into a private residential school. He completed two years at the school and then returned to public school. He was mainstreamed into a regular class, but continued to receive counseling for his emotional problems. During seventh grade his emotional problems resurfaced and he began to display disruptive behavior. When he brought a loaded gun to a school basketball game, the student was suspended from school. After a hearing before the school board, he was expelled. Later his expulsion was modified to an indefinite suspension and he was placed in a residential school at district expense. The student's parents filed suit in federal court on his behalf, charging that the school district violated his procedural due process rights, violated the EHA by expelling him for behavior attributed to his emotional disorder, and violated the Rehabilitation Act by expelling him solely because of his emotional disability. The parents sought monetary damages for these alleged constitutional and statutory violations under 42 U.S.C. § 1983. The parents also sought damages for intentional infliction of emotional distress. The school district moved to dismiss the parents' claims or in the alternative for summary judgment.

The court first considered the due process claim. It found that the student had been afforded the minimum requirements of due process. The school district also argued that the parents' claims under the EHA should be dismissed for failure to exhaust administrative remedies. The court stated that the only circumstance in which administrative procedures may be bypassed is where pursuing such remedies would either be futile or inadequate. The parents claimed that since the only issue in their claim under the EHA was that of damages, it would be futile to pursue such remedies since damages cannot be awarded in an administrative procedure. However, the court held that it was unable to determine whether the student's placement was appropriate without an adequate factual record developed at the administrative level. Accordingly, it dismissed the parents' claims under the EHA. It also dismissed the parents' claims under the Rehabilitation Act since the provisions of the Act were not intended to be used to expand the scope of remedies which are available under the EHA. Since the court had dismissed all of the parents' federal law claims it lacked jurisdiction to consider the parents' state law claim for intentional infliction of emotional distress. Accordingly, the state law claims were dismissed without prejudice. *Carey on behalf of Carey v. Maine School Admin. Dist. No. 17*, 754 F.Supp. 906 (D.Me.1990).

In a Mississippi case, a student's sexual misconduct prevented his return to the classroom. The behaviorally disabled student admitted to school officials that while in a special education class he had unbuttoned a girl's blouse and touched her breast. As a result, the school suspended him for three days and he was sent before the County Youth Court. Because this was the boy's third instance of school-related sexual misconduct, the Youth Court sent him to a state hospital for one month of treatment. After he lived at home for seven months following his hospitalization, the boy's mother sought to re-enroll him at his school under his former IEP program. However, school officials claimed that the old IEP was inapplicable in light of the boy's continuing sexual misconduct and proposed that he be placed in a closely supervised group home.

The boy's mother then brought suit in U.S. district court seeking a preliminary injunction to compel school officials to allow her son to attend class under his former IEP. The court ruled in favor of the school district, noting that in order to grant a preliminary injunction there must be an immediate threat of irreparable harm to the plaintiff. However, in this case the boy's mother had delayed for seven months before seeking to once again enroll her son in the school. Also, school officials had evidenced a genuine concern for the boy's welfare by offering to provide home tutoring during the time in which a new appropriate IEP could be formulated. The court held that because the boy had neither a current IEP nor a current educational placement, and because of the danger that he presented to others, there were insufficient grounds to order that he be returned to the classroom. On appeal by the boy's mother, the U.S. Court of Appeals, Fifth Circuit, affirmed the district court, holding that when a disabled student presents a substantial danger to himself or others, immediate removal from the classroom may be justified. The school's decision to provide the boy with home tutoring was upheld. *Jackson v. Franklin County School Bd.*, 765 F.2d 535 (5th Cir.1985).

The boy and his mother appealed again to the court of appeals. They argued that the district court was wrong in not finding that the boy's due process rights were violated by being excluded from school during the spring of 1984 and the first two months of the 1984-85 school year. The court of appeals held that when the school failed to convene an IEP conference in the spring of 1984 it had violated the EHA. The EHA specifically required that "written prior notice to the parents or guardian" be provided whenever a school "proposes to initiate or change . . . the identification, evaluation, or educational placement of the child or the provision of a free appropriate public education to the child." The court observed that the U.S. Supreme Court has held that even a short suspension of up to ten days required notice of charges and some type of informal hearing. It stated that a failure on the part of the school to follow the procedural requirements of the EHA amounted to a failure by the school to provide a free appropriate education for the boy. The court concluded that, under the EHA, the burden rested on the school or agency to safeguard disabled children's rights by informing the parents or guardians of those rights. Both the EHA and the Fourteenth Amendment required the school to provide the boy with notice and a hearing regarding his continued exclusion from school. The case was remanded to the district court. *Jackson v. Franklin County School Bd.*, 806 F.2d 623 (5th Cir.1986).

In an Illinois case when a seventeen-year-old "exceptional" child told his teacher, "I'm not serving your fucking detention. Fuck you," he was promptly suspended for five days. A federal district court held that the child knew, or should have known, that his behavior was unacceptable. Further, the court pointed to the U.S. Supreme Court decision *Goss v. Lopez*, 419 U.S. 565, 95 S.Ct. 729, 42 L.Ed.2d 725 (1975), which held that "suspension is considered not only to be a necessary tool to maintain order but a valuable educational device." The court concluded by noting that a five-day suspension should not be equated to expulsion or termination, and that federal law permits the enforcement of ordinary classroom discipline through such suspensions. *Bd. of Educ. of the City of Peoria, School Dist. 150 v. Illinois State Bd. of Educ.*, 531 F.Supp. 148 (C.D.Ill.1982).

The following case illustrates that a suspension can constitute a "change in placement" if it is to last for an indefinite period. Here a school for the blind in New York suspended a deaf, blind and emotionally disturbed residential student who engaged in persistent self-abusive behavior. The reason for the suspension was that the school lacked the staff to supervise the fourteen-year-old girl, who needed to be watched continually. Without the proper supervisory staff the girl was a danger to herself. In fact, at one time during her enrollment at the school the girl had to be hospitalized because of self-inflicted injuries. The suspension was to last "until such time it appeared to be in the best interests of the child and the school to revoke the suspension." The student's mother brought suit against the school to compel it to reinstate her daughter as a residential student and to force it to provide a hearing in compliance with the EHA. Shortly after the suit was commenced the girl was reinstated in the school and the school argued that the mother's claim was then moot.

The U.S. district court disagreed with the school's claim, saying that the actions of the school were unlawful. The court observed that the time during which the child had been hospitalized as a result of self-inflicted injuries stemming from her self-abusive behavior did not constitute a "change in placement" triggering procedural safeguards. However, the indefinite suspension period which was to last until such time as "it appeared to be in the best interests of the child and the school to revoke the suspension" was unlawful within the meaning of the EHA. The indefinite suspension constituted a "change in placement" within the meaning of the EHA and thus required a hearing. *Sherry v. New York State Educ. Dep't*, 479 F.Supp. 1328 (W.D.N.Y.1979).

The following cases illustrate that expulsions are not viewed in the same light as suspensions. Expulsions trigger the procedural safeguards of the EHA and require a showing that the behavior leading to the expulsion was not the result of an expelled child's disability.

A law student at the University of Wisconsin completed his first semester with below standard grades. He was dismissed during his second semester because he failed to furnish certification of his undergraduate degree. The school allowed him to return the following spring despite knowledge that he was an alcoholic. Sensing that he was doing poorly, the student asked to withdraw. The school later learned that while drunk, he had harassed and threatened a classmate. The school readmitted the student for a third time the following spring. He completed the semester with below standard grades and the school expelled him. The student sued the school in a Wisconsin federal court alleging § 504 violations of the Rehabilitation Act, by discriminating against him on account of alcoholism. The district court granted the school's dismissal motion because the student was not "otherwise qualified" to continue as a law student. He then appealed to the U.S. Court of Appeals, Seventh Circuit.

The appeals court noted that § 504 provided that an institution receiving federal funds may not discriminate against an "otherwise qualified disabled individual." It also noted that previous cases had held that "an otherwise qualified person is one who is able to meet all of a program's requirements in spite of his disability." The Rehabilitation Act did not forbid decisions based on the actual attributes of the disabled individual. It also recognized that the school's decision was based on evaluations of how the student had previously performed and how he could be expected to perform in the future. In this case the school acted on the basis of the student's past performance rather than his alcoholism. The appeals court upheld the district court decision to dismiss the case. *Anderson v. Univ. of Wisconsin*, 841 F.2d 737 (7th Cir.1988).

A learning disabled Mississippi high school student was found with marijuana cigarettes and knives at school. A local school district recommended that he be expelled for the remainder of the school year and that he receive no academic credit for the year. It also offered the student homebound instruction during the expulsion period. A hearing officer concluded that the expulsion was impermissible because the student did not present an immediate danger to himself or other students, and the school district appealed.

The Mississippi Supreme Court held that a student with a disability could be expelled based upon a reasonable conclusion that the student would otherwise disrupt the educational process of other students. The school district, however, would have to provide quality educational services to the student during the expulsion period.

The test in expelling a student, stated the court, was whether the behavior for which the student was expelled was caused in some way by his disability. It held that school districts could expel disabled students so long as less harsh forms of discipline are considered and proper procedures are followed under the EHA. *Bd. of Trustees v. Doe*, 508 So.2d 1081 (Miss.1987).

The Nebraska Supreme Court has held that the expulsion of a disruptive student with a disability violated the EHA. In this case a student expelled for disruptive behavior from a school for the trainable mentally retarded was found by the court to have been denied a free appropriate education. After the expulsion the student, who suffered from autism, mental retardation and epilepsy, was placed in regional institutions by his parents. While in the institutions, many of the skills the child previously learned were lost, but the school district made no attempt to relocate the student. The Nebraska Supreme Court held that the expulsion constituted a change in placement which was subject to the procedural protections of the EHA. It further stated that under the Act, local school officials were prohibited from expelling students whose disabilities were the cause of their disruptive behavior. The school's only course of action in such circumstances was to transfer the disruptive student to an appropriate, more restrictive environment. The court ordered that the school district reimburse the parents for the cost incurred in the institutionalization of their child. *Adams Cent. School Dist. No. 690 v. Deist*, 334 N.W.2d 775 (Neb.1983).

A U.S. district court in Florida granted a preliminary injunction against state and local school officials preventing them from enforcing the expulsion of nine disabled students. The students, expelled for alleged misconduct, were all classified as "educable mentally retarded," "mildly mentally retarded," or "EMR/dull normal." The Florida school district which had expelled the students did so on the ground that the students knew right from wrong.

The students sued the school district alleging they were denied a free appropriate education under the EHA as a result of their expulsions. The district court agreed with the students finding that under § 504 of the Rehabilitation Act and the EHA, no disabled student could be expelled for misconduct related to the disability. The court found that no determination was made as to the relationship between the students' disabilities and their behavioral problems. The court also found that an expulsion is a change in educational placement. The students' request for an injunction was granted.

The school district appealed to the U.S. Court of Appeals, Fifth Circuit, which affirmed the district court ruling. The court of appeals held that the determination that a disabled student knows the difference between right and wrong is not sufficient to support a determination that his misconduct was or was not a manifestation of his disability. Only a trained, knowledgeable group of persons should determine whether a student's misconduct bears a relationship to his disabling condition. Because no such determination was made in this case, the court found the expulsion of the nine students to have constituted a change in placement invoking the procedural protections of the EHA and § 504 of the Rehabilitation Act. *S-1 v. Turlington*, 635 F.2d 342 (5th Cir.1981).

CHAPTER THREE

IDEA PROCEDURAL SAFEGUARDS

I. DUE PROCESS HEARING

The procedural safeguards of the IDEA are designed to ensure that parents and children are able to enforce their rights under the Act. The safeguards include the right to an " impartial due process hearing" under § 1415(b)(2) when parents or guardians are dissatisfied with any matter relating to the identification, evaluation, or educational placement of the child, or the provision of a free appropriate public education to the child. These hearings most often occur when parents or guardians are dissatisfied with their child's IEP. These hearings are to be conducted by the state or local educational agency responsible for providing services. The hearing must be conducted by an impartial hearing officer. The initial due process hearing may be provided at the state or local educational agency level. If the initial hearing is held at the local level, either party may appeal "to the State educational agency which shall conduct an impartial review of such hearing" [section 1415(c)] . The decision of the initial hearing officer is final unless appealed; the decision of the state officer is likewise final unless either party brings an action in state court or federal district court [section 1415(e)(1)].

A District of Columbia student suffered from weak motor skills and a short attention span. His parents sought a special education placement for the student, but a multi-disciplinary team determined that he was ineligible. His parents then enrolled him in a full-time special education school, after which they sought to recover their educational costs from the school district. The district refused to pay, and the parents requested an administrative hearing under the IDEA. The hearing officer found that the school district's notice that the student was ineligible for special education had been insufficient and had excluded proposed evidence offered by the district. However, the officer shifted the burden of proof from the school district to the parents and ruled that the parents had failed to show that the student was eligible. Both parties appealed to the U.S. District Court for the District of Columbia. The district court ruled that the hearing officer's procedural errors required a remand of the case to the hearing officer for further consideration. District of Columbia regulations required that the school district bear the burden of proving its case at all administrative hearings under the IDEA. The hearing officer had erroneously excluded evidence. The due process hearing under the IDEA is the parents' primary procedural protection and school districts must provide exhaustive explanations of the reasons for their decisions. In keeping with the desire to have a hearing officer with expertise in special education determine educational issues, the court remanded the case for further consideration. *Kroot v. Dist. of Columbia*, 800 F.Supp. 976 (D.D.C.1992).

The District of Columbia Public Schools (DCPS) sent notices to parents of students with disabilities regarding changes in their individualized education programs (IEPs). Contained in the notices was a reference to the parents' statutory right to request a due process hearing. The notice indicated that the parents' right must be exercised within 15 days or deemed waived. Upon initiation of the due process hearings, the hearing officers found that the IEPs were invalid. Additionally, the hearing officers held that the 15 day time limit was improper. The DCPS appealed, arguing that the time limit had to prejudice the parents' rights to be improper. On appeal to a federal district court, the court affirmed the hearing officers' findings. The court held that neither the IDEA nor the regulations contain a time limit within which a due process hearing must be requested. Moreover, the court held that the time limit violated the parents' procedural rights, and that proof of actual prejudice was not required for the time limit to be invalidated. *Smith v. Hensen,* 778 F.Supp. 43 (D.D.C.1992).

The parents of a disabled eight-year-old District of Columbia child filed a request for special education and related services with their school district. The district's multidisciplinary team determined that the child was multiply disabled and eligible for a free appropriate public education. The district convened an IEP meeting which was attended by the parents and their consultant. The district IEP proposed placement in a public special education school for multiply disabled students. The notice indicated that the district had considered private school placements but had rejected them in favor of an appropriate public placement. The parents requested a hearing at which a hearing officer determined that the district's notice had failed to meet the procedural requirements of 34 C.F.R. §§ 300.504 and 505. The hearing officer ruled that the district should have explained why the student was classified as multiply disabled and why the child could not be placed in programs which were designed solely to meet a single disability. Although the district issued a revised notice within two days explaining that the district had evaluated the child as both learning disabled and other health impaired, the notice explained that the disabilities were "concomitant." Therefore, the district believed the child would have difficulty achieving educational benefits in programs designed to deal with only one disability. A second hearing was held at which a hearing officer determined that the notice was statutorily deficient. Because of the deficient notice, the hearing officer did not permit the district to present evidence concerning the appropriateness of its proposed placement. However, he permitted the parents to present evidence concerning the two private schools. The hearing officer ruled that one of the private schools was an appropriate placement and ordered the district to place him there at the school district's expense. The school district appealed to the U.S. District Court for the District of Columbia.

The court cited C.F.R. § 300.505(a), which requires notices to include "a description of the action proposed or refused by the agency, an explanation of why the agency proposes or refuses to take the action, and a description of any option the agency considered and the reasons why those options were rejected." Under that standard, the court ruled that the hearing officer had erroneously found the school district's notices deficient. The original notice had not been deficient because the term "multiply disabled" properly notified the parents that the student had more than one disability. The district's notices also clearly identified that an appropriate public placement was available. Because of the hearing officer's errors, the court granted the school district's motion for summary judgment. *Smith v. Squillacote*, 800 F.Supp. 993 (D.D.C.1992).

A multidisciplinary team proposed an individualized educational program (IEP) for an Oregon student. It included 85% of each day in regular classes and 15% in a resource room where the student would receive special assistance in math. His mother contested the proposed IEP and the recommended placement. She requested a hearing pursuant to Oregon law. A local hearing officer approved the IEP. The mother then sought review of the hearing officer's decision. The Superintendent of Public Instruction appointed a reviewing officer. Oregon law provided that the hearing officer's decision could be reversed only if the reviewing officer found that the hearing officer's decision was not supported by "substantial evidence in the record." The reviewing officer affirmed the hearing officer's decision. The mother then appealed to the Oregon Court of Appeals.

The court of appeals observed that EHA § 1415(c) required reviewing officers to make independent decisions upon completion of their case review. It also noted that the federal regulation governing review procedures required reviewing officers to "make an independent decision on completion of the review." The court of appeals reversed the reviewing officer's decision because his review wrongly relied on state law. The reviewing officer merely reviewed the local hearing officer's decision to determine whether there was sufficient evidence in the record to support his decision. He failed to make an independent decision based on the record. The court of appeals remanded the case to the superintendent so that he could independently review the record and make appropriate findings of fact consistent with the EHA and the regulation. *Tompkins v. Forest Grove School Dist.*, 740 P.2d 186 (Or.App.1987).

The Michigan Court of Appeals reversed on procedural grounds a state review officer's decision in favor of the parents of a child with a disability, citing a lack of impartiality on the part of the review officer. The court's opinion also indicated that it was displeased with the review officer's disregard of financial burdens on school districts. In this case a girl suffered a stroke at the age of ten which left her with a full scale I.Q. of 47 and a potential I.Q. of 64. When her parents approached their local school district requesting a free appropriate public education for their daughter, the district evaluated her and proposed placement in a classroom for the "educable mentally impaired." The parents disagreed and a due process hearing was held. The hearing officer, rejecting the parents' claim that the girl required a two-to-one student-teacher ratio, approved the school district's proposed EMI placement. The parents appealed to the state review officer, who exercised his statutory power to allow neither the school nor the parents to file written briefs or present oral arguments. After examining the evidence which had been presented to the hearing officer, the review officer ruled that the girl was entitled to a student-teacher ratio of not more than three to one, and the school district appealed.

The state court of appeals held that because the parents had written arguments attacking the hearing officer's decision on the appeal form they filed with the review officer, the review officer had, in effect, allowed the parents to file a written brief. The review officer had therefore been obligated to allow the school district to present its position as well. Since the review officer had improperly allowed only one side to file a brief, his decision was vacated and the case was remanded to the review officer with instructions that oral arguments be allowed. *Nelson v. Southfield Pub. Schools*, 384 N.W.2d 423 (Mich.App.1986).

The New Hampshire Supreme Court decided a case in which a fourteen-year-old girl, who suffered from a severe learning disability coupled with speech and language disorders, was placed in a private residential school in Massachusetts. The reason for this placement was the inability of the girl's New Hampshire school district to provide an appropriate educational program for her. During the summer, after the child's second year at the school in Massachusetts, the local school district in New Hampshire formulated an IEP for the child which utilized public resources. The girl's mother appealed the school district's decision to place the child in a public program, which resulted in a determination that the public program offered was both "free and appropriate," and that the school district would no longer be obliged to pay for the child's education at the school in Massachusetts or any other private facility. The determination also denied tuition reimbursement to the mother for the four month period following the proposed IEP. (The mother had enrolled the child for a third year at the private school pending the resolution of the appeals process.) The mother then asked the New Hampshire Supreme Court to order the school district to pay the expenses incurred for the four months.

The court declined to rule on the matter since the child's mother had not appealed the final administrative decision to a state trial court or federal district court. Petitioning the supreme court of a state is not the appropriate method for seeking review of a decision of a state board of education. Although the court declined to hear the merits of the mother's complaint, it noted that if a school district can provide satisfactory assurance that its programs meet EHA standards for "free appropriate public education" of children with disabilities, it will only be liable for the costs resulting from the placement of disabled children in its own public programs and not for the cost incurred in private placements. *Petition of Darlene W.*, 469 A.2d 1307 (N.H.1983).

Where state law regarding the role of a hearing officer contradicts the EHA, the EHA controls. Following the private evaluations of their two children, North Carolina parents informed the principal of the public school in which the children were enrolled that the children were being placed in a private educational facility for half of each school day. Subsequently, the parents asked that the board of education provide the children with an IEP comparable to that of the private institution or, alternatively, that the board provide transportation and tuition for the children to continue at the private facility for the 1984-85 school year. They asked to be reimbursed for expenses incurred by them resulting from the children's private school placement during the 1983-84 year. The board of education denied their request and the parents requested a due process hearing. The hearing officer determined that he had no authority under North Carolina state law to grant an award of reimbursement and no hearing was held. When the state board of education denied a request by the parents that the hearing officer be granted such authority, the parents appealed to a U.S. district court.

The parents claimed that the board of education, through the appointed administrative hearing officer, deprived them of their EHA procedural rights. They also contended that the state board of education refused to interpret or amend state regulations to be consistent with the EHA. The state board argued that reimbursement costs were monetary penalties that could only be imposed by the courts. The district court noted that the EHA contained a detailed procedural component with which local and state boards were required to comply. It concluded that to allow a state hearing officer to conduct a hearing on the issue of reimbursement and to enter findings of fact based on that hearing, but to refuse to order reimbursement even when appropriate, made the EHA less than complete. To the extent North Carolina's interpretation of the authority of a hearing officer contradicted the EHA, the terms of the EHA must control. The local board of education was ordered to conduct another hearing and order reimbursement costs if appropriate. *S-1 v. Spangler*, 650 F.Supp. 1427 (M.D.N.C.1986).

A hearing officer is not charged with the responsibility of choosing between an educational program offered by a school district and counterproposals submitted by parents. To give the hearing officer such powers would be to diminish the role of the school districts in selecting the best possible educational program appropriate to the needs of children with disabilities. This ruling was handed down by a federal district court in the District of Columbia in a case in which the parents of a child with a disability challenged District of Columbia hearing procedures. The court observed that the EHA requires a due process hearing if the parents of a disabled child objected to the placement of their child in a program they deemed inappropriate to the child's needs.

Here, the parents were dissatisfied with the program offered by the school district. They asked the court to order the hearing officer to weigh the proposals of both the school district and the parents and then to determine which of the two proposals was most appropriate for their child. The court refused to grant such powers to the hearing officer. Instead the court reiterated the duties of the hearing officer in such cases—the officer was required to hear the school district's proposal. If the parents were dissatisfied with that proposal they could offer alternative suggestions to the school district. If, after hearing the proposal and the counterproposals, the hearing officer deemed the school district's proposal to be inadequate, the hearing officer was required to remand the district's proposal to the district with instructions to submit a new proposal within 20 days. *Davis v. Dist. of Columbia Bd. of Educ.*, 530 F.Supp. 1215 (D.D.C.1982).

A U.S. district court in Connecticut has dealt with the procedural problem of whether testimony of a hearing officer regarding her mental processes while making a decision could be allowed in a case involving an administrative determination that a minor's placement in a private residential facility was not necessary for educational reasons. The case arose on appeal of a state administrative determination to the district court. The defendant school board was excused from any financial obligation in excess of tuition costs by the administrative determination and the minor, through his parents, appealed.

At the appeal stage the state listed as its sole witness the hearing officer whose decision was being appealed. The minor's motion to preclude her testimony at trial was granted. The court noted that in reviewing a decision of an administrative agency, it was not the proper function of the court to probe the mental processes of the agency or its members, particularly if the agency made a considered decision upon a full administrative record. Such probing should ordinarily be avoided and there must be a strong showing of bad faith or improper behavior before such inquiry may be made.

In this case, the state based its opposition to the motion on the premise that the mental processes rule had little or no application in a case where the officer was testifying voluntarily and the purpose of the testimony was not to contradict or impeach the record which had already been established.

The court stated that this proposition was supported neither by logic nor authority. The objectivity and independence of the hearing officer in her role as administrative adjudicator would likely be undermined by her being offered by the state as a probative witness in support of its case. Cross examination and the court's assessment of the testimony would involve, necessarily, a review of the mental processes of the adjudicative officer. Such an examination of a judge would be destructive of judicial responsibility. Just as a judge's mind should not be subjected to scrutiny, so the integrity of the administrative process must be equally respected. The court, therefore, granted the motion to exclude the hearing officer's testimony. *Feller v. Bd. of Educ. of State of Connecticut*, 583 F.Supp. 1526 (D.Conn.1984).

Two disabled children in Alabama, dissatisfied with the educational plans that had been prescribed for them, sought and were afforded due process hearings. Prior to the hearings, the children, through their parents, filed written objections to the method used by the state for selecting due process hearing officers. They alleged that the selection of hearing officers who were officers or employees of local school systems in which the children were enrolled or who were university personnel involved in the formulation of state policies concerning special education violated the EHA and its implementing regulations. Despite these objections, due process hearings were conducted and in each case a determination adverse to the children was reached. The children's claims were then evaluated by a review panel which was selected by the same method as the due process panel. Prior to the second hearing the children filed a second set of written objections to the method of selecting hearing officers. The review panel affirmed the adverse ruling of the due process panel and the children brought suit in federal court.

A U.S. district court enjoined the local school superintendent from selecting, as due process hearing officers under the EHA, individuals who were officers or employees of local school systems which the children attended, or university personnel who had been or were involved in the formulation of state policies on educating disabled children.

The school district appealed to the U.S. Court of Appeals, Eleventh Circuit, which affirmed the district court ruling. The court of appeals found that officers and employees of local school boards in Alabama were employees of agencies "involved in the education and care of the child" under § 1415(b)(2) with a personal or professional interest in the type of educational assistance extended to disabled children, and thus were not eligible to serve on due process hearing panels. Further, university personnel involved in the formulation of state policies for the education of the disabled were not sufficiently impartial to serve as due process hearing officers under the EHA. *Mayson v. Teague*, 749 F.2d 652 (11th Cir.1984).

A hearing officer in Rhode Island ordered a school district to fund the special education of two learning disabled children at a private school in Massachusetts. A U.S. district court upheld the hearing officer's order. The school district appealed claiming that because the hearing officer was an employee of the Department of Education, the hearing did not satisfy the EHA requirement that it not "be conducted by an employee of the local or state educational agency . . . involved in the education or care of the child." [§ 1415(b)(2)]. The U.S. Court of Appeals, First Circuit, upheld the district court ruling saying that the school district was not within the "protected class" of children with disabilities and their parents that Congress envisioned when it prohibited employees of a state educational agency from acting as review officers. *Colin K. v. Schmidt*, 715 F.2d 1(1st Cir.1983).

Section 1415(e)(3) gives any party at any hearing the right to a written or electronic verbatim record of the hearing. The next two cases deal with the form this record can take.

A thirteen-year-old child afflicted with dyslexia attended a private school in New Hampshire. The school district offered an IEP which was to be implemented by placing the student in one of the district's public schools. Her parents rejected the plan and requested an impartial due process hearing to resolve the dispute. A prehearing conference was held and all parties were represented by counsel. The hearing officer took notes and tape recorded the proceeding. Thereafter, he issued an order stating that the district could employ a court reporter to supplement the hearing officer's effort to record the hearing. At the hearing, the district's counsel brought a private court reporter certified by the state of New Hampshire to record the proceedings at the district's expense. The parents announced their intention to appeal the prehearing order allowing the district to employ a court reporter. A complaint was filed in a federal district court. The district court dismissed the action and the parents appealed to the U.S. Court of Appeals, First Circuit.

The court noted that there had been gaps and inaudible tapes at previous administrative hearings. Therefore the court concluded that in order to secure its entitlement to a verbatim record of the hearing, the district had a right to ensure that a quality recording was made. The attendance of a court reporter was a reasonable and necessary means for the district to secure its statutory right. The parents contended that the use of the court reporter denied them their rights under the EHA. By statute, public access to a special education hearing is permitted only with the permission of the parents or child. The court, however, found no meaningful distinction between permitting a court reporter to attend a hearing to make a verbatim recording and exposing that same person to the recording at the completion of the hearing in order to make a transcript of the proceeding. Therefore, the court affirmed the trial court's decision allowing the court reporter to attend the administrative hearing. *Caroline T. v. Hudson School Dist.*, 915 F.2d 752 (1st Cir.1990).

A thirteen-year-old Connecticut student with Down's Syndrome received special education in the public schools of Groton, Connecticut. The student's mother's native language was Danish, making it difficult for her to follow written and spoken English. Pursuant to the EHA, the mother, the teacher, and others participated in the development of the individualized education program (IEP) for the student at a yearly meeting. Because of her difficulty with English, the mother requested to tape record the meeting. She believed that a recording would let her listen to the meeting again along with a dictionary. The teacher, however, did not wish to be taped. She felt that it would make her uncomfortable and create unnecessary tension. The board of education then denied the mother permission to tape record the meeting. After the mother requested a due process hearing, the board of education ruled that the mother would be permitted to take notes of the teacher's statements and could tape record the others if they did not object. The mother felt, however, that the notes of the meeting were unsatisfactory. The teacher then refused to attend an annual review meeting when she learned that the mother intended to tape record the meeting. The mother refused to proceed without the teacher present and requested a due process hearing. The hearing officer concluded that the mother did not as a matter of law have a right to tape record the meetings. Further, the hearing officer found that there was no evidence that the tape recording was necessary for the student to receive an appropriate education. The mother appealed to a U.S. district court. Both parties moved for summary judgment.

The EHA, the court noted, emphasized the importance of parental participation in developing the IEP. The EHA provided safeguards "that guarantee parents both an opportunity for meaningful input into all decisions affecting their child's education and the right to seek review of any decisions they think inappropriate." However, the Office of Special Education Programs (OSEP), addressed this issue stating that "although taping is clearly not required, it is permissible at the option of either the parents or the agency," 34 CFR Part 300. The OSEP noted, however, that it did not have authority to require or prohibit recordings. The court determined that the EHA is "designed to help implement individualized and personalized educational plans for disabled children and their parents." Since the mother had difficulty understanding what took place at the meetings, a tape recording would allow the mother to go home and review what was said at the meeting until she was clear what her child's IEP entailed. The court determined that the tape recording was an essential part of her participation in the planning and evaluation of the IEP. The court then addressed the second issue, whether the teacher could refuse to be taped. The court determined that since the teacher's participation is extremely important to the success of the meetings, she would have to have an objective reason why her comments should not be taped. Her argument that such taping would make her uncomfortable, the court determined, was completely self-serving. The parents' summary judgment motion was granted and the mother was allowed to tape record the meetings. *E. H. v. Tirozzi*, 735 F.Supp. 53 (D.Conn.1990).

II. EXHAUSTION OF ADMINISTRATIVE REMEDIES

The doctrine of exhaustion of remedies provides that "no one is entitled to judicial relief for a supposed or threatened injury until the prescribed administrative remedy has been exhausted." This was pointed out by the U.S. Supreme Court in the case of *Myers v. Bethlehem Shipbuilding Corp.*, 303 U.S. 41, 58 S.Ct. 459, 82 L.Ed. 638 (1938). The reasons supporting the exhaustion of remedies doctrine were advanced in a later Supreme Court case, *McKart v. U.S.*, 395 U.S. 185, 89 S.Ct. 1657, 23 L.Ed.2d 194 (1968). Among the reasons given were the development of an accurate factual record, thus allowing more informed

judicial review, encouraging "expeditious decision making," and furthering Congressional intent.

A. Operation of the Exhaustion Doctrine

IDEA § 1415 provides for an initial independent review of a contested IEP at the agency level. Section 1415(e)(2) provides that an "aggrieved party" may bring a separate civil action in state or federal court to challenge the final decision of a state educational agency. Normally the parents or guardians of a child with a disability have the duty to exhaust all administrative channels before resorting to a state or federal court. However, some courts have excused the "exhaustion" requirement under certain exceptional circumstances.

A group of parents of children with disabilities became dissatisfied with the extended school year programming offered by the Tucson school district. They felt their children were not receiving enough instruction in the summer months, causing regression between conventional school years. They filed a complaint with the Arizona Department of Education pursuant to the state's complaint procedure, alleging that the school district was violating the IDEA because of its extended year policies and because it had failed to provide formal written notice of the denial of extended year services. EDGAR (the U.S. Education Division General Administrative Regulations) requires states to adopt a formal procedure for receiving and resolving complaints that the state or local education agency is violating the IDEA or its regulations. In this case, the state did not respond to the EDGAR complaint within 60 days, as it was supposed to, and the group of parents brought a class action suit in federal district court against the Tucson School District. The court dismissed their complaint because they had failed to exhaust their administrative remedies, and they appealed to the U.S. Court of Appeals, Ninth Circuit. The court of appeals affirmed the district court's decision. Here, the parents had not shown that resort to the administrative process would be futile or inadequate. Neither had they shown that the school district had adopted a policy or pursued a practice of general applicability that was contrary to the law. Further, they could not escape the exhaustion requirement just by bringing a class action lawsuit for injunctive relief. The court upheld the dismissal. *Hoeft v. Tucson Unified School Dist.*, 967 F.2d 1298 (9th Cir.1992).

A Louisiana special education student's parents desired to record their daughter's individualized education program conference. The school board, however, had adopted a formal policy regulating the recording of parent conferences. Under this policy, recordings were permitted only when all conference participants consented. One of the IEP conference participants objected and the conference proceeded without being recorded. The parents complained that the policy was illegal. In response, the board amended the policy to allow taping when it is necessary to ensure that the parents fully understand the IEP process. Under the new policy, whether taping is necessary is a determination to be made by the school authorities. Dissatisfied with the amendment, the parents sued in federal court, seeking an injunction against enforcement of the policy. The district court held for the parents and the school board appealed to the U.S. Court of Appeals, Fifth Circuit. On appeal, the school board argued that the district court ruling was improper since the parents had not exhausted their administrative remedies. The parents argued that pursuing administrative remedies was futile because the board was obviously not going to change its policy. The court of appeals, however, agreed with the school board. It noted that any civil action brought concerning the "identification, evaluation, or educational placement" of a child must be preceeded by administrative proceedings on the same issue. Such proceedings may only be bypassed when they would be futile or inadequate. In this case, the proceedings would not be futile, even though the school board had obviously predetermined its policy, because the state administrative agency would review any decision of the school board on the issue. *Gardner v. School Bd. of Caddo Parish,* 958 F.2d 108 (5th Cir.1992).

The District of Columbia Public Schools (DCPS) and the School for Contemporary Education (SCE) became embroiled in a contract dispute over the amount of funds owed the SCE by the DCPS for special education students in attendance at the SCE. The SCE consequently notified the DCPS that it would not reserve spaces for DCPS students without assurances that a certain sum would be paid for the following year. The grandmother of a student at the school, believing SCE to be the only appropriate placement for her grandson, sought a temporary restraining order to require the DCPS to agree to pay tuition and related services for the upcoming year.

The U.S. District Court for the District of Columbia dismissed the case for lack of subject matter jurisdiction. It noted that the Individuals with Disabilities Education Act established an elaborate procedural mechanism by which the rights of children with disabilities were protected. Here, the grandmother did not exhaust the process; she made no complaint to the DCPS, nor did she request a due process hearing. Thus, she had to show that exhaustion of her administrative remedies would be futile or inadequate for the lawsuit to be maintained. This, she was unable to do. In addition, the DCPS had offered an alternative placement which she had not shown was inappropriate. *Moss by Mutakabbir v. Smith,* 794 F.Supp. 11 (D.D.C.1992).

Thirteen Pennsylvania school districts received notice from the state department of education that the department had "capped" the excess costs of special education reimbursement at a level of eight percent of the school districts' total budget, thus denying them $154,403 in reimbursement funds. The school districts sued, claiming that there was no statutory or regulatory authority on the part of the department to impose the cap. The department objected to the suit, claiming that the districts had not exhausted their administrative remedies. The school districts admitted that they had failed to pursue their administrative remedies, but claimed that the department had prejudged the facts and the law making any administrative remedy futile. The Pennsylvania Commonwealth Court dismissed the districts' petition for review. It stated that courts should presume that the administrative process will, if given a chance, discover and correct its own errors. Regulations provided the school districts with the opportunity for a hearing which they had not pursued. *Colonial School Dist. v. Dep't of Educ.,* 602 A.2d 455 (Pa.Cmwlth.1992).

A twelve-year-old New York student suffered from Tourette's Syndrome, which often results in uncontrolled violent behavior. A committee on special education recommended that he be placed in a self-contained special education class. The parents disagreed with this placement and brought an Article 78 proceeding in a New York trial court requesting that their son be placed in a 12-month residential private school. The trial court dismissed the complaint, stating that the parents would have to exhaust their administrative remedies before seeking redress in the courts. The parents appealed to the Supreme Court, Appellate Division, of New York. In order to bypass administrative remedies the parents would have to demonstrate that pursuing administrative remedies would be futile or would cause irreparable harm to their son. The court determined that the parents in this case failed to produce any evidence of either harm to their son or that the administrative remedies would be futile. Therefore, the appellate court upheld the decision of the trial court and dismissed the complaint. *Dawson v. Gibson*, 575 N.Y.S.2d 517 (A.D.1991).

A District of Columbia student had severe language, emotional and behavioral problems. Her parents sent her to a private school. The student's parents then contacted the District of Columbia Public Schools (DCPS) for special education placement. However, the DCPS's first evaluation concluded that the student required no special education. The DCPS also failed to develop an individualized education program (IEP) or recommend placement by the beginning of that school year. The parents then enrolled their daughter in a private school where she had attended summer school. The district then developed an IEP for the student, recommending that 25% of her school hours be mainstreamed with nondisabled students. The parents disagreed with the IEP and requested a due process hearing before an administrative hearing officer. The parties were unable to reach a settlement and three hearings were held.

As the following school year approached, the parents requested a fourth due process hearing but then withdrew the request in favor of a federal lawsuit filed in the U.S. District Court for the District of Columbia. The court granted the DCPS's summary judgment motion. The parents filed a motion to amend the judgment, and the court reversed itself, vacating its prior opinion and ruling for the parents. The court held that further administrative appeals by the parents would have been futile. The private school was an appropriate placement for the current and following school years because the DCPS had failed to participate in IEP meetings for that year. Because the DCPS had already paid for the student's private school tuition for the current school year, the court ordered the DCPS to reimburse the parents for the upcoming school year. The DCPS then appealed to the U.S. Court of Appeals, District of Columbia Circuit. According to the court, the law clearly required that all administrative remedies be exhausted before an EHA lawsuit could be filed in a federal district court. An exception existed if exhaustion of remedies would be futile or inadequate. The parents had not exhausted their administrative remedies in this case because the administrative hearings had ended in only a determination for the prior school year, whereas the final order had pertained to the current and upcoming academic years. The court reversed the district court's decision. *Cox v. Jenkins*, 878 F.2d 414 (D.C.Cir.1989).

A learning disabled Rhode Island student with attendance and behavior problems required special education services and speech therapy. He was placed in a self-contained classroom in a local school where he continued to have tardiness and behavior problems. The school district developed an IEP, which the student's mother approved. The IEP called for the student's enrollment as a special education student. He continued to miss classes and was frequently placed on suspension. Because of the school's policy regarding absences, the student did not receive academic credit for any of his courses. The student's mother claimed that she was never informed of her right to challenge the school's disciplinary system through an administrative process. The student filed a complaint with the Rhode Island Department of education, alleging that the department had failed to comply with federal and state regulations regarding procedural safeguards. The department notified the school's superintendent that the disciplinary actions taken against the student violated the law because the school had not met to determine whether there was a causal relationship between the student's misbehavior and his disability. The superintendent stated that the school had determined that the student was behaviorally disordered but that not all of his inappropriate behavior was due to his disabling condition. The student continued to experience attendance problems and eventually quit school. He then sued the school board in a federal district court under the EHA, the Rehabilitation Act and the Civil Rights Act, challenging the school's disciplinary sanctions. The court found that it lacked jurisdiction because the student had failed to exhaust state administrative remedies. The student appealed to the U.S. Court of Appeals, First Circuit. The court of appeals noted that the student would have to exhaust the administrative remedies outlined in the EHA before proceeding with any action in the district court. The student had not pursued any administrative remedies, other than his initial complaint. No evidence was presented which suggested that asking for a due process hearing would have been futile. The student would not be irreparably harmed in the absence of immediate action by the federal court. The student was required to exhaust his administrative remedies before he could bring an action in the district court. The court of appeals affirmed the district court's decision. *Christopher W. v. Portsmouth School Comm.*, 877 F.2d 1089 (1st Cir.1989).

A fifteen-year-old student was an exceptional child within the meaning of Maine education laws. He attended public school special education classes, but began to suffer from severe psychological problems. He eventually had suicidal thoughts, and was admitted to a medical center for depression. He then attended a children's hospital in Boston and underwent psychiatric diagnosis, care and treatment. While the student was still in the children's hospital, the school district considered placement for the upcoming school year. The student's parents supported the recommendations of the doctor who had treated the student at the children's hospital, but the school district refused to do so. The Maine Department of Mental Health and Mental Retardation then funded a sixty-day evaluation at a New Hampshire rehabilitation facility. While the student was at the New Hampshire facility the parents twice attempted to reconvene the IEP meeting and then requested an impartial due process hearing under the Maine education statute and the EHA.

Meanwhile, the New Hampshire facility's staff attempted to develop an appropriate IEP. The school district refused to attend the meeting. The facility's IEP team recommended residential treatment and placement at the facility for six to twelve months. The district refused to comply with the IEP and the student returned to Maine. The student's parents then sued the district in a federal district court, requesting a temporary restraining order to prevent the district from denying placement at the New Hampshire facility. The school district argued that the student had failed to exhaust his administrative remedies as required by the EHA. The court ruled that the student's parents had failed to show that the student would be severely harmed by a failure to be placed in the New Hampshire facility. While the parents alleged that there had been significant developments following the development of the IEP, this was no reason to avoid the administrative remedies doctrine. The court denied the parents' motion and dismissed the lawsuit. *Harper v. School Admin. Dist. No. 37*, 727 F.Supp. 688 (D.Me.1989).

A sixteen-year-old student with a language disorder attended a Tennessee public school. His parents became dissatisfied with the implementation of his IEP and requested a due process hearing. The hearing officer found that the school had provided the student with an appropriate education as required by the EHA. The parents did not appeal this decision. The following year a meeting was held to develop a new IEP. The parents requested that the student be placed in a private school but their request was denied. They later enrolled the student in a private school and sued the public school in a federal district court, alleging that it had failed to provide the student with an appropriate education. In the meantime, the parents sought another due process hearing requesting reimbursement for the student's private school costs. The hearing officer denied their request because they had bypassed the EHA's procedural requirements. The school proposed another IEP, which the parents rejected. Rather than requesting a due process hearing, they filed a supplemental complaint and requested the district court to find the private school an appropriate placement. They also sought tuition reimbursement. The district court held that the private school was an appropriate placement and ordered the public school to pay the student's private school tuition. The state appealed this decision to the U.S. Court of Appeals, Sixth Circuit.

The court of appeals held that the parents had not waived their right to seek reimbursement under the EHA by unilaterally removing the student from the public school and placing him in the private school. Although the parents had not waived their right to seek redress under the EHA, they were required to exhaust administrative procedures before seeking reimbursement for the student's private school costs. The parents were procedurally required to request a due process hearing instead of going directly to the district court. The court of appeals reversed the district court's decision and remanded the case for further proceedings. *Doe by and through Doe v. Smith*, 879 F.2d 1340 (6th Cir.1989).

A fourteen-year-old Indiana student had serious emotional disabilities. His IEP called for regular class attendance with outside counseling for his behavioral problems. The junior high school which the student attended used a demerit system for regular students which imposed a maximum sanction of expulsion. The student was suspended several times during one semester and received a sufficient number of demerits to justify expulsion. The school suspended the student under procedures for regular students, but when school administrators learned that he was receiving special education services, the suspension was lifted. A case conference was held, but the parents walked out of the meeting. The school later determined that the student's conduct was related to his emotional condition. As a result, the student was not expelled. Prior to the conference, the parents had requested a due process hearing. The hearing officer ordered a new IEP conference. The parents made a written request for review of this decision before the state Board of Special Education Appeals. The board held a hearing and upheld the hearing officer's order. The parents then sued the school district in a federal district court, claiming that the IEP was inadequate. The court noted that the EHA explicitly required the use of administrative remedies and procedures and required states to develop adequate procedures for providing due process to disabled students. The parents and student had failed to exhaust their administrative remedies and were precluded from review in a federal court. The court granted the school district's motion to dismiss the case. *Browning v. Evans*, 700 F.Supp. 978 (S.D.Ind.1988).

The Association for Retarded Citizens of Alabama sued the Alabama Superintendent of Education on behalf of 6,000 children with disabilities. The association asserted that the superintendent violated the EHA by failing to provide sufficient funding to support necessary facilities and programs for the children. It also contended that the superintendent had violated the Due Process Clause of the Constitution because he failed to establish an effective administrative review process. The association claimed the children were entitled to relief under § 1983 of the Civil Rights Act. The association did not employ EHA administrative remedies before it initiated the lawsuit. A U.S. district court held for the superintendent and the association appealed to the U.S. Court of Appeals, Eleventh Circuit. The court of appeals observed that under the EHA, complaining parties were required to utilize the act's elaborate administrative scheme before challenging the actions of local school authorities in the courts. This administrative review process provided for a factual record and full development of technical issues. It also prevented deliberate disregard of congressionally-established agency procedures. Initial review at the administrative level was required to determine whether the superintendent was providing the educational facilities and programs to which the children were entitled. Permitting the association to bypass EHA administrative procedures would violate Congress' mandate that parents and school officials formulate individualized educational plans together. The due process claim did not require exhaustion of administrative remedies since it was brought under § 1983. The association was required to exhaust the EHA administrative procedures if it desired to contest the alleged insufficient funding and facilities. *Ass'n for Retarded Citizens of Alabama v. Teague*, 830 F.2d 158 (11th Cir.1987).

A disabled child was confined to a juvenile detention center in Florida. He sued the local school board in a U.S. district court under § 504 of the Rehabilitation Act and the EHA. He alleged that the detention center was overcrowded, unsanitary, lacked adequate staffing and was deficient in special education opportunities. The school board moved for dismissal. It contended that the child's claims under § 504 were invalid because the EHA provided all the remedies and procedures which Congress afforded disabled children. It also claimed that the child's lawsuit should be dismissed because he failed to exhaust administrative remedies. The child contended that exhaustion of administrative remedies would be futile. The court held for the child with respect to his § 504 claim. Under the Handicapped Children's Protection Act the child could assert claims under both § 504 and the EHA. However, the court held for the school board regarding its exhaustion of administrative remedies argument. The child failed to show that exhaustion of administrative remedies would be futile or cause him irreparable harm. The school board's motion to dismiss the child's claim was granted. *G.C. v. Coler*, 673 F.Supp. 1093 (S.D.Fla.1987).

The father of a student with a disability in Virginia sued the county school board in a U.S. district court alleging that it had failed to develop a proper IEP for his son. He argued that because the school board had violated federal and state law in its failure to provide appropriate educational services for his son, he did not need to exhaust EHA administrative remedies prior to commencing court proceedings. The school board asked the court to dismiss the father's lawsuit, claiming that he had failed to first seek all of his remedies at the administrative level.

The court observed that administrative remedies must be exhausted prior to any lawsuit filed to vindicate the rights of disabled students. When the father sought to bring suit under other laws he was required to exhaust EHA administrative remedies to the same extent that this exhaustion would be required if the suit had been brought under the EHA. This exhaustion doctrine, observed the court, serves the "interest of accuracy, efficiency, agency autonomy, and judicial economy." Here, although the father disagreed with the IEP developed for his son by the school board, he had made no attempt to invoke the administrative procedures available to him. Further, he had not shown that the exhaustion of administrative remedies would be futile. The court granted the school board's motion for dismissal and ruled that the father could seek relief in federal court if he was still dissatisfied with the IEP after he had fully exhausted his administrative remedies. *Davenport v. Rockbridge County School Bd.*, 658 F.Supp. 132 (W.D.Va.1987).

A severely disabled Wisconsin child, through her parents, brought suit in U.S. district court against the local school district and its special education director, alleging that her right to an appropriate special education and other constitutional rights had been violated by the school district. The child's IEP called for one-to-one instruction which the parents claimed was suspended without notice to them. The school district responded that this action was an "experiment" designed to determine whether the child would benefit by a program change. The parents appealed the child's IEP to the state superintendent of instruction.

Pending the result of the appeal the parents, dissatisfied with the child's educational program, had her independently evaluated and enrolled her at a special rehabilitation facility. When the superintendent finally ruled on the parents' claim, he concluded that the child was entitled to a full-day educational program. The case was tried and the court held that the parents' suit would be dismissed for their failure to exhaust state administrative remedies. The parents were not entitled to reimbursement for the expenses they incurred in having their child independently evaluated and for unilaterally enrolling their child in a special facility. This, said the court, was "self help" activity precluding reimbursement.

The court also found that the parents were not denied due process of law with regard to the change in the child's IEP without notification to the parents. The court stated that although the imposition of a change in an IEP without parental consent may deprive them of "liberty with finality," it was apparent in this case that the alleged damage as a result of the change was minimal. The parents' claim that their equal protection rights under the U.S. Constitution had been violated was without merit because the child had never been totally excluded from any program offered by the school district. The court noted that the parents' argument that exhaustion of remedies should be excused on the ground that the superintendent had failed to reach a final decision within thirty days as required by law was also without merit. This, the court said, would not excuse the parents' failure to exhaust their administrative remedies. The case was dismissed. *Williams v. Overturf*, 580 F.Supp. 1365 (W.D.Wis.1984).

The exhaustion doctrine was also applied in a New York case which involved a blanket decision by the New York Commissioner of Education that learning disabled children were not eligible for residential placement unless their learning disability was accompanied by an additional problem, such as an emotional disturbance. Eighteen learning disabled children who were denied residential placement sued the commissioner in a U.S. district court without first requesting a hearing. The court enjoined the commissioner from adhering to the policy and did not require the parents of the children to exhaust administrative remedies. The commissioner appealed to the U.S. Court of Appeals, Second Circuit, which reversed the district court ruling.

The Court of Appeals held that the district court acted too hastily, and should have required that the children exhaust state administrative remedies before bringing suit in federal court. The court was not persuaded by the parents' argument that exhaustion might prove "futile." There was, according to the court, always the possibility that, during the hearing process, the commissioner might reverse himself in a compelling case if he were proved wrong and a residential placement was shown to be necessary for a learning disabled child. The court stated that exhaustion may well have afforded relief to the children. Accordingly, the parents were not entitled to judicial relief when administrative relief might be available. *Riley v. Ambach*, 668 F.2d 635 (2d Cir.1981).

A Nebraska case involved a mentally retarded child who also suffered from muscular dystrophy. The child, who eventually became confined to a wheelchair, was unable to continue his then current educational placement because of the school's inability to accommodate students in wheelchairs. The child's parents, dissatisfied with the alternate placement provided, brought suit in federal district court challenging the appropriateness of the placement decision. The boy and his parents never requested a due process hearing prior to bringing suit.

At the time the suit was commenced there existed inconsistencies between state and federal administrative procedures. At that time, therefore, the student was under no duty to exhaust administrative remedies. However, at the time the case went to trial the inconsistencies had been resolved. The court held that because the inconsistencies had been rectified there was no longer any justification for permitting the child to circumvent the exhaustion requirement. The court observed that a state hearing officer is in the best position to make an initial determination on a child's placement. Here, there was no reason to believe that the state would not proceed in an expeditious manner if the parents opted for a due process hearing. The parent appealed to the U.S. Court of Appeals, Eighth Circuit. The court of appeals agreed with the district court ruling. No relief could be provided by a federal court where the child's father had failed to exhaust administrative remedies. The boy and his father never invoked the impartial hearing process provided by state law. *Monahan v. State of Nebraska*, 687 F.2d 1164 (8th Cir.1982).

A blind Kentucky child who suffered from other disabilities, including mental retardation, was not making adequate progress in his current placement. His parents and the school district met to discuss the student's IEP placement. The Admission and Release Committee (ARC) recommended that he be placed in a residential school and specifically the Kentucky School of the Blind (KSB), an institution for visually impaired school-aged children. KSB admission criteria requires that a prospective student demonstrate the ability for academic and vocational learning, self-care, and independent functioning. Therefore, the student was denied admission because he required extensive medical care. His parents requested a due process hearing. They sought to have the hearing officer determine if the student should be placed at KSB. In response to the request, the former head of the Kentucky Department of Education's Office of Education for Exceptional Children (OEEC) took the position that KSB was not the proper respondent and also that the hearing officer had no authority to order placement in a particular facility. The parents then instituted an action in a federal district court. Specifically, they asked that the action be styled as a class action for all visually impaired students who have one or more additional disabilities.

The court determined that the action would be certified as a class action. It then decided that if placement at the KSB was the only means by which an appropriate education could be obtained, the school would be required to accept students who did not otherwise meet the school's criteria. The court, however, did determine that the school's admission criteria did not violate due process or equal protection. It also ruled that the parents must exhaust their administrative remedies before filing suit. It then remanded the case so that the parents could exhaust their administrative remedies. *Eva N. v. Brock*, 741 F.Supp. 626 (E.D.Ky.1990).

A New York kindergartner participated in class testing at her school. Because of her poor performance on the psychological and auditory portions, her scores were reported to the district's committee on special education (CSE). The student's mother consented to weekly speech and language services. The school also tried to determine whether the student was disabled within the meaning of state education laws. The officials did not obtain written consent from the student's parent. Several months later, when the school's speech teacher told the student's mother that the student needed to undergo more evaluations, the mother refused permission. She obtained a psychologist at her own expense. The reports were then submitted to the school district, which determined that the student needed special education services. This required classification of the student as a disabled child. The mother objected to the classification, and offered to pay for private education for her daughter. Shortly thereafter, the CSE unanimously classified the student as speech impaired, assigning her to regular classrooms. This was to be supplemented by private speech services at the mother's expense.

The mother objected again to the disabled child designation, and the district's assistant superintendent suggested retesting. The CSE then held another meeting, at which the assistant superintendent discovered that the mother had never previously consented to her daughter's evaluation. The assistant superintendent then nullified all previous CSE findings. The assistant superintendent stated to the mother that he would destroy the student's file if she so desired. When the student's mother did not respond, the assistant superintendent destroyed the file. The mother then filed a civil rights lawsuit in a federal district court, alleging violations of the Rehabilitation Act, the EHA and 42 U.S.C. § 1983. She claimed that the school district had incorrectly classified her daughter without consent. The school district argued that the mother had failed to exhaust her administrative remedies, that the statute of limitations barred her claims, and that the complaint failed to state a claim upon which relief could be granted. The court considered the EHA's requirement for exhaustion of administrative remedies and noted that administrative review was proper if any party was dissatisfied with the results of impartial hearings. Only then could a lawsuit proceed in federal district court. While parties may also seek redress under other acts such as the Rehabilitation Act and § 1983, they are still required to exhaust administrative remedies as if the suit had been brought under the EHA. There were no facts in this case to indicate that the mother should have been excused from exhausting her administrative remedies and the school district was entitled to summary judgment on those grounds. *Buffolino v. Bd. of Educ. of Sachem Central School Dist.*, 729 F.Supp. 240 (E.D.N.Y.1990).

In another New York case the mother of a child with a disability, concerned about her son's lack of progress in his second year of kindergarten, asked that he be evaluated by a psychologist. The mother claimed that a school representative who came to her home with a parental permission form put a check mark on the form in the box indicating that she denied the district permission to conduct an evaluation of her child. The mother later brought suit in a U.S. district court claiming that as a result of being denied the special education to which he was entitled, her son suffered damages to his intellect, emotional capacity and personality, and was impeded in acquiring necessary training. In addition, she alleged that she moved to a different school district to obtain the services her child needed and that she herself had suffered emotional distress. The court held in favor of the mother and the school district appealed. The U.S. Court of Appeals, Second Circuit, held that because the mother had not availed herself of her EHA administrative remedies, she was not entitled to relief under the Act. However, the court did find that the mother had a claim under the Civil Rights Act. *Quakenbush v. Johnson City School Dist.*, 716 F.2d 141 (2d Cir.1983).

B. Exceptions to the Exhaustion Doctrine

The following cases illustrate that exhaustion of administrative remedies is not required when it is clear that the exhaustion of the administrative remedies would be futile or cause irreparable harm. There are cases in which courts deem state administrative remedies inadequate and thus not subject to the exhaustion requirement. Such things as delay by an agency in making a decision, or the fact that the agency may not be empowered to grant relief, will excuse the "exhaustion" requirement. The unavailability of a state or local remedy or a predetermined result by an agency will also excuse the requirement.

A family with a teenage student moved into a school district in New York. The school district's Committee on Special Education (CSE) classified the student as learning disabled and recommended a public school placement, augmented by special education classes. After the student failed to adjust, the CSE recommended a private school placement. A month later the CSE changed the student's classification from learning disabled to emotionally disturbed, in order to expedite state approval of the private placement recommendation. The placement was approved, but the parents withdrew their son from school three days after he began attending classes. When an emergency CSE meeting failed to resolve the parents' concerns, they requested an impartial hearing to challenge the student's classification and placement. The parents, however, were dissatisfied with the method by which New York law allowed selection of hearing officers. According to New York education laws, and the implementing regulations, the board of education selects the hearing officer. The student's father sued, claiming that the method created an economic incentive for hearing officers to rule for the school in order to ensure further work as hearing officers. A federal district court dismissed the action, stating that the father had no standing to challenge the statute, and that he had failed to exhaust his administrative remedies. The father appealed to the U.S. Court of Appeals, Second Circuit.

The court stated that in order for an individual to invoke the power of the federal judiciary an individual: (1) must allege a personal injury or threat of injury; (2) the injury must be traced to the action challenged, and; (3) the injury must be redressed by the requested relief. If these elements are satisfied an individual is said to have "standing." The court noted that all the elements were satisfied here. First, Congress had created a statutory right to due process in the IDEA, a violation of which constitutes injury in fact. Even though the father challenged the choosing of hearing officers on a system-wide basis, he was still personally affected. Second, the injury was traceable to the statute and regulation. Third, an injunction against the use of the statute would redress the alleged harm. Therefore, the district court's ruling on standing was erroneous. In addition, the court stated that seeking administrative remedies would have been futile. As such, they need not have been pursued prior to an action in federal court. The court reinstated the action and remanded the case for further proceedings. *Heldman v. Sobol*, 962 F.2d 148 (2d Cir.1992).

A Florida Court of Appeal clarified the role of appellate courts reviewing cases brought under Florida's plan for the education of children with disabilities. The court noted that the Florida legislation basically followed the Education of the Handicapped Act (now the IDEA) with one important exception — review of the state administrative agency's action may be brought directly to the court of appeal without first bringing a civil action at the trial court level. Such an action would be a necessary prerequisite to appellate review under § 1415(e) of the IDEA, but not under Florida law. The court stated that the importance in this distinction is that the trial court may hear additional evidence, while the court of appeal must be restricted to the record transmitted to it. In effect, if a separate civil action is brought at a trial court level, the case will receive full review as if it were being heard for the first time, whereas a case brought directly to the appellate court would be given traditional appellate review. This means the decision would be overturned only if it lacked competent substantial evidence to support it. *Dist. School Bd. of Putnam County v. Roderick*, 593 So.2d 1174 (Fla.App.1992).

A Virginia student attended a private special education school. The local school district paid his tuition. The student's mother requested that her son be transferred to a neighborhood public school. When the district denied the request, the mother initiated an administrative hearing. A hearing officer affirmed the private school placement. The mother appealed the decision to a state reviewing officer who affirmed the placement. The mother and the district met to develop an individualized education program (IEP). The district sought to have the student placed in a program at a different high school.

The mother rejected the change in placement pending the outcome of a lawsuit she had filed in a Virginia federal district court. She sought to have the court overturn the district's original decision to have the student remain at the private school. At trial, the mother informed the court that she no longer wished to pursue the question of whether the private school placement constituted an appropriate education for her son. She wanted the court to decide the appropriateness of placing her son at the new high school. The court refused to hear the case because the IEP for which administrative proceedings had been conducted was not before it. The mother appealed the district court's dismissal to the U.S. Court of Appeals, Fourth Circuit. The appeals court held that the mother did not have to re-exhaust all administrative remedies. The new IEP continued to provide for the student's education at a place other than where the mother wished. Therefore, her complaint remained the same. It returned the case to the district court to determine if the student should be placed at his neighborhood high school. *DeVries by DeBlaay v. Spillane*, 853 F.2d 264 (4th Cir.1988).

The parents of several students with disabilities in New York filed a class action lawsuit against the New York State Department of Education, the local school board and other local defendants alleging that they had violated the EHA by failing to properly identify, evaluate, and place disabled students. The parents entered into a consent judgment with the local school board and the other local defendants which provided the parents with the relief they had sought in correcting the violations. The parents then sought attorney fees, which were awarded by a U.S. district court. The local school district appealed this award of attorney fees to the U.S. Court of Appeals, Second Circuit.

The court of appeals considered the local school district's argument that attorney fees could not be awarded under the EHA because the parents in this case were not challenging a final decision of a state administrative agency relating to the evaluation or placement of a specific student. The court noted that the generalized procedural violations challenged by the parents "lend themselves well to class action treatment," and that administrative remedies need not be exhausted where they would not provide adequate relief. The court of appeals then noted that the consent judgment in this case provided substantial relief to the parents which could not have been obtained through administrative appeal processes. It therefore concluded that the parents were entitled to attorney fees. It decided that since the parents had sought relief under §§ 1983 and 1988 of the Civil Rights Act as well as the EHA, the award of attorney fees would be made under § 1988. The court of appeals also ruled that the award of attorney fees should be reduced by the amount of such fees which were spent by the parents in suing the state since the state had not participated in the consent judgment. *J.G. v. Rochester City School Dist. Bd. of Educ.*, 830 F.2d 444 (2d Cir.1987).

A severely learning disabled Massachusetts student received special education services since the first grade. When she was fourteen, the school offered her an IEP providing for placement at a learning disabled school. Her parents rejected the IEP and requested an administrative hearing. The hearing officer determined that the IEP would not serve to assure the student's maximal educational benefit and ordered the school district to procure a placement at another school. Despite the hearing officer's order, the school district failed to place the student at the school. The parents then sought injunctive relief in a federal district court to prevent the school district from delaying her enrollment at the school. The school district contended that the girl was not an aggrieved party under the Individuals with Disabilities Education Act (IDEA). The court agreed stating that the student and her mother prevailed before the hearing officer; therefore they were not aggrieved parties under the act. However, the court noted that it did have jurisdiction under 42 U.S.C. § 1983 to enforce the hearing officer's order. The school district objected to the motion for a preliminary injunction. First, it argued that the court should deny the motion because the girl failed to exhaust her administrative remedies. The court disagreed, and indicated that to force her to exhaust her administrative remedies would result in irreparable harm. The affidavit clearly demonstrated that the parents lacked the financial means to provide such placement. Therefore, the court granted the preliminary injunction, forcing the school district to comply with the hearing officer's ruling. *Grace v. Lexington School Committee*, 762 F.Supp. 416 (D.Mass.1991).

In October 1984, a hearing officer found four procedural violations of the EHA by the Baltimore City Schools relating to an eighteen-year-old disabled student. The hearing officer found that the student was a seriously emotionally disturbed adolescent who required a residential placement and ordered the city to permanently place the student in a residential setting by November 20, 1984. On December 5, 1984, the student sued the city in a U.S. district court because the student had not received any change in his educational program. The district court dismissed the student's claims and he appealed to the U.S. Court of Appeals, Fourth Circuit.

The student claimed that he was denied a free appropriate public education when the city school system failed to implement the hearing officer's decision in a timely manner. The district court had dismissed the complaint, holding that the student had failed to exhaust his EHA administrative remedies. The court of appeals disagreed, noting that the student had received a final administrative decision and that he had neither the responsibility nor the right to appeal the favorable decision by the local hearing officer since he was not an aggrieved party. The student had exhausted all administrative remedies and when the city did not appeal the hearing officer's decision, it became the final administrative decision of the state.

The court of appeals also concluded that since the EHA did not contain any provision for enforcing final administrative orders by a hearing officer, the student was entitled to a § 1983 claim. When the city refused to enforce the hearing officer's decision to put the student in a residential placement the city had, under color of state law, violated the EHA. The district court was therefore wrong in dismissing the student's § 1983 claim. His § 1983 claim was remanded to the district court for further proceedings. *Robinson v. Pinderhughes*, 810 F.2d 1270 (4th Cir.1987).

The U.S. Court of Appeals, Second Circuit, reversed a district court's decision to dismiss a case because of the plaintiff's failure to exhaust her administrative remedies. The controversy originally centered on whether a school district was liable for the transportation cost of the plaintiff's son. The school district declined to provide transportation reimbursement, because the tests necessary to determine whether the child was in fact disabled were never made due to the parent's rejection of the school district's psychologists. A final administrative decision then was rendered in favor of the school district. When the case was appealed to a U.S. district court, the judge held that the plaintiff had not exhausted her administrative remedies because the testing data had not been provided. The U.S. Court of Appeals reversed the lower court, stating that the absence of the testing data did not mean that the proper administrative route was not followed by the plaintiff. The court concluded that if a final administrative decision has been rendered, it is to be reviewed on its merits. The case was remanded for further proceedings. *Dubois v. Connecticut State Bd. of Educ.*, 727 F.2d 44 (2d Cir.1983).

The U.S. Department of Education's Office of Civil Rights (OCR) responded to parental complaints about the education of their disabled children against the Georgia State Board of Education and two local school districts by investigating the districts and the state education department. When county special education administrators and state education department officials refused to cooperate with the investigation, the OCR began an administrative proceeding to terminate federal funding of state and local special education. The state board of education and local districts sued the U.S. Department of Education in a federal district court, alleging that the OCR had acted outside its powers. The OCR argued that the case should be dismissed because the Georgia educators had failed to exhaust their administrative remedies. The district court granted the OCR's motion and the Georgia educators appealed to the U.S. Court of Appeals, Eleventh Circuit.

The appeals court agreed with the OCR, ruling that the Georgia educators had failed to exhaust their administrative remedies. The appeals court then amended its decision, giving further grounds for the judgment favoring the OCR's right to challenge the Georgia educators. According to the court, Congress intended federal agencies to implement § 504 of the Rehabilitation Act by appropriate means of regulation and enforcement. This included investigation and review of federal funding recipients. Termination of federal funding was an appropriate sanction, according to a congressional report. The OCR was not plainly outside its jurisdiction by investigating the Georgia educators. Additional grounds for affirming the district court's dismissal of the Georgia educator's complaint were that the EHA did not prohibit federal supervisory action as taken by the OCR, and that the Georgia educators had failed to exhaust their administrative remedies. The appeals court affirmed the judgment, as modified. *Rogers v. Bennett*, 873 F.2d 1387 (11th Cir.1989).

III. STATUTE OF LIMITATIONS

The IDEA does not specify a time limitation in which parties may bring suit in state or federal court after exhausting administrative remedies or appeal an adverse administrative decision. Administrative procedures are generally governed by state laws which usually specify a thirty-day limitation on appeals. However, state laws for other types of actions usually set a longer time limitation. Conflicts arise when one party files a lawsuit or appeals a decision outside what the other party perceives to be the applicable statute of limitations.

A Texas high school student was disabled by formaldehyde sensitization, a medical condition which made it impossible for her to tolerate substances containing formaldehyde, such as smoke, paint, and pesticides. Two years after she reached the age of eighteen, she sued the school district and several of its officers alleging that they had failed to provide her with a learning environment which accommodated her disability, in violation of the Rehabilitation Act. She further charged that they exposed her to harmful chemicals while she was a student at the high school. The defendants moved to dismiss her suit on the grounds that it was barred by the statute of limitations. A federal district court dismissed the claim as time-barred, and the student appealed to the U.S. Court of Appeals, Fifth Circuit. On appeal, the student argued that the statute of limitations should have been tolled until she reached the age of eighteen years. Thus, under the state's two-year limitations period for personal injury claims, her lawsuit would not be untimely because it had been filed exactly two years after she reached the age of eighteen. The appellate court agreed with the student's argument, holding that the district court should have considered the possibility that the statute of limitations was tolled on account of the student's minority. Accordingly, it reversed the district court's decision and remanded the case for a determination of whether the student's birthday was in fact on the date that she alleged it was. *Hickey v. Irving Independent School District*, 976 F.2d 980 (5th Cir.1992).

A Virginia student, with severe learning disabilities, was entitled to receive a free appropriate public education under the IDEA. In June 1989, the local school board awarded the student her high school diploma, and notified her that its obligation to provide her with special education services had terminated. In February 1991, the student's mother filed an administrative complaint, and in June 1991, the Virginia Department of Education issued a Letter of Findings which stated that the school board had complied with state and federal law when it terminated the student's special education. In June 1992, the student and her parents brought suit in federal court, alleging violations of the Rehabilitation Act, 42 U.S.C. § 1983, the IDEA, and the Virginia Regulations Governing Special Education. The school board (and the other school defendants) moved to dismiss the claims as untimely. The U.S. District Court, Eastern District of Virginia, noted that the limitations period under the IDEA was one year. IDEA claims accrue when students and their parents learn of the injury, "whether or not they know the injury is actionable." Here, the injury alleged by the plaintiffs was the premature denial of special education benefits. The student and her parents knew the facts which gave rise to this injury three years earlier, in June 1989, when the student was graduated. The IDEA claim was thus time-barred as were all the other claims. The court dismissed the case. *Richards v. Fairfax County School Bd.*, 798 F.Supp. 338 (E.D.Va.1992).

After a medical student was dismissed from a private school, he brought suit against the school in a federal district court, seeking reinstatement, and alleging that he had been discriminated against in violation of the Rehabilitation Act of 1973. He also alleged that the school breached its contract with him. The school moved to dismiss the action as untimely filed, to strike the claims for compensatory and punitive damages, and to make the complaint more definite. The court, in ruling on the motions, assumed every allegation in the complaint to be admitted by the school. It noted first that the student, at the age of twenty, was diagnosed with a hereditary neuroendocrine condition known as "Panic Disorder." However, a resident in training at the medical school, who was treating him, determined that he was addicted to the medication he was taking to control the condition. He then switched to an alternative medication prescribed by the resident. Due to problems associated with the new medication, he had problems in his second year, and, after failing a class in his third year, was dismissed. His requests for readmittance were denied.

The court noted that the Rehabilitation Act did not contain a provision which specified a controlling statute of limitations. However, the U.S. Supreme Court has held that where a federal civil rights statute does not contain a statute of limitations, "federal courts should select the most appropriate or analogous state statute of limitations." Under federal law, a claim under the Rehabilitation Act in Virginia is analogous to a claim for an injury to a person, held the court. Thus, since that time period was two years, the claim was timely filed. The court went on to find that the claim for breach of contract needed to be made more certain and definite, and that the motion to strike the claims for compensatory and punitive damages (with respect to the breach of contract action) had to be deferred until the more definite statement was filed. *Wolsky v. Eastern Virginia Medical Authority*, 795 F.Supp. 171 (E.D.Va.1992).

A New Hampshire student and the student's parents were dissatisfied with the student's individualized education plan (IEP) and sued in federal court for review of a state hearing officer's decision to uphold the plan. They claimed that the IEP was not promulgated in compliance with procedures established by the IDEA and that it violated the protections guaranteed by the Rehabilitation Act and its implementing regulations. However, the claim was brought 32 days after the hearing officer's decision was issued. The school district argued that the claim was brought two days too late and should be dismissed, citing the 30 day statute of limitations for review of administrative decisions. The student argued that the limitation period begins to run when the hearing officer's decision is received, not when it is issued. The U.S. District Court, District of New Hampshire, stated that the limitation period begins to run upon issuance of the administrative decision. The court also stated that there was no reason not to apply the statute of limitations in this case. The student and parents had the assistance of counsel, who admitted familiarity with the 30-day rule. The court dismissed the IDEA action, leaving intact the Rehabilitation Act claim. *I.D. v. Westmoreland School Dist.*, 788 F.Supp. 632 (D.N.H.1991).

In a motion for reconsideration, the parents and student argued that a new cause of action accrued when they received notice of the hearing officer's decision complete with its own 30-day limitation period. They also argued that the 30-day statute of limitation should be equitably tolled in this case, and that the court should not retroactively apply the statute of limitation. The court renewed its dismissal. The receipt of the hearing officer's decision did not create a new cause of action with its own 30-day limitation period. The petition was still untimely. The court also stated that there remained no reason to equitably toll the statute of limitation. Finally, the court stated that the New Hampshire federal court which originally announced the 30-day limitation period applied it to its own litigants — therefore, there was no reason not to apply it in this case. Again, the court allowed only the student's claim under the Rehabilitation Act to continue. *I.D. v. Westmoreland School Dist.*, 788 F.Supp. 634 (D.N.H.1992).

A New Hampshire Department of Education hearing officer found that a student's individual education plan (IEP) was both procedurally and substantively in compliance with the Individuals with Disabilities Education Act (IDEA), 20 U.S.C. § 1400, *et seq.* The hearing officer rendered his decision on August 29. The student's attorney received the decision on September 4, and commenced a district court suit pursuant to §1415(e)(2) of the IDEA for review of the administrative decision on October 4. The school district argued that the suit was untimely because the 30-day limitation period for court review of administrative decisions began to run at the date of the decision. The student argued that the 30-day limitation started to run when the decision was received and not when it was issued. The court held that the suit was untimely. Cases decided in New Hampshire federal court after this lawsuit had been brought had determined that a 30-day limitation period applied to §1415(e)(2) actions in New Hampshire, and that this period began to run when the decision was issued. Despite the student's argument that it would be unfair to apply the reasoning in those cases to this lawsuit, since they were decided after this suit was brought, the court applied the limitation period to this case. In general, courts will apply a new rule of law to pending cases if the rule was also applied to the case in which it was actually announced. The courts in the preceding cases had applied the new rules of limitations to the litigants in those cases, so they would be applied in this case as well. *G.D. v. Westmoreland School Dist.*, 783 F.Supp. 1532 (D.N.H.1992).

A learning disabled cognitive impaired 14-year-old student attended a Massachusetts school from kindergarten through sixth grade. Her school district proposed an individualized educational plan (IEP) for the 1989-90 school year. The IEP called for the student's placement in a special education class in the district. The student's parents, however, placed their daughter in a private school and formally rejected the proposed IEP. The parents requested a hearing from the state Bureau of Special Education Appeals (BSEA). The BSEA determined that the school district could provide the student with an appropriate education. The BSEA denied the parents' motion for reconsideration.

Pursuant to § 1415(e)(2) of the Individuals with Disabilities Education Act (IDEA), the parents brought an action in federal district court to review the BSEA's decision. The action was brought over six months later and the school district moved to dismiss the complaint based on the 30-day Massachusetts statute of limitations for review of administrative decisions. The parents argued that the limitation did not apply. The U.S. District Court for the District of Massachusetts held that a 30-day limitation period did apply. The court noted that the IDEA does not specify a limitation period for bringing actions under § 1415(e)(2). In such cases, the federal courts borrow an appropriate statute of limitation derived from state law. The limitation is chosen from the "most analogous" state cause of action, so long as the limitation period is consistent with federal policies. The court stated that the most analogous period was the 30-day limitation period for appellate review of administrative actions. The court also held that this period was not inconsistent with the purposes of the IDEA. The court dismissed the complaint. *Gertel v. School Comm. of Brookline School Dist.*, 783 F.Supp. 701 (D.Mass.1992).

Since the first grade, a New Hampshire student had been identified as an educationally disabled student. He was both learning and emotionally disabled. Over the next four years, the student's varying IEPs called for a self-contained classroom or, in the alternative, mainstream classes with a resource room supplementation. However, his behavior and progress deteriorated over these years. Finally, two different doctors evaluated the student and determined that his progress was restricted substantially by his language disorder. On the basis of these reports, his parents rejected the IEP. It had outlined a program similar to the one which was unsuccessfully completed previously because it had not adequately addressed his learning disability. When an impasse was reached, the parents unilaterally placed him in a private school and requested a due process hearing. The hearing officer concluded that the student's IEP and proposed placement were inappropriate, that the parents' unilateral placement was appropriate, and that the parents should be reimbursed for the expenses. The school district appealed to a federal district court.

The court determined that the first issue to be addressed was whether the school district's action, instituted ninety-four days after the decision of the hearing officer, was time-barred. The court noted that Congress had not established a statute of limitations for actions under the EHA. Federal courts must borrow one from an analogous state cause of action, provided that the state limitations are consistent with the underlying federal policies. The court determined that the applicable statute of limitations was the thirty-day statute governing appeals from administrative decisions. Therefore, the claim was time barred and the parents' motion to dismiss was granted. *Bow School Dist. v. Quentin W.*, 750 F.Supp. 546 (D.N.H.1990).

A Michigan father brought suit in a federal district court on behalf of his disabled daughter and himself against their school district. His complaint sought review of two due process hearings held in the spring of 1985 and early 1986 to resolve disputes concerning the IEP established for his daughter. In 1989, the father sought a due process hearing reviewing the 1985 and 1986 hearings, but the school district denied the request. The Michigan Department of Education investigated the request and ordered the district to hold a due process hearing. The decision was appealed to the U.S. Department of Education's Office of Special Education and Rehabilitative Services which denied the appeal. When the due process hearing was not held the father instituted this action in a federal district court.

The school district objected to the father representing the interest of his daughter since he was not licensed to practice law. The court noted that while a litigant has the right to act as his own counsel he may not be permitted to represent the interest of his minor child. Therefore, the court dismissed all of the daughter's claims without prejudice. The court next turned to the claims under the EHA on behalf of the father. The school district contended that the statute of limitations had run out and that the claims must fail. The court noted a two-step analysis had been developed to determine which state statute of limitations should be applied to a federal cause of action that lacks an express limitations period. The court must first determine which state cause of action is most analogous and then decide whether the state statute of limitations governing that action is consistent with the policies of the EHA. The court determined that the three year statute of limitations that is applicable to all claims against the state of Michigan was the most analogous here. Therefore, the disputes over the student's IEP that were resolved in the spring of 1985 and early 1986 were time barred. The court further found that the father failed to exhaust his administrative remedies and dismissed the lawsuit. *Lawson v. Edwardsburg Public School*, 751 F.Supp. 1257 (W.D.Mich.1990).

A learning-disabled student completed fourth grade in a mainstream class at a private school. His parents then requested the District of Columbia Public Schools (DCPS) to provide special education services. The DCPS proposed an IEP which included placement in a special education program in their public school in which students with disabilities were placed with nondisabled students for a quarter of their curriculum. The parents disagreed with the IEP and requested a hearing. They claimed that the private school was an appropriate educational environment because it did not involve contact with nondisabled students. A hearing officer approved a modified version of the DCPS's IEP but the parents kept their son at the private school and paid his expenses for the next three years. The DCPS advised the parents that the hearing officer's determination was final but that an appeal could be made to an appropriate court. The notice did not advise the parents of any applicable statute of limitations. Nearly three years later the parents sued the DCPS in a federal district court under the EHA for an order declaring the IEP inappropriate. They also sought approval of the student's current private school placement and tuition expenses. The court applied a local thirty-day statute of limitations, which barred review of the hearing officer's order. The parents appealed to the U.S. Court of Appeals, District of Columbia Circuit.

The appeals court noted that the EHA did not specifically provide a statute of limitations for appeals from final administrative determinations. Where Congress did not establish a statute of limitations for federal lawsuits, federal courts could "borrow" local statutes of limitation provided they did not conflict with underlying federal policies. Whenever the school district made a new placement decision, a new thirty-day period would begin in which parents could file a claim. The court noted that while other federal circuits had approved longer statutes of limitation, the thirty-day period was consistent with federal law. However, the DCPS had failed to advise the parents that they had only thirty days to file an appeal in the appropriate court. For this reason, the court reversed the district court's decision. *Spiegler v. Dist. of Columbia*, 866 F.2d 461(D.C.Cir.1989).

A mentally disabled North Carolina student attended a local public school. Due to psychological difficulties, the student was then placed in a Texas private school. In the meantime, the board of education placement committee for the student's North Carolina school district recommended placement at another North Carolina institution. The board informed the parents of their right to appeal the decision and stated that they would not be reimbursed for the Texas private school tuition. The parents paid for the student's private education. The student was insured under a group health insurance policy provided by her father's employer. A special self-insurance plan benefited the student individually. It provided a $100,000 maximum lifetime benefit for therapeutic services relating to mental and nervous disorders. When the student turned eighteen, a legal guardian was appointed for her. The student then sued the board seeking reimbursement for the depletion of health insurance benefits which had been used to pay for her education. A federal district court granted summary judgment for the board, finding that although the statute of limitations had been tolled, the student lacked standing. The student then appealed to the U.S. Court of Appeals, Fourth Circuit.

The court of appeals held that the district court had correctly determined that the state's three-year statute of limitations was tolled by the student's infancy and incompetence. The student's claim was not time barred. She had timely filed the complaint after she attained majority. The court also held that the student had standing to seek reimbursement for the depletion of health insurance benefits used to pay for her education. Although none of the student's own funds were used, her remaining insurance benefits had been reduced from $100,000 to $36,000. Under state law, the student was deemed a third-party beneficiary of the insurance contract between her father, his employer and the employer's group health insurer. The student had standing to prosecute her claim under the EHA. The court of appeals remanded the district court's decision for further proceedings. *Shook v. Gaston County Bd. of Educ.*, 882 F.2d 119 (4th Cir.1989).

An educationally disabled New Hampshire student attended a day school program. The student's parents requested the school district to place the student in a residential program. The district denied their demand and the parents requested a hearing before the state Department of Education. The hearing officer determined that the student should be placed in a residential facility, which was done at the district's expense. At the time, attorney's fees were not available to prevailing parties under the EHA so the parents did not apply for them. In 1986, Congress amended the act permitting prevailing parties in EHA claims to recover attorney's fees. The parents did not apply for them at that time. Two years later, the district sought to place the student in a day program. The parents' attorney discovered that they were entitled to recover attorney's fees for the earlier action and filed a lawsuit in federal district court. Both parties moved for summary judgment.

The district court held that the state's three year statute of limitations for personal actions governed the EHA claim for attorney's fees. The scope of judicial review under the EHA was the same as that required in personal injury actions. The court also ruled that the delay of nearly twenty-seven months was unreasonable, but did not prejudice the city or the school district. The attorneys who participated in the initial action were available for discovery purposes. The court also found that the city and school district had no standing to challenge the retroactive application of attorney's fees. The district court found the parents entitled to attorney's fees and denied the city and school district's motion for summary judgment. *James v. Nashua School Dist.*, 720 F.Supp. 1053 (D.N.H.1989).

A disabled New York student attended special education classes for which the school district sought tuition reimbursement from another New York school district. The district claiming compensation failed to notify the other school district of any claim or lawsuit until two years after the expenses were incurred. New York education law sets a statute of limitations for an action to recover money from a school district at one year, and requires lawsuits filed after one year to be dismissed. The Supreme Court of Westchester County determined that there was no basis for finding the one year statute of limitations inapplicable. *Bd. of Educ. of the Katonah-Lewisboro School Dist. v. Bd. of Educ. of the Carmel Central School Dist.*, 549 N.Y.S.2d 322 (Sup.Ct.1989).

A mother placed her autistic son in a private school in California from February 1974, through February 1975. Her son entered his local school district's program in September 1977, but was suspended in December 1978, for disciplinary reasons. Without obtaining her consent the school district notified the mother that her son would be taught at home pending evaluation. However, the school district delayed his evaluation until May 1979, and failed to hold an IEP meeting until June 1979. The IEP recommended a special day school for her son but a teachers' strike delayed the school's opening until October 1979.

Her son continued in the day school until 1985 when he was notified that he was no longer eligible for public education because he was 22 years of age. The mother requested a hearing to contest the decision to terminate his education. She alleged that the school district had violated § 504 of the Rehabilitation Act in 1974-75 by excluding her son from the public school. She requested total reimbursement for all private school expenses or a compensatory education. She also contended that the school district violated the EHA in 1979 by not timely providing her son with an appropriate education. After the hearing officer ruled for the school district the mother appealed to a U.S. district court, which upheld the hearing officer's decision. She then appealed to the U.S. Court of Appeals, Ninth Circuit.

Because § 504 contains no statute of limitations, the court borrowed the statute of limitations governing similar disputes under California law, which provided for a three-year limitation. Because the statute of limitations began to run when the mother knew or had reason to know of the injury, she was too late in filing her claim. Her EHA claim was also barred because she waited six years to assert it. The district court's decision in favor of the school district was affirmed. *Alexopulos v. San Francisco Unified School Dist.*, 817 F.2d 551 (9th Cir.1987).

A disabled nine-year-old New York boy who suffered from speech and motor difficulties was evaluated by his school district's committee on the handicapped

(COH). The COH then made a recommendation for an educational placement of the boy which his parents believed to be inappropriate. They appealed the placement decision to the New York Commissioner of Education, who ruled in favor of the parents. However, the Commissioner declined to order that the parents be reimbursed for the boy's educational expenses incurred as a result of the parents' decision to unilaterally place their child in a private school. The private school had provided an appropriate education for the boy during the ten-month period from the time of the initial, incorrect COH evaluation to the time the Commissioner's decision was rendered.

Fifteen months after the Commissioner's decision denying reimbursement, the parents sued in U.S. district court seeking reimbursement for the private school tuition. The district court held that the suit was barred by the statute of limitations, a decision upheld by the U.S. Court of Appeals, Second Circuit. While noting that the EHA contains no statute of limitations, the appeals court stated that the applicable state statute of limitations will be applied in EHA lawsuits. In this case there was a conflict between a New York statute governing educational proceedings in state courts which called for a four-month limit, and a more general New York statute providing for a three-year limit on any suit "to recover upon a liability . . . created or imposed by statute."

The district court had relied upon the law providing for a four-month limit because it was the one most closely analogous to the present cause of action had it arisen under state law. The Court of Appeals sanctioned this approach, noting that to allow the longer three-year statute of limitations to govern lawsuits seeking reimbursement for educational expenses would conflict with the EHA requirement that a child remain in his current educational placement during the pendency of any proceedings to review the appropriateness of a child's placement. Said the court, "this 'status quo' provision hardly contemplates a period of three years plus pendency of the proceedings. After all, it is a child's education we are talking about." The court therefore refused to allow the three-year general statute of limitations to govern the case and stated that because the parents had failed to appeal the Commissioner's decision within four months, their suit had been properly dismissed. *Adler v. Education Department of State of New York*, 760 F.2d 454 (2d Cir.1985).

The mother of a twenty-year-old mentally disabled, speech impaired and emotionally disturbed girl filed suit in U.S. district court against the Board of Education of Wood County, West Virginia. Since 1969, the girl had been enrolled at a private school in Wichita, Kansas. For several years the mother paid the entire cost of this education. After Congress enacted the EHA, the Board of Education assumed responsibility for the bulk of her educational and residential costs at the Institute. However, when the girl reached the age of eighteen the board concluded that she could be appropriately educated in the Wood County public school system. The mother was told that the board would no longer pay the cost of her private school education.

The mother objected and requested a due process hearing. The hearing officer agreed with the Board of Education that the girl should be transferred from the private school to the Wood County public school. The mother appealed the hearing officer's decision to the West Virginia State Board of Education which agreed with Wood County's decision to place the girl in the public school system. The mother filed suit in U.S. district court nearly one year after the State Board's decision and the school board asked that the suit be dismissed because it had been filed more than 120 days after the State Board's decision. The 120-day limitation would be applied only to West Virginia special education cases filed after the present decision. *Thomas v. Staats*, 633 F.Supp. 797 (S.D.W.Va.1985).

A twelve-year-old boy with a disability was enrolled at the Achievement Center, a private school for the learning disabled in the Roanoke, Virginia, area. Previously, he had been enrolled in Roanoke County public schools in which he had only taken special education classes in one area, mathematics. His parents were unhappy with a single math class being the only special education class provided. During the 1983-84 school year, the child's academic and social problems became severe and his parents filed a complaint against the superintendent for failure to develop a sufficient IEP. A hearing officer held that the IEP was adequate and the parents were denied tuition reimbursement. The state review board affirmed the hearing officer's decision. Seventy-six days after the state board's decision, the parents filed a complaint under the EHA against the school superintendent claiming that the school district was denying their son an appropriate education. The school moved for dismissal on the ground that the complaint had been filed too late.

The U.S. district court noted that because the EHA does not specify a time limit in which to bring a lawsuit, the courts must determine the time limit based on the "most analogous" state cause of action. It found the Virginia Supreme Court Rules 2A:2 and 2A:4 analogous to EHA proceedings, but held that the thirty-day limit contained in the Rules was not in keeping with EHA policy. Instead, the court found that the one-year statute of limitations provided for tort actions under a state statute (Va. Code secs. 8.01-248) was the appropriate time limit. Congress' policy in EHA cases was that placement disputes be given as fair and complete a hearing as possible. Finding that the one-year statute of limitations for tort cases was more conducive to fairness, the court denied the school's motion to dismiss the complaint. *Kirchgessner v. Davis*, 632 F.Supp. 616 (W.D.Va.1986).

A thirty-day statute of limitations period did not bar a suit brought against the Pennsylvania Department of Education and a local school district. A disabled student requiring clean intermittent catheterization to enable her to attend school challenged a school district policy which denied such services. The U.S. Court of Appeals, Third Circuit, affirmed a district court ruling in favor of the child. The court of appeals agreed with the district court's decision to apply either a two-year or a six-year statute of limitations period to the child's claim under the EHA. Finding that the thirty-day limitations period was incompatible with the EHA, the court held that it did not apply. The court of appeals decided that the two-year state statute of limitations which applied to actions to recover damages for injuries caused by the wrongful act or negligence of another, and controlled in medical malpractice cases, was the most analogous statute. Because the child's claim was brought within the two-year period, her action was not barred. *Tokarcik v. Forest Hills School Dist.*, 665 F.2d 443 (3d Cir.1981).

In a Texas case, a child with a disability was placed by her school district in a public facility which was equipped to treat children with emotional disturbances and autism. She made progress during her first year there. However, during the second year she regressed significantly. The parents removed her from the facility and placed her in another institute. After tuition expenses were denied by the child's school district, the parents sought relief in a U.S. district court which held that because the parents had brought suit nine months after the denial, their claim was barred by a thirty-day statute of limitations. In addition, said the court, the parents forfeited all rights to recover tuition for the private residential facility by unilaterally withdrawing the child from the school district's program. The parents appealed this decision to the U.S. Court of Appeals, Fifth Circuit, which agreed with the district court ruling that the parents were not entitled to reimbursement, but reversed the thirty-day statute of limitations ruling, saying that the limitation was inconsistent with the EHA policy of investing parents with discretion to take action regarding their children's education. *Scokin v. State of Texas*, 723 F.2d 432 (5th Cir.1984).

In Hawaii, a thirty-day statute of limitations period did apply to a suit brought outside that period by the Hawaii Department of Education. The Department had filed two suits in federal court challenging adverse hearing officer decisions on the issue of responsibility for the costs of educating two disabled children. The U.S. Court of Appeals, Ninth Circuit, held that the Department's suit was barred by its failure to appeal the hearing officer's decision within the thirty-day limitation period set by the Hawaii Administrative Procedures Act. The court found the APA to provide a more comprehensive standard of review than the EHA. Further, the need to avoid delays in resolving disputes over education plans for disabled children supported the application of a thirty-day statute of limitations period for a state agency to appeal an adverse decision. The court affirmed a U.S. district court decision to dismiss the cases. However, the court noted that it was not being asked to decide whether the same thirty-day rule would apply to parents or guardians seeking judicial review of a disabled child's placement. The thirty-day rule may not apply in those cases. *Dep't of Educ., State of Hawaii v. Carl D.*, 695 F.2d 1154 (9th Cir.1983).

IV. FAILURE TO COMPLY WITH THE IDEA

Due process of law is contingent upon a school district's adherence to IDEA procedural safeguards. The failure to adhere to the IDEA will generally result in a favorable ruling for the parents or guardians of students with disabilities.

A functionally retarded, learning disabled student resided at a Massachusetts private school until he was twenty years old. The student and his social worker reached an agreement to terminate the student's placement at the school. The student expressed a desire to live with his mother. He was then discharged from the school and into the custody of his mother. The student's termination occurred without the involvement of either his surrogate parent, appointed by the state, or his mother. Neither party was provided with notice or an opportunity to participate in the termination decision. Within a few weeks, the living arrangement fell apart. The family services agency placed the student in a structured home. The placement lasted twenty-four hours. The student then moved into a homeless shelter and a series of temporary living arrangements. Thereafter, he began supporting himself through prostitution. The student's mother challenged the termination in an administrative hearing. The hearing officer determined that the student terminated the placement himself and was not entitled to compensatory education. The mother then brought an action in a federal district court. The district court dismissed an EHA claim determining that the EHA procedural safeguards such as the stay-put provision are not applicable when a legally competent adult chooses to leave an institution. The mother then appealed to the U.S. Court of Appeals, Second Circuit.

The EHA provides that if there is any proposed change in a child's IEP, the parent or guardian must be notified in writing. The parent or guardian then has the right to contest the matter in an impartial due process hearing conducted by the state educational agency. During the pendency of these proceedings, the child must be allowed to remain in his current educational placement under the stay-put provision of the act [§ 1415(e)(3)]. The court determined that the issue was whether the state must comply with the EHA procedural safeguards before terminating the educational placement of a disabled student who is between eighteen and twenty-one, on the basis of the student's consent. The court noted that the EHA and the U.S. Department of Education make it clear that if a state provides education to an eighteen to twenty-one-year-old disabled child, the requirements of the EHA apply. Thus, the statute and the relevant state regulations apply to an eighteen to twenty-one-year-old even though there has been no determination of incompetency. The court held that the state was required to comply with the EHA procedural safeguards before it terminated, on the basis of consent, the educational placement of a student. The court reversed the decision of the trial court and remanded the case to determine the amount of compensatory education to which the student was entitled. *Mrs. C. v. Wheaton*, 916 F.2d 69 (2d Cir.1990).

An emotionally disabled New York student attended a vocational school as a part of his mainstreaming. His parents were notified that the school district intended to graduate him at the end of the school year. When the vocational school notified the parents that the student should continue in its program for another year, the parents requested an impartial hearing. They objected to their son being graduated because he had not attained targets established by the vocational school. Following the hearing but prior to the hearing officer's decision, the student was graduated. The hearing officer agreed that graduation was appropriate and the parents appealed to the Commissioner of Education. They requested that their son be allowed to continue the vocational program until a final decision was reached. The commissioner denied the request and determined that the student had been properly graduated.

The parents sued the school district in a New York federal district court. They asserted that the school district violated the EHA stay-put provision by graduating their son. They sought to have their son reinstated to the vocational program pending a final decision. The court noted that one of the purposes of the stay-put provision was to prevent school officials from removing a child from the classroom over the parents' objection pending completion of review proceedings. It then noted that what had to be determined was whether graduation constituted a change in placement. The court equated graduation to a long-term suspension because it resulted in the total exclusion of the student from his educational placement. Therefore, EHA procedural safeguards should be enforced. The court ordered the school district to reinstate the student to the vocational program during the pendency of the proceedings. *Cronan v. Bd. of Educ. of East Ramapo Cent. School Dist.*, 689 F.Supp. 197 (S.D.N.Y.1988).

The procedures outlined in the EHA bind the parents or guardians of students as well as schools.

A Michigan child received special education services under an emotional impaired (EI) label. His school district suspended him in April 1985, due to the increasing severity of his emotional problems. In May 1985, the school district convened an IEP meeting for him. His parents approved of the May 1985 IEP. The child was hospitalized for a suicide attempt in the fall of 1985. He never returned to the district's school. The child's parents independently obtained several professional evaluations which recommended a twelve month residential placement in a highly structured environment. On November 4, 1985, the parents unilaterally placed him in the Devereux Foundation School in Pennsylvania. After numerous procedural steps, a state hearing officer affirmed a local hearing officer's decision which required the child to submit to an evaluation in Michigan. The parents sued the school district in U.S. district court. At a February 1986 IEP meeting the parents asked the school district to conduct an evaluation of the child in Pennsylvania.

The parents contended that the school district waived its right to compel evaluation since it refused their February 1986 request to evaluate the child at Devereux. They also argued that the state level decision compelling evaluation violated the child's due process rights. The parents claimed that only the Devereux evaluations should be considered in determining his IEP. The district court held for the school district. It was undisputed that the child was in Pennsylvania when his parents offered him for evaluation. The school district was under no duty to go to Pennsylvania to conduct an evaluation of the child who had been unilaterally removed from the school district without the prior knowledge or acquiescence of school officials. His due process rights were not denied since the school district requested an evaluation of the child before rendering a final decision. Having overlooked EHA procedures, the parents could not now seek to have the school district place the child at Devereux. *Lenhoff v. Farmington Pub. Schools*, 680 F.Supp. 921 (E.D.Mich.1988).

A fourth grade boy displayed signs of disruptive behavior and his teacher suggested that he receive psychological help. To avoid having such information on his school records, his parents enrolled him in a private school outside of the district. After he was expelled from the private school and had attended a series of public schools unsuccessfully, his grandmother contacted the Seattle school district to ask if the district could help with the costs of his private school enrollment. She was told the school district would have to do a "complete workup" to find out what his needs were and what could be done. The district psychologist contacted the boy's mother and told her that based on his limited information, he could not find the boy eligible for special education services but that the school district would evaluate his needs should he return to the area. The mother requested a hearing. The Seattle superintendent of public instruction reversed the decision and the mother initiated a lawsuit.

The Court of Appeals of Washington stated that the issue was whether a school district must reimburse a parent for tuition costs when the parent unilaterally places a child in an out-of-state private school before the school district has had an opportunity to assess the child's needs and make a recommendation. The EHA authorizes tuition reimbursement, in appropriate cases, when the parents and the district disagree as to which educational placement is appropriate for the child. In this case, however, such disagreement was absent. The mother's unilateral placement of her son in the private school without the district's assessment prevented recovery of her expenses for his private school education. *Hunter v. Seattle School Dist. No. 1*, 731 P.2d 19 (Wash.App.1987).

The U.S. Court of Appeals, Fourth Circuit, ruled that a school district's failure to fully advise the parents of a dyslexic child of their EHA procedural rights justified unilateral private school placement by the parents. In this North Carolina case, the child, who had been enrolled in his local public elementary school, had extreme difficulty in reading. Although he was required to repeat second grade, the child was thereafter advanced due to the school district's practice of making "social promotions." When the child reached the third grade, an IEP was developed which identified him as having reading deficiencies only and called for placement in a regular classroom 90% of the time, and placement in a learning disabilities resource room for the remainder of the time. When the child reached the fifth grade he still could not read. In desperation, his parents enrolled him in a private residential facility. At this time a private evaluation of the child was performed which finally disclosed that although he was of above average intelligence, the child suffered from dyslexia. The parents also discovered for the first time that under federal law their school district might be obligated to pay for their child's placement at the private school. The parents filed suit and a U.S. district court ruled in their favor.

On appeal, the U.S. Court of Appeals upheld the district court's ruling, ordering that the school district must pay the cost of the child's placement at the private school. The child had made no educational progress while in the public schools and the IEP developed by public school officials was utterly inadequate, said the court. The school district's contention that the child had achieved educational benefits because he had advanced from grade to grade was dismissed by the appellate court, due to the school's policy of making social promotions. Furthermore, the school district's failure to fully inform the parents of their rights under the EHA constituted a *per se* breach of its statutory duties. The appellate court also noted that the child had finally begun to make educational progress after his placement at the private residential school. The child's parents were thus entitled to recover the costs of his placement from the school district. *Hall v. Vance County Bd. of Educ.*, 774 F.2d 629 (4th Cir.1985).

The parents of a learning disabled boy claimed that the Mississippi Board of Education violated the EHA by not having an impartial state review team decide whether to reimburse them for their son's tuition at a private school during the 1984-85 school year and to provide a private education for the next school year. The parents had become dissatisfied with the IEP developed for their son, a learning disabled child. They sought an administrative hearing concerning the child's proper placement and reimbursement for the tuition they had paid at a private school. The hearing officer ruled that the parents should be reimbursed for the 1984-85 school year, but that the child should return to the public school system. On appeal, however, the state review board ruled that the parents should not receive tuition reimbursement and that the boy should return to public school.

The parents filed suit in federal district court, requesting a new hearing before the state review board. The district court granted the request because it found that the State Board of Education had violated the EHA. The court held that officers of local school boards and personnel active in state policy for the education of disabled children should not serve on the state review panel. These individuals were too closely involved with the State Board of Education and could not provide the parents with an impartial hearing. Also, the court ruled that a state review team must make specific findings of fact in support of their conclusions under the EHA. *Kotowicz v. Mississippi State Bd. of Educ.*, 630 F.Supp. 925 (S.D.Miss.1986).

Another school district was found to have violated the procedural safeguards of the EHA by the failure to provide an impartial hearing officer. This case arose in Iowa and involved a challenge to a local school district's decision to place a child in special education classes. The child's guardian brought suit against the Iowa State Superintendent of Public Instruction alleging that the superintendent violated the "impartial hearing officer" provision of the EHA by presiding over the due process hearing which the child had received. A U.S. district court held that the superintendent violated the EHA provision barring employees of agencies involved in the education of a child from serving as hearing officers in due process hearings required by the Act. The district court remanded the case for a new hearing which was to be presided over by an outside hearing officer and the superintendent appealed to the U.S. Court of Appeals, Eighth Circuit.

The court of appeals was asked to decide whether the superintendent, as Superintendent of Public Instruction and an employee of the State Board of Public Instruction, was employed by a direct provider of educational services, the local school board, or whether he merely exercised supervisory authority over the direct provider. The court affirmed the district court ruling, declaring the superintendent to be statutorily disqualified from serving as a hearing officer. The EHA's clear language and history indicate that "no hearing may be conducted by an employee of the State or local educational agency involved in the education or care of the child." *Robert M. v. Benton*, 634 F.2d 1139 (8th Cir.1980).

The parents of an emotionally and learning disabled child with severe behavioral problems brought suit against an Oregon school district alleging that an appropriate education program was not being made available to their child and that the school district had violated statutes and regulations it was legally bound to follow. They requested and received a complaint hearing before the state Department of Education (DOE). The DOE found that the school district had violated applicable state and federal laws and awarded the parents partial reimbursement of tuition costs they had incurred by enrolling their son in a private school. However, it denied the parents' request for attorney fees. Both the parents and the school district appealed to the Court of Appeals of Oregon.

The court held that the DOE was the correct forum in which to bring the complaint. Had the parents' complaint alleged only that they disagreed with the district's IEP or educational placement for their child, the proper forum for resolution of that matter would have been a due process hearing. However, it alleged that an appropriate educational program was not made available to the child and also that the district violated various other federal statutes and regulations. Accordingly, the correct forum was a "complaint hearing." Such a hearing is governed by Oregon state law, which requires that local school districts comply with the EHA, that school districts have complaint procedures available for alleged violations and that sanctions be imposed against noncomplying districts. However, the DOE, after finding violations, did not have the authority to require the school district to reimburse the parents' expenses. The district had a duty, said the court, to provide the child with a free appropriate education and, its having failed in that duty, the DOE only had the authority to withhold funds from it. The court went on to hold that the DOE had the power to award attorney fees even though it had not done so in this case, and that the DOE's findings of fact were supported by substantial evidence. *Laughlin v. School Dist. No. 1*, 686 P.2d 385 (Or.App.1984).

The parents of an eleven-year-old learning disabled child in the District of Columbia, dissatisfied with a local school district's placement of the child, expressed their concern to the school staff. A meeting with school staff followed in which the parents again reiterated the concerns they had expressed earlier regarding the appropriateness of the child's education. After the meeting the school sent the parents a "Notice of Continuing Special Education Services," which stated that the child was to continue in the current program at the school. The notice did not inform the parents of the need to file any form, not did it state any way by which a dissatisfied parent could challenge the school's decision. A hearing was scheduled, but it was later canceled by the school. A letter to the parents' attorney stated that "since the school was 'unaware' of the parents' desire to change the child's program, no formal evaluation procedure had been initiated for the child." Accordingly, the letter continued, "the public schools will not be ready, nor are they required to participate at a hearing until they are given an opportunity to complete the formal evaluation/placement process."

The parents then brought suit against the school in federal court requesting the court to order the school to provide a due process hearing in which their objections to their child's continued placement at the school would be "fully ventilated." Without the hearing, claimed the parents, they were being denied due process guarantees mandated by the EHA and the Act's regulations which require that the parents or guardian of a child be afforded a hearing whenever they have a complaint about a school district's proposal to change or refusal to change a child's educational placement or any matter concerning the child's placement.

The school also argued that the parents had failed to submit a "Form 205" request which would have given the school notice of their objections. Noting that a school must be afforded reasonable notice of any parent's desire for a change of placement before the school is required to act upon the request, the court nevertheless found that the notice of placement to the parents did not inform them that filing "Form 205" was the proper procedure for objecting to their child's placement. Accordingly, the court denied the school's motion to dismiss the case and ordered that a hearing be held within five days of the court's order to address the parents' complaints about their child's IEP. *Pastel v. Dist. of Columbia Bd. of Educ.*, 522 F.Supp. 535 (D.D.C.1981).

A child with a disability and his mother brought suit on behalf of themselves and all disabled children not receiving an appropriate education by reason of delays of the Illinois Superintendent of Education in resolving placement appeals. A severely emotionally disturbed twelve-year-old child was recommended for placement by his school district in a self-contained classroom for behavior disorder students. His mother objected to the recommendation and said that she had been advised by experts that a highly structured residential program would be an appropriate placement for the child. The mother appealed the decision but after five months the superintendent had made no decision. The mother claimed that the superintendent was obligated to decide within thirty days. She alleged that the long delay and inappropriate educational setting had caused the deterioration of the child's condition to the extent that he had to be placed in a mental hospital. The superintendent sought to dismiss the suit, arguing that the EHA creates no substantive rights for children with disabilities.

A U.S. district court in Illinois disagreed, saying that the EHA is the source of a federal statutory right to a free appropriate education in every state electing to receive financial assistance, and that it is more than merely a "funding statute." The court then applied due process analysis and said that the passage of time caused the deprivation of the child's substantive right to an appropriate education; timeliness of review is an essential element of due process. The superintendent's motion to dismiss was denied. *John A. v. Gill*, 565 F.Supp. 372 (N.D.Ill.1983).

A Pennsylvania case resulted in a determination that a local school district failed to meet its legal responsibility to provide an appropriate program of education in training for an exceptional child. The court based its ruling on the fact that the district, instead of making an initial placement recommendation, merely provided the parents with a list of "approved private schools" and took twenty-one months to make an official recommendation of appropriate educational placement. *Pires v. Commonwealth of Pennsylvania, Dep't of Educ.*, 467 A.2d 79 (Pa.Cmwlth.1983).

CHAPTER FOUR

PRIVATE SCHOOL TUITION

I. REIMBURSEMENT FOR TUITION EXPENSES

Parents or guardians of children with disabilities who unilaterally change the placement of their child during the pendency of any review proceedings often seek reimbursement from their school district for private school tuition expenses. In *Burlington School Committee v. Department of Education of Massachusetts*, below, the U.S. Supreme Court ruled that parents who violate the IDEA's status quo provision may nevertheless receive private tuition reimbursement from the school district if the IEP proposed by the school is later found to be inappropriate. However, they do so at their own risk because if the proposed IEP is found to be appropriate, the parents will not be entitled to reimbursement for expenses incurred in unilaterally changing their child's placement.

A. Unilateral Placement by Parents

In the *Burlington* case, the father of a learning disabled third grade boy became dissatisfied with his son's lack of progress in the Burlington, Massachusetts, public school system. A new IEP was developed for the child which called for placement in a different public school. The father, however, followed the advice of specialists at Massachusetts General Hospital and unilaterally withdrew his son from the Burlington school system, placing him instead at the Carroll School, a state-approved private facility in Lincoln, Massachusetts. He then sought reimbursement for tuition and transportation expenses from the Burlington School Committee, contending that the IEP which proposed a public school placement was inappropriate.

The state Board of Special Education Appeals (BSEA) ruled that the proposed IEP was inappropriate and that, therefore, the father had been justified in placing his son at the Carroll School. The BSEA ordered the Burlington School Committee to reimburse the father for tuition and transportation expenses, and the School committee appealed to the federal courts. A federal district court held that the parents had violated the EHA status quo provision by enrolling their child in the private school without the agreement of public school officials. Thus, they were not entitled to reimbursement. The U.S. Court of Appeals, First Circuit, reversed the district court's ruling, and the Burlington School Committee appealed to the U.S. Supreme Court.

In upholding the court of appeals, the Supreme Court ruled that parents who place a disabled child in a private educational facility are entitled to reimbursement for the child's tuition and living expenses, *if* a court later determines that the school district had proposed an inappropriate IEP. The Court stated that reimbursement could not be ordered if the school district's proposed IEP was later found to be appropriate. The Supreme Court observed that to bar reimbursement claims under all circumstances would violate the EHA, which favors proper interim placements for children with disabilities. In addition, under the School Committee's reading of the EHA status quo provision, parents would be forced to leave their child in what might later be determined to be an inappropriate educational placement, or would obtain the appropriate placement only by sacrificing any claim for reimbursement. This result, found the Court, was not intended by Congress. However, the Court noted that "this is not to say that this provision has no effect on parents." Parents who unilaterally change their children's placement during the pendency of proceedings do so at their own financial risk. If the courts ultimately determine that a child's proposed IEP was appropriate, the parents are barred from obtaining reimbursement for an unauthorized private school placement. *Burlington School Comm. v. Dep't of Educ. of Massachusetts*, 471 U.S. 359, 105 S.Ct. 1996, 85 L.Ed.2d 385 (1985).

A New Hampshire school district developed an IEP for a learning disabled child which placed the student in mainstream classes for all subjects and made a resource room available for up to three hours per week as needed. However, the student did not make much use of the resource room the first semester and his grades fell. The following summer, the student's parents placed their son at a private special education day school where he made significant progress. The next year's IEP provided for an increase in resource room time as well as modifying the student's mainstream academic classes. However, the parents disagreed with this IEP. They unilaterally placed their son at the private school. The parents then requested a due process hearing, challenging the IEPs that had been prepared for their son and seeking reimbursement for the cost of tuition and transportation to the private school. A hearing officer found that the IEPs were inappropriate and ordered reimbursement.

The school district appealed that decision to the U.S. District Court, District of New Hampshire. The court reversed the hearing officer's decision, finding that a preponderance of the evidence indicated that the IEPs had been reasonably calculated to yield educational benefits in the least restrictive environment. Appeal was taken to the U.S. Court of Appeals, First Circuit. The court of appeals affirmed the district court's decision, holding that the district court had committed no mistake of law in its assessment of the appropriateness of the proposed IEPs. Even though the private school's program may have provided the student with a better education than that offered by the public school, the IEPs proposed by the school district met the minimum federal standard of appropriateness. Accordingly, the school district was not required to reimburse the parents for the "superior placement of their child." *Hampton School District v. Dobrowolski*, 976 F.2d 48 (1st Cir.1992).

An Arizona girl, profoundly deaf since birth, was considered a disabled child under the Individuals with Disabilities Education Act (IDEA). Her local school district developed an individualized education plan for her, and decided to place her at the Arizona School for the Deaf and Blind. Her parents disagreed with the proposed placement, and requested an impartial due process hearing to determine whether the placement would deprive their daughter of a free appropriate public education. The hearing officer determined that the district's proposed placement was appropriate, and the parents appealed to the Arizona Department of Education which upheld the hearing officer's decision. The parents then unilaterally enrolled their daughter at an institute for the deaf in St Louis, Missouri, and requested that the school district reimburse them for the speech therapy services provided at that private school. They also sought the costs of such services to be provided in the future. When the school district refused, they requested another due process hearing to contest the denial of reimbursement. The district refused to schedule a hearing, and the state department of education upheld the district's refusal to reimburse and to provide a hearing. The parents brought suit in a federal district court and both parties moved for summary judgment.

The court first noted that the school district and the state of Arizona had provided the student with an opportunity to receive a public education designed for her unique needs. The hearing officer specifically found that the method of speech therapy preferred by the parents would not facilitate the student's ability to learn and receive an education. Further, the IEP proposed by the school district and upheld by the hearing officer was based upon an accepted, proven methodology for facilitating speech communication of profoundly deaf students. However, the court then noted that even where a student is unilaterally placed in a private school at the choice of the parents, school officials are not relieved of their responsibility to that child. The state and local education agencies must still provide the disabled students with special education and related services where necessary. In this case, it was agreed by the parties that speech therapy was a related service covered under the IDEA, but they disagreed as to what the defendants had to do in order to fulfill their obligations under the IDEA and its regulations. The school district and the state maintained that they continued to provide speech therapy services at the Arizona school and that the service remained open to the student; thus, they had fulfilled their obligation under the IDEA. The parents, however, contended that because the student was in Missouri, she could not both attend that school and receive speech therapy in Arizona; thus, the student had effectively been denied the right to receive such services. The court determined that the regulations did not provide that the local and state agencies had to pay for related services when parents unilaterally placed their children in private schools outside the state. Here, by providing speech therapy services at the Arizona school, the defendants had complied with the requirements of the IDEA. Accordingly, the parents' claim for reimbursement of past and future costs of speech therapy services was denied. The parents, noted the court, could not compel the school district to provide a specific program to educate their child. The court granted summary judgment to the defendant state and local agencies. *Dreher v. Amphitheatre Unified School District*, 797 F.Supp. 753 (D.Ariz.1992).

A learning disabled District of Columbia student and her parents requested an evaluation for the upcoming school year. The results of the evaluation were that the student "required a fulltime program of special education" and her parents were advised that she would be placed in the secondary learning disabilities program. The parents rejected the proposed placement. Subsequently, the student was enrolled in a private school and tutored at home. The parents proceeded to request a due process hearing and tuition reimbursement. The due process hearing was held but the hearing officer did not require the school to pay for the private schooling. The hearing officer held that for that school year the student had not been placed nor was a placement proposed by the public school. Thus, the student was not under the public school's special education program. Additionally, due process does not apply where an appropriateness hearing is requested and the student has not been evaluated and placed for that year. The parents sought review of the hearing officer's decision in a federal district court.

The United States District Court for the District of Columbia found against the school and reversed the hearing officer's decision. The court explained that the IDEA required review of individualized education programs once a year. Although the duty to revise is "owed to children receiving special education from that agency," the court held that "her parents put the school system on 'reasonable notice' of their desire for a change of placement"; therefore, the system had to act. The court found that the parents' request for a due process hearing served to put the school on notice. Consequently, the school was obligated under the IDEA to review and possibly to revise the student's IEP. Additionally, a later hearing by a different officer determined that the student's placement in the private school was appropriate and ordered the public school to reimburse tuition. The court applied the later decision holding that it could attach retroactively if "it continues to be appropriate." Hence, the court ordered the payment of tuition for the school year and attorney's fees. *Edwards-White v. District of Columbia*, 785 F.Supp. 1022 (D.D.C.1992).

A New York school district prepared an IEP for a student with a learning disability, who experienced behavioral and academic problems. Although the IEP called for resource room education and some counseling, his behavioral and academic problems continued. However, the school did not recommend any change in his IEP. Consequently, his parents withdrew him and enrolled him in another school district where he began to improve. His parents requested reimbursement for the subsequent placement which the school denied. The denial of reimbursement was later upheld at a hearing. The parents appealed to the Commissioner of Education. The commissioner held that the original placement was inappropriate, the parents' subsequent placement was appropriate, and the parents were entitled to reimbursement for tuition and transportation. The commissioner, however, felt he lacked authority to award attorney's fees. The school appealed, and the supreme court upheld the commissioner's findings, but did not address the issue of attorney's fees. On appeal, a New York appellate division court modified the holding, finding that the commissioner could not order reimbursement for payments "prior to commencement of the process." It granted reimbursement only from the time subsequent to the start of the administrative review process. Otherwise, the court upheld the supreme court's decision. Both parties appealed to New York's highest court, the Court of Appeals.

On appeal, the Court of Appeals of New York reinstated the commissioner's judgments, including the retroactive reimbursements. The court held that the commissioner had the authority to make the determinations. Additionally, the court returned the case to the supreme court for a determination of attorney's fees to be awarded to the parents, absent any "special circumstances" causing denial of the fees. *NE School District v. Sobol*, 584 N.Y.S.2d 525 (Ct.App.1992).

A Connecticut three-year-old suffered from a sensorineural hearing loss and speech and language delays. A planning and placement team (PPT) recommended that the student be placed in a public preschool program for hearing impaired students and that he attend the school's summer school program for the disabled. The student's parents disagreed with the PPT's recommendation and placed him in a summer program at a private nursery school which enrolled both hearing impaired and nonhearing impaired students. After completion of the summer program, a second PPT meeting was held in which the PPT recommended that the student be placed in the public school's segregated preschool hearing impaired program. The parents disagreed with the placement and returned the student to the private school. The parents then requested an administrative hearing before the Connecticut Department of Education. The hearing officer concluded that the program developed by the PPT was reasonably designed to meet the student's special education needs and was therefore appropriate. The hearing officer also found that the parents were not entitled to tuition reimbursement. The parents sued the board of education in a federal district court seeking review of the hearing officer's decision. The district court found that the public school program was inappropriate and ordered tuition reimbursement. The board appealed to the U.S. Court of Appeals, Second Circuit.

The court of appeals held that the district court had failed to give proper deference to the agency experts' judgment when it concluded that the board had failed to offer the student an appropriate educational program. The court noted that the student's IEP was geared toward providing him with the best possible education. The PPT had conducted a thorough analysis of the student's disability and his special needs with full knowledge of the legislative preference for mainstreaming. The court agreed with the PPT that the proposed program was appropriate to meet the student's special education needs in the least restrictive environment. The public school was an appropriate placement for the student and he was not entitled to tuition reimbursement. The court of appeals reversed the district court's decision. *Briggs v. Bd. of Educ. of State of Conn.*, 882 F.2d 688 (2d Cir.1989).

A Massachusetts child began receiving special education at the age of three. Through the fifth grade he spent up to 24% of his school week outside of the regular classroom in special education. His mother became concerned that he was not progressing adequately by the end of his fifth grade year. The results of the standardized test indicated that he was at a second to third grade level in reading and language skills. The boy was then to undergo a full evaluation in order to understand the full extent of his learning problems. The evaluation indicated that he had severe speech disarticulation and a significant reading and language disability. Further, he had significant difficulty with pencil control, attention deficit disorder, and poor motor planning skills. A new IEP was developed which provided for academic support for three periods per week and typing twice a week. His mother was still concerned about the adequacy of his educational program. An expert educational consultant was retained who recommended that the boy be placed in a private facility. The parents then unilaterally placed their son in a private facility. A due process hearing was held and the hearing officer determined that the child's IEP's were inappropriate and tuition reimbursement was ordered for the parents. The school district then appealed to a federal district court.

When a school fails to provide a child with an appropriate education, the court is authorized to grant whatever relief it deems appropriate. Two requirements must be met in order for parents to be eligible for reimbursement: first, it must be demonstrated that the school's proposed IEP was inappropriate to meet the student's educational needs; and second, even if the parents show that the IEP was inappropriate, they must still demonstrate that the placement they chose was appropriate.

The court determined that in view of the child's severe problem with language and writing skills, five and one-half hours of special education per week were insufficient to provide him with an appropriate education. Therefore, the court determined that the IEP was inappropriate. Next, the court had to decide whether the private facility was appropriate. The student's program, and student teacher ratio was as follows: auditory-oral expression, 7:1; language arts, 5:1; small engine repair, 4:1; math, 4:1; tutorial, 1:1; physical education, 11:1; life science, 7:1. In addition, the student voluntarily received one period of speech therapy each week. The court determined that this program adequately addressed the student's needs. The parents were then reimbursed for tuition expenses for the school year. However, they could not be reimbursed for the current school year, because all the facts were not in yet. *Norton School Committee v. Massachusetts Department of Education*, 768 F.Supp. 900 (D.Mass.1991).

A student with a disability was placed at a private school which subsequently closed. Despite objections from the mother of the student, the local school district would not produce an IEP for the student until the next school year began. By that time the mother had already placed the student in another private school. The IEP then called for public school placement. The mother appealed and a hearing was held well after the beginning of the school year. It resulted in a fact finding that the public school would be an appropriate placement. However, the hearing officer ordered the school district to reimburse the mother for the tuition expenses for the entire year. The school district then appealed this ruling to a federal district court.

On appeal, the school argued that the mother's unilateral placement of the student in the private school should not be rewarded with tuition reimbursement. The court faced the issue of determining what was required of the school district in formulating an IEP under the EHA. The intent of the EHA was to provide a free appropriate education for the child. Therefore, the child's interests must come first. The court opined that requiring the mother to wait for an appropriate IEP until the school year began would deprive her of a right to appeal which is granted by the EHA. Delayed determination on the student's placement would also hinder the child's learning for that year. Even though the public school placement may have been appropriate at the beginning of the year, a switch would not now be beneficial. Indeed, it could harm the student. The school's delays in preparing an IEP had "forced the mother's hand." The hearing officer's order requiring the school district to pay the tuition to the private school was upheld. *Block v. Dist. of Columbia*, 748 F.Supp. 891 (D.D.C.1991).

The parents of a Massachusetts child with a disability were denied reimbursement for past tuition expenses at a private school which their child attended by the choice of the parents, and the local school district was also absolved from having to pay for any future tuition. The child had attended local public schools through the third grade but the following year, at the suggestion of a learning disabilities specialist, his parents enrolled him in a remedial program at a private school. The student remained there for several years. At approximately the same time as the child began his private schooling, the public school devised an IEP for him. However, the parents rejected the plan, preferring to place the child in the private school. Following an administrative determination, disputed by both the parents and the school district, a lawsuit was brought. A lower court entered judgment dismissing the parents' action for reimbursement and declaring that the school was not responsible for tuition at the private school.

On appeal to the Court of Appeals of Massachusetts, the lower court's determinations were affirmed. After resolving a number of procedural problems the court went on to say that "private placements are authorized only when the appropriate special education program . . . is not available within the public school system. . . . The private placement provisions of the statute only apply to a child who seeks services in the public school system and who is then identified as requiring special services which the school system either cannot, or chooses not to, provide." It was noted that parents who undertake a private placement unilaterally assume a financial risk because school authorities very possibly could recommend a different placement. The court also commented on both federal and state laws which encourage a mainstreaming policy. It stated that the common objective of these laws is the prompt provision of needed services to learning disabled children through the free local public school system except where the resources of those schools cannot appropriately meet the children's needs. In this case, following that policy required a public school program for the child if one could be developed which would meet his special needs. Here the parents took the position that he would be better served by a private school education. This, of course, was their right but, subject to the limited exceptions, no public obligation to pay for this private education could arise unless a school authority determined that the public school system could not meet the child's special needs. Thus, the parents were obligated to pay their child's tuition costs. *School Comm. of Franklin v. Comm'r of Educ.*, 462 N.E.2d 338 (Mass.App.1984).

The U.S. Court of Appeals, Fifth Circuit, reversed a trial court ruling which granted a preliminary injunction to the parents of a disabled child they placed in a private school pending the outcome of their action against a local Texas school district. The parents had requested the district court to issue the injunction ordering the school district to pay, pending resolution of the case, the costs of the private school. The Court of Appeals held that under federal law, maintenance of the present placement of a child with a disability (or the "status quo") during the pendency of proceedings demands only that school districts and state educational agencies maintain financial commitments to continue to fund an educational placement that they already funded prior to commencement of proceedings. Nothing requires a school district to pay the costs of parent-chosen private schooling pending judicial review of placement procedures and decisions by a state agency. *Stacey G. v. Pasadena Indep. School Dist.*, 695 F.2d 949 (5th Cir.1983).

A South Carolina learning disabled student had a reading grade level of 5.4 in the 9th grade. The school district then proposed an IEP where the student would attend regular class but would also participate in a resource room for emotional and mentally retarded students part-time. The parents rejected this placement as they believed it would be inappropriate to place the student alongside students with emotional illness and mental retardation. The school district then proposed to mainstream the student and provide three periods per week of special instruction. The goals set forth in the IEP were to increase the student's reading level from 5.4 to 5.8 for the year. The parents were dissatisfied with the IEP and requested a due process hearing. The hearing officer determined the placement to be appropriate and the parents placed their daughter in an unapproved private school which specialized in the education of children with learning disabilities. The parents then filed suit in a federal district court seeking reimbursement for the tuition costs at the private school. The trial court awarded the parents tuition costs and the school district appealed to the U.S. Court of Appeals, Fourth Circuit.

The school district contended that it had provided the student with an appropriate education that was reasonably calculated to enable the student to receive educational benefit (which was all that was required under the EHA). The court noted that the EHA states that the advancement from grade to grade will be one important factor in determining educational benefit. Therefore, it determined that the district court did not err in finding that a goal of four months' progress over a period of a year was rather modest for this particular student and was unlikely to permit her to advance from grade to grade with passing marks. Next, the school district contended that the EHA did not permit reimbursement for an unapproved school. The court, however, disagreed and awarded reimbursement stating that the EHA puts no restrictions on the court's ability to award relief as it "deems" appropriate. *Carter v. Florence County School Dist. Four*, 950 F.2d 156 (4th Cir.1991).

An Ohio child received public special education until the sixth grade. His parents then removed him and placed him in a private boys' school for learning disabled children through the eighth grade. In the ninth grade, his parents returned him to the public high school. At his parents' request, he was mainstreamed in all of his classes with some support help. After he did not pass all of his classes, an IEP was developed calling for the boy to be put in a learning disabled class, which the parents rejected. They requested an impartial due process hearing and again enrolled their son in the boys' learning disabled school. The hearing officer held for the school district and denied the parents tuition reimbursement. The state level reviewing officer affirmed the decision and the parents filed suit in a federal district court. The court reversed and granted the parents tuition reimbursement for the tenth and eleventh grade years. The school district then appealed to the U.S. Court of Appeals, Sixth Circuit.

On appeal, the school district contended that the trial court did not give due deference to the hearing officer's decisions. The court noted that removal of a disabled child to private school at public expense is allowed under the EHA only when the public school is unable to provide the child with an appropriate education and the private school is able to do so. The court determined that in this case, the removal of the boy from a public school when the only objection was the failure to fully mainstream and the decision to then place him in a private school would not satisfy the requirements of the EHA. The court reversed the trial court's decision and held for the school district. *Gillette v. Fairland Bd. of Educ.*, 932 F.2d 551 (6th Cir. 1991).

B. Residential School Placement

In order for parents to obtain tuition reimbursement when they have placed their disabled child in a residential home, they must show that the IEP placement was inappropriate and that the residential placement was appropriate. The parents will then be reimbursed for all necessary related costs.

A North Dakota couple and their daughters lived within the boundaries of the Southwest School District. One of the daughters had a profound sensori-neural hearing loss and began attending the North Dakota School for the Deaf in Devils Lake pursuant to an approved education program. During this time, the mother and her two daughters moved to Devils Lake where the two girls went to school. The father stayed in the Southwest district where his job was. For the first two years of this arrangement, the parents received boarding care payments from the Southwest district for their disabled daughter. At the beginning of the third year, rather than continue renting a place, the parents purchased a house in Devils Lake for the mother and her two daughters. The Southwest district denied the application for boarding care payments for this school year. The parents then requested a due process hearing under the Individuals with Disabilities Education Act (IDEA). The hearing officer denied boarding care payments to the parents, finding that although the father legally resided within the Southwest district, both daughters had established residency within the Devils Lake district. A state trial court affirmed this decision, and the parents appealed to the North Dakota Supreme Court.

The supreme court first noted that boarding care payments were related services which were provided to students with disabilities who required boarding care away from the family residence in order to receive special education and related services in an approved program. The court then stated that, under North Dakota law, where a child moved into a school district merely for the purpose of obtaining school privileges, the child would be considered a nonresident of the district for school purposes. Here, the student with a disability had moved to Devils Lake solely to obtain schooling at the school for the deaf. If suitable facilities had existed in the Southwest district, the student would still be living there. Further, the fact that the disabled student's sister also attended school in Devils Lake and was considered a resident there was not contradictory because she had not moved there solely to obtain school privileges. Rather, she had moved there to be with her mother and sister. Next, the court addressed the issue of whether the parents needed to obtain a registration certificate to be eligible for boarding care payments. The court stated that the registration requirements did not apply in this case because boarding home care for the student was provided in the home of a relative. Even though the statute did not include parents in the definition of relative, it would not be logical to require a parent to obtain a certificate but not require a more distant relative to do so. Accordingly, the parents were entitled to boarding care payments. The court reversed the trial court's decision and remanded the case for further proceedings, including an award of reasonable attorney's fees to the prevailing parents as allowed under the IDEA. *Lapp v. Reeder Public School District No. 3,* 491 N.W.2d 65 (N.D.1992).

A nineteen-year-old Tennessee student with disabilities was placed in a developmental center where an IEP was developed. A multidisciplinary team (m-team) meeting regarding an appropriate education plan for the student took place. The m-team recommended placement in a group home. Although the group home was not considered educational, it offered vocational experiences and the director agreed to follow the IEP. The student was transferred; however, her mother began receiving bills for the expenses in excess of the Medicaid coverage. The mother requested a due process hearing, stating that the student's eligibility under the IDEA entitled her daughter to a free, appropriate public education. After a due process hearing, an administrative law judge (ALJ) did not issue written findings of fact; however, his ruling resulted in nullifying the decision to keep the student in the group home. As a result, the mother was notified of the discharge of her daughter. To invoke the IDEA's "stay put" provision, the mother filed suit in a federal district court. The court denied the motions for summary judgment and granted the "stay put" order. The court rejected the ALJ's finding that the placement was not educational, therefore preventing funding from the Department of Mental Health and Retardation or the Department of Education. Even though the group home was not an educational institution, the placement there constituted an educational placement. *Mclain v. Smith*, 793 F.Supp. 756 (E.D.Tenn.1989).

Another suit was then brought to determine whether or not the placement was "educationally necessary." The same federal district court affirmed the ALJ's decisions regarding the school district's financial responsibility, the requirement of residential placement, that the group home was not an appropriate educational placement and that the school district had to find an appropriate placement. However, the court rejected the ALJ's determination that the student's mother knowingly waived her daughter's rights under the IDEA. Even though she knew the group home was not a school, she was told that there was no other opening for her daughter. *Mclain v. Smith*, 793 F.Supp. 761 (E.D.Tenn.1990).

A New Jersey teenager had a range of disabilities including communication and learning problems and emotional problems indicative of Obsessive Compulsive Disorder. Her parents requested a due process hearing to challenge the day-school placement proposed by a local school board. At the hearing, a settlement was entered into in which the school board agreed to place the student at a residential education facility for nine months and the parents agreed to make no further demands for funding of residential placement against the school board. At this same time, the parents were seeking funding of the residential portion of their daughter's placement from various state agencies. The parents eventually filed suit, alleging that the state and local entities had violated the IDEA by failing to fund the residential part of the placement. All the parties moved for summary judgment.

The federal district court first denied the parents' motion for summary judgment because it had not yet been determined whether the residential placement was necessary in order to meet the standards of a free appropriate public education. Until this was determined, the court could not decide if the state defendants were liable to fund that aspect of the placement. Next, the court denied the state entities' motions for summary judgment for the same reason. Finally, the court denied the school board's motion for summary judgment. Even though the settlement provided that the parents agreed to forego their daughter's rights against the board, the board still had a duty under the IDEA and under New Jersey law to provide the student with a free appropriate public education. Since everything hinged on the necessity of the placement, the case had to be tried. *Woods on Behalf of T.W. v. New Jersey Dep't of Education*, 796 F.Supp. 767 (D.N.J.1992).

A neurologically impaired New Jersey student was placed in a perceptually impaired program. An IEP was designed with five goals. The following year the IEP was reviewed and the school agreed to provide a more intensive reading and writing program. The student's parents rejected the proposed IEP because they were concerned that the student was still reading at a second-grade level and that he had not received proper training to overcome his dyslexia. The parents enrolled the student at a private Massachusetts school which specialized in teaching students with severe dyslexia. The parents then requested a due process hearing seeking reimbursement for tuition and residential costs at the private school. The hearing officer found that the public school's IEP failed to clearly specify the student's educational goals and objectives or provide a means of measuring his progress. The officer also found that the parents had unilaterally placed the student in the private school without any indication that the student required residential placement. The parents' request for reimbursement was denied and they appealed to a new Jersey trial court. The court found that the school had failed to design an appropriate IEP for the student and that his parents should be reimbursed for tuition but not his room and board. Both parties then appealed to the Superior Court, Appellate Division, which vacated the trial court's order and remanded the case for a new trial. On remand, the trial court dismissed the parents' claim and they appealed to the Appellate Division, which affirmed the dismissal. The Supreme Court of New Jersey granted certification.

The supreme court noted that the school district had the burden to prove that the IEP was adequate. Because the district's IEP was nonspecific in its written aspirations and evaluation of effectiveness, it was incapable of review and inappropriate. The court held that the parents were entitled to tuition reimbursement, but not residential expenses. The student could have remained at the public school if it had provided the level of education provided by the private school. Residency at the private school was unnecessary. The supreme court reversed the appellate division and remanded the case to the trial court. *Lascari v. Bd. of Educ.*, 560 A.2d 1180 (N.J.1989).

A Massachusetts child suffered from learning disabilities which included difficulties with visual motor skills, visual perception, visual tracking and motor coordination. He attended the Concord School but made little progress, especially in his social skills. The parents unilaterally placed the student into a private residential school in Massachusetts and sought to have the child's IEP changed to include placement at the school. The school district refused and the parents instituted an administrative hearing with the Bureau of Special Education which ruled that Concord had offered the student an appropriate education but ordered the parents reimbursed for certain interim expenses including the residential school tuition. The parents brought suit in a federal district court and they assigned an error to the bureau's determination that Concord was an appropriate placement. Concord then cross claimed contending that the bureau exceeded its authority by ordering any reimbursement. At trial, the district court accepted the administrative record as evidence and prevented the parents from calling certain additional witnesses. The court found that the IEP was appropriate and affirmed the defendant's placement but reversed the bureau's order for reimbursement of the interim costs. The parents appealed to the U.S. Court of Appeals, First Circuit.

The appellate court determined that the issue was whether the trial court's ruling was clearly erroneous. Massachusetts provides that special education programs assure the maximum possible development of disabled students. The parents contended that because the student had been doing better at the residential school, it was the appropriate placement. The appellate court disagreed, stating that the school district properly determined the appropriate education to assure the maximum possible development of the student under Massachusetts law. The trial court did not abuse its discretion in precluding the testimony of the parents' expert witnesses, because the testimony was deliberately withheld at the administrative level. Therefore, the parents were not entitled to be reimbursed for their costs of the residential placement. *Roland M. v. Concord School Committee*, 910 F.2d 983 (1st Cir.1990).

A severely multiply disabled Ohio student was evaluated at a center for developmental disorders. The center diagnosed the student as "basically retarded with a language delay." The center concluded that the student suffered from a severe language disorder, had difficulty with interactive skills, demonstrated inconsistent eye contact, inconsistent reaching out, and an inappropriate gesturing system. Upon the recommendation of the center, the student was enrolled in several placements based on his IEP, but the parents were consistently unhappy with them. Finally, the center recommended a residential placement and encouraged the parents to investigate residential homes, suggesting a particular residence. The parents decided that the resident home was unsatisfactory. The school district also provided names of other possible residential homes. The parents rejected this IEP and instead enrolled the student in a Japanese resident home. They then commenced a due process proceeding seeking reimbursement for the student's tuition and expenses. The impartial hearing officer rendered an opinion in favor of the district and denied the parents reimbursement for the tuition and expenses. The parents appealed to the state level review officer who also found in favor of the district. The parents then sued in a federal district court.

The court noted that the parents must show that the Japanese school was an appropriate placement and the proposed IEP was inappropriate. The court then found that the Japanese school was not appropriate for four reasons. First, it preferred not to work with severely mentally retarded children. Second, the parents' involvement was minimal due to the distance between the U.S. and Japan. Third, there were language difficulties which would hinder the student's communicative development. And finally, the extreme cost of the Japanese school would act to the detriment of many other students. The parents contended that since the student became more compliant, the Japanese school was appropriate. The court noted that there was no evidence to suggest that the student's behavior was the product of the Japanese school or merely his being in a well-structured residential setting. Under the EHA, the placement need only give some educational benefit, it need not maximize the child's abilities. The district court affirmed the decision of the state level review officer, and held for the school district. *Matta v. Bd. of Educ.-Indian Hill Ex. Vil. Schools*, 731 F.Supp. 253 (S.D.Ohio 1990).

A ten-year-old Washington special education student was seriously emotionally disturbed due to an unstable childhood, including neglect and abuse. After adoption, the student began her public education in Washington; then when the adoptive parents moved to Riverside, California, they enrolled the child in a mental health day treatment program. Shortly thereafter, because of her destructive behavior, she was placed in a mental health residential treatment program. The parents then moved to Fresno. They continued, however, to educate their daughter in Riverside. Then the mental health director of the Riverside facility informed the parents that the child's behavior had deteriorated to such an extent that the staff could no longer control her, even with medication. The staff recommended placement in an acute care facility where the child was eventually placed. The costs were paid primarily through the parents' medical insurance until their policy was exhausted. The parents then asked their school district to provide an appropriate educational placement for their daughter. The district provided a number of options which the parents rejected. Instead the parents requested that the school district fund the student's placement at the acute care facility. When the district refused to do so, the parents sought an administrative hearing to determine whether the student was entitled to be educated at the district's expense at the acute care facility. The administrative hearing officer ruled in favor of the student's parents, ordering the district to pay for the student's hospitalization. The school district appealed to a federal district court. The trial court ruled in favor of the student and ordered the school district to pay all costs. The school district appealed to the U.S. Court of Appeals, Ninth Circuit.

On appeal, the school district argued that it was not required to pay for the student's placement because the child was not hospitalized for purely educational reasons. The court noted that, thus far, the student was hospitalized primarily for medical and psychiatric reasons and therefore the district was not responsible for the costs of placement under the EHA. The court determined that the district was, however, responsible for maintaining placement of the child at the acute care facility through the pendency of court review proceedings. The court of appeals reversed the district court's decision and determined that the school district was not responsible for the residential placement costs. *Clovis Unif. v. Office of Administrative Hearings*, 903 F.2d 635 (9th Cir.1990).

A New York father placed his thirteen-year-old daughter who suffered from anorexia nervosa at the Hedges Treatment Center, a Pennsylvania residential treatment facility. He placed her at Hedges due to several placement delays by a school district's committee on the handicapped (COH). A federal district court denied his request for tuition reimbursement because he had failed to exhaust administrative remedies. He then sought an administrative hearing and the hearing officer ordered placement at Hedges. However, the New York Commissioner of Education refused to provide tuition reimbursement because Hedges was approved only for fourteen-year-olds and older. The father appealed to the same federal district court. It upheld the placement. The daughter received all of the benefits and rights at Hedges that she would have received at a New York school even though Hedges was not approved for her age.

On appeal before the U.S. Court of Appeals, Third Circuit, the commissioner contended that the district court exceeded its authority by ordering the placement. The court of appeals agreed with the commissioner. EHA § 1401(18)(B) required that the daughter receive special education and related services which met the state educational agency standards. EHA § 1413(a)(4)(B)(ii) provided that the state determine whether private facilities like Hedges met those standards. Thus, the EHA incorporated state educational standards. It was the state of New York's obligation (through the commissioner) to ensure that private facilities met applicable state educational standards. No court or agency could approve a placement at a private facility consistent with the EHA unless the commissioner approved the facility prior to the placement. The hearing officer and the district court wrongly placed the daughter at Hedges without the commissioner's approval. The district court decision was reversed and the father was denied reimbursement. *Antkowiak v. Ambach*, 838 F.2d 635 (2d Cir.1988), *U.S. cert. denied sub nom Doe v. Sobel*, 109 S.Ct. 133 (1988).

A special education dispute of fourteen years' duration was settled by the U.S. Court of Appeals, Third Circuit. The court of appeals upheld a federal district court's ruling that the Westfield, New Jersey, Board of Education was not liable for the cost of nine years of private school placement. The child in this case was first identified as disabled in 1968. At that time the Westfield Board of Education placed the child at the Midland School, a private facility. In 1972, further testing was performed by outside experts as well as Westfield's child study team. The child was thereafter labeled "mentally retarded-educable" by the child study team, and an IEP was formulated which called for placement at a different institution, the Tamaques

School. Objecting to the label "mentally retarded-educable," as well as the change in placement, the parents kept him at Midland and paid the tuition themselves.

In 1975, the parents filed a petition with the New Jersey Department of Education seeking review of Westfield's 1972 reclassification decision. The parents contended that during the pendency of all review proceedings, Westfield was obligated to pay for their child's tuition at Midland, since EHA § 1415(e)(3) requires that a child remain in his or her "then current" placement until review is completed. Due to the department's failure to comply with EHA procedural requirements, a proper hearing on the merits of the parents' claim was not held until June 9, 1983.

At the due process hearing in 1983, the parents claimed that they were entitled to tuition reimbursement for their child's education at the Midland school from 1972 to 1981, since they were entitled to leave their child at Midland during all review proceedings. They also claimed that the Westfield Board of Education was liable for the period their child attended school in Jerusalem. The hearing officer denied the parents' claims and they filed an action in federal district court, seeking review, but the court upheld the hearing officer's decision. The parents appealed their case to the U.S. Court of Appeals, Third Circuit, which similarly agreed with the hearing officer. The appeals court stated that since § 1415(e)(3) had not become effective until 1977, the Westfield Board of Education was relieved of responsibility for its 1972 decision to change the child's educational placement from Midland to Tamaques. Thus, the parents' decision to keep their child at Midland was not protected by § 1415(e)(3). The appeals court ruled that the parents should have placed the child at Tamaques in accordance with Westfield's 1972 recommendation.

The court also held that under EHA § 1412(2)(B), the Westfield Board of Education would be responsible for the post-graduation education of the child only if the board made it a regular practice to educate children even after they had graduated. Since the board did not, and since the child had already graduated when his parents sent him to the school in Jerusalem, the board was not liable for those expenses. Noting that all the classifications and placements proposed by Westfield's child study team were appropriate, the court of appeals affirmed the prior rulings against the parents. *Wexler v. Westfield Bd. of Educ.*, 784 F.2d 176 (3d Cir.1986).

In 1978, the state of New York agreed to pay the tuition costs of a schizophrenic boy who had been placed in a private residential psychiatric hospital which operated an accredited academic high school. Behavioral problems prevented the boy from attending the high school, but he continued to reside at the hospital. His doctors hoped that the behavior problems could be overcome. The boy's parents, after petitioning state officials in vain, sought to compel the state to pay the cost of the boy's residential care at the hospital from the time of his placement, July 1978, through June 1983, when the boy turned twenty-one years old. The state argued that as long as the child's behavioral problems prevented him from attending the high school at the institution, he was in effect uneducable and therefore the state had no responsibility for any of his expenses.

The court ruled that once the state placed the boy at the psychiatric hospital, it became obligated to pay the entire expense of the placement. The state could not escape its responsibility for costs of the boy's residential care simply by stating that those costs did not directly address educational problems. As long as the boy could be educated (however little) through a residential placement, the state remained responsible for the cost of that placement. *Vander Malle v. Ambach*, 667 F.Supp. 1015 (S.D.N.Y.1987).

The town of Henniker, New Hampshire, was not entitled to reimbursement from a local school district for the placement expenses of a child with a disability adjudged delinquent, according to the New Hampshire Supreme Court. When the boy entered the Henniker school system, he was diagnosed as educationally disabled and an IEP was established for him. When he entered junior high school in the Hillsboro-Deering school district, the district found the boy was emotionally disturbed. It decided that his problem could be addressed within the school system under an IEP that provided for psychological counseling, parent consultations and academic monitoring. The student was later adjudicated a delinquent child by a New Hampshire district court. The court ordered that he be placed in a foster home and put him on probation. He violated probation and was placed by the court in the Chamberlain School. The town of Henniker was billed for the cost of the student's educational and residential fees at the Chamberlain School. The town sought reimbursement for these costs from the Hillsboro-Deering school district in state district court. The court found that the school district was liable for the educational portion of the expenses. The school district appealed the decision.

The Supreme Court of New Hampshire held that the district court had exceeded its authority. When a disabled child is involved in delinquency proceedings a court can only order a review of the IEP by the school district; it has no authority to order a school district to assume financial responsibility for a placement not addressed or provided for in a child's IEP. Since the child's placement arose out of his delinquency adjudication, his residential and educational cost at Chamberlain had to be paid by the town in which he resided, with a right of reimbursement from the person legally responsible for the child's support. The school district was held not liable for the cost of the child's private residential school placement. *In re Todd P.*, 509 A.2d 140 (N.H.1986).

Reimbursement was denied to the parents of an Oklahoma youth, who brought suit in federal district court after their local school district refused to fund their son's placement at a residential facility. The youth, who was classified as "educable mentally handicapped" and who had serious emotional and behavioral problems, had been enrolled at the age of eighteen in his local school district's EMH program. An IEP was developed at this time with the approval of his parents, in which it was agreed that if the boy became "unmanageable" he would be suspended for three-day intervals. Although his educational program included both high school instruction and vocational instruction, he was soon expelled from the vo-tech program due to his emotional outbursts. When these outbursts continued at the high school, school officials notified his parents that an alternative to classroom placement was necessary. Homebound instruction was suggested, but the parents rejected the proposal. For the next several months the parents considered residential placement; during this period the youth received no educational services. His parents also failed to bring him to school for testing to aid in the formulation of a new IEP, as requested by school officials.

The parents then requested funding for their child's placement at an out-of-state residential facility. When their school district refused they requested a due process hearing under the EHA. The parents, after discovering the name of the hearing officer, believed that he would find in favor of the school district and withdrew their request for a hearing. At the beginning of the next school year they appeared once again at the high school to enroll their son, and school officials, who had not expected the youth to enroll, requested a week to formulate an IEP. Several days later school officials attempted to arrange a meeting with the parents to discuss a new IEP for the youth, but the parents refused because a new teacher had not yet been hired to instruct him. The school officials explained that a new teacher would not be hired unless the parents approved the new IEP and assured them that they would enroll their son. This impasse caused the parents to unilaterally enroll their son in the out-of-state residential facility. A due process hearing resulted in approval of the school district's decision not to reimburse the parents for the cost of his placement, and the parents sought judicial review. The U.S. Court of Appeals, First Circuit, upheld the denial of tuition reimbursement and found that the district had taken all steps necessary to provide the child with a free appropriate public education. The appeals court stated that "although the residential facility undoubtedly offered . . . a superior educational program, an education which maximizes a child's potential is not required by the EHA." *Cain v. Yukon Pub. Schools, Dist. I-27*, 775 F.2d 15 (10th Cir.1985).

C. Placement in Unapproved Schools

Tuition reimbursement will almost never be granted when parents place their children in an unapproved school, unless the school district's placement was "woefully inadequate." However, this is a difficult burden for the parents to meet.

A Florida student suffered from dyslexia and attention deficit disorder. He was classified as learning disabled. His parents became dissatisfied with his progress because in the tenth grade he was only reading at a third grade level. They challenged his IEP and sought to place him in a residential school in New York, which had a high degree of success in teaching dyslexic children to read. Shortly after the hearing commenced, the school district entered into negotiations indicating that it had approved placement of their son at the residential school. Subsequently, the school district informed the parents that it could not recommend that placement as the residential school was not approved. The parents then placed their son in the school. An administrative hearing was begun in which the hearing officer determined that the IEP was inadequate but that the student could not be placed in an unapproved private school. The hearing officer further stated that there was no private school either within or without the state dealing with this child's severe learning disability which had been approved by the state. The parents then filed this suit in a federal district court. The school district moved to dismiss the case.

The defendants asserted that the court could not order them to place the student in an unapproved school, nor could the court order tuition reimbursement. The court agreed, stating that:

> A federal district court cannot order either placement of a child in an unapproved school or reimbursement for funds spent on an unapproved school because such remedies would violate the [IDEA's] requirement that placement "meet the standards of the State educational agency."

The court, however, determined that if the school district failed to comply with the IDEA and if, indeed, no approved school was available to meet the educational needs of the student, it had broad discretion to order appropriate relief to support the purposes of the IDEA. A determination of whether the educational authorities have met their obligations must be made. The IDEA requires that the school's program "meet the standards of the State." The court noted that this did not mean that the school had to appear on a list of preapproved schools. Whether Florida's approval process is consistent with the demands of the IDEA was an issue to be decided by the court. The motion to dismiss was therefore denied. *Straube v. Florida Union Free School Dist.*, 778 F.Supp. 774 (S.D.N.Y.1991).

The principal of an Illinois school district enrolled a learning disabled student as a resident student. He was unaware that the student's residence was outside of his district's boundaries. Sometime later, the mistake was discovered, and the student's mother was informed that she should either transfer her daughter or pay tuition. The mother refused to pay tuition. She also sought an injunction to stop the transfer, alleging that it would cause irreparable harm to her daughter. Lastly, the mother announced that she was soon to purchase a home within the district. The district then agreed to maintain the child's enrollment. Alleged family concerns later led the mother to purchase a home outside the district. The student was transferred to her new residence's district based upon that district's request. Her previous school district subsequently sought unpaid tuition as well as legal sanctions in a federal district court. Although Illinois allows nonresident tuition, it does not mandate that it be charged. The court determined that public policy weighed against the district's tuition recovery. The school then alleged that the injunction sought by the mother had been conceived in bad faith, and thus justified legal sanctions. Because of the reasons forwarded for the change in home selection, and the later transfer being based on the request of the student's new district, the court declined to impose sanctions. *Cohen v. Wauconda Community Unit Sch. Dist. 118*, 779 F.Supp. 88 (N.D.Ill.1991).

The parents of a mentally disabled New Jersey student filed an IDEA action to determine his appropriate placement. The student was enrolled in a public school's mentally disabled class, but the parents wanted to enroll him in an unaccredited private school in which he could be mainstreamed. An administrative law judge for the New Jersey Department of State, Office of Administrative Law, ruled that the district's obligation to educate the child would not be satisfied by enrollment in the unaccredited private school. The parents appealed to the Superior Court of New Jersey, Appellate Division, which ruled that it was without jurisdiction to hear administrative appeals in IDEA matters. It held that appeal must be taken in either a state trial court or U.S. District Court. The court allowed the parents ten days to file an appropriate appeal in a New Jersey trial court or a federal district court. *C.S. v. Middletown Township Bd. of Educ.*, 613 A.2d 492 (N.J.Super.A.D.1992).

The parents of a New York student with a disability unilaterally placed their son in an unapproved school when their son's school district recommended a placement which the parents found unacceptable. The parents requested a hearing claiming that the placement was inappropriate and untimely. They also requested tuition reimbursement for expenses at the unapproved school. A hearing officer overruled the district's recommendation, finding it untimely and insufficient. Although the hearing officer found that the placement at the unapproved school was appropriate, he denied tuition reimbursement because the school had never been approved by the state education commissioner. The parents appealed to the commissioner, who upheld the decision denying tuition reimbursement. The parents then sued the school district in a federal district court which dismissed the lawsuit. The parents then appealed to the U.S. Court of Appeals, Second Circuit.

The parents argued that to obtain reimbursement they need only show that the district's proposed IEP was inappropriate, and not that the unapproved school met state educational requirements. The court held that the parents could not obtain tuition reimbursement because the unapproved school was ineligible to contract for the education of disabled students. Under the EHA, children with disabilities may be educated at public expense only where private schools meet state educational standards. Placement in an unapproved school, whether by state officials or parents, was improper under the EHA because it violated the requirement that placement of disabled students meet state educational agency standards. The court of appeals affirmed the district court's decision denying tuition reimbursement. *Tucker v. Bay Shore Union Free School Dist.*, 873 F.2d 563 (2d Cir.1989).

The parents of a learning disabled child placed their daughter in a private day school. The school district was then required to either approve this placement or propose a more appropriate placement within fifteen days. When the school district failed to propose an alternative placement, the parents requested a due process hearing. The hearing officer ordered the school district to place the student within fifteen days. The district again failed to comply and the parents requested another hearing. The hearing officer found that the school district had failed to comply with the order, but refused the parents' request for tuition reimbursement. The hearing officer found that the private school was not certified under the EHA during the 1989-90 school year; therefore, tuition reimbursement could not be awarded. The parents then filed a claim in federal court seeking tuition reimbursement. The parents moved for summary judgment and the district moved to dismiss.

In support of the summary judgment motion, the parents argued that the school was certified for nearly the entire school year in question. The school's certification was suspended in April 1990, but was later reinstated. Additionally, the school district agreed to reimburse the tuition expenses for twelve other disabled children at the same school during the 1989-90 school year. The court noted that the EHA provides for placement in private schools at public expense where it is deemed "appropriate." Since the school district failed to provide the student with an appropriate placement in a timely manner, the parents' only alternative was a private placement. Because the school was certified when their daughter was placed, the court stated that it was reasonable for them to expect a tuition reimbursement. The court held that the student's placement at the day school was appropriate under the EHA. It granted the parents' motion for summary judgment and ordered the school to repay the parents for their daughter's tuition expenses. *Shirk v. District of Columbia*, 756 F.Supp. 31 (D.D.C.1991).

The mother of a disabled Fairfax, Virginia, student unilaterally placed him in the East Hill Farm and School in Vermont. She then requested a due process hearing to resolve the questions of tuition reimbursement and living expenses. Two due process hearings found that the Fairfax County Public Schools' (FCPS) recommendation of placement at the Little Keswick School, Inc., was appropriate and the mother appealed to a U.S. district court. The district court ruled in favor of FCPS and the mother appealed to the U.S. Court of Appeals, Fourth Circuit.

The court of appeals affirmed the district court's decision to deny tuition reimbursement to the mother for the East Hill education. It noted that when a disabled child is educated at a private school under the EHA, the state or local school district has an obligation to ensure that that school meets applicable state educational standards. Here, East Hill was not approved by Virginia to offer special education. Therefore, FCPS could not place the boy and fund his education at East Hill without violating the EHA's requirement that children with disabilities be educated at public expense only in those private schools that met state educational standards. The court of appeals observed that "when a disabled child is educated at a private school under the EHA, the State has an obligation to ensure that the school meets applicable State educational standards." Therefore, the EHA did not require FCPS to place the student in the unapproved Vermont school. The district court decision was affirmed. *Schimmel v. Spillane*, 819 F.2d 477 (4th Cir.1987).

An emotionally disabled New York child and his parents sued their local school district and various state officials under the EHA to recover tuition and costs incurred during the year and one-half the child spent at a private school in Maine. The child had been placed in a private school in New York by his school district but was expelled. He then returned home where he received four months of home tutoring. Then, concluding that no good faith effort was being made to place the child, the parents sent him to the Maine school from which he graduated. Because the out-of-state school was not on New York's list of approved facilities the parents were denied reimbursement for expenses for this placement. Suit was then brought, but a U.S. district court in New York granted the defendants' motion to dismiss. The court said that parents are generally entitled to an impartial due process hearing if they disagree with a local placement recommendation. However, this procedure is not available to review the state Commissioner of Education's refusal to contract with an out-of-state facility. *Smrcka v. Ambach*, 555 F.Supp. 1227 (E.D.N.Y.1983).

A Pennsylvania learning disabled student's IEP provided for a learning disabled resource room and contemplated a search for a potential fulltime placement in an appropriate private school. A private school was found by the school district but was rejected by the parents. The school district then revised the IEP and recommended a parttime learning disabled program. The parents rejected the proposal and requested a hearing. The hearing officer found that the proposed IEP was inappropriate because the proposed parttime program was not yet in existence. The parents then placed the student at their own expense at a private school in Vermont. They obtained counsel and asked for another hearing. The hearing officer found the school district's IEP for the parttime learning disabled classroom program to be appropriate. The decision of the hearing officer also denied reimbursement for the tuition expense at the private school in Vermont. The parents then filed this action in a federal district court. The court noted that the Eleventh Amendment barred tuition reimbursement from the Commonwealth of Pennsylvania. The 1990 Amendments to the EHA abrogated the Eleventh Amendment immunity of the states but since they were not retroactive the court granted the state immunity. Further, the court determined that there was no claim alleged against the school district upon which relief could be granted and, accordingly, it dismissed the complaint. *David H. v. Palmyra Area School Dist.*, 769 F.Supp. 159 (M.D.Pa.1990).

II. RELIGIOUS SCHOOLS

Public aid to private religious schools implicates the Establishment Clause of the First Amendment. Such aid must have a secular purpose which neither advances nor inhibits religion and does not entangle the state with religion.

The U.S. Supreme Court ruled unanimously on the issue of state aid to students with disabilities at private religious schools. The Court held that the First Amendment to the U.S. Constitution does not prevent a state from providing financial assistance to a disabled individual attending a Christian college. The plaintiff in this case, a blind person, sought vocational rehabilitative services from the state of Washington's Commission for the Blind pursuant to state law [Wash.Rev. Code sec. 74.16.181 (1981)]. The law provided that visually disabled persons were eligible for educational assistance to enable them to "overcome vocational handicaps and to obtain the maximum degree of self-support and self-care." However, because the plaintiff was a private school student intending to pursue a career of service in the church, the Commission for the Blind denied him assistance. The Washington Supreme Court upheld this decision on the ground that the First Amendment to the U.S. Constitution prohibited state funding of a student's education at a religious college.

The U.S. Supreme Court took a different, much less restrictive view of the First Amendment and reversed the Washington court. The operation of Washington's program was such that the commission paid money directly to the student, who would then attend the school of his or her choice. The fact that the student in this case chose to attend a religious college did not constitute state support of religion, because "the decision to support religious education is made by the individual, not the state." The First Amendment was therefore not offended. The case was remanded to the Washington Supreme Court. *Witters v. Washington Dep't of Servs. for the Blind*, 471 U.S. 481, 106 S.Ct. 748, 88 L.Ed.2d 846 (1986).

On remand, the Washington Supreme Court reconsidered the matter under the Washington State Constitution, which is far stricter in its prohibition on the expenditure of public funds for religious instruction than is the U.S. Constitution. Vocational assistance funds for the student's religious education violated the state constitution because public money would be used for religious instruction. The court rejected the student's argument that the restriction on public expenditures would violate his right to free exercise of religion. The court determined that the commission's action was constitutional under the free exercise clause because there was no infringement of the student's constitutional rights. Finally, denial of the funds to the student did not violate the Fourteenth Amendment's equal protection clause because the commission had a policy of denying any student's religious vocational funding. The classification was directly related to the state's interest in ensuring the separation between church and state as required by both state and federal constitutions. The court reaffirmed its denial of the student's tuition. *Witters v. State Comm'n for the Blind*, 771 P.2d 1119 (Wash.1989).

A profoundly deaf Arizona student, who met the requirements of the IDEA and the Arizona adaptation of that statute, requested state funds to provide a sign language interpreter for school. The student attended a private, religious high school. Upon the parents' request for an interpreter at the private school, the school district questioned the constitutionality of providing the interpreter. The deputy county attorney and Arizona attorney general agreed that providing the interpreter would violate "constitutional prohibitions against a state establishment of religion." The parents sought an injunction requiring the school district to provide the interpreter. The district court denied the parents' request and granted summary judgment against them. Specifically, the district court held that the service would violate the First Amendment of the U.S. Constitution. The parents appealed.

On appeal to the U.S. Court of Appeals, Ninth Circuit, the appellate court affirmed the lower court's holding in favor of the school district. The appellate court applied the three-part Lemon test found in *Lemon v. Kurtzman,* 403 U.S. 602, 91 S.Ct. 2105, 29 L.Ed.2d 745 (1971), finding that providing the interpreter would violate the Establishment Clause. Specifically, the pervasive religious encounters throughout the classes and general attendance at the school as conveyed by a public employee (the interpreter) would serve to promote sectarian beliefs. The court stated that the "presence and function of an employee paid by the government in sectarian classes could create a 'symbolic union'" between the government and religion. This appearance that the government jointly sponsored the school's activities would violate the Constitution. Additionally, the court held that the denial of the interpreter would not violate the Free Exercise Clause. The court determined that the state interest in not violating the Establishment Clause provided a compelling interest to "impose a burden on their [the parents'] free exercise rights." *Zobrest v. Catalina Foothills School District,* 963 F.2d 1190 (9th Cir.1992).

A Maine student with a disability attended a private, religious school that required special education services to be brought to the school by the local school district. The public school district providing the services informed the student and his parents that the services as currently being provided violated the Maine Special Education Regulation. The school further notified the parents and student that the student would be bussed to a public school to receive his services. The parents appealed the decision to a hearing officer who held that the services should be provided at the public school, because the student's current school was not a religiously neutral site. The Supreme Court affirmed. The parents further appealed to the Supreme Judicial Court of Maine which further affirmed the hearing officer's decision. Under the U.S. Supreme Court's interpretation of the Establishment Clause of the First Amendment, it was not error to require the services to be provided at a religiously neutral site. *Wright v. Saco School Dep't.,* 610 A.2d 257 (Me.1992).

Parents of disabled children who lived in a New York Jewish community requested that their local school district furnish special education services at their private schools. The parents and children adhered to the practices of Hasidism which generally requires that males and females be separated. The male and female Hasidic students attended separate private schools. Initially the district provided special education services at the individual schools. It later determined that it would only furnish special education services at the public schools. The parents refused to allow their children to attend public school to receive special education services. They sought administrative review of the school district decision.

A New York trial court ordered the district to provide services to the Hasidic children in a "mobile or other appropriate site not physically or educationally identified with but reasonably accessible to the Hasidic children." The school district appealed this decision to a New York appellate court which overturned the trial court decision because it had the primary effect of advancing religion. After the appellate court determined that the school district only need provide services at the public schools, the parents appealed to the New York Court of Appeals.

The New York high court determined that a school district must offer the same services to nonpublic school students as it does to public school students. It noted that the Education for All Handicapped Children Act declared that each disabled child is to have a free appropriate public education. Congress had recognized that not all services could be furnished in regular public school classes. In effect, the high court held that the district was not required to provide services at the private school or at a neutral site. It simply had to make the services available to all students residing within district boundaries. It modified the appellate court decision that the district was not allowed to provide services outside of the public school. *Bd. of Educ. v. Wieder*, 527 N.E.2d 767 (N.Y.1988).

A Virginia student became profoundly hearing impaired after an attack of meningitis at age three. He was identified as disabled and provided with special education services. He attended a preschool class in a regional special education school through the first grade. Then his parents voluntarily placed him at a private religious school to further his religious education and development. The school was a sectarian, religious school in which Christian teachings together with nonreligious subjects were woven into the curriculum. The parents then asked the county to provide a full-time cued speech interpreter at the Christian school. The county denied their request but offered to provide a cued speech interpreter to the student at a public school. The parents requested a due process hearing. The hearing officer determined that the county was not responsible for providing a cued speech interpreter to the student because he was unilaterally placed in a private sectarian school by his parents for personal reasons. The hearing officer further held that if the county was to provide a cued speech interpreter at the religious school it would violate the Establishment Clause of the U.S. Constitution. The parents then appealed the hearing officer's decision to the Virginia Department of Education. The department affirmed the decision of the hearing officer and the parents filed this case in a federal district court. The district court granted summary judgment in favor of the county and the parents appealed to the U.S. Court of Appeals, Fourth Circuit.

The first issue to be addressed was whether Virginia or the federal special education laws required the county to provide a cued speech interpreter to a student at a private, sectarian school. The court determined that under the EHA the local school district need not pay for a child's related services when the child's parents choose to place that student in a private school. Next, the parents claimed that the county's denial of publicly funded cued speech interpretation at the Christian school burdened their religious belief that "they are to provide their children with Christian education and to educate their children in Christian schools." The court determined that such infringements were subject to strict scrutiny and could be justified only by a compelling state interest. The court found a compelling state interest to educate the disabled and found that the Free Exercise Clause had not been violated. Further, the court addressed the Establishment Clause issue and determined that because religion permeated every aspect of the daily curriculum at the Christian school, and the student's cued speech interpreter would be interpreting for him at all times, allowing a cued speech interpreter at the school would violate the Establishment Clause. Therefore, the court affirmed the decision of the trial court. *Goodall by Goodall v. Stafford County School Bd.*, 930 F.2d 363 (4th Cir.1991).

Relying on the EHA's status quo provision, a federal district court ordered the New York City Board of Education to fund a disabled child's placement at a private educational facility. The city's school system, explained the court, had been operating since 1972 under a federal court order which mandates that an offer of a public school placement must be made by the school system within sixty days of a child's identification as a disabled individual. Under the court order, if the child is not offered such a placement within sixty days the parents have the right to place the child in a private facility at the board's expense. *Bd. of Educ. v. Ambach*, 628 F.Supp. 972 (E.D.N.Y.1986).

A Virginia case resulted in a ruling that that state will not fund the education of students with disabilities at out-of-state religious institutions. Here, a twenty-year-old citizen of Vietnam who was a permanent resident alien of the United States graduated from a Virginia high school in 1984. He applied to and was accepted for admission to St. Andrews Presbyterian College, a nonprofit liberal arts college affiliated with the Presbyterian Synod of North Carolina. Its primary purpose is to provide collegiate or graduate education and not to provide religious training through a theological education. The student and his foster father sought financial assistance from the state of Virginia under its program of financial aid to the disabled, which is 80% federally financed and 20% Virginia financed. Virginia denied financial aid to the student to attend St. Andrews solely because it was a church-affiliated school located outside Virginia.

Until 1969 Virginia could not provide assistance to any church-affiliated schools through tuition grants to students. In 1969, the Virginia Constitution was amended to provide for loans to students attending in-state church-affiliated schools so long as the primary purpose of those schools was to provide collegiate or graduate education. The student sued the state of Virginia in a U.S. district court claiming that the denial of financial aid violated the Establishment Clause of the First Amendment to the U.S. Constitution. He also contended that even if tuition aid was properly denied, he should still receive payments for incidental expenses to attend St. Andrews. The district court ruled for the state and the student appealed to the U.S. Court of Appeals, Fourth Circuit. For a state law to be consistent with the Establishment Clause its primary effect must neither advance nor hinder religion. The student contended that distinguishing out-of-state schools on the basis of religious affiliation violated the primary effect standard because it disfavored church-affiliated schools. The appeals court disagreed, noting that the U.S. Supreme Court has recognized that a decision to fund religious studies, along with other postsecondary education, lies within a permissible zone of accommodation of religion but is not mandatory.

The student also claimed that the Virginia policy infringed upon his right to the free exercise of religion since it forced him to forfeit attendance at an out-of-state religious institution in order to receive tuition aid. The court dismissed this allegation, observing that Virginia was not obligated to provide the student with an ideal learning situation. The state was only prohibited from forcing him to give up essential beliefs and practices in order to obtain tuition aid. The student's free exercise of religion needs and physical needs could be met in Virginia schools.

Further, the court of appeals noted that the Virginia Constitution did not prohibit the student's reimbursement for incidental expenses (books, transportation costs, living expenses, etc.) should he still choose to attend St. Andrews. Such subsidies would be to the student and not to a disqualified school. The appeals court remanded the case to the district court to determine how the state determines the primary purpose of in-state church-affiliated schools and how it provides for their monitoring so as to insure that Virginia is not advancing religion. *Phan v. Commonwealth of Virginia*, 806 F.2d 516 (4th Cir.1986).

In a New York case the U.S. Court of Appeals, Second Circuit, held that a plan to provide remedial education classes on public school property for private parochial school students violates the Establishment Clause. Chapter One of the Education Consolidation and Improvement Act established a federally funded program to provide remedial instruction and related support services to elementary and secondary school children who were "educationally deprived" and who lived in an area having a high concentration of low income families. The purpose of the program was to meet the remedial educational needs of students that could not otherwise be met by the schools they attended. States receiving Chapter One funding were required to provide such remedial services to private as well as public school students.

In order to comply with a 1985 U.S. Supreme Court decision which held that sending federally supported public school teachers to teach in private religious schools violated the Establishment of Religion Clause of the First Amendment *Aguilar v. Felton*, 473 U.S. 402, 105 S.Ct. 3232 (1985), the city of New York adopted a new plan. One aspect of the plan called for the city to conduct remedial education classes for girls from a Hasidic Jewish school on public school premises. Specifically, the plan provided for a section of the public school to be completely closed off for use by the Hasidic girls by constructing a wall in a previously open corridor. It also provided for the girls to be taught only by women (in accordance with Hasidic tradition) who spoke Yiddish. Before the plan was implemented, a local parents' association sued the New York City School District in a federal district court seeking a preliminary injunction against the plan. When the injunction was denied, the parents appealed to the U.S. Court of Appeals.

The court of appeals disagreed with the district court's observation that an injunction against the plan would hinder the free exercise of religion on the part of the Jewish girls. "The Free Exercise Clause of the First Amendment . . . does not prohibit a government from forcing a choice between receipt of a public benefit and a pursuit of a religious belief if it can show a compelling reason for doing so." Avoiding a violation of the Establishment Clause that would otherwise result from an apparent endorsement of the tenets of a particular faith was ample reason for compelling that choice. The court of appeals reversed the lower court decision and held that the parents were entitled to preliminary injunctive relief on the ground that the city plan had the primary effect of establishing religion through a federally funded program. *Parents' Ass'n of P.S. 16 v. Quinones*, 803 F.2d 1235 (2d Cir.1986).

CHAPTER FIVE

RELATED SERVICES

The IDEA requires school districts to provide special education students a free appropriate education. This may include related services, which are defined in IDEA § 1401(17) as transportation, speech pathology, psychological services, physical and occupational therapy, medical and counseling services and others, so long as they relate to diagnoses for special education purposes.

I. PSYCHOLOGICAL SERVICES

Although expressly included within the IDEA definition of related services, psychological services are not defined in the act. This has made the area of psychological services a highly litigated one.

A Tennessee student who had a history of behavioral and academic problems was evaluated by his school district to determine if he was disabled. The school deemed the student not to be seriously emotionally disturbed. Consequently, he was not qualified as disabled and could not receive special services. Although the student's mother signed a statement agreeing with the assessment and an acknowledgment that she understood her rights, she later learned that her son was near expulsion because of his behavior. Consequently, she removed him and enrolled him in a private hospital with a special education program for emotionally disturbed children. The hospital determined that the student was emotionally disturbed. The student's parents then proceeded with a due process hearing to determine whether he was emotionally disabled. Additionally, the parents sought tuition reimbursement. The hearing officer found against the parents and student. The district court affirmed the hearing officer's conclusions. The parents appealed.

On appeal, the U.S. Court of Appeals, Sixth Circuit, reversed the lower court's decision against the student. The appellate court held that the student was disabled and entitled to special services including the psychological services he received at the private hospital. Additionally, the appellate court found that the student and parents were entitled to reimbursement because of the school's failure to properly

135

assess the student's disability which led to the failure to design an appropriate individualized educational plan. Thus, the school's inadequate educational plan allowed the parents to pursue an appropriate choice. Hence, the school district was required to pay for psychological expenses incurred as a part of the IDEA requirement of providing a free appropriate public education. *Babb v. Knox County School System*, 965 F.2d 104 (6th Cir.1992).

A Virginia first grade student began to do poorly in school and showed signs of learning and emotional disabilities. His teacher recommended that the student be evaluated to determine if he was disabled. A child study committee met and, 200 days after the initial referral, the committee determined that the child was not disabled. The parents requested that the child be referred to an outside professional to be evaluated. The committee agreed and the child was diagnosed as having emotional and learning disabilities. Three days after the report from the outside professional was sent to the school the child became hysterical. That night the child became progressively worse, and the parents admitted him to a hospital. While the child remained at the hospital he received educational and psychological counseling as well as medical services. After the child was released from the hospital, the committee met and developed an IEP for the child with the parents' consent. The IEP did not provide for one-on-one counseling but the parents provided the counseling at their own expense. The parents then demanded reimbursement for the psychological counseling and the hospital stay. The school district refused and the parents then requested a due process hearing. The hearing officer found for the school district and the parents appealed to a federal district court. After the court found for the school district, the parents appealed to the U.S. Court of Appeals, Fourth Circuit.

On appeal, the court affirmed the district court's decision to deny reimbursement. As for the hospital claim, clearly the child was not given a free and appropriate education by the school district while he was in the hospital. The court did, however, remand the case to the district court to determine if the placement in the hospital was an appropriate placement and if so to determine which expenses were incurred for special education and related services and to order reimbursement for related services expenses only. *Tice v. Botetourt County School Bd.*, 908 F.2d 1200 (4th Cir.1990).

After failing the seventh grade, a disabled Tennessee student attended a private school for children with learning disabilities. After one year, the student had outgrown the school academically. The parents and local school officials met and agreed that the student would attend regular classes and receive special support from the school staff. After a short time, the student started having trouble in his classes and began to skip school. His behavior became so irrational that his parents sent him to a psychiatrist. When the student's behavior did not improve, the parents admitted him into a private psychiatric hospital. The parents requested a due process hearing to determine reimbursement for the hospital expenses. The hearing officer found the placement at the hospital appropriate and necessary for the student to benefit educationally and ordered the school to reimburse the student's parents for all expenses. The school appealed to a Tennessee trial court which reversed the hearing officer's decision, holding that it was not supported by substantial and material evidence. The parents then appealed to the Court of Appeals of Tennessee.

The court of appeals held that payment for the student's psychiatric services was expressly excluded by the EHA. Under the EHA a physician's services are covered only when necessary to provide diagnosis or evaluation. The physician's services were not necessary for diagnosis or evaluation. The court found that the student's placement in the psychiatric hospital was for medical reasons, rather than for educational purposes. The school was not responsible for the student's hospitalization expenses. The court of appeals affirmed the trial court's decision denying reimbursement. *Metropolitan Gov't v. Dep't of Educ.*, 771 S.W.2d 427 (Tenn.App.1989).

A thirteen-year-old girl suffering from anorexia nervosa and various other emotional problems was placed at a Pennsylvania treatment center by her father. This placement occurred after the local school district committee on the handicapped (COH) had determined that the girl could be categorized as an "emotionally disturbed" child with medical problems. The father placed the girl at the Pennsylvania center because of placement delays by the COH. After being denied tuition reimbursement by the New York Commissioner of Education, the father sued in U.S. district court. The court denied reimbursement because the father had failed to comply with EHA procedures. The father then sought and received a ruling by a hearing officer that his daughter was emotionally disabled. However, the commissioner refused to provide tuition reimbursement because the Pennsylvania treatment center was approved by the commissioner only for children age fourteen or older. The father once again sought review in the same U.S. district court.

The district court held that the decisions of the hearing officer that the girl was emotionally disabled, and that she required placement at the Pennsylvania center, were not reviewable by the commissioner. The court also observed that the girl had applied to nine in-state approved institutions, and had been rejected by all nine, indicating that the father had been reasonable in attempting to place her at a school acceptable to the commissioner. The commissioner claimed that under the EHA, the state was required to provide special education and related services which are a part of a "free public education" but that other services, such as medical services, are not provided for in the EHA. The district court ordered a trial to determine what portion of the girl's expenses at the Pennsylvania treatment center were related services to be paid by the state of New York. After trial, the district court concluded that counseling, psychological services, and periodic psychiatric evaluations for medication purposes were "related services when provided by a psychologist, social worker, or other professional." The father was entitled to reimbursement for both these expenses and tuition, according to the court.

The commissioner appealed to the U.S. Court of Appeals, Second Circuit. Although the court of appeals did not dispute that the tasks performed for the girl's benefit were related services under the EHA, it reversed the district court decision. It concluded that the court and the hearing officer wrongly placed the girl at the Pennsylvania treatment center without the commissioner's prior approval. *Antkowiak v. Ambach*, 838 F.2d 635 (2d Cir.1988), *cert. den. sub nom Doe v. Sobel*, 109 S.Ct. 133 (1988).

During the 1983-84 school year the teacher of a first grade student referred him to a psychologist for testing in order to determine if the student was in need of special education. In January 1984, a psychologist for the Roanoke (Virginia) County Schools (RCS) tested the student and informed his mother that he did not require testing for a learning disability (LD). On March 1, 1984, RCS conducted an eligibility meeting to determine if the student was disabled and to discuss an appropriate educational placement for him. A private school psychologist, who had evaluated the student on the mother's behalf, testified that the student should be placed in an LD classroom. However, RCS placed him in a "behavioral adjustment" (BA) classroom. The student's mother then removed him to a private school for learning disabled children.

Prior to the student's second grade year (1984-84) RCS held another eligibility meeting. RCS recommended a dual placement IEP in which the student would spend a part of each day in a BA classroom, an LD classroom and a regular classroom. The mother sued RCS seeking tuition reimbursement for the student's private school placement. After a U.S. district court concluded that she was entitled to reimbursement for the last three months (beginning March 1) of the 1983-84 school year only, she appealed to the U.S. Court of Appeals, Fourth Circuit.

The court of appeals agreed with the district court that the mother was entitled to tuition reimbursement for the last three months of 1983-84 but not the 1984-85 year. It reasoned that the 1984-85 dual placement was a reasonable judgment by RCS. It agreed with the district court's conclusion that the 1984-85 IEP enabled the student to "benefit" (as required under the EHA) from the IEP. The mother was also entitled to reimbursement for the costs of the evaluation by the private school's psychologist. *Hudson v. Wilson*, 828 F.2d 1059 (4th Cir.1987).

An emotionally disturbed student in Connecticut sought an injunction requiring the state to pay the full cost of her attendance at a private school, including psychotherapy. The student's school district had denied such services on the ground that the psychotherapy was not a "related service" under the EHA because the definition of related service excludes medical services that are not diagnostic or evaluative. A federal district court disagreed with the school district's characterization of related services. The plain meaning of the EHA distinguishes between "medical services" and other supportive services, including speech pathology and audiology, physical therapy and recreation, as well as psychological services. Only medical services are singled out as limited to services for diagnostic and evaluative purposes. Thus, the court concluded that psychological services required to assist the student to benefit from her special education were related services required to be provided by the state, without cost to the student or her parents. *Papacoda v. State of Connecticut*, 528 F.Supp. 68 (D.Conn.1981).

II. MEDICAL SERVICES

Generally, medical services are excluded from "related services" under the IDEA unless the services are for diagnostic or evaluative purposes relating to education.

In the following case, the U.S. Supreme Court ruled that clean intermittent catheterization (CIC) is a related service not subject to the "medical service" exclusion of the EHA. The parents of an eight-year-old daughter born with spina bifida brought suit against a local Texas school district after the district refused to provide catheterization for the child while she attended school. The parents pursued administrative and judicial avenues to force the district to train staff to perform the simple procedure. After a U.S. district court held against the parents they appealed to the U.S. Court of Appeals, Fifth Circuit, which reversed the district court ruling. The school district then appealed to the U.S. Supreme Court.

The Supreme Court affirmed that portion of the court of appeals decision which held that CIC is a "supportive service," not a "medical service." The court was not persuaded by the school district's argument that catheterization is a medical service because it is provided in accordance with a physician's prescription and under a physician's supervision, even though it may be administered by a nurse or trained layperson. The court listed four criteria to determine a school's obligation to provide services that relate to both the health and education of a child. First, to be entitled to related services, a child must be disabled so as to require special education. Second, only those services necessary to aid a child with disabilities to benefit from special education must be provided, regardless of how easily a school nurse or layperson could furnish them. Third, EHA regulations state that school nursing services must be performed by a nurse or other qualified person, not by a physician. Fourth, the child's parents in this case were seeking only the *services* of a qualified person at the school, they were not asking the school to provide *equipment.* The Court reversed those portions of the court of appeals ruling which held the school district liable under the Rehabilitation Act and which held that the parents were entitled to attorney's fees. *Irving Indep. School Dist. v. Tatro*, 468 U.S. 883, 104 S.Ct. 3371, 82 L.Ed.2d 664 (1984).

A six-year-old Utah student suffered from congenital neuromuscular atrophy and severe scoliosis and was confined to a motorized wheelchair. She breathed through a tracheostomy tube in her windpipe, which needed to be suctioned to loosen mucous and reduce the chances of a mucous plug. The student's tracheostomy tube was typically suctioned five times during a three-hour school day. Despite this suction, the tube occasionally would plug. For this reason, and others, the student required constant nursing care. When the student was to begin first grade, the student's parents requested that the school district provide the student with the necessary nursing care to allow her to attend classes. The school district refused, stating that the nursing care was a medical service excluded under the IDEA. Instead, the school decided to provide home instruction to the student. The parents argued that the tracheostomy care was a support service necessary to allow the student to receive educational benefit. Such support services are covered by the IDEA. The parents sued the school district to force it to provide nursing care.

The U.S. District Court, District of Utah, held for the school district. It first stated that the school district was only obligated to provide "an appropriate education," not the best education possible. The district's plan of providing home instruction to the student, which would not require it to provide nursing care, was reasonable, even if the student would get a better education at the school. The instruction need only be calculated to give the student educational benefit. Second, the court stated that the nursing care was a "medical service" excluded by the Act and not a related support service. The burden of the cost of medical services should not be shifted to the school district under the guise of related services. *Granite School Dist. v. Shannon M.*, 787 F.Supp. 1020 (D.Utah 1992).

Parents of a seventeen-year-old student with severe mental and physical impairments claimed that a Pennsylvania school district violated the Education of the Handicapped Act (EHA) because it failed to provide their child with adequate special education. For several years the school district had provided the student with direct physical therapy from a licensed therapist. Thereafter a physical therapist came in once a month to train the student's teacher to integrate physical therapy with the student's education. The student's parents acknowledged that the school program had benefited the student to some degree, but argued that his educational program was not providing him a meaningful benefit as the EHA required.

The parents first challenged the student's IEP before a Commonwealth of Pennsylvania Department of Education hearing officer who found that the student was benefiting from his education and that his education was appropriate. The Pennsylvania Secretary of Education affirmed this finding. The parents then appealed to a federal district court which dismissed the case. The district court concluded that because the student had received some benefit from his education the provisions of the EHA had been met. The parents appealed to the U.S. Court of Appeals, Third Circuit. On appeal the court found that the purpose of the EHA is to provide "full educational opportunity to all [disabled] children." Congress' use of this phrase indicated an intent to afford more than a trivial amount of educational benefits. One of the chief concerns of the EHA was to foster self-sufficiency for children with disabilities. Implicit in this emphasis is the notion that states must provide some sort of meaningful education. Physical therapy was an essential part of the student's appropriate education. The court of appeals ruled in favor of the parents and remanded the case to the district court for a determination of whether the student's physical therapy was meaningful as required under the EHA. *Polk v. Cent. Susquehanna Intermediate Unit 16*, 853 F.2d 171 (3d Cir.1988).

After a New Jersey student was classified as emotionally disturbed, he attended classes half-time at an alternative school and half-time at another high school. As a result of disciplinary problems he encountered at the alternative school, his parents sought to have him enrolled full-time at the high school. The child study team agreed. However, as a condition of enrollment, he and his parents had to sign a performance contract which provided that he would be suspended from the school and transferred to the alternative program if he failed to comply with his performance requirements. He was suspended from the high school as a result of an altercation he had with a teacher. At that time, the child study team recommended that he be placed as a day student at the alternative school. The parents did not consider that to be an appropriate placement. They then consulted with an educational consultant who recommended a residential placement. They filed a due process petition against the board. Because the parties were unable to resolve the dispute, a hearing was scheduled before an administrative law judge. The parties agreed to resolve the classification and placement issue by way of an independent evaluation. However, the parents reserved their right to pursue the issue of expunging his records and reimbursement of counseling and attorney's fees. The independent evaluator concluded that the student could receive an appropriate education through a day program rather than a residential placement.

The parties then agreed to a consent order which provided that the student would be placed in another alternative school and the parents would receive reimbursement for counseling and the student's record would be expunged. The student's behavior at this new school deteriorated. He was found with drugs and admitted to smoking marijuana and occasionally drinking. He was expelled and in order to return to school, he would have to attend a substance abuse program. The parents then asked the board of education to pay for the program. The board denied this request and the parents requested a due process hearing. The hearing officer found that the care in question was medical in nature and thus did not fall under the EHA. Further, the parents' request for attorney's fees was denied. The parents then appealed to a federal district court.

The court looked to whether the student's placement in a substance abuse program was a related service or whether it was excluded as a medical service. The only medical services covered are those which are diagnostic or for evaluation purposes. The parents argued that where a child's education is adversely affected by substance abuse, successful completion of a substance abuse program would increase the effectiveness of the child's educational program. However, the court stated that the fact that "a particular program may benefit a classified child's special education program clearly does not ipso facto compel the conclusion that the program was a related service." The court noted that there were medical services provided by the substance abuse program which were not diagnostic or for evaluation purposes. Therefore, the court denied reimbursement to the parents. The court however, awarded attorney's fees to the parents because they were the prevailing party at the administrative level. Although the issue of residential placement was not decided in their favor, other issues which were nonetheless significant resulted in a benefit to them. *Field v. Haddonfield Board of Education*, 769 F.Supp. 1313 (D.N.J.1991).

A Tennessee student suffered from brain damage since birth and was afflicted with a serious emotional disturbance and mental retardation. Her condition was aggravated by a severe behavioral disorder which caused bizarre and uncontrollable outbursts endangering both herself and others. These outbursts were unpredictable and could last for hours. The student's behavior rendered placement in mainstream educational facilities provided by the school district impractical. Therefore, the student's parents and special education personnel worked together for years to find an appropriate individualized education program. The student had received educational services at four different schools. None were successful in meeting the student's specific educational goals or improving the student's behavior. Since an effective residential program could not be found, the student's IEP consisted of homebound instruction. The student's parents learned of Cedarbrook's Fresh Approach Program. Cedarbrook is a residential rehabilitation facility in Tennessee for brain injury victims. The Fresh Approach program addresses significant behavioral problems which interfere with the student's rehabilitation. After placement in the program, the student's behavior improved significantly.

After the parents were denied reimbursement, they instituted this action in a federal trial court. The court determined that the IEP offered by the district did not provide educational benefit to the student. The student deteriorated rather than benefitted under the IEP which consisted of three hours per week of homebound instruction. The court then determined that Cedarbrook represented an appropriate educational placement for which the district was liable. The issue in determining the appropriateness of Cedarbrook placement was whether it was educational or medical in nature. The occupational therapy, psychological services, recreational therapy, physical therapy and medical evaluations provided by Cedarbrook were all specifically listed as special education and related services in the EHA. Therefore, the residential placement was educational and not medical in nature. Finally, the court determined that the school district was not required to provide compensatory education because neither the student nor the district were previously aware that the Cedarbrook program existed. Thus, a compensatory education was not warranted. *Brown v. Wilson County School Bd.*, 747 F.Supp. 436 (E.D.Tenn.1990).

A Pennsylvania child was injured in an automobile accident which resulted in the permanent implantation of a tracheostomy. He required ready access to a trained attendant to maintain the tracheostomy. An insurer paid for the cost of the attendant. When the child returned to school the insurer demanded that the child's school district pay the cost of the attendant during the school day. It contended that the presence of the attendant was a "related service" under the EHA and the Rehabilitation Act. The school district refused to pay.

The insurer sued the school district in a federal district court seeking a declaration that the attendant was a "related service" for which the school district was obligated to pay. The school district contended that the EHA required administrative agency procedures through which "related service" must be determined. The insurer argued that there were no special education issues involved so as to require referral to an agency. It contended that the real issue concerned whether the health needs of the child must be provided for by the school district pursuant to the EHA and Rehabilitation Act. The court held for the school district because the insurer lacked legal standing to press its claim. The insurer's relationship with the child's parents through the insurance contract in no way altered the EHA. The insurer's lawsuit was dismissed. *Allstate Ins. Co. v. Bethlehem Area School Dist. and BB*, 678 F.Supp. 1132 (E.D.Pa.1987).

A U.S. district court in New York ruled that school districts are not required to pay for in-school nursing care. The mother of a severely disabled seven-year-old student requested that her local school district provide in-school nursing care for her daughter. After the school district denied her request she asked for an impartial hearing and the hearing officer found that because the nursing care constituted "related services" under the EHA, the local school district was required to provide and pay for the special nursing services. The school district appealed the decision and the New York State Commissioner of Education reversed the hearing officer's order. The commissioner determined that the in-school nursing care was not a related service. The mother appealed to a U.S. district court.

The district court observed that the EHA mandates a "free appropriate public education," including "related services," and requires that an individualized education program be developed for each disabled child providing for his or her specific educational needs. The issue before the district court was the extent to which school health support services are mandated by the EHA. The mother contended that the extensive medical attention required by her daughter qualified as a related service under the EHA. The school physician testified that the services required by the daughter would require the expertise of a licensed practical nurse or a registered nurse. The school district argued that the medical care required did not constitute related services because the EHA excludes from the definition of "related services" medical services required for purposes other than diagnosis or evaluation. The court concluded that the child's daily medical needs did not qualify as related services and that the EHA does not require that school districts provide a severely physically disabled child with constant, in-school nursing care. The mother's request for relief in the form of payment for the daily nursing care of her child was denied. The mother appealed to the U.S. Court of Appeals, Second Circuit. The mother contended that the district court gave "insufficient deference" to the decision in *Department of Education v. Katherine D.*, 727 F.2d 809 (9th Cir.1983). Although the student in that Hawaii case needed special care, she only required the intermittent services of a lay person. Here, the disabled daughter needed a full-time person with special training, and thus the decision of the district court was affirmed. *Detsel v. Bd. of Educ.*, 820 F.2d 587 (2d Cir.1987).

III. INTEGRATED TREATMENT PROGRAMS

Other services, such as occupational therapy, family counseling and extracurricular activities are sometimes requested by parents or guardians of children with disabilities. Whether a court will order a school district to provide such services seems to depend upon the particular facts of the case.

A South Dakota student, who suffered from Williams Syndrome, was enrolled in special education as soon as she started school. At a conference, the student's parents were informed that she was regressing in her motor skills, visual tracking, and sequencing skills. An IEP meeting was held to address the problem. When a dispute arose regarding the student's program, her parents enrolled her in a private occupational therapy program. A few months later, after a second IEP evaluation was made, the school district agreed that the student's needs would best be met by her continued placement in the private program. The school district agreed to pay the student's future tuition in the program, but denied the parents' request for reimbursement of the expenses incurred from the student's initial placement in the program. An administrative hearing officer ordered the school district to reimburse the parents. The school district appealed to a federal trial court. The trial court affirmed the hearing officer's order and also awarded attorney's fees to the parents. The school district appealed to the U.S. Court of Appeals, Eighth Circuit.

On appeal, the school district argued that the parents were not entitled to reimbursement for their daughter's private placement since she was appropriately placed after the initial IEP and her parents unilaterally removed her without proper notice. The court noted that parents may obtain reimbursement for private placement if such placement was determined by the court to be proper under the EHA. Also, proper notice requires only that the parents make clear to the school district that they want a change in placement. The court held that the parents gave the school district adequate notice of their objections to their daughter's placement and it affirmed the lower court's award of attorney's fees and tuition reimbursement. *Rapid City School Dist. v. Vahle*, 922 F.2d 476 (8th Cir.1990).

The parents of two children with disabilities who received physical therapy as related services in conjunction with the mandated education required under the Education of the Handicapped Act (EHA) were covered by health insurance policies issued by the same insurer. The students attended two intermediate educational units formed as part of the Pennsylvania public school system. Physical therapy was provided by licensed physical therapists either employed by or affiliated with the units. Both sets of parents and the two intermediate educational units sought coverage from the insurer, which was denied. The insurer's basic coverage provided that the policy would pay for "physical therapy prescribed by the attending provider as to type and duration when performed by a duly qualified physical therapist." The parents and educational units filed a class action suit in a Pennsylvania federal district court. The insurer moved to dismiss their case, contending that the policy covered only "medically necessary hospitalization and medical benefits," and that the physical therapy which had been provided to the children would never have been prescribed by doctors without the EHA. It further argued that the policies excluded coverage for services which the insureds were not legally obligated to pay or which they were entitled to receive from a governmental unit or agency without cost. The district court granted the motion for dismissal, and the parents and educational units appealed to the U.S. Court of Appeals, Third Circuit.

The court of appeals refused to accept the insurer's position that the EHA does not authorize shifting of costs to private insurers when intermediate educational units have a statutory duty to provide an appropriate public education for children with disabilites at public expense. Under some circumstances, the insurer would be obliged to pay for physical therapy services furnished under a disabled student's individualized education program. However, the court noted that the parents were entitled under the EHA to the physical therapy services provided, and that the parents were not legally obligated to pay for those services. Since the insurer had contractually excluded coverage for services which were provided free under the EHA, the court refused to hold it liable for the costs of the physical therapy at issue. The court thus affirmed the district court's decision, and dismissed the case. *Chester County Intermediate Unit v. Pennsylvania Blue Shield*, 896 F.2d 808 (3d Cir.1990).

A Pittsburgh child was paralyzed from the chest down as a result of spina bifida. Prior to kindergarten, the child was evaluated by a multidisciplinary team which recommended that he be placed in a program for physically disabled students and that he receive physical and occupational therapy. However, in September of the following year, the board terminated the physical and occupational therapy without notice to the student's parents. His parents were then notified of the board's intent to reclassify him from exceptional to nonexceptional. The student's mother rejected the intended change. At the request of the board, a due process hearing was held before a hearing officer, who found that the student was an exceptional child in need of special education and related services. He ordered the board to prepare an IEP for the student which included physical and occupational therapy. The secretary of the Department of Education upheld the hearing officer's decision. The board appealed to the Commonwealth Court of Pennsylvania.

On appeal, the board contended that the student was not exceptional, and was not entitled to compensatory physical and occupational therapy. Physically disabled means orthopedic or other health impairments of sufficient magnitude to limit the classroom accommodation and educational performance. The court noted that the student's paralysis limited his educational performance. The student was unable to perform physical activities which were required of other students. The physical education teacher modified the instructions to the student to accommodate his impairment. The court determined that the child was an exceptional child and that he was in need of a regular physical and occupational therapy program. The court also determined that he was entitled to compensatory physical and occupational therapy as a result of the board's denial of an appropriate program. The court affirmed the Department of Education's decision. *Bd. of Educ. v. Commonwealth Dep't of Educ.*, 581 A.2d 681 (Pa.Cmwlth.1990).

A child in California suffered from mental retardation and infantile autism. The Regional Center for the East Bay (RCEB) was a nonprofit community agency created under the California Welfare and Institutions Code. The child was eligible for the services RCEB provided. RCEB placed the child at the Behavior Research Institute of California (BRI). BRI was licensed as a community care facility by the California Department of Social Services. RCEB funded the child's residential program at BRI and a school district paid his educational costs. In October 1987, RCEB terminated the child's placement and funding at BRI due to his self-abusive behavior. RCEB claimed that the California Administrative Code permitted it to remove the child when his health or safety was threatened. The child's parents asked a U.S. district court for a temporary order to prevent RCEB from terminating their child's placement and funding at BRI pending a hearing. The court denied their request. The parents then requested a preliminary injunction against the change in placement.

The court noted that it had authority over noneducational state agencies that provide related services under the EHA. Residential placements qualify as "related services" under the EHA if they are made for educational purposes. Here, the child's residential placement at BRI was not a related service under the EHA. It was an independent residential placement made pursuant to state law. There was no evidence that the child's placement at BRI was made for educational purposes. Because RCEB's placement of the child at BRI was not protected by EHA safeguards, the parents' request for a preliminary injunction was denied. *Corbett v. Regional Center for the East Bay*, 676 F.Supp. 964 (N.D.Cal.1988).

The parents then moved for reconsideration. The district court reversed its previous decision. The child's placement at BRI was made for educational purposes and was therefore protected by EHA "stay-put" provisions. A member of the child's IEP team testified that the child's educational, behavioral, social and developmental needs were all "intertwined." When residential placement is necessary to provide a disabled child with a free appropriate education, residential placement is a "related service" under the EHA. The child's placement at BRI was jointly recommended by the IEP team and RCEB in part to enable him to receive a free appropriate education. The court had authority over RCEB. The court held that EHA § 1415(e)(3) created a presumption in favor of the child's current educational placement. This presumption could only be overcome by showing that maintaining the child at RCEB was "substantially likely to cause injury either to himself ... or to others." RCEB failed to overcome the presumption. The parents prevailed and the court vacated its previous denial. The child could remain at BRI pending any appeals. *Corbett v. Regional Center for the East Bay*, 699 F.Supp. 230 (N.D.Cal.1988).

The U.S. Court of Appeals, Sixth Circuit, has affirmed a district court ruling that the EHA did not obligate school districts to provide continuous occupational therapy to a student with a disability in Ohio. The court of appeals also held that the inclusion of nonacademic extracurricular activities once per week was not automatically required. The court observed that the EHA, in and of itself, does not require that states maximize the potential of children with disabilities commensurate with the opportunity provided to other children. These programs, the court found, were not necessary to permit the child to benefit from his instruction. *Punikaia v. Clark*, 720 F.2d 463 (9th Cir.1983).

IV. TRANSPORTATION

The IDEA expressly authorizes expenditure of public funds for transportation as a related service.

The four-year-old child of an Alabama couple was born with Down's Syndrome— a condition which made him mentally disabled and speech impaired. He was thus entitled to special education and related services under the IDEA. The local board of education developed an individualized education program which called for a three-day per week program. The parents, after expressing their preference for a five-day program, contacted a private school about placing their son there. They were notified by a state official that related services would not be provided if they unilaterally placed their son in the private school. Nevertheless, they enrolled their son at the private school and requested a due process hearing to determine whether their son was entitled to related services. A hearing officer denied the parents the relief they sought; they appealed.

Before the U.S. District Court, Middle District of Alabama, they asserted that the board was denying their son the appropriate public education due him under the IDEA. The board contended that it had met its obligations under the act by offering the student special education and related services in the public setting. It further argued that the Director of the Office of Special Education Programs in the U. S. Department of Education agreed with its position that related services did not have to be provided for unilaterally-placed students. The court looked to the regulations which implement the IDEA (located at 34 CFR Part 300). The regulations state that if a child with a disability had available a free appropriate public education and the parents chose to place the child in a private school, the public agency would not be required to pay for the child's education at the private school. However, the public agency would still have to "make services available to the child." 34 CFR § 300.403. According to the court, this clearly indicated that the board remained responsible for providing related services (including transportation) to the child. The court ruled in favor of the parents. *Tribble v. Montgomery County Bd. of Educ.*, 798 F.Supp. 668 (M.D.Ala.1992).

Following a scandal in which more than 25 people representing some 36 school bus companies were indicted on charges of attempting to bribe an undercover police officer posing as a state bus inspector to overlook safety and other infractions, the New York City Department of Transportation required all applicants for school transportation contracts for the transportation of preschool children with disabilities to certify that none of their employees had been convicted of a misdemeanor or felony relating to pupil transportation service within two years of such certification. The bus companies sued, claiming it was unreasonable to include such a requirement. A New York trial court agreed, and the city appealed to the New York Supreme Court, Appellate Division. The appellate court reversed. The city had acted reasonably in requiring the certification. It was legitimate to take into consideration the criminal records of the bus company employees. The city had wide discretion when choosing a safe and responsible bidder. *Positive Transportation, Inc. v. City of New York*, 584 N.Y.S.2d 51 (A.D.1st Dep't 1992).

The Utah Division of Rehabilitative Services determined that a woman was eligible to receive benefits for educational rehabilitation services. It developed an individual work rehabilitation plan to help her complete a social work degree from Utah State University. Subsequently, the woman qualified for public assistance and federal education assistance in the form of a Pell Grant, which paid $2,300 per academic year. The divisions then informed her that it would no longer allow reimbursement for transportation expenses under the plan. She requested a hearing where it was determined that the Pell Grant was a "comparable" benefit and thus ought to be used to meet her transportation costs. Accordingly, transportation cost reimbursement was denied. The woman appealed to the Court of Appeals of Utah which noted that Pell Grant money could be spent on transportation costs as well as tuition, room and board, and books and supplies. It held that the division had acted reasonably in finding the Pell Grant to be a comparable benefit. As such, it had to be used to meet the costs of transportation according to the federal regulations. The court affirmed the division's denial of reimbursement. *Holland v. State Office of Education, Division of Rehabilitation Services*, 834 P.2d 596 (Utah App.1992).

A hearing impaired Ohio student and her parents sued their local school district under the Education of the Handicapped Act (EHA). They sought a determination that the district had to provide the student with transportation to and from a private school for the deaf. An independent hearing officer found that the student met the time and distance requirements for free public transportation. The school district appealed to a federal district court. The court found that because the student had no disability which precluded her from using nondisabled transportation services, she was not entitled to free transportation. The student's parents appealed to the U.S. Court of Appeals, Sixth Circuit.

The court held that under the EHA when a student is voluntarily placed in a private school, a public school district does not need to provide a related service to that student if that particular service is not designed to meet the unique needs of the student. In order to obtain transportation as a related service under the EHA, parents must establish that the student is disabled, that transportation is a related service and that the related service is designed to meet the unique needs of the student caused by the disability. Parents must also prove that the school district must be responsible under the EHA for providing the related services. In this case, the student was disabled and, under the statute, transportation was a related service. The need for transportation, although a related service, was no more unique to the student because she was deaf than it would have been had she not been deaf. Since the statute specifically required a relationship between the related service and the unique needs of the student, the requirements were not met. The district was not required to provide the student with transportation to the private school. The appeals court affirmed the district court's decision for the school district. *McNair v. Oak Hills Local School Dist.*, 872 F.2d 153 (6th Cir.1989).

A severely multiply impaired Michigan student was placed at a school within his school district. The student's IEP indicated that the student's education could take place either in his home or at a school but it did not require the district to provide transportation. The student's parents objected to the IEP because it denied the student transportation. A hearing was held and the local hearing officer found that the district was not required to provide transportation due to the student's medically fragile nature. The parents appealed and the state reviewing officer reversed, finding that, given proper training, an aide could place the student in his wheelchair and suction his tracheostomy tube during transportation. The district sought review in a federal district court to determine whether it was obligated to provide the student with transportation to and from school.

The court held that transportation represented a supportive service which the district was required to provide under the EHA. The EHA required schools to provide related services, which included transportation and other supportive services except medical services for diagnostic and evaluation purposes. The court found that the medical services exclusion was limited to services provided by licensed physicians and did not include services of other trained medical professionals. There was no evidence which indicated that the complications surrounding transportation of the student required the attention of a licensed physician. The district was required to provide transportation to the student and to use a medical professional, other than a physician, if necessary to safely transport the student. *Macomb County Intermediate School Dist. v. Joshua S.*, 715 F.Supp. 824 (E.D.Mich.1989).

A "trainable mentally handicapped" (TMH) student attended a special educational facility in Florida. The school board operated both a southern facility, which the student attended, and a geographically distant northern facility. During the school year, the student's parents became concerned with the possibility of sexual abuse occurring at the southern facility. A counselor at that facility had been arrested and charged with sexual abuse. Although the sexual abuse charges were later dropped, the student's parents withdrew her from the facility for approximately six months. After returning to the southern facility, the parents requested a hearing to determine whether the student was properly classified as a TMH student. At the hearing, the school board established that the student was properly classified. However, the hearing officer further found that the student's parents had lost confidence in the southern facility and ordered that the student attend the northern facility. The school board was to also provide transportation for the student to that facility. The school board appealed the hearing officer's decision to a Florida district court of appeal.

The court held that the board was not required to pay the additional expense of transporting the student to the northern facility. The hearing had not been conducted for the purpose of determining whether the student should be transferred from the southern facility to the northern facility. It was conducted for the sole purpose of considering the student's reclassification into a different category of mentally disabled student. The hearing officer had found that she was properly classified. The student had been provided a free appropriate public education at the southern facility as required by state law. The board was not required to pay the additional expense of transporting the student to the northern facility. *School Bd. of Pinellas County v. Smith*, 537 So.2d 168 (Fla.App.2d Dist.1989).

A hearing-impaired Philadelphia student received a scholarship for bi-weekly hearing treatment at a therapy clinic. His mother requested that the school district provide her son with transportation to the clinic. When the district refused, the mother requested a due process hearing. The hearing officer determined that the district was not obligated to provide transportation to the clinic. The mother appealed to the Pennsylvania Secretary of Education. The secretary determined that additional therapy would allow the student to make better use of his residual hearing. He also held that additional therapy would assist the student in his current classroom and ensure that he continued to function independently and successfully in the future. The secretary determined that the district must provide transportation because the combination of the student's regular education and the additional therapy constituted "sufficient services reasonably calculated to give real educational benefit." The district appealed this decision to the Pennsylvania Commonwealth Court.

On appeal, the district argued that it was already providing the student with an appropriate education. In upholding the secretary's decision, the court determined that the combined therapies constituted services calculated to afford the student real educational benefit. Since the additional therapy program was approved by the Department of Education, the school district was obligated to provide free transportation. The court noted that although the student was progressing satisfactorily, evidence showed that students with the same problem require additional assistance later on in their education and that providing additional therapy now would allow the student to become more independent. Thus, the district was required to provide transportation to the clinic. *School Dist. of Philadelphia v. Dept. of Educ.*, 547 A.2d 520 (Pa.Cmwlth.1988).

A disabled Virginia child brought suit against a school district alleging that the district failed to provide her with an appropriate education. The child, through her parents, requested reimbursement for the cost of summer programs which the child had attended as well as placement at a private school of the parents' choice. In addition, the child's parents requested reimbursement for their travel expenses incurred while the child was a patient and student at a home for crippled children in Pennsylvania. The U.S. district court held that neither state law nor the EHA required the state to pay all of the expenses incurred by parents in educating a child, whether the child is disabled or not. Thus, the parents were not entitled to reimbursement for their travel expenses. *Bales v. Clarke*, 523 F.Supp. 1366 (E.D.Va.1981). See also *Helms v. Indep. School District No. 3*, 750 F.2d 820 (10th Cir.1984), a similar Florida case in which the parents of a disabled child enrolled in a Georgia residential school were denied reimbursement for their travel expenses incurred as a result of visits to their son in Georgia.

An individualized education program committee meeting was held to review a Michigan hearing impaired student's special education program. The student's mother disagreed with the committee's placement and requested local and state level administrative hearings. Both hearing officers supported the committee's report. They found that the committee's local school placement would best develop the student's potential in the least restrictive environment. The mother however placed the student in the Model Secondary School for the Deaf (MSSD) in Washington, D.C. because she believed that both the EHA and the Michigan Mandatory Special Education Act (MMSEA) required placement there. MSSD is a federally funded program which does not require tuition or residence charges. The student's mother then sought reimbursement from her local school district in the amount of $2,500 per year for transportation expenses to and from MSSD. The district refused and she sued various state and local school officials in a Michigan federal district court.

The central issue was the degree to which the school district program and the MSSD program fulfilled EHA requirements and the MMSEA. Under the MMSEA, school districts were to provide special education programs and services that were designed to develop the "maximum potential" of each disabled student within the least restrictive environment. The EHA incorporated the MMSEA standard by reference. The school officials contended that the committee's IEP adhered to EHA and MMSEA standards. They further argued that the mother's objection to its IEP rested upon her philosophical disagreement with mainstreaming. She allegedly failed to consider the merits of the education the student would receive at the local district school. The mother argued that the school district's IEP failed to maximize the student's potential as a disabled student.

The court upheld the hearing officer's decisions. It agreed with the school officials that the mother's argument turned upon a discussion of the merits of mainstreaming versus placement in a segregated setting. The court refused to substitute its judgment for that of the committee on decisions of this nature. Although the state of Michigan had not defined "maximum potential" there were geographical and physical limits to its commitment to educate students with disabilities to their maximum potential. Michigan law indicated that "maximum potential" meant neither "utopian" nor the best education possible. Although other hearing-impaired students had been placed at MSSD, their placements were deemed the least restrictive placement for them. This was not the case here. Because the mother had not met her burden of proving that the committee's IEP failed to meet EHA requirements including the MMSEA's "maximum potential" requirement, she was not entitled to transportation costs. *Barwacz v. Michigan Dep't of Educ.*, 681 F.Supp. 427 (W.D. Mich.1988).

A deaf girl in Ohio was provided with special education and transportation at no cost by a school district for three years. The child's parents then unilaterally enrolled the child in a private school for the deaf for the 1985-86 school year. Both the parents and the school district agreed that the child had been provided a free appropriate education in public school as required by the EHA. The parents nevertheless requested that the school district pay for the child's transportation to and from the private school and reimburse them for transportation costs that they had already paid. They asserted that the transportation was a related service for which the school district was liable under the EHA. The school district refused to pay and this refusal was upheld by the state education agency. The child's parents appealed.

A U.S. district court declared that "'special education' means the educational program established and monitored by the state, financed with authorized state and federal funds as expressly mandated by the EHA to appropriately educate the disabled." Required related services therefore "are those required to be provided to the disabled child with regard to the child's 'special education' program." The court determined that the EHA required the state to provide related services only for programs that the state has designed and offered as "special education." Because the parents unilaterally chose to place the child in private school for their own reasons, that placement was not "special education" within the meaning and intent of the EHA. The court concluded that "Congress did not intend the public to bear the additional expense of a private education for disabled children where those children have already been provided a free, appropriate special education program and services related to that program by the state." It ruled that the school district did not have to pay for the child's transportation to and from the private school. *McNair v. Cardimone*, 676 F.Supp. 1361 (S.D.Ohio 1987).

The mother of a multi-disabled girl requested special education and related services for the girl in March 1986. However, the District of Columbia Public Schools (DCPS) did not propose an educational program for the girl until August 1986. The mother unilaterally placed the girl in the Lab School (a private special education day school) claiming that because DCPS failed to timely propose an appropriate placement for the girl she was forced to seek an appropriate program on her own. The mother then sought a U.S. district court order that DCPS provide the girl with transportation from home to the Lab School.

The mother argued that a federal regulation implemented pursuant to the EHA [34 CFR § 300.451(a)] required DCPS to provide transportation to the Lab School as a related service even though the girl had been unilaterally placed. DCPS argued that the federal regulation cited by the mother to support her claim only applied to cases where a child was placed in a private school by his or her parents and required a particular program that was not offered by the public school. The district court observed that 34 CFR § 300.451(a) had to be construed in light of § 300.403. The latter section made it clear that when the public agency (DCPS) provided a free appropriate education and the mother chose to place the girl in a private school nevertheless, "the regulations relating to payment for a private school are not involved and therefore the public agency is not required ... to pay for the child's education at the private school." Section 300.451(a) merely clarified that DCPS was not relieved of *all* responsibility for the girl. The court concluded that neither the EHA nor the implementing regulation required DCPS to provide transportation for the girl to attend the Lab School. *Work v. McKenzie*, 661 F.Supp. 225 (D.D.C.1987).

The individualized education program (IEP) developed for an orthopedically disabled child recommended that he be educated in a regular class because he was functioning at or above his grade level in all of his academic subjects. It also provided that a special vehicle was needed for his transportation in order to meet his special physical needs. Though the child's local school district offered an appropriate education in and transportation to a public school, his father voluntarily placed him in a private school. After two hearing officers determined that the school district only had to pay $406 per year (considerably less than the actual cost) for the child's transportation to the private school, his father sued the New Jersey Department of Education seeking the actual cost.

The issue before the Superior Court of New Jersey, Appellate Division, was whether the child was entitled to transportation as a "related service" under the EHA even though his IEP did not indicate the need for special education. The court held that the child was not entitled to transportation as a "related service." It reasoned that, although the child had a disability, he did not have a disability that required special education. Therefore, stated the court, related services auxiliary to special education were not mandated by the EHA. The court accepted the school district's argument that under New Jersey law, if a school district provided transportation for students to and from public schools, it was also required to do so for private school students. Since the child was being transported as a private school student and not as a disabled student, he was held to be entitled only to the fixed amount of $406 under New Jersey law. *A.A. v. Cooperman*, 526 A.2d 1103 (N.J.Super.A.D.1987).

The West Virginia Supreme Court of Appeals held that under state law, two disabled children were entitled to transportation to school. In this case, two families lived on a dirt road, located in rural West Virginia, known as Dry Monday Branch. The road, which was often traversable only by four-wheel drive vehicle, was owned by a timber company which never objected to its use by the two families. The families had, respectively, a seven-year-old boy and a six-year-old girl who were both afflicted with spina bifida. Both children wore orthopedic braces from waist to feet and were unable to walk to the established school bus stop, which was located on a regular road one-half to nine-tenths of a mile from the children's homes. The county school board refused to send a school bus up Dry Monday Branch because of the road's poor condition, and the children's parents did not own a reliable vehicle in which to transport them to the established bus stop. As a result, the children were unable to attend school during the 1984-85 school year.

Throughout the summer of 1985, the children's parents attempted to persuade school officials to provide transportation for their children. Finally the superintendent sent them a letter informing them that because Dry Monday Branch was a privately owned road, was poorly maintained and was unsafe for a school bus, the parents would have to provide transportation themselves.

Because the laws of West Virginia [W.Va.Code 18-5-13(6)(a)] require that county boards of education provide "adequate" transportation to any student living more than two miles from school, the parents sought an order that the board provide their children with transportation down Dry Monday Branch. The West Virginia Supreme Court of Appeals agreed and issued a writ of mandamus directing the county school board to provide proper transportation. The court held that poor road conditions could not excuse the board from providing adequate transportation to all students. Since neither child was able to walk to the established school bus stop, the board's arrangements were inadequate as a matter of law. As further justification for its decision, the court noted that the timber company which owned Dry Monday Branch regarded it as a public road. *Kennedy v. Bd. of Educ., McDowell County*, 337 S.E.2d 905 (W.Va.1985).

V. REIMBURSEMENT FOR OTHER EXPENSES

In addition to tuition reimbursement, parents sometimes request reimbursement for related expenses, such as sign language interpreters, rehabilitative services, independent evaluators and therapy.

A West Virginia man contacted a private rehabilitation facility in Pennsylvania to negotiate the admittance of his son for rehabilitation. Concerned about the man's ability to pay, the private facility only permitted the youth to be admitted on a thirty-day basis with care to be terminated if it became clear that no funding would be available. Later, at the individualized education program meeting, the father's attorney took the county superintendent of schools aside and offered to mediate the case (with respect to funding). In the mediation, everything was conducted through the attorney; as a result, there was a misunderstanding about whether the superintendent promised to pay for care. However, the private facility understood that the superintendent promised to fund the care. When care was not paid for, the facility sued in federal court, alleging breach of contract and that it had relied on the superintendent's promise to pay for the rehabilitative services. The West Virginia Board of Education argued that it had never approved the financing of rehabilitative care for the boy; thus, it was not bound under West Virginia law. The court agreed with the board. It stated that, even if a commitment to pay was made, "the procedures requisite to using state funds to pay for [the youth's] rehabilitation mandated by state law and regulations were not followed." Accordingly, the alleged promise made by the superintendent was beyond his authority. The board could not be bound by these actions. The court granted summary judgment to the board. *Lake Erie Institute of Rehabilitation v. Marion County, West Virginia, Board of Educ.*, 798 F.Supp. 262 (W.D.Pa.1992).

A multiply-disabled Idaho student was classified as trainable mentally retarded. He was placed in a public school's disabled contained classroom, taught by special education teachers. The student's parents then decided to place him in a private school, but all the schools contacted required a full-time aide as a prerequisite. The parents enrolled him in a parochial school for the following school year. They then commenced an administrative proceeding to obtain reimbursement for the aide. The district's child study team met to determine financial responsibility for the full-time aide. The team was advised by its counsel that it had no financial responsibility and it then informed the parents about the public education system's educational opportunities. The district offered placement in a segregated special education program. The parents argued that the student was entitled to mainstreaming under the EHA. The district then offered to fund educational services in a private school, but refused to pay for the aide. The parents kept their son in the parochial school and began an administrative appeal for the cost of the aide and tuition. The hearing officer ruled in favor of the school district, and the parents appealed to an Idaho county court. The court overturned the hearing officer's determination and ruled in favor of the parents. The district then appealed to the Idaho Supreme Court.

The supreme court noted that the district had failed to rebut the parents' argument that mainstreaming was appropriate. Free appropriate education must be provided in the least restrictive environment and there was a strong preference for mainstreaming in conformity with the EHA. The court noted that school district documents did not qualify as an IEP, because they set forth no goals or other evaluation procedures for determining whether EHA educational objectives were being met. Because there was no appropriate IEP, the district was not in compliance with the EHA and the hearing officer's determination was erroneous. The court ordered the school district to reimburse the parents for their son's tuition and for his aide. *Thornock v. Boise Indep. School Dist. 1*, 767 P.2d 1241 (Idaho 1988).

A five-year-old District of Columbia multiply-disabled student was eligible for special education services. Her parents requested private special education from the District of Columbia Public Schools (DCPS). They unilaterally placed her in a private daycare center. Each week the student received speech and occupational therapy from an outside source. The DCPS completed an IEP for the student, identifying her as multiply-disabled with motor and speech communication problems. The DCPS placed the student in a public school program for children with disabilities. The student's parents challenged the public school placement and requested two EHA due process hearings. The hearing officer refused to award tuition expenses to the parents, and later determined that the school district's placement was appropriate. The hearing officer also stated that the student's placement at her private daycare program was inappropriate and did not provide the services described in her IEP. The hearing officer held that the DCPS should pay for the student's outside occupational and speech therapy because they were appropriate and because the DCPS had failed to timely place the student.

The parents appealed the decision to the U.S. District Court, District of Columbia, claiming that the DCPS placement was inappropriate. The district court ruled in the parents' favor because the DCPS program was inadequate and the district was completely incapable of providing occupational therapy. The district lacked adequate funding and had a lengthy waiting list for occupational therapy. The court approved the educational alternative proposed by the parents, which was a private special education school in Maryland specializing in educating children with severe sensory integration deficiencies and occupational therapy. The court also awarded attorney's fees to the parents under the EAHCA. *Kattan by Thomas v. Dist. of Columbia*, 691 F.Supp. 1539 (D.D.C.1988).

A learning disabled New York third-grader attended regular classes with supplemental resource room support. Her school district's committee on special education considered placing her in a self-contained classroom based upon a reevaluation. It also recommended neurological testing. However, the student's parents rejected the test results and had the student evaluated independently. They then sought reimbursement for the costs of the independent evaluation from the school district. A hearing officer ruled for the district because the parents had failed to request or notify the school district of their wish to obtain the evaluation. The parents served the district with a notice of intent and petition seeking review by the Commissioner of Education of New York. A New York special education law authorizing review of this type of determination by a state education department review officer took effect several days later and the petition was served upon the state review officer. The officer conducted a hearing and determined that placement in the self-contained classroom was inappropriate and that the student's parents should be reimbursed. The district appealed to a New York trial court, which ruled that the state review officer had jurisdiction to rule on the matter. The district appealed to the New York Supreme Court, Appellate Division, Third Department, which ruled that the state review officer was without jurisdiction to hear the matter and that the state commissioner of education had review authority under prior legislation. The appellate division court reversed the trial court's decision. *Bd. of Educ., Commack Union Free School Dist. v. Fernandez*, 590 N.Y.S.2d 310 (A.D.3d Dept.1992).

A New York child, born prematurely, required visual stimulation treatments. She was diagnosed as having a combination of optic neuropathy with superimposed cerebral dysfunction. In effect, she acted like she was blind because her brain could not process visual stimulation. Accordingly, the parents obtained the services of a certified and licensed teacher, who had special expertise in the teaching and treatment of visually impaired children. The teacher was certified by the New York Board of Education as a special education teacher of the blind and partially sighted in the public schools. The parents sought coverage from their medical insurance company but were denied reimbursement. The company claimed that visual stimulation therapy was not a covered medical service and further, that the special education teacher was only licensed to provide therapy in a public school. The parents then filed a reimbursement action in a New York small claims court. The court noted that all of the experts who testified, stated that the infant required visual stimulation therapy. Therefore, the court determined that the service was medically necessary and within the scope of coverage. The court also noted that the teacher's license provided that it was "valid for service in the public schools," but it did not contain any language limiting it to that kind of facility. Thus, the teacher was licensed to provide the visual stimulation therapy outside the public school and the court awarded coverage for the special education teacher's services. *Saxe v. Metropolitan Life Ins. Co.*, 577 N.Y.S.2d 570 (N.Y.City Civ.Ct.1991).

CHAPTER SIX

ATTORNEY'S FEES

Prior to 1986 there was no provision in the EHA for attorney's fees. Accordingly, the U.S. Supreme Court held in *Smith v. Robinson*, 468 U.S. 992 (1984), that attorney's fees were not recoverable for special education claims made under the EHA. It also held that attorney's fees were not recoverable under 42 U.S.C. § 1983 or the Rehabilitation Act. With the passage of the Handicapped Children's Protection Act (HCPA) of 1986, Congress expressly provided for attorney's fees to a prevailing parent or guardian in cases that were pending on or after July 4, 1984.

I. COURT PROCEEDINGS

Under the Handicapped Children's Protection Act (HCPA), part of the IDEA, attorney's fees are recoverable where a student or guardian prevails in a court proceeding pending on or after July 4, 1984.

A Texas man owned and operated a school for delinquent, disabled, and disturbed teens. After one of the school's students died in 1973, a county grand jury returned a murder indictment charging the owner with wilful failure to administer proper medical treatment and failure to provide timely hospitalization. After the state closed the school, the owner sued for monetary and injunctive relief under 42 U.S.C. §§ 1983 and 1985. The complaint ultimately asked for damages of $17 million. The owner died in 1983, and the administrators of his estate continued the case. The case was tried before a jury, which found that although the defendants had committed acts that deprived the owner of a civil right, this deprivation was not the proximate cause of any damages. Therefore, it held that the owner's estate should take nothing.

The U.S. Court of Appeals for the Fifth Circuit affirmed in part and reversed in part. The court affirmed the failure to award compensatory or nominal damages against the conspirators because the complainants had not proved an actual deprivation of a constitutional right. Because the jury found that the lieutenant governor had deprived the owner of a civil right, however, the court remanded for entry of judgment against the lieutenant governor for $1 in nominal damages. The owner's estate then sought attorney's fees under 42 U.S.C. § 1988, which allows prevailing parties in civil rights actions to be awarded reasonable attorney's fees. The district court entered an award ordering the estate to be paid $280,000 in fees, $27,000 in expenses, and $10,000 in prejudgment interest. A divided Fifth Circuit panel reversed the fee award stating that an award of $1 was insufficient to justify an award as a prevailing party. The U.S. Supreme Court than granted review.

The Supreme Court held that a plaintiff who wins nominal damages is a prevailing party under § 1988. A plaintiff prevails when actual relief on the merits of his claim materially alters the legal relationship between the parties by modifying the defendant's behavior in a way that directly benefits the plaintiff. Here, the estate was entitled to nominal damages because it was able to establish liability for denial of procedural due process. The prevailing party inquiry does not turn on the magnitude of the relief obtained or whether a nominal damages award is a technical, insignificant victory. However, even though the estate was the prevailing party it was not entitled to a fee award. While the technical nature of nominal damages does not affect prevailing party inquiry, it does bear on the fees awarded under § 1988. The most critical factor in determining a fee award's reasonableness is the degree of success obtained, since a fee based upon the hours expended on the litigation as a whole may be excessive if a plaintiff achieves only partial or limited success. Since the estate failed to prove the essential element of its claim for monetary relief, the only reasonable fee was no fee at all. *Farrar v. Hobby*, 506 U.S. —, 113 S.Ct. 566, 121 L.Ed.2d 494 (1992).

A Minnesota sixth-grader began to experience academic and emotional problems. His school district requested permission to conduct an assessment of his ability, achievement and social-emotional skills. Eventually, the district conducted three evaluations, which resulted in a program of complete mainstreaming. The student still received poor grades, but the IEP team saw no need to modify the program. The team decided to mainstream the student for the eighth grade. However, before the school year, the student moved to a different town to live with his father. The new school district then sought to place him in special education. The student's mother refused to give her consent to special education placement, and the student attended regular classes. Soon, the student returned to live with his mother. The district attempted to make another assessment for special education services, but the mother refused to give her consent. She requested a conciliation conference, then obtained an attorney and requested a due process hearing. The hearing officer held that the proposed fourth assessment of the student was appropriate, and its decision was affirmed by a deputy commissioner of education. The mother then filed a lawsuit under the EHA and 42 U.S.C. § 1983, seeking an order to reverse the hearing officer's decision and a declaratory judgment that the EHA permitted her son to obtain a full due process hearing on any issue relating to his evaluation or placement. A federal district court granted the mother's motion. The mother then made a motion in the court for an award of attorney's fees under the EHA. The court held that the mother was a prevailing party under the EHA and awarded attorney's fees in excess of $10,000. This represented only one half of the fees requested.

The mother then failed to appear for court-ordered depositions, and the district court issued a final order dismissing the complaint. The school district then appealed the attorney's fees award to the U.S. Court of Appeals, Eighth Circuit. The court noted that an award of attorney's fees under the EHA could only be reversed for an abuse of discretion. It rejected the school district's argument that special circumstances existed which made the attorney's fees award unjust. The court noted that the school district had continually opposed the mother's request for a due process hearing, effectively denying her an opportunity to present her objections. The district had operated under an unreasonable interpretation of state law, which, like the EHA, provided parents an opportunity to present their complaints about evaluation and placement of special education students. The district court had not abused its discretion by awarding attorney's fees as there were no special circumstances in support of the district's argument. The court of appeals affirmed the district court's order awarding attorney's fees. *ISD 623, Roseville, Minnesota v. Digre*, 893 F.2d 987 (8th Cir.1990).

A California school district decided to transfer a severely disabled student to another school. After a hearing officer upheld the district's decision, the student sued it in a federal district court under the Education of the Handicapped Act (EHA). Before trial the parties settled the case. The district agreed not to transfer the student to a different school, and to create a special day class for the student at her current school. The settlement did not mention attorney's fees. At the time of the settlement, the U.S. Supreme Court had determined that attorney's fees were not available to prevailing parties. *Smith v. Robinson*, 468 U.S. 992 (1984). After that decision, Congress enacted the HCPA which overruled *Smith*, and provided for recovery of attorney's fees retroactively to the date of *Smith*.

Because the student in this case had initially sought relief at the administrative level after the *Smith* decision was rendered, the student petitioned the district court for attorney's fees. The district court found for the school district and the student appealed to the U.S. Court of Appeals, Ninth Circuit. The appeals court held that the district court had abused its discretion in denying attorney's fees to the student. When the parties settled, the student had no right to receive fees. Although the school district had no expectation of paying fees and might not have entered the settlement had it known it could be liable for fees, these reasons failed to justify the denial of attorney's fees. The HCPA applied retroactively to any action brought after July 3, 1984, the date of the *Smith* decision. The unfairness of retroactivity did not justify the denial of attorney's fees. The appeals court remanded the case to determine whether special circumstances existed which would allow denial of attorney fees under the EHA. *Abu-Sahyun v. Palo Alto Unified School Dist.*, 843 F.2d 1250 (9th Cir.1988).

The parents of a child with a disability sued an Illinois school district under the EHA, seeking compensation for the education of their disabled son. Their case was pending on July 4, 1984, and was resolved in March of 1986. In August 1986, Congress passed an amendment to the EHA (HCPA) which made attorney's fees available to litigants prevailing under the EHA if their cases were pending on July 4, 1984. The student's parents then sought attorney's fees in a federal district court. The district court awarded the parents attorney's fees and the school district appealed to the United States Court of Appeals, Seventh Circuit. The court of appeals held that the student was not barred from seeking attorney's fees which were initially not available when the case was decided. The student's original complaint had requested attorney's fees. However, the district court did not address that issue because there was no legal basis for an award of fees until Congress passed the amendments in August 1986. Ordinarily, failing to rule on the request would have precluded it in later litigation. However, the U.S. Constitution permitted Congress to alter this principle by providing retroactive recovery of attorney's fees. The appeals court affirmed the district court's decision. *Max M. v. New Trier High School Dist. No. 203*, 859 F.2d 1297 (7th Cir.1988).

A group of three students with disabilities sued the District of Columbia in order to ensure their educational placement in time for the new school year. The U.S. District Court for the District of Columbia agreed to hold a hearing on the students' claims. One student had not been given a suitable placement program when the lawsuit was brought. However, the district determined the student's placement by the time the hearing was to be held. The second student was unable to procure timely due process hearings from the district. The third was not given a placement before the start of the school year. By the time the hearing was held, the district had agreed to accommodate each of these students' needs. Two of the students later returned to court to ensure that the district provided them with transportation to school. The district admitted its duty to provide bus service, but claimed that bureaucratic problems impeded it from providing service.

The court ordered the district to provide adequate transportation, stating that the district's bureaucratic morass did not excuse its failure to meet its legal obligations. The students then applied for attorney's fees under 20 U.S.C. § 1415 (e)(4)(B). The district opposed an award of attorney's fees, arguing that the students were not "prevailing parties" as required by the statute. According to the district, the court proceedings merely constituted a "technical victory" and did not clothe the students with "prevailing party" status.

The court disagreed. The students were prevailing parties as required by federal law. Thus, they were entitled to attorney's fees. It noted that the students had not received appropriate educational placements through the school system. The facts indicated that the instant lawsuit prompted the district to take action. The court stated that "[w]ithout the intervention of this Court, it is doubtful that the District would have arisen from its slumber in time for the [students] to attend classes with their peers." In addition, the students had to go to court to ensure that they were provided with transportation. The court awarded attorney's fees. However, it held that the students were only entitled to $49 for expert witnesses — a $40 attendance fee and $9 travel expenses. Any additional expert fees could not be considered attorney's fees. *Aronow v. Dist. of Columbia*, 780 F.Supp. 46 (D.D.C.1992).

Two sets of parents of severely disabled students sued the New York education commissioner for placement costs at an out-of-state facility for severely disabled persons. A New York trial court agreed with the parents' decision to place the children at the out-of-state facility. Although the parents had failed to exhaust their administrative remedies, further appeal to the commissioner would have been futile given his previous refusal to implement each student's special committee recommendation. The parents then made a motion for attorney's fees under the HCPA. Both children's parents were represented by the same attorneys from the same law firm. The trial court granted the motion for attorney's fees totaling over $34,000 in the first case and $43,803.25 in the second. The commissioner appealed, claiming that HCPA counsel fees were not available under the EHA, and that the fees were improperly determined.

The appellate division court ruled that under the U.S. Supreme Court decision in *Honig v. Doe*, 108 S.Ct. 592, parents are permitted to seek EHA review by a court where the administrative process was futile or inadequate. Therefore, the parents had properly filed the matter in court. However, the parents' attorneys had failed to submit sufficient evidence to determine their fees. Because the attorneys had represented the parents of both children, there was a possibility that they were being paid twice for the same research. The court remanded the case to the trial court and directed the attorneys to submit their time sheets, taking precautions to protect confidential material. *Behavior Research Institute v. Ambach*, 535 N.Y.S.2d 465 (A.D.3d Dep't 1988).

After an Illinois special education student was hospitalized for behavioral problems, the school district conducted multidisciplinary staff conferences to further evaluate his special education needs. Representatives of the Illinois Department of Mental Health and Developmental Disabilities (DMHDD) were invited but did not attend the conferences. Following the conferences, the school district recommended that the student be placed at the behavior education center, a more restrictive program than his previous special education program. The parents disagreed with the placement believing that the student's special education needs required a residential placement. They requested a due process hearing and the hearing officer determined that his educational needs were so complex as to require residential placement which was to be paid by the school district. The school district then filed suit in an Illinois trial court against the student, his parents, the Illinois State Board of Education and DMHDD seeking reversal of the residential placement decision or in the alternative a declaration of funding responsibility to the state board of education or DMHDD if the placement decision was upheld by the court.

The court ordered the board of education and the DMHDD to share in the cost of room and board along with the school district. The parents then filed an application for attorney's fees. Thereafter, the school district moved to allocate the attorney's fees either in whole or in part to the state board of education and DMHDD on the grounds that the parents had prevailed against those agencies. The court granted the parents' motion for attorney's fees against only the school district. The school district then appealed to the Appellate Court of Illinois.

The school district contended that since the board of education and the DMHDD were ordered to pay room and board, the school district was a prevailing party. The trial court had refused to apportion the attorney's fees, finding that the school district had unreasonably prolonged the proceedings leading to the student's placement. The court noted that it would be contrary to the language of the education act to determine that the school district was the prevailing party. However, the record indicated that the attorney's fees were incurred as a result of the refusal of the board of education and DMHDD to accept responsibility for their costs of the residential placement. Therefore, the court ordered allocation of attorney's fees among the three parties responsible for paying the residential placement. *Community Consolidated School Dist. v. Illinois State Board of Education*, 576 N.E.2d 250 (Ill.App.1st Dist.1991).

An orthopedically disabled student at the Louisiana Special Education Center (LSEC) was transferred to a hospital in March 1985, to be treated for respiratory problems. When he attempted to return to the LSEC, it refused to admit him, arguing that it was not equipped to deal with his medical problems. The student subsequently sued the LSEC under the EHA. A federal district court ordered the school to admit the student who subsequently sought attorney's fees. The district court denied attorney's fees on the basis of *Smith v. Robinson*, in which the Supreme Court declared attorney's fees unavailable in EHA cases. He appealed, but before the appeal reached the court, Congress passed the Handicapped Children's Protection Act of 1986 which overruled the *Smith* decision by expressly providing for attorney's fees in EHA cases. The U.S. Court of Appeals, Fifth Circuit, ruled that he was entitled to attorney's fees and remanded the case to the district court. The district court awarded attorney's fees to the student in the amount of $9,300 and the LSEC appealed.

The court of appeals first determined that the LSEC could not avoid paying the attorney's fees on the ground that it had acted in good faith when it refused to admit the student. It also rejected the LSEC's argument that he could not sue for attorney's fees because the EHA allows payment of such fees only to "the parents or guardian of a disabled child or youth." The student in this case was eighteen years or older while the suit was in progress and he therefore sought attorney's fees in his own name. The court declared that the EHA legislative history indicated that disabled children can seek attorney's fees on their own behalf if they are old enough and are otherwise competent to bring suit. Because the district court had not abused its discretion in awarding attorney's fees, the award was proper. The court of appeals ruled in the student's favor and remanded the case to the district court for a determination of the amount of additional attorney's fees that he should receive for the appeal. *Fontenot v. Louisiana Bd. of Elementary & Secondary Educ.*, 835 F.2d 117 (5th Cir.1988).

A North Dakota child eligible for special education services under the EHA enrolled in the Bismarck public school system. At the end of the year, his mother became concerned about the adequacy of her son's educational services. She hired an attorney who failed to attend scheduled meetings. After the attorney then filed a due process complaint citing a number of procedural errors, the parties signed a consent agreement. The mother then filed this action in a federal district court for the sole purpose of obtaining attorney's fees. The trial court awarded a reduced fee and she appealed to the U.S. Court of Appeals, Eighth Circuit. The EHA provides for attorney's fees to parents who prevail in any action or proceeding including administrative hearings. However, the court may reduce the amount of attorney's fees if the court finds that the parents unreasonably protracted the final resolution of the controversy. The court noted that the attorney failed to attend meetings and filed a due process complaint without any attempt at informal negotiation. The appellate court determined that a denial of the entire fee award was warranted for unreasonably protracting a resolution. *Johnson v. Bismarck Public School Dist.*, 949 F.2d 1000 (8th Cir.1991).

II. ADMINISTRATIVE PROCEEDINGS

Where a student or parent prevails in an administrative proceeding, a lawsuit may be brought for the sole purpose of obtaining attorney's fees.

A sixteen-year-old student who had been identified as disabled under the Individuals with Disabilities Education Act (IDEA) attended public school in Maine. In 1991, the local school held a Pupil Evaluation Team (PET) meeting to prepare an individualized education plan for the upcoming school year. The parents, who were present at the meeting, were dissatisfied with the resulting IEP and asked the school district to convene another PET meeting. After the next meeting, the school district issued a revised IEP. However, the parents continued to be dissatisfied with it, and unilaterally placed their son in a private residential school program for the following school year. They requested an administrative due process hearing at which the hearing officer found that the school had to increase services, goals and objectives in the IEP. The hearing officer denied the parents' request to replace their son at the residential school. After the school district denied the parents' request for attorney's fees and costs, they brought an action under 20 U.S.C. § 1415.

The issue before the federal district court was whether the parents could recover attorney's fees and costs arising from attorney and expert witness participation in PET meetings. The language of the statute provided that attorney's fees could be awarded in "any action or proceeding brought under this subsection." The court noted that treating PET meetings as part of the administrative hearing/litigation process would simply encourage adversarial conduct. This was not the purpose of the meetings. Accordingly, no fees or costs could be recovered by the parents in connection with the PET meetings.

Next, the court noted that the parents could recover fees and costs if they were considered a prevailing party at an administrative due process hearing. Prevailing party status requires the parents to obtain relief on a significant claim in litigation, requires a material alteration in the parties' legal relationship, and requires success that is not merely technical or minor in nature. Here, the parents had satisfied all three criteria and thus were prevailing parties at the administrative hearing. The court noted that even though the parents did not achieve their ultimate goal of having the IEP declared wholly inadequate, they did succeed in obtaining an increase in services, goals and objectives. Further, despite the fact that they ultimately chose to keep their son in a private residential program specifically rejected by the hearing officer, they won benefits at the administrative hearing which were available to their son if he returned to the public school system. Moreover, even though their success was small in relation to what they had asked for, the quality of the relief obtained was significant. The court therefore awarded a percentage of the fees and costs asked for with respect to the administrative hearing. *Fenneman v. Town of Gorham*, 802 F.Supp. 542 (D.Me.1992).

Tennessee parents of a child with disabilities requested the school district to place their child in a residential program where they claimed the child's educational needs would be better met. The school refused residential placement and offered another program. The parents appealed the school's decision to the Tennessee Department of Education. An administrative law judge (ALJ) denied residential placement and rejected the school's alternative plan as insufficient. The ALJ ordered the school to increase therapy services and provide behavior management and "living skills" education. Both the parents and the school appealed. The district court affirmed the ALJ's judgments regarding increased therapy and rejection of the residential placement, but did not adopt the other relief the ALJ had granted. It also denied the parents' motion for payment of attorney's fees.

On appeal to the U.S. Court of Appeals, Sixth Circuit, the appellate court reversed the district court's denial of attorney's fees. The court held that the amended Individuals with Disabilities Education Act (IDEA) allowed recovery of attorney's fees for prevailing parents of students with disabilities. Following the Supreme Court interpretation, the central issue test was rejected; the new standard requires "a resolution of the dispute which changes the legal relationship." The ordered additional therapy services produced a change in the school's legal relationship with the parents. Thus, the court held that the parents should be awarded attorney's fees. *Krichinsky v. Knox County Schools*, 963 F.2d 847 (6th Cir.1992).

A special education student and his parents sought and were granted a temporary restraining order which compelled the District of Columbia to comply with the decision of an administrative hearing officer. The hearing officer had ordered the student to be removed from a hospital and placed in a residential school, but the District of Columbia had delayed in complying with the order. The student and his parents then brought a motion before the U.S. District Court for the District of Columbia for an award of costs and attorney's fees under § 1415(e)(4)(B) of the Individuals with Disabilities Education Act. The District of Columbia opposed the motion, asserting that the plaintiffs were only entitled to recover attorney's fees where they had lost at the administrative level and had successfully appealed to a federal district court. Here, the plaintiffs had prevailed at the administrative level. The court, however, noted that the law of the D.C. Circuit did not support that position.

In *Moore v. District of Columbia*, 907 F.2d 165 (D.C.Cir.1990), the court of appeals had held that a plaintiff (student) could recover attorney's fees incurred when the plaintiff won at a due process special education hearing. Similarly, when a plaintiff has to go to court to enforce the decision of a hearing officer, attorney's fees may be awarded. Since the statute says that the court may award attorney's fees to a prevailing party "in any action or proceeding," there was no necessity that the student have lost at the administrative level and won on appeal in order to be eligible for such an award. The purpose of the statute was to compensate plaintiffs who "have had to fight a legal battle" to obtain services for which they have a legal entitlement. Since the plaintiffs in this case had won at the administrative level on paper, but had been forced to use the court to get a meaningful decision, they were entitled to an award of attorney's fees. The court granted the plaintiff's motion. *Capiello v. District of Columbia*, 779 F.Supp. 1 (D.D.C.1991).

In two separate cases, the parents of two disabled children sought to have them put in a residential setting for educational purposes. The respective school districts refused. For a while an attempt at education was made at the schools and when that proved ineffective, the children were placed in day schools specifically for the disabled. Eventually the parents asked for an administrative hearing in which their requests were granted. They then sought attorney's fees, costs and expenses, which were denied. They filed suit in a California federal district court which ruled against them, and they appealed to the U.S. Court of Appeals, Ninth Circuit.

The court of appeals noted that at the time of the district courts' decisions, there were few cases available which spoke to the subject of attorney's fees. However, with the enactment of the Handicapped Children's Protection Act of 1986 cases had been decided which interpreted the Act. The court followed the Fifth Circuit's decision in *Duane M. v. Orleans Parish School Bd.*, 861 F.2d 115 (1988) and the Sixth Circuit's holding in *Eggers v. Bullitt County School District*, 854 F.2d 892 (1988), and held that the parents could recover attorney's fees and appropriate costs plus expenses. The court recognized that the overwhelming majority of cases now supported awarding fees to parents who prevailed in administrative hearings as well as at trial. It thus reversed the district courts' decisions. *McSomebodies v. San Mateo City School Dist.*, 897 F.2d 975 (9th Cir.1989) and *McSomebodies v. Burlingame Elementary School Dist.*, 897 F.2d 974 (9th Cir.1989).

Several Washington, D.C., students with disabilities and their parents instituted administrative proceedings in which they prevailed. They then instituted this action in a federal district court for recovery of attorney's fees and costs incurred in the administrative proceedings. The trial court found for the parents, and the school district appealed to the U.S. Court of Appeals, D.C. Circuit, which reversed. The parents then filed a suggestion for en banc consideration and the court decided to rehear the case.

On appeal, the court noted that the four circuit courts that have addressed the issue have concluded that the Handicapped Children's Protection Act (HCPA) does authorize an award of attorney's fees to a parent who prevails in an EHA administrative proceeding. The court, through an in-depth analysis of the statutory content and legislative history, determined that the HCPA does authorize an award of attorney's fees to a prevailing party. The court of appeals affirmed the trial court's decision to grant attorney's fees. *Moore v. District of Columbia*, 907 F.2d 165 (D.C.Cir.1990).

The parents of a disabled California student requested an administrative hearing to determine whether the individualized education program (IEP) proposed by the student's school district was appropriate under the Individuals with Disabilities Education Act (IDEA). A California statute gave parties the right to a mediation conference prior to the state-level hearing in addition to the procedural safeguards of the IDEA. The parents agreed to a mediation conference and there they reached an agreement under which the student was placed in a private residential facility for a thirty-day period. When the student's private school counselors recommended continued treatment at the facility, the school district first sought a continuation of the administrative hearing, but ultimately agreed to continue funding the private school placement. The parents dismissed the administrative proceeding but requested reimbursement of $3,200 in attorney fees, which the school district rejected. The parents brought an IDEA suit for attorney's fees and expenses in the U.S. District Court for the Central District of California.

The court noted that while there was no IDEA equivalent of the California mediation conference statute, it was clear that the federal IDEA took precedence over any California statutes. There was overwhelming support for the parents' claim for attorney's fees under the IDEA's history in the legislature and in the courts. The parents were entitled to recover their attorney's fees for work done prior to a hearing, which included the mediation process and the action for enforcement of the claim for attorney's fees in federal court. This was consistent with the line of federal court cases awarding parents attorney's fees and other costs when settlements were reached prior to due process hearings and parents were deemed "prevailing parties" under the IDEA. *Masotti v. Tustin Unified School Dist.*, 806 F.Supp. 221 (C.D.Cal.1992).

Parents of a disabled Ohio student requested a formal IDEA due process hearing to determine appropriate educational programs and services for their child. Prior to the hearing, the parties identified and substantially resolved five issues. The hearing officer granted the student an extended school year and other relief. The parents then requested payment of their attorney's fees, which the school district refused to pay. The parents sued the district in the U.S. District Court for the Northern District of Ohio. A federal judge granted the parents summary judgment, and referred the matter to a federal magistrate for a determination of appropriate attorney's fees. The magistrate awarded the parents approximately $22,000 in fees and costs. The school district then argued to the federal district judge that there should be no recovery of attorney's fees because the parties had settled the matter and there were no prevailing parties under the IDEA. The judge disagreed, reasoning that the parents had been granted the majority of their requests. The parents should be awarded attorney's fees because they had been forced to litigate the prevailing party issue. An award of attorney's fees was justified because it was a second major litigation for the parents due to the school district's inflexibility. The court modified the magistrate's award resulting in a recovery of over $44,000 for the parents. *Moore v. Crestwood Local School Dist.*, 804 F.Supp. 960 (N.D.Ohio 1992).

A Tennessee four-year-old was diagnosed as hearing impaired with speech and language disabilities. Her parents notified the local school board and negotiations began to determine the correct educational program. Following a multidisciplinary team meeting, the parents stated their dissatisfaction with the board's educational options and stated their preference for comprehensive full-day, five-day-a-week classes with specific therapies and services. The board then proposed that the student attend a public school where she would receive help from a deaf education specialist one hour per day, see a speech therapist for a half-hour three days a week, and consult a vision specialist twice a week. The parents rejected this proposal and requested a due process hearing, which resulted in a finding that the school board had denied the student special education and related services and had negligently attempted to identify and evaluate appropriate services. However, the hearing officer found that the board had not violated federal regulations for offering a placement not based on an IEP or for failing to maintain a continuum of alternative placements. Neither party appealed the hearing officer's decision, but the parents filed a lawsuit in a federal district court for their attorney's fees.

The district court outlined the appropriateness of attorney's fees under the Handicapped Children's Protection Act (HCPA). The HCPA permits reasonable attorney's fees to parents of children with disabilities who are prevailing parties under the act. Because the hearing officer had ruled that the school board was negligent, the court stated that the student was the prevailing party. However, attorney's fees are unavailable for actions performed after a written offer of settlement if the final relief granted is no more favorable than a written offer of settlement. The court noted a letter from the board's special education services director offering the public school placement with speech therapy and other specialists which did not materially differ from the eventual result of the hearing. The court also noted that the attorney had delayed almost one month in rejecting the board's offer. Because the settlement offer was as favorable as the final award, the court disallowed attorney's fees and dismissed the lawsuit. *Hyden v. Bd. of Educ. of Wilson County*, 714 F.Supp. 290 (M.D.Tenn.1989).

The parents of a Massachusetts learning disabled student disapproved of the IEP proposed for the student by the Boston School Committee. The parents appealed the committee's IEP proposal to the Massachusetts Department of Education. The department rejected the IEP and granted the educational services the parents had requested. During the proceedings, the parents were represented by an attorney at a rate of $150 per hour for a total of 51.5 hours. The parents sued the committee in federal district court to recover attorney's fees under the 1986 Handicapped Children's Protection Act (HCPA).

The committee argued that the HCPA did not authorize the award of attorney's fees when parents prevailed only at the administrative level. It contended that the parents must be "aggrieved parties," unsuccessful in the administrative process, and must pursue their claim in federal district court before the court had jurisdiction to consider an award of attorney's fees. The court rejected the committee's argument and held that the parents were entitled to reasonable attorney's fees. The HCPA's legislative history demonstrated that Congress intended to award attorney's fees to parents for legal representation in any action or proceeding. Under the HCPA prevailing parties may recover reasonable fees based on rates prevailing in the community. The time the parents' attorney spent on the administrative process was found reasonable. However, the attorney did not submit supporting documentation concerning the prevailing hourly rate attorneys received in the community. The court found that the parents were therefore entitled to reasonable attorney's fees limited to $125 per hour. *Williams v. Boston School Comm.*, 709 F.Supp. 27 (D.Mass.1989).

A mildly retarded young adult initiated administrative proceedings against his Connecticut school district. He sought additional education as compensation for a two-year period during which he was hospitalized and received little or no education. After unsuccessful administrative hearings, the young adult appealed to a U.S. district court. The lawsuit was settled by a consent decree signed by both the state and the local school district. The decree granted the young adult two years of compensatory education at the state's expense. The young adult sued both the state and the school district in a U.S. district court after passage of the HCPA. He sought attorney's fees incurred in the earlier lawsuit at the administrative level. The court held that because the young adult had obtained limited success against the school district at the administrative level (in that the school district was fiscally responsible for the young adult's education during his two-year hospitalization) it was liable for twenty percent of the attorney's fees. The school district appealed to the U.S. Court of Appeals, Second Circuit.

The school district argued that attorney's fees were unavailable for administrative hearings under the HCPA. Furthermore, the young adult failed to prevail against it as required by the HCPA. The young adult argued that he was entitled to attorney's fees from both the state and the school district due to the "relative culpability" of both defendants. The court of appeals held for the school district although it rejected the district's argument that the HCPA failed to afford attorney's fees for work done in connection with administrative hearings. Under the HCPA a court may award attorney's fees to any disabled youth who is a "prevailing party." A youth is considered a prevailing party if he or she succeeds on any significant issue in litigation. The young adult clearly prevailed against the state with respect to the consent decree but the court concluded that he did not prevail against the school district either at the administrative level or in the consent decree. Although a hearing officer found that the school district was fiscally responsible for the young adult's education during his hospitalization, she refused to award compensatory education. The consent decree imposed no obligations or expenses on the school district. The state alone was liable for attorney's fees. *Counsel v. Dow*, 849 F.2d 731 (2d Cir.1988).

A Michigan student was born with a syndrome known as "Fragile X," a neurological disability which manifests itself behaviorally as a sensory integration dysfunction. His school district determined that he was eligible for special education services. Before the student's entry into kindergarten, his school convened an "Individualized Education Placement Committee" to develop the student's required "individualized education program" (IEP). The entire committee agreed that the most appropriate and least restrictive environment was an integrated kindergarten program, in which disabled children were integrated into a class of children with no disabilities. The program was team-taught by both special and regular education teachers. The school district offered such a program at only one of its schools, which was approximately eight miles from the student's home. The parents, however, wanted the integrated program to be moved or duplicated at their neighborhood school. As a result, the parents disagreed with the IEP and requested a due process hearing. Thereafter, the parents retained an attorney. The school district met with the parents and their attorney to resolve their differences prior to the hearing. At this meeting, the attorney insisted that the legal requirement of the least restrictive environment required placement in the local school, a principle which the school district disputed. The parents, however, presented a list to the school district of their desires. The school district, based on this list, made a settlement offer which became the basis of the eventual agreement. The integrated program was not duplicated, and the student enrolled at the neighborhood school, though at the price of provision of fewer services than the school district had initially offered. The attorney demanded that the school district pay her fees, but the district refused. The parents filed suit in federal district court for an award of attorney's fees under the Handicapped Children's Protection Act.

The district court noted that in order to collect attorney's fees, the parents must have been the prevailing party, they must have obtained a more favorable result than initially offered, and they must not have unreasonably protracted the proceeding. Under these standards, no award was appropriate. First, the parents were not prevailing parties. Although the student was enrolled in his neighborhood school, it was at the sacrifice of the full program at the more distant school, which would have best met the student's needs. The court found that the list was a concession from the parents' initial position. Second, the court stated that the attorney caused the parents to unreasonably protract final resolution of the controversy. The attorney did not improve the position of either the student or his parents and unnecessarily aggravated and protracted the misunderstanding. The court dismissed the suit. *Fischer by Fischer v. Rochester Comm. Schools*, 780 F.Supp. 1142 (E.D.Mich.1991).

A Rhode Island student was diagnosed as having a behavioral disorder and a learning disability. The school devised some individualized education programs for him. The student's parents questioned the diagnosis because it focused on the behavioral disorder rather than the learning disability. Later, the parents requested an independent evaluation. Subsequently, they sought a due process hearing, alleging a possible violation of the student's right to a free, appropriate education under the IDEA. The school district provided two written settlement offers, both of which were rejected. After a hearing, the hearing officer found in favor of the school, finding no violation, although the hearing officer did require reimbursement for the independent evaluation. The parents appealed and sought attorney's fees, costs and expenses.

The district court held that the parents were not entitled to attorney's fees, costs or expenses. It found that rejection of an offer more favorable than the litigated outcome resulted in the denial of attorney's fees, costs and expenses. Additionally, the court found that the student's parents were not justified in rejecting the offer made by the district. *Mr. L. & Mrs. L. on Behalf of Matthew L. v. Woonsocket Education Dept.*, 793 F.Supp. 41 (D.R.I.1992).

An Indiana child attended a public school and was classified as physically disabled. After the child entered the second grade, her parents, teacher, and other school officials met to develop her IEP. At that time, an agreement was reached on a number of issues, but there remained disagreements on others. Throughout that school year and the following summer, the teachers and the child's parents continued to disagree on several issues. The parents wanted full control over who was to deliver the physical therapy and occupational services given to their daughter. The school, however, offered to provide the physical and occupational therapy services through its own personnel. The parents filed for an administrative hearing. During the hearing, the school attempted to make an interim settlement. The school offered to have its occupational therapist work with the child. This was agreed to and for the first time, the school's occupational therapist was permitted to work with the child. The mother, however, would not allow the school's physical therapist to work with the child. She continued to have her own physical therapist work with her child. The administrative officer entered her decision which indicated that the parents could use their own physical therapist and that the school must reimburse them for the amount not covered by insurance. The parents, however, would be responsible for the costs of the private evaluations by their own physical therapist. The parents then sought reimbursement of the legal fees incurred in the administrative proceeding in a federal district court.

In order for the parents to recover their legal fees, they must show that they prevailed (i.e., in some way won) at the administrative level. At trial, the hearing officer who rendered the administrative decision stated that the decision was in favor of the school authorities because no significant relief was granted to the parents of the child. The district court, however, determined that the administrative decision was slightly in favor of the parents. The parents did not receive all the attorney's fees that they requested because their lawyer acted adversarially which the court determined to be unnecessary. The court then awarded reduced attorney's fees based on this decision. *Howey by Howey v. Tippecanoe School Corp.*, 734 F.Supp. 1485 (N.D.Ind.1990).

A severely disabled New York student attended a private school for the blind and retarded at public expense pursuant to the EHA. After the school closed, the student instituted administrative proceedings to obtain placement at another school. The administrative proceedings were protracted which caused the student to lose nearly two years of academic education. The New York State Commissioner of Education refused to provide compensatory education beyond the student's twenty-first birthday to make up for the delay. The student then appealed that decision to a federal district court claiming that the delays in the hearing process violated his rights under the EHA. The federal district court dismissed the case on the grounds that the Eleventh Amendment barred the action. The U.S. Court of Appeals, Second Circuit, reversed the decision and granted the plaintiff one year of compensatory education past the age of twenty-one. The U.S. Supreme Court granted a writ of certiorari and remanded the case for consideration in light of its decision in *Dellmuth v. Muth*, 109 S.Ct. 2397 (1989). The Supreme Court held that the EHA did not itself state an intent to abrogate sovereign immunity. The second circuit reformed its prior holding and restated its judgment granting the student one year of compensatory education. The student then instituted an action to recover attorney's fees and costs of $100,000. The defendants argued that the attorney's fees should be substantially reduced and suggested the amount of $14,000.

Under the EHA, a plaintiff must be a prevailing party to recover attorney's fees. In regard to related claims, the court noted that even if they did not succeed on all the claims, the attorney's fees were to be awarded by looking at the case as a whole. The court noted that the accepted system for determining a reasonable fee was to start with the number of hours worked and multiply this by an appropriate hourly rate. Furthermore, the court noted that any errors due to recordkeeping were more than accounted for by discounting the billable hours. The court found that the fees charged by the plaintiff were a little excessive and reduced the amount to $96,000 plus costs. *Burr by Burr v. Sobol*, 748 F.Supp. 97 (S.D.N.Y.1990).

After a Texas first grade student encountered difficulty mastering her subjects, her teacher recommended that she receive special education services. The school district assessed the student for disabilities and recommended that she receive special therapy services but concluded that she suffered no disabling conditions. The student subsequently failed all of her courses and was retained in the first grade. The parents obtained an independent assessment of their daughter's abilities from a center for developmental pediatrics which determined that the student was mildly retarded and required special education services. After the district again concluded that her condition did not justify special education services, the parents sought a due process hearing. The parties entered into a settlement agreement whereby most of the parents' relief was granted, except the student was not classified as mentally retarded. The parents then filed an action in a federal district court for reimbursement of their attorney's fees. The trial court ruled that the parents were the "prevailing party" under the terms of the EHA, and therefore entitled to recover attorney's fees from the school district. The school district appealed to the U.S. Court of Appeals, Fifth Circuit.

The court noted that there were only two prerequisites of prevailing party status under the EHA: 1) the remedy received under the EHA must alter the legal relationship between the parties, and 2) the nature of the remedy must foster the purposes of the EHA. The school district argued that the parents could not demonstrate either of the two conditions for prevailing party status. The court noted that although the items of relief obtained in the settlement were available to general students, it appeared that the district did not previously offer these items of relief to the student. The court also noted that the legislative history of the EHA suggested that Congress intended the fee statute to cover any beneficial extension of educational opportunity to disabled children. The district court judgment was affirmed and attorney's fees were awarded to the parents. *Angela L. v. Pasadena Indep. School Dist.*, 918 F.2d 1188 (5th Cir.1990).

A blind New York student sought admission to the New York Institute for the Education of the Blind. The institute rejected him and he appealed. A hearing officer appointed by the New York State Commissioner of Education ordered the student's admission to the institute and awarded him a year of free compensatory public education. The institute appealed the decision to the commissioner, who upheld the admission. However, he ruled against the student concerning the compensatory education. The student then sued the commissioner in a U.S. district court. The court dismissed the case. However, the student's claim for attorney's fees for the administrative level proceedings which resulted in his institute admission was still pending before the court. The commissioner contended that the HCPA provided no attorney's fees to parties who prevailed at the administrative level. He also claimed that he was not a party against whom the student prevailed at the administrative level. The student argued that he prevailed against the commissioner for the purpose of attorney's fees because the commissioner was the only official with the authority to appoint students to the institute.

The court held that the student was entitled to recover attorney's fees on the issue of admission to the institute, but was not entitled to recover attorney's fees from the commissioner. Even though the commissioner unlawfully reviewed the hearing officer's decision, it did not follow that the student was entitled to attorney's fees from him. The EHA does not contemplate an award of attorney's fees against a decisionmaker such as the commissioner. The student could only recover attorney's fees from the institute. *Burr v. Ambach*, 683 F.Supp. 46 (S.D.N.Y.1988).

A Pennsylvania school district provided a deaf student with a sign language interpreter. The parents initiated a due process hearing asking for a new interpreter because they were convinced that the skills of the interpreter were inadequate. The interpreter requested a transfer shortly thereafter and the school immediately began searching for a new interpreter. The hearing officer rejected the parents' claim that the student's poor performance was due solely to the interpreter. He found that many other factors, such as poor attendance and low motivation, led to her poor performance. The hearing officer then ordered the school district to make all efforts to locate a new interpreter. The state hearing officer affirmed the decision and denied the parents' request for attorney's fees. The parents then filed for attorney's fees in a federal district court. The trial court awarded summary judgment to the school district and the parents appealed to the U.S. Court of Appeals, Third Circuit.

In order to receive an award of attorney's fees the parents must have succeeded on "any significant issue in litigation which achieved some of the benefit the plaintiffs sought in bringing the suit." The court applied a two-part test: whether the plaintiffs achieved relief and whether there was a causal connection between the litigation and the relief. The court noted the first prong of the test involved a common sense comparison between the relief sought and that obtained. Although the girl obtained a different interpreter, the parents did not prevail on any of their legal claims. They had asked for a finding that her interpreter was not qualified, but the hearing officer rejected this argument. Nonetheless, the hearing officer had ordered a search for a new interpreter; the court therefore found that the parents had obtained some benefit. Thus, the court applied the second prong of the test, causation. It determined that the parents did not show a causal connection under either theory between their lawsuit and the hiring of a new interpreter. Thus, the court upheld the decision of the trial court and denied attorney's fees. *Wheeler by Wheeler v. Towanda Area School Dist.*, 950 F.2d 128 (3rd Cir.1991).

An emotionally disturbed New Jersey student required a shared-time program to meet the goals set out in his IEP. The student was involved in several incidents which resulted in indefinite suspension. The parents then retained an attorney and sought to have the student readmitted to the shared-time program through an administrative hearing. Prior to the hearing the administrative law judge met with the parties and facilitated the reaching of a settlement. The settlement provided that the student would be admitted to a shared-time program with a different high school and also provided other relief. The parents then instituted this action in a federal district court solely for the purpose of recovering attorney's fees in connection with the settlement, the administrative hearing and the instant action. The parents moved for summary judgment.

The court noted that a prevailing party must "succeed on any significant issue in the proceedings that achieved some of the benefit plaintiff sought from administrative review." Since the parents' main objective was to have their son readmitted to a shared-time program, they were deemed to be prevailing parties under the HCPA. The court thus awarded reasonable attorney's fees. *E.P. by P.Q. v. Union County Reg. High Sch. Dist. 1*, 741 F.Supp. 1144 (D.N.J.1989).

In 1985, the U.S. Court of Appeals, Fourth Circuit, held that a school board wrongly expelled a student for behavior which resulted from his disability. After the passage of the Handicapped Children's Protection Act of 1986 (HCPA) his parents asked the court of appeals for an award of attorney's fees. The HCPA provides that a court may award reasonable attorney's fees to parents of children with disabilities who are prevailing parties under EHA § 1415(e)(4)(B)-(D). The court of appeals remanded the question to a U.S. district court in Virginia.

The school board resisted the application of the HCPA on several theories. It contended that a violation of the separation of powers doctrine would occur if the HCPA's retroactive application formed the basis of a decision in a pending case. It also argued that retroactive application of the HCPA to award attorney's fees to the parents would exceed the spending power of Congress. Specifically, it argued that Congress' power to impose liabilities on recipients of federal aid was limited since attorney's fees had not been available to parents when the board accepted EHA funds. It also claimed that the parents were too late in filing their request for attorney's fees. Finally, it contended that the HCPA only provided for an award of attorney's fees to parties who prevailed in court proceedings as opposed to those who prevailed in due process hearings.

Concerning the school board's separation of powers argument, the court observed that here the law was changed only generally. Although the change had broad application, it only affected this case incidentally (i.e., attorney's fees, not the decision itself). The court held that the only limitation on Congress' power to impose liabilities on federal aid recipients was that Congress must do so unambiguously as it did here. The court also concluded that the parents had requested attorney's fees three months after passage of the HCPA which was not an unreasonable period of time. Finally, the court held that the HCPA only clearly prohibited an award of attorney's fees when court-obtained relief was less than any settlement offer. It also noted that the HCPA provided for fee awards in "any action or proceeding," implying the possibility of fee recovery for due process hearings. The court therefore ordered that the parents recover attorney's fees. *School Bd. v. Malone*, 662 F.Supp. 999 (E.D.Va.1987).

An Oregon student had severe epilepsy along with related behavior and learning problems. After the student assaulted two other students and an employee of the school district, the school district assembled a multidisciplinary team to assess the situation. The team concluded that the behavior could be related to his disabling condition. As a result, the school was precluded from automatically expelling him because that would constitute a change in placement. However, the school district sought injunctive relief in order to change the student's placement prior to exhausting its administrative remedies. The parents objected to the school district's proposed change of placement and requested a due process hearing. Prior to the final hearing date, the parties reached an agreement. Pursuant to an IEP recommendation made by the school district's multidisciplinary team, the parents agreed to enroll the student in a newly created program at the high school. Subsequently, the parents filed an application for attorney's fees in a federal district court. The court granted the attorney's fees and the school district appealed to the U.S. Court of Appeals, Ninth Circuit.

The school district argued that the district court erred when it determined that there were no special circumstances sufficient to justify denial of attorney's fees. It maintained that an award of attorney's fees to the parents would effectively penalize it for its exemplary behavior in response to the life threatening emergency posed by the student's violent behavior. Ordinarily, a prevailing party should recover attorney's fees unless special circumstances would render such an award unjust. To determine whether special circumstances exist, the court must consider two factors: whether an award of attorney's fees would further the congressional purpose in enacting the EHA and the balance of equities. Clearly, the congressional intent in regard to the EHA and the HCPA was to provide parents of children with disabilities with a substantive right that should be enforced through the procedural mechanisms in the act, including a right to attorney's fees if the parents prevail. Therefore, the school district argued only the second prong of the special circumstances test, the balance of the equities. The school district properly utilized the mechanisms available to it to defuse a very difficult situation. However, in doing so, it attempted to effect a permanent unilateral change in the student's placement. It sought to terminate all services by the school district. Further, the prior notice indicated an intent to change permanently the student's placement. Under the circumstances of this case, the appellate court could not say that the district court abused its discretion when it found no special circumstances sufficient to justify the denial of attorney's fees. *Barlow-Gresham Union Dist. 2 v. Mitchell*, 940 F.2d 1280 (9th Cir.1991).

After the parents of four disabled children were successful in challenging a decision by the New York Commissioner of Education to terminate their children's placement, they moved in a New York trial court for an order awarding attorney's fees under EHA § 1415(e)(4)(B). This subsection is part of the Handicapped Children's Protection Act of 1986. The commissioner contended that § 1415 did not authorize any fees in this case since the original lawsuit was not brought under it. Specifically, he claimed that the administrative action attacked in the original lawsuit did not involve a determination made by the commissioner after an appeal to him, but rather dealt with a claim that the commissioner's wrong interpretation of New York law was denying the students the placement they deserved under the EHA. Such a distinction required the denial of attorney's fees according to the commissioner.

The court disagreed, concluding that, because the commissioner had recognized from the outset of the original lawsuit (according to statements made by his attorney) that the theory behind the lawsuit was a violation of the EHA he was therefore liable for attorney's fees. The court also ruled that the EHA should be broadly construed to "effect its purpose of providing appropriate free public education for disabled students" and that any remedy (including attorney's fees) which encouraged parents to protect the child's interests should be "viewed expansively." The trial court awarded attorney's fees to the parents. *Esther C. by Ephraim C. v. Ambach*, 515 N.Y.S.2d 997 (Sup.1987).

Both parties then appealed the attorney's fee issue to the New York Supreme Court, Appellate Division, Third Department. The court noted that Congress enacted the Handicapped Children's Protection Act (HCPA) specifically to award attorney's fees to parents prevailing in EHA lawsuits. Although the trial court had awarded over $11,000 in attorney's fees to the parents, it had awarded only $750 for its appeal to the court for attorney's fees despite the parents' allegation that their attorneys had worked over thirty hours on the application. The appellate division court assessed the trial court's determination of a $90 hourly rate as reasonable and modified the trial court's decision to reflect attorney's fees on that basis. The appellate court remanded the case to the trial court for further proceedings to determine appropriate attorney's fees. *Esther C. by Ephraim C. v. Ambach*, 535 N.Y.S.2d 462 (A.D.3d Dep't 1988).

A New Jersey special education lay advocate sued the New Jersey State Board of Education in a U.S. district court. She sought compensation for her services. The court held that she was not entitled to compensation for her services as a lay advocate in due process hearings under the EHA. She then appealed to the U.S. Court of Appeals, Third Circuit.

On appeal she contended that the EHA preempted a New Jersey Court Rule which required that lay advocates represent the disabled free of charge. The no-fee provision was preempted because it hindered the fulfillment of the goals set out by Congress in the EHA. The advocate argued that because the EHA gave parents the right to representation by lay advocates, Congress intended that lay advocates charge fees. She also claimed that the no-fee provision violated her rights under the Equal Protection Clause of the U.S. Constitution.

The court of appeals upheld the district court decision. The EHA did not support the advocate's contention that Congress intended no distinction between lay advocates and attorneys. The EHA, which permitted a prevailing party to recover attorney's fees, contained no express provision granting fees to lay advocates.

The advocate's equal protection argument failed because the court found the New Jersey no-fee provision rationally related to New Jersey's interest in maintaining high ethical and fiduciary standards among attorneys. According to the court, permitting lay advocates to charge fees for their representation would likely encourage an abundance of unlicensed legal practitioners to the detriment of the public. *Arons v. New Jersey State Bd. of Educ.*, 842 F.2d 58 (3d Cir.1988).

CHAPTER SEVEN

SCHOOL LIABILITY

I. LIABILITY FOR INJURIES

Courts have generally held schools and their agents liable for injuries received by students with disabilities during the course of the regular school day which resulted from the schools' or their agents' failure to provide a reasonably safe environment, failure to warn participants of known hazards or to remove known dangers where possible, failure to properly instruct participants in an activity, or failure to provide supervision adequate for the type of activity, the ages of the participants involved and their physical and mental capabilities.

A. Negligent Supervision

A twenty-one-year-old mentally disabled Tennessee student traveled regularly with his class to the YMCA to use its swimming pool. The trips were supervised by a teacher and an aide, both school employees, and while at the pool, by a YMCA lifeguard. Some of the trips involved Special Olympics training. The student's mother had signed a document which released county employees from liability as a result of any injuries that might occur in connection with the Special Olympics Program. Near the end of a training excursion at the YMCA, the teacher instructed all of the students to get out of the pool. No one saw the student exit from the pool and he was later found on the floor of the pool. The lifeguard revived the student and he was taken to the hospital. The student suffered injuries and incurred medical expenses as a result of the incident. The student and his parents sued the county and the county board of education in a Tennessee trial court alleging negligent student supervision. The trial court found for the county. The student and his parents appealed to the Court of Appeals of Tennessee.

The court of appeals held that the county was negligent in failing to adequately supervise the student. The evidence indicated that neither the teacher, aide or lifeguard were watching the student after he was told to get out of the pool. The court also found that the release signed by the mother relieved the county of liability, but did not waive the student's rights. Under state law a guardian cannot waive the rights of an infant or incompetent. The student's mother could not execute a valid release of the rights of her son against the Special Olympics or anyone else. The court of appeals ruled the release void and remanded the case for further proceedings. *Childress v. Madison County*, 777 S.W.2d 1 (Tenn.App.1989).

In a similar case involving negligent supervision, a Florida man was instructed by school administrators to enroll his nine-year-old son in a particular elementary school for special speech therapy classes. The district promised the man that bus transportation would be provided for the child. The bus transportation did not materialize so the man took his son to a public bus stop. After two weeks the man let the child go to the bus stop alone and the child was killed while crossing an intersection. The man sued the school, asserting that it had negligently supervised his son. The court granted summary judgment for the school because the parent had also failed to supervise his son. The father appealed to the Court of Appeal of Florida.

On appeal, the issue was whether the school could be held liable for negligent supervision even if the father was found to be negligent. The court of appeal reversed and ordered a trial since the failure of the man to supervise his son could not preclude liability for negligent supervision on the part of the school district. *Brunson v. Dade County Sch. Bd.*, 559 So.2d 646 (Fla.App.3d Dist.1990).

An Illinois student suffered from spinal muscle atrophy with scoliosis and was confined to a wheelchair. She attended a school which was owned and operated by the school district. Across the street from the school was the school's playground which the district also controlled and maintained. While being transported in her wheelchair by a classmate on a walkway between the school and the playground, the student's chair hit a crevice. The student was thrown on the pavement and was injured. Although the student's parents had advised the district to always secure the student in the wheelchair they had provided, the student's seatbelt had not been fastened. The student sued the school district and the city in an Illinois trial court alleging that the district had negligently failed to provide adequate equipment and that it was guilty of wilful and wanton misconduct. The student also claimed that the city had been negligent in failing to keep the walkway in a reasonably safe condition. The city filed a counterclaim against the school district for contribution. The trial court dismissed the student's claim against the school district and the city's counterclaim for contribution. The student and the city appealed to the Appellate Court of Illinois, Fifth Circuit.

The appellate court held that the student had a claim against the district based on the district's alleged failure to furnish adequate equipment. If the equipment provided by the parents was not adequate for a particular activity, the district was required to provide alternative adequate equipment. The appellate court also ruled that the trial court erred when it dismissed the claim based on wilful and wanton misconduct. The district had been notified that the student must be fastened in her wheelchair whenever she was moved. The district, however, had allowed the student to be pushed by a classmate without being secured with the seatbelt. The court also found that the city's allegations sufficiently alleged a cause of action for contribution based on the district's wilful and wanton misconduct. The appellate court reversed the trial court's decision and remanded for further proceedings. *Bertetto v. Sparta Comm. Unit Dist. 140*, 544 N.E.2d 1140 (Ill.App.5th Dist.1989).

An emotionally handicapped and learning disabled student who was 14 years old attended a Florida high school. She functioned on a third or fourth grade level and was extremely naive and socially immature. One morning, the student twice changed out of her conservative dress into a mini-skirt. Each time, a teacher forced her to change back into her school clothes. During the student's lunch period, a male student took her to the school parking lot and drove her to a house. Other male students also left the school and went to the house. The disabled student was raped by five male students.

Her parents then sued the school board, alleging that it had breached its duty to provide reasonably safe conditions and supervision while the student was under the school's control. A Florida trial court granted summary judgment to the school board, and the parents appealed to the District Court of Appeal of Florida, which reversed and remanded the case. The appellate court held that the parents' claim was not one for lack of adequate security — a discretionary function for which the school board would be entitled to the defense of sovereign immunity. Instead, the claim was for negligent supervision. There existed questions of fact as to whether the school board had breached its duty to adequately supervise both the disabled student and the male students who raped her. The case was sent back for a jury trial. *Doe v. Escambia County School Bd.*, 599 So.2d 226 (Fla.App.1st Dist.1992).

In 1986, an educable, mentally disabled, fifteen-year-old student was assigned to a South Carolina sixth grade class. The following year he was advanced to the ninth grade, where he became a discipline problem. As a result, he was placed in a self-contained special education classroom. The student was injured while wrestling with another student in the school hallway. The students were in the company of a school janitor at the time of the injury. The student's parents sued the school, claiming that the principal had instructed the student to report to a school janitor whenever he felt like he was unable to behave. They also claimed that the school janitor merely watched the students wrestle. A trial court granted summary judgment to the school district, stating that the parents had presented no evidence that the school district exercised its discretion in a grossly negligent manner. The parents appealed to the South Carolina Court of Appeals.

The court of appeals reversed. The court stated that summary judgment (that is, a grant of judgment before trial) is only appropriate when there is no genuine issue of fact. If all the claims of the student's parents were true, gross negligence might exist. Therefore, a genuine issue of fact existed regarding whether the school district exercised its duty in a grossly negligent manner. The court remanded the case to the trial court for a determination of the necessary issues. *Grooms v. Malboro County School Dist.*, 414 S.E.2d 802 (S.C.App.1992).

Schools may be found liable for injuries caused by the criminal acts of others where supervision is inadequate. A nineteen-year-old mentally retarded student, who functioned at a five-year-old level, was a student at a Louisiana residential training school operated by a Roman Catholic diocese. The girl participated in a co-educational training program for mentally disabled students offered at a nearby parish school. When at the parish school, the students were under the supervision of the school's employees and took regularly scheduled breaks. At the beginning of a break, the boys and girls were taken separately to the bathroom and were supposed to be under constant supervision. One afternoon after assembling the boys for a break, the boy's supervisor left and went to the office which had a glass wall to allow observation. When he looked back, he noticed two of the boys missing. He found one of the students guarding a door and the other inside leaning over the nineteen-year-old girl with his pants down. The girl was returned to the residence home and examined by a nurse who did not check for signs of sexual activity. After the girl's guardians removed her from the home a few weeks later, she was withdrawn, seemed afraid of men, had nightmares, crying spells, and suffered a loss of appetite. As a result, the girl's guardians sought counseling for her. The guardians then filed this suit against the parish school board, the residence training school and the Roman Catholic diocese in a state trial court for the costs of the counseling and other damages. The trial judge dismissed the claims because the guardians had failed to prove sexual intercourse occurred. The guardians appealed to the Court of Appeal of Louisiana.

The appellate court disagreed, stating that it was not necessary to prove actual intercourse under a negligence theory. The guardians only needed to prove that as a result of the defendants' negligence the girl suffered harm. The guardians met this requirement because the symptoms occurred after the incident. The court reversed the trial court's decision and found the parish school board negligent. The appellate court affirmed the trial court's decision with respect to the training school and the Roman Catholic diocese because they were not the cause of the girl's injuries. *Guidry v. Parish School Bd.*, 560 So.2d 125 (La.App.3d Cir.1990).

An emotionally disabled male student at a Florida public school was mixed with regular students in a shop class as part of the federal mainstreaming requirement. On a day when a substitute teacher was entrusted with supervision of the shop class the student was sexually assaulted in class by another student. The assailant was a youth who was known by school officials to be prone to sexually assaultive behavior. The disabled student was forced into performing oral sex on the assailant for ten minutes at the rear of the classroom. The substitute teacher claimed that he was unaware of this incident but that he had been diligently monitoring the classroom at the time of the assault. The assaulted student sued the school district in state court contending that the district had breached its duty of reasonable care owed to him. The jury found in favor of the student. However, the trial judge threw out the verdict and the student appealed. The Florida District Court of Appeal reversed the trial judge and reinstated the jury verdict in favor of the student. Only when there is no evidence upon which a jury could properly rely should its verdict be set aside. The case was remanded to the trial court with orders to reinstate the jury verdict and to act on other post-trial motions. *Collins v. School Bd. of Broward County,* 471 So.2d 560 (Fla.App.4th Dist.1985).

Several Missouri students with disabilities complained to their school district that their bus driver had physically and sexually abused them. They sued the district in a Missouri federal district court for violating their constitutional right to privacy and bodily security. They alleged that the district failed to take sufficient action to prevent the bus driver from continuing his abusive behavior. The district sought to have the suit dismissed by claiming that district officials had not been deliberately indifferent to the driver's acts. Nor did the district have a policy of ignoring and failing to act upon these types of complaints.

In considering the dismissal motion the court noted that the district's negligence in supervision was not sufficient to establish liability. It also noted that in order to impose personal liability on district officials, students would have to show that the officials were personally involved in the violation. The students asserted that the officials' inaction made them liable. The officials argued that their failure to act did not amount to a deliberate indifference or to tacit authorization of the alleged abuse. The court determined that most of the complaints failed to establish the necessary pattern of unconstitutional conduct. The court also noted that the officials responded to the complaints by questioning the bus driver and counseling him about physical interaction with children. The court dismissed the case against the officials in their individual capacities and the suit against the district. The students failed to show that the district had an official policy or custom which led to the harm caused. Thus, the school district's dismissal motion was granted. *Jane Doe (A) v. Special School Dist. of St. Louis County*, 682 F.Supp. 451 (E.D.Mo.1988).

The parents appealed to the U.S. Court of Appeals, Eighth Circuit. They contended that the school district's official policy did not allow the officials to adequately investigate prior complaints of the bus driver's conduct. The court, however, determined that the school district did not have any knowledge of, nor had the district been indifferent to, the rights of the disabled children. The parents further contended that the individual defendants failed to adequately respond to a known risk of physical and emotional harm by the bus driver. Individual defendants will be subject to liability only if it can be proven that they received notice, demonstrated indifference, failed to take sufficient action and that such failure caused the injury to the children. The court determined that the evidence did not support a finding that the individual defendants had notice of a pattern of unlawful acts by the bus driver. The school district and its officials were at most guilty of negligence. The court of appeals affirmed the trial court's decision, granting summary judgment to the school district. *Jane Doe A v. Special School District*, 901 F.2d 642 (8th Cir.1990).

Liability may also arise from a school's failure to detect or treat students' injuries. In a New York case, a fourteen-year-old deaf girl contracted rheumatic fever while attending a summer camp operated by the National Council of Beth Jacob Schools. Due to the camp's negligence, the girl's disease was neither detected nor treated until she returned home at the end of the summer. As a result, she developed polyarthritis, an enlarged heart, a heart murmur and a leakage of her aortic valve. The girl was forced to miss two and one-half months of school. At the time the case went to trial (three years after she contracted the disease) the girl tired easily and had a susceptibility to heart problems. Her medical expenses totaled $2,900. The trial court, sitting without a jury, awarded the girl $30,000 in damages and her mother $2,000. The girl's mother appealed, contending that the trial court's award of damages was insufficient. The New York Supreme Court, Appellate Division, noted that under state law, nonjury damage awards are freely reviewable by an appellate court. It agreed with the mother's contentions and modified the award to $50,000 for the child and $5,000 for the mother. The appellate court reasoned that the trial court's award was inadequate because the child, who already had been afflicted with one disability, now had to deal with a heart condition that showed no signs of improving. *Berman v. Nat'l Council of Beth Jacob Schools, Inc.*, 501 N.Y.S.2d 413 (A.D.2d Dept.1986).

A nineteen-year-old New York student was injured while participating in a work study program. The student was learning disabled and his mother persuaded him to join a work study program so that he would have enough credits to graduate. He worked with lumber under the direct supervision of a company. During his work study the student severed two of his fingers and injured a third one when using a saw he was familiar with. Alleging negligent supervision, the student sued the school in a New York trial court.

The school asserted that it had no duty to exercise control over the student because he was of majority age and because his mother encouraged him to participate in the program. The New York state court held that schools were not insurers for the safety of students. Further, the court stated that a less demanding standard of reasonable care was warranted when a student was nineteen years old. The court also stated that there was no evidence that any of the machinery was unfit. Thus, the trial court ruled in favor of the school. *Kennedy v. Waterville Cent. Sch. Dist.*, 555 N.Y.S.2d 224 (Sup.1990).

A Louisiana student attended a school for the mentally disabled. While walking toward his bus, the student was struck in the jaw by another student who was a foster child in the custody of the Louisiana Department of Health and Human Resources (DHHR). Upon arriving at home, the student began to experience pain in his jawbone which subsequently required surgery. The student sued the state of Louisiana, through the DHHR, its insurer, the school board and the foster child. A Louisiana trial court directed a verdict for the state and the school board. The student then appealed to the Court of Appeal of Louisiana, Third Circuit.

On appeal, the student argued that the DHHR and its insurer were strictly liable for the foster child and that the school board, through its employees, negligently failed to supervise the bus loading procedures. The court found that the state was not strictly liable. There was no language under state law which suggested that the state could be held strictly liable for the acts of a foster child. The court also found that the school board was not negligent in failing to prevent the foster child from striking the student. The incident was of a sudden and unforeseeable nature and therefore unavoidable. There was no reason to anticipate any trouble between the two students. Because the altercation happened so quickly teachers who were assigned to supervise the boarding of the buses were unable to prevent the injury. The spontaneous, unpredictable act of the foster child did not create liability on behalf of the school board or its employees. The court of appeal affirmed the trial court's decision. *Gooden v. State DHHR*, 546 So.2d 279 (La.App.3d Cir.1989).

A severely disabled New York infant was placed on a bus equipped for disabled children and then taken to a school for mentally retarded children. Although the child could not communicate by speech, he cried or whined when he was in pain. On the day in question, the child did not cry or whine either in school or on the bus. However, when the mother put the infant to bed right after he returned from school, she noticed that the child had a broken leg. She sued the school district and the bus company in a New York trial court alleging negligence in her son's care. The defendants moved to dismiss the complaint.

The mother relied on a legal principle (*res ipsa loquitur*) that allows recovery for negligence even if one cannot point to the exact person or persons responsible for the negligence. The three requirements which must be proved are as follows: the event must be of a kind which ordinarily does not occur in the absence of negligence, it must be caused by an agency or instrumentality (i.e., source of injury) within the exclusive control of the defendant, and it must not have been due to any voluntary action or contribution on the part of the injured plaintiff. Although the mother met the first and third requirements, she did not meet the second. The court noted that in this case neither the injury nor the circumstances pointed to the instrumentality. Therefore, in the absence of proof of negligence, the mother could not recover and the trial court dismissed the case. *Rabena v. City of New York*, 556 N.Y.S.2d 807 (N.Y.C.Civ.Ct.1990).

A quadriplegic student at the Southwest Louisiana State School brought a negligence lawsuit against the school after suffering a spiral-type fracture of his right femur. On the morning of the injury the student's mother bathed him, fed him and strapped him into his wheelchair. She then gave him his usual dosage of phenobarbital. The school bus arrived and he was wheeled out to meet it without apparent incident. The bus driver testified that the student was in his usual good spirits as he transported him to the State School. He said that he strapped the student's wheelchair down securely that morning. Upon his arrival at the State School, the student, who weighed only thirty-two pounds, was wheeled into class where two of his instructors noticed that he was "crying and fussing." They sought to alleviate his discomfort by placing him on a mat. When this proved unsuccessful, one instructor lifted him off the mat and placed him on a table. She testified that as she did so, she heard a loud "pop." The student was immediately taken to a doctor, and the spiral fracture was diagnosed. He was hospitalized for three weeks and he recovered completely. Believing that the State School and its employees had somehow been negligent, causing the student's injury, his parents brought a lawsuit in state district court. They pointed to a statement one of the teachers had made immediately after taking the student to the doctor. She had said that she did not understand how the student's leg could have broken unless she had accidently knelt on it.

However, evidence was also presented of an incident which occurred one year after the original fracture. The student, while strapped in his wheelchair at home, became excited and pushed his leg until it became caught in the chair, then twisted it, causing the same type of spiral fracture as had occurred the previous year. He was using the same wheelchair at the time of this later incident. In light of this evidence, the district court ruled in favor of the State School and its employees, stating that a number of other explanations existed for the student's injury besides negligence on the part of a State School employee. On appeal by the parents, the Louisiana Court of Appeal upheld this ruling. Stated the court: "The mere fact that an accident occurred does not necessarily mean that someone was negligent." The court held that the parents had failed to meet their burden of proving by a preponderance of the evidence that a State School employee had caused their son's injury. *Henry v. State*, 482 So.2d 962 (La.App.3d Cir.1986).

In this case, the issue was not whether the institution was liable for negligent supervision, but whether it was entitled to insurance coverage resulting from the injuries. A Wisconsin mother sued a facility on behalf of her severely mentally retarded daughter who was sexually molested and became pregnant while in the insured facility's custody. The insured diagnosed the daughter's pregnancy during the fifteenth or sixteenth week of gestation. The insurer brought a declaratory judgment action to determine its obligations under the policy. The policy contained a sexual abuse exclusion which stated that the coverage would not apply to any claim, demand, or causes of action arising out of or resulting from sexual abuse.

The complaint filed by the mother in the underlying lawsuit alleged failure to supervise and untimely detection of pregnancy. The insured, seeking to obtain defense costs from the insurer, argued that it might be found solely liable under the ultimate detection of pregnancy claim. However, the court found that the language "arise out of or relate to" with respect to sexual abuse included all claims brought by the mother. Therefore, the court held that the exclusion applied to deny coverage, and the insurer had no duty to defend or indemnify the facility. *IPCI Ltd. v. Old Republic Ins. Co.*, 758 F.Supp. 478 (E.D.Wis.1991).

B. Negligent Placement

In a Maryland case, as part of a disabled female student's new IEP she was placed in a regular eighth grade physical education class, with no restrictions placed upon her participation. Her parents failed to express any dissatisfaction or challenge this new IEP. Midway through the school year she was seriously injured while maneuvering on a "Swedish Box." Her parents filed suit in state court against the school board and the physical education teacher, claiming that they had been negligent in placing the student in a regular physical education class without adequate safeguards. The parent's complaint did not allege negligent supervision, but negligent placement in the class.

The circuit court ruled that the parents could not base their lawsuit on negligent placement. The parents had not contested the revised IEP when it was initially implemented, and thus they were barred from contesting it now in a civil lawsuit. The court's ruling was based on the elaborate state procedural system through which disputes over special education placements could be contested. The parents had not availed themselves of this system and the circuit court refused to allow the parents to do in a civil lawsuit what they should have done through established procedures. This ruling effectively destroyed the parents' case since they would now have to prove that the teacher failed to use "reasonable care" in supervising the student. The circuit court therefore rendered a decision in favor of the school board and teacher.

The parents appealed to the Maryland Court of Special Appeals, which affirmed the circuit court decision. When the parents failed to contest the IEP which placed the student in the regular physical education class, they placed her in the same legal position as any other student in the class and no suit for "negligent placement" would be possible. Because the parents were unable to prove that the teacher had failed to exercise reasonable care in the supervision of the student the appeals court upheld the lower court's ruling against the parents. *Alban v. Bd. of Educ. of Harford County*, 494 A.2d 745 (Md.App.1985).

In a New York case, a severely disabled individual sustained serious injuries after being placed in a residential facility. Suit was brought on his behalf, alleging negligence on the part of the facility's employees. The suit alleged that employees at the residential facility had allowed the individual to participate in a normalization program designed to allow familiarization with tasks of daily living. During the program he accidently overturned a covered pot of hot water used to demonstrate the preparation of tea and coffee, causing him to be severely burned.

Reversing a lower court, the New York Court of Appeals dismissed the claim that employees had negligently placed him in the therapy program, stating that the decision to place him in the program involved medical judgment for which no liability could be imposed. The lower court's ruling that the use of a covered pot of hot water to instruct severely disabled persons was so negligent that a trial was not even necessary was reversed by the Court of Appeals, which stated that while a residential facility owes a duty of reasonable care to severely disabled persons, it is not required to maintain constant surveillance of each individual. After noting that "there are certain risks inherent in any therapeutic program, especially, as in this case, one which is designed to provide a normal homelike setting," the Court of Appeals remanded the case to the lower court for reconsideration of whether the lawsuit should be allowed to proceed. *Killen v. State*, 498 N.Y.S.2d 358 (1985).

The mother of a blind, deaf and mute student in the District of Columbia, who had been sexually assaulted by the coordinator of a program for blind and deaf students, sued the coordinator and the District of Columbia. She contended that the district was liable for damages arising from the assault on her daughter due to the district's negligence in hiring or failing to supervise the coordinator. The District of Columbia Court of Appeals affirmed a trial court ruling in favor of the school district. The court of appeals found that although an employer may be held liable for the acts of employees committed within the scope of their employment, there was no showing that the coordinator's assault of the child was within that scope.

The court rejected the mother's argument that the assault was a direct result of the coordinator's job assignment since his employment necessarily included some physical contact with the child. The mother argued that a deaf, blind and mute child can be taught only through the sense of touch and, therefore, the fact that physical touching was necessarily a part of the teacher-student relationship made it foreseeable that sexual assaults would occur. The court found that a sexual assault cannot be deemed a direct result of a school official's authorization to take a student by the hand or arm in guiding her past obstacles in the building. Here, the attack was "unprovoked," had not arisen from the coordinator's instructions or job assignment and was not an integral part of the school's activities, interests or objectives. The coordinator's acts could not be viewed as being within the scope of his employment, and thus the school district was not liable. *Boykin v. Dist. of Columbia*, 484 A.2d 560 (D.C.App.1984).

II. GOVERNMENTAL IMMUNITY

Governmental immunity is a doctrine which prohibits a lawsuit against any governmental entity or its officials. The doctrine, which has its roots deep in Anglo-American common law, has suffered a great decline in the last century. While some states retain the doctrine in full force, others have partially or completely eliminated it by legislative or judicial decision. Congress has at least partially authorized lawsuits against the U.S. Government through passage of the Federal Tort Claims Act.

A. Eleventh Amendment Immunity

Where a lawsuit is brought against state officials in *federal* court, the Eleventh Amendment to the U.S. Constitution comes into play. Generally, a private citizen is barred by the Eleventh Amendment from seeking in federal court an award of money damages against a state or against state officials in their official capacities. However, the federal courts may issue injunctions ordering states and state officials to conform their future conduct to the dictates of federal law; this is known as "prospective relief" and is not barred by the Eleventh Amendment.

Local political subdivisions, unlike states and official state departments, are fully subject to lawsuits brought by private citizens in federal court because they are not considered "states" under the Eleventh Amendment. Further, the Eleventh Amendment is inapplicable to suits brought by the federal government against a state, and is inapplicable to any lawsuit brought in a state court. In addition, Congress may remove a state's Eleventh Amendment protection by specifically abrogating it for particular and specified purposes.

In 1989, the Supreme Court in *Dellmuth v. Muth*, 491 U.S. 223, 109 S.Ct. 2397, 105 L.Ed.2d 181 (1989), ruled that while local school districts could be sued under the EHA, states were immune from EHA liability under the Eleventh Amendment. In response, Congress passed the Education of the Handicapped Act Amendments of 1990—known as the Individuals with Disabilities Education Act (IDEA), which included a new section, § 604, which specifically abrogates a state's Eleventh Amendment immunity to suit in federal court for violations of the EHA. This section, as part of the IDEA, allows suit against a state for both legal and equitable remedies in federal court. However, the provisions of the IDEA which abrogate sovereign immunity only effect violations which occur in whole or in part after the date of enactment of the Education of the Handicapped Act Amendments of 1990, or October 30, 1990. As such, sovereign immunity is still available for acts occurring before that date.

An Illinois student filed suit in federal district court claiming that the state failed to provide the student with a free appropriate public education. The state moved to dismiss the complaint based upon Eleventh Amendment immunity. The Eleventh Amendment to the U.S. Constitution prohibits the naming of the state as a defendant in a suit. This has led the U.S. Supreme Court to require plaintiffs to meet a stringent standard demonstrating Congress's intent that a state may be sued in federal court. Congress's intention must be unmistakably clear to nullify the Eleventh Amendment immunity. The Education of the Handicapped Act confers upon disabled children the right to a free appropriate public education. In 1989, the U.S. Supreme Court held that the statutory language of the EHA did not evince an unmistakably clear intention to abrogate the state's immunity from suit.

In October of 1990, Congress passed the Individuals with Disabilities Education Act (IDEA) which significantly abridged the states' sovereign immunity rights. The IDEA explicitly provided that states would not be immune under the Eleventh Amendment from suit in federal court for a violation. However, only violations that occurred after October 30, 1990, were affected. Since, the violations occurred in part after October 30, 1990, the state could not claim a sovereign immunity defense, and the motion to dismiss was denied. *Joshua B. v. New Trier Township High School Dist. 203*, 770 F.Supp. 431 (N.E.Ill.1991).

However, even in cases where the abrogation does not yet apply, the Eleventh Amendment does not bar claims against state officials in their individual capacities. A New York paraplegic student had been a client of the Office of Vocational Rehabilitation (OVR). OVR operated rehabilitation programs established under the Federal Vocational Rehabilitation Act of 1983. The purpose of the Act was the development and implementation of programs of vocational rehabilitation for disabled individuals, designed to help them obtain employment. The Act required states receiving funding under the Act to develop an individualized written rehabilitation program (IWRP) for each person in the program. The IWRP was to be tailored to each client's individual needs and potential with an emphasis placed on the determination and achievement of a vocational goal. The student maintained that since his IWRP had employment as a practicing attorney as his goal, the OVR should have funded his higher education, including law school. The OVR funded the student's undergraduate tuition and living expenses. However, during law school the OVR then limited its expenditures on behalf of each of its clients to $1,500 for tuition and $1,300 for maintenance per year. As a result, the student had to borrow more than $25,000 to cover the costs of law school. The student then commenced this action based on his belief that the OVR was required to individualize service to rehabilitation clients. He sued the state agency and state officials in a federal district court claiming an equal protection violation of the Rehabilitation Act and a violation of § 1983 of the Civil Rights Act. After the defendants moved to dismiss the action, the motion was referred to a magistrate for a recommendation.

The magistrate determined that all claims but the § 1983 claim against the individual defendants were barred by the Eleventh Amendment. Under the Eleventh Amendment, a private person may not sue a state agency in a federal court. The court agreed with the magistrate's decision except that it determined that the other claims against the officials in their individual capacities did not constitute a suit against the state and were therefore not barred by the Eleventh Amendment. Accordingly, the trial court denied the motion to dismiss. *McGuire v. Switzer*, 734 F.Supp. 99 (S.D.N.Y.1990).

A Navajo student, suffering from severe arthritis, was confined to a wheelchair at the age of thirteen. She successfully completed her junior high school education without any delays resulting from her illness, and she then sought admission to the only high school in her neighborhood. The school was administered by the U.S. Bureau of Indian Affairs. School officials allegedly denied admission to the student for four consecutive academic years because the school's facilities could not accommodate her disability. During her attempts to attend the local high school, she attended a high school ten miles away along poorly surfaced roads which, due to her severe arthritis, caused her great pain. The roads also became impassable in bad weather and the student eventually withdrew from school because of poor academic performance brought on by excessive absences. She then sued the federal school officials in an Arizona federal district court. The court ordered her admittance to the school and she finally graduated two years later than she should have. However, she continued her lawsuit against the officials, asserting claims under the Education of the Handicapped Act (EHA), under the Rehabilitation Act and under the Fifth Amendment Due Process Clause.

The school officials sought to dismiss the student's claims on the grounds of sovereign immunity. Further, they argued that the Rehabilitation Act did not place the burden of making schools accessible on individual defendants. They also argued that the student's Fifth Amendment due process claim should be dismissed because the EHA was the student's exclusive remedy. The court, however, disagreed. It first stated that because the student sought damages against the officials in their individual rather than representative capacities, her claims were not directed against the United States. Thus, the officials were not entitled to sovereign immunity. The court also noted that Congress had intended other claims to be pursued in conjunction with the EHA and that the student's constitutional claim should not be dismissed. However, the court noted that mere negligence would not be sufficient to hold the school officials liable under the due process clause. The court thus held that there were material questions of fact to be determined and denied the school officials' motion to dismiss the case. *Begay v. Hodel*, 730 F.Supp. 1001 (D.Ariz.1990).

A U.S. district court in Wisconsin applied the doctrine of Eleventh Amendment governmental immunity in a claim against the Milwaukee public school system. A disabled child brought suit in federal court against the school system on behalf of himself and all other similarly situated children in Milwaukee who were placed in day treatment facilities. After the state proposed termination of the day service placements, the parents of the children alleged that their children were being denied educational facilities in violation of the EHA. The court held that the parents' claim for damages against the Wisconsin state superintendent of public instruction was essentially a claim against state funds, and that no congressional authorization existed to abrogate the state's Eleventh Amendment immunity from retroactive monetary claims payable from the state treasury. *Editor's Note: See introduction to this section.* However, the court did grant an injunction to the children against the superintendent of public instruction in her official capacity. The injunction restrained the Milwaukee public schools from terminating the current placement of the children and removing the children from those schools until completion of a full and impartial evaluation of their education needs. The injunction, said the court, was prospective in nature and thus was not barred by governmental immunity. *M.R. v. Milwaukee Public Schools*, 495 F.Supp. 864 (E.D.Wis.1980).

B. Qualified Immunity

The doctrine of qualified immunity shields government officials, whether local, state or federal, from liability arising out of their discretionary acts. This immunity generally extends only to officials acting at the planning level, not the operational level.

A Connecticut eight-year-old suffered from a seizure disorder, learning disabilities and behavioral disturbances that rendered him disabled within the meaning of the EHA. The student was admitted to the Greater Bridgeport Children's Services Center (GBCSC) for psychiatric treatment. In order to provide educational services to children residing in or receiving day treatment at the institution the state had established Unified School District No. 2, known as the family school. A child became eligible to attend the family school upon admission to GBCSC. Once the treatment team determined that a child no longer required GBCSC care, he was discharged and became ineligible for services from the family school. The student remained at the family school for the 1984-85 school year. He was discharged from the medical facility at the end of the school year and became ineligible for services at the family school. His parents then demanded an administrative hearing to review the discharge decision and requested that he be allowed to attend the family school pending the conclusion of the hearing. This request was denied and his parents filed a lawsuit alleging that the medical and school officials violated the student's rights under the EHA. The district court granted summary judgment to the defendants holding that, although the EHA was applicable to the family school, the defendants were entitled to qualified immunity. The district court also awarded the parents attorney's fees. Both parties appealed to the U.S. Court of Appeals, Second Circuit.

Government officials performing discretionary functions generally are shielded from liability for civil damages insofar as their conduct does not violate clearly established statutory or constitutional rights of which a reasonable person would have known. The defendants maintained that it was not clear when this action arose that the EHA applied to GBCSC discharge decisions. The court agreed. The court noted that the student's discharge was not from the family school but from the GBCSC, a medical facility. Therefore, the court determined that since the law was not clearly established at the time of the discharge the defendants were entitled to the protection of qualified immunity. The court, however, reversed the order for reimbursement of attorney's fees as the parents were not prevailing parties. *Christopher P. by Norma P. v. Marcus*, 915 F.2d 794 (2d Cir.1990).

A Michigan child was born with a congenital heart defect which left him with symptoms of dizziness, fainting, chest pain, exhaustion and rapid heart palpitations. As an infant, he also contracted meningitis which left him with orthopedic and learning disabilities. Because of his heart condition, his physician directed that he was not to participate in competitive contact sports or any forced exertion. The school district was also informed of his medical history and physical limitations. During recess, the boy was instructed to perform the "gut run" as punishment for talking with another classmate. The "gut run" was a 350-yard sprint that was required to be completed in under two minutes. While making the run, the boy suffered cardiac arrhythmia and died. The school district then concealed the true circumstances of the boy's death; the parents were informed that their son died while voluntarily playing football. The parents then brought this action in a federal district court alleging a violation of substantive due process. The defendants filed a motion to dismiss.

The Due Process Clause of the Fourteenth Amendment provides that no state may "deprive any person of life, liberty, or property, without due process of law." The parents claimed that the defendants had an obligation not to harm their son. For the parents to prevail, the action taken must amount to a deliberate decision of a government actor to deprive a person of life, liberty, or property. An abuse of governmental power can only arise in situations where a custodial relationship exists between the individual harmed and the state actor who inflicted the harm. It is clear that the boy was in a custodial relationship with his teacher. The high school teacher stood *in loco parentis* (in the place of the parents) which heightened the teacher's responsibility for the student's well-being. Accordingly, punishment which was not disciplinary in nature or which clearly exceeded reasonable discipline could amount to a substantive due process violation. The parents also alleged that the other defendants knew or should have known of the teacher's practice of using the "gut run" as discipline and chose not to interfere. This failure could show such "deliberate indifference" to the rights of the boy as to rise to the level of a violation. The defendants contended that they were protected by Eleventh Amendment qualified immunity. They asserted that the legal standard making their actions a substantive due process violation was not clearly established at the time of the boy's death. However, the court noted that as early as Sept. 17, 1987, the defendants were on notice that in the public school context, physical punishment which was not disciplinary in nature or which was so disproportionate to the need presented amounted to a "brutal and inhumane abuse of official power literally shocking to the conscience" which violated an individual's substantive due process rights. The court denied the motion to dismiss. *Waechter v. School Dist. No. 14-030*, 773 F.Supp. 1005 (W.D.Mich.1991).

A mildly retarded Vermont young man had been in the custody of the state since the age of three. He had lived in nine foster homes and schools prior to turning eighteen. After his eighteenth birthday, he was placed under the guardianship of the Department of Mental Health (state). While in a foster home, the man threatened a member of the household with a screwdriver and then stayed away overnight. The caretakers notified the state that they could not handle the student and that he would have to leave within two days. The man was uncooperative, so the state ordered the police to transport the man pursuant to Vermont's emergency admissions procedure law. An administrative hearing was held to determine if the statutory requirements for short term emergency admission to the residential educational facility had been met. Admission was denied. Because the state did not have a residential placement available, he remained at the school for approximately two years. He received only sporadic educational services largely because he resisted attempts to develop an individual education program for him. This action was filed on his behalf seeking a declaratory judgment and injunction requiring state officials to place him in an appropriate, professionally supervised community facility and develop a long range treatment, residential and educational plan. The state officials moved to dismiss the case against them citing their qualified immunity. The federal district court denied the motion for summary judgment. The defendants then appealed to the U.S. Court of Appeals, Second Circuit.

Qualified immunity is the doctrine that shields government officials performing discretionary functions from liability for civil damages. The mentally retarded young man claimed that the EHA was violated because his ability to succeed educationally was linked to his residential placement and frequent changes in residence led to inconsistent and sporadic schooling that limited his ability to receive an appropriate education. In order to defeat a qualified immunity defense, the man was required to show that his right was clearly established. The court determined that it was not clearly established that state employees had any duty to provide a consistent residential placement. The EHA requires the local education agency to provide for appropriate education but makes no mention of any other state agencies or their possible duty. Therefore, the court of appeals granted qualified immunity to the defendants and reversed the district court's decision. *P.C. v. McLaughlin*, 913 F.2d 1033 (2d Cir.1990).

An Indiana special education student was subjected to at least three incidents of sexual abuse by other students in her classes. The incidents occurred in separate years, culminating with an attempt by another student to have sexual intercourse with her on a field trip. The teacher in charge of the field trip had permitted the student to accompany three male students to the lavatory unsupervised. In both of the previous instances, the teacher had notified parents of the students involved, and in this case the teacher wrote letters to the students' parents and punished the students. The abused student was transferred to a private school by her parents the following year. None of the incidents were ever reported to the county welfare department or law enforcement agency. Indiana law directs individuals with knowledge that children are victims of abuse to make oral reports to local child protection or law enforcement agencies.

The student sued the school corporation, the teacher, the principal and other officials in an Indiana trial court for the expense of psychological counseling following the third incident. The school corporation initially responded with a request for a jury trial, then amended its answer with a motion for summary judgment. The student responded with a motion to strike the corporation's governmental immunity defense because it had not been raised in the initial answer. The court granted the school corporation's summary judgment motion as a final judgment in favor of the corporation and officials. The student appealed to the Indiana Court of Appeals, Third District.

The appeals court ruled that the student was not prejudiced by the corporation's failure to raise the affirmative defense of governmental immunity in its initial answer. It also rejected the student's argument that the corporation must be liable for the sexual abuse incidents because of its prior knowledge of past incidents. The school corporation had not violated a duty of care to the student. However, the teacher's and principal's actions were not protected under any governmental immunity doctrine. Although Indiana statutes required reporting of child abuse, they did not provide a basis for civil lawsuits against governmental officials. The case was remanded for determination of whether the teacher breached a duty to reasonably supervise the students, and whether the principal had failed to reasonably supervise students. In neither case would civil liability be premised upon the child abuse reporting statute. *Borne v. Northwest Allen County School Corp.*, 532 N.E.2d 1196 (Ind.App.3d Dist.1989).

C. State Statutory Immunity

Congress has enacted the Federal Tort Claims Act which allows individuals to sue the federal government in limited circumstances. Many states have enacted similar legislation wherein they effectively consent to be sued in certain instances.

A special needs student at a Massachusetts junior high school was injured while fleeing from an altercation with another student. The injury occurred in the presence of the student's teacher in the school cafeteria. At the time of the injury, the student was attending the public schools pursuant to his individualized education plan (IEP). The teacher and school officials were aware that the special needs student was impulsive, erratic, and combative (and thus likely to get into fights). The student sued the city, claiming negligent educational programming and negligent supervision of students. A superior court dismissed the claim and the student appealed to the Appeals Court of Massachusetts. The appeals court noted that the Massachusetts Tort Claims Act exempts from liability any public employee who is exercising a "discretionary function." The court stated that the negligent educational programming claim must fail because the adoption of a plan to integrate pupils with disabilities into the public schools is purely discretionary. The claim for negligent supervision also failed. The court stated that student discipline and school decorum fall readily within the discretionary function exception in the Tort Claims Act. Therefore, the appeals court affirmed the superior court's decision. *Bencic v. City of Malden*, 587 N.E.2d 795 (Mass.App.Ct.1992).

An Ohio high school student had difficulty learning and also experienced behavioral problems. As a result, he was disciplined by school authorities. He also underwent psychological testing at the request of the school. The testing did not reveal any disability. The student withdrew from the school and was later diagnosed as having epilepsy. The student's parents sued the school district, claiming that as an epileptic their son was considered a child with a handicap under state law. The parents claimed that the school district negligently failed to identify the student as handicapped as it was required to do under state law. They also claimed that the actions violated the student's constitutional rights. The school district and its employees moved to dismiss the negligence charges, claiming sovereign immunity. The trial court granted the request, and the parents appealed to the Court of Appeals of Ohio.

The court noted that political subdivisions in Ohio are immune from liability for damages incurred as a result of an act or omission of the subdivision or one of its employees. The employee is also immune, with certain exceptions. An exception exists where another portion of Ohio law expressly provides for liability for an action. Although the parents argued that this exception applied because Ohio law required identification of students with handicaps, the court held that it did not. Imposing *responsibility* for an action is not the same as imposing *liability* for that action. The law must expressly state that violation of a duty can form the basis of a civil action for damages. Likewise, an exception for employee negligence on governmental grounds was only intended for claims arising from the maintenance of government property. *Zellman v. Kenston Bd. of Educ.*, 593 N.E.2d 392 (Ohio App.1991).

A Wyoming student suffered from physical and mental disabilities. He and his family resided within the boundaries of a school district which had entered into a special education residential services agreement with the Board of Cooperative Educational Services (BOCES). BOCES members were selected by the board of trustees of participating school districts. Its purpose was to provide special educational services for member school districts. BOCES agreed to pay for the student's education including room and board. The student was placed at a facility owned and operated by BOCES. At BOCES the student was severely burned while being bathed by a staff member. The student's parents sued the school district in a Wyoming district court. The district court held that BOCES employees were not employees of the school district and the school district could not be liable for acts of BOCES employees. The student's parents appealed to the Supreme Court of Wyoming.

On appeal, the school district argued that BOCES was a governmental agency. The student's parents contended that although BOCES was an agent of the school district, this relationship did not make it a governmental entity under the Wyoming Governmental Claims Act. The court found that under the act, a governmental entity was any local government unit including school districts and their agents. BOCES was a governmental entity and its employees were immune from liability. The school district was not liable for BOCES employees' acts. The district court's decision was affirmed. *Sykes v. Lincoln County School Dist. 1 & 2*, 763 P.2d 1263 (Wyo.1988).

An educable mentally handicapped (EMH) student in Chicago was struck by a chalkboard clip thrown by another EMH student and was injured. The incident occurred during a twenty-minute recess break, during which the regular EMH classroom teacher was absent. The class was unsupervised at the time because a teacher's aide who was assigned to simultaneously supervise both the regular classroom and the EMH classroom was not in the room. The student sued the teacher's aide, the teacher and the city board of education in an Illinois trial court. The teacher's aide testified that during the recess period she went back and forth between the classrooms, leaving each class unattended for only a minute at a time. She also stated that when she heard yelling from the EMH classroom she immediately returned. Some of the students in the classroom testified that there had been no supervision in the EMH classroom for one half-hour before and twenty minutes after the accident occurred. There was no evidence that the student who threw the chalkboard clip had prior behavioral problems. The school psychologist testified that EMH students were placed there because of low I.Q. and not for behavioral disorders. The trial court granted the school district and officials' summary judgment motion, applying a wilful and wanton standard for the conduct of school board personnel. The injured student appealed to the Illinois Appellate Court.

The court noted that under Illinois law, teachers and other educational employees who are responsible for supervising students were immune from negligent conduct. Because the teacher and assistant were immune from liability for ordinarily negligent conduct, it was required to show that they had been wilful or wanton in order to impute liability to them. Thus, the trial court had applied the proper legal standard for evaluating school employees' conduct. The court rejected the injured student's argument that this standard should not apply to EMH classroom settings. The court also noted that teaching assistants were entitled to immunity from lawsuit and were protected from liability under the Local Governmental and Governmental Employees Tort Immunity Act. Illinois courts consistently have held that there is no wilful or wanton misconduct where the teacher merely leaves children unsupervised. The requisite standard was for injured parties to show that the teacher or school was aware of a high probability of serious harm or unreasonable risk of harm. Because there was no such evidence in this case, no factual question existed about whether the school or its employees should have known of a high probability of impending danger to the EMH students. The appellate court affirmed the trial court's summary judgment for the school board and its employees. *Jackson v . Chicago Bd. of Educ.*, 549 N.E.2d 829 (Ill.App.1st Dist.1989).

A behaviorally disturbed Kansas student was injured in a high school industrial arts class while using a table saw. The school district had developed an IEP which included enrollment in regular classes. The student's woodworking teacher was allegedly notified that he was a special education student and advised of his particular problem. However, the teacher denied receiving any such notice. The student's father sued the school district and its employees in a federal district court. The father contended that the district and the teacher had failed to take reasonable steps to protect the safety of the student and were negligent in failing to properly supervise him in the woodworking class. The school district moved for summary judgment, arguing that its actions were discretionary and that it was therefore entitled to immunity under the Kansas Tort Claims Act.

The court found that under the Tort Claims Act a governmental entity or its employee shall not be liable for damages resulting from any claim based upon the exercise, performance or failure to perform a discretionary function or duty. The school board was entitled to immunity only if its actions were not governed by any readily ascertainable standard, or if no legal duty existed to act in a certain manner. The court held that the school district and the teacher were under a legal duty to properly supervise the student in the woodworking class. They also had to take reasonable steps to protect his safety, including properly instructing him on safety procedures and providing proper guards and warning signs. These matters were not discretionary and the teacher and the school district were not entitled to immunity.

In addition, the district would not have been immune if it failed to notify the teacher of the student's IEP, as it was under a legal duty to do so. The district court denied the school district's motion for summary judgment. *Greider v. Shawnee Mission Unified School Dist.*, 710 F.Supp. 296 (D.Kan.1989).

A Texas elementary school student who suffered from cerebral palsy was pushed into a stack of chairs and sustained a head injury while a group of students were left unsupervised. The student had mild convulsions, developed cold sweats and became dazed and incoherent, but the teacher did not call for help or send her to the school nurse. When the student was later taken to the nurse by an occupational therapist, the nurse told her to stay in school. On the way to her daycare center on a school bus at the end of the day the student suffered severe convulsions. The bus driver contacted his supervisor requesting that a school nurse be provided at the next stop, but he was told to take the student to the daycare center, where she finally received medical treatment. The student's mother filed a lawsuit against the school district and school employees alleging that their grossly negligent failure to provide adequate care decreased the student's life expectancy. After the lawsuit was dismissed before trial the mother appealed.

The Texas Supreme Court considered whether the lawsuit was barred by the Texas Tort Claims Act. The court noted that the act provides an exception from immunity for professional school employees when in "disciplining a student the employee uses excessive force or negligence which results in bodily injury to the student." The mother argued that under this exception school employees could be held liable both for using excessive force when disciplining a student *and* for any "negligence which results in bodily injury to the student." Although the language of the exception was ambiguous because negligence isn't "used," the court observed that it has been interpreted by Texas courts to apply only when a student's bodily injury is a result of some form of punishment. Because the student in this case was not being punished when she incurred her injuries, the court determined that the exception did not apply.

The court next turned to the mother's assertion that the student's injuries fell within another exception to sovereign immunity for damages arising from the "use or operation of a motor vehicle." The court concluded that this exception did not apply because although the girl suffered convulsions on the school bus, those convulsions were not "the proximate result of the use or operation of the school bus." The supreme court affirmed the dismissal of the case. *Hopkins v. Spring Indep. School Dist.*, 736 S.W.2d 617 (Tex.1987).

D. Exceptions

A trainable mentally retarded six-year-old girl was allegedly sexually molested by her bus driver for over a year. The principal and her teachers had witnessed the girl sitting on his lap. The child exhibited other behavior commensurate with sexual abuse at school. The bus driver denied the allegations and claimed that he asked the girl to sit up front because she had behavioral problems on the bus. The school district failed to institute a bus incident reporting program which was required by the state. The girl's mother brought this action in a Kansas trial court for negligence against the driver, the school bus transportation service, and the school district. The trial court denied summary judgment for the defendants and they appealed to the Supreme Court of Kansas.

School authorities are required by law to exercise reasonable care and supervision for the safety of the children under their control. A school is required to act when a child, while in its charge, is threatened by a third party, and it must make reasonable efforts to avoid injury to the child. The mother claimed that because the school district failed to institute the bus incident reporting program her child was injured. The court noted that this was a close case, but that the risk of harm was a jury question. The school district also asserted that it should have been granted immunity under the discretionary function exception to the Kansas Tort Claims Act. It argued that the day-to-day supervision and retention of the bus driver was based on individual judgment. The burden was on the governmental entity to establish immunity under the exception. The child finally told of the molestation when asked by her mother why she would not behave on the bus. If the proper incident report procedures were followed, presumably the mother would have asked the child earlier and the sexual molestation would have been reported earlier. The court noted that recent court decisions have held that the discretionary function exception is not applicable where a legal duty exists. Therefore, the school district was not entitled to discretionary immunity and the court remanded the case back to the trial court to determine if the school district breached its duty of care. *Kansas State Bank & Trust Co. v. Specialized Trans. Services, Inc.*, 819 P.2d 587 (Kan.1991).

An instructional aide helped in the education and training of developmentally disabled children attending a Montana school district's special education program. A four-year-old student was allegedly sexually assaulted by the aide and received serious injuries that would require reconstructive surgery in adulthood. She suffered continual nightmares and became fearful of school. The school district maintained an insurance policy insuring against liabilities arising from its negligence. The student's parents, on her behalf, brought suit against the school district under 42 U.S.C. § 1983 and alleged negligence in hiring and supervision in a Montana trial court. The trial court dismissed the complaint, granting immunity to the school district, and the parents appealed to the Supreme Court of Montana.

The parents contended that the trial court erred in three ways in dismissing the suit. First, the parents alleged that Montana immunity statutes and case law resulted in an ambiguity disallowing governmental immunity. They argued that the Montana Supreme Court had previously ruled that there was no governmental immunity for negligence in a special education program. In that case, the court held that it was the court's duty to permit an action for negligence when the statute granting immunity was unclear. However, in the instant case, the court concluded that this statute clearly granted immunity. The parents also contended that the purchase of insurance waived governmental immunity. The court agreed and determined that the purchase by the school district of liability insurance waived its immunity to the extent of the coverage.

Lastly, the parents contended that the district court improperly failed to rule on their claims under 42 U.S.C. § 1983. The appellate court noted that in consideration of the § 1983 claims of the parents, the trial court was required to analyze the complaint and the facts, and to apply the law in reaching a decision as to whether the § 1983 claims were barred. The trial court did not make any such analysis. Apparently, it was assumed that the § 1983 claims would be barred because of the governmental immunity. However, the court noted that in *Howlett v. Rose*, 110 S.Ct. 2430 (1990) the U.S. Supreme Court concluded that a state immunity defense was not available in a § 1983 action brought in a state court. Therefore, the court remanded the case to the district court to rule on the § 1983 claim and to determine the extent of liability. *S.M. v. R.B.*, 811 P.2d 1295 (Mont.1991).

A physically-disabled Pennsylvania student with cerebral palsy fell backwards after refusing to use his walker and struck his head on the sidewalk. The accident occurred under a classroom aide's supervision on school grounds. His injuries included permanent paralysis and respiratory disability. The student's parents sued the school, claiming the injuries resulted from the dangerous condition of the school property. The school moved to have the case dismissed by claiming governmental immunity under § 8542(b) of the Judicial Code. The trial court found the allegations made by the parents to amount to no more than "a claim for negligent supervision which had been repeatedly denied as a cause of action under § 8542." The court dismissed the case and the parents appealed.

On appeal, the parents argued that the school had not adapted the school grounds so that it would be safe for use by disabled students. The failure to do so resulted in a "dangerous condition" which fell within an exception to the governmental immunity doctrine. The court held that the exception could only be applied where the alleged negligence made the property itself unsafe for activities for which it was used. The student's fall was not caused by the condition of the school's property. It was not connected in any way to the property, sidewalk or street. There had been no prior incidents which would have placed the school on notice that a dangerous condition existed which required correction. The school was entitled to dismissal of the case on the basis of governmental immunity under § 8542(b). *Houston v. Cent. Bucks School Auth.*, 546 A.2d 1286 (Pa.Cmwlth.1988).

A Pennsylvania student who was mentally retarded drowned in a Pennsylvania university's pool while he was participating in a Recreation for Exceptional Citizens Program (REC). He was eighteen-years-old and suffered from cerebral palsy since birth. The student's parents sued the university and the REC in a Pennsylvania trial court for negligently creating a dangerous condition on real property and for not following proper safety procedures for a swimming pool. The trial court ruled in favor of the university and the organization stating that the pool, unattended by a lifeguard, was not a dangerous condition created by the school's negligence. The parents then appealed to the Pennsylvania Supreme Court.

The university and the REC asserted the defense of sovereign immunity. However, the parents alleged that their claim fell within the real property exception to sovereign immunity. The court stated that the real property exception extended to injuries arising out of the care, custody or control of real estate. Thus, the exception did not apply to claims of negligent supervision. Since the swimming pool itself did not cause the injury, the school and the REC were not liable. The supreme court affirmed the trial court's decision. *Nusheno v. Lock Haven Univ.*, 574 A.2d 129 (Pa.Cmwlth.1990).

III. REMEDIES AVAILABLE TO STUDENTS UNDER THE IDEA

Upon violations of the IDEA, students may seek either monetary or equitable relief (in the nature of an injunction). Relief may be awarded by an administrative officer or it may come from the courts. Generally, monetary damages are disfavored, but they can be awarded in proper circumstances.

A. Monetary Damages

In January 1984, a disabled Mississippi boy was suspended from school for unbuttoning a girl's blouse and he was sent to a state hospital for evaluation and treatment with his mother's consent. After the boy returned home he was refused admission to school but his mother was not informed officially of the refusal. The boy was refused admission again in September 1984, and the mother filed complaints with local and state education authorities but received no satisfaction. She sued the school board in a U.S. district court alleging that the boy's due process rights were violated. She also sought a court order to readmit her son to school.

The district court held a due process hearing in December 1984, in which it upheld an October 1984, school board IEP determination that the boy should be placed in a residential setting. The U.S. Court of Appeals, Fifth Circuit, upheld the decision and after further proceedings in the district court the mother appealed again to the court of appeals. She contended that the boy's due process rights were violated when he was excluded from school in the winter and fall of 1984.

The court of appeals held that when the school board failed to convene an IEP conference in the spring of 1984 it violated the EHA. The EHA specifically required that "written prior notice to the parents" be provided whenever the school proposes to initiate or change . . . the . . . educational placement of the child. . . ." The U.S. Supreme Court has held that even a short suspension of ten days requires notice and some type of formal hearing. Also, both the EHA and the Fourteenth Amendment require the school to provide the boy with notice and a hearing regarding his continued exclusion from school. The court held that this procedural violation gave rise to a claim by the boy for compensatory damages under the "due process" exception to *Smith v. Robinson*. It also observed that the Handicapped Children's Protection Act of 1986 provides for compensatory damages. The case was remanded to the district court to determine the extent of the boy's loss caused by the school's failure to provide notice and a hearing in April and August 1984. The court of appeals also instructed the district court to determine what damages, either monetary or in remedial educational services, would be appropriate for the boy. *Jackson v. Franklin County School Bd.*, 806 F.2d 623 (5th Cir.1986).

A California state hospital patient was developmentally disabled. Between 1977 and 1981, California received federal funds to provide education to disabled children under the EHA. However, between 1977 and 1981 the state allocated no EHA funds for eligible students in the state hospital system, including the hospital in which the patient resided. The patient was a child during those years. He instituted a class action lawsuit against the state of California. He alleged that the state's failure to allocate EHA funds for the education of children in state hospitals deprived members of the class of their "liberty interests" in a free appropriate public education. This allegedly violated the due process clauses of the state and federal constitutions. He sought $20 million in damages and attorney's fees under the Civil Rights Act for violations of the EHA.

One of the issues before a California appellate court was whether money damages were an appropriate remedy if he proved that he and his class were unlawfully excluded from EHA services. The patient claimed the Handicapped Children's Protection Act (HCPA) provided for money damages. The court rejected the patient's argument. Compensatory educational services were available to the patient and other members of the class. The court noted that if the patient's parents had furnished the special education services he claimed he was wrongfully denied between 1977 and 1981, the decision in *Burlington School Comm. v. Dep't of Educ.* authorized reimbursement. *Burlington* required that compensatory educational services be furnished to children who were entitled to EHA services but were now beyond the age of ordinary entitlement. Money damages were inconsistent with Congress' intent to allow the limited financial resources of states to be spent on the education of disabled children rather than damages. Although the HCPA provided for the retroactive award of attorney's fees, it expressly excluded the retroactive recovery of money damages. The patient could not obtain money damages if he prevailed on his civil rights claims. *White v. State*, 240 Cal.Rptr. 732 (Cal.App.3d Dist.1987).

A Connecticut case demonstrates other circumstances where monetary damages are allowed under pre-1986 law. It involved a multi-disabled boy who required a highly structured but flexible school program. A June 1982, study found that the boy was making no academic progress in the Trumbull, Connecticut Public School program and recommended placement in the Foundation School. The parents unilaterally placed the boy in the Foundation School in December 1982. When Trumbull proposed a new program for the boy for the 1983-84 school year, which was modeled after Foundation's program, a hearing officer found it to be appropriate but the parents insisted on leaving him at Foundation. They sued Trumbull seeking a court order requiring the school board to pay reasonable costs of tuition and transportation for the boy's attendance at Foundation. They also requested that the board be required to maintain the boy in his Foundation School placement during the pendency of the court proceedings. They sought damages of $10 million and costs incurred by the exhaustion of their EHA remedies. The board moved for a dismissal before a hearing officer who denied the motion, and the board then appealed to a U.S. district court.

The issue before the court was whether the parents were entitled to money damages under § 1983 of the federal Civil Rights Act and § 504 of the Rehabilitation Act of 1973. The court noted that prior to passage of the Handicapped Children's Protection Act of 1986, (Pub.L.No. 99-372, 100 Stat. 796) the exclusive remedy of the parents was the EHA, but that is no longer true. The court therefore had to determine whether the 1986 legislation should be given retroactive application in this case. Applying the law in effect at the time it rendered its decision would be appropriate, held the court, unless doing so would result in injustice or if there was statutory direction or legislative history to the contrary. All three exceptions were operative here. Congress did not intend to give retroactive effect to § 3 of the Handicapped Children's Protection Act of 1986 which provides that plaintiffs must exhaust all administrative procedures before seeking resolution in a civil action. The parents had to rely on prior law for relief. The motion to dismiss with respect to the parents' § 3 claim was granted to Trumbull.

The court noted that under pre-1986 law, monetary damages are generally denied but are allowed under two exceptional circumstances: (1) "where the child's physical health would have been endangered if the parents had not made alternative arrangements; and (2) where defendants acted in bad faith by failing, in an egregious fashion, to comply with the procedural provisions of the EHA ." The court reasoned that the parents might qualify for the "bad faith" exception and accordingly it refused to dismiss this portion of the parents' lawsuit. *Silano v. Tirozzi*, 651 F.Supp. 1021 (D.Conn.1987).

In a Georgia case, a young child, through his parents, brought an action against his school district, board of education and certain of its administrators seeking declaratory, injunctive and monetary relief for alleged violations of the EHA. When the child started school he was tested and it was determined by school authorities that he should be assigned to a self-contained learning disability classroom. The parents agreed to this placement. Approximately one year later the child's progress was reviewed and placement was changed to "research learning disability" which gave him part-time assistance. Again, the parents approved. Shortly thereafter, the parents insisted that their child be placed in a regular first grade class without resource assistance. This request was denied by the school board.

A hearing was later held at which the hearing officer determined that assistance was unnecessary, thus clearing the way for regular classroom placement. The school rejected this decision, prompting an automatic appeal to the state board of education. That board determined that the current school board placement was appropriate. Suit was then filed in federal court by the child and his parents. During pendency of the suit, the child was placed in a regular classroom. The trial court entered summary judgment for the local school board, and appeal was taken to the U.S. Court of Appeals, Eleventh Circuit, which ruled that the parents' monetary claims under the EHA were moot due to the child's removal from all special education during pendency of the action. *Powell v. Defore*, 699 F.2d 1078 (11th Cir.1983).

Money damages were allowed in a case in New York. The parents of a seventeen-year-old deaf child brought suit in a U.S. district court, seeking to compel their local school district and the New York State Commissioner of Education to pay for their child's education since 1973-1974 at a special school for the deaf in Massachusetts. The suit was brought under the EHA with the parents claiming that the defendants' failure to bear such costs deprived their child of a free appropriate public education in violation of the Act. Up to the time of the suit the parents paid the expenses of sending the child to the school. The defendants claimed that adequate schools existed in New York, that the Massachusetts school was not approved by the Commissioner and that money damages may not be awarded in an action under the Act.

The court disagreed and held that money damages may be awarded under the Act, "at least to the extent of reimbursement for tuition and expenses related to providing an appropriate educational placement for the disabled child. The statute's language authorizing the court to fashion such relief as it determines to be 'appropriate' grants a substantial amount of discretion to the court." However, the court did state that such damages could be awarded against the school district only and not against the Commissioner. The mere fact that the school was not approved by the commissioner did not necessarily preclude the plaintiffs from maintaining the present action but they were told by the court that they could not maintain an action for school years for which they had not made a prior request that the school district pay. The net result of the lawsuit was that a motion by the defendants to dismiss was denied, but the parents were required to undergo additional administrative proceedings to further clarify the issues involved. In the meantime, court action was stayed. *Matthews v. Ambach*, 552 F.Supp. 1273 (W.D.N.Y.1982).

B. Compensatory Education

Although compensatory education is not usually awarded under the IDEA, it may be awarded where benefits which Congress intended to protect under the IDEA were not granted. A student with disabilities does not have a right to demand public education beyond age twenty-one, unless the student is found entitled to educational services to compensate for the deprivation of a free appropriate education.

A Pennsylvania student was identified as socially and emotionally disturbed (SED) by her school district's multi-disciplinary team. She attended SED classes at a neighboring school district because her own school had no SED program. When the neighboring district discontinued its SED classes, the student was assigned to a learning disabled (LD) class in her own district. During the school year, the district suspended the student for a total of approximately thirty days for disruptive behavior and cutting classes. A high school vice principal and a teacher who eventually became one of the student's teachers for the following school year met with the student's mother and presented her with an IEP changing the student's classification from LD to SED. However, the district had not formulated an IEP and it contained only general goals for all students in the class. There was no IEP team meeting and the student's mother had no input into the plan.

The student's mother requested a hearing, after which the hearing officer concluded that the district had violated IDEA procedural safeguards by failing to complete a current multidisciplinary evaluation, failing to develop an IEP and suspending the student for more than fifteen days without giving notice to her parents. The mother appealed the hearing officer's finding that the district's actions did not violate Pennsylvania law and the IDEA. She also appealed the hearing officer's failure to award her attorney's fees in the matter. A state department of education appeals panel substantially upheld the hearing officer's findings and awarded the student compensatory education. The school district appealed to the Commonwealth Court of Pennsylvania. The court rejected the district's argument that the student's mother had participated in the IEP by meeting with school personnel on her own initiative. She had not been given an opportunity to provide real input as a part of an IEP team. Participation by one of the student's teachers for the following school year was also a deficiency under the IDEA because the IEP team must include teachers from the current year. The award of compensatory education was appropriate because it remedied school violations of the student's statutory rights. Compensatory education required school districts to belatedly pay expenses they should have paid all along. The court held for the student. *Big Beaver Falls School District v. Jackson*, 615 A.2d 910 (Pa.Cmwlth.1992).

In a Pennsylvania case, a profoundly retarded student was afflicted with severe behavior problems. The school district, the student's mother and the Delaware County intermediate unit agreed that he should be placed at a special education day facility, known as Summit School. He remained at Summit throughout the year and progressed with his IEP. The next fall, the student's behavior deteriorated significantly. Summit officials and the student's teacher determined that he could no longer be provided with an appropriate education and they recommended that he be placed in a residential program. After three years of inappropriate education, the student's parents contacted the Department of Education requesting that it assist in locating an appropriate special education program for the student. The bureau suggested that the student be placed in an out of state residential school. Meanwhile, the student's mother filed a declaratory judgment action against the Commonwealth of Pennsylvania, the Secretary of Education and the school district. A federal district court awarded the student compensatory education. The school district appealed to the U.S. Court of Appeals, Third Circuit.

The school district contended that a compensatory remedy required the court to ascertain the student's future educational needs and that these needs were not ripe for decision. The appellate court, however, noted that the trial court had merely determined that it was unable to predict the student's future, specific educational needs and left the components of the instructional program to be determined once he reached the age of twenty-one. Next the district contended that it was entitled to Eleventh Amendment immunity from the student's EHA claims. The court determined, however, that although there was a significant amount of state funding it was not established that the district was acting under color of state law. The district acted in an independent nature in determining special education services and other educational services. Therefore, the school district did not fall within the state's Eleventh Amendment immunity. Finally, the district contended that compensatory education was not a remedy available under the EHA. The court concluded that Congress empowered the courts to grant a compensatory remedy. And since the school district did not place the student in an appropriate school, the student was harmed by its failure to do so. The U.S. Court of Appeals upheld the district court's decision and granted the student a compensatory education of two and one-half years beyond age twenty-one. *Lester H. by Octavia P. v. Gilhool*, 916 F.2d 865 (3d Cir.1990).

A disabled New Hampshire student entered a public school in 1982 and took numerous tests to determine an appropriate Individualized Education Program (IEP). The tests indicated borderline intelligence, so the student was placed in a self-contained facility for the mentally disabled. When he was tested in 1988, the evaluator concluded that there was no change in his IEP. The student's mother expressed concern over the student's placement but her requests for an independent evaluation were denied. The school district then conducted an evaluation which resulted in the student's placement in a program for the emotionally disturbed. While in this program, the student complained of severe abuse by other students and was subsequently returned to the program for the mentally disabled. The student's parents obtained an independent evaluation and the evaluator's recommendations were only partially incorporated into the school district's 1989-90 IEP. Contrary to the independent evaluator's recommendations, it called for extensive mainstreaming.

At the end of the 1989-90 school year, the student was performing at a substandard level in both reading and math. The school district's proposed IEP for the 1990-91 school year was substantially similar to the previous IEP and again provided for extensive mainstreaming. The parents rejected the proposed IEP and sought a due process hearing. The hearing officer determined that the student was entitled to "intensive, individual instruction" at a qualified private facility for two years at school district expense. The school district appealed the decision to the U.S. District Court for the District of New Hampshire. The court determined that the hearing officer's award was not compensatory but rather part of the student's "free appropriate education." The award was not compensatory because it was to occur during the school year and before the student reached 21 years of age. Expert testimony had shown that the public school's IEPs involving mainstreaming caused the student extensive frustration and ultimately failed to provide him with an appropriate education. Therefore, private placement of the student was necessary to ensure that the student received a "free appropriate education." However, given the requirement that IEP's be evaluated annually, the hearing officer's two-year award of private education was reduced to one year.

Next, the court stated that numerous circuits, pursuant to *Burlington School Comm. v. Dept. of Educ.*, 471 U.S. 359, 105 S.Ct. 1996, 85 L.Ed.2d 385 (1985), had concluded that compensatory education was available under the IDEA. Compensatory education was merely the school district's belated provision of required educational services. Because the student had not received an adequate IEP for two and one-half years, the district was obligated to provide such compensatory education. Thus, the student was entitled to both private placement and compensatory education. *Manchester School District v. Christopher B.*, 807 F.Supp. 860 (D.N.H.1992).

A New Hampshire boy with disabilities was entitled to special educational services under the Individuals with Disabilities Education Act. His disabilities included spastic paraplegia, cortical blindness, tactile agnosia, and mild mental retardation. In December 1981, the student suffered a seizure at home, and his parents decided not to return him to school after the winter break ended. The school superintendent and the state department of education authorized home-based instruction, but the school district did not provide such services. For two years, there were a number of disagreements over the appropriateness of different proposed placements and evaluations. During this time, the student did not receive special education or related services. However, a placement was finally agreed upon, and the student returned to school. Five years later, when the student turned twenty-one, his parents were notified that he was being discharged as a special education student. His parents appealed the discharge, seeking compensatory education beyond the statutorily required age of twenty-one because of the school district's failure to provide special educational services for the two years in which the placement was disputed. An administrative hearing officer found that the doctrine of laches barred the parents' claim (laches is a defense to a claim where the claimants have delayed in bringing suit, and 1) the delay is unreasonable, and 2) the delay is prejudicial). A federal district court affirmed the hearing officer's decision, and appeal was taken to the U.S. Court of Appeals, First Circuit.

On appeal, the court reversed the district court's grant of summary judgment to the school district. First, it noted that the parents' delay in filing their claim was not so unreasonable as to make the laches defense available unless there was a clear showing of prejudice. Second, genuine issues of material fact existed as to whether the school district was prejudiced by the delay. Since the parents had not been certain that the school district was going to end their son's education when he reached twenty-one, their delay in filing suit was not unreasonable. Further, even if it was unreasonable, the court below should have looked at all the facts to determine if there was prejudice to the school district as a result of the delay. Accordingly, the court remanded the case for further proceedings. *Murphy v. Timberlane Regional School District*, 973 F.2d 13 (1st Cir.1992).

A New Hampshire woman suffering from cerebral palsy, blindness and severe mental retardation brought a civil action against several school districts, the state and the state's commissioner of education, alleging that the defendants deprived her of a free appropriate public education and related procedural protections in contravention of the Individuals with Disabilities Education Act (IDEA). When she filed this suit, she was 21 years old. The crux of her complaint was that she had not received any educational services during her lifetime. Both the hearing officer and the magistrate judge determined that she was barred from any action because she was over 21. She appealed both decisions to the U.S. District Court, District of New Hampshire.

The magistrate judge and the hearing officer reached the same conclusion, but for different reasons. The hearing officer concluded that he did not have jurisdiction to grant compensatory relief to a plaintiff who was over 21. The magistrate, on the other hand, suggested that the plaintiff was simply barred from seeking compensatory education after her 21st birthday under the ruling of *Honig v. Doe*, 484 U.S. 305, 108 S.Ct. 592, 98 L.Ed.2d 686 (1988). However, the court noted that, in the *Honig* case, the student was asking the court to enforce the "stay put" provisions of the IDEA (then called the EHA) in the future. The U.S. Supreme Court determined that the EHA only gave rights to the student and not the right to demand that the school comply with the EHA either presently or in the future. Here, the court noted, the plaintiff sought compensation for an alleged deprivation of rights which occurred between the ages of three and 21 at a time when she was entitled to those rights. Accordingly, the court found that the plaintiff's present age was no bar to an award of compensatory education. Further, the court determined that a hearing officer may grant compensatory education to a plaintiff over the age of 21. The court determined that the hearing officer's ability to award relief must be coextensive with the court due to the importance the IDEA places on the protections afforded by the administrative process. *Cocores v. Portsmouth, N.H., School Dist.*, 779 F.Supp. 203 (D.N.H.1991).

A Blind New York student sought admission to the state institute for the education of the blind. When the institute rejected his application, the student appealed to the state commissioner of education. A hearing officer determined that the student should be admitted to the institute with a year of free compensatory public education. The commissioner upheld the admission in a subsequent administrative appeal brought by the institute, but determined that the student was not entitled to compensatory education. The student then sued the commissioner in a federal district court, which dismissed the part of the complaint concerning compensatory education, but allowed the student to recover attorney's fees from the institute. The student appealed to the U.S. Court of Appeals, Second Circuit.

The court of appeals ruled that the student was entitled to a year and one-half of compensatory education. The court remanded the case to the district court to vacate the commissioner's decision. The U.S. Supreme Court granted the New York education commissioner's petition for a writ of certiorari. The Court vacated and remanded the case to the court of appeals for further consideration in light of its decision in *Dellmuth v. Muth*, 491 U.S. 223, 109 S.Ct. 2397, 105 L.Ed.2d 181 (1989). In *Dellmuth*, the Court ruled that states could not be liable for tuition reimbursement in lawsuits filed under the Education of the Handicapped Act due to the Eleventh Amendment of the Constitution.

On remand, the court of appeals noted that in its previous decision, it had reinstated the compensatory education award to the student despite the fact that he was over the age of twenty-one. This was because he had been denied his right to a free appropriate education during the extensive delays caused by the state administrative hearings. The appeals court stated that it did not base its previous holding in this case on the abrogation of a state's Eleventh Amendment immunity because it did not believe that argument was necessary to reach its outcome. Rather, its decision had merely vacated a decision by the state commissioner of education. The relief granted was prospective in nature and would be permissible despite the Eleventh Amendment. The court reaffirmed its previous holding. *Burr by Burr v. Sobol*, 888 F.2d 258 (2d Cir.1989).

In January 1990, attorneys for the New York State Commissioner of Education filed a new petition for certiorari with the U.S. Supreme Court, again arguing that the award of compensatory education imposed against the state violated the Eleventh Amendment. The Court vacated the court of appeals' decision and remanded the case for further consideration in light of *Dellmuth v. Muth*, see Section II, above. *Sobol v. Burr*, 109 S.Ct. 3209 (1990).

In November 1985, a mildly retarded young adult sued his local school district and the state of Connecticut. He claimed that he was being denied his right to an education under the EHA. The case was settled through a consent decree which was signed by both the state and local defendants. The consent decree granted the young adult two years of compensatory education at the state's expense.

After passage of the Handicapped Children's Protection Act of 1986 (HCPA), the young adult sued both the school district and the state seeking the attorney's fees he incurred in the earlier lawsuit ($2,633). The school district argued that because the state had to pay the expense of the young adult's compensatory education he had "prevailed" only against the state and not against the school district. According to the district, this meant that the state was solely liable for the young adult's attorney's fees.

The court rejected the school district's arguments. It observed that the young adult did obtain limited success against the school district at the administrative level. Before filing the lawsuit, he had sought a compensatory education through the EHA's due process hearing procedures. The school district was involved in that administrative process. Even though a hearing officer denied the young adult's request for a compensatory education, that denial resulted in the lawsuit which in turn produced the consent decree favorable to him. Therefore, the young adult was deemed to have "prevailed" in the administrative process. The court ruled that the school district should pay twenty percent, and the state eighty percent, of the young adult's attorney's fees. *Counsel v. Dow*, 666 F.Supp. 366 (D.Conn.1987).

The school district then appealed to the U.S. Court of Appeals, Second Circuit. The school district argued that attorney's fees were unavailable for administrative hearings under the HCPA. Furthermore, the young adult failed to prevail against it as required by the HCPA. The young adult argued that he was entitled to attorney's fees from both the state and the school district due to the "relative culpability" of both defendants. The court of appeals held for the school district although it rejected the district's argument that the HCPA failed to afford attorney's fees for work done in connection with administrative hearings. Under the HCPA a court may award attorney's fees to any disabled youth who is a "prevailing party." A youth is considered a prevailing party if he or she succeeds on any significant issue in litigation. The young adult clearly prevailed against the state with respect to the consent decree but the court concluded that he did not prevail against the school district either at the administrative level or in the consent decree. Although a hearing officer found that the school district was fiscally responsible for the young adult's education during his hospitalization, she refused to award compensatory education. The consent decree imposed no obligations or expenses on the school district. The state alone was liable for attorney's fees. *Counsel v. Dow*, 849 F.2d 731 (2d Cir.1988).

A twenty-five-year-old California man with Down's Syndrome brought suit against the California education commissioner on the grounds that he had been excluded from the educational system prior to 1973. The lawsuit alleged that for several years his mother had unsuccessfully tried to enroll him in a San Francisco public school special education class. In 1973, at the age of twelve, he was finally allowed to enroll in the special education program. When he reached the age of twenty-one, his school district sought to terminate his placement in the special education program as provided by § 1415(b)(2) of the EHA. He claimed, however, that he should be allowed to stay in the program to compensate for the seven years he was wrongfully denied a special education prior to 1973. A federal district court denied his request, and he appealed to the U.S. Court of Appeals, Ninth Circuit, which affirmed the district court's decision.

The appeals court ruled that even though the man had been denied access to a special education prior to the enactment of the EHA in 1975, he was barred from bringing suit under any other statute, including the Rehabilitation Act. The court cited the U.S. Supreme Court's 1984 decision of *Smith v. Robinson*, 468 U.S. 992, 104 S.Ct. 3457, 82 L.Ed.2d 746 (1984), which stated that all special education lawsuits must be brought under the EHA. In *Smith* the Supreme Court held that Congress, having passed the EHA, had removed all other Acts as possible bases for special education lawsuits. Extending this doctrine to lawsuits which arose even before 1975, the court of appeals held that the man could make no claim under any Act but the EHA. Since the EHA contains no provision authorizing "compensatory educations" for pre-1975 denials of special educational services, and explicitly states that persons over the age of twenty-one are not entitled to such services, the man's lawsuit was dismissed. *Alexopulos v. Riles*, 784 F.2d 1408 (9th Cir.1986).

The parents of a student with a disability in Georgia sought in federal court a compensatory education for their child, whom they claimed was inappropriately placed. The child had been attending a special education program which had been recommended by his school district. The parents insisted that he be placed in a regular classroom. A series of administrative appeals resulted in a determination that a special education environment would be best for the child. However, the parents disagreed and filed suit in a U.S. district court, which entered summary judgment for the local school board. The parents appealed to the U.S. Court of Appeals, Eleventh Circuit, arguing that their child was entitled to a compensatory education so he could catch up to his age group, having fallen behind his nondisabled peers because of a year spent in the special education program. The court ruled against the parents, stating that there is nothing in the EHA requiring a school board to remediate a previously disabled child. *Powell v. Defore*, 699 F.2d 1078 (11th Cir.1983).

The governor of Illinois and state education officials appealed a court order reinstating the parents' claim for a compensatory education for their child. The officials alleged that the order should be amended on four grounds: 1) the parents' failed to assert the compensatory educational claim at the state level administrative hearing; 2) the requested relief was moot because the child had turned twenty-one and was no longer eligible for special education services; 3) the parents failed to allege sufficient wrongdoing on the part of the school district, i.e., that the school district had acted in bad faith; and 4) state educational officials should not be held legally responsible for the acts of a local educational agency.

A U.S. district court held that the record of the administrative proceedings revealed that the parents did raise the compensatory education issue at the state level hearing. Second, the issue was not moot because Congress did not intend to prevent compensatory educational relief in cases where a child may have passed the age where he is legally entitled to special education services. A contrary holding, said the court, could result in school districts intentionally delaying services until the districts are no longer responsible for the child's education. Third, the state's argument that the plaintiffs had failed to allege sufficient wrongdoing on the part of the state was invalid. The court held that the pre-*Burlington* "exceptional circumstances" test, where parents are entitled to reimbursement only when a school district has acted in bad faith or somehow endangered or threatened the health and safety of the child, did not apply. Here, the parents were asking for prospective relief, and the exceptional circumstances test applied only when retroactive relief is requested.

Finally, the court did not absolve the state defendants from liability for the local school district's actions. The court noted that Congress intended that responsibility for the implementation of all services under the EHA be at the state level. However, the plaintiffs could only sue the state defendants in their official, not individual, capacity. The court held that there was no basis for holding the governor liable. The state's motion to amend the previous order was thus granted in part and denied in part. *Max M. v. Thompson*, 592 F.Supp. 1450 (N.D.Ill.1984). See also *Max M. v. Thompson*, 592 F.Supp. 1437 (N.D.Ill.1984).

CHAPTER EIGHT

SCHOOL DISTRICT OPERATIONS

I. EMPLOYMENT

The following cases address issues involving special education employees. Employee misconduct, discrimination, teachers' constitutional privacy rights, hiring practices, salary, termination, seniority, tenure, and unemployment compensation benefits represent the range of special education employee-related concerns which have been before the courts.

A. Dismissals for Cause

1. Employee Misconduct

A South Carolina teacher was terminated for slapping a student with a disability and for failure to maintain classroom control. The principal at the teacher's elementary school testified that the teacher had been hired to teach five to seven students between the ages of eleven and twelve who had learning disabilities. The teacher had difficulty disciplining her students and frequently called on the principal for aid. The principal stated that the problems should have been handled in the classroom. The teacher also apparently slapped one unruly student with a disability. The teacher appealed her termination to a South Carolina trial court which reversed the school board's decision and ordered reinstatement. The school district appealed to the Court of Appeals of South Carolina.

The court of appeals stated that the board's decision should only be overturned if it was not supported by substantial evidence. The court stated that there was substantial evidence to support the termination. The principal's testimony, as well as that of the school superintendent and a school psychologist, all suported the decision to discharge. The court reversed the trial court's ruling and reinstated the board's decision to terminate. *Hendrickson v. Spartanburg County School Dist.,* 412 S.E.2d 871 (S.C.App.1992).

An assistant teacher was employed at a Florida residential treatment center for emotionally disturbed and mentally disabled children. Two months after he was hired, the teacher struck a student with a pointer. He was cited for violations of school policy and child abuse, and given a final written warning which stated that similar actions would be grounds for immediate dismissal. Nine months later the teacher was involved in another incident in which he threw a cup of coffee at a student. The teacher was dismissed for child abuse. He then applied for unemployment compensation benefits which an appeals referee denied because he had been dismissed for misconduct. Under a Florida statute misconduct was defined as a "substantial disregard of the employer's interests." The teacher contended that his actions did not constitute misconduct and that he should not have been denied benefits. The Florida Unemployment Appeals Commission affirmed the referee's denial of benefits. The teacher then appealed to the District Court of Appeal of Florida, claiming that the referee's decision was not supported by substantial evidence.

The court noted that the appeals referee had found that the teacher exhibited blatant disregard of his employer's interests. This constituted misconduct which warranted denial of unemployment benefits. The court held that the appeals referee's conclusion was supported by substantial evidence, and it upheld the appeals referee's decision. *Sturaitis v. Montanari Clinical School,* 522 So.2d 429 (Fla.App.4th Dist.1988).

In a Maryland case, reinstatement was ordered for a teacher who was also a Catholic priest. The teacher, who had taught in Japan for over twenty years, took employment teaching groundskeeping and home maintenance to severely retarded males of secondary school age at a center for the mentally disabled. His teaching objective was to train students to enter the employment market as handymen or custodial workers. The teaching program consisted of working with a small group of students in the classroom for several days a week, and at various outdoor worksites on the remaining school days.

One day, without authorization, the teacher left four of his six students under a teaching aide's supervision at a recreational center, where they were to clean the building and the adjacent grounds. He took the two remaining students with him to work on other groundskeeping projects. When it began to snow the teacher took the boys to a work shed located behind his home and directed them to work on a project at this site. One of the boys became disruptive and began throwing glass bottles and mishandling the saw he was using. The teacher ordered him to stop his disruptive behavior but to no avail. At this point, the teacher decided that the boy needed to be "timed out," a behavior modification technique used by some special education teachers whereby a misbehaving student is isolated and kept still, in order to calm him and to cause him to reflect on his misbehavior. The teacher ordered the boy to leave the shed and kneel outside on two wooden blocks under a plastic-covered picnic table for an extended period in below-freezing snowy weather. Throughout the incident, the other boy remained inside the shed shivering and shaking from the cold. A neighbor who witnessed the episode called the police, who found the boy sobbing and crying.

The County Board of Education terminated the teacher's employment and the teacher appealed to the State Board of Education, which modified the disciplinary sanction from dismissal to suspension. The County Board appealed and the case finally reached the Court of Appeals of Maryland, which held that the dismissal was not warranted and that the State Board did not exceed its statutory power in imposing a lengthy suspension instead of dismissal. The court took note of the teacher's excellent teaching record and stated that the teacher's action, although improper, was motivated by and intended to modify the behavior of a student whom he could not reach by verbal direction. *Bd. of Educ. of Prince George's County v. Waeldner*, 470 A.2d 332 (Md.1984).

A woman taught in a Missouri school district for thirty-six years. In the 1983-84 academic year she taught remedial math in an elementary school during which there were in effect board of education regulations, which included a provision regarding corporal punishment of students. Teachers were only to administer corporal punishment by blows to the child's "fleshy posterior" in the presence of the principal or a principal's designee. The provision also stated that a teacher should never hit a child on the head. These regulations were placed in the teacher's lounge and/or library of each school building in the district.

In the fall of 1983, the principal received a report from a mother that the teacher had slapped her ten-year-old son. The principal also received at least one other complaint from a parent who stated that the teacher had struck her son in the back with her hand. In March 1984, the district superintendent sent a letter to the teacher alleging that she had violated the board's corporal punishment regulations by striking children without the presence of the principal and by hitting students about the head. It further stated that if any of the shortcomings still existed by May 1, 1984, the teacher's contract would be terminated. After receiving another similar letter from the superintendent the teacher requested a school board hearing on the matter. The board found that the teacher had persistently violated the corporal punishment regulations and her teaching contract was terminated as of October 30, 1984. The teacher appealed the decision to a Missouri circuit court, which ruled for the school board. She appealed this decision to the Missouri Court of Appeals. The court held that the board's decision to terminate the teacher's contract was valid. The lower court decision was upheld. *Shepard v. South Harrison R-II School Dist.*, 718 S.W.2d 195 (Mo.App.1986).

A teacher employed at a Georgia state hospital was terminated for allegedly having sexual relations with a developmentally disabled female resident at the hospital. The teacher requested a hearing. The hearing officer found that a preponderance of the evidence showed no misconduct by the teacher and ordered that he be reinstated. The Georgia Department of Human Resources (DHR) requested a review of the hearing officer's decision by the state personnel board. The board found that the teacher had had sexual intercourse with the resident and this was sufficient cause for dismissal.

The teacher filed a petition in a Georgia trial court seeking review of the board's decision. The trial court found that the record contained no "reliable, probative and substantial evidence" that the teacher had engaged in the alleged misconduct. It reversed the decision of the board and ordered that the teacher be reinstated. The DHR filed an appeal with the Court of Appeals of Georgia. The appeals court held that a trial court may reverse the decision of the state personnel board only where the board's decision is clearly erroneous. It noted that the court may not substitute its judgment for that of the board as to the weight of the evidence on questions of fact. Accordingly, if a court can find any evidence in the record to sustain the board's decision, it must uphold that decision. The question of the credibility of the resident's testimony was to be resolved by the board as finder of fact, and not by the trial court on appeal. The court affirmed the board's findings and held that the trial court erred in reversing the board's decision. *Dep't of Human Resources v. Horne*, 401 S.E.2d 556 (Ga.App.1991).

An Oregon teacher was discharged for gross unfitness and sexual misconduct. He sought reinstatement from the Teachers Standards and Practices Commission. The commission found that the teacher lacked good moral character to serve as a teacher and to hold an Oregon Teaching Certificate. The lack of good moral character was evidenced by the teacher's repeated acts of inappropriate contact with female students. The commission denied his application for reinstatement. The teacher appealed to the Court of Appeals of Oregon.

On appeal, the teacher contended that the commission had not defined its interpretation of "good moral character." The court concluded, however, that the commission offered a "reasoned interpretation" of the term by reference to gross unfitness and to gross neglect of duty. The teacher next contended that the commission erred because the students who complained about him were not called to testify, but rather, the students' allegations were admitted through police reports and testimony of others. Oregon admitted evidence in administrative proceedings of a type commonly relied upon by reasonably prudent persons. The court determined that the hearsay evidence of students' complaints and statements was admissible because it could be relied on by reasonably prudent persons. The court affirmed the commission's decision and denied the teacher reinstatement. *Reguero v. Teachers Standards and Practices*, 789 P.2d 11 (Or.App.1990).

2. Qualification Requirements

An Indiana psycometrist was employed under annual contracts with a city school system for five consecutive years. She was then laid off under an administrative reduction policy adopted by the city school board. The reduction policy eliminated guidance counselor and psycometrist positions and created a new combined position for psycometrist/counselors. However, the school district's attorneys advised the district to reemploy the psycometrist for the following school year because proper cancellation procedures were not followed. Having served five successive yearly contracts, the psycometrist had achieved permanent teacher status under Indiana education law. The district again notified the psycometrist that it would consider her termination at a board meeting. The reasons it stated for termination were declining student enrollment, uncertain funding and lack of seniority. The board based its termination findings on the rescinded administrative reduction policy of the previous year, in which psycometrists were required to obtain certification both as psycometrists and guidance counselors in order to perform in the new job designation. At the same time the psycometrist's contact was cancelled a second time, the school district retained two nontenured employees in psycometrist/counselor positions, allegedly because they both had classroom teacher licenses. The psycometrist appealed her contract cancellation to an Indiana trial court which affirmed the school board's decision. The psycometrist appealed to the Indiana Court of Appeals.

The court found that the school board had illegally created new licensing requirements for its teachers. Under Indiana law, this responsibility was exclusively the state board of education's. The appeals court overturned the trial court's conclusion that the psycometrist was less qualified than the two retained employees. The psycometrist's license satisfied the requirements of the state Commission on Teacher Training and Licensing for School Psychologists I and she was therefore a "teacher" under the state's statutory definition. The two retained employees were not properly licensed and the psycometrist's contract should not have been cancelled. Because the board had cancelled the psycometrist's contract arbitrarily, it had deprived her of a property interest secured by the Due Process Clause of the Fourteenth Amendment. She was entitled to damages and equitable relief under § 1983 of the Civil Rights Act, along with attorney's fees under § 1988 of the same act. The court reversed and remanded the trial court's decision. *Stewart v. Fort Wayne Comm. Schools*, 545 N.E.2d 7 (Ind.App.3d Dist.1989).

A Montana man began his teaching career in 1963. He taught until 1981 when his position was changed to school psychologist. Problems between the psychologist and certain school district employees arose and these problems eventually culminated in his termination by the board of trustees. The psychologist appealed his termination and eventually won a settlement in which he was awarded back pay and fringe benefits due to the improper discharge procedures used by the school district. A proper termination hearing was then held and the board of trustees voted to terminate the psychologist for incompetence. The psychologist appealed to the Montana Supreme Court after a Montana trial court affirmed the board of trustees' decision.

The psychologist contended that the district was required to offer him a teaching position in other areas of his certification. The psychologist was certified to teach science, biology, chemistry and guidance counseling. The court noted that it would be against public policy to require the district to reinstate the psychologist to another teaching position. The district would have been required to terminate a nontenured teacher to make room for the psychologist. The court determined that the goals of the state in educating its students would not be served by such a result. The psychologist next contended that there was insufficient evidence to determine that he was incompetent. The court, however, noted that there was sufficient evidence to support the conclusion of incompetency in his position as school psychologist. Numerous complaints had been lodged by teachers and parents concerning his work. The other psychologist employed by the district reviewed the psychological evaluations, and noted deficiencies in his psychological reports. Four experts reviewed 109 of the 400 cases prepared by the psychologist. As a result of their review, all the experts agreed that the psychologist was incompetent. Therefore, the Supreme Court of Montana upheld the trial court's decision. *Harris v. Bailey*, 798 P.2d 96 (Mont.1990).

Since 1975, a Louisiana school board had employed a woman as a special education supervisor. In 1982, after becoming dissatisfied with her performance, the board obtained an opinion from the Louisiana Attorney General which stated that because the supervisor was not certified for the position, she was not tenured under the state's tenure laws. The board then notified her that her contract would not be renewed for the following year. No dismissal hearing was held. She sued the board in state court, contending that she was tenured, and the court ordered the board to hold a dismissal hearing. When it was done the board once again voted to dismiss, but failed to follow proper procedures. Once again the supervisor successfully sued the board, winning reinstatement and back pay. She then commenced the present lawsuit in federal court, claiming that her federal civil rights had been violated by the board's failure to adhere to state notice and hearing requirements. In essence, she claimed that this failure had deprived her of her federal due process rights.

The U.S. Court of Appeals, Fifth Circuit, disagreed with her claims. The fact that the state courts had forced the board to hold a dismissal hearing completely satisfied all federal due process requirements. Under the U.S. Constitution, due process requires only compliance with minimal notice and hearing requirements; the fact that state law provided greater protection was irrelevant. The court stated: "There is not a violation of due process every time a . . . government entity violates its own rules. Such action may constitute a breach of contract or violation of state law, but unless the conduct trespasses on federal constitutional safeguards, there is no constitutional deprivation." The dismissal of the special education supervisor's federal claims was thus affirmed. *Franceski v. Plaquemines Parish School Bd.*, 772 F.2d 197 (5th Cir.1985).

3. Procedural Improprieties

The Arizona State School for the Deaf and Blind (ASDB) placed a physical education instructor on administrative leave pending investigation by the superintendent of schools. The instructor was then sent a letter notifying him of possible termination for improper attitude, inefficiency and physical assault. The instructor responded by mail rebutting each allegation. However, he was terminated for cause one month later. He then requested a post-termination hearing. The school denied his request. He filed a complaint in an Arizona trial court. The trial court denied the instructor's request for a post-termination hearing and the instructor appealed to the Court of Appeals of Arizona.

On appeal, the instructor contended that the trial court abused its discretion in denying him the right to a post-termination hearing. Before a public employee can invoke the Fourteenth Amendment's guarantee of procedural due process, he must first assert a constitutionally protected interest. Continued employment with a state agency has been recognized as a constitutionally protected claim. The Supreme Court in *Cleveland Bd. of Educ. v. Loudermill*, 470 U.S. 532, 105 S.Ct. 1487, 84 L.Ed.2d 494 (1985), held that before termination, at a minimum, an employee is entitled to oral or written notice of the charges against him, an explanation of the employer's evidence, and an opportunity to present his side of the story. In *Loudermill*, the court held that due process was satisfied if informal pre-termination procedures were followed by a full post-termination hearing. The court determined that the ASDB would be required to provide adequate notice and a hearing before it fired the instructor. Therefore, the instructor was entitled to a due process post-termination hearing. *Deuel v. ASDB*, 799 P.2d 865 (Ariz.App.1990).

A probationary Wisconsin special education teacher's contract was not re-newed. The teacher sued for reinstatement and money damages in a Wisconsin trial court. She asserted that the board violated a provision of the law providing for a private conference between the members of the board and the affected teacher prior to the nonrenewal. The teacher also claimed bias on the part of a board member who was also the parent of a special education student in the teacher's class. The trial court granted summary judgment to the school district, dismissing the complaint. She appealed to the Court of Appeals of Wisconsin.

The appellate court determined that the board was immune from suit for damages because the acts complained of were discretionary rather than ministerial. However, the court determined that there were material issues of fact precluding summary judgment on the claim for reinstatement. A Wisconsin statute provides that a teacher has a right to a private conference with the board prior to nonrenewal of his or her contract. Her complaint alleged that one of the board members voting with the four to three majority not to renew her contract was a student's mother. Therefore, the court concluded that the teacher was entitled to a trial on her claim for reinstatement. Her complaint raised issues of disputed fact material to her claim that the private conference provisions were not properly followed and that there may have been bias on the part of a board member. *Harkness v. Palmyra-Eagle School Dist.*, 460 N.W.2d 769 (Wis.App.1990).

An Iowa woman worked at a school for the deaf as an industrial arts teacher. She was also certified to teach science, math, social studies, and language arts in grades 7-12. Due to a dramatic decline in enrollment, the school superintendent sent the teacher a letter which terminated her contract as a teacher, but gave no reasons for the termination. The letter did, however, notify the teacher of her right to meet with the superintendent privately regarding the termination. At this meeting, the superintendent told the teacher that he was retaining two other teachers with similar seniority because of their additional credentials in driver's education and physical education which made them more versatile staff members. The Iowa Board of Regents affirmed the superintendent's decision to terminate the teacher's contract. She brought an action under 42 U.S.C. § 1983 alleging deprivation of her procedural and substantive due process rights, and asserting a claim of gender-based employment discrimination. The § 1983 claims were tried to a jury, which returned verdicts in the teacher's favor.

On appeal to the Supreme Court of Iowa, the superintendent conceded that his initial letter did not tell the teacher why she had been singled out as the object of the staff reduction. However, he maintained that the termination was not effective until a final decision was made by the regents. The court, however, agreed with the teacher's argument that the letter was a final action by the superintendent to terminate her employment. Further, since she was a tenured employee, she was entitled to oral or written notice of the charges which precipitated the termination and an opportunity to be heard. The court noted that a reasonable jury could determine that she had been denied this opportunity because of the letter written by the superintendent. Further, she had shown that twenty-seven other faculty members with less seniority than herself had not been terminated. Accordingly, the court upheld the jury's verdict in favor of the teacher and held that the award of $150,000 was not excessive. *Lee v. Giangreco*, 490 N.W.2d 814 (Iowa 1992).

In an Arkansas case, the state's supreme court refused to set aside a tenured special education teacher's dismissal, where her attorney did not adequately prove the case in the lower court. Here a special education teacher had been employed in a school district for thirteen years. She had never received an unsatisfactory evaluation and in the past had been used as a model for new teachers. However, soon after a new principal arrived at her school he informed her that her performance was inadequate. He recommended dismissal, and her employment was terminated by the school board shortly thereafter. The teacher sued in county court seeking reinstatement to her position on the ground that her dismissal had been politically motivated. Evidence was presented that the teacher's husband had been a former school employee and had twice engaged in disputes with the superintendent. Also, her husband had twice (unsuccessfully) run for the school board, and a board member had once stated that he wanted to "get a shot" at the teacher. The county court, however, found that the school board had acted out of dissatisfaction with the special education teacher's classroom performance, and she appealed.

The Arkansas Supreme Court upheld the county court. Although admitting that the teacher's attorney had presented strong evidence of political reasons for her dismissal, he had not sufficiently explored during trial the bases for her principal's unsatisfactory evaluations. Without proof that the principal had possessed political motives, the school board was entitled to rely upon his recommendation of dismissal. The Supreme Court declined to intervene. *Kirtley v. Dardanelle Pub. Schools*, 702 S.W.2d 25 (Ark.1986).

After the New York City Board of Education caused the A.C.J. Transportation Corp., a private contractor providing private bus transportation to children with disabilities on behalf of the board, to terminate the contract of a male bus driver following complaints of sexual misconduct, a federal court jury awarded him $15,000 in damages plus attorney's fees. The U.S. Court of Appeals, Second Circuit, reversed the damage award and sent the case back to the district court with instructions to award only nominal damages to the bus driver.

The U.S. Court of Appeals upheld the determination that the bus driver had been deprived of due process, but reversed the award of damages. The district court had acted improperly when it failed to consider that even if the bureau had afforded due process to the disabled student bus driver, he probably would have been fired anyway.

Thus, the compensation for lost salary may have been erroneous. The court of appeals remanded the case for further proceedings with instructions that if the district court concluded that the bus driver would have been fired even if a proper hearing notice had been given to him, the court could award him nominal damages only. *Stein v. Bd. of Educ. of City of New York*, 792 F.2d 13 (2d Cir.1986).

B. Employment Discrimination

Under Title VII of the Civil Rights Act of 1964 (42 U.S.C. § 2000e *et seq.*), a plaintiff has the initial burden to establish that he or she was not hired or promoted due to racial or sexual discrimination by the employer. The plaintiff must show that he or she 1) is a member of a protected minority class; 2) applied and was qualified for the position sought; 3) was not hired or promoted; and 4) that a non-minority was hired or promoted to the position the plaintiff was seeking. Once the plaintiff makes this initial showing, the burden shifts to the employer to articulate a legitimate, nondiscriminatory reason for not hiring the plaintiff. If the employer is able to do so, then the courts will rule in favor of the employer.

1. Disability Discrimination

Discrimination on the basis of handicap by employers receiving federal financial assistance is prohibited by § 504 of the Rehabilitation Act. Such employers must "reasonably accommodate" individuals with handicaps who are "otherwise qualified" for employment.

The U.S. Supreme Court ruled that tuberculosis is a handicap under § 504 of the Rehabilitation Act. Federal law defines an individual with handicaps as "any person who (i) has a physical or mental impairment which substantially limits one or more of such person's major life activities, (ii) has a record of such impairment or (iii) is regarded as having such an impairment." It defines "physical impairment" as disorders affecting, among other things, the respiratory system and defines "major life activities" as "functions such as caring for one's self . . . and working."

The case involved a Florida elementary school teacher who was discharged because of the continued recurrence of tuberculosis. The teacher sued the school board under § 504 but a U.S. district court dismissed her claims. However, the U.S. Court of Appeals, Eleventh Circuit, reversed the district court's decision and held that persons with contagious diseases fall within § 504's coverage. The school board appealed to the U.S. Supreme Court.

The Supreme Court ruled that tuberculosis was a handicap under § 504 because it affected the respiratory system and affected her ability to work. The school board contended that in defining an individual with handicaps under § 504, the contagious effects of a disease can be distinguished from the disease's physical effects. However, the Court reasoned that the teacher's contagion and her physical impairment both resulted from the same condition: tuberculosis. It would be unfair to allow an employer to distinguish between a disease's potential effect on others and its effect on the afflicted employee in order to justify discriminatory treatment. Allowing discrimination based on the contagious effects of a physical impairment would be inconsistent with the underlying purpose of § 504. That purpose is to ensure that persons with handicaps are not denied jobs because of prejudice or ignorance. The Court noted that society's myths and fears about disability and disease are as handicapping as the physical limitations that result from physical impairment, and concluded that contagion cannot remove a person from § 504 coverage. The Supreme Court remanded the case to the district court to determine whether the teacher was "otherwise qualified" for her job and whether the school board could reasonably accommodate her as an employee. *School Bd. of Nassau County v. Arline*, 480 U.S. 273, 107 S.Ct. 1123, 94 L.Ed.2d 307 (1987).

On remand, the Florida federal district court held that the teacher was "otherwise qualified" to teach. The teacher posed no threat of spreading tuberculosis to her students in 1978. When she was on medication, medical tests indicated a limited number of negative cultures. Her family members tested negative and she had limited contact with students. The court ordered reinstatement or front-pay in the amount of $768,724 for earnings until retirement. *Arline v. School Bd. of Nassau County*, 692 F.Supp. 1286 (M.D.Fla.1988).

A Virginia school district employed a recent college graduate as a probationary special education teacher subject to her passing the National Teacher Examination (NTE). The teacher failed the communications skills portion of the NTE six times and was not rehired. Although the teacher was hired as a temporary special education substitute teacher in the following school year, she was removed from that position because school administrators found her classroom management skills weak. The teacher sued the Virginia Board of Education in a federal district court, alleging that she had a learning disability covered by the Rehabilitation Act, and that she had been improperly removed from her position. The court granted the board's summary judgment motion. The U.S. Court of Appeals, Fourth Circuit, reversed, remanding the case to the district court.

On remand, the court noted that the Rehabilitation Act was not intended to eliminate academic requirements or to modify basic academic standards. The teacher had failed to establish that she had an impairment that substantially limited a major life activity, which was required to gain relief under the Rehabilitation Act. This was because psychological opinions at the trial indicated that the alleged learning disability from which the teacher suffered could not be found in *DSM-3RN*, the nationally recognized directory of mental illnesses. The teacher had failed the NTE communications skills test two more times since the lawsuit was filed, and the board of education had reasonably accommodated the teacher by allowing her an extra hour to complete the test, permitting her to use a transcript of the tape and use a tape recorder to listen to recordings more slowly. The teacher was not "otherwise qualified" under the Rehabilitation Act because she could not perform essential functions of a public school teacher, including the ability to comprehend written and spoken communication and manage a classroom effectively. The court awarded judgment to the board. *Pandazides v. Virginia Bd. of Educ.*, 804 F.Supp. 794 (E.D.Va.1992).

The U.S. Court of Appeals, Ninth Circuit, applied *Arline* in a recent case. A teacher of hearing-impaired children was relegated to an administrative position when the school district discovered that he had AIDS. The teacher sued the school board asserting that it had violated his rights under the Rehabilitation Act of 1973 by removing him from the classroom. The teacher's request for a preliminary injunction which would have allowed him to teach until the court could hold a trial and issue a ruling was denied by a U.S. district court. The U.S. Court of Appeals, Ninth Circuit, reversed and issued the preliminary injunction. The court of appeals later issued a decision which sets out the reasons for the issuance of the preliminary injunction.

The court noted that to acquire the preliminary injunction the teacher had to demonstrate a combination of probable success at trial and a possibility of irreparable injury. Under the Rehabilitation Act the teacher could not be dismissed because of his handicapping condition (AIDS) if he was otherwise qualified to teach. The court then applied a test devised by the U.S. Supreme Court in *Arline*. The test provided that "a person who poses a significant risk of communicating an infectious disease to others in the workplace will not be otherwise qualified for his or her job if reasonable accommodations will not eliminate that risk." The court then pointed out the district court's finding that transmission of AIDS was unlikely to occur in the classroom. The court held that the teacher was otherwise qualified for his position because his presence in the classroom would not pose "a significant risk of communicating an infectious disease to others." This finding meant that the teacher would probably succeed at trial.

The court then noted that although the teacher's salary was not reduced when he was transferred to the administrative position, the transfer removed him from a job for which he had developed special skills and from which he derived "tremendous personal satisfaction and joy." The administrative position, on the other hand, involved no student contact and did not utilize the teacher's skills, training or experience. The court also observed that the teacher's ability to work would surely be affected in time by AIDS which has proved fatal in all reported cases. The court concluded that any delay in returning the teacher to the classroom caused an irretrievable loss of the teacher's productive time. This established the possibility of irreparable injury if the preliminary injunction was not awarded.

Because the teacher had shown 1) that he would probably succeed at trial, and 2) that the denial of a preliminary injunction in his favor could cause him irreparable injury the court awarded the preliminary injunction. The teacher was returned to the classroom. *Chalk v. U.S. Dist. Court*, 840 F.2d 701 (9th Cir.1988).

A sixty-one-year-old speech pathologist for the Ohio Mental Retardation and Developmental Disabilities Board became ill, and the board determined that she could no longer perform her job. Because of her age, her supervisor told her that under Ohio law she had only two options: an unpaid medical leave, which would not entitle her to any benefits, or a length-of-service retirement, which would entitle her to a monthly payment. Had she been under sixty, the Ohio plan would have given her a third option: disability benefits with the possibility of returning to work if her condition sufficiently improved. Under this third option, she would have been entitled to receive double the amount of money per month as she would have under the retirement option. Faced with the two choices put to her, she chose the length-of-service retirement. She sued the board in federal district court claiming age discrimination. The district court determined that the employer's conduct constituted "involuntary retirement" because of age. The board appealed to the U.S. Court of Appeals, Sixth Circuit.

The school board contended that the speech therapist was retiring in order to obtain health benefits and that this was not actionable. The court, however, concluded that she was not retiring because of health reasons but that her benefits were limited because of her age. The court of appeals determined that in administering retirement plans employers may not force older workers involuntarily into less desirable retirement programs on the basis of age. The court of appeals affirmed the trial court's decision. *Betts v. Hamilton County*, 897 F.2d 1380 (6th Cir.1990).

A physically disabled Nevada student received a teaching degree in special education and was then licensed by the state of Nevada as a special education teacher. She applied for a teaching position with a Nevada school district and also placed herself on the list of persons available for substitute teaching. She worked as a substitute teacher for over three years and received high praise for her performance. However, she was not offered permanent employment. She then worked as a substitute teacher under a federally-funded temporary contract at another school. The following spring the school had four teaching positions available and offered the teacher a temporary contract. When the teacher received her one-year temporary contract, a permanent position was open in the school district but was given to a student teacher with no teaching experience. The teacher received the most difficult and demanding class assignment at the school. She then filed a discrimination lawsuit against the school district in a U.S. district court.

The court found that under § 794 of the Rehabilitation Act, an otherwise qualified individual with handicaps could not be discriminated against under any program or activity receiving federal financial assistance. The teacher fell within the Act's definition of a person with handicaps and was otherwise qualified to serve as a special education teacher. The court found that the school district never made an affirmative effort to recognize the teacher's disabilities or to accommodate them. Thus she was discriminated against solely on the basis of her disability. The court found for the teacher and awarded her compensatory damages. *Recanzone v. Washoe County School Dist.*, 696 F.Supp. 1372 (D.Nev.1988).

An Iowa residential treatment center for emotionally troubled adolescents employed two women as youth service workers in the girls' cottage. In 1985, the management converted the girls' cottage into a boys' cottage and discontinued providing a residential facility for girls. As a part of this conversion the staff was converted to an all-male staff. After the two women were laid off, they filed complaints with the civil rights commission which awarded backpay and reinstatement. The facility filed a review in an Iowa trial court which found for the employees. The facility then appealed to the Court of Appeals of Iowa. On appeal, the facility contended that it had a legitimate nondiscriminatory reason for not employing women as youth service workers. All the residents were adolescent boys and needed an all-male staff as role models. The court, however, found that there was not sufficient evidence of a bona fide occupational qualification that the youth service workers be male. Therefore, the court upheld the decision of the trial court. *Children's Home v. Civil Rights Comm'n*, 464 N.W.2d 478 (Iowa App.1990).

An applicant for a special education teaching position in Iowa sued a local education agency under the federal Rehabilitation Act and Iowa law alleging that the agency refused to hire him due to his physical disability. The teacher, a resident of Vermont, suffered from several severe disabilities but was able to walk without assistance and to lift children and drive. The teacher applied to the Iowa agency for a job, and was scheduled for an interview in Iowa at his own expense, with possible reimbursement if he were hired.

After arranging the interview, the teacher became concerned that he had not disclosed his disabilities. Because of limited financial resources, he did not wish to fly to Iowa only to be rejected because of his disabilities. He called the Iowa school, explained his disabilities and was told that the job involved transporting children which, in turn, required a bus driver's permit that the teacher probably could not get because of his disabilities. The agency suggested a trip to Iowa would probably be futile.

The teacher then sued in a U.S. district court, which found in his favor. The test of proof for a discrimination claim under the Rehabilitation Act is: 1) that the plaintiff is an individual with handicaps under the terms of the Act; 2) that the plaintiff is otherwise qualified to participate in the program or activity at issue; 3) that the plaintiff was excluded from the program or activity solely by reason of her or his handicap; and 4) that the program or activity receives federal financial assistance.

Here, there was no dispute that the plaintiff was an individual with handicaps within the meaning of the Rehabilitation Act. The court also had little difficulty in finding that the plaintiff was otherwise qualified for the position, because of his superior credentials. The court also found that the plaintiff had satisfied the third and fourth prongs of the test, in that the defendant agency was a recipient of federal financial assistance, including funds received pursuant to the EAHCA and that, with a minimum of accommodation, the school district could have arranged an alternative situation whereby the teacher would not have had to transport children. The court awarded the teacher $1,000 in damages for mental anguish, and $5,150 for loss of earnings. *Fitzgerald v. Green Valley Educ. Agency*, 589 F.Supp. 1130 (S.D.Iowa 1984).

A Kansas school district employed a high school principal who served as its principal for grades seven through twelve. The district also employed the principal's wife, who had contracts to drive a school bus and to sell concessions at school sporting events. The principal had been employed for a period of almost nine years. In the middle of a two-year contract for employment, the district authorized the principal to take a leave of absence due to his alcohol-related problems. The principal was admitted to a hospital for drug and alcohol rehabilitation. He underwent treatment until he received a work release permit nearly two months later. The school board decided to pay the principal for his leave of absence. However, within two months, the school board adopted a resolution consolidating the school district into a one-principal system and resolving not to renew the principal's contract. The board notified the principal that his position had been abolished for economic reasons. The principal accused the board of failing to renew his contract because of his status as a recovering alcoholic. Within several months of the district's nonrenewal of the principal's contract, it advised his wife that her bus driving position had also been eliminated. This was because her bus route had been combined with another route for the following school year. The district also stated that concessions would be operated by high school students and that her contract to sell concessions at sporting events for the school year was terminated.

The couple filed a lawsuit against the district in a federal district court, claiming that it had wrongfully discharged both of them. The lawsuit was filed under several federal statutes, including the Rehabilitation Act of 1973, 29 U.S.C. § 794. The husband stated that the reasons given for nonrenewal by the district were pretextual and that the termination constituted unlawful discrimination under the Rehabilitation Act. The school district filed a motion for summary judgment, stating that the husband and wife had failed to state any claims upon which relief could be granted. According to the court, a party claiming discrimination under the Rehabilitation Act must prove that he is a person with handicaps under the act, that he is otherwise qualified for the position sought, that he is being excluded from the position solely by reason of his disability, and that the program or activity maintaining the position received federal funding. The principal's claims failed because he did not claim that he had been dismissed solely because of his alcoholism. The principal himself had stated other issues, including general dissatisfaction by the district about his job performance. Therefore, the court granted the district's motion for summary judgment. It also dismissed his state law claims for wrongful discharge and the wife's complaint that she had been discriminated against for associating with a person with alcohol-related problems. Noting that the district had not violated the constitutional rights of either the husband or wife, the court granted the district's motions to dismiss the lawsuit. *Pierce v. Engle*, 726 F.Supp. 1231 (D.Kan.1989).

2. Retaliatory Discharge

A New York teacher had various health problems including visual and mobility problems. He was assigned to teach a support skills program to a small group of students who were deficient in mathematics. Shortly after the teacher (in his capacity as the grievance coordinator for the teachers' association) advised his colleagues that they were not obligated to attend an after-school meeting called by the principal, he was informed that the support skills program was being discontinued for lack of space. He was then reassigned as a regular classroom teacher. The teacher requested a hearing with the New York State Public Employment Relations Board (PERB) which determined that the school district had violated the Public Employees Fair Employment Act by eliminating the support skills program in retaliation against the teacher for engaging in a protected activity. The PERB directed the school district to reinstate the teacher in his former position as support skills instructor. The school district appealed to the New York Supreme Court, Appellate Division.

On appeal, the district disputed the factual findings made by the PERB. The court noted that in order to annul an administrative determination, the court must find that the record lacks substantial evidence to support the determination. The court concluded that there was ample evidence to support the PERB's finding. Most convincing was the fact that the support skills program was terminated almost immediately after the teacher advised his colleagues that they were not obligated to attend the after-school meeting. The district's stated reason for terminating the program, lack of space, was clearly pretextual, according to the court, since the program used only the rear corner of a classroom which was shared with another class. The court upheld the PERB's determination that the school district had retaliated against the teacher in reassigning him and ordered him reinstated to his previous position. *Uniondale Union Free School v. Newman*, 562 N.Y.S.2d 148 (A.D.2d Dep't 1990).

A Minnesota social worker employed by a school district was suspended with pay pending an investigation of her work behavior. She instituted a lawsuit alleging defamation and retaliatory discharge. Later that year, the school district terminated her after the hearing examiner concluded that the social worker's suspension was supported by substantial and competent evidence. She appealed her discharge to the Minnesota Court of Appeals. The court of appeals affirmed the termination and the Minnesota Supreme Court denied further review. She then sought to amend her claim to add a charge of violation of her free speech rights. The school district then moved to amend its answer to allege collateral estoppel and moved for summary judgment. The trial court allowed the amendment and granted summary judgment to the school district. After the Court of Appeals of Minnesota affirmed the decision, she appealed to the Supreme Court of Minnesota.

The main issue on appeal was whether the doctrine of collateral estoppel applied to issues adjudicated in a school board proceeding to terminate a teacher so as to defeat her claim for defamation, retaliatory discharge and deprivation of free speech rights. For collateral estoppel to apply, the issue must be identical to the issue raised in the prior agency adjudication, the issue must have been necessary to the agency adjudication, the agency determination must be a final adjudication, the estopped party must have been a party to the prior agency determination, and the estopped party must have been given a full and fair opportunity to be heard on the adjudicated issue. In a termination proceeding, the school board acts in a quasi-judicial capacity. The decision was subject to judicial review; indeed, in this case the school board decision was reviewed and affirmed by the court of appeals. The court determined that the doctrine of collateral estoppel precluded relitigation of the truth of the alleged defamatory statements concerning the social worker's conduct because the issue raised before the board was identical to the issue then before the court. However, the court found that collateral estoppel did not apply to the social worker's retaliatory discharge and free speech claims. "Since no discharge had occurred at the time of the hearing, the school board could not decide the lawfulness of its own conduct as an employer." The court reversed and remanded the case to conduct a trial on those issues. *Graham v. Special School Dist. 1*, 472 N.W.2d 114 (Minn.1991).

3. Racial Discrimination

A black Maryland speech and language pathologist indicated she wished to become an elementary school principal. She had been working as a fulltime speech pathologist, dividing her time between two elementary schools. She had never held a position that involved administrative or supervisory duties. After she received her doctoral degree, she submitted an application to the Elementary Principal Assessment Center (center) which was the first stepping stone for persons interested in becoming an elementary school principal. Applications were reviewed by a screening committee. The committee members worked independently and were not told the names or races of the applicants. The speech pathologist was ranked very low and not admitted to the center. She then filed this suit in a federal district court alleging race discrimination and that her failure to be accepted was in retaliation for her previous filing of a discrimination lawsuit. The school moved for summary judgment.

The court noted that in order to succeed on a claim of retaliation the plaintiff must prove that there was some causal connection between the failure to be accepted and the protected activity. Since members of the selection committee did not know of her previous claims, there was no connection to her nonacceptance. To succeed on her discrimination claim the speech pathologist must show that she was not hired even though she was qualified. At this point the defendant must articulate a legitimate, nondiscriminatory reason for its action, and then the plaintiff must show that the reason given was pretextual. The court noted that the school district showed that it had a nondiscriminatory reason for not admitting the speech pathologist. The race-neutral selection process produced far better qualified applicants which included 26% minorities. Since the speech pathologist failed to produce evidence indicating that the reason given was pretextual, she failed to establish a case of race discrimination. The court granted summary judgment to the school. *Featherson v. Montgomery County Public Schools*, 739 F.Supp. 1021 (D.Md.1990).

The Pulaski County, Arkansas, Special School District decided to have a "head teacher" serve as a liaison to represent the needs of special education students. Two teachers from the special education staff applied for the position: a black male and a white female. When the white female was awarded the head teacher position after being recommended by a two-person selection committee, the black male sued the school district in a U.S. district court claiming racial discrimination. After the district court ruled for the school district the man appealed to the U.S. Court of Appeals, Eighth Circuit.

The court of appeals observed that the district court had determined that the school district selected the white female teacher for legitimate, nondiscriminatory reasons. The school district relied on her prior experiences as a head teacher, the higher evaluations of her overall teaching skills, her flexibility and her superior grasp of the fundamentals of developing individualized educational plans. The appellate court observed that the district court's choice to believe an employer's account of its motivations is a factual finding which may be overturned on appeal only if that decision was "clearly erroneous." The court was convinced that the district court carefully considered all the testimony and exhibits and that its findings had ample support in the trial court record. In ruling that the district court's decision was not clearly erroneous the court of appeals stated that "a factfinder's choice between two permissible views of the evidence cannot be clearly erroneous."

The man also argued that the district court was wrong in ruling that the ultimate burden of proving intentional discrimination remained with him. He said that in light of the school district's past history of racial discrimination, the district court should have shifted the burden to the district to prove by clear and convincing evidence that the reasons were nondiscriminatory for its selection of the white female. The court of appeals refused to apply the higher standard.

A further argument presented by the man was that the district court mistakenly admitted into evidence teacher evaluations of the two teachers made *after* the selection of the white female as head teacher. The court of appeals ruled, however, that even if it was a mistake to admit the postdecision evaluations into evidence, the district court did not consider them in making its findings. Instead, it relied on the testimony of the selection committee members concerning the areas in which they felt the white female was superior. The decision of the district court denying the man's racial discrimination claim was upheld. *Nelson v. Pulaski County Special School Dist.*, 803 F.2d 961 (8th Cir.1986).

C. Collective Bargaining

Two special education teachers taught primary and elementary language for the 1986-87 school year. For the 1987-88 school year, one teacher was reassigned to teach a higher level of language and the other was reassigned to teach intermediate skills development. Both assignments required new classroom preparation. The teachers' association viewed this assignment as a violation of the collective bargaining agreement (cba). The cba stated that involuntary transfers may be made, but they must be unavoidable and should be held to a minimum. A grievance on behalf of the two teachers was submitted to arbitration. The arbitrator determined that the reassignment had been in violation of the cba, and that the school district must reassign the teachers to their previously held positions. The school district filed this action to vacate the arbitrator's award in a New York trial court. After the trial court granted the petition, the association appealed to the Appellate Division. The appellate court affirmed the trial court's decision, and the association appealed to the Court of Appeals of New York. The court of appeals held that, once the arbitrator determined that the involuntary transfer positions violated the cba, it was within his power to order the teachers reassigned. The court of appeals reversed the decision of the trial court and reinstated the arbitrator's award. *Bd. of Educ. v. Arlington Teachers,* 574 N.E.2d 1031 (N.Y.1991).

A Washington special education aide was accused of inappropriately fondling a student with disabilities. The aide was suspended and an investigation was conducted by the school district. The district, later confirmed by the board of directors, decided to discharge him. The aide sought an arbitration proceeding under his collective bargaining agreement. The arbitrator found that the aide did not inappropriately fondle the student and ordered reinstatement, restoration of wages and benefits, and removal of the incident from his file. The aide, upon the arbitrator's judgment, sought damages for emotional distress, defamation and attorney's fees. The trial court granted summary judgment in favor of the district regarding the emotional distress and defamation claims. Additionally, the trial court denied attorney's fees. The aide appealed.

On appeal to the Court of Appeals of Washington, the appellate court affirmed the lower court's decision. Regarding attorney's fees, the court found that the Washington statute did provide for such a recovery. Specifically, the statute encompassed arbitration proceedings as an action and arbitrators' awards as judgments. However, the court held that the right to attorney's fees could be waived by a collective bargaining agreement. In this case, the aide's right to attorney's fees was bargained away through the collective bargaining agreement, and he was not entitled to such an award. *Hitter v. Bellvue School Dist.,* 832 P.2d 130 (Wash.App.Div.1 1992).

A tenured teacher was laid off because of a staff reduction in a Michigan school district. She was covered by a collective bargaining agreement which contained a provision governing layoff/ recall procedures and qualification standards. During her layoff, she completed all state requirements for learning disabilities certification. The teacher sent the school district a teaching certificate showing a new learning disabilities endorsement. The teacher filed petitions with the State Tenure Commission, contending that she should have been recalled to learning disabilities positions which were given to probationary teachers with less seniority and for whom the school district had to seek temporary approval. The commission found that the school district was obligated to recall the teacher for learning disabilities positions before applying for a permit or a renewal for temporary approval of probationary teachers. Both parties sought review of the commissioner's decision in a Michigan circuit court, which affirmed the decision and remanded the matter to the commission for further administrative proceedings. Both parties then appealed to the Court of Appeals of Michigan.

The court held that the school district could fill a position with a person on "temporary approval" only when a fully certified teacher was unavailable. Because the teacher was fully certified, she should have been chosen for any learning disabilities positions ahead of any temporarily approved candidate. Michigan law further provided that a tenured teacher who had been terminated because of a reduction in staff should be appointed to the first vacancy for which she was certified and qualified. A teacher could not waive any of these rights and privileges under state law by signing a collective bargaining agreement. The appeals court affirmed the commission's decision and remanded the matter to the commission for further administrative proceedings. *Hodgeson v. Bd. of Educ. of Buena Vista*, 438 N.W.2d 295 (Mich.App.1989).

An Ohio woman was hired to tutor children with disabilities for the 1985 and the 1986 school years. She agreed to work for seven hours per day at nine dollars per hour for the 1985 school year and ten dollars per hour for the 1986 school year. She agreed to teach for 180 days. According to the comprehensive agreement between the board and the Indian Lake Education Association (teachers bargaining unit), a teacher with her qualifications and experience should have earned $15,585 in 1985 and $19,795 in 1986. By virtue of her contract, she was earning well under those amounts. She then filed a complaint with the Court of Appeals of Ohio which awarded her backpay. The school board appealed to the Supreme Court of Ohio. The board claimed that the ruling that a tutor is a teacher should be interpreted to be prospective only, which would preclude recovery in this case. The court disagreed. It affirmed the appellate court's decision and awarded the teacher backpay, holding that the tutor was a teacher and should be paid the same as other teachers. *State, Ex Rel Travenner v. Indian Lake Local School Dist.*, 578 N.E.2d 464 (Ohio 1991).

An Illinois private school received funding from the state to operate a special education and therapy program for its students. The school also received federal funding to operate a Head Start program. The funds received were kept separate and the school operated each program independent of the other. The school employed 45 individuals, of which approximately 20 were assigned to work in the school's therapeutic program. The National Labor Relations Board (NLRB) found that the school had violated the National Labor Relations Act by threatening and then discharging two psychotherapists because they had repeatedly protested the school's delay in paying their wages and the announcement of imminent layoffs. The school did not dispute these facts but contended that the NLRB lacked jurisdiction over the school's operation since the school received funding from state and federal sources. The NLRB petitioned the U.S. Court of Appeals, Seventh Circuit, for enforcement of the NLRB's order requiring the private school to remedy its unfair labor practices.

The court of appeals held that the school's relationship to state agencies for funding purposes was insufficient to deprive the NLRB of jurisdiction. The unfair labor practices at issue evolved from the state funded therapeutic day school program which was independently operated, funded from separate revenues and staffed with their own employees. The NLRB's jurisdiction was not limited by the fact that the school was operated in part through public funds. The court of appeals ordered enforcement of the NLRB's order requiring the private school to remedy its unfair labor practices. *NLRB v. Potential School for Exceptional Children*, 883 F.2d 560 (7th Cir.1989).

After a collective bargaining agreement between a teachers' union and a school district expired, a series of selective teacher strikes was called by the union. The school district asked for a preliminary injunction prohibiting further strikes which was granted by a Pennsylvania common pleas court. The union appealed to the Commonwealth Court of Pennsylvania, which ruled that the common pleas court was wrong in holding that the strike activity posed a threat to the health, safety or welfare of the public. The school district had argued that the strike infringed upon the right to an education guaranteed to all children with disabilities under the EAHCA. Although the selective strikes did not violate the rights of disabled students in this case, the commonwealth court conceded that the same facts could become aggravated by "some unexpected circumstances or [if] continued for such a period of time" so as to violate the rights of disabled students. Such circumstances, however, were not yet present, and the lower court decision favoring the school district was reversed. *Wilkes-Barre Area Educ. Ass'n v. Wilkes-Barre Area School Dist.*, 523 A.2d 1183 (Pa.Cmwlth.1987).

A group of twelve Indiana school districts and corporations joined together to address the special education needs of school children within their boundaries. Each year, the members of this cooperative entered into a contract governing the cooperative for that particular year. Each year, one member district acts as the cooperative's administrator, known as the LEA. The cooperative's special education teachers then enter into individual teaching contracts with the LEA. This is also done on an annual basis. Each special education teacher is categorized based on how his or her working assignment is apportioned between members of the cooperative. Once categorized, each teacher has the same rights and benefits as if employed by that member school district. According to the cooperative agreement, teachers are to be allowed to retain the salary and insurance benefits of the previous year's assignment if a change in categories or assignment occurs. However, teachers' salaries are calculated separately for each individual's teaching contract by the LEA.

For the 1984-85 school year, a group of special education teachers were assigned to a school corporation that had a 180 day school year. Their previous assignment was to a school corporation that offered a higher salary, but which had a 183 day school year. Their individual salaries were calculated by dividing the higher salary by 183 and multiplying this *per diem* rate by the 180 contract days of their new assignment. This prorated salary was incorporated into each individual teacher's contract with the LEA. Desiring the full contract salary from their previous assignment, the teachers filed a grievance. Their grievance was granted by their principal at an interim level. The disposition by the principal was that pay withheld should be restored. That interim disposition was later rescinded by the superintendent of schools. The teachers sued, claiming that the grievance disposition was valid and binding, and that the salary proration violated the teachers' rights. An Indiana trial court found for the cooperative and the teachers appealed to the Indiana Court of Appeals.

The court of appeals held that the interim level grievance disposition was not binding. The principal had no actual authority to fix or pay the salaries of the teachers, nor was there any reason for the teachers to believe that he had such authority. The court further held that the salary proration did not violate the teachers' rights. The direct benefits the teachers were seeking to draw was pay for three days not actually worked. The amount the teachers received was in line with what they had been promised in both their own contracts and the cooperative agreement between the districts. The court of appeals affirmed the trial court's decision. *Prairie Heights Educ. v. Bd. of School Trustees*, 585 N.E. 289 (Ind.App.1992).

A probationary Wisconsin special education teacher's contract was not re-newed. The teacher sued for reinstatement and money damages in a Wisconsin trial court. She asserted that the board violated a provision of the law providing for a private conference between the members of the board and the affected teacher prior to the nonrenewal. The teacher also claimed bias on the part of a board member who was also the parent of a special education student in the teacher's class. The trial court granted summary judgment to the school district, dismissing the complaint. She appealed to the Court of Appeals of Wisconsin.

The appellate court determined that the board was immune from suit for damages because the acts complained of were discretionary rather than ministerial. However, the court determined that there were material issues of fact precluding summary judgment on the claim for reinstatement. A Wisconsin statute provides that a teacher has a right to a private conference with the board prior to nonrenewal of his or her contract. Her complaint alleged that one of the board members voting with the four to three majority not to renew her contract was a student's mother. Therefore, the court concluded that the teacher was entitled to a trial on her claim for reinstatement. Her complaint raised issues of disputed fact material to her claim that the private conference provisions were not properly followed, and that there may have been bias on the part of a board member. *Harkness v. Palmyra-Eagle School Dist.*, 460 N.W.2d 769 (Wis.App.1990).

In 1978, the Leonard Kirtz Mahoning County School for the Retarded hired a woman as a special education teacher. She was assigned to Developmental Class-room I, which consisted of students who were the least fortunate in terms of educational potential. After three years, she discovered that three teachers for students with the most potential were leaving the school. She made a request to both the superintendent and the principal that she be transferred to one of the vacant positions. However, the county board denied her request and immediately transferred two other teachers, neither of whom had requested reassignment, and hired one new teacher, in order to fill the three vacancies.

The Ohio Supreme Court rebuked the county board for its blatant disregard of its own collective bargaining agreement. Reversing an errant lower court, the Supreme Court reinstated an arbitrator's ruling that because the agreement required the county board to respect a teacher's transfer requests, the board was bound to transfer her. Held the court: "The board argues, and the court of appeals decided, that collective bargaining agreements are not as binding upon public employers as they are upon private employers. It is time to put an end to that notion and categorically reject the argument. Today's decision gives notice that negotiated collective bargaining agreements are just as binding upon public employers as they are upon private employers." The county board was ordered to honor its contractual obligation to the teacher. *Mahoning County Bd. of Mental Retardation and Developmental Disabilities v. Mahoning County TMR Educ. Ass'n*, 488 N.E.2d 872 (Ohio 1986).

The Supreme Judicial Court of Massachusetts vacated a preliminary injunction entered by a three-judge panel of the Superior Court, which had enjoined a strike by bus drivers for special needs children. The case arose when several bus companies, with whom the Boston School Committee had contracted, failed to negotiate a mutually acceptable collective bargaining agreement. The bus drivers, who were affiliated with the AFL-CIO, declined to work without a contract. Parents of children with disabilities were left to make their own arrangements for their children's transportation to and from school. As a result, the parents commenced a class action suit and asked the Superior Court for an injunction ordering the striking school bus drivers back to work, which was granted. On appeal by the school bus drivers' union, the Supreme Judicial Court reversed and held that under Massachusetts law [M.G.L.A. ch. 150E, sec. 9A(b)] the parents could not sue to enjoin the strike because the bus drivers, although ostensibly employed by private bus companies, were public employees. As such, only the public employer could petition the court to enjoin the strike. The court also noted that although state law clearly outlaws any strike by public employees, it just as clearly forbids anyone but the relevant public employer from seeking a back-to-work order. The Superior Court's injunction was therefore vacated. *Allen v. School Comm. of Boston*, 487 N.E.2d 529 (Mass.1986).

The Board of Trustees of the Florida School for the Deaf and the Blind entered into a three-year collective bargaining agreement with its teachers' union, effective July 1, 1983, to June 30, 1986. The agreement contained annual reopeners on salary, insurance benefits and any other two articles chosen by each. Less than one year after the contract had been in effect, the Board of Trustees and the teachers' union reached an impasse over the number of hours teachers were to work each day. A special master was consulted in an attempt to work out a solution, but the board rejected his report. Under Florida law, the board was required to submit the dispute to its legislative body for resolution [F.S.A. sec. 447.403(4)]. The term "legislative body" is defined as the state legislature, any county board of commissioners, any district school board, or the governing body of any municipality. The term also includes any body having authority to make appropriations of public funds. [447.203(10)]. The Board of Trustees informed the teachers' union that in its opinion the board itself was a legislative body. The board claimed that since it transferred monies between categories of appropriations, it was a body that appropriates public funds. Therefore the Board of Trustees unilaterally changed the working hours of its special education teachers from seven to seven and one-half hours per day.

The teachers' union filed a complaint with the Public Employees' Relations Commission and received a ruling that the board had committed an unfair labor practice by unilaterally increasing the working hours of its special education teachers. On appeal, this ruling was affirmed. The court stated that just because the Board of Trustees transferred monies into different categories did not mean it was a legislative body. The board only acted pursuant to statutory authority; it was the legislature itself which did the actual appropriating. Since it was not a "legislative body," the Board of Trustees was without authority to unilaterally modify the collective bargaining agreement with the special education teachers' union. The court upheld the Commission's award of penalties and attorney's fees against the board. *Florida School for the Deaf and the Blind v. Florida School for the Deaf and the Blind, Teachers United, FTP-NEA*, 483 So.2d 58 (Fla.App.1st Dist.1986).

D. Tenure, Seniority, Salary and Benefits

1. Achieving Tenure Status

An Arizona man worked as a special education teacher for a school district for three years, attaining tenure status. He was then informed by the school district that it would be unable to renew his teaching contract due to a reduction of certified staff necessitated by a reduction in enrollment. The teacher then found new employment, signing a one-year contract with another school district. Subsequently, the first school district's director of personnel learned of the availability of a teaching position for which the teacher might be qualified. She called the teacher's residence but received no answer. She then made no other effort to contact the teacher about the position because she knew that he had signed a contract to teach elsewhere. Although the teacher began his new job at the start of the school year, he was allowed to resign during the year when he had the opportunity to start a private school. However, the private school failed. The teacher then sued the first school district, alleging that it had violated Arizona law by failing to offer him the open position. A state trial court determined that the law did not require the school district to offer the position when it knew that he had already entered into a valid and binding contractual obligation with another district. After the trial court granted summary judgment to the school district, the teacher appealed.

On appeal to the Court of Appeals of Arizona, the teacher maintained that the position should have been offered to him. The Arizona law states that certified teachers dismissed for reasons of economy *"shall* have a preferred right of reappointment in the order of original employment." The court found this language to be mandatory, and the school district could not act in derogation of the teacher's right to reappointment. Accordingly, the court reversed the trial court's decision and remanded the case. *Hampton v. Glendale Union High School District*, 837 P.2d 1166 (Ariz.App.1992).

A West Virginia special education school devoted itself primarily to mentally retarded students. Federal law required the school district which operated the school to provide certain students with serious disabilities with education and related services beyond the normal 180 day school year to prevent educational regressions during the long summer vacation. The school could not charge tuition or fees for this summer session. The school's principal posted the job vacancies for the special education summer program, and then conducted interviews with the applicants. The principal's decision on whom to hire focused on the applicants' relationship with the students, giving preference to those who had existing relationships with the students. An applicant who was not hired brought a grievance, claiming that his seniority required the principal to hire him. A hearing examiner ordered the board of education to pay the teacher back wages and benefits. A West Virginia trial court reversed, holding the examiner's decision to be contrary to the law. The teacher appealed to the Supreme Court of Appeals of West Virginia.

On appeal, the teacher argued that West Virginia law on summer schools mandated that the more experienced teacher be hired. The supreme court disagreed. The court stated that the special education summer session was not a traditional summer school and was not governed by the normal hiring mandates of West Virginia law. IDEA hiring requirements for special education summer programs are governed by West Virginia law. Under that law, vacant teaching positions are filled according to the applicants' qualifications. Seniority is only considered for otherwise equal applicants. The principal had made a diligent, professional, and reasonable attempt to hire the best qualified teachers. Therefore, there was no basis for an award of backpay or benefits. *Bd. of Educ. v. Enoch*, 414 S.E.2d 630 (W.Va.1992).

A Michigan county school district decided to reorganize its special education services for hearing-impaired students. Prior to the reorganization, two constituent school districts had provided these services. After the reorganization, the services were discontinued and the Dearborn Board of Education provided them. Five special education teachers who had lost their jobs in the reorganization were hired by the board of education. The teachers were given credit for seniority earned with other districts. A teachers' union representative challenged the propriety of granting teachers credit for seniority earned in other districts. The trial court held in favor of the board of education and the union appealed to the Court of Appeals of Michigan.

The appeals court noted that the Michigan State School Aid Act provided that if special education personnel were transferred from one district to another they would be "entitled to the rights, benefits and tenure to which the person would otherwise be entitled had that person been employed by the receiving district originally." The overall statutory scheme did not recognize a transfer procedure different from the arrangement used in this case. Thus, the five teachers were "transferred" within the meaning of the statute and they were entitled to benefits including retention of their seniority. The court of appeals affirmed the trial court's decision. *Local 681 v. Dearborn Bd. of Educ.*, 431 N.W.2d 253 (Mich.App.1988).

In 1977, a Louisiana teacher began teaching remedial reading and math to slow learners in the fifth and sixth grades. She was employed under the funding of a federal program called Chapter I. In 1985, school authorities were advised of budget cuts in the program. They were given permission to cut Chapter I expenses immediately for the upcoming school year. The principal informed the teacher that she would be dismissed; however, the cut was reconsidered. The next spring the teacher received a letter from the school superintendent telling her that her position would be eliminated due to spending cuts in the Chapter I program. After she unsuccessfully contacted the principals of other schools for employment, the teacher formally requested employment by writing a letter to the superintendent. The superintendent offered her an opportunity to present her grievances at a school board meeting. At the meeting, the teacher complained of her dismissal, but the school board refused to change its procedure for removing probationary teachers. The teacher then filed suit in a Louisiana trial court, alleging the board had failed to follow the procedure required by state law for removing tenured teachers. She also alleged discrimination and sought damages for her injured reputation. In addition, she claimed that if she was not a tenured teacher, the board had not followed its "reduction in force" policy when it terminated her. The trial court found that the teacher was not tenured for purposes of state law. However, the court determined that she was not a probationary teacher, either. She was in a separate category of teacher, each employed under a federal grant. Thus, she was not entitled to the termination procedures under state law. The teacher appealed to the Louisiana Court of Appeal.

The court of appeal held for the school board and affirmed the trial court's decision. It held that she was neither a tenured nor probationary teacher. Therefore, state requirements did not apply. The court also held that the board's "reduction in force" policy did not apply. The policy required the layoffs be used as a last resort, based on seniority, qualifications, and performance. The teacher was in a special position, having been employed under a federal grant. The court upheld the trial court's decision, affirming the layoff. *Abbott v. Claiborne Parish School Bd.*, 550 So.2d 294 (La.App.2d Cir.1989).

A Louisiana civil service employee taught special education classes at a state school operated by the state Department of Health and Human Resources (DHHR). A year after the commencement of her employment by the DHHR, the state legislature created a special school district into which all state special schools were consolidated. The special school district was governed by the state Board of Elementary and Secondary Education (BESE). After the legislative change, state school employees were given the option of remaining classified civil service personnel or becoming probationary teachers under the BESE. The latter option, which the special education instructor selected, would bring the employees under the state tenure laws, which generally require probationary terms of three contract years in order to obtain tenure. Under the statute, the word "teacher" implied a certified employee at a special school who had served the mandatory three contract years. Probationary employees were not entitled to the tenure protection afforded to "teachers," and untenured employees could be terminated upon a simple recommendation of a supervisor. Tenured status required a notice and hearing before any termination action could commence accompanied by valid reasons.

The special education employee served for two years under the BESE, when her employment was terminated. She sued BESE in a Louisiana trial court, asserting that she had served in the same position for over three years. She claimed that her year of service under the DHHR should be considered a contract year with BESE and credited toward her acquisition of tenure. The court granted the BESE's motion for summary judgment, and the employee appealed to the Louisiana Court of Appeal. The court of appeal refused to consider the employee's argument that her year of service with DHHR should be considered a contract year. The court specifically found that the employee was not a "teacher" as defined by Louisiana education law. The tenure provisions of the Louisiana statute applied only to teachers who were certified and met the other requirements of state law. In this case the DHHR employment did not require a teaching certificate, and the employee had not served the mandatory three years of contract service to become a "teacher" in Louisiana. The BESE's motion for summary judgment was correct and the court of appeal affirmed it. *Perkins v. State Bd. of Elem. and Secondary Educ.*, 552 So.2d 735 (La.App.1st Cir.1989).

A West Virginia woman had worked with a university-affiliated organization for developmental disability for thirteen years. Each year she entered into one-year contracts. In 1986, she entered into a one-year contract which appointed her to a position with the university-affiliated Center for Developmental Disabilities. The program was funded solely through grants and contracts from the federal and state governments and was staffed solely by temporary employees who, according to the university, were hired on one-year contracts with no expectation of continued employment. The West Virginia Department of Human Services indicated that the funding for the employee's position would be eliminated in the ensuing fiscal year. The director notified her that her position would be eliminated. She filed a grievance and the hearing examiner determined that she should be reinstated and given backpay, concluding that a program reduction was governed by the university's policies and procedures for program change, which provided that employees with the greatest seniority will be retained when a program is reduced. The hearing examiner found that the woman was the most senior faculty member assigned to the program and that the university, in failing to renew her annual appointment, acted contrary to the policy. After a West Virginia trial court affirmed the hearing examiner's decision, the university appealed to the Supreme Court of Appeals of West Virginia.

On appeal, the university contended that the court incorrectly interpreted its policies. The policies defined a program change as:

> any modification, reorganization, or adjustment of a program
> which involves the anticipated release of a tenured faculty
> member during the term of appointment.

The university argued that the woman was neither a tenured faculty member nor a nontenured faculty member who was released during the term of her appointment, and that the nonrenewal of her contract did not constitute a program change. The court noted that, with respect to nontenured faculty members, for a protected property interest to arise there must be rules, understandings, and a relationship between the employee and the institution. The record indicated that although the employee was hired under a contract which provided for one year of employment only, she had been hired under such contracts for many years. She had worked at the university's affiliated Center for Developmental Disabilities from 1976 to 1980. She had always been offered a new contract, even though at times grants had been terminated. Thus, the court determined that she had a reasonable expectation that her employment would continue. However, due to the unavailability of grant money, she was not entitled to an award of backpay. Unlike an ordinary case, this unavailability eliminated any pool of money from which an award of backpay could be made. *West Virginia Univ. v. Sauvgeot*, 408 S.E.2d 286 (W.Va.1991).

2. Transferring Tenure Status

An Indiana teacher held a public school teacher's certificate with elementary and disabled endorsements. The teacher signed a regular teacher's contract with an Indiana School. The school board assigned the teacher to a special education class. A month later the teacher requested medical leave from the special education position because of stress related problems. The leave was to last only as long as it took to reassign her to a regular education class. The board denied the teacher's request to be transferred, but approved her request for immediate medical leave. After the board failed to assign her to a regular class which became available in January, she sued the board in an Indiana trial court. The court found for the teacher, and the board appealed to the Court of Appeals of Indiana, Third District.

The court of appeals held that the teacher was entitled to compensation for the salary she would have received had the board assigned her to the elementary teaching position. The court noted that state law required that where a board had granted a leave of absence, the teacher had the right to return to a teaching position for which she was certified. The teacher was certified, qualified and had a statutory right to return to the elementary teaching position. Because the board did not transfer her to the open position, it had failed to honor her statutory right. The court of appeals affirmed the trial court's decision. *Jay School Corp. v. Cheeseman*, 540 N.E.2d 1248 (Ind.App.3d Dist.1989).

When an Arkansas school district delayed and hindered the implementation of a special education program, the principal of a school and several teachers discussed these problems with the administrator of the program, then with school district administrators and the school board. When these efforts proved fruitless, the principal and teachers sent a letter to the state department of education. The letter enumerated instances of failure to follow established procedures relating to the education of disabled students. The department of education conducted an investigation which resulted in a conclusion that the school district had not followed proper procedures in the placement of students with disabilities.

Afterward, several of the teachers' contracts were not renewed, and the principal and one teacher resigned under pressure by the school board. The principal and teachers sued the school district and various administrators seeking money damages for the retaliation they suffered in response to the letter. They claimed the retaliation was a violation of their First Amendment right of free speech on a matter of public concern in their community. When a U.S. district court ruled in favor of the principal and teachers, the school district and administrators appealed.

The U.S. Court of Appeals, Eighth Circuit, determined that the letter concerned the quality of education in the community and the school district's observance of federal policy as prescribed by Congress for the welfare of children with disabilities. The letter therefore involved a matter of public concern and was protected by the First Amendment. The lower court's ruling was upheld. *Southside Pub. Schools v. Hill*, 827 F.2d 270 (8th Cir.1987).

The following case illustrates that, for purposes of tenure, a transfer from a position not related to special education to one involving special education responsibilities is not a lateral transfer. After an "excessed" elementary school principal in New York was assigned to a position as assistant to the director of special education, he filed suit against the school district claiming that his tenure rights had been violated. Following dismissal of his case by a lower court, he appealed to the Supreme Court, Appellate Division. The major issue before the appellate court was whether the new assignment, which would have required the principal to serve a 3-year probationary term, was outside the area in which he was granted tenure. The school district argued that the two positions were essentially the same because both included implementation of the curriculum and supervision of the teachers. The court rejected this argument, pointing to the unique responsibilities in special education and the need to focus on the remedial needs of certain groups of students in accordance with federal and state law. The court ordered the plaintiff appointed to a suitable position. *Cowan v. Bd. of Educ. of Brentwood Union*, 472 N.Y.S.2d 429 (A.D.2d Dept.1984).

3. Salary Disputes

A learning disabilities consultant was hired in March 1980 by the Trenton, New Jersey, Board of Education. At the time of hiring he was placed at step eleven of the learning consultants' salary guide. Beginning in the fall of 1980, and for each academic year thereafter, the consultant was moved up one step on the salary guide. By 1983 he was at step 15, was being paid an annual salary of $27,227 and was scheduled for an increase to $28,569.

The school board and the teacher's association, however, had negotiated an agreement before the learning disabilities consultant was hired which provided that any employee hired after February 1 of any year would remain at his or her step on the salary guide during the following academic year. The school district, which had erroneously advanced the consultant on the salary guide in the fall of 1980 even though he had been hired after February 1, did not realize its error for three years; it then reduced the teacher to step fourteen and made a reduction in his salary from $28,569 to $27,751 a year. When the consultant received his first reduced check he contacted the personnel office immediately. His check was not corrected. On January 30, 1984, he informed the Board of Education that he had retained an attorney and requested back pay and reinstatement to his proper salary level. On February 8, 1984, the board sent him a letter refusing his request.

The consultant filed a complaint with the New Jersey Commissioner of Education. The case was heard by an administrative law judge (ALJ), who ruled that the complaint had not been filed within the required ninety days of the date the consultant first received notice of his salary reduction. The ALJ held that notice of the salary reduction had been accomplished by the consultant's receipt of his paycheck. The State Board of Education affirmed the ALJ's decision, and the consultant appealed to the New Jersey Superior Court, Appellate Division.

The court found that under the New Jersey Teacher Tenure Act the consultant had a vested right in his salary. Therefore, it held that the unilateral decision by the school district to reduce his salary violated his rights under the Act. It said that the fact that the consultant's paycheck was less than what he expected did not constitute proper notice that his salary was being reduced. It was not until the school board's letter of February 8, 1984, denying his requests for back pay and reinstatement to his proper salary that he was put on notice that a "dispute" existed. The court remanded the case to the Commissioner of Education for resolution of the dispute on the merits. *Stockton v. Bd. of Educ. of City of Trenton*, 509 A.2d 264 (N.J.Super.A.D.1986).

A group of special education teachers instituted a proceeding challenging the constitutionality of the compensation structure of their collective bargaining agreement in a New York trial court. The agreement gave increased wages and benefits to special education teachers who taught severely disabled students in state mandated year-round education programs, while teachers who taught mildly disabled students during the school year and in optional summer programs were paid less. The teachers claimed that this distinction was arbitrary, capricious, and in violation of their right to equal pay for equal work. An administrative review board dismissed the action, finding that a rational basis existed for the distinction. The teachers appealed to the New York Supreme Court, Appellate Division. On appeal, the court held that a classification which benefits one group of individuals economically, but does not benefit members of a similar classification, can be constitutional. The court concluded that the state's objective, to encourage those teachers with experience teaching the most profoundly disabled to participate in the year-round education program, was a valid objective. The court affirmed the administrative panel's dismissal of the teachers' suit. *Litman v. Bd. of Educ. of City of New York*, 565 N.Y.S.2d 93 (A.D.1st Dep't 1991).

4. Seniority and Tenure Benefits

Special education employees in New York challenged the infringement of their seniority rights in the following two cases. In the first, two tenured teachers employed by the New York Board of Cooperative Educational Services (BOCES) in the special education area brought suit alleging that after two school districts for which BOCES provided special education services established their own special education programs, no longer utilizing the BOCES program, BOCES improperly dismissed them. The teachers were hired as of the date of their dismissal by the respective school districts as teachers in their programs. The teachers sought to have themselves reinstated to their former positions as tenured BOCES teachers. The court held that because BOCES retained teachers in the special education tenure area having less seniority than the dismissed teachers, the abolition of the teachers' positions may have violated teacher tenure law. The New York Supreme Court, Appellate Division, reversed a lower court ruling dismissing the teachers' complaint and remanded the case to the lower court, which was to reinstate the teachers if it found that teachers with less seniority than the dismissed teachers were retained by BOCES, in violation of New York tenure law. BOCES would then be directed to follow an appropriate procedure for correctly determining the teachers with less seniority to be made eligible for hiring by the school districts which had established their own special education program. *Koch v. Putnam-Northern Westchester Bd. of Coop. Educ. Serv.,* 470 N.Y.S.2d 651(A.D.2d Dept.1984).

A former special education classroom teacher brought a claim for disability retirement benefits against the Teachers' Retirement System of New York. The teacher suffered from an emotional disorder and right eye dysfunction which she claimed were causally related to the physical injuries and stress she suffered while employed. The Teachers' Retirement System denied benefits and the teacher brought an Article 78 proceeding seeking to vacate its determination in a New York trial court. The teacher argued that she was entitled to disability benefits on the ground that the accumulated on-the-job stress of her ordinary work activities caused her present disabilities. The court noted that the teacher must prove that an employment-related accident caused her disabilities. She had presented no expert medical opinion linking her present disabilities to her employment. Therefore, because an activity performed in the ordinary course of employment does not constitute accidental injury, the court denied her disability retirement benefits. The decision of the Teachers' Retirement System was upheld. *Impellizeri v. Teachers' Retirement System,* 570 N.Y.S.2d 20 (A.D.1st Dep't 1991).

The Director of Special Education Services for a local school district in South Dakota alleged that the board of education acted illegally in not finding him another position in the district after his position was eliminated due to economic necessity. The director argued before the state supreme court that the board was obligated to follow the state's staff reduction policy. Under the statute, he argued, he was classified as a "teacher" and thus was protected from termination under the circumstances. The board insisted that despite the fact that the director held a teaching certificate and was employed under a "Teaching Contract," only certain provisions of the statute were applicable to him because his employment was administrative in nature. The director, continued the board, was an "other administrative employee" under the statute. The director's other certifications, claimed the board, were not taken into account. The court held in the director's favor. The board acted illegally in not following the staff reduction procedures applicable to continuing contract teachers. Though the director may have been classed as an "other administrative employee" under the statute, the statute also provided that such persons were "teachers" for purposes of tenure. *Burke v. Lead-Deadwood School Dist. No. 40-1,* 347 N.W.2d 343 (S.D.1984).

A different result was reached by the Supreme Court of Iowa in a case involving a teacher who had filled a special education teaching vacancy for one year. The teacher was not special education-certified but was given special permission by the State Department of Public Instruction to teach a special education class, because of the school district's inability to find a replacement for a special education teacher who had resigned. At the close of the school year, the "substitute" teacher expressed an interest in returning the following year either in the same capacity or as a regular classroom teacher. He also offered to receive special education training over the summer months. However, he was not reemployed. The state Supreme Court affirmed a lower court ruling in the district's favor, finding that the teacher was a "temporary substitute" and therefore did not have probationary teaching status. The statutory tenure provisions thus did not apply to the teacher and his termination was upheld. *Fitzgerald v. Saydel Consol. School Dist.*, 345 N.W.2d 101 (Iowa 1984).

In a case arising in the state of Washington, unemployment compensation benefits were claimed by employees of a state school for the deaf and blind. The noninstructional employees appealed a decision of the Washington Commissioner of the Department of Employment Security who denied them unemployment benefits during the summer closure of the schools. Washington Unemployment Compensation law prescribes that to deny unemployment benefits to an employee off work during the summer months, written notices to the employee must state that he or she will perform services at the end of the summer months. The civil service employees claimed that written notices they received advising them of the summer closure of the schools, informing them that they were being placed on "leave without pay," and stating that they would be expected to resume their positions at a time to be specified later, were ineffective when applied to civil service employees to exempt them from the unemployment compensation statute. The schools argued that the employees were noninstructional employees rendering services for an educational institution, thus making them ineligible for unemployment benefits while not working during summer recess. The Court of Appeals of Washington was persuaded by the schools' argument and found that the employees were not entitled to unemployment benefits. The written notices the employees received satisfied the unemployment compensation statute's exemption requirement by being "reasonable assurances" of reemployment and were consistent with civil service law. *Alexander v. Employment Security Dep't of the State of Washington*, 688 P.2d 516 (Wash.App.1984).

A West Virginia county board of education advertised for a teaching position for the gifted, grades five through eight and for the learning disabled, grade six. After the board hired one applicant, another applicant claimed she was better qualified and filed a petition for a writ of mandamus in a West Virginia trial court directing the board to appoint her. A writ of mandamus issues where there is a clear legal right. The court denied the petition and the applicant appealed to the Supreme Court of Appeals of West Virginia.

Courts have granted boards of education broad discretion in matters relating to the hiring of school personnel. However, this discretion must be exercised in a manner which "best promotes the interest of the schools." The court determined that the interest of the schools would be promoted when the hiring decisions were made on the basis of the qualifications of the persons hired. The court then compared the qualifications of the applicants and noted that the plaintiff applicant had fourteen years teaching experience, a master's degree, was certified to teach grades kindergarten through eight, and was in the process of receiving her certificate to teach gifted children. The applicant who was hired had only a bachelor's degree, was certified to teach grades kindergarten through six, and was not in the process of receiving a certificate to teach gifted children. Since the position in the present case was to teach gifted and learning disabled students grades kindergarten through eighth, the court found the plaintiff applicant clearly had the superior qualifications. Accordingly, the court ordered the board to hire the plaintiff, and awarded backpay and attorney's fees. *Egan v. Bd. of Educ. of Taylor County*, 406 S.E.2d 733 (W.Va.1991).

II. BUDGET AND FINANCE

The following cases concern litigation over special education budget and finance. The first cases deal with disputes concerning state and federal funding.

A. State and Federal Funding

The U.S. Department of Education regulates funds allocated to states under the Individuals with Disabilities Education Act (IDEA). A state receives federal funds based on the number of children with disabilities receiving special education and related services. The IDEA also includes provisions to ensure that federal funds are used to defray the excess costs of educating children with disabilities and to supplement the amount spent by the state for this purpose. The Spokane School District received federal funds for the purpose of educating its disabled children. Prior to the 1980-81 school year, Spokane taught disabled children in self-contained classrooms. Because self-contained classrooms were not available in all schools, extensive transportation was necessary. The Association of Retarded Citizens challenged the use of self-contained classrooms as a violation of the EHA requirement of the "least restrictive environment." In response, Spokane changed its system to teach all but the most severely disabled children in regular classrooms. As a result, the district spent less for the special education of disabled children in the 1981-82 school year than in the 1980-81 school year. In 1983, the Department of Education audited Spokane's use of the federal funds and determined that the federal funds were used to "supplant" state funds rather than supplement them because the amount spent in 1981-82 was less than in 1980-81. The district appealed to the U.S. Court of Appeals, Ninth Circuit.

On appeal, Spokane contended that so long as it did not use federal funds to displace state funds for particular costs, the statute was satisfied. The Department of Education, however, argued that the statute prohibited local agencies from using federal funds without using state funds in a particular program and further required local agencies to maintain the same level of funding efforts each year. The court determined that Spokane's interpretation would allow a local agency to reduce its own expenditures for educating children with disabilities without losing federal funds by simply eliminating particular programs. Therefore, the court determined that this reading of the statute was unreasonable. The court affirmed the Department of Education's decision to require maintenance of local funding efforts each year. *State of Washington v. U.S. Dep't of Educ.*, 905 F.2d 274 (9th Cir.1990).

Under the Rehabilitation Act, 29 U.S.C. § 701 *et seq.*, the U.S. Department of Education is responsible for administering the federal vocational rehabilitation (VR) program. Accordingly, the department distributes grant money to states to assist them in providing services to individuals with disabilities. The department awarded the state of Missouri a grant which was administered by the state Department of Social Services (DSS). During the fiscal year of the grant, some DSS employees worked both on the federally-funded VR services and on state-funded programs under the Missouri Bureau of the Blind (BOB). The DSS channeled over $190,000 in VR grant money to its employees' salaries in that year. No records were kept, however, of attendance or the proportionate amount of time the employees spent on these two separate cost objectives, although the DSS did conduct a time study of employee activity during four nonconsecutive weeks during the year. A state auditor determined that the DSS accounting procedures did not meet the standards of federal regulation, and an administrative law judge eventually ordered the DSS to repay the $190,000. The Secretary of Education affirmed the order, and the DSS petitioned the U.S. Court of Appeals, Eighth Circuit, for review.

On appeal, the DSS argued that a cost allocation plan it had submitted to the U.S. Department of Health and Human Services (HHS) for the relevant time period authorized the DSS's VR expenditures for employee salaries since the cost allocation plan included salary distribution procedures for employees working on BOB programs and the plan had been approved by HHS. Therefore, the normal accounting procedures were not necessary. The court disagreed. An HHS-approved cost allocation plan can only be applied, according to federal regulations, to "indirect costs." Indirect costs are those which cannot be specifically identified with a particular cost objective. The court found that federal regulations clearly showed that employee compensation is a direct cost, that is, one that can be identified with a particular cost objective. Since the DSS's employees were either working on VR or BOB projects at any particular time, their compensation could be identified with one particular cost objective. As such, they were direct costs. Therefore, the cost allocation plan could not be a substitute for proper accounting procedures. Finally, the court held that there were no mitigating circumstances to relieve the DSS of its obligation to return the funds in dispute. *Missouri D.S.S. v. U.S. Dep't of Educ.*, 953 F.2d 372 (8th Cir.1992).

The Department of Education sought to terminate federal education funds to a Georgia school district because the school district refused to cooperate with an investigation by the Office of Civil Rights (OCR) in eight parental complaints of discrimination against children with disabilities. The school district contended that the Office of Civil Rights did not have the authority to investigate the complaints at issue. The issue was the relationship between the Education of the Handicapped Act and the Rehabilitation Act. In 1984, OCR began an investigation of the school district's special education program based on parental complaints concerning possible violations.

The school district refused to cooperate with the investigation, contending that the residential placement regulation was contrary to the Rehabilitation Act and thus could not authorize a lawful investigation because by requiring residential placement of children with disabilities it imposed an obligation to engage in affirmative action (which went beyond the scope of § 504 of the Rehabilitation Act). Further, the school district contended that the alleged violations of the right to a free appropriate education, including residential placement, must be addressed through EHA procedures rather than through § 504. The OCR insisted that the school district was obligated to cooperate with the investigation and, faced with continued resistance, it initiated fund termination proceedings. The school district initiated court proceedings to prevent the OCR from terminating its funds. A federal district court dismissed the action on the grounds that the school district had failed to exhaust its administrative remedies and the appellate court affirmed, holding that the county was required to exhaust administrative remedies before the court could address the merits of the case. The remand accomplished little towards the parties' basic dispute over the proper interpretation of the EHA and the Rehabilitation Act.

The school district contended that the court should strike down the residential placement regulation and order the OCR to restore its terminated funds because the regulation was beyond the scope of § 504. The court rejected the school district's contentions and affirmed the OCR's termination of its funds because the administrative law judge correctly determined that the school district violated the OCR's regulation requiring grantees to cooperate with investigations. Thus, the school district could prevail only if it could establish that the residential placement action required affirmative action in violation of § 504. The court rejected the county's contention that the residential placement action was invalid. It affirmed the decision of the trial court because in the absence of a further developed record and the application of OCR's actual cases of discrimination, the court could not say that the EHA deprived the OCR of the jurisdiction to investigate the complaints of discrimination at issue in this case. *Freeman v. Cavazos*, 939 F.2d 1527 (11th Cir.1991).

Before the passage of an amendment to the Louisiana Constitution, the state's public educational system was under the control of the state superintendent of education. The amendment created the Board of Elementary and Secondary Education (BESE). The board was supposed to take over most of the superintendent's duties, but power conflicts between the two often arose. Before the superintendent's position was eliminated in 1988, the BESE and the superintendent jointly applied to the U.S. Department of Education (DOE) for funds under the Education of the Handicapped Act (EHA). After the DOE approved the funds, they were distributed, as was customary, to the superintendent. The BESE discovered that the superintendent planned to use the funds on a program it believed did not fulfill federal requirements. The BESE contacted the DOE about the alleged misexpenditures. After the DOE completed an audit, it ordered the BESE to repay the funds, concluding they had been misspent. The BESE contended that it was not responsible because it had not received the funds. After the Education Appeal Board ordered it to return the funds, the BESE appealed to the U.S. Court of Appeals, Fifth Circuit.

The court of appeals affirmed the order. It held that since the BESE was a "recipient" under applicable regulations, the DOE could order it to repay the funds. The BESE had significantly not denied the finding that the funds had been misspent. DOE could not be estopped from ordering repayment because the BESE had warned it that the funds were going to the superintendent. *Louisiana State Bd. of Educ. v. U.S. Dept. of Education*, 881 F.2d 204 (5th Cir.1989).

The U.S. Department of Education (DOE) awarded funds to the Michigan Department of Education under a grant program administered by the DOE's Rehabilitative Services Administration. The grant was intended to fund vocational rehabilitation and independent living programs to help individuals with disabilities find employment. The DOE inspector general's office conducted an audit of the Michigan education department and determined that thirteen of 259 audited authorizations for client service expenditures were to be disallowed. On the basis of the audit, the DOE demanded a refund of $465,732. The amount demanded reflected a recalculation for possible error. The Michigan department challenged the audit determination in an administrative hearing conducted by the DOE's Education Appeals Board (EAB). The EAB upheld the audit and the Michigan education department appealed to the U.S. Court of Appeals, Sixth Circuit.

On appeal, the Michigan department argued that the DOE's determination was without authority. It also complained that the audit was based upon an erroneous sampling and that the refund demand was incorrect as a result. The DOE argued that its decision was supported by substantial evidence and that its random sampling technique was appropriate. The appeals court agreed with the DOE. The administrative hearing was supported by substantial evidence and was within the Rehabilitation Act's statutory scheme. It would be impossible for the EAB to audit the over 6,600 cases coming under the grant. The amount demanded had been reduced to compensate for possible errors and the state had had an opportunity to present its own evidence of possible errors in the administrative hearing. Because the administrator had not used an arbitrary statistical sample for the audit, there was no basis for disallowing it. The court affirmed the decision for the DOE. *Michigan Dep't of Educ. v. U.S. Dep't of Educ.*, 875 F.2d 1196 (6th Cir.1989).

State educational agencies must allocate federal funds in a timely fashion or risk forfeiture. Under the EHA, states receive grants of federal funding which are then subgranted to qualified local educational authorities (LEAs) for use in providing educational services to children with disabilities. Each LEA is entitled to a share of the state's grant based on its proportionate share of the state's population of disabled children. If an LEA does not spend its subgrant in a timely fashion, the funds revert to the state. Also, if the state fails to obligate funds to LEAs by the end of the fiscal year succeeding the fiscal year for which the funds were appropriated, those funds have to be returned to the U.S. Department of Education.

Several LEAs returned unspent 1979 funds to the state of Massachusetts four days before the deadline for state obligation of funds to LEAs. The state, however, directed these funds to LEAs which had received only partial subgrants for 1979 after the obligation period had ended. Because these LEAs had been less than fully funded by 1979 subgrants the state allowed them to apply the reallocated funds to expenditures that they had paid for themselves prior to the deadline. The U.S. Department of Education determined that Massachusetts had impermissibly retained and reallocated the funds and Massachusetts petitioned for review of this determination in the U.S. Court of Appeals, First Circuit. The court noted that the department's interpretation was reasonable and "entirely consistent" with the EHA plan for fund allotment. The court upheld the department's decision that Massachusetts had impermissibly retained and reallocated the funds. *Massachusetts Dept. of Educ. v. U.S. Dept. of Educ.*, 837 F.2d 536 (1st Cir.1988).

In New York prior to July 1, 1989, tuition rates for educational services for preschool children with disabling conditions were set through the family court. Since the system was found not to comply with federal law, the legislature authorized the Commissioner of Education to annually determine the tuition rate beginning with the 1990-91 school year. The interim rate for the 1989-90 school year was to be selected by the commissioner. The commissioner issued a letter to the providers of the services giving them two options to set the interim rate. The providers chose one, but the commissioner did not set the rates based upon these options. Further, the commissioner directed the rates to differ based upon whether the child was from inside or outside Suffolk County. Several providers then instituted this action to annul the interim tuition rate determination. The trial court granted partial relief to the providers and they appealed to the Supreme Court, Appellate Division.

The commissioner had based his interim rate on the previous contracts. However, the court noted that the legislative enactment superseded any earlier contracts. Therefore, the court determined that the commissioner acted arbitrarily and capriciously in basing the rates on these previous contracts. Further, the court determined that the difference in tuition rate based upon residence in Suffolk County violated the Equal Protection Clause. The court modified the district court's decision and directed the trial court to grant the providers' request for an entire rate adjustment. *Long Island Ass'n for Children v. Sobol*, 572 N.Y.S.2d 787 (A.D.3d Dep't 1991).

B. Local Funding Disputes

A Pennsylvania school district submitted a special education plan and budget to its intermediate unit as required by Pennsylvania law. The intermediate unit, which was composed of several local school districts, in turn submitted the plan and budget to the state special education bureau. The bureau reviewed the plan and budget, and disapproved several items, including the district's claim for reimbursement of costs for personnel in related services such as occupational and physical therapy and psychiatric services. The special education bureau conducted a hearing at the district's request, and the state secretary of education granted the bureau's motion for summary judgment. The secretary determined that the state legislature had specifically omitted reimbursement for the claimed expenses, by excluding them from the statute under which the district sought reimbursement. Personnel costs for assistance in the related services of occupational therapy, physical therapy and psychiatric services were not properly reimbursed by the state. The school district appealed to the Commonwealth Court of Pennsylvania.

The court reviewed Pennsylvania state legislation and administrative regulations which were based on both state and federal laws. Although school districts were required to provide a free appropriate education for exceptional students based upon their unique needs, state regulations did not require reimbursement to districts for all related services personnel. The court agreed with the secretary's finding that the failure by the legislature to identify specific related services personnel in the statute was an intentional omission. The Pennsylvania statutory scheme required the education bureau to reimburse intermediate units rather than individual school districts. The intermediate units had no individual taxing powers like local districts and were directly funded by the state. Accordingly, it was reasonable to reimburse the intermediate unit for special education related services costs performed by the intermediate unit while at the same time not approving related services expenses at the school district level. The court affirmed the secretary's decision for the special education bureau. *Bethlehem Area School Dist. v. Carroll*, 616 A.2d 737 (Pa.Cmwlth.1992).

A provider of educational services to children with disabilities applied to the New York State Commissioner of Education and the New York City School District for a tuition rate increase for the preschool-age and school-age children with disabilities it serviced. An increase was granted, raising the rate from $24,831 to $31,098, an increase of about 25%. The service provider then applied for a tuition rate increase for the children with disabilities under the age of three that it serviced. The service provider was given a 5% increase for those children. The service provider appealed that rate increase to the state Board of Education, claiming it was inadequate compared to the 25% increase it had received for the older students. The board held that the rate was adequate.

The service provider sued, seeking a declaration that the district's and board's actions were arbitrary and capricious. It sought an order directing the department to increase the tuition rate for children with disabilities under the age of three to the same rate as three to five-year-old children. However, the trial court held that only the Family Court was authorized to approve tuition expenses for children under the age of three. The service provider appealed to the New York Supreme Court, Appellate Division.

The appellate court stated that the New York Family Court Act authorizes the Family Court to issue an order to provide for a disabled child's education including the expenses incurred for any child in need of special education services. While state law requires the state commissioner of education to determine the tuition rate for approved special programs or services provided for preschool children, that authority is specifically limited to children between the ages of three and five. Hence, only the Family Court, not the commissioner, is vested with the authority to set tuition rates for children with disabilities under the age of three. Since no order had yet been issued by the Family Court, the current proceeding was premature and had to be dismissed. *United Cerebral Palsy of New York City, Inc. v. Sobol*, 582 N.Y.S.2d 558 (A.D.1992).

C. Residence Disputes

Disputes have arisen when a child is temporarily institutionalized within the boundaries of one school district and the parents reside in another. A child afflicted with Down's Syndrome was placed in a "family home at board" since birth. The home provided room, board, medical and incidental expenses to the child. The parents' home school district reimbursed the school district of the family home until the parents moved. They then sought to have the student's tuition paid by the district in which the student resided. They claimed that the student was a resident of that school district. An impartial hearing officer found for the school district and the parents filed suit in federal court and eventually the U.S. Court of Appeals, Second Circuit, remanded with the instruction that this was an issue of state law. The New York state trial court granted summary judgment to the parents, and the school district appealed to the Court of Appeals of New York.

On appeal, the school district contended that the parents had not overcome the presumption that the child's residence was that of his parents. Residence is defined as the place that the parents or legal guardians reside. This presumption may be overcome by a showing that the parents have given up parental control and that the child's permanent domicile is within the district. To date, the parents had maintained parental control over the student. Therefore, the appellate court affirmed the decision of the hearing officer and found for the school district. *Catlin by Catlin v. Sobol*, 569 N.Y.S.2d 353 (Ct.App.1991).

A Pennsylvania statute established an irrebuttable presumption that students were residents of the school district in which their parents resided. The act provided no opportunity for a hearing to contest the presumption. Although state regulations permitted parents of exceptional children to challenge the type of education received, the regulations did not permit a challenge to the denial of tuition-free education because of the nonresidency presumption. A New York student moved to Pennsylvania and began public school attendance. His parents paid tuition, but soon commenced a class action suit in a federal district court challenging the statute.

The court considered U.S. Supreme Court cases dealing with school district residency requirements. It determined that the Pennsylvania statute was identical to a Connecticut statute which the Supreme Court had found unconstitutional. This was because there were reasonable alternatives for determining residency besides an irrebuttable presumption of nonresidence based upon parental residence. Under the Supreme Court cases, residence in the school context required only physical presence and an intention to remain in the school district. A Texas statute upheld by the Supreme Court permitted free education regardless of parental residence so long as the student could establish that transfer to the school district was not for the primary purpose of obtaining a free public education there. The court noted that Pennsylvania was permitted to establish reasonable criteria for determining in-state status. The Pennsylvania statute was unconstitutional because it denied the class members their procedural due process rights. The court ordered the state education secretary to convene a residency hearing as well as to consider all the complaining students' Rehabilitation Act and EHA complaints. Other class members were also to be afforded individual opportunities to establish residency. *Steven M. v. Gilhool*, 700 F.Supp. 261 (E.D.Pa.1988).

In a New York case the New York Supreme Court, Appellate Division, has issued a ruling which interprets § 4004(2)(a) of that state's Education Law. This section declares that "the school district in which a child resided at the time the social services district . . . assumed responsibility for the support and maintenance of the child . . . shall reimburse the state toward the state's expenditure on behalf of such child." The dispute in this case arose when custody of a child with a disability was surrendered by his mother to a county social services department. He was later returned to the custody of his mother. At that time he began to attend school in the Brentwood school district, his district of residence.

When the mother once again surrendered custody of her child to the county social services department, the state sought reimbursement from the Brentwood district. Brentwood refused, arguing that the school district where the child resided at the time of his first placement with the social services department was his school district of origin for the purpose of § 4004(2)(a). This interpretation would mean that any subsequent residence was irrelevant. The state Commissioner of Education had previously ruled that "when a child is returned to the custody of his parents and then subsequently replaced with the Department of Social Services, the financial burden of such care falls on the school district in which the child resided at the time of placement, regardless of his residence at the time of any earlier placement." The Appellate Division agreed with the Commissioner, holding that § 4004(2)(a) requires that whatever school district in which a child resides at the time of his placement in a social services program must bear the financial burden. The five-judge panel concluded that the Commissioner's ruling that Brentwood reimburse the state was practical because it "relieves a former school district of the responsibility for underwriting the expenses of a subsequently relocated child with whom the district may not have had any contact for years." *Brentwood Union Free School Dist. v. Ambach*, 495 N.Y.S.2d 513 (A.D.3d Dept.1985).

In a New Hampshire case a declaratory judgment action was brought to determine which school district was liable for the special education expenses of an educationally disabled child. The child had lived for nearly one year with a married couple who wished to adopt him. However, later the couple decided not to adopt him and the child then became a patient at a New Hampshire state hospital. He later lived at a group home and at a training center in Massachusetts. A New Hampshire trial court placed all responsibility for the child's educational expenses on the school district in which the child had lived with the couple who had wished to adopt him. The school district appealed to the Supreme Court of New Hampshire, which affirmed the trial court ruling, saying that a state statute which obligated "the district in which the child last resided" to pay his special education expenses referred to the place where a child actually lived outside of a facility. Because the evidence was sufficient to support a finding that the child's residence for nearly one year with the couple who had wished to adopt him was bona fide, that district was liable for his special education expenses incurred after his leaving the couple's home. *In re Gary B.*, 466 A.2d 929 (N.H.1983).

A research institute operated seven group homes in Massachusetts licensed by the Department of Mental Retardation. Twenty-one of its students were from Massachusetts; five of the Massachusetts students were funded by the Department of Education. Fifteen of the students were funded by the Department of Mental Retardation, and one was funded by the Department of Mental Health. The case began with a complaint filed by the institute in which the institute sought declaratory injunctive relief effectively requiring payment of the $150,000 reimbursement rate for 1991 (set in settlement of an administrative appeal). However, the Executive Office for Administration and Finance advised the rate setting commission that the regulations on which the 1991 rates were set were subject to prior administrative and finance approval. The Department of Mental Retardation, one of the sources of the funding, informed the institute that it would not pay the settlement figure, because it was not approved by the Executive Office of Administration and Finance. The institute then filed a complaint in a Massachusetts trial court asserting its right to the $150,000 rate. The court determined that a special needs student was not entitled by the Education of the Handicapped Act to have a facility's reimbursement rate set at a particular figure. The court further stated that the students' rights to services under mental retardation and mental health laws were expressly conditioned on available resources. And finally, the court agreed that the settlement agreement between the facility and the rate setting commission did not give the facility a contractual right to receive the rate established in that agreement. *Behavior Research v. Secretary of Administration*, 577 N.E.2d 297 (Mass.1991).

In a Colorado case, a juvenile court terminated the parent-child relationship between an emotionally disabled child and his parents and granted custody of the child to the Denver Department of Social Services (DDSS). The department then placed the child with a set of foster parents. The child was enrolled in a special education program for children with emotional disorders in the school district in which he resided with his foster parents. Because the child experienced great difficulty in school adjustment, the school district recommended that he be placed in a twenty-four-hour residential child care facility. The foster parents objected to this proposal because they believed he was doing well living in their home and because they believed it would destroy the bonding which had developed between them and the child. The foster parents unilaterally enrolled the child in the Denver Academy, a private day school specializing in the treatment of children with learning disabilities. The child's guardian ad litem then filed a motion with the juvenile court seeking to compel the DDSS to pay the $5,400 annual tuition at the Denver Academy. The juvenile court held that it lacked authority to consider such matters and the guardian ad litem appealed.

The Colorado Court of Appeals affirmed the juvenile court's ruling. The child's guardian ad litem argued that since the juvenile court had placed the child in the custody of the department, the court had authority to review all aspects of the child's care, including his educational program. This argument was rejected on the ground that Colorado's Exceptional Children's Act provides that a student's school district of residence is completely responsible for providing and paying for special educational services. Thus, although the juvenile court had jurisdiction over the child's welfare, the responsibility for his special education lay with his school district. The DDSS was not the responsible party and could not be compelled to fund the child's education at the private academy. *A.C.B. v. Denver Dep't of Social Servs.*, 725 P.2d 94 (Colo.App.1986).

III. STUDENTS WITH DISABILITIES IN SCHOOL ATHLETICS

Students with disabilities may not be excluded from any athletic activity conducted by a school receiving federal financial assistance as long as the student is "otherwise qualified" to participate. "Otherwise qualified" means that the student is qualified to participate in spite of his or her disability.

A. Athletes' Eligibility

A learning disabled Tennessee student transferred from a private Christian school to a public high school. The Tennessee Secondary School Athletic Association (TSSAA) ruled the student ineligible to participate in interscholastic sports for twelve months based upon TSSAA rules. The student's requests for a hardship waiver were repeatedly denied by the TSSAA. The student's parents filed a civil rights action in a federal district court, where they were granted an injunction restraining the TSSAA from applying the transfer rule. The U.S. Court of Appeals, Sixth Circuit, dissolved the injunction and dismissed the matter because the student had failed to exhaust his administrative remedies. The student's parents then followed IDEA procedures by requesting an IEP which would include participation in interscholastic sports. The school district refused to include interscholastic sports competition in the IEP and the parents appealed to the Tennessee State Department of Education. A state hearing officer determined that the student should be granted a hardship waiver because his transfer had been motivated by his learning disability and the desire to gain access to remedial education programs which were unavailable at the private school. The hearing officer further determined that failure to grant the hardship waiver amounted to discrimination on the basis of disability, but failed to rule that interscholastic sports participation was a "related service" under the IDEA. The student was forced to sit out two football games following the hearing because the TSSAA maintained that the IEP was not binding upon it as the TSSAA had not participated in the IEP meetings.

The student's parents again obtained a federal district court injunction permitting his participation in interscholastic sports. The parents also sought a punitive damage award of $1.5 million, claiming that the TSSAA had taken retaliatory action against the student in violation of his constitutional rights. The court granted the

TSSAA's summary judgment motion on the damage award issue and the parents appealed to the U.S. Court of Appeals, Sixth Circuit. The court of appeals ruled that the school and student could rely on the injunction granted by the district court and that the games in which the student played should not be forfeited. However, the district court had properly dismissed the civil rights, constitutional and general damage claims filed by the student. General damages for emotional anguish for the pain and suffering of missing two high school games did not constitute appropriate judicial relief under the IDEA. *Crocker v. Tennessee Secondary School Athletic Ass'n*, 980 F.2d 382 (6th Cir.1992).

An Illinois student confined to a wheelchair wished to compete against regular students in track and field. The school district granted the parents' request for a due process hearing. The hearing officer concluded that the student must be allowed to compete on the school's teams. When safety warranted it, the student should participate in a separate wheelchair division. The hearing officer ruled that the district was under no obligation to provide services beyond those offered to nondisabled students. The officer ordered the school district to establish a wheelchair division for any sport offered to nondisabled students in the district. The district held a multidisciplinary conference (MDC) to decide whether the student could safely participate with nondisabled athletes. The MDC participants determined that the student could only compete with nondisabled students in golf and tennis. His participation at track events should be limited to a wheelchair division.

The student filed a lawsuit against the school district in a federal district court, claiming violation of 42 U.S.C. § 1983 and the Education of the Handicapped Act (EHA). The court noted a number of procedural deficiencies in the administrative proceedings. The court also noted that most of the MDC participants were not knowledgeable about wheelchair athletics and many were unfamiliar with the student's disabilities. The EHA's regulations permitted persons having significant information regarding the student to participate in MDCs. This included parents. The school district had not sought out such evidence. The district had violated the hearing officer's order for a case study and medical examination. The MDC lacked qualified personnel and failed to comply with the hearing officer's order. The district violated the student's rights under the EHA and § 1983. *Hollenbeck v. Bd. of Educ. of Rochelle Township*, 699 F.Supp. 658 (N.D.Ill.1988).

A New York school district attempted to prevent a junior high school girl from participating in contact sports by reason of her visual impairment, which resulted from a congenital cataract. New York law provides that upon a school district's determination that a student shall not be permitted to participate in an athletic program by reason of physical impairment, the student may commence a special proceeding to enjoin the school district from prohibiting such participation. Further, if the court finds that it is in the best interests of the student to participate in the athletic program and that it is reasonably safe to do so, the court shall grant permission to participate. The law further protects a school district from liability for any injury sustained by a student participating pursuant to such a court determination.

In this case, the lower court determined that with protective eyewear it would be reasonably safe for this student to participate in the athletic program, but denied her application on the grounds that it would not be in her best interests to participate, because of the immunity from liability granted to the school district should an injury occur. The New York Supreme Court, Appellate Division, rejected this lower court finding and granted the student permission to participate. Whatever immunity from liability is enjoyed by a school district is not to be weighed by the court in considering the best interests of the student. Here, ample evidence suggested that with protective eyewear it would be in the best interests of this student to participate in the athletic program. *Kampmeier v. Harris*, 411 N.Y.S.2d 744 (A.D.4th Dept.1978).

B. Transfer and Age Restrictions

A nineteen-year-old emotionally disabled student wanted to play on the school basketball team during his senior year. However, because he was over eighteen he was ineligible under the rules of the Michigan High School Athletic Association. His parents and the school brought suit against the athletic association seeking to have the student declared eligible to play. A Michigan trial court issued a temporary restraining order barring the association from enforcing the eligibility rules against the student. During the time the order was in effect, the student played a series of games. However, the trial court eventually ruled in favor of the association, finding that the eligibility rule was valid. The trial court ordered the association not to penalize the school or the basketball team for the student having played during the time the restraining order was in effect. The Court of Appeals of Michigan affirmed the trial court's decision. The association appealed to the Supreme Court of Michigan.

The association contended that the court had no authority to bar the association from declaring invalid any games the boy played in while ineligible. The supreme court agreed stating that the association's regulation was valid. It was reasonably designed to rectify the competitive inequities that would inevitably occur if schools were permitted without penalty to field ineligible athletes under the protection of a temporary restraining order. The supreme court reversed the decision of the lower courts and granted relief to the association. *Cardinal Mooney High School v. MHSAA*, 467 N.W.2d 21 (Mich.1991).

A high school athletic regulatory agency in Texas barred a male high school student from participating in high school football because he had moved to another district to live with his grandparents. The student had suffered emotional problems and was disabled within the meaning of the Rehabilitation Act. The student sued alleging that there were compelling medical reasons why he should be permitted to participate in the football program. The U.S. district court issued a preliminary injunction restraining the athletic regulatory agency from enforcing its rule. The court said that the purpose of the rule was to prevent recruiting abuses and to prevent an athlete from irresponsibly shopping around for a school or coach. These evils were not present here. To deny the student the opportunity to play football would violate his rights as an individual with a handicap. *Doe v. Marshall*, 459 F.Supp. 1190 (S.D.Tex.1978).

A nineteen-year-old neurologically impaired high school senior challenged a New York Department of Education regulation prohibiting students over eighteen years of age from participating in interscholastic athletics. The boy had entered the public school system at the ninth grade level after leaving a private school, where he had failed the ninth grade. His participation in wrestling from the ninth grade until his senior year appeared to have significantly improved his self image. The boy brought suit in U.S. district court, alleging he had been discriminated against on the basis of his disability and had been unlawfully denied the opportunity to participate in interscholastic wrestling in violation of the equal protection provisions of the U.S. Constitution and the Rehabilitation Act. The court held that because the student had reached the age of nineteen and had not been treated any differently than any other nonphysically disabled nineteen-year-old student, there was no violation of equal protection, nor was there unfair discrimination. *Cavallaro v. Ambach*, 575 F.Supp. 171 (W.D.N.Y.1983).

IV. STUDENT RECORDS

Generally, access to disabled students' records will not be allowed when the privacy interest of the students outweighs the asserted need for inspection of the records.

An Illinois high school student suffered from a behavioral disorder. The school district proposed placing the student in a self-contained behavioral disorder program at the high school. The student's parents disagreed with this placement proposal and placed him in a private residential facility pending a hearing. A hearing officer approved of the school district's proposed placement. On appeal, a reviewing officer concluded that a private residential facility was the appropriate placement. However, he denied the parents' request for partial reimbursement of expenses since the private residential facility the student had been sent to was not approved by the Illinois State Board of Education. The school district appealed to an Illinois circuit court.

The school district's attorneys attached copies of the hearing officer's order and the reviewing officer's decision to the complaint they filed with the circuit court. Several months later, articles concerning the case appeared in two local newspapers. Eventually, the lawsuit was settled and dismissed. However, the parents then sued the school district, claiming that it had violated the Illinois School Student Records Act by allowing its attorneys access to copies of the review and hearing officers' decisions, and by revealing the contents of those decisions to the Lake County Circuit Court Clerk. They also claimed that the district had revealed information to the local newspapers. The circuit court dismissed the claims, and the parents appealed to the Appellate Court of Illinois.

The court noted that under Illinois law, student records may not be disclosed except in specified circumstances. The Student Records Act did not authorize the disclosure of student records to attorneys at the hearings. But since the law allowing attorneys to be present at placement hearings was passed later than the Student Records Act, the legislature must have intended to allow attorneys to have access to those records. The law also required the district to deliver the decisions to the circuit court clerk. Therefore such delivery could not violate the Act. Finally, the newspaper articles were based on public information from court files which the parents had made no effort to impound. They therefore waived any right to prevent disclosure. *Aufox v. Bd. of Educ. of Tp. High School Dist.*, 588 N.E.2d 316 (Ill.App.1992).

A Maryland special education student was sexually abused by her grandfather. He was charged with child abuse and prior to his trial attempted to subpoena his granddaughter's school records. The student participated in a special education program because of emotional problems. The school district refused to turn over the records and filed a motion for a protective order. A hearing was held at which the attorney for the defendant argued that the records were relevant since they might reveal a physical impairment which could relate to the student's capacity to observe and understand or a mental deficiency which could result in an inability to control her actions. The judge examined the records privately and determined that there was nothing in them which could be admissible for purposes of impeaching the student's testimony. The grandfather was subsequently convicted and he appealed his conviction to the Court of Special Appeals of Maryland.

A Maryland law requires the permission of the student's parents or a court order before a student's records may be disclosed. A court may refuse to grant such an order unless the information sought is both favorable to the accused and material to his case. The Sixth Amendment of the Constitution requires that a criminal defendant be allowed to confront and cross-examine his accusers. The defendant argued that he needed the information contained in the school records to adequately cross-examine the student. The court held that the defendant's right to cross-examine the student was not violated since he was not prevented from doing so and that the Sixth Amendment requires that the defendant only be given access to material evidence. It is the court's role to determine what evidence is material, not the defendant's. The trial court's refusal to grant the court order was upheld. *Zall v. State*, 584 A.2d 119 (Md.App.1991).

A human rights advocacy committee in Florida petitioned for access to confidential school records which it considered pertinent to its investigation of the alleged abuse of four developmentally disabled students by public school personnel. A Florida trial court denied the committee's request and appeal was taken to the District Court of Appeal of Florida. The court affirmed the trial court rulings. It found that the committee was not entitled to access to the confidential school records of the students because a state statute limited the committee's area of jurisdiction, for the purpose of obtaining client records, to matters occurring solely within a program or facility operated, funded or regulated by the Department of Health and Rehabilitative Services. The court also based its decision on a school code provision protecting the privacy interests of every student with regard to his or her educational records. *Human Rights Advocacy Comm. v. Lee County School Bd.*, 457 So.2d 522 (Fla.App.2d Dist.1984).

The Human Rights Authority of the State of Illinois Guardianship and Advocacy Commission appealed an order of an Illinois district court denying the enforcement of a subpoena issued by the commission. Acting on a complaint which alleged that a local school district was not providing occupational and physical therapy for its students, the commission began an investigation and asked the district superintendent to produce the students' educational program records. The records were to be masked so as to delete any information by which students could be identified. When the school district failed to turn over the information, the commission issued a subpoena for the masked records. Again, the school district refused to comply. The commission then sought judicial enforcement of the subpoena.

The district court ruled that the commission had no right to examine the records because it did not satisfy the access requirements of Illinois state law regarding student records. After the commission appealed to the Appellate Court of Illinois, the school district argued that, along with the access provisions of the Student Records Act, the commission had no authority to investigate or review special education programs, and that the commission's right to investigate did not apply to all of the disabled students in a school district, but was limited to individual cases. The thrust of the school district's first argument was that the commission was somehow usurping the role of the State Board of Education by investigating the special education program of the school district. The commission's inquiry was "tantamount to the control and direction of special education which makes local school authorities accountable to the Commission rather than the State Board of Education as required by the School Code."

The appellate court disagreed. The statutory authority of the commission to investigate complaints concerning violations of the rights of persons with disabilities, including the right to special education programs, was not subordinate to that of the State Board of Education. Further, the commission's investigation of the school district's overall special education program, and not merely individual students, was within the bounds of the commission's statutory authority. *Human Rights Authority of the State of Illinois Guardianship Comm. v. Miller*, 464 N.E.2d 833 (Ill.App.3d Dist.1984).

Staff at a Washington residential school for children with disabilities noticed bruises on one of the students and suspected that she may have been the victim of sexual abuse. The school superintendent ordered a series of medical tests to determine whether she had been sexually assaulted. Her parents sued the school claiming its medical tests had violated the student's rights under the state and federal constitution. They alleged that school personnel had committed various tortious acts including assault, battery, and rape. At a pretrial hearing, the school moved to exclude the expert witness testimony of the girl's psychiatrist. He was to testify regarding her emotional state before and after the tests were conducted and also as to what was said at a staff meeting concerning the student. The psychiatrist was an employee of the school, but also had a private practice. The school asserted that a state law which prevents state employees from assisting others in any transaction involving the state barred the psychiatrist from testifying. The trial court agreed and excluded his testimony from trial.

The parents appealed to the Court of Appeals of Washington. The appeals court examined the statute relied upon by the state and concluded that it did not apply. A further section in the law provided that it was not intended to prevent a state employee from giving testimony under oath. The court held that the state could not assert a testimonial privilege over its employees. The state conceded that the psychiatrist could not be prevented from giving testimony regarding facts, but could be prevented from giving expert testimony regarding the student's mental state. The court also rejected this argument since the statute which allows state employees to testify does not place any restrictions on the subject matter of their testimony. The trial court's order excluding the psychiatrist's testimony was reversed. *Drewett v. Rainier School*, 806 P.2d 1260 (Wash.App.1991).

V. SPECIAL EDUCATION FOR PRESCHOOL CHILDREN AND CHILDREN OVER EIGHTEEN YEARS OF AGE

The IDEA requires that states provide a free appropriate education to children between the ages of three and twenty-one. However, § 1412(B) of the Act states that with respect to children with disabilities aged three to five and eighteen to twenty-one, the requirement to provide an education shall not apply if to do so would conflict with state law regarding public education for such age

groups. Additionally, a 1986 amendment established a discretionary funding program encouraging states to develop "early intervention services" for children with disabilities from birth until their third birthday. The 1986 amendment also established a new preschool grant program which created incentives for states to ensure that all children with disabilities ages three to five receive special education services.

A twenty-three-year-old Texas student with a disability had received special education services in a Houston, Texas, school district until she was twenty-one-years-old. The school district implemented the student's individualized education plan (IEP) which indicated specific goals for her educational and behavioral progress. The child never attained these goals. Since the child had reached twenty-one, she was due to graduate from school. The parents then instituted a due process hearing to determine if their child had received an appropriate education. The hearing officer determined that the child did not make any significant educational progress and that her behavioral problems had not been adequately addressed. The parents then sued the school district in a federal district court alleging civil rights and EHA violations. The parents claimed that the school district denied the student a free appropriate education under the EHA and that it also failed to provide an adequate IEP for their child. The defendant moved to dismiss the case.

The court dismissed all claims against the school district, noting three factors in its ruling. First, the statute of limitations barred all claims before 1986, and the parents had not provided any reason why the statute of limitations should be tolled. Next, the court discussed the parents' § 1983 claim. Specifically, the parents contended that the student had made no significant educational progress and that her behavioral problems were not addressed; therefore, she was discriminated against due to her disability. The court, however, determined that it was not enough to show a failure of an educational program. The plaintiff must show that the educators failed to adequately administer a program based on a bias because the plaintiff was disabled. Since these allegations were not made and no evidence was given in support of the claim, the student could not recover on the discrimination claim. Further, the court dismissed the EHA claim stating that due to the U.S. Supreme Court's decision in *Honig v. Doe*, 484 U.S. 305 (1988), the twenty-three-year-old's claims were moot. The *Honig* court stated that because the plaintiff was twenty-four-years-old, he was "no longer entitled to the protections and benefits of the EHA which limits eligibility to disabled children under twenty-one." Since this student was twenty-three-years-old, she was no longer entitled to the protections of the EHA and the court dismissed all the claims. *McDowell v. Fort Bend Indep. Sch. Dist.*, 737 F.Supp. 386 (S.D.Tex.1990).

A multiply-disabled student filed a complaint with the state school superintendent for a due process hearing five weeks before she reached the age of twenty-one. The school district advised the student that she would no longer be eligible for free public education after her twenty-first birthday. She sought an order from the state superintendent which would require her school district to continue her free education. Although the hearing occurred after the student's twenty-first birthday, the hearing officer ruled that the school district must provide her with free education until her twenty-second birthday. The school district then sought a ruling on state funding. The superintendent ruled that the school district could use federal funds to comply with the hearing officer's decision, but no state funds were to be expended. The school district appealed to the Wyoming County Court, which sent the appeal to the Wyoming Supreme Court.

The supreme court noted that the EHA adopted state educational standards to determine an individual state's obligation to provide free appropriate public education. The Wyoming constitution acknowledged the right to an education and state statutes required free and appropriate education for disabled students of school age. The language did not apply to adults who had reached age twenty-one. The student was not entitled to a due process hearing and was not entitled to any relief. School districts were not permitted to expend either federal or state funds for students over twenty-one-years-old. The district's policy stated that students with disabilities could be considered for graduation whenever the IEP had been completed or upon reaching age twenty-one. The hearing officer had incorrectly ruled that because the student had a continuing need for educational services, the district was committed to continue her free education. The district was not responsible for the student's failure to complete the district's disabled students' graduation requirements. The court reversed the hearing officer's decision. *Natrona County School Dist. 1 v. Ryan*, 764 P.2d 1019 (Wyo.1988).

The Wyoming Supreme Court considered a student with a disability who had finished his education after reaching age twenty-one. He submitted a claim for maintenance and tuition costs for his vocational activity program after his twenty-first birthday. The hearing officer determined that the state obligation ended at his twenty-first birthday. His parents appealed to a Wyoming county court which reversed the hearing officer's decision and ruled that the state had contracted for an additional year's educational costs, and that the school district had an obligation to continue funding. During the course of the administrative proceedings, the student completed his educational program. When the matter came before the Wyoming Supreme Court, the court noted that the disposition in the *Ryan* case (above) prohibited expenditure of funds on a student over twenty-one. However, as the student had completed his educational program the court determined that the educational expenses should be allocated between the school district and the state board as if the services had been rendered before his twenty-first birthday. *State v. Cochran*, 764 P.2d 1037 (Wyo.1988).

The parents of a disabled student filed a complaint under the EHA challenging the appropriateness of their child's IEP. They requested a hearing one day before the student turned twenty-two. An impartial hearing officer was appointed to hear the case. The school district filed a writ of prohibition in the Ohio Court of Appeals, alleging that the hearing officer had no jurisdiction over the case since the student was over the age of entitlement. The court granted the writ based on the U.S. Supreme Court's decision in *Honig v. Doe*, in which the Court held that a student's case was moot because he was over the age of entitlement. The hearing officer appealed to the Supreme Court of Ohio.

The supreme court held that the lower court had wrongly applied the standard set forth in *Honig*, since that case involved a suspension and not compensatory education. In a similar case involving compensatory education, a federal appeals court held that *Honig* does not bar an award of compensatory education beyond the age of entitlement. The court held that compensatory education should be granted to an overage student if he is able to show that the school district failed to provide a free appropriate education during the years that the student was entitled to it. Since there existed a possibility that the student would be granted compensatory education, the hearing officer had jurisdiction over the case. The court reversed the decision of the court of appeals and remanded the case for the requested hearing. *Bd. of Educ. of Strongsville v. Theado*, 566 N.E.2d 667 (Ohio 1991).

A Nebraska special education student petitioned the state education department, claiming he was entitled to remain in his school district's special education programs until his twenty-second birthday. The education department's hearing officer dismissed the petition because the student had already reached age twenty-one. The student appealed to a Nebraska trial court, which affirmed the hearing officer's decision but permitted the student to stay in school pending further appeal. The student appealed to the Nebraska Supreme Court.

On appeal, the student claimed that the Rehabilitation Act required school districts using federal funds to provide free education to persons over twenty-one years old. The district claimed that the trial court, by allowing the student to stay in school pending appeal, had erroneously required it to maintain the student's placement beyond his twenty-first birthday. The supreme court ruled that according to the applicable Nebraska statutes and the state constitution, free instruction was mandated for all persons between the ages of five and twenty-one years but not to students over twenty-one years old. The court also ruled that EHA regulations specifically required that state law determine public education age groups. States had the right to determine when educational services to students with disabilities could terminate. The supreme court affirmed the trial court's decision. Because Nebraska law stated that free education to disabled students was available only until the student's twenty-first birthday the district was not required to maintain the student in a special education program. *Monahan v. School Dist. 1 of Douglas County*, 425 N.W.2d 624 (Neb.1988).

Under Indiana law, a disabled child is entitled to a free education until and including the child's eighteenth year. Under federal law, the maximum age at which a child with a disability can receive appropriate education is twenty-one. An Indiana girl was placed in a special education program at a private school. The school denied a renewal application for the student because she had reached the age of nineteen. Under Indiana regulations, state-financed private education placements for children with disabilities terminate when the child reaches the age of nineteen. The parents then requested an administrative hearing challenging the termination of her current placement and seeking reimbursement of tuition expenses for their earlier unilateral placement at a hospital. The hearing officer denied both claims. The parents then brought this action in a federal district court requesting tuition reimbursement and compensatory damages.

The school district contended that the issue was moot because she was beyond the mandatory age under both Indiana law and federal law. A controversy must exist at every stage of the proceedings, including the appellate stages. The court noted that there were two reasons why this case was now moot. First, the student had reached the maximum age under Indiana and federal law. Therefore, the issues presented were no longer live. Second, the parents could not avoid the statutory age limit by seeking compensatory damages because neither the hearing officer nor the board of special education appeals reviewed the issue of compensatory damages, and without a decision below, the appellate court had no authority to rule on the issue. The court denied the parents the relief they requested. *Merrifield v. Lake Central School Corp.*, 770 F.Supp. 468 (M.D.Ind.1991).

The U.S. Court of Appeals ruled that a twenty-three year old man had no EHA claims. The case involved a Michigan man, born in 1954, who was able to communicate only through limited use of sign language. He was enrolled in three different special education programs from 1973 until he reached the age of twenty-five in 1979. The man was never excluded from attending any of the schools or from participating in special education programs, and he was never enrolled in a program that received federal financial assistance. He sued the three school districts in a U.S. district court alleging that the school districts had deprived him of a meaningful education. Specifically, the man claimed that his due process and equal protection rights under the Fourteenth Amendment had been violated. He also claimed that the school districts had failed to afford him a free appropriate education according to the EHA and the Rehabilitation Act. The district court ruled against the man and he appealed to the U.S. Court of Appeals, Sixth Circuit.

At the time, the EHA was the exclusive avenue through which a person could assert an equal protection claim to a publicly financed special education. The court had to determine whether the EHA had been available to the young man. The man claimed that the EHA became effective in 1975, but the court found that the EHA's requirement to make a free appropriate public education available did not become effective until 1977. It also noted that when the man entered one of the school district's programs in the fall of 1977 he was twenty-three years old. The EHA only requires an appropriate public education for children with disabilities between ages three and twenty-one. The man thus had no legitimate equal protection claims under the EHA.

The court of appeals stated that in order to establish a deprivation of an interest protected by the due process clause, the man had to show that he was excluded from the school districts' special education programs. He argued that he was in effect excluded from the districts' programs because he had no communicative skills and sat in classrooms where he was unaware of what was happening. In ruling for the school district, the court noted that other courts have repeatedly rejected the idea that the due process clause secures a right to the "most appropriate" education. Even though the man was limited in what he gained from the special education classes he was not excluded from those classes and did receive an appropriate education. Thus, the school district did not infringe upon the man's due process rights.

The court also denied the man's Rehabilitation Act claim since none of the programs that he participated in received federal financial assistance. It was not enough to show that the schools that the man attended were federally financed because the most common standard applied is whether the specific program was federally financed. The EHA and Rehabilitation Act claims were inapplicable and the court found no constitutional violations. The district court decision against the man was upheld. *Gallagher v. Pontiac School Dist.*, 807 F.2d 75 (6th Cir.1986).

When a Kentucky girl with congenital cataracts began to have vision loss, she was provided with home instruction. The Education of the Handicapped Act (EHA) required the school district to provide an appropriate education to the child beginning Sept. 1, 1978. No Individualized Education Program (IEP) was prepared for the girl until more than four years after the 1978 deadline. Neither were her parents apprised of their due process rights. The girl attained the age of 21 in 1982. For the remainder of that year the school district provided her with home instruction. On May 5, 1983, a conference was held for the purpose of developing an IEP for her and she was graduated from the high school on May 30, 1983, at the age of 22. She requested permission to participate in the public graduation exercises, but her request was denied. She commenced this action in a federal district court against the board of education alleging that they had violated the statutory provisions by failing to establish an individualized education program for her and that through lack of due diligence and failure to follow statutorily mandated procedures the defendants had failed to discover that the girl was capable of learning "sighted reading" with the aide of specialized equipment. She further alleged that her earning power had been impaired by a deficient education. She asked for a money judgment for the loss of wages and the cost of appropriate remedial education. The court dismissed the case and she appealed to the U.S. Court of Appeals, Sixth Circuit.

The girl asserted that the board should be denied the statute of limitations defense because it failed to abide by the EHA by informing her parents of their procedural rights. The court disagreed, stating that the parents knew that the girl was not being educated with other students and they were aware that she was not receiving instruction in sighted reading. The court affirmed the trial court's dismissal. In a dissenting opinion, the senior circuit judge stated that the board should be estopped from raising the statute of limitations defense because it failed in four consecutive years to provide the student with the statutorily mandated appropriate education. Further, the judge noted that the parents could not file a timely action to assert rights to which they were not informed they were entitled. *Hall v. Knott County Bd. of Educ.*, 941 F.2d 402 (6th Cir.1991).

A disabled child in Oklahoma who was about to be graduated by her school district brought suit against the school district alleging that she was in the tenth, not the twelfth, grade and was therefore entitled to two additional years of special education. The school district argued that any notations in the student's individual education program (IEP) or her report card indicating that she was in the tenth grade were a mistake and that the child was in the twelfth grade and thus eligible for graduation. The district further argued that Oklahoma state law did not obligate school districts to provide education to students with disabilities from eighteen through twenty-one years of age nor did the EHA impose such a requirement. A U.S. district court in Oklahoma held in the child's favor and the school district appealed.

The U.S. Court of Appeals, Tenth Circuit, affirmed the district court ruling finding that since nondisabled children in the eighteen to twenty-one age group may be entitled to additional years of education when one or more grades are failed, disabled children within this age group are similarly entitled to continue their education.

The court found evidence of the school district's different methods used to determine when disabled and nondisabled children are in the twelfth grade and found that certain standards for the evaluation of disabled children, as with nondisabled children must be met before a disabled child can be deemed to have advanced a grade. A nondisabled student's performance was evaluated by standardized course content whereas a disabled student's progress was measured by whether the goals in his or her IEP were met. The court found that the EHA contemplates that a disabled child's progress in school should be measured by objective, if not standardized, criteria. It would make a farce of the clear intent of Congress to interpret the EHA as allowing a disabled child to fail to meet his or her IEP objectives and yet advance a grade level.

Here, the court found a failure on the part of the school district to adequately measure the child's progress. A notation in the child's IEP and in her report card indicating that she was in tenth grade prompted the court to rule that the child was entitled to two additional years of special education. *Helms v. Indep. School Dist. No. 3*, 750 F.2d 820 (10th Cir.1985).

VI. GIFTED PROGRAMS

A Pennsylvania school district used a "pull-out" program for its gifted students in kindergarten through seventh grade. In this program, students with outstanding intellectual and creative abilities are removed from the regular classroom and provided certain identified programming in addition to the regular curricula. From eighth to twelfth grade, the district used an "enrichment" program, whereby all qualified students, whether or not gifted, are placed in separate enriched classes for given subjects. A student who had been in the pull-out program entered the eighth grade. She was placed in the enrichment program.

Her father objected and he requested a due process hearing as provided by Pennsylvania law. He requested the school district to perform an evaluation of his daughter at its expense. He also wanted his daughter to remain in the "pull-out" program pending the outcome of the hearing and he wanted an award of attorney's fees. The hearing officer ordered the school district to develop an IEP, but ordered no reimbursement for the evaluation the father had requested. The father appealed to a state board which ordered the school district to develop an IEP and leave the child in the "pull-out" program. The board also held that the father was not entitled to an independent evaluation at district expense, nor was he entitled to attorney's fees. The father appealed to the Pennsylvania Commonwealth Court.

On appeal, the father argued that he was entitled to recovery of attorney's fees and to obtain an independent evaluation of his daughter at public expense pursuant to the Individuals with Disabilities Education Act (IDEA), 20 U.S.C. § 1400 *et seq.* He also argued that under the IDEA he should be reimbursed for materials and services he purchased to replicate his daughter's prior educational program during the pendency of the proceedings. The court disagreed, stating that it was not bound by the IDEA in this case. The IDEA was enacted for the benefit of children with disabilities. Nowhere in the IDEA does it provide that gifted children fall within its protections. The court affirmed the rulings. *Huldah A. v. Easton Area School Dist.*, 601 A.2d 860 (Pa.Cmwlth.1992).

A Pennsylvania school district devised an IEP for an exceptional student. It recommended that the district include the student in its "enrichment" program. The enrichment program added certain materials to the regular curriculum but did not attempt to provide accelerated instruction. The student's parents requested a due process hearing in which they asserted that the enrichment program was insufficient. The hearing officer concluded that the student should be given specialized instruction in addition to the enrichment program. Both the state secretary of education and the Pennsylvania Commonwealth Court affirmed the hearing officer's decision. The school district appealed to the Pennsylvania Supreme Court.

The issue before the supreme court was whether the secretary and the commonwealth court had exceeded the provisions of the Pennsylvania Public School Code in requiring the school district to provide the student with an IEP beyond the enrichment program. The code required that schools provide gifted students with plans for individualized instruction designed to meet the "unique needs of the child." The school district argued that this subjective standard would lead to its bankruptcy. It argued that providing a program for exceptional children which addressed their needs to some degree was sufficient. The supreme court affirmed the lower court and administrative decisions. Public school code regulations promulgated by the state education board required individualized planning and education for exceptional children. School districts were required to prepare an IEP for each exceptional child. However, districts were not required to provide individual tutors for exclusive individual programs outside the school district's existing special education curriculum. The student was entitled to specialized instruction beyond the enrichment program. *Centennial School Dist. v. Commonwealth Dep't of Educ.*, 539 A.2d 785 (Pa.1988).

A Connecticut student attended regular classes and participated in the gifted program in the public school from kindergarten through fifth grade. Although he did well academically, he had behavioral problems. After beginning sixth grade he had deteriorated emotionally and was hospitalized. While the student was in the hospital, the school district contracted with a school district near the hospital to provide the student with an education. When the student was released from the hospital, his parents and the school district met to discuss his educational placement. His parents requested that the school district pay for a residential treatment facility recommended by a social worker from the hospital. The school board offered to pay for the educational costs if the placement was for medical reasons. The parents requested a due process hearing and a mediation was held which did not resolve the dispute. The parents then instituted this action in a federal trial court.

The parents contended that their son was an exceptional child and therefore entitled to services under the EHA. An exceptional child is defined as "a child who deviates either intellectually, physically, socially or emotionally so markedly from normal expected growth and development patterns that he or she is or will be unable to progress effectively in a regular school program and needs a special class, special instruction, or special services." Several psychologists, social workers, and teachers testified that the student exhibited signs of depression and violent behavior. However, the court concluded that the student was not a disabled student entitled to special education under the EHA. The court ruled that although the child had some emotional difficulties, these difficulties did not adversely affect his educational performance. The student was able to progress and do exceptionally well in school despite his behavioral problems. The court thus held that the school district need not pay the residential facility's expenses. *Doe v. Bd. of Educ. of State of Connecticut*, 753 F.Supp. 65 (D.Conn.1990).

In Pennsylvania a student who had scored 121 on an I.Q. test sued her school district in U.S. district court claiming that her exclusion from a gifted student program violated her rights under the EHA. Pennsylvania law provides that "Persons shall be assigned to a program for the gifted when they have an IQ of 130 or higher. A limited number of persons with IQ scores lower than 130 *may* be admitted to gifted programs when other educational criteria in the profile of the person strongly indicates gifted ability." In addressing the student's arguments, the district court held that although Pennsylvania law extended the same due process guarantees to gifted students as it did to students with disabilities, the student was not entitled to EHA procedural protections as a matter of federal law. The court also rejected the student's claim that she had been denied due process of law under the Fourteenth Amendment. It reasoned that because she had not achieved an I.Q. score of 130 or higher, the student had no "property interest" in being admitted to the gifted student program. Although under Pennsylvania law a student with a I.Q. score of less than 130 "may" be admitted to a gifted student program, this did not mean that such a student was entitled to admittance. Also, the court rejected the argument that the student's equal protection rights had been violated by the school district. It observed that because there is no fundamental right to an education under the U.S. Constitution, Pennsylvania's I.Q. regulations were only required to be "rationally related" to some legitimate state purpose. Accordingly, the district court ruled in favor of the school district. *Student Roe v. Commonwealth*, 638 F.Supp. 929 (E.D.Pa.1986).

A Pennsylvania student was determined to be "mentally gifted" within the definition found in Pennsylvania law. His school district developed an interim individualized educational program for him, which his parents approved. In addition, however, the student's parents contended that he had a specific learning disability which required special education. The school district disagreed and turned down the parents' request for special education services. A hearing officer concluded that the student did not have a learning disability that required special education. A state department of education review panel reversed that decision, concluding that the student had a specific learning disability in the area of written expression which required special education. The school district appealed to the Commonwealth Court of Pennsylvania.

On appeal, the district argued that the student's success in regular education classes precluded his classification as an exceptional student with a specific learning disability. It also argued that the student could be accommodated by modifications to his regular education program. The court disagreed. It held that a student who requires supplementary aids and services to guarantee a successful performance level must be able to receive special education services despite his classification as gifted. Since there was sufficient evidence to support the review panel's decision, it was affirmed. *Weiser Area School Dist. v. Dep't of Educ.*, 603 A.2d 701 (Pa.Cmwlth.1992).

VII. CASES ARISING UNDER STATE LAW

The IDEA, while paramount in the field of special education, leaves many issues to state law. The cases which follow were decided on the basis of state law. The subjects of these cases vary widely.

An emotionally disturbed Texas sixth grader who attended special classes for emotionally disabled children and who had a history of aggressive behavioral problems became disruptive during classroom instruction. The teacher then sent the student to the principal's office. The student received corporal punishment from the school's principal for misbehaving in class. Shortly after the child returned home, he complained of pain and of having been beaten by the principal. The parents called the sheriff's department and a police officer took pictures of the welts and scrapes on the child's body. The sheriff's department investigated the incident, but no criminal action was instituted. The parents claimed the injuries were the result of the corporal punishment. They filed an action against the school's principal, the teacher and the school district in a federal district court. The court dismissed all claims except the state law excessive-force charge directed at the principal. It then remanded the case to the state court. The parents appealed to the U.S. Court of Appeals, Fifth Circuit.

Fifth Circuit cases dictated that injuries sustained incidentally to corporal punishment do not implicate the due process clause if the state affords post-punishment remedies for the student. The court noted that Texas law has authorized educators to impose a reasonable measure of corporal punishment upon students when necessary to maintain school discipline, and the state affords students post-punishment criminal or civil remedies if teachers are unfaithful to this obligation. The parents contended that the Fifth Circuit had an overly rigid rule and did not contemplate cases of student discipline such as physical disfigurement or severe emotional injury. The court held that Texas law provided adequate post-punishment relief in favor of students. The court of appeals thus affirmed the trial court's decision and remanded the claim to state court. *Fee v. Herndon*, 900 F.2d 804 (5th Cir.1990).

A Rhode Island boys' home provided private residential facilities for dependent and neglected children. The students residing in the home were provided an on-grounds educational program conducted through an elementary and special education school. The state Department of Children and Their Families (DCF) contracted with the home to provide tutorial and remedial help when appropriate. However, no agreement was made for providing speech therapy services. The DCF and the home requested a local public school to provide speech therapy services. The school initially agreed to allow the children to participate in its speech therapy program, but later discontinued the services. The home's director requested a hearing to determine whether the children residing in the home had the right to participate in speech therapy services conducted through the public school system.

The State Commissioner of Education ruled that the public school was not required to allow children to participate in speech therapy services. He claimed that the home was a "closed facility" because some children were not allowed to enroll as fulltime students in the public school system. Under a state statute, the public school was relieved of its obligation to provide speech therapy services whenever children were "confined" to a state-supported or state-operated "closed" facility. The DCF appealed the commissioner's decision to a Rhode Island trial court which vacated the previous decision and found that the home was not a "closed" facility under the statute. The children were entitled to the public school system's speech therapy services. The school then appealed to the Supreme Court of Rhode Island.

The supreme court held that the home was not a "closed" facility within the meaning of the statute. The fact that the children were not allowed to enroll fulltime in the public school system did not, by itself, make the home a closed facility. There was no evidence that the children were unable to leave the facility. Some students had been enrolled part-time outside the facility in the public school system. The court held that only when students are unable to leave a facility to attend public schools, even on a part-time basis, will a facility be "closed" within the scope of the statute. The school was obligated to provide the students with speech therapy services. The supreme court affirmed the trial court's decision. *In re Children Res. at St. Aloysius Home*, 556 A.2d 552 (R.I.1989).

A truant officer for a Massachusetts public school instigated a juvenile court proceeding at which a thirteen-year-old student was determined to be a "child in need of services." Such a determination is made under the authority of Massachusetts law, specifically under G.L. c.119, § 39J. The judge at the proceeding ordered the student to be enrolled in special education classes at a private school and also ordered the county to pay for the schooling. The student attended the school for a three month period, but the county treasurer refused to pay the student's tuition. As a result, the student attended no school for 6 months, until he resumed public schooling. The student sued, seeking an order directing the treasurer to pay the expenses the student incurred at the school. A trial court concluded that G.L. c.119 did not govern special education programs or assignments and held for the county. The student appealed to the Supreme Judicial Court of Massachusetts.

The supreme judicial court stated that the "children in need of services" statute is concerned with social and family problems. It does not make a child's education a central judicial concern. Even more importantly, Massachusetts law provides a very substantial and detailed process for the determination at the local level of the educational needs of students, for the possibility of review of such determination by a state agency, and for judicial review of the various decisions. A judge may not bypass these detailed provisions. The supreme judicial court held for the county. *Oscar F. v. County of Worcester*, 587 N.E.2d 208 (Mass.1992).

A fifty-eight-year-old mentally disabled woman had resided at a Vermont training school since 1949. In 1983, she was conditionally discharged from the school and placed in a staffed apartment unit. Six months later, she broke her hip and was hospitalized. She was then placed in a convalescent center by her guardian and the state department of mental health. Following her conditional discharge from the center, the mental health department filed a petition with a Vermont trial court to determine the appropriateness of discharge from the training school. No action was taken until 1986, when the trial court reactivated its review. The court found the training school placement insufficient, citing a lack of an individual program plan to meet her needs. An individual program plan resembles an IEP for adults. The mental health department's commissioner then unconditionally discharged the student from the training school without a hearing. The trial court dismissed the proceedings and the department ended its support services. The student then sued the department for review of the absolute discharge, claiming that the department had failed to fulfill its duty to provide adequate care. The department then made a motion to dismiss the matter, which the court denied. However, the court granted the department's motion for appeal to the Vermont Supreme Court.

The supreme court noted an insufficient record for it to make a decision since the court had not previously interpreted the Vermont statute under which the case was filed. Additionally, it had never ruled on the question of arbitrary discharge from care, or on the argument that the department had failed to meet a legal duty to provide adequate care. The court dismissed the appeal, and remanded the case to the trial court for further consideration. *In re A.G.*, 559 A.2d 656 (Vt.1989).

The New Hampshire Department of Health and Human Services (HHS) is responsible for ensuring that services are provided to the developmentally disabled. The Department of Education (DOE) is responsible for ensuring that schools give children with disabilities a free appropriate education. Because a person may be both developmentally disabled and educationally disabled, the HHS and DOE regulations may overlap. The New Hampshire legislature ordered the commissioners of each agency to enter into an agreement defining each other's procedural role. Two developmentally disabled and educationally disabled students sued to force the commissioners to settle the procedural dispute between the two officials. Each had been turned down for residential placement at public expense. After a New Hampshire trial court dismissed their complaint, they appealed to the New Hampshire Supreme Court.

The court upheld the dismissal. It refused to issue an order forcing the commissioners to settle the dispute, holding that such discretionary acts could not be ordered. It held that the students' opportunity for review by the state agencies did not violate the EHA because they could directly appeal to a federal court, instead of following the state agency's route of appeal. Thus, the state procedure for dealing with inter-agency disputes did not violate the EHA. *Guy v. Comm'r, New Hampshire Dep't of Educ.*, 565 A.2d 397 (N.H.1989).

In 1989, the New York legislature passed a law transferring the responsibility of determining the special educational needs of three-to-four-year-olds from the family court to a local preschool special education committee (CPSE). The statute provides that although the law becomes effective July 1, 1989, the family court retains jurisdiction over petitions filed with it prior to August 1, 1989. A petition for special educational services for a three-year-old preschooler was not received until August 8, 1989. The family court determined it no longer had jurisdiction to decide the case, given the date it had received the petition. It acknowledged that although the child's placement would be significantly delayed as a result, the legislature's decree must be followed. The family court referred the case to the local CPSE. *Matter of Martin K.*, 545 N.Y.S.2d 897 (Fam.Ct.1989).

A New Jersey man, J.R., had attended several different school settings over the years and his behavior had worsened. Eventually he was placed in a residential facility in Pennsylvania. His diagnoses ranged from autism and schizophrenia to avoidant personality. He had also been found to be substantially limited in three areas: self-direction, capacity for independent living, and learning. Until 1988, his father's insurance paid the cost of the placement. The father then sought to have his son declared developmentally disabled and eligible for services under the Developmental Disabilities Act (Act). An administrative law judge (ALJ) determined that J.R. was developmentally disabled and in need of services. However, the Director of the Division of Developmental Disabilities rejected the ALJ's conclusions. Instead, he relied upon the opinion of the division's expert, that J.R. was schizophrenic and in need of psychiatric treatment rather than the services provided by the division. The father appealed the order in the Superior Court of New Jersey.

On appeal, the court noted that it could not substitute its own opinion for that of an agency head, but the court could reverse if it concluded that the agency's findings were unsupported by the evidence. The Act states that the definition of developmental disability is a severe disability which
    1) is attributed to a mental or physical impairment or combination of
       mental or physical impairments;
    2) is manifested before age twenty-two;
    3) is likely to continue indefinitely;
    4) results in substantial functional limitations in three or more of the
       following areas of major life activity, self-care, receptive and expressive
       language, learning, mobility, self-direction and capacity for independent
       living or economic self-sufficiency; and
    5) reflects the need for a combination and sequence of special interdisciplinary
       or generic care, treatment or other services which are life long or extended
       duration and are individually planned and coordinated.

The court determined that the agency's decision that J.R. was not in need of services was unsupported by the evidence. J.R. met the Act's criteria and should receive services. Therefore, the court reversed the decision of the director and awarded services to J.R. under the Developmental Disabilities Act. *T.R. v. Division of Developmental Disabilities*, 592 A.2d 13 (N.J.1991).

A second grade Pennsylvania student had difficulty reading and keeping up with her class. She was tested by school officials to determine if she was learning disabled. Some of the tests identified her as learning disabled. Her mother requested permission to teach her at home but the school district denied the request. The student suffered daily illnesses because of frustration about her problems. The mother unilaterally removed her from school and then sued school officials in a federal district court. She claimed the student had been denied equal protection under the Fourteenth Amendment because school officials had failed to provide her with an appropriate individualized educational program (IEP). She sought monetary damages for the alleged physical and emotional harm to the student and herself. The court dismissed the complaint, holding that the school officials violated no equal protection rights by failing to provide the student an IEP. Pennsylvania law clearly indicated that neither parents nor children who are not disabled may bring a lawsuit for damages based on claims that the child received an inadequate or inappropriate education. Although the mother failed to rely upon the EHA the court stated that the case also would have been dismissed under the EHA, which does not provide for damages for physical or emotional harm. *Smith v. Philadelphia School Dist.*, 679 F.Supp. 479 (E.D.Pa.1988).

After the Illinois State Superintendent of Education ordered that several disabled children be given their diplomas, an Illinois school district appealed to a U.S. district court challenging the order. The school district argued that the superintendent had allowed the issuance of the diplomas despite the fact that the children failed to pass a minimum competency test as required by the local school board. The district court held that school boards have the right to develop reasonable means to determine the effectiveness of their educational programs with respect to all individual students to whom they issue diplomas and the use of the minimum competency tests is a reasonable means of measuring that effectiveness. The court held that nothing in the EHA or other federal or state law stands in the way of such testing. The court did advise schools to modify tests in order to minimize the effect of physical capacity. To that end, the court suggested that a blind student not be given a competency test which was printed in a normal manner. However, the court stated that the test should not be modified to avoid measuring a student's mental capabilities since to do so would fail completely to measure the results of the educational process. *Brookhart v. Illinois State Bd. of Educ.*, 534 F.Supp. 725 (C.D.Ill.1982).

After the New York Commissioner of Education and a local board of education invalidated diplomas received by two students with disabilities enrolled in public school, the students' guardian brought suit to enjoin the commissioner and the board of education from invalidating the diplomas. The guardian objected to the requirement of basic competency tests as a prerequisite to obtaining a high school diploma. The Court of Appeals of New York affirmed two lower court rulings in favor of the school. The court stated that the students had no reasonable expectation of receiving a high school diploma without passing the competency test. The competency testing program had been in effect for three years prior to the completion of the students' studies and, thus, the students were not denied adequate notice of the requirement. *Bd. of Educ. v. Ambach*, 457 N.E.2d 775 (N.Y.1983).

The following cases illustrate the principle that any state statutory scheme which assesses parents or guardians or other relatives and requires reimbursement to the state for educating a child with a disability will not stand as valid law. This is due to the IDEA *free* appropriate education requirement for children with disabilities and the supremacy of federal law over state law.

An Illinois child resided in facilities operated by the Illinois Department of Mental Health and Developmental Disabilities until his death. Prior to his death, his father was appointed guardian of his estate. The estate included a large sum of money obtained in a medical malpractice settlement. After the child's death, the department claimed $48,725 was due to it pursuant to the Illinois Mental Health and Developmental Disabilities Code. Under the code, the estates of disabled educational services recipients were required to reimburse the department for its services. Reimbursement was based upon ability to pay. The father refused to pay. The department then filed a lawsuit against the state in an Illinois trial court, seeking reimbursement. The court held that the EHA prevented recovery by the department. The court dismissed the claim and the department appealed to the Appellate Court of Illinois, Fourth District.

The appellate court held that the EHA preempted state law. The department could not obtain reimbursement from the minor's guardianship account. The EHA assured all children with disabilities the right to a free appropriate public education. Free education included the right to receive free nonmedical care and room and board if placement in a public or private residential program was necessary to provide special education and related services. The minor was in such programs in order to receive special education. The Appellate Court affirmed the lower court's decision. The state could not seek reimbursement under the EAHCA. *Matter of Guardianship Estate of Zarse*, 529 N.E.2d 50 (Ill.App.4th Dist.1988).

The parents of a disabled child appealed from an order of the Illinois Department of Mental Health and Developmental Disabilities assessing them a "responsible relative liability charge" for the care of their child. The department's decision was based upon its belief that this was mandated by the Illinois Mental Health and Developmental Disabilities Code. The Appellate Court of Illinois upheld a lower court decision reversing the department's order, ruling that the department's decision was in violation of the EHA.

The court observed that federal law requires maintenance by the state of "a policy that assures all [children with disabilities] the right to a free appropriate public education." This education is to include both "special education" and "related services." The state's contention was that federal statutes should not prevent the assessment of charges pursuant to state law. The court disagreed, observing that there is a strong insistence by federal law on the requirement that all expenditures of every kind for the education and welfare of the child are to be borne by the educational authorities of the state. The assessment was therefore prohibited. *Parks v. Illinois Dep't of Mental Health and Developmental Disabilities*, 441 N.E.2d 1209 (Ill.App.1st Dist.1982).

A U.S. district court held that an Illinois statute requiring relatives to reimburse the state for payments made to support the residential placement of developmentally disabled children was contrary to the EHA and invalid under the Supremacy Clause of the U.S. Constitution. The EHA requires that states provide children with disabilities with a free appropriate public education, which includes both special educational and related services. The court characterized the Illinois scheme as a blatant violation of federal law. In overturning the "responsible relatives" statute, the court ordered that relatives who had paid prior assessments be reimbursed for the $100 monthly contribution fee they had paid (back to the year 1978) for the residential care of their developmentally disabled children.

On appeal by the state, the U.S. Court of Appeals, Seventh Circuit, affirmed the ruling that Illinois violated the EHA by requiring parents to pay any part of the living expenses of disabled children who are placed in a private residential facility on the ground of developmental disability rather than of educational need. The court rejected the state's argument that the class of developmentally disabled children are placed in residential institutions for reasons other than education and, therefore, those children fall outside the EHA. It noted that "if the child is so far disabled as to be unconscious, and is thus wholly uneducable, he falls outside the Act even though his disability is more rather than less severe than that of the children protected by the Act." However, the court continued that "in light of the close connection between mental retardation and special educational need . . . developmental disability, far from being an exempted category, is an important subcategory of the disabilities covered by the Act." What Illinois had done, found the court, was to carve out a class of disabled children and deny them the full reimbursement to which they were entitled.

The appellate court, however, reversed that portion of the district court's ruling which ordered the state to reimburse the parents for expenses they had paid back to the year 1978. The parents were only entitled to reimbursement necessary to clear outstanding bills, thus preventing the expulsion of children from their residential placements. *Parks v. Pavkovic*, 753 F.2d 1397 (7th Cir.1985).

New Jersey's department of education issued detailed regulations governing private schools which educate disabled children. The regulations applied only to private schools to which local school boards sent children with disabilities in order to satisfy the local board's educational obligations. These private schools were required to submit detailed budgets, establish strict bookkeeping and accounting procedures, submit to annual audits by the state, and most objectionably, a school's profit was limited to 2.5% of its per pupil costs. Several private school associations sued the department seeking to have the regulations declared invalid. They claimed that the regulations were "confiscatory" and had been enacted without proper authority.

The New Jersey Superior Court, Appellate Division, upheld the regulations as within the scope of the department's powers. Especially persuasive to the court was the argument that private schools, by choosing to accept disabled students on referral from local school boards, should expect to relinquish a degree of privacy and autonomy over their affairs. The 2.5% profit ceiling is a reasonable exercise of department authority over private schools which, said the court, have voluntarily submitted to department control. However, the court left open the possibility that in the future, if a private school were able to show that due to its financial condition the regulations were unreasonable as applied to it, then a waiver of the regulations might be justified. *Council of Private Schools for Children with Special Needs v. Cooperman*, 501 A.2d 575 (N.J.Super.A.D.1985).

A New York school district provided special education services to a disabled student. After one year, the school district sought tuition reimbursement in a New York trial court from another school district pursuant to Education Law § 3202. The court granted the defendant school district's motion to dismiss because the claiming school district had not filed a notice of claim within three months pursuant to Education Law § 3813(1). The claimant school district appealed to the Supreme Court, Appellate Division.

On appeal, the school district contended that it did not have to comply with the notice of claim requirement when the action was one to "vindicate a public interest." The court agreed. However, it noted that the public interest exception did not permit the school district to commence an action after the one year statute of limitation set out in Education Law § 3813(2-b). Therefore, the action was properly dismissed as time-barred. *Katonah-Lewisboro School v. Carmel School*, 571 N.Y.S.2d 333 (A.D.1991).

CHAPTER NINE

DISCRIMINATION

The Rehabilitation Act of 1973 prohibits discrimination against individuals with disabilities in programs receiving federal financial assistance. Under the Act, no otherwise qualified individual with a disability is to be excluded from employment, programs, or services to which he or she is entitled. Additionally, claims for alleged discrimination are sometimes brought under the Equal Protection Clause of the U.S. Constitution, which also prohibits discrimination by guaranteeing that laws will be applied equally to all citizens.

I. DUTY NOT TO DISCRIMINATE AGAINST THE DISABLED

The duty not to discriminate against individuals with disabilities may arise by statute and/or may be concomitant with the receipt of federal funding. Where a state's asserted interest in discriminating against the disabled is outweighed by the liberty interests of the disabled, the state must affirmatively act to eliminate the source of discrimination, or, in other cases, must refrain from acting when doing so would promote unfair discrimination.

A. Students, Patients and other Individuals under the Rehabilitation Act and the Equal Protection Clause

The U.S. Supreme Court ruled recently that mental retardation is not a "suspect classification" calling for heightened protection under the U.S. Constitution. This case arose when the operator of a proposed group home for mentally disabled individuals was denied a building-use permit by the city council of Cleburne, Texas. The city council determined that the group home would be classified as a "hospital for the feebleminded" under the zoning laws and proceeded to deny a permit to the group home. The operator sued the city in federal court, claiming that the council's action unlawfully discriminated against mentally retarded citizens in violation of the Equal Protection Clause of the U.S. Constitution.

The Supreme Court, while ordering the group home to be granted a permit, held that government regulations regarding mentally retarded individuals are not to be subjected to rigorous judicial analysis as are classifications based on race, alienage or sex. The Equal Protection Clause, held the Court, does not afford the same protection to disabled citizens as it does to minorities. Although in this case the group home won its building-use permit, the Supreme Court's holding limited the scope of the Equal Protection Clause to cases involving irrational, unfounded or arbitrary action against the disabled. *City of Cleburne, Texas v. Cleburne Living Center,* 473 U.S. 432, 105 S.Ct. 3249, 87 L.Ed.2d 313 (1985).

A student with a disability enrolled in a college of optometry. He suffered from retinitis pigmentosis and an associated neurological condition. As a result, he had a restricted field of vision and impaired motor skills, sense of touch and manual coordination. The college's policy was that each school year was governed by its current catalog. The student enrolled in the college, under the terms of a catalog effective for the 1978-79 academic year. The catalog language cautioned that it did not create a contract between the college and any student. During the student's first year of study, the college introduced a pathology clinic proficiency requirement involving use of special equipment. The clinic requirement was not listed in the 1978-79 catalog. The student failed his tests on the equipment, and requested a waiver. The college's board of trustees denied his request, but granted him an extra quarter to practice on the equipment. Despite his extra practice, the student failed to satisfy the proficiency requirements. The college refused to award the student a degree.

The student sued the college in a federal district court, claiming that it violated § 504 of the Rehabilitation Act, 42 U.S.C. § 1983, and that the college breached his educational contract under state law. The court dismissed the § 1983 claim and conducted a trial on the other matters. The college prevailed in the § 504 claim, but the student prevailed on the breach of contract claim. The student appealed to the U.S. Court of Appeals, Sixth Circuit, on his § 504 claim and the college cross-appealed on the breach of contract claim. The student claimed that the college used the test as a pretext for discrimination because it applied a higher standard to him by requiring mechanical proficiency with equipment. The court held that the college could reasonably set standards for its program to ensure competence. Section 504 did not require the college to lower its academic requirements to accommodate students with disabilities. The college had not failed to reasonably accommodate the student, and it prevailed on the § 504 claim. The court also held that students should reasonably anticipate changes in academic requirements after enrolling. The college's addition of new degree requirements was reasonable. There was no evidence that the college had deliberately introduced the clinical proficiency requirement to prevent the student's graduation. The case was reversed in part and affirmed in part so that the college prevailed in all matters. *Doherty v. Southern College of Optometry,* 862 F.2d 570 (6th Cir.1988).

An Alabama college admitted a schizophrenic student even though she failed to meet the college's admission standards. The college was apparently unaware of the student's condition until the first week of classes when her roommate's father called the school to complain; the student was then transferred to a different dormitory room. The student alleged that the college subsequently began to treat her in a hostile manner, stating that she was "constructively dismissed," in other words, forced to resign. The student filed a Rehabilitation Act complaint in the U.S. District Court for the Southern District of Alabama, which held for the college. Because § 504 of the Rehabilitation Act prohibits the exclusion of disabled students from participation in or denial of benefits of programs receiving federal financial assistance and protects them from discrimination, the district court had instructed the jury to return a verdict for the student only if it found that her dismissal was the result of intentional discrimination or discriminatory animus. The student appealed to the U.S. Court of Appeals, Eleventh Circuit.

On appeal, the student argued that the jury instructions were incorrect and resulted in the decision against her. The court of appeals disagreed, finding that the instructions were consistent with the Rehabilitation Act and with previous decisions of the Eleventh Circuit. Compensatory damages under the Rehabilitation Act were precluded in cases of unintentional discrimination, but were permissible in cases of intentional discrimination. The jury had determined that there was no intentional discrimination against the student, so she could not obtain compensatory damages under the Rehabilitation Act. Accordingly, the jury instructions were appropriate and the district court's decision was affirmed. *Wood v. President and Trustees of Spring Hill College*, 978 F.2d 1214 (11th Cir.1992).

A Vermont woman suffered from hypothyroidism (an endocrinological disorder producing symptoms of apathy, difficulty concentrating, and fatigue). She qualified as a person with handicaps under § 504 of the Rehabilitation Act. She entered the University of Vermont's Masters of Education in Counseling program in 1976. However, she did not complete the required course work in five years, so in October 1982, the university informed her that her Masters degree work was terminated. For the next two years, the student enrolled in courses at the university while seeking reinstatement as a Masters degree candidate. The university notified the student that it would accept her as a candidate for its new Masters of Science in Counseling degree, but the student did not find the terms of readmission acceptable. In 1984, the university withdrew its offer of readmission. It determined that the student's hypothyroidism was a treatable medical condition and that it had reasonably accommodated her by its offer of readmission. In 1990, the student brought suit against the university in federal district court. The court granted summary judgment to the university on the ground that the student's claim was time-barred because of Vermont's 3-year statute of limitations for personal injury actions.

On appeal, the U.S. Court of Appeals, Second Circuit, held that the district court had properly decided the case. Section 504 of the Rehabilitation Act was a discrimination law and, like other federal discrimination laws which did not have a stated limitations period, ought to be governed by the same state limitations period for personal injury actions that apply to other federal laws. The court affirmed the lower court's grant of summary judgment to the university on the student's § 504 claim. *Morse v. University of Vermont*, 973 F.2d 122 (2d Cir.1992).

The University of Alabama, Board of Trustees (UAB) denied auxiliary aids to hearing impaired disabled students because of their financial ability to pay or their enrollment in noncredit courses. UAB adopted a policy that provided aids such as note-takers and transcriptions of tape recordings of classes, but would not provide costly aids such as interpreters. UAB directed such disabled students to the Vocational Rehabilitation Service to provide the costly aids. Then the students were directed to apply for financial aid. If the students could demonstrate the financial need and an inability to pay they would receive the free interpreter or aid. The policy excluded students taking noncredit or nondegree courses from receiving auxiliary aids. The federal district court ruled that the UAB policy violated § 504 of the Rehabilitation Act when it failed to provide an interpreter to students who were unable to procure such services elsewhere free of charge and when it failed to provide any auxiliary aids to students in nondegree programs. UAB appealed to the U.S. Court of Appeals, Eleventh Circuit.

On appeal, the court sought to determine the statutory intent and the legislative history of § 504. The court noted that the Department of Health, Education and Welfare published a notice of proposed rules which indicated that universities could refer students to state vocational rehabilitation agencies as a first step in obtaining auxiliary aids. However, where no resource exists the university must provide the needed auxiliary aid. Next, the court analyzed the reasonableness of the auxiliary aid policy. Other courts have determined that § 504 does not impose an affirmative action on the part of universities who receive federal funds. However, the court determined that in this case it was not an affirmative action on the part of the university to provide an interpreter because the lack of an interpreter effectively denies the disabled person an opportunity to learn. The court also determined that noncredit and nondegree courses are also covered by § 504 because they are a part of "all of the operations of ... a college, university, or other post-secondary institution." The court of appeals affirmed the trial court's decision requiring UAB to provide aids to hearing impaired students free of charge. *U.S. v. Bd. of Trustees for Univ. of Ala.*, 908 F.2d 740 (11th Cir.1990).

A Pennsylvania medical student's back problems made attending medical school difficult due to the uncomfortable chairs and the school's parking arrangements. She requested and received a deferral from the school for a year during which time she received notification from another school that she had been accepted. However, in the application to that medical school, she did not indicate that she had matriculated at the first medical school. When the first medical school found out about the acceptance it notified the student, the other school, and the AMCAS. The other medical school then denied her acceptance and the student sued the first medical school for violations of the Rehabilitation Act and tortious interference with her present and future contracts with other medical schools. The trial court granted summary judgment to the college, and the student appealed to the U.S. Court of Appeals, Third Circuit.

On appeal, the court noted that in order to be held liable under the Rehabilitation Act, the previous medical school must know or be reasonably expected to know of the student's disability. Neither the Rehabilitation act, not the regulations specify what notification was necessary to adequately inform the school of her disability or what constituted awareness of the disability. Under the act, a person with handicaps is any person who: 1) has a physical or mental impairment which substantially limits one or more of such person's major life activities, 2) has a record of such impairment, or 3) is regarded as having such impairment. Although the district court determined that the student never sufficiently demonstrated to the school that one of her major life activities had been impaired, the apppellate court determined that there was sufficient evidence to create a material issue of fact as to whether the medical school knew or had reason to know that the student met the standards of a disabled individual. Therefore, the court of appeals reversed this part of the district court's decision.

However, the appellate court determined that the medical school had not interfered with the student's acceptance at a second college by contacting and disclosing her matriculation at the first college because it was following AMCAS rules and there was sufficient evidence to support the district court's conclusion that the student matriculated at the first college. *Nathanson v. Medical College of Pa.*, 926 F.2d 1368 (3d Cir.1991).

An Illinois case resulted in a ruling that a disabled student may not sue the U.S. Secretary of Education. Here, a graduate student pursuing an MBA at Chicago's Roosevelt University failed to inform university officials that he was handicapped, and did not tell them that he was learning disabled. Instead, the university thought that he was recovering from a serious illness. In view of the student's "illness," the university allowed him to continue in its MBA program even though he received his third "C," which usually results in academic dismissal. Eventually, the student was unable to meet the MBA program's requirements. He attempted to bring suit under the Rehabilitation Act directly against the U.S. Secretary of Education, seeking damages due to the secretary's refusal to review his claim that the university had discriminated against him on the basis of his disability.

The federal district court observed that the student had never informed the university that he was disabled by a learning disability. Unquestionably, he had no claim against the university since the Rehabilitation Act imposes no duty upon institutions which are unaware of a person's disability, said the court, and this no doubt explained why he had attempted to sue the secretary instead. The student's lawsuit was thus dismissed by the court, which stated: "There is no doubt that a recipient or applicant of federal funds has a cause of action against the Secretary under Section 603 [of the Rehabilitation Act]. There is also no doubt that a beneficiary in [the disabled student's] position has a private right of action against the recipient institution. But no private cause of action exists under Section 504 [of the Act] for a beneficiary against the Secretary." The student's complaint against the secretary was dismissed, and he appealed to the U.S. Court of Appeals, Seventh Circuit.

The question before the court was whether the student could force the secretary to review his case or force the secretary to cut off the university's federal funding. The court held that "a request for damages against administrative adjudicators is not supported by any statute.... A request for damages against the Secretary of Education, who personally played no role in the administrative adjudication, also is not provided by any other statute." The court concluded that a private person had no legal interest in public enforcement of matters such as the termination of federal funding. The student had to be content with his own remedies against the university. The lower court's ruling that the student could not maintain a lawsuit against the secretary of education was upheld. *Salvador v. Bennett,* 800 F.2d 97 (7th Cir.1986).

A New York woman who had been blind from birth filed a request for sponsorship under the Rehabilitation Act of 1973 to attend undergraduate college and law school. The Commission for the Blind and Visually Handicapped of the New York State Department of Social Services, which administered the Act in New York, refused the request, citing the applicant's current employment as a paralegal and the grant she had received to train for that position. An administrative law judge held that, although the applicant's career might not be the highest level obtainable by her, it was suitable employment and consistent with her capacities or her abilities and the goals of the Vocational Rehabilitation Program. The applicant then sued in state court for review of the decision.

The New York Supreme Court, Appellate Division, held for the applicant. It stated that the Rehabilitation Act was enacted to provide vocational rehabilitation services for persons with disabilities in order to maximize their employability. In light of this goal, the commission must provide services which enable the applicant to reach her highest achievable vocational goal, rather than simply assure that she has suitable employment. The administrative law judge did not utilize this as the standard for approval, so the judge's decision was in error. The case was remanded for further proceedings based on this ruling. *Polkabla v. Comm. for the Blind*, 583 N.Y.S.2d 464 (A.D.1992).

A profoundly deaf student received a bachelor's degree in English from a District of Columbia university. After graduating, he sought to employ his writing skills in the fields of advertising, marketing, and technical writing. However, after sending out eighteen resumes and receiving no offers to interview, he chose to enter law school at Notre Dame. He applied to the Indiana Department of Human Service's Office of Vocational Rehabilitation (OVR) for assistance in defraying the cost of an interpreter to assist him in his law classes. The OVR agreed to finance an interpreter, but the particular interpreter chosen did not suit the student. He found a more expensive alternative interpreter, but the OVR refused to pay the additional fee. The student wrote a letter to the OVR stating his intention to appeal the decision, as well as requesting tuition, book, transportation, and maintenance expenses.

A hearing officer decided that the OVR improperly denied the student's request to pay the alternate interpreter, but did not rule on the other expenses since they had never been formally requested. The director of the OVR ordered a new hearing at which the same conclusion was reached. However, the director entered a final order denying the student's eligibility. He stated that since the student was employable within the fields of advertising, marketing, and technical writing, he did not meet the requirements for eligibility. On appeal, an Indiana trial court reinstated the hearing officer's decision. The OVR appealed.

The Court of Appeals of Indiana stated that in order to be eligible for assistance under the Rehabilitation Act of 1973, an individual must be handicapped and his or her disability must result in a "substantial handicap to employment." The question thus presented was whether the student's deafness impeded his occupational performance by preventing the obtaining, retaining, or preparing for employment consistent with his capacities and abilities. The court used a forward-looking test and stated that since the student was potentially employable as an attorney, his deafness prevented his preparation for employment as such. The court remanded for a determination of which services the student should receive. *Indiana Dep't of Human Services v. Firth*, 590 N.E.2d 154 (Ind.App.1992).

The Texas legislature instituted an education law which required students to maintain a 70% average in their course work in order to be eligible to participate in extracurricular activities. A learning disabled third grader with dyslexia was excluded from a trip to Astroworld. He brought a suit challenging the statute as unconstitutional as applied against persons with handicaps. A Texas trial court denied relief and the boy appealed to the Court of Appeals of Texas. By the time the case came to trial the legislature had amended the statute to include the following:

(c) Suspension of a disabled student whose disability significantly interferes with the student's ability to meet regular academic standards shall be based upon the student's failure to meet the requirements of the student's individual education plan. The determination of whether a disability significantly interferes with a student's ability to meet regular academic standards shall be made by the student's admission, reviews and dismissal committee..."

The court noted that prior to the amendment the statute was unconstitutional as applied to students with handicaps. However, currently the statute met constitutional standards and the court ruled that the case was moot, i.e., there was no longer a case in controversy. *Texas Educ. Agency v. Stamos*, 817 S.W.2d 378 (Tex.App.1991).

The next two cases summarize how the courts treat alcoholism with respect to the Rehabilitation Act.

Two honorably discharged veterans who were recovering alcoholics sought an extension of the ten-year Veterans' Administration (V.A.) limitation for the receipt of educational assistance under the G.I. Bill. The ten-year limitation on educational benefits can be extended by the V.A. if the veteran can show he was prevented from using his benefits earlier because of "physical or mental disability which was not the result of ... [his] own willful misconduct." V.A. regulations state that the deliberate drinking of alcohol is considered willful misconduct.

Both veterans requested extension of benefits after expiration of their respective ten-year limitation periods. These requests were based on grounds that they were disabled by alcoholism. The V.A. denied their requests, stating that their alcoholism was due to willful misconduct. One veteran sued the V.A. in a New York district court. The other veteran sought review in the District Court for the District of Columbia.

The New York district court held for the V.A., but its decision was reversed by the U.S. Court of Appeals, Second Circuit. The District of Columbia district court ruled that the V.A. regulation was contrary to the Rehabilitation Act. The Act prohibits federal programs from discriminating against individuals with handicaps solely because of their handicaps. The District of Columbia Court of Appeals reversed the district court's decision.

Noting the disagreement between two federal courts of appeal, the U.S. Supreme Court granted review and heard the cases together. The Court held that the Rehabilitation Act does not preclude a lawsuit against the V.A. Congress had changed the time limit for benefits several times, most recently in 1977. However, the Rehabilitation Act did not repeal the willful misconduct provision of the 1977 regulations. Nothing in the act required that any benefit extended to one category of persons with handicaps also be extended to all other categories of disabled persons. Congress had the right to establish the allocation priorities for veterans' benefits. The District of Columbia Court of Appeals decision was affirmed, and the Second Circuit Court of Appeals was reversed. The V.A. prevailed in both matters. *Traynor v. Turnage*, 485 U.S. 535, 108 S.Ct. 1372, 99 L.Ed.2d 618 (1988).

A law student at the University of Wisconsin completed his first semester with below standard grades. He was dismissed during his second semester because he failed to furnish certification of his undergraduate degree. The school allowed him to return the following spring despite knowledge that he was an alcoholic. Sensing that he was doing poorly, the student asked to withdraw. The school later learned that while drunk, the student had harassed and threatened a classmate. The school readmitted the student for a third time the following spring. He completed the semester with below standard grades and the school expelled him. The student sued the school in Wisconsin federal court alleging § 504 violations of the Rehabilitaion Act, by discriminating against him on account of alcoholism. The district court granted the school's dismissal motion because the student was not "otherwise qualified" to continue as a law student. He then appealed to the U.S. Court of Appeals, Seventh Circuit.

The appeals court noted that § 504 provided that an institution receiving federal funds may not discriminate against an "otherwise qualified disabled individual." It also noted that previous cases had held that "[a]n otherwise qualified person is one who is able to meet all of a program's requirements in spite of his disability." The Rehabilitation Act did not forbid decisions based on the actual attributes of the individual. It also recognized that the school's decision was based on evaluations of how the student had previously performed and how he could be expected to perform in the future. In this case, the school acted on the basis of the student's past performance rather than on his alcoholism. The appeals court upheld the district court decision to dismiss the case. *Anderson v. Univ. of Wisconsin*, 841 F.2d 737 (7th Cir.1988).

A Kansas school district used a 3' x 5' "time-out" room for in-school suspensions of a disabled student. The student had a history of truancy, violent behavior and willful disobedience of school rules. The student was placed in the time-out room when he was disruptive so he could regain his composure and not disturb other students. He was to engage in classroom work while in the time-out room. The student sued the school district in a federal district court. He alleged that use of the time-out room violated his due process rights under the Fourteenth Amendment to the U.S. Constitution. He also claimed that use of the time-out room violated the Eighth Amendment's prohibition against cruel and inhumane punishment. The school district argued that the student's fundamental contention was that it had violated the EHA's change-in-placement provision. Therefore, the student's claim should fail because he had not exhausted his administrative remedies under the EHA.

The court held for the student concerning the exhaustion of remedies argument. The use of the time-out room was not an activity the EHA was intended to prevent. Therefore, the EHA was not the exclusive avenue through which the student could bring his lawsuit. The student could sue alleging deprivation of his constitutional rights under § 1983 of the Civil Rights Act.

The court also concluded that the use of the time-out room did not constitute cruel and inhumane punishment. The Supreme Court held that the Eighth Amendment protection against such punishment should not be extended to lawsuits brought by public school students.

The court held for the school district regarding the student's due process claim. The student was not deprived of his constitutional interest in education when he was placed in the time-out room. In fact, the use of the time-out room ensured that the student would not be deprived of his right to a public education when he was suspended because it kept him in school during that time. The student was not deprived of due process because he was placed in the time-out room only after three documented disciplinary violations. He was given sufficient prior notice of the reason for the placement in the time-out room. The school sent written notice to his parents when use of the time-out room was contemplated. His parents were notified about time-out room use in conferences with school officials. The school district was not liable for violating the student's constitutional rights. *Hayes v. Unified School Dist. No. 377*, 669 F.Supp. 1519 (D.Kan.1987).

A university medical student had failed numerous courses in his second attempt at completing a first year program, and was dismissed. The student suffered from dyslexia and claimed that the school had discriminated against him because of his disability. Specifically, he complained that the university's refusal to alter its method of testing by multiple choice exams led to his failure. The student filed a lawsuit in a federal district court claiming a violation of § 504 of the Rehabilitation Act. The district court granted summary judgment to the university and the student appealed to the U.S. Court of Appeals, First Circuit, which agreed to hear the case en banc.

Section 504 prohibits any entity which receives federal financial assistance from denying the benefits of an activity because of disability. The student was required to show that in spite of his disability he was otherwise qualified for the program. The school was required to make reasonable accommodations for a qualified individual, but need not make fundamental changes in its program. The court focused on what was required of the university. It was ruled to have an obligation to seek a reasonable accommodation. In the absence of finding a reasonable accommodation, it must submit a factual record which shows that it "considered alternative means, their feasibility, costs, and effect on the academic program, and came to a rationally justifiable conclusion that the available alternatives would result. . . in lowering academic standards requiring substantial program alterations."

The university submitted, in the form of an affidavit from the dean, an explanation that the tests measure a student's ability to memorize and assimilate complicated material and are important as a matter of substance as opposed to only a matter of form. In order to further show the importance of the abilities tested by multiple choice questions, it also cited a modern day physician's duties which include making emergency choices based on a quick reading of complicated material. The court felt that the dean's affidavit was completely insufficient. There was no mention of alternatives considered, or who participated in the decision. "Were the simple conclusory averment of a head of an institution to suffice, there would be no way of ascertaining whether the institution had made a professional effort to evaluate the possible ways of accommodating a disabled student or had simply embraced what was most convenient." The court reversed the summary judgment which the district court had granted for the school, and remanded the case to the district court. *Wynne v. Tufts Univ. School of Medicine*, 932 F.2d 19 (1st Cir.1991).

B. Students, Parents and Other Individuals under the IDEA

A 16-year-old California high school student, suffering from cerebral palsy, learning disabilities and right side deafness, used a wheelchair for mobility. She participated in a two-week training program with an organization which trains service dogs for use by people with disabilities. At the end of the training period, she received a service dog of her own. She then sought to bring the dog to school with her, but the school district refused to allow her to do so. She sued the school district in a federal district court, seeking injunctive and declaratory relief, and emotional distress damages. The district sought to dismiss her claim, and she moved for a preliminary injunction to allow her, during the course of the trial, to be accompanied by her service dog at school.

The district court first determined that the student's claim should not be dismissed because of her failure to exhaust her administrative remedies. The student did not contend that the service dog was educationally necessary, but merely asserted that she had a right to be accompanied by her service dog in places of accommodation. Thus, the relief that she sought was not specifically available under the Education of the Handicapped Act (EHA). The court ruled that the student need not exhaust her EHA administrative remedies to bring the lawsuit. It then determined that facilities which were open to members of the general public, like schools, were required to make access equally available to disabled and able-bodied persons alike.

The court then looked to the student's motion for a preliminary injunction. It recognized that preliminary relief would require an alteration of the status quo and decided that if the student could show that she would likely be successful in her case, and that the harm she would suffer by not having her dog with her would be much greater than the harm to the school by the dog's presence, she would be entitled to preliminary relief. Here, the school was a facility required by law to be nondiscriminatory and the student's chances of success were good. Further, the school district had shown only that it would suffer a minor inconvenience by having to restructure the student's educational program to accommodate her service dog. The student's injuries would far outweigh those of the school and, accordingly, the court granted the preliminary injunction in favor of the student. *Sullivan v. Vallejo City Unified School District*, 731 F.Supp. 947 (E.D.Cal.1990).

A West Virginia man enrolled his two hearing-impaired children in a public school. Since there were no other hearing-impaired children in the school system, it did not have an adequate program for such children. When the children were not being privately taught by a speech therapist, they were placed in a regular classroom. The children were then placed in a school for the deaf and the blind, until one child was expelled for behavioral problems. After another attempt to place the children in different hearing-impaired schools, the children were again placed in the same public school. School authorities determined that the children also had speech, learning and behavioral problems. After the father rejected the school's attempt to institutionalize the children, he filed a complaint with the state Human Rights Commission. He alleged that his children had been denied an appropriate education and thus had been discriminated against. Pending a determination, the children were finally given individualized educational programs. The commission determined that the board had violated the Human Rights Act by failing to provide an appropriate education. It ordered monetary damages and compensatory education until the children reached age 24. After a West Virginia trial court vacated the order, the father appealed to the West Virginia Supreme Court of Appeals.

The court reinstated the commission's order. It held that the board was a "person" within the meaning of state law and thus had violated prohibitions against disability discrimination. Further, state law imposes a duty on the board to establish an appropriate education for children with disabilities. The federal Education of the Handicapped Act (EHA) also required placement of the children in the least restrictive environment. The board had not done so because it sought to send the children to out of state institutions. It had discriminated against the children on the basis of disability. *Board of Education v. Human Rights Comm'n*, 385 S.E.2d 637 (W.Va.1989).

The deaf parents of two New York public school students who had normal hearing repeatedly requested the school district to provide qualified sign-language interpreters for school meetings. The district denied requests to provide or pay for interpreters to assist the parents in communicating with teachers and counselors. The parents claimed that they had been unable to participate in some school events and had expended $2,000 in one academic year for their own interpreter. They claimed that they were being denied equal access to school services in violation of the Rehabilitation Act of 1973, 29 U.S.C. § 794 and the Civil Rights Act, 42 U.S.C. § 1983. They sued the school district in a federal district court for declaratory, injunctive and monetary relief.

The court held that the parents were otherwise qualified persons with handicaps who were entitled to meaningful access to school-initiated meetings. It also held that the superintendent of schools was entitled to qualified immunity from liability. The court refused to grant a school district motion to dismiss the case. It then held a trial to determine the extent of the school district's obligation under § 504 of the Rehabilitation Act. According to the court, the parents had been effectively barred from participation in school district programs for parents due to a lack of a sign language interpreter. The parents were entitled to an interpreter for all school-sponsored activities designed for parental involvement which focused on academic progress or discipline. The parents would have to provide their own interpreters for participation in voluntary extracurricular activities. *Rothschild v. Grottenthaler*, 725 F.Supp. 776 (S.D.N.Y.1989).

A New Hampshire father alleged that his daughter, a child with a disability, was not receiving a free appropriate education. He was granted an administrative due process hearing by the state. Dissatisfied with the results of the hearing, he sued the New Hampshire State Board of Education in a federal district court. After the state refused to provide him with a free written transcript of the administrative hearing, he brought a separate lawsuit against it in the same court. The court ruled that the state did not have to provide a free written transcript of the hearing, so he appealed to the U.S. Court of Appeals, First Circuit.

The court of appeals observed that, although a written transcript of the hearing would be more helpful than a recording for purposes of an EHA lawsuit, EHA § 1415(d)(3) only granted the right to receive either a written transcript or electronic verbatim record of the hearing. Since the state had provided an electronic verbatim record of the administrative due process hearing, it had fulfilled its responsibility. The father's claim that because he could not afford the $3,000 for a written transcript, his due process rights had been violated, was rejected by the court of appeals. It concluded that the administrative due process hearing itself satisfied the father's basic due process rights.

The father also contended that the failure to provide a transcript violated his rights under the Equal Protection Clause. He claimed that the refusal to provide the transcript was the result of unconstitutional discrimination based upon either his daughter's disability or his lack of wealth. The court of appeals did not accept the first argument since the father had failed to show that the EHA provision infringed upon the rights of any "suspect class." A "suspect class" is a group of persons who are afforded special protection under the Equal Protection Clause (e.g., racial minorities). The U.S. Supreme Court has held in *City of Cleburne v. Cleburne Living Center*, 473 U.S. 432, 105 S.Ct. 3249, 87 L.Ed.2d 313 (1985), that persons with disabilities are not a suspect class. Thus, legislative classifications based upon disabilities will not be given rigorous examination by the courts. Further, the court of appeals held that a classification based upon indigence received closer examination only if indigents were "completely unable to pay for some desired benefit [which results in] an absolute deprivation of a meaningful opportunity to enjoy that benefit." Here, the alleged classification based upon wealth only made recourse to the court more difficult rather than impossible. The district court's decision was upheld. *Edward B. v. Paul*, 814 F.2d 52 (1st Cir.1987).

A group of mentally retarded children in Virginia brought suit against the Virginia Commissioner of the Department of Welfare, and other state officials, seeking injunctive relief enjoining the defendants from maintaining them in an institution or state hospital. The children claimed that these placements were made in lieu of providing them with an appropriate education and services in a foster home or other community-based facility in their home communities. A federal district court held that the children had a valid claim under the Developmentally Disabled Assistance and Bill of Rights Act, the EHA and the Rehabilitation Act. These statutes afford personal civil rights to beneficiaries under the statutes, which were intended to promote equal treatment of and equal opportunity to the beneficiaries. The defendants' motion for summary judgment on the ground that the children had failed to state a valid claim was denied. *Medley v. Ginsberg*, 492 F.Supp. 1294 (S.D.W.Va.1980).

C. Teachers

Teachers and other school employees are protected by the Rehabilitation Act against discrimination on the basis of disability.

The U.S. Supreme Court ruled that tuberculosis is a disability under § 504 of the Rehabilitation Act. Federal law defines an individual with a handicap as "any person who (i) has a physical or mental impairment which substantially limits one or more of such person's major life activities, (ii) has a record of such impairment or (iii) is regarded as having such an impairment." It defines "physical impairment" as disorders affecting, among other things, the respiratory system and defines "major life activities" as "functions such as caring for one's self . . . and working."

The case involved a Florida elementary school teacher who was discharged because of the continued recurrence of tuberculosis. The teacher sued the school board under § 504 but a U.S. district court dismissed her claims. However, the U.S. Court of Appeals, Eleventh Circuit, reversed the district court's decision and held that persons with contagious diseases fall within § 504's coverage. The school board appealed to the U.S. Supreme Court.

The Supreme Court ruled that tuberculosis was a disability under § 504 because it affected the respiratory system and affected her ability to work. The school board contended that in defining an individual with a handicap under § 504, the contagious effects of a disease can be distinguished from the disease's physical effects. However, the Court reasoned that the teacher's contagion and her physical impairment both resulted from the same condition: tuberculosis. It would be unfair to allow an employer to distinguish between a disease's potential effect on others and its effect on the afflicted employee in order to justify discriminatory treatment. Allowing discrimination based on the contagious effects of a physical impairment would be inconsistent with the underlying purpose of § 504. That purpose is to ensure that persons with handicaps are not denied jobs because of prejudice or ignorance. The Court noted that society's myths and fears about disability and disease are as handicapping as the physical limitations that result from physical impairment, and concluded that contagion cannot remove a person from § 504 coverage. The Supreme Court remanded the case to the district court to determine whether the teacher was "otherwise qualified" for her job and whether the school board could reasonably accommodate her as an employee. *School Bd. of Nassau County v. Arline*, 480 U.S. 273, 107 S.Ct. 1123, 94 L.Ed.2d 307 (1987).

On remand, the Florida federal district court held that the teacher was "otherwise qualified" to teach. The teacher posed no threat of spreading tuberculosis to her students in 1978. When she was on medication, medical tests indicated a limited number of negative cultures. Her family members tested negative and she had limited contact with students. The court ordered reinstatement or front-pay in the amount of $768,724 for earnings until retirement. *Arline v. School Bd. of Nassau County*, 692 F.Supp. 1286 (M.D.Fla.1988).

A teacher of hearing-impaired children was relegated to an administrative position when the school district discovered that he had AIDS. The teacher sued the school board asserting that it had violated his rights under the Rehabilitation Act of 1973 by removing him from the classroom. The teacher's request for a preliminary injunction (which would have allowed him to teach until the court could hold a trial and issue a ruling) was denied by a U.S. district court. The U.S. Court of Appeals, Ninth Circuit, reversed and issued the preliminary injunction. The court of appeals later issued a decision which set out the reasons for the issuance of the preliminary injunction.

The court noted that to acquire the preliminary injunction the teacher had to demonstrate a combination of probable success at trial and a possibility of irreparable injury. Under the Rehabilitation Act the teacher could not be dismissed because of his handicapping condition (AIDS) if he was otherwise qualified to teach. The court then applied a test devised by the U.S. Supreme Court in *Arline*. The test provided that "a person who poses a significant risk of communicating an infectious disease to others in the workplace will not be otherwise qualified for his or her job if reasonable accommodations will not eliminate that risk." The court then pointed out the district court's finding that transmission of AIDS was unlikely to occur in the classroom. The court held that the teacher was otherwise qualified for his position because his presence in the classroom would not pose "a significant risk of communicating an infectious disease to others." This finding meant that the teacher would probably succeed at trial.

The court then noted that although the teacher's salary was not reduced when he was transferred to the administrative position, the transfer removed him from a job for which he had developed special skills and from which he derived "tremendous personal satisfaction and joy." The administrative position, on the other hand, involved no student contact and did not utilize the teacher's skills, training or experience. The court also observed that the teacher's ability to work would surely be affected in time by AIDS which has proved fatal in all reported cases. The court concluded that any delay in returning the teacher to the classroom caused an irretrievable loss of the teacher's productive time. This established the possibility of irreparable injury if the preliminary injunction was not awarded.

Because the teacher had shown 1) that he would probably succeed at trial, and 2) that the denial of a preliminary injunction in his favor could cause him irreparable injury, the court awarded the preliminary injunction. The teacher was returned to the classroom. *Chalk v. U.S. Dist. Court*, 840 F.2d 701 (9th Cir.1988).

A physically disabled Nevada student received a teaching degree in special education and was then licensed by the state of Nevada as a special education teacher. She applied for a teaching position with a Nevada school district and also placed herself on the list of persons available for substitute teaching. She worked as a substitute teacher for over three years and received high praise for her performance. However, she was not offered permanent employment. She then worked as a substitute teacher under a federally-funded temporary contract at another school. The following spring the school had four teaching positions available and offered the teacher a temporary contract. When the teacher received her one-year temporary contract, a permanent position was open in the school district but was given to a student teacher with no teaching experience. The teacher received the most difficult and demanding class assignment at the school. She then filed a discrimination lawsuit against the school district in a U.S. district court.

The court found that under § 794 of the Rehabilitation Act, an otherwise qualified individual with a handicap could not be discriminated against under any program or activity receiving federal financial assistance. The teacher fell within the Act's definition of a person with a handicap and was otherwise qualified to serve as a special education teacher. The court found that the school district never made an affirmative effort to recognize the teacher's disabilities or to accommodate them. Thus she was discriminated against solely on the basis of her disability. The court found for the teacher and awarded her compensatory damages. *Recanzone v. Washoe County School Dist.*, 696 F.Supp. 1372 (D.Nev.1988).

An applicant for a special education teaching position in Iowa sued a local education agency under the federal Rehabilitation Act and Iowa law alleging that the agency refused to hire him due to his physical disability. The teacher, a resident of Vermont, suffered from several severe disabilities but was able to walk without assistance and to lift children and drive. The teacher applied to the Iowa agency for a job, and was scheduled for an interview in Iowa at his own expense, with possible reimbursement if he were hired.

After arranging the interview, the teacher became concerned that he had not disclosed his disabilities. Because of limited financial resources, he did not wish to fly to Iowa only to be rejected because of his disabilities. He called the Iowa school, explained his disabilities and was told that the job involved transporting children which, in turn, required a bus driver's permit that the teacher probably could not get because of his disabilities. The agency suggested a trip to Iowa would probably be futile.

The teacher then sued in a U.S. district court, which found in his favor. The test of proof for a discrimination claim under the Rehabilitation Act is: 1) that the plaintiff is an individual with a handicap under the terms of the Act; 2) that the plaintiff is otherwise qualified to participate in the program or activity at issue; 3) that the plaintiff was excluded from the program or activity solely by reason of her or his disability; and 4) that the program or activity receives federal financial assistance.

Here, there was no dispute that the plaintiff was an individual with a handicap within the meaning of the Rehabilitation Act. The court also had little difficulty in finding that the plaintiff was otherwise qualified for the position, because of his superior credentials. The court also found that the plaintiff had satisfied the third and fourth prongs of the test, in that the defendant agency was a recipient of federal financial assistance, including funds received pursuant to the EAHCA and that, with a minimum of accommodation, the school district could have arranged an alternative situation whereby the teacher would not have had to transport children. The court awarded the teacher $1,000 damages for mental anguish, and $5,150 for loss of earnings. *Fitzgerald v. Green Valley Educ. Agency*, 589 F.Supp. 1130 (S.D.Iowa 1984).

A Louisiana hospital required a nurse to divulge medical information about his human immunodeficiency virus (HIV) status. The nurse had failed to report that he was a hepatitis B carrier and that he had once had a syphilis infection. The hospital suspended the nurse pending disclosure of information and later discharged him when he refused to provide the information. The hospital's infection control policies required employees to report infectious or communicable diseases to its employee health service. The nurse claimed that the policy violated his rights under § 504 of the Rehabilitation Act, 29 U.S.C. § 794. Section 504 provides that: "no otherwise qualified individual with a handicap . . . shall, solely by reason of his handicap, ... be subjected to discrimination under any program or activity receiving federal financial assistance." Congress defined an "individual with a handicap" to include individuals who are perceived as being impaired as well as individuals who are actually impaired. The nurse claimed that the hospital perceived him as being HIV positive and thus handicapped. The nurse sued the hospital in federal district court.

According to the court, there was no evidence to show that the hospital had perceived the nurse to be HIV positive. The nurse was informed at the termination hearing that he was being discharged for failure to follow hospital policy. He was discharged because he had violated the hospital's infection control policies, not because he was regarded as HIV positive. The nurse's refusal to comply with the hospital's policies rendered him "not otherwise qualified" to perform his job. The court held that the discharge of the nurse for refusal to provide HIV test results did not violate § 504 of the Rehabilitation Act. *Leckelt v. Bd. of Comm'rs of Hospital Dist. No. 1*, 714 F.Supp. 1377 (E.D.La.1989).

In 1979, the Council for the Hearing Impaired of Long Island and others brought suit in a federal district court against the Commissioner of Education of the State of New York, and several federal officials, alleging that the offering of lower salaries at educational institutions for students with disabilities was unlawful. Specifically, the plaintiffs contended that because teaching salaries at these institutions were lower than those found in other schools, there existed a relatively high staff turnover rate which had an adverse impact on disabled students' education. The plaintiffs charged that this violated the EHA, § 504 of the Rehabilitation Act, § 1983 of the Civil Rights Act and the First and Ninth Amendments to the U.S. Constitution.

On a motion for summary judgment, the district court dismissed the claim that a high staff turnover rate violated the EHA, noting that nothing in the EHA requires the education of children with disabilities to be "equal" to that of other children. All that is required is that children with disabilities be provided with an "educational benefit." Also dismissed were the plaintiffs' claims under the First and Ninth Amendments, since education is not guaranteed by the U.S. Constitution. However, the plaintiffs were allowed to proceed with their claims under the Rehabilitation Act and the Civil Rights Act, insofar as they alleged the state of New York had unlawfully discriminated between disabled and nondisabled children in the provision of educational services. The district court then proceeded to admonish the plaintiffs for failing to diligently prosecute their case, stating that they "have been content to file repetitive motions with this Court without developing the factual basis necessary to support their claims." The court stated that unless the plaintiffs brought new evidence establishing their claims, the case would be dismissed for lack of prosecution. *Council for the Hearing Impaired v. Ambach*, 610 F.Supp. 1051 (E.D.N.Y.1985).

II. RACIAL DISCRIMINATION IN PLACEMENT PROGRAMS

The *de facto* overrepresentation of minority students in special education programs, or underrepresentation of such students in gifted programs is insufficient to prove racial discrimination in placement programs. A plaintiff must prove that the alleged overrepresentation or underrepresentation is the result of purposeful discriminatory intent.

In 1976, a desegregation order made busing mandatory in Dallas, Texas. Despite the order, minority scores on national achievement tests remained low, and the Dallas area school districts wanted to improve minority education scores. However, they were ordered by the federal district court not to disturb the present levels of desegregation in the schools brought about by the 1976 order because the court deemed the levels acceptable. Three South Dallas Education Centers for remedial learning were then developed for minorities by the school districts and were approved by a federal district court and Court of Appeals as complying with the desegregation order.

The school districts made another proposal for four remedial education centers for West Dallas minority students. Students in the fourth through sixth grades who were currently being bused would attend a center in their own attendance zone. The centers would have a teacher-pupil ratio of 1:18 rather than the required 1:27. Although salaries would be higher, requirements for teachers in the centers would be more stringent. In order to avoid disruptions due to "pull-outs" for special lessons and tutoring, students would attend the school for extended hours. In addition, enhanced programs in special fields such as science were also planned.

Opponents of the proposed centers questioned the progress that the school districts claimed to have made in the existing South Dallas Centers, contending that the methodology used to tabulate improvements among the students attending the centers was flawed. However, the district court approved the West Dallas plan in spite of the opponents' objections. The court determined that providing remedial learning did more to prevent segregation than busing because it improved the quality of minority education. Furthermore, stated the court, the centers were the best educational opportunity available to the students. The proposal for the remedial education centers was therefore approved. *Tasby v. Wright*, 630 F.Supp. 597 (N.D.Tex.1986).

The Georgia chapter of the NAACP commenced a class action lawsuit in a federal district court on behalf of all black children in the state, claiming that the Georgia State Board of Education and a number of local school districts were assigning black students to programs for the educable mentally retarded in a racially discriminatory manner. The NAACP produced uncontroverted statistical evidence that a disproportionately high number of black students had been taken out of regular classrooms and placed in EMR programs. Depending on the school district, this was done on the basis of state I.Q. tests, the Metropolitan Achievement Test, the Development Indicators for the Assessment of Learning Tests, the MacMillan Placement Test, as well as other familiar evaluation devices and procedures. The NAACP made two basic allegations: 1) the use of these placement methods was intended to produce intraschool racial segregation, and 2) black children were assigned to the EMR programs in a discriminatory manner. Thus, the essence of the plaintiff's lawsuit was that since a disproportionately large number of black children were assigned to EMR programs, racial segregation had been the inevitable result. The methods of assignment to the programs, as well as the programs themselves, were alleged to be in violation of the U.S. Constitution, the Civil Rights Act and the Rehabilitation Act. The district court ruled against the plaintiffs on all counts and an appeal was taken to the U.S. Court of Appeals, Eleventh Circuit.

The appellate court held that ability grouping *per se*, and placement of black students in special education programs, did not violate federal law "even when it results in racial disparity in a school district's classrooms." The problem, said the court of appeals, stemmed from past racial segregation. Georgia's black children had previously been confined to grossly inferior "black" schools, receiving substandard public educations. When integration took place, "lack of prior educational quality would predictably cause black students from the inferior system to immediately be resegregated" within special education classes. The court of appeals had previously struck down this practice, holding that a newly-integrated school district may not use ability groupings if the result is racial segregation.

However, in the present case none of the black children had ever attended racially segregated public schools; all of Georgia's public schools had been integrated since the early 1970's. Therefore, the black children in this case could not claim that they had been placed in special education classes due to their past attendance at substandard schools. Past segregation had not caused them to be assigned to special education classes. Indeed, the court found that "family background and hard work, rather than race, had the most powerful and consistent relationship to scholastic success." Accordingly, the court declared that the grouping of students on the basis of ability or achievement was permissible, even if the impact of such ability grouping was not racially neutral, as long as the school district had operated a nonsegregated school system "for a period of at least several years."

The NAACP also argued that "ability grouping exacerbates, rather than relieves, the problem of disproportionately lower achievement by black students." This argument was dismissed by the court, which found that ability grouping was educationally sound and "permits more resources to be routed to lower achieving students in the form of lower pupil-teacher ratios and additional instructional materials." Although nearly all of the district court's rulings against the NAACP were affirmed, the court of appeals remanded the case to the district court for a hearing on whether the NAACP was entitled to relief under the Rehabilitation Act for the school district's misinterpretation of state I.Q. regulations. *Georgia State Conference of Branches of NAACP v. State of Georgia*, 775 F.2d 1403 (11th Cir.1985).

Black parents in Maryland sought to reopen a school desegregation case which had been decided in 1972. The parents, who had been plaintiffs in the earlier case, now alleged that the school district was not in compliance with the 1972 desegregation order. The parents claimed that the district was intentionally discriminating on racial grounds in the area of special education. They claimed that statistical evidence showed that racial imbalances existed in the district's special education and talented and gifted education programs.

The same federal district court held that despite the statistical overrepresentation of blacks in special education programs, the procedures followed by the school system in placing children in special education programs did not discriminate against black children. The district utilized a checklist which included physical, emotional and academic evaluations and from which, once a handicapping condition was verified, it formulated an individualized education program. If parents objected to the proposed IEP or any part of the process of identification, diagnosis or formulation of an IEP, they were afforded administrative hearings as required by the Education for All Handicapped Children Act. The court also upheld the district's use of the California Achievement Test and the Cognitive Abilities Test for admission into the district's gifted student program. It also found that there had been a constant effort on the part of the district's staff to include greater numbers of black children in the gifted program. Accordingly, it concluded that the district had not intentionally discriminated against black children in the area of special education.

The case was appealed to the U.S. Court of Appeals, Fourth Circuit, which partially upheld the district court. The lower court had properly noted that usually, where numerical racial disparities exist in special programs, it is presumed that such disparities are the result of "chance" and not illegal racial discrimination. However, the rule is different in school districts that have a past history of racial segregation. The appeals court held that in such districts, the burden of proof is on the district to show that the disparities in the number of minority youths assigned to special and gifted programs is not the result of racial discrimination. Because the Maryland school district in this case had, in the past, operated a racially segregated school system, the Court of Appeals remanded the case to the lower court with instructions to force the school district to meet its higher standard of proof in determining whether the placement of students in special programs was discriminatory. *Vaughs v. Bd. of Educ. of Prince George's County*, 758 F.2d 983 (4th Cir.1985).

III. AVAILABILITY OF CIVIL RIGHTS REMEDIES

Section 1983 of the federal Civil Rights Act and the Rehabilitation Act of 1973 are sometimes invoked by plaintiffs as a remedy where the IDEA does not provide one. Both Acts prohibit unfair discrimination against individuals with disabilities. The 1984 U.S. Supreme Court case *Smith v. Robinson* barred recourse to the Rehabilitation Act in cases where the relief sought was available under the IDEA. The Handicapped Children's Protection Act of 1986 reversed *Smith v. Robinson* by amending the IDEA to state that the other federal civil rights laws may be relied upon by children with disabilities.

A. <u>When a Claim May be Brought</u>

The cases in this section deal with when claims, other than under the IDEA, may be brought.

Parents of children with disabilities sued the Connecticut state board of education in a U.S. district court under § 1983 of the Civil Rights Act. They alleged that the board failed to make meaningful attempts to resolve their complaints against a local school district. In addition, they claimed that the school district had violated § 1983 by failing to provide an adequate psychologist and staff and by failing to conduct evaluations of the disabled children. They sought an injunction that would require the board to formulate and implement adequate complaint resolution procedures. The court ruled that since the EHA was a comprehensive remedial statute, the parents could not sue under § 1983. The parents appealed to the U.S. Court of Appeals, Second Circuit.

The state board argued that the parents failed to exhaust their EHA administrative remedies. It also contended that it had fully complied with EHA requirements. The court of appeals observed that the right of the parents to assert a § 1983 claim was limited by two exceptions. Section 1983 claims are not available when Congress has foreclosed enforcement of the statute in the statute itself or when a statutory remedial scheme provided an exclusive remedy. The court of appeals reversed the district court decision. The district court wrongly dismissed the parents' complaint on the ground that no civil rights lawsuit could be maintained by them outside the EHA. The Handicapped Children's Protection Act of 1986 (HCPA) codified a congressional purpose to provide for such lawsuits. In light of the HCPA's clear legislative history, the parents were entitled to bring a § 1983 lawsuit based on alleged EHA violations. *Mrs. W., Mrs. B. v. Tirozzi*, 832 F.2d 748 (2d Cir.1987).

On remand to a federal district court, the board moved for judgment on the pleadings, contending that the court of appeals had not addressed the main issue as to whether there was a right to the complaint resolution procedures (CRPs) which could be enforced under § 1983. The district court held that the parents of the children had stated a § 1983 claim for violation of the EHA. The Connecticut Board of Education had failed to meaningfully attempt to resolve the parents' complaints and had failed to fully implement federally required informal CRPs. Parents are allowed to pursue EHA violations by invoking procedures provided in § 1983. The board was required to provide CRPs to address complaints of violations of federal law. The court found for the parents and denied the board's motion for judgment on the pleadings. *Mrs. W. v. Tirozzi*, 706 F.Supp. 164 (D.Conn.1989).

A student with a disability in Oregon sued his school district, seeking attorney's fees and civil rights remedies under the EHA, the Rehabilitation Act and § 1983 of the Civil Rights Act. A federal district court held for the school district because the EHA provided the only remedy available to the student when he commenced his lawsuit. However, the EHA did not afford the relief sought by the student. The student moved that the court reinstate his lawsuit due to passage of the Handicapped Children's Protection Act (HCPA). He claimed that the HCPA permitted him to sue for attorney's fees and for relief under § 1983. His motion was granted. The school district then moved that the court reconsider its decision to reinstate the student's lawsuit.

The school district claimed that the HCPA did not form the basis for reinstatement of the student's § 1983 claim. Because Congress specifically provided that § 2 of the HCPA (providing for attorney's fees awards) be retroactive, it intended that § 3 of the HCPA not be retroactive. Section 3 provided that students with disabilities may sue state and local educational agencies under the Constitution, the Rehabilitation Act and other federal civil rights statutes (§ 1983). The court held for the student, citing *Jackson v. Franklin County School Bd.*, 806 F.2d 623 (5th Cir.1986) and *Bd. of Educ. v. Diamond*, 808 F.2d 987 (3d Cir.1986). Congressional silence regarding the retroactivity of § 3 was insufficient to imply congressional intent to limit retroactivity to § 2. Because § 3 had retroactive effect, the student's § 1983 civil rights claim could proceed to trial along with his § 2 claim for attorney's fees. The school district's motion was denied. *Dodds v. Simpson*, 676 F.Supp. 1045 (D.Or.1987).

The U.S. Court of Appeals, Eleventh Circuit, held that where a school district deprives a disabled child of a due process hearing under the EHA a lawsuit may be brought under § 1983 of the Civil Rights Act. This case involved an emotionally and physically impaired high school girl in Florida who was placed in a county special education school pursuant to her IEP. Although the girl made excellent progress at school she fought incessantly with her family. As a result her mother decided that placement at an out-of-state residential facility was warranted, and she requested a due process hearing on this matter. The school district special education director forwarded the mother's request for a due process hearing to the school district attorney, but no hearing was provided within the Act's 45-day limit.

The child's parents then unilaterally placed the girl in the private facility and filed suit against the school district seeking to recover their tuition costs and attorney's fees. The parents' lawsuit was based upon the EHA, the Rehabilitation Act and § 1983. A U.S. district court held that 1) the EHA cannot provide the basis for an award of compensatory damages; 2) the Rehabilitation Act provides no private cause of action for money damages; and 3) § 1983 is inapplicable to special education cases because Congress intended EHA remedies to be exclusive.

The parents appealed to the U.S. Court of Appeals, Eleventh Circuit, which reversed in part and affirmed in part. The court held that § 1983 may provide the basis for a lawsuit in special education cases where, as here, the plaintiff has been denied the procedural protections of the EHA. This was significant because of the relative ease of obtaining money damages and attorney's fees under § 1983. The appeals court affirmed the district court ruling with regard to the claim under the Rehabilitation Act and remanded the case to the district court for a determination of money damages. *Manecke v. School Bd. of Pinellas County, Florida*, 762 F.2d 912 (11th Cir.1985).

A Massachusetts student received a high school diploma at the end of the 1985-86 academic year. She contended (at state administrative hearings) that the issuance of this diploma was a violation of her right to obtain special education services. The State Advisory Commission for Special Education (SAC) ordered the school to rescind the diploma and provide the student whatever special educational services were appropriate. The school filed this action in a federal district court to oppose SAC's decision. The court determined that no liability attached under the civil rights statute for issuance of a diploma. However, it noted that her procedural rights had been violated. Therefore, the school was ordered to provide remedial services to compensate her for those services she would have received had the procedural process been followed. *Puffer v. Raynolds*, 761 F.Supp. 838 (D.Mass.1990).

The mother of a disabled child in New York claimed that she and her son suffered damages as a result of a local school district's failure to evaluate the child and provide him the special education to which he was entitled. The child allegedly suffered damages to his intellect, emotional capacity and personality, and was impeded in acquiring necessary training. In addition, the mother alleged that she moved to a different school district to obtain the services her child needed and that she herself suffered emotional distress. A federal district court held in favor of the mother and child, and the school district appealed.

The U.S. Court of Appeals, Second Circuit, held that because the mother had not availed herself of her administrative remedies under the EHA, she was deprived of her means of relief under that Act. However, the court found it unthinkable that Congress would have intended that a parent in this situation, where the district had refused to evaluate the child, should be left without any remedy. Accordingly, the court permitted the Civil Rights Act to supply the remedy for the mother who had been denied EHA procedural safeguards. The court viewed the absence of any prescribed remedy in the EHA as a "gap" to be filled by § 1983 of the Civil Rights Act. The case was remanded to determine the amount of damages. *Quakenbush v. Johnson City School Dist.*, 716 F.2d 141 (2d Cir.1983).

The New Mexico Association for Retarded Citizens and others commenced a class action against the state of New Mexico, seeking declaratory and injunctive relief on behalf of children with disabilities allegedly denied certain federally guaranteed special education services. The case, decided by the U.S. Court of Appeals, Tenth Circuit, involved the interpretation of § 504 of the Rehabilitation Act. Section 504 provides that "no otherwise qualified individual with a handicap in the United States . . . shall, solely by reason of his handicap, be excluded from participation in, be denied the benefits of, or be subjected to discrimination under any program or activity receiving federal financial assistance." Under the regulations to this act schools are required to provide "free appropriate public education" to all disabled students within their territorial jurisdiction.

The court of appeals observed that the U.S. Supreme Court has held, in interpreting § 504, that its purpose is to prohibit discrimination against the disabled rather than mandate affirmative relief for them. This is distinguished from the affirmative duties required under the EHA, which makes the receipt of federal money contingent on a state's performing affirmative duties with respect to the education of the disabled. The state of New Mexico had chosen not to participate in the EHA program. Against this legislative and regulatory backdrop, citizens in New Mexico contended that the state's entire program in dealing with the special needs of children with disabilities was deficient. The court, while recognizing that discrimination against children with disabilities could require the fashioning of a judicial remedy, remanded the case to a lower court, stating that § 504 violations must be evaluated in light of the Supreme Court's decision that the statute and its regulations are designed to prohibit discrimination rather than to require action. *New Mexico Ass'n for Retarded Citizens v. State of New Mexico*, 678 F.2d 847 (10th Cir.1982).

The mother of an eleven-year-old girl with cerebral palsy, who challenged the proposed transfer of her child from a traditional elementary school to an elementary school specially designed to meet the needs of children with disabilities, was denied relief under the EHA and the Rehabilitation Act. In holding that the child could not receive a satisfactory education in a traditional school, even with the use of supplementary aids and services to the maximum extent possible, a federal District Court in Michigan stated that there was no valid claim under the Rehabilitation Act because, under this Act, there must be an intentional, bad faith denial of education resources, or a grossly negligent placement decision. This was not the case here.

Thus, the transfer decision was upheld. *Johnston v. Ann Arbor Pub. Schools*, 569 F.Supp. 1502 (E.D.Mich.1983).

B. The Claim's Likelihood of Success

These cases address the likelihood of the claim's success.

A Texas first grade special education student was sexually abused by his bus driver on a number of occasions. Allegedly, the school principal knew that the driver was suspected of abusing the student, but took no action. When the student's mother learned what happened, she sued the principal and the school district under 42 U.S.C. § 1983 alleging that the district's policy of leaving the investigation of alleged sexual abuse to the discretion of the school principal violated the student's constitutional right to be free from such conduct. A federal district court found for the mother and the district appealed to the U.S. Court of Appeals, Fifth Circuit. The court of appeals stated that a school district cannot be held liable solely because it employs an individual. The court stated that the repetition of the student's injury was not caused by the district's policy. Instead it was caused by the failure of the employee to properly exercise the discretion given him by the district. The court of appeals reversed the district court's decision. *Spann v. Tyler Indep. School Dist.*, 876 F.2d 437 (5th Cir.1989).

After passage of the Handicapped Children's Protection Act of 1986 (HCPA) three disabled children in New Hampshire asked a federal district court to reinstate their civil rights claims. The court held that since § 3 of the HCPA (which made § 1983 civil rights lawsuits and money damages available to disabled students) was not expressly made retroactive, their civil rights claims could not be reinstated. On reconsideration, the district court found that § 3 of the HCPA was to be applied to cases that were pending as of the HCPA's effective date (August 5, 1986). It observed that "while section 3 is not to be applied retroactively, section 3 is to be applied to cases pending at the time of its enactment." It also noted that "a court is to apply the law in effect at the time it renders its decision, unless doing so would result in manifest injustice or there is statutory direction or legislative history to the contrary." Since no manifest injustice would occur if the children were allowed to reinstate their civil rights claims under § 1983, the court vacated its earlier decision not to reinstate the claims. It held that the children could bring a civil rights lawsuit against the local school officials. *Edward B. v. Brunelle*, 662 F.Supp. 1025 (D.N.H.1986).

In *Robinson v. Pinderhughes*, the U.S. Court of Appeals, Fourth Circuit, held that because the Baltimore City Schools failed to implement a hearing officer's decision in a timely manner and had not appealed the decision, it had violated the EHA. The court of appeals also concluded that since the EHA did not contain any provision for enforcing final administrative orders by a hearing officer, the student was entitled to a § 1983 claim. When the Baltimore City Schools refused to enforce the hearing officer's decision to put him in a residential placement the Baltimore City Schools had, under color of state law, violated the EHA. The district court was therefore wrong in dismissing the student's § 1983 claim. His § 1983 claim was remanded to the district court for further proceedings. *Robinson v. Pinderhughes*, 810 F.2d 1270 (4th Cir.1987).

The U.S. Court of Appeals, Ninth Circuit, upheld a federal district court's issuance of an injunction against various California education officials prohibiting the use by any public school of standardized I.Q. tests to aid in placing students in EMR (educable mentally retarded) classrooms. The opinion of the court of appeals also upheld the district court's order that any California school district with a black EMR enrollment greater than one standard statistical deviation above its white student EMR enrollment must prepare a plan to rectify the racial imbalance. The case was filed as a class action suit in 1971 two years after the rapid implementation by California education officials of standardized I.Q. testing for EMR placement purposes. The district court found that the overrepresentation of black children in California EMR classrooms violated the EHA, Title VI of the Civil Rights Act of 1964 and other state and federal laws. The State Education Superintendent's argument that the overrepresentation was due to a higher incidence of mental retardation in black children (due to their adverse socioeconomic positions) was discounted by the district court.

The case followed a tortuous procedural history and was eventually appealed to the U.S. Court of Appeals, Ninth Circuit, which held several hearings and rehearings and finally issued the present decision affirming the district court's judgment. The court of appeals agreed that the superintendent's explanation of the overrepresentation of black children in EMR classrooms was erroneous because extremely poor or culturally disadvantaged black children had the same level of EMR placement as black children generally. The court thus believed that the superintendent's logic was inconsistent, and it adopted the district court's conclusion that the standardized I.Q. testing mistakenly placed black children in EMR classes. It emphasized the evil inherent in disproportionate black student EMR placements and upheld the district court's order that standardized I.Q. testing for placement purposes be stopped. *Larry P. v. Riles*, 793 F.2d 969 (9th Cir.1984), as amended after denial of rehearing 6/25/86.

A fifteen-year-old New York girl, three and one-half feet tall with a partially amputated right arm, a functionally impaired left arm and hand, and legs of approximately one foot in length, asked for and received from her school district a special van to transport her to school and the help of an aide during the school day. The school sponsored a Spanish class trip to Spain for which this student was academically qualified. The trip involved tours of historical sites which required the students to walk many miles. The school denied this student permission to go on the trip on the ground that she would endanger herself by attending. She sued the school seeking to enjoin it from enforcing its ban on her attendance. She argued that because the school was receiving federal funding for this trip she could not be barred from going simply on the ground that she was disabled.

A federal district court in New York noted that the Rehabilitation Act of 1973 specifically states that a student with a handicap may not be excluded from participation in a program receiving federal funding solely on the basis of his or her disability if that student is otherwise qualified. However, in this case, after the court itself witnessed the difficulty this child had even climbing onto the witness stand, it held that she was not otherwise qualified since she could not fulfill the physical requirements of the trip. Her complaint against the school district was dismissed. *Wolff v. South Colonie School Dist.*, 534 F.Supp. 758 (N.D.N.Y.1982).

APPENDIX A

THE INDIVIDUALS WITH DISABILITIES EDUCATION ACT
AS AMENDED THROUGH 1992

[The IDEA (20 U.S.C. § 1400 *et seq.*), previously known as the EHA, is reproduced here in its entirety, fully compiled, as amended by Congress through 1992. No separate section on amendments is included in this volume because all amendments have been placed in the appropriate location in the statutory text, and any repealed sections have been deleted from the text. The Handicapped Children's Protection Act of 1986 appears in § 1415(e)(4) and § 1415(f). The major provisions of the Education of the Handicapped Act Amendments of 1986 appear in § § 1408, 1411, 1413, 1418, 1419, 1433, and 1471-85.]

CHAPTER 33—THE INDIVIDUALS WITH DISABILITIES EDUCATION ACT

SUBCHAPTER I—GENERAL PROVISIONS

SUBCHAPTER II—ASSISTANCE FOR EDUCATION OF ALL CHILDREN WITH DISABILITIES

SUBCHAPTER III—CENTERS AND SERVICES TO MEET SPECIAL NEEDS OF INDIVIDUALS WITH DISABILITIES

SUBCHAPTER IV—TRAINING PERSONNEL FOR THE EDUCATION OF INDIVIDUALS WITH DISABILITIES

educating deaf or deaf-blind students; assurance required; training of regular education teachers.

(c) Special projects for preservice training, regular educators, and inservice training of special education personnel.

(d) Grants for career advancement and competency-based training for current workers.

(e) Parent training and information programs.

1432. Grants to State educational agencies and institutions for traineeships.

1433. Clearinghouses.

(a) Establishment of national clearinghouses.

(b) National clearinghouse for children and youth.

(c) National clearinghouse on postsecondary education for individuals with disabilities.

(d) National clearinghouse on careers in special education.

(e) Considerations governing awards.

(f) Annual report to Congress.

1434. Reports to the Secretary.

1435. Authorization of appropriations.

(a) In general.

(b) Personnel training for careers in special education and early intervention.

1436. Omitted.

SUBCHAPTER V—RESEARCH IN THE EDUCATION OF INDIVIDUALS WITH DISABILITIES

1441. Research and related activities.

(a) Grant and contract authority; statement of objectives; description of specific activities.

(b) Qualifications of applicants.

(c) Publication of research priorities in Federal Register.

(d) Index of projects.

(e) Coordination with other research; information to other agencies.

(f) Attention deficit disorder.

(g) Model demonstration programs.

(h) Research grants for unique needs, specialized instruction, and progress measurement; family involvement; adult role models.

1442. Research and demonstration projects in physical education and recreation for children with disabilities.

1443. Repealed

1444. Authorization of appropriations.

SUBCHAPTER VI—INSTRUCTIONAL MEDIA FOR INDIVIDUALS WITH DISABILITIES

SUBCHAPTER VII—TECHNOLOGY, EDUCATIONAL MEDIA, AND MATERIALS FOR INDIVIDUALS WITH DISABILITIES

SUBCHAPTER VIII—INFANTS AND TODDLERS WITH DISABILITIES

SUBCHAPTER I—GENERAL PROVISIONS

§ 1400. Congressional statements and declarations

(a) Short title

This chapter may be cited as the "Individuals with Disabilities Education Act".

(b) Findings

The Congress finds that—
(1) there are more than eight million children with disabilities in the United States today;
(2) the special educational needs of such children are not being fully met;
(3) more than half of the children with disabilities in the United States do not receive appropriate educational services which would enable them to have full equality of opportunity;
(4) one million of the children with disabilities in the United States are excluded entirely from the public school system and will not go through the educational process with their peers;
(5) there are many children with disabilities throughout the United States participating in regular school programs whose disabilities prevent them from having a successful educational experience because their disabilities are undetected;
(6) because of the lack of adequate services within the public school system, families are often forced to find services outside the public school system, often at great distance from their residence and at their own expense;
(7) developments in the training of teachers and in diagnostic and instructional procedures and methods have advanced to the point that, given appropriate funding, State and local educational agencies can and will provide effective special education and related services to meet the needs of children with disabilities;
(8) State and local educational agencies have a responsibility to provide education for all children with disabilities, but present financial resources are inadequate to meet the special educational needs of children with disabilities; and
(9) it is in the national interest that the Federal Government assist State and local efforts to provide programs to meet the educational needs of children with disabilities in order to assure equal protection of the law.

(c) Purpose

It is the purpose of this chapter to assure that all children with disabilities have available to them, within the time periods specified in section 1412(2)(B) of this title, a free appropriate public education which emphasizes special education and related services designed to meet their unique needs, to assure that the rights of children with disabilities and their parents or guardians are protected, to assist States and localities to provide for the education of all children with disabilities, and to assess and assure the effectiveness of efforts to educate children with disabilities.

§ 1401. Definitions

(a) As used in this chapter—

(1)(A) The term "children with disabilities" means children—

(i) with mental retardation, hearing impairments including deafness, speech or language impairments, visual impairments including blindness, serious emotional disturbance, orthopedic impairments, autism, traumatic brain injury, other health impairments, or specific learning disabilities; and

(ii) who, by reason thereof, need special education and related services.

(B) The term "children with disabilities" for children aged 3 to 5, inclusive, may, at a State's discretion, include children—

(i) experiencing developmental delays, as defined by the State and as measured by appropriate diagnostic instruments and procedures, in one or more of the following areas: physical development, cognitive development, communication development, social or emotional development, or adaptive development; and

(ii) who, by reason thereof, need special education and related services.

(2) Repealed. Pub. L. 98-199, § 2(2), Dec. 2, 1983, 97 Stat. 1357.

(3) Repealed. Pub. L. 100-630, § 101(a)(2), Nov. 7, 1988, 102 Stat. 3289.

(4) The term "construction", except where otherwise specified, means (A) erection of new or expansion of existing structures, and the acquisition and installation of equipment therefor; or (B) acquisition of existing structures not owned by any agency or institution making application for assistance under this chapter; or (C) remodeling or alteration (including the acquisition, installation, modernization, or replacement of equipment) of existing structures; or (D) acquisition of land in connection with activities in clauses (A), (B), and (C); or (E) a combination of any two or more of the foregoing.

(5) The term "equipment" includes machinery, utilities, and built-in equipment and any necessary enclosures or structures to house them, and includes all other items necessary for the functioning of a particular facility as a facility for the provision of educational services, including items such as instructional equipment and necessary furniture, printed, published, and audio-visual instructional materials, telecommunications, sensory, and other technological aids and devices, and books, periodicals, documents, and other related materials.

(6) The term "State" means any of the several States, the District of Columbia, the Commonwealth of Puerto Rico, the Virgin Islands, Guam, American Samoa, the Commonwealth of the Northern Mariana Islands, or the Trust Territory of the Pacific Islands.

(7) The term "State educational agency" means the State board of education or other agency or officer primarily responsible for the State supervision of public elementary and secondary schools, or, if there is no

such officer or agency, an officer or agency designated by the Governor or by State law.

(8) The term "local educational agency" means a public board of education or other public authority legally constituted within a State for either administrative control or direction of, or to perform a service function for, public elementary or secondary schools in a city, county, township, school district, or other political subdivision of a State, or such combination of school districts or counties as are recognized in a State as an administrative agency for its public elementary or secondary schools. Such term also includes any other public institution or agency having administrative control and direction of a public elementary or secondary school.

(9) The term "elementary school" means a day or residential school which provides elementary education, as determined under State law.

(10) The term "secondary school" means a day or residential school which provides secondary education, as determined under State law, except that it does not include any education provided beyond grade 12.

(11) The term "institution of higher education" means an educational institution in any State which—

(A) admits as regular students only individuals having a certificate of graduation from a high school, or the recognized equivalent of such a certificate;

(B) is legally authorized within such State to provide a program of education beyond high school;

(C) provides an educational program for which it awards a bachelor's degree, or provides not less than a two-year program which is acceptable for full credit toward such a degree, or offers a two-year program in engineering, mathematics, or the physical or biological sciences which is designed to prepare the student to work as a technician and at a semiprofessional level in engineering, scientific, or other technological fields which require the understanding and application of basic engineering, scientific, or mathematical principles or knowledge;

(D) is a public or other nonprofit institution; and

(E) is accredited by a nationally recognized accrediting agency or association listed by the Secretary pursuant to this paragraph or, if not so accredited, is an institution whose credits are accepted, on transfer, by not less than three institutions which are so accredited, for credit on the same basis as if transferred from an institution so accredited: *Provided, however,* That in the case of an institution offering a two-year program in engineering, mathematics, or the physical or biological sciences which is designed to prepare the student to work as a technician and at a semiprofessional level in engineering, scientific, or technological fields which require the understanding and application of basic engineering, scientific, or mathematical principles or knowledge, if the Secretary determines that there is no nationally recognized accrediting agency or association qualified to accredit such institutions, the Secretary shall appoint an advisory committee, composed of persons specially qualified to evaluate training provided by such institutions, which shall prescribe the standards of content, scope, and quality which must be met in order to qualify such institutions to participate under this Act and shall also determine whether particular institutions meet such standards. For the purposes of this paragraph the Secretary shall publish a list of nationally recognized accrediting agencies or associations which the Secretary determines to be reliable authority as to the quality of education or training offered.

The term includes community colleges receiving funding from the Secretary of the Interior under the Tribally Controlled Community College Assistance Act of 1978.

(12) The term "nonprofit" as applied to a school, agency, organization, or institution means a school, agency, organization, or institution owned and operated by one or more non-profit corporations or associations no part of the net earnings of which inures, or may lawfully inure, to the benefit of any private shareholder or individual.

(13) The term "research and related purposes" means research, research training (including the payment of stipends and allowances), surveys, or demonstrations in the field of education of children with disabilities, or the dissemination of information derived therefrom, including (but without limitation) experimental schools.

(14) The term "Secretary" means the Secretary of Education.

(15) The term "children with specific learning disabilities" means those children who have a disorder in one or more of the basic psychological processes involved in understanding or in using language, spoken or written, which disorder may manifest itself in imperfect ability to listen, think, speak, read, write, spell, or do mathematical calculations. Such disorders include such conditions as perceptual disabilities, brain injury, minimal brain dysfunction, dyslexia, and developmental aphasia. Such term does not include children who have learning problems which are primarily the result of visual, hearing, or motor disabilities, of mental retardation, of emotional disturbance, or of environmental, cultural, or economic disadvantage.

(16) The term "special education" means specially designed instruction, at no cost to parents or guardians, to meet the unique needs of a child with a disability, including—

(A) instruction conducted in the classroom, in the home, in hospitals and institutions, and in other settings; and

(B) instruction in physical education.

(17) The term "related services" means transportation, and such developmental, corrective, and other supportive services (including speech pathology and audiology, psychological services, physical and occupational therapy, recreation, including therapeutic recreation, social work services, counseling services, including rehabilitation counseling, and medical services, except that such medical services shall be for diagnostic and evaluation purposes only) as may be required to assist a child with a disability to benefit from special education, and includes the early identification and assessment of disabling conditions in children.

(18) The term "free appropriate public education" means special education and related services that—

(A) have been provided at public expense, under public supervision and direction, and without charge,

(B) meet the standards of the State educational agency,

(C) include an appropriate preschool, elementary, or secondary school education in the State involved, and

(D) are provided in conformity with the individualized education program required under section 1414(a)(5).

(19) The term "transition services" means a coordinated set of activities for a student, designed within an outcome-oriented process, which promotes movement from school to post-school activities, including post-secondary education, vocational training, integrated employment (including supported employment), continuing and adult education, adult services, independent living, or community participation. The coordinated set of activities shall be based upon the individual student's needs, taking into account the student's preferences and interests, and shall include instruction, community experiences, the development of employment and other post-school adult living objectives, and, when appropriate, acquisition of daily living skills and functional vocational evaluation.

(20) The term "individualized education program" means a written statement for each child with a disability developed in any meeting by a representative of the local educational agency or an intermediate educational unit who shall be qualified to provide, or supervise the provision of, specially designed instruction to meet the unique needs of children with disabilities, the teacher, the parents or guardian of such child, and, whenever appropriate, such child, which statement shall include—

(A) a statement of the present levels of educational performance of such child,

(B) a statement of annual goals, including short-term instructional objectives,

(C) a statement of the specific educational services to be provided to such child, and the extent to which such child will be able to participate in regular educational programs,

(D) a statement of the needed transition services for students beginning no later than age 16 and annually thereafter (and, when determined appropriate for the individual, beginning at age 14 or younger), including, when appropriate, a statement of the interagency responsibilities or linkages (or both) before the student leaves the school setting.

(E) the projected date for initiation and anticipated duration of such services, and

(F) appropriate objective criteria and evaluation procedures and schedules for determining, on at least an annual basis, whether instructional objectives are being achieved. In the case where a participating agency, other than the educational agency, fails to provide agreed upon services, the educational agency shall reconvene the IEP team to identify alternative strategies to meet the transition objectives.

(21) The term "excess costs" means those costs which are in excess of the average annual per student expenditure in a local educational agency during the preceding school year for an elementary or secondary school student, as may be appropriate, and which shall be computed after deducting

(A) amounts received—

(i) under this part,

(ii) under chapter 1 of title I of the Elementary and Secondary Education Act of 1965, or

(iii) under title VII of the Elementary and Secondary Education Act of 1965, and

(B) any State or local funds expended for programs that would qualify for assistance under such part, chapter, or title.

(22) The term "native language" has the meaning given that term by section 7003(a)(2) of the Bilingual Education Act [20 U.S.C. 3223(a)(2)].

(23) The term "intermediate educational unit" means any public authority, other than a local educational agency, which is under the general supervision of a State educational agency, which is established by State law for the purpose of providing free public education on a regional basis, and which provides special education and related services to children with disabilities within that State.

(24)(A) The term "public or private nonprofit agency or organization" includes an Indian tribe and the Bureau of Indian Affairs of the Department of the Interior (when acting on behalf of schools operated by the Bureau for children and students on Indian reservations) and tribally controlled schools funded by the Department of the Interior.

(B) The terms "Indian," "American Indian," and "Indian American" mean an individual who is a member of an Indian tribe.

(C) The term "Indian tribe" means any Federal or State Indian tribe, band, rancheria, pueblo, colony, or community, including any Alaskan native village or regional village corporation (as defined in or established under the Alaska Native Claims Settlement Act).

(25) The term "assistive technology device" means any item, piece of equipment, or product system, whether acquired commercially off the shelf, modified, or customized, that is used to increase, maintain, or improve functional capabilities of individuals with disabilities.

(26) The term "assistive technology service" means any service that directly assists an individual with a disability in the selection, acquisition, or use of an assistive technology device. Such term includes—

(A) the evaluation of the needs of an individual with a disability, including a functional evaluation of the individual in the individual's customary environment;

(B) purchasing, leasing, or otherwise providing for the acquisition of assistive technology devices by individuals with disabilities;

(C) selection, designing, fitting, customizing, adapting, applying, maintaining, repairing, or replacing of assistive technology devices;

(D) coordinating and using other therapies, interventions, or services with assistive technology devices, such as those associated with existing education and rehabilitation plans and programs;

(E) training or technical assistance for an individual with disabilities, or, where appropriate, the family of an individual with disabilities; and

(F) training or technical assistance for professionals (including individuals providing education and rehabilitation services), employers, or other individuals who provide services to, employ, or are otherwise substantially involved in the major life functions of individuals with disabilities.

(b) For purposes of subchapter III of this chapter, "youth with a disability" means any child with a disability (as defined in subsection (a)(1) of this section) who

(1) is twelve years of age or older; or

(2) is enrolled in the seventh or higher grade in school.

§ 1402. Office of Special Education Programs

(a) Administration and execution of programs and activities

There shall be, within the Office of Special Education and Rehabilitation Services in the Department of Education, an Office of Special Education Programs which shall be the principal agency in the Department for administering and carrying out this and other programs and activities concerning the education and training of individuals with disabilities.

(b) Deputy Assistant Secretary: selection and supervision, General Schedule and Senior Executive Service status; Associate Deputy Assistant Secretary and minimum assistantships: establishment, General Schedule status

(1) The office established under subsection (a) of this section shall be headed by a Deputy Assistant Secretary who shall be selected by the Secretary and shall report directly to the Assistant Secretary for Special Education and Rehabilitative Services. The position of Deputy Assistant Secretary shall be in grade GS-18 of the General Schedule under section 5104 of Title 5 and shall be a Senior Executive Service position for the purposes of section 3132(a)(2) of such Title.

(2) In addition to such Deputy Assistant Secretary, there shall be established in such office not less than six positions for persons to assist the Deputy Assistant Secretary, including the position of the Associate Deputy Assistant Secretary. Each such position shall be in grade GS-15 of the General Schedule under section 5104 of Title 5.

§ 1403. Abrogation of sovereign immunity

(a) State immunity abrogated

A State shall not be immune under the eleventh amendment to the Constitution of the United States from suit in Federal court for a violation of this Act.

(b) Availability of remedies

In a suit against a State for a violation of this Act, remedies (including remedies both at law and in equity) are available for such a violation to the same extent as such remedies are available for such a violation in the suit against any public entity other than a State.

(c) Effective date

The provisions of subsections (a) and (b) shall take effect with respect to violations that occur in whole or part after the date of the enactment of the Education of the Handicapped Act Amendments of 1990.

§ 1404. Acquisition of equipment and construction of necessary facilities

(a) Authorization for use of funds

In the case of any program authorized by this chapter, if the Secretary determines that such program will be improved by permitting the funds authorized for such program to be used for the acquisition of equipment and the construction of necessary facilities, the Secretary may authorize the use of such funds for such purposes.

(b) Recovery of payments under certain conditions

If, within twenty years after the completion of any construction (except minor remodeling or alteration) for which funds have been paid pursuant to a grant or contract under this chapter, the facility constructed ceases to be used for the purposes for which it was constructed, the United States, unless the Secretary determines that there is good cause for releasing the recipient of the funds from its obligation, shall be entitled to recover from the applicant or other owner of the facility an amount which bears the same ratio to the then value of the facility as the amount of such Federal funds bore to the cost of the portion of the facility financed with such funds. Such value shall be determined by agreement of the parties or by action brought in the United States district court for the district in which the facility is situated.

§ 1405. Employment of individuals with disabilities

The Secretary shall assure that each recipient of assistance under this chapter shall make positive efforts to employ and advance in employment qualified individuals with disabilities in programs assisted under this chapter.

§ 1406. Grants for removal of architectural barriers; authorization of appropriations

(a) The Secretary is authorized to make grants and to enter into cooperative agreements with the Secretary of the Interior and with State educational agencies to assist such agencies in making grants to local educational agencies or intermediate educational units to pay part or all of the cost of altering existing buildings and equipment in accordance with standards promulgated under the Act entitled 'An Act to insure that certain buildings financed with Federal funds are so designed and constructed as to be accessible to the physically handicapped,' approved August 12, 1968.

(b) For the purposes of carrying out the provisions of this section, there are authorized to be appropriated such sums as may be necessary.

§1407. Regulation requirements

(a) Minimum period for comment before effective date

For purposes of complying with section 1232(b) of this title with respect to regulations promulgated under subchapter II of this chapter, the thirty-day period under such section shall be ninety days.

(b) Lessening of procedural or substantive protections as in effect on July 20, 1983, prohibited

The Secretary may not implement, or publish in final form, any regulation prescribed pursuant to this chapter which would procedurally or substantively lessen the protections provided to children with disabilities under this chapter, as embodied in regulations in effect on July 20, 1983 (particularly as such protections relate to parental consent to initial evaluation or initial placement in special education, least restrictive environment, related services, timeliness, attendance of evaluation personnel at individualized education program meetings, or qualifications of personnel), except to the extent that such regulation reflects the clear and unequivocal intent of the Congress in legislation.

(c) Repealed.

§ 1408. Eligibility for financial assistance

Effective for fiscal years for which the Secretary may make grants under section 1419(b)(1) of this chapter, no State or local educational agency or intermediate educational unit or other public institution or agency may receive a grant under subchapters III through VII of this chapter which relate exclusively to programs, projects, and activities pertaining to children aged three to five, inclusive, unless the State is eligible to receive a grant under section 1419(b)(1) of this chapter.

§ 1409   Administrative provisions applicable to subchapters III through VII and section 1418

(a) Plan for implementation of authorized programs

The Secretary shall maintain a process for developing a program plan for the implementation of each of the programs authorized under section 1418 of this title and subchapters III through VII of this chapter. The plan shall include program goals, objectives, strategies, and priorities. In conducting the process, the Secretary shall involve individuals with disabilities, parents, professionals, and representatives of State and local educational agencies, private schools, institutions of higher education, and national organizations who have interest and expertise in the program.

(b) Needs of minority children and youth

In awarding grants, contracts, and cooperative agreements under subchapters III through VII of this chapter, the Secretary, where appropriate, shall require applicants to demonstrate how they will address, in whole or in part, the needs of infants, toddlers, children, and youth with disabilities from minority backgrounds.

(c) Transitions facing children with disabilities during years in school

In awarding grants, contracts, or cooperative agreements under subchapter III through VII of this chapter, the Secretary, where appropriate, may require applicants to address the various transitions that a child with a disability may face throughout such child's years in school, including—

(1) the transition from medical care to special education for those children with disabilities, including chronic health impairments, who may require individualized health-related services to enable such children to participate in, or benefit from, special education;

(2) the transition between residential placement and community-based special education services; and

(3) the transition between a separate educational placement and the regular classroom setting.

(d) Program evaluations

The Secretary shall conduct directly, or by contract or cooperative agreement with appropriate entities, independent evaluations of the programs authorized under section 1418 of this title and under subchapters III through VII of this chapter and may for such purpose use funds appropriated to carry out such provisions. The findings of the evaluators shall be utilized in the planning process under subsection (a) of this section for the purpose of improving the programs. The evaluations shall determine the degree to which the program is being conducted consistent with the program plan and meeting its goals and objectives. The Secretary shall submit to the appropriate committees of the Congress the results of the evaluations required by this subsection.

(e) Report on program plans and evaluations

The Secretary shall report on the program plans required in subsection (a) of this section and findings from the evaluations under subsection (d) of this section in the annual report to the Congress required under section 1418 of this title.

(f) Acquisition and dissemination of information

The Secretary shall develop effective procedures for acquiring and disseminating information derived from programs and projects funded under subchapters III through VII of this chapter, as well as information generated from studies conducted and data collected under section 1418 of this title.

(g) Dissemination of reports to other recipients

The Secretary shall, where appropriate, require recipients of all grants, contracts, and cooperative agreements under subchapters III through VII of this chapter to prepare reports describing their procedures, findings, and other relevant information in a form that will maximize the dissemination and use of such procedures, findings, and information. The Secretary shall require their delivery, as appropriate, to the Regional and Federal Resource Centers, the Clearinghouses, and the Technical Assistance to Parents Programs (TAPP) assisted under subchapters III and IV of this chapter, as well as the National Diffusion Network, the ERIC Clearinghouse on the Handicapped and Gifted, and the Child and Adolescent Service Systems Program (CASSP) under the National Institute of Mental Health, appropriate parent and professional organizations, organizations representing individuals with disabilities and such other networks as the Secretary may determine to be appropriate.

(h) Evaluation panels

(1) The Secretary shall convene, in accordance with paragraph (2), panels of experts who are competent, by virtue of their training or experience, to evaluate proposals under section 1418 of this title and subchapters III through VII of this chapter.

(2) Panels under paragraph (1) shall be composed of individuals with disabilities, parents of such individuals, individuals from the fields of special education, related services, and other relevant disciplines.

(3) The Secretary shall convene panels under paragraph (1) for any application that includes a total funding request exceeding $60,000 and may convene or otherwise appoint panels for applications that include funding requests that are less than such amount.

(4) Panels under paragraph (1) shall include a majority of non-Federal members. Such non-Federal members shall be provided travel and per diem not to exceed the rate provided to other educational consultants used by the Department of Education and shall be provided consultant fees at such a rate.

(5) The Secretary may use funds available under section 618 and parts C through G to pay expenses and fees of non-Federal members of the panels.

(i) Site visits

The Secretary shall conduct at least 1 site visit for each grant, contract, and cooperative agreement receiving $300,000 or more annually under subchapters III through VII of this chapter.

(j) Discretionary programs

(1) With respect to the discretionary programs authorized by subchapters III through VII of this chapter, the Congress finds as follows:

(A)(i) The Federal Government must be responsive to the growing needs of an increasingly more diverse society. A more equitable allocation of resources is essential for the Federal Government to meet its responsibility to provide an equal educational opportunity for all individuals.

(ii) America's racial profile is rapidly changing. While the rate of increase for white Americans is 3.2 percent, the rate of increase for racial and ethnic minorities is much higher: 38.6 percent for Hispanics, 14.6 percent for African-Americans, and 40.1 percent for Asians and other ethnic groups.

(iii) By the year 2000, this Nation will have 260,000,000 people, one of every three of whom will be either African-American, Hispanic, or Asian-American.

(iv) Taken together as a group, it is a more frequent phenomenon for minorities to comprise the majority of public school students. Large city school populations are overwhelmingly minority, e.g., Miami, 71 percent; Philadelphia, 73 percent; Baltimore, 80 percent.

(v) Recruitment efforts within special education at the level of preservice, continuing education, and practice must focus on bringing larger numbers of minorities into the profession in order to provide appropriate practitioner knowledge, role models, and sufficient manpower to address the clearly changing demography of special education.

(vi) The limited English proficient population is the fastest growing in our Nation, and the growth is occurring in many parts of our Nation. In the Nation's 2 largest school districts, limited-English students make up almost half of all students initially entering school at the kindergarten level. Studies have documented apparent discrepancies in the levels of referral and placement of limited-English proficient children in special education. The Department of Education has found that services provided to limited-English proficient students often do not respond primarily to the pupil's academic needs. These trends pose special challenges for special education in the referral, assessment, and services for our Nation's students from non-English language backgrounds.

(B)(i) Greater efforts are needed to prevent the intensification of problems connected with mislabeling and high dropout rates among minority children with disabilities.

(ii) More minority children continue to be served in special education than would be expected from the percentage of minority students in the general school population.

(iii) Poor African-American children are 3.5 times more likely to be identified by their teacher as mentally retarded than their white counterpart.

(iv) Although African-Americans represent 12 percent of elementary and secondary enrollments, they constitute 28 percent of total enrollments in special education.

(v) The drop out rate is 68 percent higher for minorities than for whites.

(vi) More than 50 percent of minority students in large cities drop out of school.

(C)(i) The opportunity for full participation in awards for grants and contracts; boards of organizations receiving funds under this chapter; and peer review panels; and training of professionals in the area of special education by minority individuals, organizations, and historically Black colleges and universities is essential if we are to obtain greater success in the education of minority children with disabilities.

(ii) In 1989, of the 661,000 college and university professors, 4.6 percent were African-American and 3.1 percent were Hispanic. Of the 3,600,000 teachers, prekindergarten through high school, 9.4 percent were African-American and 3.9 percent were Hispanic.

(iii) Students from minority groups comprise more than 50 percent of K-12 public school enrollment in seven States yet minority enrollment in teacher training programs is less than 15 percent in all but six States.

(iv) As the number of African-American and Hispanic students in special education increases, the number of minority teachers and related service personnel produced in our colleges and universities continues to decrease.

(v) Ten years ago, 12.5 percent of the United States teaching force in public elementary and secondary school were members of a minority group. Minorities comprised 21.3 percent of the national population at that time and were clearly underrepresented then among employed teachers. Today, the elementary and secondary teaching force is 3 to 5 percent minority, while one-third of the students in public schools are minority children.

(vi) As recently as 1984-85, Historically Black Colleges and Universities (HBCUs) supplied nearly half of the African-American teachers in the Nation. However, in 1988, HBCUs received only 2 percent of the discretionary funds for special education and related services personnel training.

(vii) While African-American students constitute 28 percent of total enrollment in special education, only 11.2 percent of individuals enrolled in preservice training programs for special education are African-American.

(viii) In 1986-87, of the degrees conferred in education at the B.A., M.A., and Ph.D levels, only 6, 8, and 8 percent, respectively, were awarded to African-American or Hispanic students.

(D) Minorities and underserved persons are socially disadvantaged because of the lack of opportunities in training and educational programs, undergirded by the practices in the private sector that impede their full participation in the mainstream of society.

(2) The Congress further finds that these conditions can be greatly improved by providing opportunities for the full participation of minorities through the implementation of the following recommendation:

(A) Implementation of a policy to mobilize the Nation's resources to prepare minorities for careers in special education and related services.

(B) This policy should focus on—

(i) the recruitment of minorities into teaching; and

(ii) financially assisting HBCUs and other institutions of higher education (whose minority student enrollment is at least 25 percent) to prepare students for special education and related service careers.

(C)(i) The Secretary shall develop a plan for providing outreach services to the entities described in clause (ii) in order to increase the participation of such entities in competitions for grants, contracts, and cooperative agreements under any of subchapters III through VII of this chapter.

(ii) The entities referred to in clause (i) are—

(I) Historically Black Colleges and Universities and other institutions of higher education whose minority student enrollment is at least 25 percent;

(II) eligible institutions as defined in section 1058 of this title;

(III) nonprofit and for-profit agencies at least 51 percent owned or controlled by one or more minority individuals; and

(IV) underrepresented populations.

(iii) For the purpose of implementing the plan required in clause (i), the Secretary shall, for each of the fiscal years 1991 through 1994, expend 1 percent of the funds appropriated for the fiscal year involved for carrying out subchapters III through VII of this chapter.

(3) The Secretary shall exercise his/her utmost authority, resourcefulness, and diligence to meet the requirements of this subsection.

(4) Not later than January 31 of each year, starting with fiscal year 1991, the Secretary shall submit to Congress a final report on the progress toward meeting

the goals of this subsection during the preceding fiscal year. The report shall include—

> (i) a full explanation of any progress toward meeting the goals of this subsection; and
>
> (ii) a plan to meet the goals, if necessary.

SUBCHAPTER II—ASSISTANCE FOR EDUCATION OF ALL CHILDREN WITH DISABILITIES

§ 1411. Entitlements and allocations

(a) Formula for determining maximum State entitlement

(1) Except as provided in paragraph (5) and in section 1419 of this chapter, the maximum amount of the grant to which a State is entitled under this subchapter for any fiscal year shall be equal to—

(A) the number of children with disabilities aged 3-5, inclusive, in a State who are receiving special education and related services as determined under paragraph (3) if the State is eligible for a grant under section 1419 of this chapter and the number of children with disabilities aged 6-21, inclusive, in a State who are receiving special education and related services as so determined;

multiplied by—

(B)(i) 5 per centum, for the fiscal year ending September 30, 1978, of the average per pupil expenditure in public elementary and secondary schools in the United States;

(ii) 10 per centum, for the fiscal year ending September 30, 1979, of the average per pupil expenditure in public elementary and secondary schools in the United States;

(iii) 20 per centum, for the fiscal year ending September 30, 1980, of the average per pupil expenditure in public elementary and secondary schools in the United States;

(iv) 30 per centum, for the fiscal year ending September 30, 1981, of the average per pupil expenditure in public elementary and secondary schools in the United States; and

(v) 40 per centum, for the fiscal year ending September 30, 1982, and for each fiscal year thereafter, of the average per pupil expenditure in public elementary and secondary schools in the United States:

except that no State shall receive an amount which is less than the amount which such State received under this subchapter for the fiscal year ending September 30, 1977.

(2) For the purpose of this subsection and subsection (b) through subsection (e) of this section, the term "State" does not include Guam, American Samoa, the Virgin Islands, the Commonwealth of the Northern Mariana Islands, and the Trust Territory of the Pacific Islands.

(3) The number of children with disabilities receiving special education and related services in any fiscal year shall be equal to the number of such children receiving special education and related services on December 1 of the fiscal year preceding the fiscal year for which the determination is made.

(4) For purposes of paragraph (1)(B), the term "average per pupil expenditure" in the United States, means the aggregate current expenditures, during the second fiscal year preceding the fiscal year for which the computation is made (or, if satisfactory data for such year are not available at the time of computation, then during the most recent preceding fiscal year for which satisfactory data are

available) of all local educational agencies in the United States (which, for purposes of this subsection, means the fifty States and the District of Columbia), as the case may be, plus any direct expenditures by the State for operation of such agencies (without regard to the source of funds from which either of such expenditures are made), divided by the aggregate number of children in average daily attendance to whom such agencies provided free public education during such preceding year.

(5) (A) In determining the allotment of each State under paragraph (1), the Secretary may not count—

(i) children with disabilities aged three to seventeen, inclusive, in such State under paragraph (1)(A) to the extent the number of such children is greater than 12 percent of the number of all children aged three to seventeen, inclusive, in such State and the State serves all children with disabilities aged three to five, inclusive, in the State pursuant to State law or practice or the order of any court,

(ii) children with disabilities aged five to seventeen, inclusive, in such State under paragraph (1)(A) to the extent the number of such children is greater than 12 percent of the number of all children aged five to seventeen, inclusive, in such State and the State does not serve all children with disabilities aged three to five, inclusive, in the State pursuant to State law or practice or the order of any court; and

(iii) children with disabilities who are counted under subpart 2 of part D of chapter 1 of title 1 of the Elementary and Secondary Education Act of 1965 [20 U.S.C. § 2791 et seq.].

(B) For purposes of subparagraph (A), the number of children aged three to seventeen inclusive, in any State shall be determined by the Secretary on the basis of the most recent satisfactory data available to the Secretary.

(b) Distribution and use of grant funds by States for fiscal year ending September 30, 1978

(1) Of the funds received under subsection (a) of this section by any State for the fiscal year ending September 30, 1978—

(A) 50 per centum of such funds may be used by such State in accordance with the provisions of paragraph (2); and

(B) 50 per centum of such funds shall be distributed by such State pursuant to subsection (d) of this section to local educational agencies and intermediate educational units in such State, for use in accordance with the priorities established under section 1412(3) of this chapter.

(2) Of the funds which any State may use under paragraph (1)(A)—

(A) an amount which is equal to the greater of—

(i) 5 per centum of the total amount of funds received under this subchapter by such State; or

(ii) $200,000;

may be used by such State for administrative costs related to carrying out sections 1412 and 1413 of this title;

(B) the remainder shall be used by such State to provide support services and direct services, in accordance with the priorities established under section 1412(3) of this title.

(c) Distribution and use of grant funds by States for fiscal years ending September 30, 1979, and thereafter

(1) Of the funds received under subsection (a) of this section by any State for the fiscal year ending September 30, 1979, and for each fiscal year thereafter—

(A) 25 per centum of such funds may be used by such State in accordance with the provisions of paragraph (2); and

(B) except as provided in paragraph (4), 75 per centum of such funds shall be distributed by such State pursuant to subsection (d) of this section to local educational agencies and intermediate educational units in such State, for use in accordance with priorities established under section 1412(3) of this chapter.

(2) (A) Subject to the provisions of subparagraph (B), of the funds which any State may use under paragraph (1)(A)—

(i) an amount which is equal to the greater of—

(I) 5 per centum of the total amount of funds received under this subchapter by such State; or

(II) $450,000;

may be used by such State for administrative costs related to carrying out the provisions of sections 1412 and 1413 of this chapter; and

(ii) the part remaining after use in accordance with clause (i) shall be used by the State (I) to provide support services and direct services in accordance with the priorities established under section 1412(3) of this chapter, and (II) for the administrative costs of monitoring and complaint investigation but only to the extent that such costs exceed the costs of administration incurred during fiscal year 1985.

(B) The amount expended by any State from the funds available to such State under paragraph (1)(A) in any fiscal year for the provisions of support services or for the provision of direct services shall be matched on a program basis by such State, from funds other than Federal funds, for the provision of support services or for the provision of direct services for the fiscal year involved.

(3) The provisions of section 1413(a)(9) of this chapter shall not apply with respect to amounts available for use by any State under paragraph (2).

(4) (A) No funds shall be distributed by any State under this subsection in any fiscal year to any local educational agency or intermediate educational unit in such State if—

(i) such local educational agency or intermediate educational unit is entitled, under subsection (d) of this section, to less than $7,500 for such fiscal year; or

(ii) such local educational agency or intermediate educational unit has not submitted an application for such funds which meets the requirements of section 1414 of this chapter.

(B) Whenever the provisions of subparagraph (A) apply, the State involved shall use such funds to assure the provision of a free appropriate education to children with disabilities residing in the area served by such local educational agency or such intermediate educational unit. The provisions of paragraph (2)(B) shall not apply to the use of such funds.

(d) Allocation of funds within States to local educational agencies and intermediate educational units

From the total amount of funds available to local educational agencies and intermediate educational units in any State under subsection (b)(1)(B) or subsection (c)(1)(B) of this section, as the case may be, each local educational agency or intermediate educational unit shall be entitled to an amount which bears the same ratio to the total amount available under subsection (b)(1)(B) or subsection (c)(1)(B) of this section, as the case may be, as the number of children with disabilities aged three to twenty-one, inclusive, receiving special education and related services in such local educational agency or intermediate educational unit bears to the aggregate number of children with disabilities aged three to twenty-one, inclusive, receiving special education and related services in all local educational agencies and intermediate educational units which apply to the State educational agency involved for funds under this subchapter.

(e) Territories and possessions

(1) The jurisdictions to which this subsection applies are Guam, American Samoa, the Virgin Islands, the Commonwealth of the Northern Mariana Islands, and the Trust Territory of the Pacific Islands.

(2) Each jurisdiction to which this subsection applies shall be entitled to a grant for the purposes set forth in section 1400(c) of this chapter in an amount equal to an amount determined by the Secretary in accordance with criteria based on respective needs, except that the aggregate of the amount to which such jurisdictions are so entitled for any fiscal year shall not exceed an amount equal to 1 per centum of the aggregate of the amounts available to all States under this subchapter for that fiscal year. If the aggregate of the amounts, determined by the Secretary pursuant to the preceding sentence, to be so needed for any fiscal year exceeds an amount equal to such 1 per centum limitation, the entitlement of each such jurisdiction shall be reduced proportionately until such aggregate does not exceed such 1 per centum limitation.

(3) The amount expended for administration by each jurisdiction under this subsection shall not exceed 5 per centum of the amount allotted to such jurisdiction for any fiscal year, or $35,000, whichever is greater.

(f) Indian reservations

(1) The Secretary shall make payments to the Secretary of the Interior to meet the need for assistance for the education of children with disabilities on reservations aged 5-21, inclusive, enrolled in elementary and secondary schools for Indian children operated by the Secretary of the Interior. In the case of Indian students ages 3-5, inclusive, who are enrolled in programs affiliated with Bureau of Indian Affairs (hereafter in this subsection referred to as "BIA") schools and that are required by the States in which such schools are located to attain or maintain State accreditation, and which schools have such accreditation prior to the date of enactment of the Individuals with Disabilities Education Act Amendments of 1991, the school shall be allowed to count those children for the purpose of distribution of the funds provided under this paragraph to the Secretary of the Interior. The Secretary of the Interior shall be responsible for meeting

all of the requirements of this part for these children, in accordance with paragraph (3). The amount of such payment for any fiscal year shall be 1 percent of the aggregate amounts available for all States under this section for that fiscal year.

(2) With respect to all other children aged 3-21, inclusive, on reservations, the State educational agency shall be responsible for ensuring that all of the requirements of this part are implemented.

(3) The Secretary of the Interior may receive an allotment under paragraph (1) only after submitting to the Secretary of Education an application that—

(A) meets the appropriate requirements, as determined by the Secretary of Education, of sections 1412 (including monitoring and evaluation activities), 1413, and 1414(a);

(B) includes a description of how the Secretary of the Interior will coordinate the provision of services under this part with local educational agencies, tribes and tribal organizations, and other private and Federal service providers;

(C) includes an assurance that there are public hearings, adequate notice of such hearings, and an opportunity for comment afforded to members of tribes, tribal governing bodies, and affected local school boards before the adoption of the policies, programs, and procedures required under subparagraph (A);

(D) includes an assurance that the Secretary of the Interior will provide such information as the Secretary of Education may require to comply with section 1418(b)(1), including data on the number of children and youth with disabilities served and the types and amounts of services provided and needed and this information shall be included in the annual report of the Secretary of Education to Congress required in section1418(g);

(E) included an assurance that, by October 1, 1992, the Secretaries of the Interior and Health and Human Services will enter into a memorandum of agreement, to be provided to the Secretary of Education, for the coordination of services, resources, and personnel between their respective Federal, State, and local offices and with State and local educational agencies and other entities to facilitate the provision of services to Indian children with disabilities residing on or near reservations. Such agreement shall provide for the apportionment of responsibilities and costs including, but not limited to, child find, evaluation, diagnosis, remediation or therapeutic measures, and (where appropriate) equipment and medical/personal supplies as needed for a child to remain in school or a program; and

(F) includes an assurance that the Department of the Interior will cooperate with the Department of Education in its exercise of monitoring and oversight of this application, and any agreements entered into between the Secretary of the Interior and other entities under this Act, and will fulfill its duties under this Act.

Section 1416(a) shall apply to any such application.

(4)(A) Beginning with funds appropriated under section 1411(a) for fiscal year 1992, the Secretary shall, subject to this paragraph, make payments to the Secretary of the Interior to be distributed to tribes or tribal organizations (as defined under section 4 of the Indian Self-Determination and Education Assistance Act) or consortiums of the above to provide for the coordination of assistance for special education and related services for children with disabilities aged 3-5, inclusive, on reservations served by elementary and secondary schools for Indian children operated or funded by the Department of the Interior. The amount of such payments under subparagraph (B) for any fiscal year shall be .25 percent of the aggregate amounts available for all States under this section for that fiscal year.

(B) The Secretary of the Interior shall distribute the total amount of the .25 percent under subparagraph (A) in the following manner:

(i) For the first fiscal year, each tribe or tribal organization shall receive an amount proportionate to the amount of weighted student units for special education programs for BIA operated or funded schools serving such reservation generated under the formula established under section 1128 of the Education Amendments of 1978, divided by the total number of such students in all BIA operated or funded schools.

(ii) For each fiscal year thereafter, each tribe or tribal organization shall receive an amount based on the number of children with disabilities, ages 3-5, inclusive, residing on reservations as reported annually divided by the total of such children served by all tribes or tribal organizations.

(C) To receive a payment under this paragraph, the tribe or tribal organization shall submit such figures to the Secretary of the Interior as required to determine the amounts to be allocated under subparagraph (B). This information shall be compiled and submitted to the Secretary of Education.

(D) The funds received by a tribe or tribal organization shall be used to assist in child find, screening, and other procedures for the early identification of children aged 3-5, inclusive, parent training, and the provision of direct services. These activities may be carried out directly or through contracts or cooperative agreements with the BIA, local educational agencies, and other public or private non-profit organizations. The tribe or tribal organization is encouraged to involve Indian parents in the development and implementation of these activities. The above entities shall, as appropriate, make referrals to local, State, or Federal entities for the provision of services or further diagnosis.

(E) To be eligible to receive a grant pursuant to subparagraph (A), the tribe or tribal organization shall make a biennial report to the Secretary of the Interior of activities undertaken under this paragraph, including the number of contracts and cooperative agreements entered into, the number of children contacted and receiving services for each year and the estimated number of children needing services during the 2 years following the one in which the report is made. The Secretary of the Interior shall include a summary of this information on a biennial basis in the report to the Secretary of Education required under this subsection. The Secretary of Education may require any additional information from the Secretary of the Interior.

(F) The Secretary of the Interior shall offer and, on request, provide technical assistance (especially in the areas of child find, diagnosis, and referral) to State and local educational agencies (where appropriate, intermediate educational units), and tribes and tribal organizations. Such assistance may be provided through its divisions and offices at the national and local level.

(G) None of the funds allocated under this paragraph can be used by the Secretary of the Interior for administrative purposes, including child count, and the provision of technical assistance.

(5) Before January 1, 1992, the Secretary of the Interior shall submit to the Committee on Education and Labor of the House of Representatives and the Committee on Labor and Human Resources of the Senate a plan for the coordination of services for all Indian children with disabilities residing on reservations covered under this Act. Such plan shall provide for the coordination of services benefiting these children from whatever source, including tribes, the Indian Health Service, other BIA divisions, and other Federal agencies. In developing such a plan, the Secretary of the Interior shall consult with all interested and involved parties. It shall be based upon the needs of the children and the system best suited for meeting those needs, and may involve the establishment of cooperative agreements between the BIA, other Federal agencies, and other entities. Such plan shall also be distributed upon request to States, State and local educational agencies, and other agencies providing services to infants, toddlers, children, and youth with disabilities, to tribes, and to other interested parties.

(6) To meet the requirements of section 1413(a)(12) of this Act, the Secretary of the Interior shall establish, within 6 months of the date of the enactment of the Individuals with Disabilities Education Act Amendments of 1991, under the Bureau of Indian Affairs (BIA), an advisory board composed of individuals involved in or concerned with the education and provision of services to Indian infants, toddlers, children, and youth with disabilities, including Indians with disabilities, Indian parents or guardians of such children, teachers, service providers, State and local educational officials, representatives of tribes or tribal organizations, representatives from State Interagency Coordinating Councils in States having reservations, and other members representing the various divisions and entities of the BIA. The chairperson shall be selected by the Secretary of the Interior. The advisory board shall—

(A) assist in the coordination of services within BIA and with other local, State, and Federal agencies in the provision of education for infants, toddlers, children, and youth with disabilities;

(B) advise and assist the Secretary of the Interior in the performance of the Secretary's responsibilities described in this subsection;

(C) develop and recommend policies concerning effective inter-and intra-agency collaboration, including modifications to regulations, and the elimination of barriers to inter- and intra-agency programs and activities;

(D) provide assistance and disseminate information on best practices, effective program coordination strategies, and recommendations for improved educational programming for Indian infants, toddlers, children, and youth with disabilities; and

(E) provide assistance in the preparation of information required under paragraph (3)(D).

(g) Reductions or increases

(1) If the sums appropriated under subsection (h) of this section for any fiscal year for making payments to States under subsection (a) of this section are not sufficient to pay in full the total amounts which all States are entitled to receive under subsection (a) of this section for such fiscal year, the maximum amounts which all States are entitled to receive under subsection (a) of this section for such fiscal year shall be ratably reduced. In case additional funds become available for making such payments for any fiscal year during which the

preceding sentence is applicable, such reduced amounts shall be increased on the same basis as they were reduced.

(2) In the case of any fiscal year in which the maximum amounts for which States are eligible have been reduced under the first sentence of paragraph (1), and in which additional funds have not been made available to pay in full the total of such maximum amounts under the last sentence of such paragraph, the State educational agency shall fix dates before which each local educational agency or intermediate educational unit shall report to the State educational agency on the amount of funds available to the local educational agency or intermediate educational unit, under the provisions of subsection (d) of this section, which it estimates that it will expend in accordance with the provisions of this section. The amounts so available to any local educational agency or intermediate educational unit, or any amount which would be available to any other local educational agency or intermediate educational unit if it were to submit a program meeting the requirements of this subchapter, which the State educational agency determines will not be used for the period of its availability, shall be available for allocation to those local educational agencies or intermediate educational units, in the manner provided by this section, which the State educational agency determines will need and be able to use additional funds to carry out approved programs.

(h) Authorization of appropriations.

For grants under subsection (a) of this section there are authorized to be appropriated such sums as may be necessary.

§1412. Eligibility requirements

In order to qualify for assistance under this subchapter in any fiscal year, a State shall demonstrate to the Secretary that the following conditions are met:

(1) The State has in effect a policy that assures all children with disabilities the right to a free appropriate public education.

(2) The State has developed a plan pursuant to section 1413(b) of this chapter in effect prior to November 29, 1975, and submitted not later than August 21, 1975, which will be amended so as to comply with the provisions of this paragraph. Each such amended plan shall set forth in detail the policies and procedures which the State will undertake or has undertaken in order to assure that—

(A) there is established (i) a goal of providing full educational opportunity to all children with disabilities, (ii) a detailed timetable for accomplishing such a goal, and (iii) a description of the kind and number of facilities, personnel, and services necessary throughout the State to meet such a goal;

(B) a free appropriate public education will be available for all children with disabilities between the ages of three and eighteen within the State not later than September 1, 1978, and for all children with disabilities between the ages of three and twenty-one within the State not later than September 1, 1980, except that, with respect to children with disabilities aged three to five and aged eighteen to twenty-one, inclusive, the requirements of this clause shall not be applied in any State if the application of such requirements would be inconsistent with State law or practice, or the order of any court, respecting public education within such age groups in the State;

(C) all children residing in the State who are disabled, regardless of the severity of their disability, and who are in need of special education and related services are identified, located, and evaluated, and that a practical method is developed and implemented to determine which children are currently receiving needed special education and related services and which children are not currently receiving needed special education and related services;

(D) policies and procedures are established in accordance with detailed criteria prescribed under section 417(c) of this chapter; and

(E) any amendment to the plan submitted by the State required by this section shall be available to parents, guardians, and other members of the general public at least thirty days prior to the date of submission of the amendment to the Secretary.

(3) The State has established priorities for providing a free appropriate public education to all children with disabilities, which priorities shall meet the timetables set forth in clause (B) of paragraph (2) of this section, first with respect to children with disabilities who are not receiving an education, and second with respect to children with disabilities, within each disability category, with the most severe disabilities who are receiving an inadequate education, and has made adequate progress in meeting the timetables set forth in clause (B) of paragraph (2) of this section.

(4) Each local educational agency in the State will maintain records of the individualized education program for each child with a disability, and such program shall be established, reviewed, and revised as provided in section 1414(a)(5) of this chapter.

(5) The State has established (A) procedural safeguards as required by section 1415 of this chapter, (B) procedures to assure that, to the maximum extent appropriate, children with disabilities, including children in public or private institutions or other care facilities, are educated with children who are not disabled, and that special classes, separate schooling, or other removal of children with disabilities from the regular educational environment occurs only when the nature or severity of the disability is such that education in regular classes with the use of supplementary aids and services cannot be achieved satisfactorily, and (C) procedures to assure that testing and evaluation materials and procedures utilized for the purposes of evaluation and placement of children with disabilities will be selected and administered so as not to be racially or culturally discriminatory. Such materials or procedures shall be provided and administered in the child's native language or mode of communication, unless it clearly is not feasible to do so, and no single procedure shall be the sole criterion for determining an appropriate educational program for a child.

(6) The State educational agency shall be responsible for assuring that the requirements of this subchapter are carried out and that all educational programs for children with disabilities within the State, including all such programs administered by any other State or local agency, will be under the general supervision of the persons responsible for educational programs for children with disabilities in the State educational agency and shall meet

education standards of the State educational agency. This paragraph shall not be construed to limit the responsibility of agencies other than educational agencies in a State from providing or paying for some or all of the costs of a free appropriate public education to be provided children with disabilities in the State.

(7) The State shall assure that (A) in carrying out the requirements of this section procedures are established for consultation with individuals involved in or concerned with the education of children with disabilities, including individuals with disabilities and parents or guardians of children with disabilities, and (B) there are public hearings, adequate notice of such hearings, and an opportunity for comment available to the general public prior to adoption of the policies, programs, and procedures required pursuant to the provisions of this section and section 1413 of this chapter.

§ 1413. State plans

(a) Requisite features

Any State meeting the eligibility requirements set forth in section 1412 of this chapter and desiring to participate in the program under this subchapter shall submit to the Secretary, through its State educational agency, a State plan at such time, in such manner, and containing or accompanied by such information, as the Secretary deems necessary. Each such plan shall—

(1) set forth policies and procedures designed to assure that funds paid to the State under this subchapter will be expended in accordance with the provisions of this subchapter, with particular attention given to the provisions of sections 1411(b), 1411(c), 1411(d), 1412(2), and 1412(3) of this chapter;

(2) provide that programs and procedures will be established to assure that funds received by the State or any of its political subdivisions under any other Federal program, including subpart 2 of part D of chapter 1 of title I of the Elementary and Secondary Education Act of 1965, of this chapter, under which there is specific authority for the provision of assistance for the education of children with disabilities, will be utilized by the State, or any of its political subdivisions, only in a manner consistent with the goal of providing a free appropriate public education for all children with disabilities, except that nothing in this clause shall be construed to limit the specific requirements of the laws governing such Federal programs;

(3) describe, consistent with the purposes of this Act and with the comprehensive system of personnel development described in section 1476(b)(8) of this chapter, a comprehensive system of personnel development that shall include—

(A) a description of the procedures and activities the State will undertake to ensure an adequate supply of qualified special education and related services personnel, including—

(i) the development and maintenance of a system for determining, on an annual basis—

(I) the number and type of personnel, including leadership personnel, that are employed in the provision of special education and related services, by area of specialization, including the number of such personnel who are employed on an emergency, provisional, or other basis, who do not hold appropriate State certification or licensure; and

(II) the number and type of personnel, including leadership personnel, needed, and a projection of the numbers of such personnel that will be needed in five years, based on projections of individuals to be served, retirement and other leaving of personnel from the field, and other relevant factors;

(ii) the development and maintenance of a system for determining, on an annual basis, the institutions of higher education within the State that are preparing special education and related services personnel, including leadership personnel, by area of specialization, including—

(I) the numbers of students enrolled in such programs, and

(II) the number who graduated with certification or licensure, or with credentials to qualify for certification or licensure, during the past year; and

(iii) the development, updating, and implementation of a plan that—

(I) will address current and projected special education and related services personnel needs, including the need for leadership personnel; and

(II) coordinates and facilitates efforts among State and local educational agencies, institutions of higher education, and professional associations to recruit, prepare, and retain qualified personnel, including personnel from minority backgrounds, and personnel with disabilities; and

(B) a description of the procedures and activities the State will undertake to ensure that all personnel necessary to carry out this part are appropriately and adequately prepared, including—

(i) a system for the continuing education of regular and special education and related services personnel;

(ii) procedures for acquiring and disseminating to teachers, administrators, and related services personnel significant knowledge derived from education research and other sources; and

(iii) procedures for adopting, where appropriate, promising practices, materials, and technology.

(4) set forth policies and procedures to assure—

(A) that, to the extent consistent with the number and location of children with disabilities in the State who are enrolled in private elementary and secondary schools, provision is made for the participation of such children in the program assisted or carried out under this subchapter by providing for such children special education and related services; and

(B) that

(i) children with disabilities in private schools and facilities will be provided special education and related services (in conformance with an individualized education program as required by this part) at no cost to their parents or guardian, if such children are placed in or referred to such schools or facilities by the State or appropriate local educational agency as the means of carrying out the requirements of this part or any other applicable law requiring the provision of special education and related services to all children with disabilities within such State; and

(ii) in all such instances, the State educational agency shall determine whether such schools and facilities meet standards that apply to State and local educational agencies and that children so served have all the rights they would have if served by such agencies;

(5) set forth policies and procedures which assure that the State shall seek to recover any funds made available under this subchapter for services to any child who is determined to be erroneously classified as eligible to be counted under section 1411(a) or 1411(d) of this chapter;

(6) provide satisfactory assurance that the control of funds provided under this subchapter, and title to property derived therefrom, shall be in a public agency for the uses and purposes provided in this subchapter, and that a public agency will administer such funds and property;

(7) provide for—

(A) making such reports in such form and containing such information as the Secretary may require to carry out the Secretary's functions under this part, and

(B) keeping such records and affording such access thereto as the Secretary may find necessary to assure the correctness and verification of such reports and proper disbursement of Federal funds under this subchapter;

(8) provide procedures to assure that final action with respect to any application submitted by a local educational agency or an intermediate educational unit shall not be taken without first affording the local educational agency or intermediate educational unit involved reasonable notice and opportunity for a hearing;

(9) provide satisfactory assurance that Federal funds made available under this subchapter—

(A) will not be commingled with State funds, and

(B) will be so used as to supplement and increase the level of Federal, State, and local funds (including funds that are not under the direct control of State or local educational agencies) expended for special education and related services provided to children with disabilities under this subchapter and in no case to supplant such Federal, State, and local funds, except that, where the State provides clear and convincing evidence that all children with disabilities have available to them a free appropriate public education, the Secretary may waive in part the requirement of this subparagraph if the Secretary concurs with the evidence provided by the State;

(10) provide, consistent with procedures prescribed pursuant to section 1417(a)(2) of this chapter, satisfactory assurance that such fiscal control and fund accounting procedures will be adopted as may be necessary to assure proper disbursement of, and accounting for, Federal funds paid under this subchapter to the State, including any such funds paid by the State to local educational agencies and intermediate educational units;

(11) provide for procedures for evaluation at least annually of the effectiveness of programs in meeting the educational needs of children with disabilities (including evaluation of individualized education programs), in accordance with such criteria that the Secretary shall prescribe pursuant to section 1417 of this chapter;

(12) provide that the State has an advisory panel, appointed by the Governor or any other official authorized under State law to make such appointments, composed of individuals involved in or concerned with the education of children with disabilities, including individuals with disabilities, teachers, parents or guardians of children with disabilities, State and local education officials, and administrators of programs for children with disabilities, which—

(A) advises the State educational agency of unmet needs within the

State in the education of children with disabilities,

(B) comments publicly on any rules or regulations proposed for issuance by the State regarding the education of children with disabilities and the procedures for distribution of funds under this subchapter, and

(C) assists the State in developing and reporting such data and evaluations as may assist the Secretary in the performance of the responsibilities of the Secretary under section 1418 of this chapter;

(13) set forth policies and procedures for developing and implementing interagency agreements between the State educational agency and other appropriate State and local agencies to—

(A) define the financial responsibility of each agency for providing children and youth with disabilities with free appropriate public education, and

(B) resolve inter-agency disputes, including procedures under which local educational agencies may initiate proceedings under the agreement in order to secure reimbursement from other agencies or otherwise implement the provisions of the agreement;

(14) set forth policies and procedures relating to the establishment and maintenance of standards to ensure that personnel necessary to carry out the purposes of this subchapter are appropriately and adequately prepared and trained, including—

(A) the establishment and maintenance of standards which are consistent with any State approved or recognized certification, licensing, registration, or other comparable requirements which apply to the area in which such personnel are providing special education or related services, and

(B) to the extent such standards are not based on the highest requirements in the State applicable to a specific profession or discipline, the steps the State is taking to require the retraining or hiring of personnel that meet appropriate professional requirements in the State; and

(15) set forth policies and procedures relating to the smooth transition for those individuals participating in the early intervention program assisted under subchapter VIII who will participate in preschool programs assisted under this subchapter, including a method of ensuring that when a child turns age three an individualized education program, or, if consistent with sections 1414(a)(5) and 1477(d), an individualized family service plan, has been developed and is being implemented by such child's third birthday.

(b) Additional assurances

Whenever a State educational agency provides free appropriate public education for children with disabilities, or provides direct services to such children, such State educational agency shall include, as part of the State plan required by subsection (a) of this section, such additional assurances not specified in such subsection (a) of this section as are contained in section 1414(a) of this title, except that funds available for the provision of such education or services may be expended without regard to the provisions relating to excess costs in section 1414(a) of this title.

(c) Notice and hearing prior to disapproval of plan

(1) The Secretary shall approve any State plan and any modification thereof which

(A) is submitted by a State eligible in accordance with section 1412 of this title; and

(B) meets the requirements of subsection (a) and subsection (b) of this section.

(2) The Secretary shall disapprove any State plan which does not meet the requirements of paragraph (1), but shall not finally disapprove a State plan except after reasonable notice and opportunity for a hearing to the State.

(d) Participation of children with disabilities in private schools; payment of Federal amount; determinations of Secretary: notice and hearing; judicial review: jurisdiction of court of appeals, petition, record, conclusiveness of findings, remand, review by Supreme Court

(1) If, on December 2, 1983, a State educational agency is prohibited by law from providing for the participation in special programs of children with disabilities enrolled in private elementary and secondary schools as required by subsection (a)(4) of this section, the Secretary shall waive such requirement, and shall arrange for the provision of services to such children through arrangements which shall be subject to the requirements of subsection (a)(4) of this section.

(2)(A) When the Secretary arranges for services pursuant to this subsection, the Secretary, after consultation with the appropriate public and private school officials, shall pay to the provider of such services an amount per child which may not exceed the Federal amount provided per child under this subchapter to all children with disabilities enrolled in the State for services for the fiscal year preceding the fiscal year for which the determination is made.

(B) Pending final resolution of any investigation or complaint that could result in a determination under this subsection, the Secretary may withhold from the allocation of the affected State educational agency the amount the Secretary estimates would be necessary to pay the cost of such services.

(C) Any determination by the Secretary under this section shall continue in effect until the Secretary determines that there will no longer be any failure or inability on the part of the State educational agency to meet the requirements of subsection (a)(4) of this section.

(3)(A) The Secretary shall not take any final action under this subsection until the State educational agency affected by such action has had an opportunity, for at least 45 days after receiving written notice thereof, to submit written objections and to appear before the Secretary or the Secretary's designee to show cause why such action should not be taken.

(B) If a State educational agency is dissatisfied with the Secretary's final action after a proceeding under subparagraph (A) of this paragraph, it may, within 60 days after notice of such action, file with the United States court of appeals for the circuit in which such state is located a petition for review of that action. A copy of the petition shall be forthwith transmitted by the clerk of the court to the Secretary. The Secretary thereupon shall file in the court the record of the proceedings on which the Secretary based the

Secretary's action, as provided in section 2112 of title 28.

(C) The findings of fact by the Secretary, if supported by substantial evidence, shall be conclusive; but the court, for good cause shown, may remand the case to the Secretary to take further evidence, and the Secretary may thereupon make new or modified findings of fact and may modify the Secretary's previous action, and shall file in the court the record of the further proceedings. Such new or modified findings of fact shall likewise be conclusive if supported by substantial evidence.

(D) Upon the filing of a petition under subparagraph (B), the court shall have jurisdiction to affirm the action of the Secretary or to set it aside, in whole or in part. The judgment of the court shall be subject to review by the Supreme Court of the United States upon certiorari or certification as provided in section 1254 of title 28.

(e) Prohibition on reduction of assistance

This chapter shall not be construed to permit a State to reduce medical and other assistance available or to alter eligibility under titles V and XIX of the Social Security Act with respect to the provision of a free appropriate public education for children with disabilities within the State.

§ 1414. Application

(a) Requisite features

A local educational agency or an intermediate educational unit which desires to receive payments under section 1411(d) of this chapter for any fiscal year shall submit an application to the appropriate State educational agency. Such application shall—

(1) provide satisfactory assurance that payments under this subchapter will be used for excess costs directly attributable to programs which—

(A) provide that all children residing within the jurisdiction of the local educational agency or the intermediate educational unit who are disabled, regardless of the severity of their disability, and are in need of special education and related services will be identified, located, and evaluated, and provide for the inclusion of a practical method of determining which children are currently receiving needed special education and related services and which children are not currently receiving such education and services;

(B) establish policies and procedures in accordance with detailed criteria prescribed under section 1417(c) of this chapter;

(C) establish a goal of providing full educational opportunities to all children with disabilities, including—

(i) procedures for the implementation and use of the comprehensive system of personnel development established by the State educational agency under section 1413(a)(3) of this chapter;

(ii) the provision of, and the establishment of priorities for providing, a free appropriate public education to all children with disabilities, first with respect to children with disabilities who are not receiving an education, and second with respect to children with disabilities, within each disability, with the most severe disabilities who are receiving an inadequate education;

(iii) the participation and consultation of the parents or guardian of such children; and

(iv) to the maximum extent practicable and consistent with the provisions of section 1412(5)(B) of this chapter, the provision of special services to enable such children to participate in regular educational programs;

(D) establish a detailed timetable for accomplishing the goal described in subclause (C); and

(E) provide a description of the kind and number of facilities, personnel, and services necessary to meet the goal described in subclause (C);

(2) provide satisfactory assurance that—

(A) the control of funds provided under this subchapter, and title to property derived from such funds, shall be in a public agency for the uses and purposes provided in this subchapter, and that a public agency will administer such funds and property;

(B) Federal funds expended by local educational agencies and intermediate educational units for programs under this subchapter—

(i) shall be used to pay only the excess costs directly attributable to the education of children with disabilities; and

(ii) shall be used to supplement and, to the extent practicable, increase the level of State and local funds expended for the education of children with disabilities, and in no case to supplant such State and local funds; and

(C) State and local funds will be used in the jurisdiction of the local educational agency or intermediate educational unit to provide services in program areas that, taken as a whole, are at least comparable to services being provided in areas of such jurisdiction that are not receiving funds under this subchapter;

(3) provide for—

(A) furnishing such information (which, in the case of reports relating to performance, is in accordance with specific performance criteria related to program objectives), as may be necessary to enable the State educational agency to perform its duties under this subchapter, including information relating to the educational achievement of children with disabilities participating in programs carried out under this subchapter; and

(B) keeping such records, and affording such access to such records, as the State educational agency may find necessary to assure the correctness and verification of such information furnished under subparagraph (A);

(4) provide for making the application and all pertinent documents related to such application available to parents, guardians, and other members of the general public, and provide that all evaluations and reports required under clause (3) shall be public information;

(5) provide assurances that the local educational agency or intermediate educational unit will establish or revise, whichever is appropriate, an individualized education program for each child with a disability (or, if consistent with State policy and at the discretion of the local educational agency or intermediate educational unit, and with the concurrence of the parents or guardian, an individualized family service plan described in section 1477(d)for each child with a disability aged 3 to 5, inclusive) at the beginning of each school year and will

then review and, if appropriate, revise, its provisions periodically, but not less than annually;

(6) provide satisfactory assurance that policies and programs established and administered by the local educational agency or intermediate educational unit shall be consistent with the provisions of paragraph (1) through paragraph (7) of section 1412 and section 1413(a) of this chapter; and

(7) provide satisfactory assurance that the local educational agency or intermediate educational unit will establish and maintain procedural safeguards in accordance with the provisions of sections 1412(5)(B), 1412(5)(C), and 1415 of this chapter.

(b) Approval by State educational agencies of applications submitted by local educational agencies or intermediate educational units; notice and hearing

(1) A State educational agency shall approve any application submitted by a local educational agency or an intermediate educational unit under subsection (a) of this section if the State educational agency determines that such application meets the requirements of subsection (a) of this section, except that no such application may be approved until the State plan submitted by such State educational agency under subsection (a) of this section is approved by the Secretary under section 1413(c) of this chapter. A State educational agency shall disapprove any application submitted by a local educational agency or an intermediate educational unit under subsection (a) of this section if the State educational agency determines that such application does not meet the requirements of subsection (a) of this section.

(2) (A) Whenever a State educational agency, after reasonable notice and opportunity for a hearing, finds that a local educational agency or an intermediate educational unit, in the administration of an application approved by the State educational agency under paragraph (1), has failed to comply with any requirement set forth in such application, the State educational agency, after giving appropriate notice to the local educational agency or the intermediate educational unit, shall—

(i) make no further payments to such local educational agency or such intermediate educational unit under section 1420 of this chapter until the State educational agency is satisfied that there is no longer any failure to comply with the requirement involved; or

(ii) take such finding into account in its review of any application made by such local educational agency or such intermediate educational unit under subsection (a) of this section

(B) The provisions of the last sentence of section 1416(a) of this chapter shall apply to any local educational agency or any intermediate educational unit receiving any notification from a State educational agency under this paragraph.

(3) In carrying out its functions under paragraph (1), each State educational agency shall consider any decision made pursuant to a hearing held under section 1415 of this title which is adverse to the local educational agency or intermediate educational unit involved in such decision.

(c) Consolidated applications

(1) A State educational agency may, for purposes of the consideration and approval of applications under this section, require local educational agencies to submit a consolidated application for payments if such State educational agency determines that any individual application submitted by any such local educational agency will be disapproved because such local educational agency is ineligible to receive payments because of the application of section 1411(c)(4)(A)(i) of this chapter or such local educational agency would be unable to establish and maintain programs of sufficient size and scope to effectively meet the educational needs of children with disabilities.

(2)(A) In any case in which a consolidated application of local educational agencies is approved by a State educational agency under paragraph (1), the payments which such local educational agencies may receive shall be equal to the sum of payments to which each such local educational agency would be entitled under section 1411(d) of this chapter if an individual application of any such local educational agency had been approved.

(B) The State educational agency shall prescribe rules and regulations with respect to consolidated applications submitted under this subsection which are consistent with the provisions of paragraph (1) through paragraph (7) of section 1412 and section 1413(a) of this chapter and which provide participating local educational agencies with joint responsibilities for implementing programs receiving payments under this subchapter.

(C) In any case in which an intermediate educational unit is required pursuant to State law to carry out the provisions of this subchapter, the joint responsibilities given to local educational agencies under subparagraph (B) shall not apply to the administration and disbursement of any payments received by such intermediate educational unit. Such responsibilities shall be carried out exclusively by such intermediate educational unit.

(d) Special education and related services provided directly by State educational agencies: regional or State centers

Whenever a State educational agency determines that a local educational agency—

(1) is unable or unwilling to establish and maintain programs of free appropriate public education which meet the requirements established in subsection (a) of this section;

(2) is unable or unwilling to be consolidated with other local educational agencies in order to establish and maintain such programs; or

(3) has one or more children with disabilities who can best be served by a regional or State center designed to meet the needs of such children;

the State educational agency shall use the payments which would have been available to such local educational agency to provide special education and related services directly to children with disabilities residing in the area served by such local educational agency. The State educational agency may provide such education and services in such manner, and at such locations (including regional or State centers), as it considers appropriate, except that the manner in which such education and services are provided shall be consistent with the requirements of this subchapter.

(e) Reallocation of funds

Whenever a State educational agency determines that a local educational agency is adequately providing a free appropriate public education to all children with disabilities residing in the area served by such agency with State and local funds otherwise available to such agency, the State educational agency may reallocate funds (or such portion of those funds as may not be required to provide such education and services) made available to such agency, pursuant to section 1411(d) of this chapter, to such other local educational agencies within the State as are not adequately providing special education and related services to all children with disabilities residing in the areas served by such other local educational agencies.

(f) Programs using State or local funds

Notwithstanding the provisions of subsection (a)(2)(B)(ii) of this section, any local educational agency which is required to carry out any program for the education of children with disabilities pursuant to a State law shall be entitled to receive payments under section 1411(d) of this chapter for use in carrying out such program, except that such payments may not be used to reduce the level of expenditures for such program made by such local educational agency from State or local funds below the level of such expenditures for the fiscal year prior to the fiscal year for which such local educational agency seeks such payments.

§ 1415. Procedural safeguards

(a) Establishment and maintenance

Any State educational agency, any local educational agency, and any intermediate educational unit which receives assistance under this subchapter shall establish and maintain procedures in accordance with subsection (b) through subsection (e) of this section to assure that children with disabilities and their parents or guardians are guaranteed procedural safeguards with respect to the provision of free appropriate public education by such agencies and units.

(b) Required procedures; hearing

(1) The procedures required by this section shall include, but shall not be limited to—
   (A) an opportunity for the parents or guardian of a child with a disability to examine all relevant records with respect to the identification, evaluation, and educational placement of the child, and the provision of a free appropriate public education to such child, and to obtain an independent educational evaluation of the child;
   (B) procedures to protect the rights of the child whenever the parents or guardian of the child are not known, unavailable, or the child is a ward of the State, including the assignment of an individual (who shall not be an employee of the State educational agency, local educational agency, or intermediate educational unit involved in the education or care of the child)

to act as a surrogate for the parents or guardian;

(C) written prior notice to the parents or guardian of the child whenever such agency or unit—

(i) proposes to initiate or change, or

(ii) refuses to initiate or change,

the identification, evaluation, or educational placement of the child or the provision of a free appropriate public education to the child;

(D) procedures designed to assure that the notice required by clause (C) fully informs the parents or guardian, in the parents' or guardian's native language, unless it clearly is not feasible to do so, of all procedures available pursuant to this section; and

(E) an opportunity to present complaints with respect to any matter relating to the identification, evaluation, or educational placement of the child, or the provision of a free appropriate public education to such child.

(2) Whenever a complaint has been received under paragraph (1) of this subsection, the parents or guardian shall have an opportunity for an impartial due process hearing which shall be conducted by the State educational agency or by the local educational agency or intermediate educational unit, as determined by State law or by the State educational agency. No hearing conducted pursuant to the requirements of this paragraph shall be conducted by an employee of such agency or unit involved in the education or care of the child.

(c) Review of local decision by State education agency

If the hearing required in paragraph (2) of subsection (b) of this section is conducted by a local educational agency or an intermediate educational unit, any party aggrieved by the findings and decision rendered in such a hearing may appeal to the State educational agency which shall conduct an impartial review of such hearing. The officer conducting such review shall make an independent decision upon completion of such review.

(d) Enumeration of rights accorded parties to hearings

Any party to any hearing conducted pursuant to subsections (b) and (c) of this section shall be accorded—

(1) the right to be accompanied and advised by counsel and by individuals with special knowledge or training with respect to the problems of children with disabilities,

(2) the right to present evidence and confront, cross-examine, and compel the attendance of witnesses,

(3) the right to a written or electronic verbatim record of such hearing, and

(4) the right to written findings of fact and decisions (which findings and decisions shall be made available to the public consistent with the requirements of section 1417(c) and shall also be transmitted to the advisory panel established pursuant to section 1413(a)(12)).

(e) Civil action; jurisdiction; attorney fees

(1) A decision made in a hearing conducted pursuant to paragraph (2) of subsection (b) of this section shall be final, except that any party involved in such hearing may appeal such decision under the provisions of subsection (c) and paragraph (2) of this subsection. A decision made under subsection (c) of this section shall be final, except that any party may bring an action under paragraph (2) of this subsection.

(2) Any party aggrieved by the findings and decision made under subsection (b) of this section who does not have the right to an appeal under subsection (c) of this section, and any party aggrieved by the findings and decision under subsection (c) of this section, shall have the right to bring a civil action with respect to the complaint presented pursuant to this section, which action may be brought in any State court of competent jurisdiction or in a district court of the United States without regard to the amount in controversy. In any action brought under this paragraph the court shall receive the records of the administrative proceedings, shall hear additional evidence at the request of a party, and, basing its decision of the preponderance of the evidence, shall grant such relief as the court determines is appropriate.

(3) During the pendency of any proceedings conducted pursuant to this section, unless the State or local educational agency and the parents or guardian otherwise agree, the child shall remain in the then current educational placement of such child, or, if applying for initial admission to a public school, shall, with the consent of the parents or guardian, be placed in the public school program until all such proceedings have been completed.

(4) (A) The district courts of the United States shall have jurisdiction of actions brought under this subsection without regard to the amount in controversy.

(B) In any action or proceeding brought under this subsection, the court, in its discretion, may award reasonable attorneys' fees as part of the costs to the parents or guardian of a child or youth with a disability who is the prevailing party.

(C) For the purpose of this subsection, fees awarded under this subsection shall be based on rates prevailing in the community in which the action or proceeding arose for the kind and quality of services furnished. No bonus or multiplier may be used in calculating the fees awarded under this subsection.

(D) No award of attorneys' fees and related costs may be made in any action or proceeding under this subsection for services performed subsequent to the time of a written offer of settlement to a parent or guardian, if—

(i) the offer is made within the time prescribed by Rule 68 of the Federal Rules of Civil Procedure or, in the case of an administrative proceeding, at any time more than ten days before the proceeding begins;

(ii) the offer is not accepted within ten days; and

(iii) the court or administrative officer finds that the relief finally obtained by the parents or guardian is not more favorable to the parents or guardian than the offer of settlement.

(E) Notwithstanding the provisions of subparagraph (D), an award of attorneys' fees and related costs may be made to a parent or guardian who is the prevailing party and who was substantially justified in rejecting the settlement offer.

(F) Whenever the court finds that—

(i) the parent or guardian, during the course of the action or proceeding, unreasonably protracted the final resolution of the controversy;

(ii) the amount of the attorneys' fees otherwise authorized to be awarded unreasonably exceeds the hourly rate prevailing in the community for similar services by attorneys of reasonably comparable skill, experience, and reputation; or

(iii) the time spent and legal services furnished were excessive considering the nature of the action or proceeding,

the court shall reduce, accordingly, the amount of the attorneys' fees awarded under this subsection.

(G) The provisions of subparagraph (F) shall not apply in any action or proceeding if the court finds that the State or local educational agency unreasonably protracted the final resolution of the action or proceeding or there was a violation of this section.

(f) Effect on other laws

Nothing in this chapter shall be construed to restrict or limit the rights, procedures, and remedies available under the Constitution, title V of the Rehabilitation Act of 1973 {29 U.S.C.A. § 790 et seq.}, or other Federal statutes protecting the rights of children and youth with disabilities, except that before the filing of a civil action under such laws seeking relief that is also available under this subchapter, the procedures under subsections (b)(2) and (c) of this section shall be exhausted to the same extent as would be required had the action been brought under this subchapter.

Effective Date of 1986 Amendment. Section 5 of the HCPA, Pub.L. 99-372, provided that: "The amendment made by section 2 [amending 20 U.S.C. § 1415(e)(4)] shall apply with respect to actions or proceedings brought under section 615(e) of the Education of the Handicapped Act 20 U.S.C. § 1415(e) after July 3, 1984, and actions or proceedings brought prior to July 4, 1984, under such section which were pending on July 4, 1984."

§ 1416. Withholding of payments

(a) Failure to comply with this subchapter; limitations; public notice

Whenever the Secretary, after reasonable notice and opportunity for hearing to the State educational agency involved (and to any local educational agency or intermediate educational unit affected by any failure described in clause (2)), finds—

(1) that there has been a failure to comply substantially with any provision of section 1412 or section 1413 of this chapter, or

(2) that in the administration of the State plan there is a failure to comply with any provision of this subchapter or with any requirements set forth in the application of a local educational agency or intermediate educational unit approved by the State educational agency pursuant to the State plan, the Secretary—

(A) shall, after notifying the State educational agency, withhold any further payments to the State under this subchapter, and

(B) may, after notifying the State educational agency, withhold further payments to the State under the Federal programs specified in section 1413(a)(2) within the Secretary's jurisdiction, to the extent that funds under such programs are available for the provision of assistance for the education of children with disabilities.

If the Secretary withholds further payments under clause (A) or clause (B) the Secretary may determine that such withholding will be limited to programs or projects under the State plan, or portions thereof, affected by the failure, or that the State educational agency shall not make further payments under this subchapter to specified local educational agencies or intermediate educational units affected by the failure. Until the Secretary is satisfied that there is no longer any failure to comply with the provisions of this subchapter, as specified in clause (1) or clause (2), no further payments shall be made to the State under this subchapter or under the Federal programs specified in section 1413(a)(2) of this chapter within the Secretary's jurisdiction to the extent that funds under such programs are available for the provision of assistance for the education of children with disabilities, or payments by the State educational agency under this subchapter shall be limited to local educational agencies and intermediate educational units whose actions did not cause or were not involved in the failure, as the case may be. Any State educational agency, local educational agency, or intermediate educational unit in receipt of a notice pursuant to the first sentence of this subsection shall, by means of a public notice, take such measures as may be necessary to bring the pendency of an action pursuant to this subsection to the attention of the public within the jurisdiction of such agency or unit.

(b) Judicial review

(1) If any State is dissatisfied with the Secretary's final action with respect to its State plan submitted under section 1413 of this chapter, such State may, within sixty days after notice of such action, file with the United States court of appeals for the circuit in which such State is located a petition for review of that action. A copy of the petition shall be forthwith transmitted by the clerk of the court to the Secretary. The Secretary thereupon shall file in the court the record of the proceedings upon which the Secretary's action was based, as provided in section 2112 of title 28.

(2) The findings of fact by the Secretary, if supported by substantial evidence, shall be conclusive; but the court, for good cause shown, may remand the case to the Secretary to take further evidence, and the Secretary may thereupon make new or modified findings of fact that may modify the Secretary's previous action, and shall file in the court the record of the further proceedings. Such new or modified findings of fact shall likewise be conclusive if supported by substantial evidence.

(3) Upon the filing of such petition, the court shall have jurisdiction to affirm the action of the Secretary or to set it aside, in whole or in part. The judgment of the court shall be subject to review by the Supreme Court of the United States upon certiorari or certification as provided in section 1254 of title 28.

§ 1417. Administration

(a) Duties of Secretary

(1) In carrying out the Secretary's duties under this subchapter, the Secretary shall
    (A) cooperate with, and furnish all technical assistance necessary, directly or by grant or contract, to the States in matters relating to the education of children with disabilities and the execution of the provisions of this subchapter;
    (B) provide such short-term training programs and institutes as are necessary;
    (C) disseminate information, and otherwise promote the education of all children with disabilities within the States; and
    (D) assure that each State shall, within one year after November 29, 1975 and every year thereafter, provide certification of the actual number of children with disabilities receiving special education and related services in such State.
(2) As soon as practicable after November 29, 1975, the Secretary shall, by regulation, prescribe a uniform financial report to be utilized by State educational agencies in submitting State plans under this subchapter in order to assure equity among the States.

(b) Rules and regulations

In carrying out the provisions of this subchapter, the Secretary shall issue, not later than January 1, 1977, amend, and revoke such rules and regulations as may be necessary. No other less formal method of implementing such provisions is authorized.

(c) Protection of rights and privacy of parents and students

The Secretary shall take appropriate action, in accordance with the provisions of section 1232g of this title, to assure the protection of the confidentiality of any personally identifiable data, information, and records collected or maintained by the Secretary and by State and local educational agencies pursuant to the provisions of this subchapter.

(d) Hiring of qualified personnel

The Secretary is authorized to hire qualified personnel necessary to conduct data collection and evaluation activities required by subsections (b), (c) and (d) of section 1418 of this chapter and to carry out the Secretary's duties under subsection (a)(1) of this section without regard to the provisions of title 5 relating to appointments in the competitive service and without regard to chapter 51 and subchapter III of chapter 53 of such title relating to classification and general schedule pay rates except that no more than twenty such personnel shall be employed at any time.

§ 1418. Evaluation

(a) Duties of Secretary

The Secretary shall, directly or by grant, contract, or cooperative agreement, collect data and conduct studies, investigations, and evaluations—
(1) to assess progress in the implementation of this Act;
(2) to assess the impact and effectiveness of State and local efforts, and efforts by the Secretary of the Interior, to provide—
(A) free appropriate public education to children and youth with disabilities; and
(B) early intervention services to infants and toddlers with disabilities; and
(3) to provide—
(A) Congress with information relevant to policy making; and
(B) State, local, and Federal agencies, including the Department of the Interior, with information relevant to program management, administration, and effectiveness with respect to such education and early intervention services.

(b) Collection of data

(1) In carrying out subsection (a) of this section, the Secretary, on at least an annual basis (except as provided in subparagraph (E)), shall obtain data concerning programs and projects assisted under this chapter and under other Federal laws relating to infants, toddlers, children, and youth with disabilities, and such additional information, from State and local educational agencies, the Secretary of Interior, and other appropriate sources, including designated lead agencies under subchapter VIII of this chapter (except during fiscal year 1992 such entities may not under this subsection be required to provide data regarding traumatic brain injury or autism), including—
(A) the number of infants, toddlers, children, and youth with disabilities in each State receiving a free appropriate public education or early intervention services—
(i) in age groups 0-2 and 3-5, and
(ii) in age groups 6-11, 12-17, and 18-21, by disability category;
(B) the number of children and youth with disabilities in each State, by disability category, who—
(i) are participating in regular educational programs (consistent with the requirements of sections 1412(5)(B) of this chapter and 1414(a)(1)(C)(iv) of this title);
(ii) are in separate classes, separate schools or facilities, or public or private residential facilities; or
(iii) have been otherwise removed from the regular education environment;
(C) the number of children and youth with disabilities exiting the education system each year through program completion or otherwise, by disability category, for each year of age from age 14 through 21;
(D) the number and type of personnel that are employed in the provision

of—
>   (i) special education and related services to children and youth with disabilities, by disability category served; and
>   (ii) early intervention services to infants and toddlers with disabilities; and
> (E) at least every three years, using the data collection method the Secretary finds most appropriate, a description of the services expected to be needed, by disability category, for youth with disabilities in age groups 12-17 and 18-21 who have left the educational system.

(2) Beginning with fiscal year 1993, the Secretary shall obtain and report data from the States under section 1413(a)(3)(A) of this title, including data addressing current and projected special education and related services needs, and data on the number of personnel who are employed on an emergency, provisional, or other basis, who do not hold appropriate State certification or licensure, and other data for the purpose of meeting the requirements of this subsection pertaining to special education and related services personnel.

(3) The Secretary shall provide, directly or by grant, contract, or cooperative agreement, technical assistance to State agencies providing the data described in paragraphs (1) and (2) to achieve accurate and comparable information.

(c) Studies and investigations under grants, contracts, or cooperative agreements

(1) The Secretary shall make grants to, or enter into contracts or cooperative agreements with, State or local educational agencies, institutions of higher education, public agencies, and private nonprofit organizations, and, when necessary because of the unique nature of the study, private-for-profit organizations, for the purpose of conducting studies, analyses, syntheses, and investigations for improving program management, administration, delivery, and effectiveness necessary to provide full educational opportunities and early interventions for all children with disabilities from birth through age 21. Such studies and investigations shall gather information necessary for program and system improvements including—

> (A) developing effective, appropriate criteria and procedures to identify, evaluate, and serve infants, toddlers, children, and youth with disabilities from minority backgrounds for purposes of program eligibility, program planning, delivery of services, program placement, and parental involvement;
> (B) planning and developing effective early intervention services, special education, and related services to meet the complex and changing needs of infants, toddlers, children, and youth with disabilities;
> (C) developing and implementing a comprehensive system of personnel development needed to provide qualified personnel in sufficient number to deliver special education, related services, and early intervention services;
> (D) developing the capacity to implement practices having the potential to integrate children with disabilities, to the maximum extent appropriate, with children who are not disabled;
> (E) effectively allocating and using human and fiscal resources for providing early intervention, special education, and related services;
> (F) strengthening programs and services to improve the progress of children and youth with disabilities while in special education, and to effect

a successful transition when such children and youth leave special education;

(G) achieving interagency coordination to maximize resource utilization and continuity in services provided to infants, toddlers, children, and youth with disabilities;

(H) strengthening parent-school communication and coordination to improve the effectiveness of planning and delivery of interventions and instruction, thereby enhancing development and educational progress; and

(I) the identification of environmental, organizational, resource, and other conditions necessary for effective professional practice.

(2)(A) The studies and investigations authorized under this subsection may be conducted through surveys, interviews, case studies, program implementation studies, secondary data analyses and syntheses, and other appropriate methodologies.

(B) The studies and investigations conducted under this subsection shall address the information needs of State and local educational agencies for improving program management, administration, delivery, and effectiveness.

(3) The Secretary shall develop and implement a process for the on-going identification of national program information needed for improving the management, administration, delivery, and effectiveness of programs and services provided under this chapter. The process shall identify implementation issues, desired improvements, and information needed by State and local agencies to achieve such improvements, and shall be conducted in cooperation with State educational agencies that can ensure broad-based statewide input from each cooperating State. The Secretary shall publish for public comment in the Federal Register every 3 years a program information plan describing such information needs. Such program information plan shall be used to determine the priorities for, and activities carried out under, this subsection to produce, organize, and increase utilization of program information. Such program information plan shall be included in the annual report submitted under this section every 3 years.

(4) In providing funds under this subsection, the Secretary shall require recipients to prepare their procedures, findings, and other relevant information in a form that will maximize their dissemination and use, especially through dissemination networks and mechanisms authorized by this chapter, and in a form for inclusion in the annual report to Congress authorized under subsection (g) of this section.

(d) Cooperative agreements with State educational agencies

(1) The Secretary shall enter into cooperative agreements with State educational agencies and other State agencies to carry out studies to assess the impact and effectiveness of programs assisted under this chapter.

(2) An agreement under paragraph (1) shall—

(A) provide for the payment of not more than 60 percent of the total cost of studies conducted by a participating State agency to assess the impact and effectiveness of programs assisted under this chapter, and

(B) be developed in consultation with the State Advisory Panel established under this chapter, the local education agencies, and others involved in or concerned with the education of children and youth with disabilities and the provision of early intervention services to infants and toddlers with disabilities.

(3) The Secretary shall provide technical assistance to participating State agencies in the implementation of the study design, analysis, and reporting procedures.

(e) Studies to assess progress of program

(1) The Secretary shall by grant, contract, or cooperative agreement, provide for special studies to assess progress in the implementation of this chapter, and to assess the impact and effectiveness of State and local efforts and efforts by the Secretary of the Interior to provide free appropriate public education to children and youth with disabilities, and early intervention services to infants and toddlers with disabilities. Reports from such studies shall include recommendations for improving programs and services to such individuals. The Secretary shall, beginning in fiscal year 1993 and for every third year thereafter, submit to the appropriate committees of each House of the Congress and publish in the Federal Register proposed priorities for review and comment.

(2) In selecting priorities for fiscal years 1991 through 1994, the Secretary may give first consideration to—

(A) completing a longitudinal study of a sample of students with disabilities, examining—

(i) the full range of disabling conditions;

(ii) the educational progress of students with disabilities while in special education; and

(iii) the occupational, educational, and independent living status of students with disabilities after graduating from secondary school or otherwise leaving special education.

(B) conducting pursuant to this subsection a nationally representative study focusing on the types, number, and intensity of related services provided to children with disabilities by disability category.

(C) conducting pursuant to this subsection a study that examines the degree of disparity among States with regard to the placement in various educational settings of children and youth with similar disabilities, especially those with mental retardation, and, to the extent that such disparity exists, the factors that lead such children and youth to be educated in significantly different educational settings.

(D) conducting pursuant to this subsection a study that examines the factors that have contributed to the decline in the number of children classified as mentally retarded since the implementation of this chapter, and examines the current disparity among States in the percentage of children so classified.

(E) conducting pursuant to this subsection a study that examines the extent to which out-of-community residential programs are used for children and youth who are seriously emotionally disturbed, the factors that influence the selection of such placements, the degree to which such individuals transition back to education programs in their communities, and the factors that facilitate or impede such transition.

(F) conducting pursuant to this subsection a study that examines (i) the factors that influence the referral and placement decisions and types of placements, by disability category and English language proficiency, of minority children relative to other children, (ii) the extent to which these children are placed in regular education environments, (iii) the extent to which the parents of these children are involved in placement decisions and in the development and implementation of the individualized education program and the results of such participation, and (iv) the type of support provided to parents of these children that enable these parents to understand and participate in the educational process.

(f) Integration of information

The Secretary shall make grants to, or enter into contracts or cooperative agreements with, State or local educational agencies, institutions of higher education, other public agencies, and private nonprofit organizations to support activities that organize, synthesize, interpret, and integrate information obtained under subsections (c) and (e) of this section with relevant knowledge obtained from other sources. Such activities shall include the selection and design of content, formats, and means for communicating such information effectively to specific or general audiences, in order to promote the use of such information in improving program administration and management, and service delivery and effectiveness.

(g) Annual report

(1)(A) The Secretary is authorized to conduct activities, directly or by grant, contract, or cooperative agreement, to prepare an annual report on the progress being made toward the provision of—

(i) a free appropriate public education to all children and youth with disabilities; and

(ii) early intervention services for infants and toddlers with disabilities.

(B) Not later than 120 days after the close of each fiscal year, the Secretary shall transmit a copy of the report authorized under subparagraph (A) to the appropriate committees of each House of Congress. The annual report shall be published and disseminated in sufficient quantities to the education and disability communities and to other interested parties.

(2) The Secretary shall include in each annual report under paragraph (1)—

(A) a compilation and analysis of data gathered under subsection (b) of this section and under subchapter VIII of this chapter; and

(B) a description of findings and determinations resulting from monitoring reviews of State implementation of this chapter.

(3) In the annual report under paragraph (1) for fiscal year 1991 (which is published in 1992) and for every third year thereafter, the Secretary shall include in the annual report—

(A) an index of all current projects funded under subchapters III through VII of this chapter; and

(B) data reported under sections 1422 and 1434 of this title.

(4) The Secretary shall include in each annual report under paragraph (1) the results of research and related activities conducted under subchapter V of this chapter that the Secretary determines are relevant to the effective implementation of this chapter.

(5) The Secretary shall, in consultation with the National Council on

Disability and the Bureau of Indian Affairs Advisory Committee for Exceptional Children, include a description of the status of early intervention services for infants and toddlers with disabilities from birth through age 2, and special education and related services to children with disabilities from 3 through 5 years of age (including those receiving services through Head Start, developmental disabilities programs, crippled children's services, mental health/mental retardation agencies, and State child-development centers and private agencies under contract with local schools).

(h) Authorization of appropriations

There are authorized to be appropriated $12,000,000 for fiscal year 1991 and such sums as may be necessary for fiscal years 1992 through 1994 to carry out the purposes of this section and not more than 30 percent may be used to carry out the purposes of subsection (e) of this section.

§ 1419. Preschool grants

(a) Grants for fiscal years 1987 through 1989; amount of grants

(1) For fiscal years 1987 through 1989 (or fiscal year 1990 if the Secretary makes a grant under this paragraph for such fiscal year) the Secretary shall make a grant to any State which—
> (A) has met the eligibility requirements of section 1412 of this chapter,
> (B) has a State plan approved under section 1413 of this chapter, and
> (C) provides special education and related services to children with disabilities aged three to five, inclusive.

(2) (A) For fiscal year 1987 the amount of a grant to a State under paragraph (1) may not exceed—
> (i) $300 per child with a disability aged three to five, inclusive, who received special education and related services in such State as determined under section 1411(a)(3) of this section, or
> (ii) if the amount appropriated under subsection (e) of this section exceeds the product of $300 and the total number of children with disabilities aged three to five, inclusive, who received special education and related services as determined under section 1411(a)(3) of this chapter—
> (I) $300 per child with a disability aged three to five, inclusive, who received special education and related services in such State as determined under section 1411(a)(3) of this chapter, plus
> (II) an amount equal to the portion of the appropriation available after allocating funds to all States under subclause (I) (the excess appropriation) divided by the estimated increase, from the preceding fiscal year, in the number of children with disabilities aged three to five, inclusive, who will be receiving special education and related services in all States multiplied by the estimated increase in the number of such children in such State.

> (B) For fiscal year 1988, funds shall be distributed in accordance with clause (i) or (ii) of paragraph (2)(A), except that the amount specified therein shall be $400 instead of $300.
> (C) For fiscal year 1989, funds shall be distributed in accordance with clause (i) or (ii) of paragraph (2)(A), except that the amount specified therein

shall be $500 instead of $300.

(D) If the Secretary makes a grant under paragraph (1) for fiscal year 1990, the amount of a grant to a State under such paragraph may not exceed $1,000 per child with a disability aged three to five, inclusive, who received special education and related services in such State as determined under section 1411(a)(3) of this chapter.

(E) If the actual number of additional children served in a fiscal year differs from the estimate made under subparagraph (A)(ii)(II), the Secretary shall adjust (upwards or downwards) a State's allotment in the subsequent fiscal year.

(F)(i) The amount of a grant under subparagraph (A), (B), or (C) to any State for a fiscal year may not exceed $3,800 per estimated child with a disability aged three to five, inclusive, who will be receiving, or child with a disability, age three to five, inclusive, who is receiving special education and related services in such State.

(ii) If the amount appropriated under subsection (e) of this section for any fiscal year exceeds the amount of grants which may be made to the States for such fiscal year, the excess amount appropriated shall remain available for obligation under this section for 2 succeeding fiscal years.

(3) To receive a grant under paragraph (1) a State shall make an application to the Secretary at such time, in such manner, and containing or accompanied by such information as the Secretary may reasonably require.

(b) Grants for fiscal year 1990 and thereafter; amount of grants

(1) For fiscal year 1990 (or fiscal year 1991 if required by paragraph (2)) and fiscal years thereafter the Secretary shall make a grant to any State which-

(A) has met the eligibility requirements of section 1412 of this chapter, and

(B) has a State plan approved under section 1413 of this chapter which includes policies and procedures that assure the availability under the State law and practice of such State of a free appropriate public education for all children with disabilities aged three to five, inclusive and for any two-year-old children provided services by the State under subsection(c)(2)(B)(iii) or by a local educational agency or intermediate educational unit under subsection (f)(2).

(2) The Secretary may make a grant under paragraph (1) only for fiscal year 1990 and fiscal years thereafter, except that if—

(A) the aggregate amount that was appropriated under subsection (e) of this section for fiscal years 1987, 1988, and 1989 was less than $656,000,000, or

(B) the amount appropriated for fiscal year 1990 under subsection (e) of this section is less than $306,000,000,

the Secretary may not make a grant under paragraph (1) until fiscal year 1991 and shall make a grant under subsection (a)(1) of this section for fiscal year 1990.

(3) The amount of any grant to any State under paragraph (1) for any fiscal year may not exceed $1,500 for each child with a disability in such State aged three to five, inclusive.

(4) To receive a grant under paragraph (1) a State shall make an application to the Secretary at such time, in such manner, and containing or accompanied by

such information as the Secretary may reasonably require.

(c) Distribution by State of received funds

(1) For fiscal year 1987, a State which receives a grant under subsection (a)(1) of this section shall—

(A) distribute at least 70 percent of such grant to local educational agencies and intermediate educational units in such State in accordance with paragraph (3), except that in applying such section only children with disabilities aged three to five, inclusive, shall be considered,

(B) use not more than 25 percent of such grant for the planning and development of a comprehensive delivery system for which a grant could have been made under section 1423(b) of this chapter in effect through fiscal year 1987 and for direct and support services for children with disabilities, and

(C) use not more than 5 percent of such grant for administrative expenses related to the grant.

(2) For fiscal years beginning after fiscal year 1987, a State which receives a grant under subsection (a)(1) of this section or (b)(1) of this section shall—

(A) distribute at least 75 percent of such grant to local educational agencies and intermediate educational units in such State in accordance with paragraph (3), except that in applying such section only children with disabilities aged three to five, inclusive, shall be considered.

(B) use not more than 20 percent of such grant—

(i) for planning and development of a comprehensive delivery system,

(ii) for direct and support services for children with disabilities, aged 3 to 5, inclusive, and

(iii) at the State's discretion, to provide a free appropriate public education, in accordance with this Act, to 2-year-old children with disabilities who will reach age 3 during the school year, whether or not such children are receiving, or have received, services under subchapter VIII, and

(C) use not more than 5 percent of such grant for administrative expenses related to the grant.

(3) From the amount of funds available to local educational agencies and intermediate educational units in any State under this section, each local educational agency or intermediate educational unit shall be entitled to—

(A) an amount which bears the same ratio to the amount available under subsection (a)(2)(A)(i) of this title or subsection (a)(2)(A)(ii)(I) of this chapter, as the case may be, as the number of children with disabilities aged three to five, inclusive, who received special education and related services as determined under section 1411(a)(3) of this chapter in such local educational agency or intermediate educational unit bears to the aggregate number of children with disabilities aged three to five, inclusive, who received special education and related services in all local educational agencies and intermediate educational units in the State entitled to funds under this section, and

(B) to the extent funds are available under subsection (a)(2)(A)(ii)(II) of this section, an amount which bears the same ratio to the amount of such funds of this section as the estimated number of additional children with disabilities aged three to five, inclusive, who will be receiving special education and related services in such local educational agency or intermediate educational unit bears to the aggregate number of such children in all local educational agencies and intermediate educational units in the State entitled to funds under this section.

(d) Insufficiency of appropriated amounts; reduction of maximum amounts receivable by States

If the sums appropriated under subsection (e) of this section for any fiscal year for making payments to States under subsection (a)(1) of this section or (b)(1) are not sufficient to pay in full the maximum amounts which all States may receive under such subsection for such fiscal year, the maximum amounts which all States may receive under such subsection for such fiscal year shall be ratably reduced by first ratably reducing amounts computed under the excess appropriation provision of subsection (a)(2)(A)(ii)(II) of this section. If additional funds become available for making such payments for any fiscal year during which the preceding sentence is applicable, the reduced maximum amounts shall be increased on the same basis as they were reduced.

(e) Authorization of appropriations

For grants under subsections (a)(1) of this section and (b)(1) of this section there are authorized to be appropriated such sums as may be necessary.

(f) Use of appropriated funds

Each local educational agency or intermediate educational unit receiving funds under this section—

(1) shall use such funds to provide special education and related services to children with disabilities aged 3 to 5, inclusive, and

(2) may, if consistent with State policy, use such funds to provide a free appropriate public education, in accordance with this part, to 2-year-old children with disabilities who will reach age 3 during the school year, whether or not such children are receiving, or have received, services under subchapter VIII.

(g) Nonavailability of assistance under other laws

Subchapter VIII of this Act does not apply to any child with disabilities receiving a free appropriate public education, in accordance with this part, with funds received under this section.

§ 1420. Payments

(a) Payments to States; distribution by States to local educational agencies and intermediate educational units

The Secretary shall make payments to each State in amounts which the State educational agency of such State is eligible to receive under this subchapter. Any State educational agency receiving payments under this subsection shall distribute payments to the local educational agencies and intermediate educational units of such State in amounts which such agencies and units are eligible to receive under this subchapter after the State educational agency has approved applications of such agencies or units for payments in accordance with section 1414(b) of this chapter.

(b) Advances, reimbursements, and installments

Payments under this subchapter may be made in advance or by way of reimbursement and in such installments as the Secretary may determine necessary.

SUBCHAPTER III—CENTERS AND SERVICES TO MEET SPECIAL NEEDS OF INDIVIDUALS WITH DISABILITIES

§ 1421. Regional resource centers

(a) Establishment; functions

The Secretary may make grants to, or enter into contracts or cooperative agreements with, institutions of higher education, public agencies, private nonprofit organizations, State educational agencies, or combinations of such agencies or institutions (which combinations may include one or more local educational agencies) within particular regions of the United States, to pay all or part of the cost of the establishment and operation of regional resource centers that focus on special education and related services and early intervention services. Each regional resource center shall provide consultation, technical assistance, and training, as requested, to State educational agencies and through such State educational agencies to local educational agencies and to other appropriate public agencies providing special education and related services and early intervention services. The services provided by a regional resource center shall be consistent with the priority needs identified by the States served by the center and the findings of the Secretary in monitoring reports prepared by the Secretary under section 1417 of this chapter. Each regional resource center shall—

(1) assist in identifying and solving persistent problems in providing quality special education and related services for children and youth with disabilities and early intervention services to infants and toddlers with disabilities and their families,

(2) assist in developing, identifying, and replicating successful programs and practices which will improve special education and related services to children and youth with disabilities and their families and early intervention services to infants and toddlers with disabilities and their families,

(3) gather and disseminate information to all State educational agencies within the region and coordinate activities with other centers assisted under this subsection and other relevant programs and projects conducted under subchapters III-VII and by the Department of Education.

(4) assist in the improvement of information dissemination to and training activities for professionals and parents of infants, toddlers, children and youth with disabilities, and

(5) provide information to and training for agencies, institutions, and organizations, regarding techniques and approaches for submitting applications for grants, contracts, and cooperative agreements under this subchapter and subchapters IV through VII.

(b) Considerations governing approval of application

In determining whether to approve an application for a project under subsection (a) of this section, the Secretary shall utilize criteria for setting criteria that are consistent with the needs identified by States within the region served by such center, consistent with requirements established by the Secretary under subsection (f), and, to the extent appropriate, consistent with requirements under section 1410, and shall consider the need for such a center in the region to be served by the applicant and the capability of the applicant to fulfill the responsibilities under subsection (a) of this section.

(c) Annual report; summary of information

Each regional resource center shall report a summary of materials produced or developed and the summaries reported shall be included in the annual report to Congress required under section 1418 of this chapter.

(d) Coordination technical assistance center; establishment; duties

The Secretary may establish one coordinating technical assistance center focusing on national priorities established by the Secretary to assist the regional resource centers in the delivery of technical assistance, consistent with such national priorities. Such coordinating technical assistance center is authorized to—

(1) provide information to, and training for, agencies, institutions, and organizations, regarding techniques and approaches for submitting applications for grants, contracts, and cooperative agreements under this part and parts D through G, and shall make such information available to the regional resource centers on request;

(2) give priority to providing technical assistance concerning the education of children with disabilities from minority backgrounds;

(3) exchange information with, and, where appropriate, cooperate with, other centers addressing the needs of children with disabilities from minority backgrounds; and

(4) provide assistance to State educational agencies, through the regional resource centers, for the training of hearing officers.

(e) Amounts available for coordination technical assistance center

Before using funds made available in any fiscal year to carry out this section for purposes of subsection (d) of this section, not less than the amount made available in the previous fiscal year for regional resource centers under subsection (a) shall be made available for such centers of this section and in no case shall more than $500,000 be made available for the center under subsection (d) of this section.

(f) Guidelines for resource centers

(1) The Secretary shall develop guidelines and criteria for the operation of Regional and Federal Resource Centers. In developing such criteria and guidelines, the Secretary shall establish a panel representing the Office of Special Education Programs staff, State special education directors, representatives of disability advocates, and, when appropriate, consult with the regional resource center directors.

(2) Such guidelines and criteria shall include—
    (A) a description of how the Federal and Regional Resource Centers Program will be administered by the Secretary;
    (B) a description of the geographic region each Center is expected to serve;
    (C) a description of the role of a Center in terms of expected leadership and dissemination efforts;
    (D) a description of expected relationships with State agencies, research and demonstration centers, and with other entities deemed necessary;
    (E) a description of how a Center will be evaluated; and
    (F) other guidelines and criteria deemed necessary.
(3) The Secretary shall publish in the Federal Register by July 1, 1991, for review and comment, proposed and (then following such review and comment) final guidelines developed by the panel.

§ 1422. Services for deaf-blind children and youth

(a) Grant and contract authority; types and scope of programs; governing considerations

(1) The Secretary is authorized to make grants to, or to enter into cooperative agreements or contracts with, public or nonprofit private agencies, institutions, or organizations to assist State educational agencies, local educational agencies, and designated lead agencies under subchapter VIII of this chapter to—
    (A) assure deaf-blind infants, toddlers, children and youth provision of special education, early intervention, and related services as well as vocational and transitional services; and
    (B) make available to deaf-blind youth (who are in the process of transitioning into adult services) programs, services, and supports to facilitate such transition, including assistance related to independent living and competitive employment.
(2) For purposes of this section, the term "deaf-blind", with respect to children and youth, means having auditory and visual impairments, the combination of which creates such severe communication and other developmental and learning needs that they cannot be appropriately educated in special education programs solely for children and youth with hearing impairments, visual impairments, or severe disabilities, without supplementary assistance to address their educational needs due to these dual, concurrent disabilities.
(3) (A) A grant, cooperative agreement, or contract may be made under paragraph(1)(A) only for programs providing—
    (i) technical assistance to agencies, institutions, or organizations providing educational or early intervention services to deaf-blind infants, toddlers, children, or youth;
    (ii) preservice or inservice training to paraprofessionals, professionals, or related services personnel preparing to serve, or serving, deaf-blind infants, toddlers, children, or youth;
    (iii) replication of successful innovative approaches to providing educational, early intervention, or related services to deaf-blind infants, toddlers, children, and youth;
    (iv) pilot projects that are designed to—

(I) expand local educational agency capabilities by providing services to deaf-blind children and youth that supplement services already provided to children and youth through State and local resources; and

(II) encourage eventual assumption of funding responsibility by State and local authorities;

(v) the development, improvement, or demonstration of new or existing methods, approaches, or techniques that contribute to the adjustment and education of deaf-blind infants, toddlers, children, and youth; or

(vi) facilitation of parental involvement in the education of their deaf-blind infants, toddlers, children, and youth.

(B) The programs described in subparagraph (A) may include—

(i) the diagnosis and educational evaluation of infants, toddlers, children, and youth who are likely to be diagnosed as deaf-blind;

(ii) programs of adjustment, education, and orientation for deaf-blind infants, toddlers, children, and youth; and

(iii) consultative, counseling, and training services for the families of deaf-blind infants, toddlers, children, and youth.

(4) A grant, cooperative agreement, or contract pursuant to paragraph (1)(B) may be made only for programs providing (A) technical assistance to agencies, institutions, and organizations that are preparing deaf-blind adolescents for adult placements, or that are preparing to receive deaf-blind young adults into adult living and work environments, or that serve, or propose to serve, deaf-blind individuals; (B) training or inservice training to paraprofessionals or professionals serving, or preparing to serve, such individuals; and (C) assistance in the development or replication of successful innovative approaches to providing supervised rehabilitative, semi-supervised, or independent living programs.

(5) In carrying out this subsection, the Secretary is authorized to enter into a number of grants or cooperative agreements to establish and support single and multi-State centers for the provision of technical assistance and pilot supplementary services, for the purposes of program development and expansion, for children and youth with deaf-blindness and their families.

(b) Contract authority for regional programs of technical assistance

The Secretary is also authorized to enter into a limited number of cooperative agreements or contracts to establish and support regional programs for the provision of technical assistance in the education of deaf-blind children and youth.

(c) Annual report to Secretary; examination of numbers and services and revision of numbers; annual report to Congress: summary of data

(1) Programs supported under this section shall report annually to the Secretary on (A) the numbers of deaf-blind children and youth served by age, severity, sex, and nature of deaf-blindness; (B) the number of paraprofessionals, professionals, and family members directly served by each activity; (C) the types of services provided and the setting in which the services are provided; and (D) student outcomes, where appropriate.

(2) The Secretary shall examine the number of deaf-blind children and youth (A) reported under subparagraph (c)(1)(A) and by the States; (B) served by the programs under subchapter II of this chapter and subpart 2 of part D of chapter1 of title I of the Elementary and Secondary Education Act of 1965 [20 U.S.C. 3801 et seq.]); (C) the Deaf-Blind Registry of each State. The Secretary shall revise the count of deaf-blind children and youth to reflect the most accurate count and (D) student outcomes, where appropriate.

(3) The Secretary shall summarize these data for submission in the annual report required under section 1418 of this chapter.

(d) National clearinghouse for children and youth with deaf-blindness

The Secretary shall make a grant, or enter into a contract or cooperative agreement, for a national clearinghouse for children and youth with deaf-blindness—

(1) to identify, coordinate, and disseminate information on deaf-blindness, emphasizing information concerning effective practices in working with deaf-blind infants, toddlers, children, and youth;

(2) to interact with educators, professional groups, and parents to identify areas for programming, materials development, training, and expansion of specific services;

(3) to maintain a computerized data base on local, regional and national resources; and

(4) to respond to information requests from professionals, parents, and members of the community.

(e) Country-wide availability of assistance

In carrying out this section, the Secretary shall take into consideration the availability and quality of existing services for deaf-blind infants, toddlers, children, and youth in the country, and to the extent practicable, ensure that all parts of the country have an opportunity to receive assistance under this section.

(f) Grants for purposes under other parts of this chapter

The Secretary may make grants to, or enter into contracts or cooperative agreements with organizations or public or nonprofit private agencies, as determined by the secretary to be appropriate, to address the needs of children and youth with deaf-blindness, for—

(1) research to identify and meet the full range of special needs of such children and youth; and

(2) the development and demonstration of new, or improvements in existing methods, approaches, or techniques that would contribute to the adjustment and education of children and youth with deaf-blindness.

§ 1423. Early education of children with disabilities

(a) Contracts, grants and cooperative agreements; purpose; community coordination programs; national dispersion in urban and rural areas; Federal share; non-Federal contributions; arrangements with Indian tribes

(1) The Secretary may arrange by contract, grant, or cooperative agreement with appropriate public and private nonprofit organizations, for the development and operation of experimental, demonstration, and outreach preschool and early intervention programs for children with disabilities, including individuals who are at risk of having substantial developmental delays if early intervention services are not provided, which the Secretary determines show promise of promoting a comprehensive and strengthened approach to the special needs of such children. Such programs shall include activities and services designed to—

(A) facilitate the intellectual, emotional, physical, mental, social, speech or other communication mode, language development, and self-help skills of such children,

(B) provide family education and include a parent or their representative of such child, as well as encourage the participation of the parents of such children in the development and operation of any such program,

(C) acquaint the community to be served by any such program with the special needs and potentialities of such children,

(D) offer training about exemplary models and practices including interdisciplinary models and practices, to State and local personnel who provide services to children with disabilities from birth through age 8 and to the parents of such children,

(E) support the adoption of exemplary models and practices in States and local communities, including the involvement of adult role models with disabilities at all levels of the program,

(F) facilitate and improve the early identification of infants and toddlers with disabilities or those infants and toddlers at risk of having developmental disabilities,

(G) facilitate the transition of infants with disabilities or infants at risk of having developmental delays, from medical care to early intervention services, and the transition from early intervention services to preschool special education or regular education services (especially where the lead agency for early intervention programs under part H is not the State educational agency),

(H) promote the use of assistive technology devices and assistive technology services, where appropriate, to enhance the development of infants and toddlers with disabilities,

(I) facilitate and improve outreach to low-income, minority, rural, and other underserved populations eligible for assistance under subchapters II and VIII,

(J) support statewide projects in conjunction with a State's application under subchapter VIII and a State's plan under subchapter II, to change the delivery of early intervention services to infants and toddlers with disabilities, and to change the delivery of special education and related services to preschool children with disabilities, from segregated to integrated environments, and

(K) increase the understanding of, and address, the early intervention and preschool needs of children exposed prenatally to maternal substance abuse.

(2) Programs authorized by paragraph (1) shall be coordinated with similar programs in the schools operated or supported by State or local educational agencies of the community to be served and with similar programs operated by

other public agencies in such community.

(3) As much as is feasible, programs assisted under paragraph (1) shall be geographically dispersed throughout the Nation in urban as well as rural areas.

(4)(A) Except as provided in subparagraph (B), no arrangement under paragraph (1) shall provide for the payment of more than 90 percent of the total annual costs of development, operation, and evaluation of any program. Non-Federal contributions may be in cash or in kind, fairly evaluated, including plant, equipment, and services.

(B) The Secretary may waive the requirement of subparagraph (A) in the case of an arrangement entered into under paragraph (1) with governing bodies of Indian tribes located on Federal or State reservations and with consortia of such bodies.

(b) Grants for indentifying, tracking and referring children at-risk of having developmental delays

The Secretary shall fund up to 5 grants to States for 3 years for the purpose of establishing an inter-agency, multi-disciplinary, and coordinated state wide system for the identification, tracking, and referral to appropriate services for all categories of children who are biologically and/or environmentally at-risk of having developmental delays. To the extent feasible, such grants shall be geographically dispersed throughout the Nation in urban and rural areas. Each grantee must—

(1) create a data system within the first year to document the numbers and types of at-risk children in the State and that develops linkages with all appropriate existing child data and tracking systems that assist in providing information;

(2) coordinate activities with the child find component required under subchapter II and VIII;

(3) demonstrate the involvement of the lead agency and the State interagency coordinating council under subchapter VIII as well as the State educational agency under subchapter II;

(4) coordinate with other relevant prevention activities across appropriate service agencies, organizations, councils, and commissions;

(5) define an appropriate service delivery system based on children with various types of at-risk factors;

(6) document the need for additional services as well as barriers; and

(7) disseminate findings and information in the manner prescribed in section 1409(g)

(c) Technical assistance development system

The Secretary shall arrange by contract, grant, or cooperative agreement with appropriate public agencies and private nonprofit organizations for the establishment of a technical assistance development system to assist entities operating experimental, demonstration, and outreach programs and to assist State agencies to expand and improve services provided to children with disabilities. This technical assistance development system shall provide assistance to parents of and advocates for infants, toddlers, and children with disabilities, as well as direct service and administrative personnel involved with such children. Information from the system should be aggressively disseminated through established information networks and other mechanisms to ensure both an impact and benefit at the community level. The Secretary shall ensure that the technical assistance provided under this subsection includes assistance to subchapter VIII State agencies on procedures for use by primary referred sources in referring a child to the appropriate agency with the system for evaluation, assessment, or service.

(d) Early childhood research institutes

The Secretary shall arrange by contract, grant, or cooperative agreement with appropriate public agencies and private nonprofit organizations for the establishment of early childhood research institutes to carry on sustained research to generate and disseminate new information on preschool and early intervention for children with disabilities and their families. Substitutes shall disseminate this information in the manner proscribed in section 1409(g).

(e) Grants or contracts with organizations to identify needs of children with disabilities and for training of personnel

The Secretary may make grants to, or enter into contracts or cooperative agreements under this section with, such organizations or institutions, as are determined by the Secretary to be appropriate, for research to identify and meet the full range of special needs of children with disabilities and for training of personnel for programs specifically designed for children with disabilities including programs to integrate children with disabilities into regular preschool programs.

(f) Notice in Federal Register of intent to accept applications for grants, contracts, etc.

At least one year before the termination of a grant, contract, or cooperative agreement made or entered into under subsections (c) and (d) of this section, the Secretary shall publish in the Federal Register a notice of intent to accept applications for such a grant, contract, or cooperative agreement contingent on the appropriation of sufficient funds by Congress.

(g) "Children with disabilities" defined

For purposes of this section the term "children with disabilities" includes children from birth through eight years of age including infants and toddlers with disabilities.

(h) Organization, integration, and presentation of developed knowledge

The Secretary may make grants to, or enter into contracts or cooperative agreements with, institutions of higher education and nonprofit private organizations to synthesize the knowledge developed under this section and organize, integrate, and present such knowledge so it can be incorporated and imparted to parents, professionals, and others providing or preparing to provide preschool or early intervention services and to persons designing preschool or early intervention programs.

§ 1424. Programs for children with severe disabilities

(a) Grant and contract authority

The Secretary may make grants to, or enter into contracts or cooperative agreements with, appropriate public agencies and nonprofit organizations to address the special education, related services, early intervention, and integration needs of infants, toddlers, children, and youth with severe disabilities through—

(1) research to identify and meet the full range of special education, related services, and early intervention needs of such children and youth with disabilities, including their need for transportation to and from school,

(2) the development or demonstration of new, or improvements in existing, methods, approaches, or techniques which would contribute to the adjustment and education of such children and youth with disabilities,

(3) training of special and regular education, related services, and early intervention personnel for programs specifically designed for such infants, toddlers, children and youth, including training of regular teachers, instructors, and administrators in strategies (the goal of which is to serve infants, toddlers, children, and youth with disabilities) that include integrated settings for educating such children along side their nondisabled peers,

(4) dissemination of materials and information about practices found effective in working with such children and youth by utilizing existing networks as prescribed in section 1410(g), and

(5) statewide projects, in conjunction with the State's plan under part B, to improve the quality of special education and related services for children and youth with severe disabilities, and to change the delivery of those services from segregated to integrated environments.

(b) Extended school year demonstration programs

The Secretary is authorized to make grants to, or enter into contracts or cooperative agreements with, public or private nonprofit private agencies, institutions, or organizations for the development and operation of extended school year demonstration programs for infants, toddlers, children, and youth with severe disabilities.

(c) Coordination of activities with similar activities under other subchapters of this chapter

In making grants and entering into contracts and cooperative agreements under subsection (a) of this section, the Secretary shall ensure that the activities funded under such grants, contracts, or cooperative agreements will be coordinated with similar activities funded from grants and contracts under other sections of this chapter.

(d) National geographic dispersion of programs in urban and rural areas

To the extent feasible, programs authorized by subsection (a) of this section shall be geographically dispersed throughout the Nation in urban and rural areas.

(e) Priority for programs that mainstream

In awarding such grants and contracts under this section, the Secretary shall include a priority on programs that increase the likelihood that these children and youth will be educated with their nondisabled peers.

§ 1424a. Postsecondary and other specially designed model programs

(a) Grants and contract authority; development and operation of vocational, technical, postsecondary, or adult education programs

(1) The Secretary may make grants to, or enter into contracts with, State educational agencies, institutions of higher education, junior and community colleges, vocational and technical institutions, and other appropriate nonprofit educational agencies for the development, operation, and dissemination of specially designed model programs of postsecondary, vocational, technical, continuing, or adult education for individuals with a disability. Such model programs may include joint projects that coordinate with special education and transition services.

(2) In making grants or contracts on a competitive basis under paragraph (1), the Secretary shall give priority consideration to 4 regional centers for the deaf and to model programs for individuals with disabling conditions other than deafness—

(A) for developing and adapting programs of postsecondary, vocational, technical, continuing, or adult education to meet the special needs of individuals with disabilities,

(B) for programs that coordinate, facilitate, and encourage education of individuals with a disability with their nondisabled peers, and

(C) for outreach activities that include the provision of technical assistance to strengthen efforts in the development, operation, and design of model programs that are adapted to the special needs of individuals with disabilities.

(3) Persons operating programs for disabled persons under a grant or contract under paragraph (1) must coordinate their efforts with and disseminate information about their activities to the clearinghouse on postsecondary programs established under section 1433(b) of this chapter.

(4) At least one year before the termination of a grant or contract with any of the 4 regional centers for the deaf, the Secretary shall publish in the Federal Register a notice of intent to accept applications for such grant or contract, contingent on the appropriation of sufficient funds by Congress.

(5) To the extent feasible, programs authorized by paragraph (1) shall be geographically dispersed throughout the Nation in urban and rural areas.

(6) Of the sums made available for programs under paragraph (1), not less than $4,000,000 shall first be available for the 4 regional centers for the deaf.

(b) "Individuals with disabilities" defined

For purposes of subsection (a), the term "individuals with disabilities" means individuals—

(1) with mental retardation, hearing impairments including deafness, speech or language impairments, visual impairments including blindness,

serious emotional disturbance, orthopedic impairments, autism, traumatic brain injury, other health impairments, or specific learning disabilities; and

(2) who, by reason thereof, need special education and related services.

§ 1425. Secondary education and transitional services for youth with disabilities

(a) Grant and contract authority; statement of purposes; national geographic dispersion in urban and rural areas

The Secretary may make grants to, or enter into contracts with, institutions of higher education, State educational agencies, local educational agencies, or other appropriate public and private nonprofit institutions or agencies (including the State job training coordinating councils and service delivery area administrative entities established under the Job Training Partnership Act [29 U.S.C.A. § 1501 et seq.]) to—

(1) strengthen and coordinate special education and related services for youth with a disability currently in school or who recently left school to assist them in the transition to postsecondary education, vocational training, competitive employment (including supported employment), continuing education, independent and community living, or adult services,

(2) stimulate the improvement and development of programs for secondary special education, and

(3) stimulate the improvement of the vocational and life skills of students with disabilities to enable them to be better prepared for transition to adult life and services.

To the extent feasible, such programs shall be geographically dispersed throughout the Nation in urban and rural areas.

(b) Description of specific projects

Projects assisted under subsection (a) of this section may include—

(1) developing strategies and techniques for transition to independent living, vocational training, vocational rehabilitation, postsecondary education, and competitive employment (including supported employment) for youth with disabilities,

(2) establishing demonstration models for services, programs, and individualized education programs, which emphasize vocational training, independent living, transitional services, and placement for youth with disabilities,

(3) conducting demographic studies which provide information on the numbers, age levels, types of disabling conditions, and services required for some youth with disabilities in need of transitional programs,

(4) specially designed vocational programs to increase the potential for competitive employment for youth with disabilities,

(5) research and development projects for exemplary service delivery models and the replication and dissemination of successful models,

(6) initiating cooperative models among educational agencies and adult service agencies, including vocational rehabilitation, mental health, mental retardation, and public employment, and employers, which facilitate the

planning and developing of transitional services for youth with a disability to postsecondary education, vocational training, employment, continuing education, and adult services,

(7) developing appropriate procedures for evaluating vocational training, placement, and transitional services for youth with disabilities,

(8) conducting studies which provide information on the numbers, age levels, types of disabling conditions and reasons why some youth with disabilities remain to complete school programs while others drop out,

(9) developing curriculum and instructional techniques in special education and related services that will improve the acquisition of skills by students with disabilities necessary for transition to adult life and services,

(10) specially designed or adapted physical education and therapeutic recreation programs to facilitate the full participation of youths with disabilities in community programs, and

(11) developing and disseminating exemplary programs and practices that meet the unique needs of students who utilize assistive technology devices and assistive technology services as such students make the transition to postsecondary education, vocational training, competitive employment (including supported employment), and continuing education or adult services.

(c) Coordination of non-educational-agency applicant with State educational agency

For purposes of paragraphs (1) and (2) of subsection (b) of this section, if an applicant is not an educational agency, such applicant shall coordinate its activities with the State educational agency.

(d) Applications for assistance; contents

Applications for assistance under subsection (a) of this section other than for the purpose of conducting studies or evaluations shall—

(1) describe the procedures to be used for disseminating relevant findings and data to regional resource centers, clearinghouses, and other interested persons, agencies, or organizations,

(2) describe the procedures that will be used for coordinating services among agencies for which youth with a disability are or will be eligible, and

(3) provide for the direct participation of students with disabilities and the parents of disabled students in the planning, development, and implementation of such projects.

(e) Application for one-time grant; contents

(1) The Secretary shall make one-time, 5-year grants, on a competitive basis, to States in which the State vocational rehabilitation agency and State educational agency submit a joint application to develop, implement, and improve systems to provide transition services for youth with disabilities from age 14 through the age they exit school.

(2) In the case of a State whose vocational rehabilitation agency does not

participate regarding a joint application described in paragraph (1), the Secretary may make a grant under such paragraph to the State if a joint application for the grant is submitted by the State educational agency and one other State agency that provides transition services to individuals who are leaving programs under this Act.

(3) States that receive grants shall use grant funds to:

(A) Increase the availability, access, and quality of transition assistance through the development and improvement of policies, procedures, systems, and other mechanisms for youth with disabilities and their families as such youth prepare for and enter adult life.

(B) Improve the ability of professionals, parents, and advocates to work with such youth in ways that promote the understanding of and the capability to successfully make the transition from "student" to "adult".

(C) Improve working relationships among education personnel, both within LEAs and in postsecondary training programs, relevant State agencies, the private sector (especially employers), rehabilitation personnel, local and State employment agencies, local Private Industry Councils (PICs) authorized by the Job Training Partnership Act (JTPA), and families of students with disabilities and their advocates to identify and achieve consensus on the general nature and specific application of transition services to meet the needs of youth with disabilities.

(D) Create an incentive for accessing and using the expertise and resources of programs, projects, and activities related to transition funded through this section and with other sources.

(4)(A) In order to receive funding under this subsection, a State vocational rehabilitation agency and State educational agency shall describe in their application how they will use the first year, if necessary, to plan how to implement transition services, the second through fourth years to develop and implement transition services, and the fifth year to evaluate transition services. The application shall describe how the grant funds will be used during the planning period and phased out during the evaluation period to ensure the continuation of transition services. Such applications shall also include—

(i) a description of the current availability, access, and quality of transition services for eligible youth and a description of how, over 5 years, the State will improve and expand the availability, access, and quality of transition services for youth with disabilities and their families as such youth prepare for and enter adult life;

(ii) a description of how the State will improve and increase the ability of professionals, parents, and advocates to work with such youth in ways that promote the understanding of and the capability to successfully make the transition from "student" to "adult";

(iii) a description of how the State will improve and increase working relationships among education personnel, both within LEAs and in postsecondary training programs, relevant State agencies, the private sector (especially employers), rehabilitation personnel, local and State employment agencies, local Private Industry Councils (PICs) authorized by the JTPA, and families of students with disabilities and their advocates to identify and achieve consensus on the general nature and specific application of transition services to meet the needs of youth with disabilities; and

(iv) a description of how the State will use grant funds as an incentive for accessing and using the expertise and resources of programs, projects, and activities related to transition funded through this section and with other sources.

(B) The Secretary shall give preference to those applications that, in addition to clearly addressing the requirements under subparagraph (A), describe how the State will—

(i) target resources to school settings, such as providing access to rehabilitation counselors for students with disabilities who are in school settings;

(ii) target a substantial amount of grant funds, received under this subsection, to case management, program evaluation and documentation of, and dissemination of information about transition services;

(iii) provide incentives for interagency and private sector resource pooling and otherwise investing in transition services especially in the form of cooperative agreements, particularly with PICs authorized by the JTPA and local branches of State employment agencies;

(iv) provide for early, ongoing information and training for those involved with or who could be involved with transition services—professionals, parents, youth with disabilities, including self-advocacy training for such youth, and advocates for such youth as well as PICs authorized by the JTPA and local branches of State employment agencies;

(v) provide for the early and direct involvement of all relevant parties, including PICs authorized by the JTPA and local branches of State employment agencies, in operating and planning improvements in transition services, and the early and direct involvement of all relevant parties in planning and implementing transition services for individual youth;

(vi) provide access to training for eligible youth that matches labor market needs in their communities;

(vii) integrate transition services with relevant opportunities in communities, including those sponsored by PICs authorized by the JTPA and local employment agencies;

(viii) use a transition services evaluation plan that is outcome oriented and that focuses on individual youth-focused benefits; and

(ix) ensure that, when appropriate and no later than age 22, eligible youth who participate in transition services under this program would be served as appropriate in the State section 110 and/or title VI, part C program authorized under the Rehabilitation Act of 1973.

(f) Development or demonstration of new or improved methods, approaches, or techniques

(1) The Secretary is authorized to make grants to, or to enter into contracts or cooperative agreements with, such organizations or institutions as are determined by the Secretary to be appropriate for the development or demonstration of new or improvements in existing methods, approaches, or techniques which will contribute to the adjustment and education of children and youth with disabilities and the dissemination of materials and information concerning practices found effective in working with such children and youth.

(2) The Secretary shall fund one or more demonstration models designed to

establish appropriate methods of providing, or continuing to provide, assistive technology devices and services to secondary school students as they make the transition to vocational rehabilitation, employment, postsecondary education, or adult services. Such demonstration models shall include, as appropriate—

(A) cooperative agreements with the Rehabilitation Services Administration and/or State vocational rehabilitation agencies that ensure continuity of funding for assistive technology devices and services to such students; and

(B) methods for dissemination of exemplary practices that can be adapted or adopted by transitional programs for secondary school students with disabilities; and

(3)(A) the Secretary shall award one, five-year cooperative agreement through a separate competition to an institution of higher education, or nonprofit public or private organization. The purpose of this agreement will be to evaluate and document the approaches and outcomes of the projects funded under subsection (e). The results of this agreement shall be disseminated through the appropriate clearinghouses, networks, and through direct communication with Federal, State, and local agencies.

(B) The evaluation carried out pursuant to subparagraph (A) of transition services under subsection (e) shall include an evaluation of—

(i) the outcomes of the transition services provided under such subsection, including the effect of the services regarding postsecondary education, job training, employment, and other appropriate matters;

(ii) the impact of including in the individualized education program a statement of needed transition services (as required under section 1402(a)(20)(D));

(iii) the extent to which, in the provision of the transition services, agencies are cooperating effectively, including evaluation of the extent of coordination of the staff of the agencies, of procedures regarding confidentiality, assessment of needs, and procedures regarding confidentiality, assessment of needs, and referrals, and coordination regarding data bases and training; referrals, and coordination regarding data bases and training;

(iv) the extent to which obstacles exist regarding cooperation and coordination among agencies in the provision of the transition services, and the extent to which Federal law creates disincentives to such cooperation and coordination; and

(v) the extent to which the transition services have been provided in a cost-effective manner.

(C) The evaluation carried out pursuant to subparagraph (A) shall include recommendations on the manner in which the program under subsection (e) can be improved.

(D) In the annual report required under section 1418(g), the secretary shall include a report of the activities and results associated with the agreement under subparagraph (A).

(g) Coordination of educational programs with vocational rehabilitation projects

The Secretary, as appropriate, shall coordinate programs described under subsection (a) of this section with projects developed under section 777a of Title 29, the Job Training Partnership Act (JTPA), and the Carl D. Perkins Vocational and Applied Technology Education Act.

§ 1426. Programs for children and youth with serious emotional disturbance

(a) Grants, contracts, and cooperative agreements to establish projects

The Secretary is authorized to make grants to, or enter into contracts or cooperative agreements with, institutions of higher education, State and local educational agencies, and other appropriate public and private nonprofit institutions or agencies to establish projects for the purpose of improving special education and related services to children and youth with serious emotional disturbance. Such projects may include—

(1) studies regarding the present state of special education and related services to such children and youth and their families, including information and data to enable assessment of the status of such services over time;

(2) developing methodologies and curricula designed to improve special education and related services for these children and youth;

(3) developing and demonstrating strategies and approaches to reduce the use of out-of-community residential programs and the increased use of school district-based programs (which may include day treatment programs, after-school programs, and summer programs);

(4) developing the knowledge, skills, and strategies for effective collaboration among special education, regular education, related services, and other professionals and agencies; or

(5) developing and demonstrating innovative approaches to assist and to prevent children with emotional and behavioral problems from developing serious emotional disturbances that require the provision of special education and related services.

(b) Grants to provide services

(1) The Secretary is authorized to make grants, on a competitive basis, to local educational agencies in collaboration with mental health entities to provide services for children and youth with serious emotional disturbance. Such demonstration projects shall—

(A) increase the availability, access, and quality of community services for such children and youth and their families and community mental health and other relevant personnel, families of such children and youth, and their advocates;

(B) improve working relationships among education, school and community mental health and other relevant personnel, families of such children and youth, and their advocates;

(C) target resources to school settings, such as providing access to school and/or community mental health professionals and other community resources for students with serious emotional disturbance who are in community school settings; and

(D) take into account the needs of minority children and youth in all phases of project activity.

(2) Funds received under this subsection may also be used to facilitate

interagency and private sector resource pooling to improve services for such children and youth and to provide information and training for those involved with, or who could be involved with, such children and youth.

(c) Application of existing research results; evaluations, reports, dissemination of findings

Each project assisted under this section shall—
(1) apply existing research outcomes from multi-disciplinary fields;
(2) use a grant evaluation plan that is outcome-oriented and that focuses on the benefits to individual children and youth;
(3) report on the effectiveness of such project; and
(4) disseminate the findings of such project, where appropriate, in accordance with section 1410(g).

§ 1427. Authorization of appropriations

(a) There are authorized to be appropriated to carry out section 1421 $8,525,000 for fiscal year 1991, $9,300,000 for fiscal year 1992, $10,140,000 for fiscal year 1993, and $11,052,000 for fiscal year 1994.

(b) There are authorized to be appropriated to carry out section 1422 $21,900,000 for fiscal year 1991, $24,100,000 for fiscal year 1992, $26,500,000 for fiscal year 1993, and $29,200,000 for fiscal year 1994.

(c) There are authorized to be appropriated to carry out section 142 3$31,400,000 for fiscal year 1991, $34,235,000 for fiscal year 1992, $37,325,000 for fiscal year 1993, and $40,705,000 for fiscal year 1994.

(d) There are authorized to be appropriated to carry out section 1424 $9,500,000 for fiscal year 1991, $10,500,000 for fiscal year 1992, $11,600,000 for fiscal year 1993, and $12,700,000 for fiscal year 1994.

(e) There are authorized to be appropriated to carry out section 1425 $9,470,000 for fiscal year 1991, $10,230,000 for fiscal year 1992, $11,050,000 for fiscal year 1993, and $11,930,000 for fiscal year 1994.

(f) There are authorized to be appropriated to carry out section 1426 (except subsection (e)) $9,800,000 for fiscal year 1991, $10,800,000 for fiscal year1992, $11,900,000 for fiscal year 1993, and $13,050,000 for fiscal year 1994.

(g) There are authorized to be appropriated to carry out section 1426(e) $27,500,000 for fiscal year 1991, $30,250,000 for fiscal year 1992, $33,275,000 for fiscal year 1993, and $36,602,000 for fiscal year 1994.

(h) There are authorized to be appropriated to carry out section 1427 $6,500,000 for fiscal year 1991, $8,000,000 for fiscal year 1992, $9,500,000 for fiscal year 1993, and $11,500,000 for fiscal year 1994.

SUBCHAPTER IV—TRAINING PERSONNEL FOR THE EDUCATION OF INDIVIDUALS WITH DISABILITIES

§ 1431. Grants for personnel training

(a) Careers in special education; personnel standards; training-study and fellowships-traineeships costs; contract authority for areas of personnel shortages

(1) The Secretary may make grants, which may include scholarships with necessary stipends and allowances, to institutions of higher education (including university affiliated programs and satellite centers participating in programs under part D of the Developmental Disabilities Assistance and Bill of Rights Act) and other appropriate nonprofit agencies to assist them in training personnel for careers in special education related services, and early intervention, including—

(A) special education teaching, including speech-language pathology and audiology, and adaptive physical education and instructional and assistive technology services,

(B) related services to children and youth with disabilities in educational settings, and other settings,

(C) special education and other careers in preschool and early intervention services for infants and toddlers with disabilities,

(D) special education leadership, including supervision and administration (at the advanced graduate, doctoral, and post-doctoral levels), special education research, and special education personnel preparation (at the doctoral and post-doctoral levels), and

(E) training of special education personnel and other personnel providing special services and pre-school and early intervention services for children with disabilities.

(2)(A) The Secretary shall base the award of grants under paragraph (1) on information relating to the present and projected need for special education, related services, early intervention, and other personnel to be trained based on identified State, regional, or national shortages, including the need for personnel in the provision of special education to children of limited English proficiency, and the capacity of the institution or agency to train qualified personnel, and other information considered appropriate by the Secretary.

(B) The Secretary shall ensure that grants are only made under paragraph (1) to applicant agencies and institutions that meet State and professionally recognized standards for the preparation of special education and related services personnel unless the grant is for the purpose of assisting the applicant agency of institution to meet such standards, and that include in their applications a detailed description of strategies that will be utilized to recruit and train members of minority groups and persons with disabilities.

(3) Grants under paragraph (1) may be used by institutions to assist in covering the cost of courses of training or study for such personnel and for establishing and maintaining fellowships or traineeships with such stipends and allowances as may be determined by the Secretary. Such institutions shall give priority consideration in the selection of qualified recipients of fellowships and

traineeships to individuals from disadvantaged backgrounds, including minorities and individuals with disabilities who are underrepresented in the teaching profession or in the specializations in which they are being trained.

(4) The Secretary in carrying out paragraph (1) may reserve a sum not to exceed 5 percent of the amount available for paragraph (1) in each fiscal year for contracts to prepare personnel in areas where shortages exist when a response to that need has not been adequately addressed by the grant process.

(5) In making grants under subsection (a)(1), the Secretary may determine that a portion of training supported through such grants shall be conducted on an interdisciplinary basis, and shall be designed to assist special educators in properly coordinating service provision with related services personnel. To the extent feasible, training programs funded under subsection (a)(1)(B) and(a)(1)(E) shall require practice to demonstrate the delivery of related services in an array of regular and special education and community settings.

(6) Nothing in this subsection shall be construed to prevent regular education or special education personnel from benefiting or participating in training activities conducted under this subsection on a preservice or inservice basis.

(7) The Secretary, in carrying out paragraph (1), shall make grants to Historically Black Colleges and Universities, and other institutions of higher education whose minority student enrollment is at least 25 percent.

(8)[2](A) In making grants under paragraph (1), the Secretary may make grants through a separate competition to institutions of higher education, in partnership with local educational agencies and center schools for students who are deaf, to carry out not less than 4 regional model demonstration training programs on deafness and secondary disabilities.

(B) Such programs shall provide preservice and inservice training to teachers and school administrators, and leadership personnel, in the education of students who are deaf and to related services personnel.

(8)[2] In making grants under paragraph (1), the Secretary may provide for the training or retraining of regular education teachers who are involved in providing instruction to individuals who are deaf, but who are not certified as teachers of such individuals, to meet the communications needs of such individuals.

(b) Grants for educational interpreter training programs for personnel educating deaf or deaf-blind students; assurance required; training of regular education teachers

(1) The Secretary may make grants to institutions of higher education, and other appropriate nonprofit agencies or organizations for the establishment or continuation of education interpreter training programs to train personnel to effectively meet the various communication needs of elementary and secondary students who are deaf or deaf-blind. To the extent feasible, grants shall be geographically dispersed throughout the Nation in urban and rural areas.

(2) The Secretary may make a grant under paragraph (1) only if the applicant for the grant provides an assurance that all interpreters receiving training under the grant will be provided training designed to develop skills necessary for facilitating effective communication for students who are deaf or deaf-blind.

(3) In making grants under paragraph (1), the Secretary may provide for the training or retraining (including short-term and in-service training) of regular education teachers who are involved in providing instruction to individuals who

are deaf, but who are not certified as teachers of such individuals, and other personnel who work with such individuals, on the role of educational interpreters.

(c) Special projects for preservice training, regular educators, and inservice training of special education personnel.

The Secretary may make grants to institutions of higher education, State agencies, and other appropriate nonprofit agencies and organizations to develop and demonstrate effective ways for preservice training programs to prepare regular educators to work with children and youth with disabilities and their families; for training teachers to work in community and school settings with school students with disabilities and their families; for inservice and preservice training of personnel to work with infants, toddlers, children, and youth with disabilities and their families; for inservice and preservice training of personnel to work with minority infants, toddlers, children, and youth with disabilities and their families; for preservice and inservice training of special education and related services personnel in the use of assistive and instructional technology to benefit infants, toddlers, children, and youth with disabilities; and for the recruitment and retention of special education, related services, and early intervention personnel. Both preservice and inservice training shall include a component that addresses the coordination among all service providers, including regular educators.

(d) Grants for career advancement and competency-based training for current workers

(1) The Secretary shall fund up to 5 grants to States or entities to support the formation of consortia or partnerships of public and private entities for the purpose of providing opportunities for career advancement and/or competency-based training, including but not limited to, certificate or degree granting programs in special education, related services, and early intervention for current workers at public and private agencies that provide services to infants, toddlers, children, and youth with disabilities. Recipients shall meet the requirements of section 1410(g) for the dissemination of information. The purposes for which such a grant may be expended include, but are not limited to, the following:

(A) Establishing a program with colleges and universities to develop creative new programs and coursework options and/or to expand existing programs in the field of special education, related services, or early intervention. Funds maybe used to provide release time for faculty and staff for curriculum development, instructional costs, and modest start-up and other program development costs.

(B) Establishing a career development mentoring program using faculty and professional staff members of participating agencies as role models, career sponsors, and academic advisors for experienced State, city, county, and voluntary sector workers who have demonstrated a commitment to working in the above fields and who are enrolled in higher education institution programs relating to these fields.

(C) Supporting a wide range of programmatic and research activities aimed at increasing opportunities for career advancement and competency-based training in the above fields.

(D) Identifying existing public and private agency and labor union personnel policies and benefit programs that may facilitate the ability of workers to take advantage of higher education opportunities such as leave time, tuition reimbursement, etc.

(2) To the extent feasible, projects authorized under paragraph (1) shall be geographically dispersed throughout the Nation in urban and rural areas.

(3) The Secretary shall award, for the purpose of providing technical assistance to States or entities receiving grants under paragraph (1), a cooperative agreement through a separate competition to an entity that has successfully demonstrated the capacity and expertise in the education, training, and retention of workers to serve children and youth with disabilities through the use of consortia or partnerships established for the purpose of retaining the existing workforce and providing opportunities for career enhancement.

(4) The Secretary may conduct an evaluation of projects funded under this subsection.

(5) During the period in which an entity is receiving financial assistance under paragraph (1) or (3), the entity may not receive financial assistance under the other paragraph.

(e) Parent training and information programs

(1) The Secretary may make grants through a separate competition to private nonprofit organizations for the purpose of providing training and information to parents of infants, toddlers, children, and youth with disabilities and persons who work with parents to enable such individuals to participate more effectively with professionals in meeting the educational needs of children with disabilities. Such grants shall be designed to meet the unique training and information needs of parents of infants, toddlers, children, and youth with disabilities living in the area to be served by the grant, particularly those who are members of groups that have been traditionally underrepresented.

(2) In order to receive a grant under paragraph (1) a private nonprofit organization shall—

(A) be governed by a board of directors of which a majority of the members are parents of infants, toddlers, children, and youth with disabilities, particularly minority parents, and that includes members who are professionals, especially minority professionals, in the field of special education, early intervention, and related services, and individuals with disabilities, or, if the nonprofit private organization does not have such a board, such organization shall have a membership that represents the interests of individuals with disabilities, and shall establish a special governing committee of which a majority of the members are parents of infants, toddlers, children, and youth with disabilities, particularly parents of minority children, and which includes members who are professionals, especially minority professionals, in the field of special education, early intervention, and related services, to operate the training and information program under paragraph (1), and parents and professional membership of these boards or special governing committees shall be broadly representative of minority and other individuals and groups having an interest in special education, early intervention, and related services;

(B) serve the parents of infants, toddlers, children, and youth with the full range of disabling conditions under such grant program, and

(C) demonstrate the capacity and expertise to conduct effectively the training and information activities for which a grant may be made under paragraph (1). Nothing in subparagraph (A) shall be construed to authorize or permit the denial to any person of the due process of law required by the United States Constitution.

(3) The board of directors or special governing committee of a private nonprofit organization receiving a grant under paragraph (1) shall meet at least once in each calendar quarter to review the parent training and information activities for which the grant is made, and each such committee shall advise the governing board directly of its views and recommendations. Whenever a private nonprofit organization requests the renewal of a grant under paragraph (1) for a fiscal year, the board of directors or the special governing committee shall submit to the Secretary a written review of the parent training and information program conducted by that private nonprofit organization during the preceding fiscal year, and, for purposes of paragraph (1), network with clearinghouses, including those established under § 633 and other organizations and agencies, and network with other established national, State, and local parent groups representing the full range of parents of infants, toddlers, children, and youth with disabilities, especially parents of minority children.

(4) The Secretary shall ensure that grants under paragraph (1) will—

(A) be distributed geographically to the greatest extent possible throughout all the States and give priority to grants which involve unserved areas,

(B) be targeted to parents of children with disabilities in both urban and rural areas or on a State or regional basis, and

(C) serve parents of minority children with disabilities (including parents served pursuant to paragraph (10)) representative to the proportion of the minority population in the areas being served by requiring that applicants for the grants identify with specificity the special efforts that will be undertaken to involve such parents, including efforts to work with community-based and cultural organizations and the specification of supplementary aids, services, and supports that will be made available, and by specifying budgetary items earmarked to accomplish this subparagraph, and

(D) be funded at a sufficient size, scope, and quality to ensure that the program is adequate to serve the parents in the area.

(5) Parent training and information programs assisted under paragraph (1) shall assist parents to—

(A) better understand the nature and needs of the disabling conditions of children,

(B) provide follow up support for educational programs of children with disabilities,

(C) communicate more effectively with special and regular educators, administrators, related services personnel, and other relevant professionals,

(D) participate in educational decision making processes, including the development of the individualized educational program for a child with a disability,

(E) obtain appropriate information about the range of options, programs, services, and resources available at the national, State, and local levels to assist infants, toddlers, children, and youth with disabilities and their families, and

(F) understand the provisions for the education of infants, toddlers, children, and youth with disabilities under this Act.

(6) Parent training and information programs may, at a grant recipient's discretion, include State or local educational personnel where such participation will further an objective of the program assisted by the grant.

(7) Each private nonprofit organization operating a program receiving a grant under paragraph (1) shall consult and network with appropriate national, State, regional, and local agencies and organizations, such as protection and advocacy agencies, that serve or assist infants, toddlers, children, and youth with disabilities and their families and are located in the jurisdictions served by the program.

(8) The Secretary shall provide technical assistance, by grant or contract, for establishing, developing, and coordinating parent training and information programs.

(9) After the establishment in each State of a parent training and information center, the Secretary shall provide for the establishment of 3 experimental centers to serve large numbers of parents of children with disabilities located in high density areas that do not have such centers and 2 such centers to serve large numbers of parents of children with disabilities located in rural areas.

(10)(A) In the case of a grant under paragraph (1) to a private nonprofit organization for fiscal year 1993 or 1994, the organization, in expending the amounts described in subparagraph (B), shall give priority to providing services under this subsection to parents of children with disabilities aged 0-5.

(B) With respect to a grant under paragraph (1) to a private nonprofit organization for fiscal year 1993 or 1994, the amounts described in this subparagraph are any amounts provided in the grant in excess of the amount of any grant under such paragraph provided to the organization for fiscal year 1992.

(11) Effective for fiscal year 1991 and every year thereafter, the Secretary shall obtain data concerning programs and centers assisted under this subsection on

(A) the number of parents provided information and training by disability category of their children,

(B) the types and modes of information or training provided,

(C) strategies used to reach and serve parents of minority infants, toddlers, children, and youth with disabilities,

(D) the number of parents served as a result of activities described under subparagraph (C),

(E) activities to network with other information clearinghouses and parent groups as required in subsection (c)(2)(C),

(F) the number of agencies and organizations consulted with at the national, State, regional, and local levels, and

(G) the number of parents served under this subsection who are parents of children with disabilities aged 0-5.

The Secretary shall include a summary of this information in the annual report to Congress as required in section 1418(g).

§ 1432. Grants to State educational agencies and institutions for traineeships

(a) The Secretary shall make a grant of sufficient size and scope to each State educational agency for the purposes described in subsection (c) and, in any State in which the State educational agency does not apply for such a grant, to an institution of higher education within such State for such purposes.

(b) The Secretary may also make a limited number of grants to State educational agencies on a competitive basis for the purposes described in subsection (c). In any fiscal year, the Secretary may not expend for purposes of this subsection an amount that exceeds 10 percent of the amount expended for purposes of this section in the preceding fiscal year.

(c) Grants made under this section shall be for the purpose of assisting States in establishing and maintaining preservice and inservice programs to prepare special and regular education, related services and early intervention personnel to meet the needs of infants, toddlers, children, and youth with disabilities or supervisors of such persons, consistent with the personnel needs identified in the State's comprehensive system of personnel development under section 1413 and under section 1476(b)(8), and to assist the State in developing and maintaining such systems and conducting personnel recruitment and retention activities.

(d) the Secretary is authorized to provide directly or by grant, contract, or cooperative agreement, technical assistance to State educational agencies on matters pertaining to the effective implementation of section 1413(a)(3).

§ 1433. Clearinghouses

(a) Establishment of national clearinghouses

The Secretary is authorized to make grants to, or enter into contracts or cooperative agreements with, public agencies or private nonprofit organizations or institutions for the establishment of three national clearinghouses: on children and youth with disabilities; on postsecondary education for individuals with disabilities; and on careers in special education, to—

(1) collect, develop, and disseminate information,

(2) provide technical assistance,

(3) conduct coordinated outreach activities,

(4) provide for the coordination and networking with other relevant national, State, and local organizations and information and referral resources,

(5) respond to individuals and organizations seeking information, and

(6) provide for the synthesis of information for its effective utilization by parents, professionals, individuals with disabilities, and other interested parties.

(b) National clearinghouse for children and youth

The national clearinghouse for children and youth with disabilities shall:

(1) Collect and disseminate information (including the development of materials) on characteristics of infants, toddlers, children, and youth with disabilities and on programs, legislation, and services relating to their education under this Act and other Federal laws.

(2) Participate in programs and services related to disability issues for providing outreach, technical assistance, collection, and dissemination of information; and promoting networking of individuals with appropriate national, State, and local agencies and organizations.

(3) Establish a coordinated network and conduct outreach activities with relevant Federal, State, and local organizations and other sources for promoting public awareness of disability issues and the availability of information, programs, and services.

(4) Collect, disseminate, and develop information on current and future national, Federal, regional, and State needs for providing information to parents, professionals, individuals with disabilities, and other interested parties relating to the education and related services of individuals with disabilities.

(5) Provide technical assistance to national, Federal, regional, State and local agencies and organizations seeking to establish information and referral services for individuals with disabilities and their families.

(6) In carrying out the activities in this subsection, the clearinghouse will include strategies to disseminate information to underrepresented groups such as those with limited English proficiency.

(c) National clearinghouse on postsecondary education for individuals with disabilities

The national clearinghouse on postsecondary education for individuals with disabilities shall:

(1) Collect and disseminate information nationally on characteristics of individuals entering and participating in education and training programs after high school; legislation affecting such individuals and such programs; policies, procedures, and support services, as well as adaptations, and other resources available or recommended to facilitate the education of individuals with disabilities; available programs and services that include, or can be adapted to include, individuals with disabilities; and sources of financial aid for the education and training of individuals with disabilities.

(2) Identify areas of need for additional information.

(3) Develop new materials (in both print and nonprint form), especially by synthesizing information from a variety of fields affecting disability issues and the education, rehabilitation, and retraining of individuals with disabilities.

(4) Develop a coordinated network of professionals, related organizations and associations, mass media, other clearinghouses, and governmental agencies at the Federal, regional, State, and local level for the purposes of disseminating information and promoting awareness of issues relevant to the education of individuals with disabilities after high school and referring individuals who request information to local resources.

(5) Respond to requests from individuals with disabilities, their parents, and professionals who work with them, for information that will enable them to make appropriate decisions about postsecondary education and training.

(d) National clearinghouse on careers in special education

The national clearinghouse designed to encourage students to seek careers and professional personnel to seek employment in the various fields relating to the education of children and youth with disabilities shall:

(1) Collect and disseminate information on current and future national, regional, and State needs for special education and related services personnel.

(2) Disseminate information to high school counselors and others concerning current career opportunities in special education, location of programs, and various forms of financial assistance (such as scholarships, stipends, and allowances).

(3) Identify training programs available around the country.

(4) Establish a network among local and State educational agencies and institutions of higher education concerning the supply of graduates and available openings.

(5) Provide technical assistance to institutions seeking to meet State and professionally recognized standards.

(e) Considerations governing awards

(1) In awarding grants, contracts, and cooperative agreements under this section, the Secretary shall give priority consideration to any applicant with demonstrated, proven effectiveness (at the national level) in performing the functions established in this section; and with the ability to conduct such projects, communicate with intended consumers of information, and maintain the necessary communication with national, regional, State, and local agencies and organizations.

(2) In awarding grants, contracts, and cooperative agreements under this section, the Secretary shall give priority consideration to any applicant with demonstrated, proven effectiveness (at the national level) in providing informational services to minorities and minority organizations.

(f) Annual report to Congress

(1) Beginning in fiscal year 1991, and for each year thereafter, the Secretary shall obtain information on each project assisted under this section, including

(A) the number of individuals served by disability category, as appropriate, including parents, professionals, students, and individuals with disabilities;

(B) a description of responses utilized;

(C) a listing of new products developed and disseminated; and

(D) a description of strategies and activities utilized for outreach to urban and rural areas with populations of minorities and underrepresented groups.

(2) A summary of the data required by this subsection shall be included in the annual report to Congress required under section 1418.

§ 1434. Reports to the Secretary

(a) Not more than sixty days after the end of any fiscal year, each recipient of a grant or contract under this subchapter during such fiscal year shall prepare and submit a report to the Secretary. Each such report shall be in such form and detail as the Secretary determines to be appropriate, and shall include—

(1) the number of individuals trained under the grant or contract, by category of training and level of training;

(2) the number of individuals trained under the grant or contract receiving degrees and certification, by category and level of training, and

(3) information described in section 1431(d)(11) and section 1433(f)(1), as applicable.

(b) A summary of the data required by this section shall be included in the annual report of the Secretary under section 1418 of this chapter.

§ 1435. Authorization of appropriations

(a) In general

(1) There are authorized to be appropriated to carry out this part (other than sections 1431(a)(7), 1431(d), and 1433) $94,725,000 for fiscal year 1991, $103,255,000 for fiscal year 1992, $113,580,000 for fiscal year 1993, and $123,760,000 for fiscal year 1994.

(2) There are authorized to be appropriated to carry out section 1431(a)(7) $19,250,000 for fiscal year 1991, $21,175,000 for fiscal year 1992, $23,292,500 for fiscal year 1993, and $25,621,750 for fiscal year 1994.

(3) There are authorized to be appropriated to carry out section 1431(d) $11,000,000 for fiscal year 1991, $15,100,000 for fiscal year 1992, $16,300,000 for fiscal year 1993, and $17,600,000 for fiscal year 1994.

(4) There are authorized to be appropriated to carry out section 1433 $2,900,000 for fiscal year 1991, $2,465,000 for fiscal year 1992, $2,710,000 for fiscal year 1993, and $2,960,000 for fiscal year 1994.

(b) Personnel training for careers in special education and early intervention

Of the funds appropriated pursuant to subsection (a) of this section for any fiscal year, the Secretary shall reserve not less than 65 per centum for activities described in subparagraphs (A) through (E) of section 1431(a)(1) of this section.

§ 1436. Omitted

SUBCHAPTER V—RESEARCH IN THE EDUCATION OF INDIVIDUALS WITH DISABILITIES

§ 1441. Research and related activities

(a) Grant and contract authority; statement of objectives; description of specific activities

The Secretary may make grants to, or enter into contracts or cooperative agreements with, State and local educational agencies, institutions of higher education, and other public agencies and nonprofit private organizations for the purpose of advancing and improving the knowledge base and improving the practice of professionals, parents, and others providing early intervention, special education, and related services, including professionals who work with children and youth with disabilities in regular education environments, to provide such children effective instruction and enable them to successfully learn. The activities supported under this section shall support innovation, development, exchange, and use of such advancements in knowledge and practice designed to contribute to the improvement of instruction and learning of infants, toddlers, children, and youth with disabilities. In carrying out this section, the Secretary may support a wide range of research and related activities designed to—

(1) advance knowledge regarding the provision of instruction and other interventions to infants, toddlers, children, and youth with disabilities including—

(A) the organization, synthesis, and interpretation of current knowledge and the identification of knowledge gaps;

(B) the identification of knowledge and skill competencies needed by personnel providing special education, related services, and early intervention services;

(C) the improvement of knowledge regarding the developmental and learning characteristics of infants, toddlers, children, and youth with disabilities in order to improve the design and effectiveness of interventions and instruction;

(D) the evaluation of approaches and interventions;

(E) the development of instructional strategies, techniques, and activities;

(F) the improvement of curricula and instructional tools such as textbooks, media, materials, and technology;

(G) the development of assessment techniques, instruments (including tests, inventories, and scales), and strategies for measurement of progress and the identification, location, and evaluation of infants, toddlers, children, and youth with disabilities for the purpose of determining eligibility, program planning, and placement for special education, related services, and early intervention services. Particular attention should be given to the development of alternative assessment procedures and processes for minority individuals and those with limited English proficiency;

(H) the testing of research findings in practice settings to determine the application, usability, effectiveness, and generalizability of such research findings;

(I) the improvement of knowledge regarding families, minorities, limited English proficiency, and disabling conditions; and

(J) the identification of environmental, organizational, resource, and other conditions necessary for effective professional practice; and

(2) advance the use of knowledge by personnel providing special education, related services, and early intervention services including—

(A) the improvement of knowledge regarding how such individuals learn new knowledge and skills, and strategies for effectively facilitating such learning in preservice, inservice, and continuing education;

(B) the organization, integration, and presentation of knowledge so that such knowledge can be incorporated and imparted in personnel preparation, continuing education programs, and other relevant training and communication vehicles; and

(C) the expansion and improvement of networks that exchange knowledge and practice information.

(b) Qualifications of applicants

In carrying out subsection (a), the Secretary shall consider the special education, related services, or early intervention and research experience of applicants.

(c) Publication of proposed priorities in Federal Register

The Secretary shall publish proposed priorities under this subchapter in the Federal Register not later than 12 months preceding the fiscal year for which they are being announced, and shall allow a period of 60 days for public comments and suggestions. The Secretary shall, after analyzing and considering the public comments, publish final priorities in the Federal Register not later than 90 days after the close of the comment period.

(d) Index of projects

The Secretary shall provide an index (including the title of each project and the name and address of the funded organization) of all projects conducted under this subchapter in the prior fiscal year in the annual report described under section 618.

(e) Coordination with other research; information to other agencies

The Secretary shall—

(1) coordinate the priorities established under subsection (b) with research priorities established by the National Institute for Disability and Rehabilitation Research and other appropriate agencies conducting research pertaining to the education of individuals with disabilities; and

(2) provide information concerning priorities established under subsection (b) to the National Council on Disability and to the Bureau of Indian Affairs Advisory Committee for Exceptional Children.

(f) Attention deficit disorder

(1) The Secretary shall make grants or enter into contracts or cooperative agreements for the establishment of a center or centers designed to organize, synthesize, and disseminate current knowledge relating to children with attention deficit disorder with respect to the following:

(A) Assessment techniques, instruments, and strategies used for identification, location, evaluation and for measurement of progress.

(B) Knowledge and skill competencies needed by professionals providing special and regular education and related services.

(C) Environmental, organizational, resource, and other conditions necessary for effective professional practice.

(D) Developmental and learning characteristics.

(E) Instructional strategies, techniques, and activities.

(F) Curricula and instructional tools such as textbooks, media, materials, and technology.

(G) Strategies, techniques, and activities related to involvement of families.

(2) In awarding grants, contracts, and cooperative agreements under paragraph (1), the Secretary shall give priority consideration to applicants with—

(A) demonstrated knowledge concerning the disorder;

(B) proven effectiveness in performing the functions established in this subsection; and

(C) the ability to—

(i) conduct such projects;

(ii) communicate with intended consumers of information; and

(iii) maintain the necessary communication with national, regional, State, and local agencies.

(g) Model demonstration programs

(1) The Secretary shall make grants, or enter into contracts or cooperative agreements, for the establishment of model demonstration programs, of which some will be school-based models, that provide the services of an ombudsman to assist in resolving problems that are barriers to appropriate educational, related services or other services for children and youth with disabilities.

(2) Programs under paragraph (1) shall provide or identify personnel to assist children and youth with disabilities, their parents or guardians, special and regular education teachers, State and local education administrators, and related services personnel to resolve problems in a timely manner through dispute mediation and other methods, notwithstanding due process procedures, in order to further the delivery of appropriate education and related services. Participation in this program does not preclude or delay due process under subchapter II of this Act.

(3) Ombudsman services for programs under paragraph (1) shall be provided by social workers, parent advocates, psychologists, and persons with similar qualifications designated by the Secretary.

(h) Research grants for unique needs, specialized instruction, and progress measurement; family involvement; adult role models

(1) The Secretary may make grants to institutions of higher education, in partnership with other appropriate agencies and organization such as local educational agenices and center schools for students who are deaf, to—
    (A) conduct research in unique needs of children and youth, including minority children and youth, with disabilities;
    (B) develop and evaluate specialized instructional methods, materials, curricula, and technologies for use with such children and youth; and
    (C) develop and evaluate assessment techniques, instruments, and strategies used to identify, evaluate, and measure the progress of such children and youth.
(2) Each grantee under this subsection shall provide for the meaningful involvement in its project of parents and family members and adult role models.

§ 1442. Research and demonstration projects in physical education and recreation for children with disabilities

The Secretary is authorized to make grants to States, State or local educational agencies, institutions of higher education, and other public or nonprofit private educational or research agencies and organizations, and to make contracts with States, State or local educational agencies, institutions of higher education, and other public or private educational or research agencies and organizations, for research and related purposes relating to physical education or recreation for children with disabilities, including therapeutic recreation, and to conduct research, surveys, or demonstrations relating to physical education or recreation for children with disabilities, including therapeutic recreation.

§ 1443. Repealed. Pub.L. 101-476, Title V, § 503, Oct. 30, 1990, 104 Stat. 1138

§ 1444. Authorization of appropriations

For purposes of carrying out this subchapter, there are authorized to be appropriated $21,100,000 for fiscal year 1990, $24,650,000 for fiscal year 1991, $27,400,000 for fiscal year 1992, $30,200,000 for fiscal year 1993, and $33,200,000 for fiscal year 1994.

SUBCHAPTER VI—INSTRUCTIONAL MEDIA FOR INDIVIDUALS WITH DISABILITIES

§ 1451. Purposes

The purposes of this subchapter are to promote—
(1) the general welfare of deaf and hard of hearing individuals by—
(A) bringing to such individuals understanding and appreciation of those films and television programs that play such an important part in the general and cultural advancement of hearing individuals;
(B) providing through these films and television programs enriched educational and cultural experiences through which deaf and hard of hearing individuals can be brought into better touch with the realities of their environment;
(C) providing a wholesome and rewarding experience which deaf and hard of hearing individuals may share together; and
(D) utilizing educational media to help eliminate illiteracy among individuals with disabilities;
(2) the educational advancement of individuals with disabilities by—
(A) carrying on research in the use of educational media for individuals with disabilities;
(B) producing and distributing educational media for the use of individuals with disabilities, their parents, their actual or potential employers, and other individuals directly involved in work for the advancement of individuals with disabilities; and
(C) training persons in the use of educational media for the instruction of individuals with disabilities; and
(3) the general welfare of visually impaired individuals by—
(A) bringing to such individuals an understanding and appreciation of textbooks, films, television programs, video material, and other educational publications and materials that play such an important part in the general and cultural advancement of visually unimpaired individuals; and
(B) ensuring access to television programming and other video materials.

§ 1452. Captioned films, television, descriptive video and educational media for individuals with disabilities

(a) Establishment of loan service

The Secretary shall establish a loan service of captioned films, descriptive video and educational media for the purpose of making such materials available, in accordance with regulations, in the United States for nonprofit purposes to individuals with disabilities, parents of individuals with disabilities, and other individuals directly involved in activities for the advancement of individuals with disabilities, including for the purpose of addressing problems of illiteracy among individuals with disabilities.

(b) Authority of Secretary

The Secretary is authorized to—
(1) acquire films (or rights thereto) and other educational media by purchase, lease, or gift;
(2) acquire by lease or purchase equipment necessary for the administration of this subchapter;
(3) provide, by grant or contract, for the captioning for deaf and hard of hearing individuals and video description for the visually impaired, of films, television programs, and video materials;
(4) provide, by grant or contract, for the distribution of captioned and video-described films, video materials, and other educational media and equipment through State schools for individuals with disabilities, public libraries, and such other agencies or entities as the Secretary may deem appropriate to serve as local or regional centers for such distribution;
(5) provide, by grant or contract, for the conduct of research in the use of educational and training films and other educational media for individuals with disabilities, for the production and distribution of educational and training films and other educational media for individuals with disabilities and the training of individuals in the use of such films and media, including the payment to those individuals of such stipends (including allowances for travel and other expenses of such individuals and their dependents) as the Secretary may determine, which shall be consistent with prevailing practices under comparable federally supported programs;
(6) utilize the facilities and services of other governmental agencies;
(7) accept gifts, contributions, and voluntary and uncompensated services of individuals and organizations, and
(8) provide by grant or contract for educational media and materials for deaf and hard of hearing individuals.

(c) National Theatre of the Deaf

The Secretary may make grants to or enter into contracts or cooperative agreements with the National Theatre of the Deaf, Inc. and other appropriate non-profit organizations for the purpose of providing cultural experiences to—
(1) enrich the lives of deaf and hard of hearing children and adults,
(2) increase public awareness and understanding of deafness and of the artistic and intellectual achievements of deaf and hard of hearing individuals, and
(3) promote the integration of hearing and deaf and hard of hearing individuals through shared cultural, educational, and social experiences.

(d) Authorization to provide transcribed tapes through graduate school

(1) The Secretary is authorized to make a grant or enter into a contract for the purpose of providing current, free textbooks and other educational publications and materials to blind and other print-handicapped students in elementary, secondary, postsecondary, and graduate schools and other institutions of higher education through the medium of transcribed tapes and cassettes.

(2) For the purpose of this subsection, the term "print-handicapped" refers to any individual who is blind or severely visually impaired, or who, by reason of a physical or perceptual disability, is unable to read printed material unassisted.

§ 1453. Repealed.

§ 1454. Authorization of appropriations

For the purpose of carrying out section 1452 there are authorized to be appropriated $20,010,000 for fiscal year 1991, $22,010,000 for fiscal year 1992, $24,200,000 for fiscal year 1993, and $26,600,000 for fiscal year 1994.

SUBCHAPTER VII—TECHNOLOGY, EDUCATIONAL MEDIA, AND MATERIALS FOR INDIVIDUALS WITH DISABILITIES

§ 1461. Financial assistance

(a) Authority to provide new technology, media and materials

The Secretary may make grants or enter into contracts or cooperative agreements with institutions of higher education, State and local educational agencies, or other appropriate agencies and organizations for the purpose of advancing the use of new technology, media, and materials in the education of students with disabilities and the provision of related services and early intervention services to infants and toddlers with disabilities. In carrying out this section, the Secretary may fund projects or centers for the purposes of—

(1) determining how technology, assistive technology, media, and materials are being used in the education of individuals with disabilities and how they can be used most effectively, efficiently, and appropriately,

(2) designing and adapting technology, assistive technology, media, and materials to improve the education of students with disabilities,

(3) assisting the public and private sectors in the development and marketing of technology, assistive technology, media, and materials for the education of individuals with disabilities,

(4) disseminating information on the availability and use of technology, assistive technology, media, and materials for the education of individuals with disabilities, where appropriate, to entities described in section 610(g), and

(5) increasing access to and use of assistive technology devices and assistive technology services in the education of infants, toddlers, children, and youth with disabilities, and other activities authorized under the Technology-Related Assistance for Individuals With Disabilities Act of 1988, as such Act relates to the education of students with disabilities, and

(6) examining how these purposes can address the problem of illiteracy among individuals with disabilities.

(b) Authority to provide assistance which is closed captioned

(1) With respect to new technology, media, and materials utilized with funds under this subchapter to improve the education of students with disabilities, the Secretary shall make efforts to ensure that such instructional materials are closed captioned.

(2) The Secretary may not award a grant, contract, or cooperative agreement under paragraphs (1) through (4) of subsection (a) unless the applicant for such assistance agrees that activities carried out with the assistance will be coordinated, as appropriate, with the State entity receiving funds under title I of the Technology-Related Assistance for Individuals with Disabilities Act of 1988.

§ 1462. Authorization of appropriations

For the purpose of carrying out this subchapter, there are authorized to be appropriated $11,900,000 for fiscal year 1991, $12,860,000 for fiscal year 1992, $13,890,000 for fiscal year 1993, and $15,000,000 for fiscal year1994.

SUBCHAPTER VIII—INFANTS AND TODDLERS WITH DISABILITIES

§ 1471. Findings and policy

(a) Findings

The Congress finds that there is an urgent and substantial need—

(1) to enhance the development of infants and toddlers with disabilities and to minimize their potential for developmental delay,

(2) to reduce the educational costs to our society, including our Nation's schools, by minimizing the need for special education and related services after infants and toddlers with disabilities reach school age,

(3) to minimize the likelihood of institutionalization of individuals with disabilities and maximize the potential for their independent living in society,

(4) to enhance the capacity of families to meet the special needs of their infants and toddlers with disabilities, and

(5) to enhance the capacity of State and local agencies and service providers to identify, evaluate, and meet the needs of historically underrepresented populations, particularly minorities, low-income, inner-city, and rural populations.

(b) Policy

It is therefore the policy of the United States to provide financial assistance to States—

(1) to develop and implement a statewide, comprehensive, coordinated, multidisciplinary, interagency program of early intervention services for infants and toddlers with disabilities and their families,

(2) to facilitate the coordination of payment for early intervention services from Federal, State, local, and private sources (including public and private insurance coverage), and

(3) to enhance their capacity to provide quality early intervention services and expand and improve existing early intervention services being provided to infants and toddlers with disabilities and their families.

§ 1472. Definitions

As used in this subchapter—

(1) The term "infants and toddlers with disabilities" means individuals from birth to age 2, inclusive, who need early intervention services because they—

(A) are experiencing developmental delays, as measured by appropriate diagnostic instruments and procedures in one or more of the following areas: cognitive development, physical development, language and speech development (hereafter in this part referred to as "communication development"), psychosocial development (hereafter in this part referred to as "social or emotional development"), or self-help skills (hereafter in this part referred to as "adaptive development"), or

(B) have a diagnosed physical or mental condition which has a high probability of resulting in developmental delay.

Such term may also include, at a State's discretion, individuals from birth to age 2, inclusive, who are at risk of having substantial developmental delays if early intervention services are not provided.

(2) The term "early intervention services" are developmental services which—

(A) are provided under public supervision,

(B) are provided at no cost except where Federal or State law provides for a system of payments by families, including a schedule of sliding fees,

(C) are designed to meet the developmental needs of an infant or toddler with a disability in any one or more of the following areas:

(i) physical development,

(ii) cognitive development,

(iii) communication development,

(iv) social or emotional development, or

(v) adaptive development,

(D) meet the standards of the State, including the requirements of this part,

(E) include—

(i) family training, counseling, and home visits,

(ii) special instruction,

(iii) speech pathology and audiology,

(iv) occupational therapy,

(v) physical therapy,

(vi) psychological services,

(vii) case management services (hereafter in this part referred to as "service coordination services"),

(viii) medical services only for diagnostic or evaluation purposes,

(ix) early identification, screening and assessment services,

(x) health services necessary to enable the infant or toddler to benefit from the other early intervention services,

(xi) social work services,

(xii) vision services,

(xiii) assistive technology devices and assistive technology services, and

(xiv) transportation and related costs that are necessary to enable an infant or toddler or the infant's or toddler's family to receive early intervention services,

(F) are provided by qualified personnel, including—

(i) special educators,

(ii) speech and language pathologists and audiologists,

(iii) occupational therapists,

(iv) physical therapists,

(v) psychologists,

(vi) social workers,

(vii) nurses,

(viii) nutritionists,

(ix) family therapists,

(x) orientation and mobility specialists, and

(xi) pediatricians and other physicians,

(G) to the maximum extent appropriate, are provided in natural environments, including the home, and community settings in which children without disabilities participate, and

(H) are provided in conformity with an individualized family service plan adopted in accordance with section 1477 of this title.

(3) The term "developmental delay" has the meaning given such term by a State under section 1476(b)(1) of this title.

(4) The term "Council" means the State Interagency Coordinating Council established under section 1482 of this title.

§ 1473. General authority

The Secretary shall, in accordance with this subchapter, make grants to States (from their allocations under section 1484 of this title) to assist each State to develop a statewide, comprehensive, coordinated, multidisciplinary, interagency system to provide early intervention services for infants and toddlers with disabilities and their families.

§ 1474. General eligibility

In order to be eligible for a grant under section 1473 of this title for any fiscal year, a State shall demonstrate to the Secretary (in its application under section 1478 of this title) that the State has established a State Interagency Coordinating Council which meets the requirements of section 1482 of this title.

§ 1475. Continuing eligibility

(a) First two years

In order to be eligible for a grant under section 1473 of this title for the first or second year of a State's participation under this subchapter, a State shall include in its application under section 1478 of this title for that year an assurance that funds received under section 1473 of this title shall be used to assist the State to plan, develop, and implement the statewide system required by section 1476 of this title.

(b) Third and fourth year

(1) In order to be eligible for a grant under section 1473 of this title for the third or fourth year of a State's participation under this subchapter, a State shall include in its application under section 1478 of this title for that year information and assurances demonstrating to the satisfaction of the Secretary that—

(A) the State has adopted a policy which incorporates all of the components of a statewide system in accordance with section 1476 of this title or obtained a waiver from the Secretary under paragraph (2).

(B) funds shall be used to plan, develop, and implement the statewide system required by section 1476 of this title, and

(C) such statewide system will be in effect no later than the beginning of the fourth year of the State's participation under section 1473 of this title, except that in order to comply with section 1476(b)(4) of this title, a State need only conduct multidisciplinary assessments, develop individualized family service plans, and make available case management services.

(2) Notwithstanding paragraph (1), the Secretary may permit a State to continue to receive assistance under section 1473 of this title during such third year even if the State has not adopted the policy required by paragraph (1)(A) before receiving assistance if the State demonstrates in its application—

(A) that the State has made a good faith effort to adopt such a policy,

(B) the reasons why it was unable to meet the timeline and the steps remaining before such a policy will be adopted, and

(C) an assurance that the policy will be adopted to go into effect before the fourth year of such assistance.

(c) Fifth and succeeding years

In order to be eligible for a grant under section 1473 of this title for a fifth and any succeeding year of a State's participation under this subchapter, a State shall include in its application under section 1478 of this title for that year information and assurances demonstrating to the satisfaction of the Secretary that the State has in effect the statewide system required by section 1476 of this title and a description of services to be provided under section 1476(b)(2) of this title.

(d) Exception

Notwithstanding subsections (a) and (b) of this section, a State which has in effect a State law, enacted before September 1, 1986, that requires the provision of free appropriate public education to children with disabilities from birth through age 2, inclusive, shall be eligible for a grant under section 1473 of this title for the first through fourth years of a State's participation under this subchapter.

(e) Differential funding for fourth or fifth year

(1) In general

Notwithstanding any other provision of this subchapter, a State shall be eligible for a grant under section 1473 of this title for fiscal years 1990, 1991, or 1992 if—

(A) the State satisfies the eligibility criteria described in subsection (b)(1) of this section pertaining to the State's third or fourth year of participation under this subchapter; and

(B) the Governor, on behalf of the State, submits, by a date that the Secretary may establish for each such year, a request for extended participation, including—

(i) information demonstrating to the Secretary's satisfaction that the State is experiencing significant hardships in meeting the requirements of this section for the fourth or fifth year of participation; and

(ii) a plan, including timeliness, for meeting the eligibility criteria described in subsections (b)(1) and (c) of this section for the fourth, fifth, or succeeding years of participation.

(2) Approval of request

(A) First year

The Secretary shall approve a State's request for a first year of extended participation under this subsection if the State meets the requirements of paragraph (1).

(B) Second year

The Secretary shall approve a State's request for a second year of extended participation under this subsection if the State—

(i) meets the requirements of paragraph (1); and

(ii) demonstrates to the Secretary's satisfaction that the State has made reasonable progress in implementing the plan described in paragraph (1)(B)(ii).

(3) Duration

The Secretary may not approve more than two requests from the same State for extended participation under this subsection.

(4) Payment

(A) Fiscal year 1990

Notwithstanding any other provision of law, each State qualifying for extended participation under this subsection for fiscal year 1990 shall receive a payment under this subchapter in an amount equal to such State's payment under this subchapter for fiscal year 1989.

(B) Fiscal year 1991 or 1992

Except as provided in subparagraph (C) and notwithstanding any other provision of law, each State qualifying for extended participation under this subsection for fiscal year 1991 or fiscal year 1992 shall receive a payment under this subchapter for such fiscal years in an amount equal to the payment such State would have received under this subchapter for fiscal year 1990 if such State had met the criteria for the fourth year of participation described in subsection (b)(1) of this section.

(C) Minimum payment for fiscal year 1991 or 1992 for certain States

Notwithstanding any other provision of law, each State qualifying for extended participation under this subsection for fiscal year 1991 or fiscal year 1992 shall receive a payment under this subchapter of not less than $500,000. For purposes of the preceding sentence, the term "State" means each of the 50 States, the District of Columbia, and the Commonwealth of Puerto Rico.

(5) Reallotment

(A) Fiscal year 1990

The amount by which the allotment computed under section 1484 of this title for any State for fiscal year 1990 exceeds the amount that such State may be allotted under paragraph (4)(A) of this subsection (and, notwithstanding section 1484(d) of this title, any fiscal year 1990 funds allotted to any State that such State elects not to receive) shall be reallotted, notwithstanding the percentage limitations set forth in sections 1484(a) and (b) of this title, among those States satisfying the eligibility criteria of subsection (b)(1) of this section for the fourth year of participation that have submitted an application by a date that the Secretary may establish in an amount which bears the same ratio to such amount as the amount of such State's allotment under section 1484 of this title as modified by this subsection in such fiscal year bears to the amount of all such States' allotment under section 1484 of this title as modified by this subsection in such fiscal year.

(B) Fiscal year 1991 or 1992

The amount by which a State's allotment computed under section 1484 of this title for any State for fiscal years 1991 or 1992 exceeds the amount that such State may be allotted for such fiscal year under paragraph (4)(B) of this subsection shall be reallotted, notwithstanding the percentage limitations set forth in section 1484(a) and (b) of this title—

(i) first, among those States satisfying the eligibility criteria of subsection (c) of this section for the fifth year of participation that have submitted applications by a date that the Secretary may establish for each such year in an amount which bears the same ratio to such amount as the amount of such State's allotment under section 1484 of this title of all such States' allotment under section 1484 of this title as modified by this subsection in such fiscal year, except that no such State, by operation of this clause, shall receive an increase of more than 100 percent over the amount such State would have otherwise received under section 1484 of this title for the previous fiscal year;

(ii) second, if funds remain, among those States that have—

(I) satisfied the eligibility criteria of subsection (b)(1) of this section for the fourth year of participation;

(II) qualified for extended participation under this subsection; and

(III) not received a reallotment payment under clause (i),

in an amount which bears the same ratio to such amount as the amount of such State's allotment under section 1484 of this title as modified by this subsection in such fiscal year bears to the amount of all such States' allotment under section 1484 of this title as modified by this subsection in such fiscal year, except that no State, by operation of this clause, shall receive a reallotment payment that is larger than the payment such State would otherwise have received under section 1484 of this title for such year; and

(iii) third, if funds remain, among those States satisfying the eligibility criteria of subsection (c) of this section for the fifth year of participation that did not receive a reallotment payment under clause (ii) in an amount which bears the same ratio to such amount as the amount of such State's allotment under section 1484 of this title as modified by this subsection in such fiscal year bears to the amount of all such States' allotment under section 1484 of this title as modified by this subsection in such fiscal year.

(6) Definitions

For the purposes of this subsection, the term "State," except as provided in paragraph (4)(C), means—

(A) each of the 50 States, the District of Columbia, and the Commonwealth of Puerto Rico;

(B) each of the jurisdictions listed in section 1484(a), and

(C) the Department of the Interior.

§ 1476. Requirement for statewide system

(a) In general

A statewide system of coordinate, comprehensive, multidisciplinary, interagency programs providing appropriate early intervention services to all infants and toddlers with disabilities and their families, including Indian infants and toddlers with disabilities on reservations, shall include the minimum components under subsection (b) of this section.

(b) Minimum components

The statewide system required by subsection (a) of this section shall include, at a minimum—

(1) a definition of the term "developmentally delayed" that will be used by the State in carrying out programs under this subchapter,

(2) timetables for ensuring that appropriate early intervention services will be available to all infants and toddlers with disabilities in the State, including Indian infants and toddlers with disabilities on reservations, before the beginning of the fifth year of a State's participation under this subchapter,

(3) a timely, comprehensive, multidisciplinary evaluation of the functioning of each infant and toddler with a disability in the State and the needs of the families to appropriately assist in the development of the infant or toddler with a disability,

(4) for each infant and toddler with a disability in the State, an individualized family service plan in accordance with section 1477 of this title, including service coordination services in accordance with such service plan,

(5) a comprehensive child find system, consistent with subchapter II of this chapter, including a system for making referrals to service providers that includes timelines and provides for participation by primary referral sources,

(6) a public awareness program focusing on early identification of infants and toddlers with disabilities, including the preparation and dissemination by the lead agency to all primary referral sources of information materials for parents on the availability of early intervention services, and procedures for determining the extent to which primary referral sources, especially hospitals and physicians, disseminate information on the availability of early intervention services to parents of infants with disabilities,

(7) a central directory which includes early intervention services, resources, and experts available in the State and research and demonstration projects being conducted in the State,

(8) a comprehensive system of personnel development, including the training of paraprofessionals and the training of primary referral sources respecting the basic components of early intervention services available in the State, that is consistent with the comprehensive system of personnel development described in section 1413(a)(3) and that may include—

(A) implementing innovative strategies and activities for the recruitment and retention of early intervention service providers,

(B) promoting the preparation of early intervention providers who are fully and appropriately qualified to provide early intervention services under this part,

(C) training personnel to work in rural areas, and

(D) training personnel to coordinate transition services for infants and toddlers with disabilities from an early intervention program under this part to a preschool program under section 1419 of subchapter II.

(9) a single line of responsibility in a lead agency designated or established by the Governor for carrying out—

(A) the general administration, supervision of programs and activities receiving assistance under section 1473, and the monitoring of programs and activities used by the State to carry out this subchapter, whether or not such programs or activities are receiving assistance made available under section 1473, to ensure that the State complies with this subchapter, of this title to ensure compliance with this subchapter,

(B) the identification and coordination of all available resources within the State from Federal, State, local and private sources,

(C) the assignment of financial responsibility in accordance with 1478(a)(2) to the appropriate agencies,

(D) the development of procedures to ensure that services are provided to infants and toddlers with disabilities and their families in a timely manner pending the resolution of any disputes among public agencies or service providers,

(E) the resolution of intra- and interagency disputes, and

(F) the entry into formal interagency agreements that define the financial responsibility of each agency for paying for early intervention services (consistent with State law) and procedures for resolving disputes and that include all additional components necessary to ensure meaningful cooperation and coordination.

(10) a policy pertaining to the contracting or making of other arrangements with service providers to provide early intervention services in the State, consistent with the provisions of this subchapter, including the contents of the application used and the conditions of the contract or other arrangements,

(11) a procedure for securing timely reimbursement of funds used under this subchapter in accordance with section 1481(a) of this title,

(12) procedural safeguards with respect to programs under this subchapter as required by section 1480 of this title,

(13) policies and procedures relating to the establishment and maintenance of standards to ensure that personnel necessary to carry out this subchapter are appropriately and adequately prepared and trained, including—

(A) the establishment and maintenance of standards which are consistent with any State approved or recognized certification, licensing, registration, or other comparable requirements which apply to the area in which such personnel are providing early intervention services, and

(B) to the extent such standards are not based on the highest requirements in the State applicable to a specific profession or discipline, the steps the State is taking to require the retraining or hiring of personnel that meet appropriate professional requirements in the State, and

(14) a system for compiling data on the numbers of infants and toddlers with disabilities and their families in the State in need of appropriate early intervention services (which may be based on a sampling of data), the

numbers of such infants and toddlers and their families served, the types of services provided (which may be based on a sampling of data), and other information required by the Secretary.

§ 1477. Individualized family service plan

(a) Assessment and program development

Each infant or toddler with a disability and the infant's or toddler's family shall receive—

(1) a multidisciplinary assessment of the unique strengths and needs of the infant or toddler and the identification of services appropriate to meet such needs,

(2) a family-directed assessment of the resources, priorities, and concerns of the family and the identification of the supports and services necessary to enhance the family's capacity to meet the developmental needs of their infant or toddler with a disability, and

(3) a written individualized family service plan developed by a multidisciplinary team, including the parent or guardian, as required by subsection (d) of this section.

(b) Periodic review

The individualized family service plan shall be evaluated once a year and the family shall be provided a review of the plan at 6-month intervals (or more often where appropriate based on infant or toddler and family needs).

(c) Promptness after assessment

The individualized family service plan shall be developed within a reasonable time after the assessment required by subsection (a)(1) of this section is completed. With the parent's consent, early intervention services may commence prior to the completion of such assessment.

(d) Content of plan

The individualized family service plan shall be in writing and contain—

(1) a statement of the infant's or toddler's present levels of physical development, cognitive development, communication development, social or emotional development, and adaptive development, based on acceptable objective criteria,

(2) a statement of the family's resources, priorities, and concerns relating to enhancing the development of the family's infant or toddler with a disability,

(3) a statement of the major outcomes expected to be achieved for the infant or toddler and the family, and the criteria, procedures, and timelines used to determine the degree to which progress toward achieving the outcomes is being made and whether modifications or revisions of the outcomes or services are necessary,

(4) a statement of specific early intervention services necessary to meet the unique needs of the infant or toddler and the family, including the frequency, intensity, and the method of delivering services,

(5) a statement of the natural environments in which early intervention services shall appropriately be provided,

(6) the projected dates for initiation of services and the anticipated duration of such services,

(7) the name of the case manager (hereafter in this part referred to as the "service coordinator") from the profession most immediately relevant to the infant's or toddler's or family's needs (or who is otherwise qualified to carry out all applicable responsibilities under this subchapter) who will be responsible for the implementation of the plan and coordination with other agencies and persons, and

(8) the steps to be taken supporting the transition of the toddler with a disability to services provided under subchapter II of this chapter to the extent such services are considered appropriate.

(e) Parental consent.

The contents of the individualized family service plan shall be fully explained to the parents or guardian and informed written consent from such parents or guardian shall be obtained prior to the provision of early intervention services described in such plan. If such parents or guardian do not provide such consent with respect to a particular early intervention service, then the early intervention services to which such consent is obtained shall be provided.

§ 1478. State application and assurances

(a) Application

Any State desiring to receive a grant under section 1473 of this title for any year shall submit an application to the Secretary at such time and in such manner as the Secretary may reasonably require by regulation. Such an application shall contain—

(1) a designation of the lead agency in the State that will be responsible for the administration of funds provided under section 1473 of this title,

(2) a designation by the State of an individual or entity responsible for assigning financial responsibility among appropriate agencies,

(3) information demonstrating eligibility of the State under section 1474 of this title,

(4) the information or assurances required to demonstrate eligibility of the State for the particular year of participation under section 1475 of this title,

(5)(A) information demonstrating that the State has provided (i) public hearings, (ii) adequate notice of such hearings, and (iii) an opportunity for comment to the general public before the submission of such application and before the adoption by the State of the policies described in such application, and (B) a summary of the public comments and the State's responses,

(6) a description of the uses for which funds will be expended in accordance with this subchapter and, for the fifth and succeeding fiscal years, a description of the services to be provided,

(7) a description of the procedure used to ensure an equitable distribution of resources made available under this subchapter among all geographic areas within the State,

(8) a description of the policies and procedures used to ensure a smooth transition for individuals participating in the early intervention program under this subchapter who are eligible for participating in preschool programs under subchapter II, including a description of how the families will be included in the transitional plans and how the lead agency under this subchapter will notify the appropriate local educational agency or intermediate educational unit in which the child resides and convene, with the approval of the family, a conference between the lead agency, the family, and such agency or unit at least 90 days before such child is eligible for the preschool program under subchapter II in accordance with State law, and to review the child's program options, for the period commencing on the day a child turns 3 running through the remainder of the school year, and to establish a transition plan, and

(9) such other information and assurances as the Secretary may reasonably require by regulation.

(b) Statement of assurances

Any State desiring to receive a grant under section 1473 of this title shall file with the Secretary a statement at such time and in such manner as the Secretary may reasonably require by regulation. Such statement shall—

(1) assure that funds paid to the State under section 1473 of this title will be expended in accordance with this subchapter,

(2) contain assurances that the State will comply with the requirements of section 1481 of this title,

(3) provide satisfactory assurance that the control of funds provided under section 1473 of this title, and title to property derived therefrom, shall be in a public agency for the uses and purposes provided in this subchapter and that a public agency will administer such funds and property,

(4) provide for (A) making such reports in such form and containing such information as the Secretary may require to carry out the Secretary's functions under this subchapter, and (B) keeping such records and affording such access thereto as the Secretary may find necessary to assure the correctness and verification of such reports and proper disbursement of Federal funds under this subchapter,

(5) provide satisfactory assurance that Federal funds made available under section 1473(A) of this title will not be commingled with State funds, and (B) will be so used as to supplement and increase the level of State and local funds expended for infants and toddlers with disabilities and their families and in no case to supplant such State and local funds.

(6) provide satisfactory assurance that such fiscal control and fund accounting procedures will be adopted as may be necessary to assure proper disbursement of, and accounting for, Federal funds paid under section 1473 of this title to the State,

(7) beginning in fiscal year 1992, provide satisfactory assurance that policies and practices have been adopted to ensure meaningful involvement of traditionally underserved groups, including minority, low-income, and

rural families, in the planning and implementation of all the requirements of this part and to ensure that such families have access to culturally competent services within their local areas, and

(8) such other information and assurances as the Secretary may reasonably require by regulation.

(c) Approval of application and assurances required

No State may receive a grant under section 1473 of this title unless the Secretary has approved the application and statement of assurances of that State. The Secretary shall not disapprove such an application or statement of assurances unless the Secretary determines, after notice and opportunity for a hearing, that the application or statement of assurances fails to comply with the requirements of this section.

§ 1479. Use of funds

In addition to using funds provided under section 1473 of this title to plan, develop, and implement the statewide system required by section 1476 of this title, a State may use such funds—

(1) for direct services for infants and toddlers with disabilities and their families that are not otherwise provided from other public or private sources,

(2) to expand and improve on services for infants and toddlers with disabilities and their families that are otherwise available, and

(3) to provide a free appropriate public education, in accordance with subchapter II, to children with disabilities from their third birthday to the beginning of the following school year.

§ 1480. Procedural safeguards

The procedural safeguards required to be included in a statewide system under section 1476(b)(12) of this title shall provide, at a minimum, the following:

(1) The timely administrative resolution of complaints by parents. Any party aggrieved by the findings and decision regarding an administrative complaint shall have the right to bring a civil action with respect to the complaint, which action may be brought in any State court of competent jurisdiction or in a district court of the United States without regard to the amount in controversy. In any action brought under this paragraph, the court shall receive the records of the administrative proceedings, shall hear additional evidence at the request of a party, and, basing its decision on the preponderance of the evidence, shall grant such relief as the court determines is appropriate, including the right of parents or guardians to written notice of and written consent to the exchange of information among agencies consistent with Federal and State law.

(2) The right to confidentiality of personally identifiable information, including the right of parents or guardians to written notice of and written consent to the exchange of such information among agencies consistent with Federal and State law.

(3) The right of the parents or guardian to determine whether they, their infant or toddler, or other family members will accept or decline any early intervention service under this subchapter in accordance with State law without jeopardizing other early intervention services under this subchapter.

(4) The opportunity for parents or a guardian to examine records relating to assessment, screening, eligibility determinations, and the development and implementation of the individualized family service plan.

(5) Procedures to protect the rights of the infant or toddler with a disability whenever the parents or guardian of the child are not known or unavailable or the child is a ward of the State, including the assignment of an individual (who shall not be an employee of the State agency providing services) to act as a surrogate for the parents or guardian.

(6) Written prior notice to the parents or guardian of the infant or toddler with a disability whenever the State agency or service provider proposes to initiate or change or refuses to initiate or change the identification, evaluation, placement, or the provision of appropriate early intervention services to the infant or toddler with a disability.

(7) Procedures designed to assure that the notice required by paragraph (6) fully informs the parents or guardian, in the parents' or guardian's native language, unless it clearly is not feasible to do so, of all procedures available pursuant to this section.

(8) During the pendency of any proceeding or action involving a complaint, unless the State agency and the parents or guardian otherwise agree, the child shall continue to receive the appropriate early intervention services currently being provided or, if applying for initial services, shall receive the services not in dispute.

§ 1481. Payor of last resort

(a) Nonsubstitution

Funds provided under section 1473 of this title may not be used to satisfy a financial commitment for services which would have been paid for from another public or private source but for the enactment of this subchapter, except that whenever considered necessary to prevent a delay in the receipt of appropriate early intervention services by the infant or toddler or family in a timely fashion, funds provided under section 1473 of this title may be used to pay the provider of services pending reimbursement from the agency which has ultimate responsibility for the payment.

(b) Reduction of other benefits

Nothing in this subchapter shall be construed to permit the State to reduce medical or other assistance available or to alter eligibility under title V of the Social Security Act (relating to maternal and child health) or title XIX of the Social Security Act (relating to medicaid for infants and toddlers with disabilities) within the State.

§ 1482. State Interagency Coordinating Council

(a) Establishment

(1) Any State which desires to receive financial assistance under section 1473 of this title shall establish a State Interagency Coordinating Council composed of at least 15 members but not more than 25 members, unless the State provides sufficient justification for a greater number of members in the application submitted under section 1478.

(2) The Council shall be appointed by the Governor. In making appointments to the Council, the Governor shall ensure that the membership of the Council reasonably represents the population of the State.

(3) The Governor shall designate a member of the Council to serve as the chairperson of the Council, or shall require the Council to so designate such a member. Any member of the Council who is a representative of the lead agency designated under section 1476(b)(9) may not serve as the chairperson of the Council.

(b) Composition

(1) The Council shall be composed as follows:

(A) At least 20 percent of the members shall be parents, including minority parents, of infants or toddlers with disabilities or children with disabilities aged 12 or younger, with knowledge of, or experience with, programs for infants and toddlers with disabilities. At least one such member shall be a parent of an infant or toddler with a disability or a child with a disability aged 6 or younger.

(B) At least 20 percent of the members shall be public or private providers of early intervention services.

(C) At least one member shall be from the State legislature.

(D) At least one member shall be involved in personnel preparation.

(E) At least one member shall be from each of the State agencies involved in the provision of, or payment for, early intervention services to infants and toddlers with disabilities and their families and shall have sufficient authority to engage in policy planning and implementation on behalf of such agencies.

(F) At least one member shall be from the State educational agency responsible for preschool services to children with disabilities and shall have sufficient authority to engage in policy planning and implementation on behalf of such agency.

(G) At least one member shall be from the agency responsible for the State governance of insurance, especially in the area of health insurance.

(2) The Council may include other members selected by the Governor, including a representative from the Bureau of Indian Affairs, or where there is no BIA operated or funded school, from the Indian Health Service or the tribe/tribal council.

(c) Meetings

The Council shall meet at least quarterly and in such places as it deems necessary. The meetings shall be publicly announced, and, to the extent appropriate, open and accessible to the general public.

(d) Management authority

Subject to the approval of the Governor, the Council may prepare and approve a budget using funds under this subchapter to conduct hearings and forums, to reimburse members of the Council for reasonable and necessary expenses for attending Council meetings and performing Council duties (including child care for parent representatives), to pay compensation to a member of the Council if such member is not employed or must forfeit wages from other employment when performing official Council business, to hire staff, and to obtain other services of such professional, technical, and clerical personnel as may be necessary to carry out its functions under this subchapter.

(e) Functions of Council

(1) The Council shall—
    (A) advise and assist the lead agency designated or established under section 1476(b)(9) of this title in the performance of the responsibilities set out in such section, particularly the identification of the sources of fiscal and other support for services for early intervention programs, assignment of financial responsibility to the appropriate agency, and the promotion of the interagency agreements,
    (B) advise and assist the lead agency in the preparation of applications and amendments thereto,
    (C) advise and assist the state educational agency regarding the transition of toddlers with disabilities to services provided under subchapter II, to the extent such services are appropriate, and
    (D) prepare and submit an annual report to the Governor and to the Secretary on the status of early intervention programs for infants and toddlers with disabilities and their families operated within the State.
(2) The Council may advise and assist the lead agency and State educational agency regarding the provision of appropriate services for children aged birth to 5, inclusive.

(f) Conflict of interest

No member of the Council shall cast a vote on any matter which would provide direct financial benefit to that member or otherwise give the appearance of a conflict of interest under State law.

(g) Use of existing Councils

To the extent that a State has established a Council before September 1, 1986, that is comparable to the Council described in this section, such Council shall be considered to be in compliance with this section. Within 4 years after the date the State accepts funds under section 1473 of this title, such State shall establish a council that complies in full with this section.

§ 1483. Federal administration

Sections 1416, 1417 and 1420 of this title shall, to the extent not inconsistent with this subchapter, apply to the program authorized by this subchapter, except that—

(1) any reference to a State educational agency shall be deemed to be a reference to the State agency established or designated under section 1476(b)(9) of this section,

(2) any reference to the education of children with disabilities and the education of all children with disabilities and the provision of free public education to all children with disabilities shall be deemed to be a reference to the provision of services to infants and toddlers with disabilities in accordance with this subchapter, and

(3) any reference to local educational agencies and intermediate educational agencies shall be deemed to be a reference to local service providers under this subchapter.

§ 1484. Allocation of funds

(a) Territories and insular possessions

From the sums appropriated to carry out this subchapter for any fiscal year, the Secretary may reserve 1 percent for payments to Guam, American Samoa, the Virgin Islands, the Republic of the Marshall Islands, the Federated States of Micronesia, the Republic of Palau, and the Commonwealth of Northern Mariana Islands in accordance with their respective needs.

(b) Payments to Secretary of Interior for assistance to Indians

(1) The Secretary shall, subject to this subsection, make payments to the Secretary of the Interior to be distributed to tribes or tribal organizations (as defined under section 4 of the Indian Self-Determination and Education Assistance Act) or consortium of the above entities for the coordination of assistance in the provision of early intervention services by the States to infants and toddlers with disabilities and their families on reservations served by elementary and secondary schools for Indian children operated or funded by the Department of the Interior. The amount of such payment for any fiscal year shall be 1.25 percent of the aggregate of the amount available to all States under this part for that fiscal year.

(2) The Secretary of the Interior shall distribute the total amount of the 1.25 percent under paragraph (1) in the following manner:

(A) For the first fiscal year, each tribe or tribal organization shall receive an amount proportionate to the amount of weighted student units for special education programs for BIA operated or funded schools serving such reservation generated under the formula established under section 1128 of the Education Amendments of 1978, divided by the total number of such students in all BIA operated or funded schools.

(B) For each fiscal year thereafter, each tribe or tribal organization shall receive an amount based on the number of infants and toddlers residing on the reservation as determined annually divided by the total of such children served by all tribes or tribal organizations.

(3) To receive a payment under this paragraph, the tribe or tribal organization shall submit such figures to the Secretary of the Interior as are needed to determine the amounts to be allocated under paragraph (2).

(4) The funds received by a tribe or tribal organization shall be used to assist States in child find, screening, and other procedures for the early identification of Indian children aged 0-2, inclusive, and for parent training. Such funds may also be used to provide early intervention services in accordance with this part. These activities may be carried out directly or through contracts or cooperative agreements with the BIA, local educational agencies, and other public or private nonprofit organizations. The tribe and tribal organization is encouraged to involve Indian parents in the development and implementation of these activities. The above entities shall, as appropriate, make referrals to local, State, or Federal entities for the provision of services or further diagnosis.

(5) To be eligible to receive a grant pursuant to paragraph (2), the tribe or tribal organization shall make a biennial report to the Secretary of the Interior of activities undertaken under this subsection, including the number of contracts and cooperative agreements entered into, the number of children contacted and receiving services for each year, and the estimated number of children needing services during the 2 years following the one in which the report is made. The Secretary of the Interior shall include a summary of this information on a biennial basis to the Secretary of Education along with such other information as required under section 1411(f)(3)(D) of this Act. The Secretary of Education may require any additional information from the Secretary of the Interior.

(6) None of the funds under this subsection can be used by the Secretary of the Interior for administrative purposes, including child count, and the provision of technical assistance.

(c) States

(1) For each of the fiscal years 1987 through 1994 from the funds remaining after the reservation and payments under subsections (a) and (b) of this section, the Secretary shall allot to each State an amount which bears the same ratio to the amount of such remainder as the number of infants and toddlers in the State bears to the number of infants and toddlers in all States, except that no State shall receive less than 0.5 percent of such remainder, or $500,000, whichever is greater.

(2) For the purpose of paragraph (1)—

(A) the terms "infants" and "toddlers" mean children from birth to age 2, inclusive, and

(B) the term "State" does not include the jurisdictions described in subsection (a) of this section.

(d) Election by State not to receive allotment

If any State elects not to receive its allotment under subsection (c)(1) of this section, the Secretary shall reallot, among the remaining States, amounts from such State in accordance with such subsection.

§ 1484a. Federal interagency coordinating council

(a) Establishment and Purpose.

(1) In general

The Secretary shall establish a Federal Interagency Coordinating Council in order to—

(A) minimize duplication of programs and activities relating to early intervention services for infants and toddlers with disabilities and their families, and preschool services for children with disabilities, across Federal, State, and local agencies;

(B) ensure the effective coordination of Federal early intervention and preschool programs and policies across Federal agencies;

(C) coordinate the provision of Federal technical assistance and support activities to States;

(D) identify gaps in Federal agency programs and services; and

(E) identify barriers to Federal interagency cooperation.

(2) Appointments

The council established under paragraph (1) (hereafter in this section referred to as the "Council") and the chairperson of the Council shall be appointed by the Secretary in consultation with other appropriate Federal agencies. In making the appointments, the Secretary shall ensure that each member has sufficient authority to engage in policy planning and implementation on behalf of the department, agency, or program that such member represents.

(b) Composition

The Council shall be composed of—

(1) a representative of the Office of Special Education Programs;

(2) a representative of the National Institute on Disability and Rehabilitation Research;

(3) a representative of the Maternal and Child Health Services Block Grant Program;

(4) a representative of programs assisted under the Developmental Disabilities Assistance and Bill of Rights Act;

(5) a representative of the Health Care Financing Administration;

(6) a representative of the Division of Birth Defects and Developmental Disabilities of the Centers for Disease Control;

(7) a representative of the Social Security Administration;

(8) a representative of the Special Supplemental Food Program for Women, Infants and Children of the Department of Agriculture;

(9) a representative of the National Institute of Mental Health;

(10) a representative of the National Institute of Child Health and Human Development;

(11) a representative of the Bureau of Indian Affairs of the Department of the Interior;

(12) a representative of the Indian Health Service;

(13) a representative of the Surgeon General;

(14) a representative of the Department of Defense;

(15) a representative of the Administration for Children and Families;

(16) a representative of the Alcohol, Drug Abuse and Mental Health Administration;

(17) a representative of the Pediatric Aids Health Care Demonstration Program in the Public Health Service;

(18) at least 3 parents of children with disabilities age 12 or under, of whom at least one must have a child with a disability under the age of 6;

(19) at least 2 representatives of State lead agencies for early intervention services to infants and toddlers, one of which must be a representative of a State educational agency and the other a representative of a noneducational agency;

(20) other members representing appropriate agencies involved in the provision of, or payment for, early intervention services and special education and related services to infants and toddlers with disabilities and their families and preschool children with disabilities; and

(21) other persons appointed by the Secretary.

(c) Meetings

The Council shall meet at least quarterly and in such places as the Council deems necessary. The meetings shall be publicly announced, and, to the extent appropriate, open and accessible to the general public.

(d) Functions of the Council

The Council shall—

(1) advise and assist the Secretary in the performance of the Secretary's responsibilities described in this part;

(2) conduct policy analyses of Federal programs related to the provision of early intervention services and special educational and related services to infants and toddlers with disabilities and their families, and preschool children with disabilities, in order to determine areas of conflict, overlap, duplication, or inappropriate omission;

(3) identify strategies to address issues described in paragraph (2);

(4) develop and recommend joint policy memoranda concerning effective interagency collaboration, including modifications to regulations, and the elimination of barriers to interagency programs and activities;

(5) coordinate technical assistance and disseminate information on best practices, effective program coordination strategies, and recommendations for improved early intervention programming for infants and toddlers with disabilities and their families and preschool children with disabilities; and

(6) facilitate activities in support of States' interagency coordination efforts.

(e) Conflict of Interest

No member of the Council shall cast a vote on any matter that would provide direct financial benefit to that member or otherwise give the appearance of a conflict of interest under Federal law.

§ 1485. Authorization of appropriations

There are authorized to be appropriated to carry out this subchapter $220,000,000 for fiscal year 1992, and such sums as may be necessary for each of the fiscal years 1993 and 1994.

APPENDIX B

FEDERAL REGULATIONS
AND
AMENDMENTS THROUGH 1992

[The most important federal regulations and amendments affecting the education of children with disabilities, Parts 300 and 104 of Title 34 of the Code of Federal Regulations, have been reproduced here in their entirety as promulgated by the U.S. Department of Education.]

Subpart A-General

Purpose, Applicability, and Regulations That Apply to this Program

§ 300.1 Purpose.

The purpose of this part is:

(a) To ensure that all children with disabilities have available to them a free appropriate public education which includes special education and related services to meet their unique needs;

(b) To ensure that the rights of children with disabilities and their parents are protected;

(c) To assist States and localities to provide for the education of all children with disabilities; and

(d) To assess and ensure the effectiveness of efforts to educate those children.

(Authority: 20 U.S.C. 1401 Note)

§ 300.2 Applicability to State, local, and private agencies.

(a) *States.* This part applies to each state that receives payments under Part B of the Act.

(b) *Public agencies within the State.* The State plan is submitted by the State educational agency on behalf of the State as a whole. Therefore, the provisions of this part apply to all political subdivisions of the State that are involved in the education of children with disabilities. These would include:

(1) The State educational agency;

(2) Local educational agencies and intermediate educational units;

(3) Other State agencies and schools such as Departments of Mental Health and Welfare and State schools for students with deafness or students with blindness; and

(4) State correctional facilities.

(c) *Private schools and facilities.* Each public agency in the State is responsible for ensuring that the rights and protections under this part are given to children referred to or placed in private schools and facilities by that public agency. (See §§ 300.400-300.403)

(Authority: 20 U.S.C. 1412(1), (6); 1413(a); 1413(a)(4)(B))

Note: The requirements of this part are binding on each public agency that has direct or delegated authority to provide special education and related services in a State that receives funds under Part B of the Act, regardless of whether that agency is receiving funds under Part B.

§ 300.3 Regulations that apply.

The following regulations apply to this program:

(a) 34 CFR part 76 (State-Administered Programs) except for §§ 76.780-76.782.

(b) 34 CFR part 77 (Definitions).

(c) 34 CFR part 79 (Intergovernmental Review of Department of Education Programs and Activities).

(d) 34 CFR part 80 (Uniform Administrative Requirements for Grants and Cooperative Agreements to State and Local Governments).

(e) 34 CFR part 81 (General Education Provisions Act —Enforcement).

(f) 34 CFR part 82 (New Restrictions on Lobbying).

(g) 34 CFR part 85 (Governmentwide Debarment and Suspension (Nonprocurement) and Governmentwide Requirements for Drug-Free Workplace (Grants)).

(h) 34 CFR part 86 (Drug-Free Schools and Campuses).

(i)   The regulations in this part—34 CFR part 300 (Assistance to States for Education of Children with Disabilities).

(Authority: 20 U.S.C. 1221e-3(a)(1))

Definitions

Note 1: Definitions of terms that are used throughout these regulations are included in this subpart. Other terms are defined in the specific subparts in which they are used. Below is a list of those terms and the specific sections and subparts in which they are defined:

Appropriate professional requirements in the
State (§ 300.153(a)(1))
Average per pupil expenditure in public
elementary and secondary schools in the
United States (§ 300.701(c))
Consent (§ 300.500)
Destruction (§ 300.560)
Direct services (§ 300.370(b)(1)
Evaluation (§ 300.500)
First priority children (§ 300.320(a))
Highest requirements in the State applicable to a
specific profession or discipline
(§ 300.153(a)(2))
Independent educational evaluation
(§ 300.503(a)(3)(i))
Individualized education program (§ 300.340)
Participating agency, as used in the
confidentiality requirements in §§ 300.560-
300.576 (§ 300.340(b))
Party or parties (§ 300.584(a))
Personally identifiable (§ 300.500)
Private school children with disabilities
(§ 300.450)
Profession or discipline (§ 300.153(a)(3))
Public expense (§ 300.503(a)(3)(ii))
Second priority children (§ 300.320(b))
Special definition of "State" (§ 300.700)
State-approved or recognized certification,
licensing, registration, or other comparable
requirements (§ 300.153(a)(4))
Support services (§ 300.370(b)(2))

Note 2: Below are abbreviations for selected terms that are used throughout these regulations:

"FAPE" means "free appropriate public education."

"IEP" means "individualized education program."

"IEU" means "intermediate educational unit."
"LEA" means "local educational agency."
"LRE" means "least restrictive environment."
"SEA" means "State educational agency."

As appropriate, each abbreviation is used interchangeably with its nonabbreviated term.

§ 300.4 Act.

As used in this part, "Act" means the Individuals with Disabilities Education Act, formerly the Education of the Handicapped Act.

(Authority: 20 U.S.C. 1400)

§ 300.5 Assistive technology device.

As used in this part, "assistive technology device" means any item, piece of equipment, or product system, whether acquired commercially off the shelf, modified, or customized, that is used to increase, maintain, or improve the functional capabilities of children with disabilities.

(Authority: 20 U.S.C. 1401(a)(25))

§ 300.6 Assistive technology service.

As used in this part, "assistive technology service" means any service that directly assists a child with a disability in the selection, acquisition, or use of an assistive technology device.
The term includes—

(a) The evaluation of the needs of a child with a disability, including a functional evaluation of the child in the child's customary environment;

(b) Purchasing, leasing, or otherwise providing for the acquisition of assistive technology devices by children with disabilities;

(c) Selecting, designing, fitting, customizing, adapting, applying, retaining, repairing, or replacing assistive technology devices;

(d) Coordinating and using other therapies, interventions, or services with assistive technology devices, such as those associated with existing education and rehabilitation plans and programs;

(e) Training or technical assistance for professionals (including individuals providing education or rehabilitative services), employers, or other individuals who provide services to, employ, or are otherwise substantially involved in the major life functions of children with disabilities.

(Authority: 20 U.S.C. 1401(a)(26))

Note: The definitions of "assistive technology device" and "assistive technology service" used in this part are taken directly from section 602(a)(25)-(26) of the Act, but in accordance with Part B, the statutory reference to "individual with a disability" has been replaced with "child with a disability." The Act's definition of "assistive technology device" and "assistive technology service" incorporate verbatim the definitions of these terms used in the Technology-Related Assistance for Individuals with Disabilities Act of 1988.

§ 300.7 Children with Disabilities.

(a)(1) As used in this part, the term "children with disabilities" means those children evaluated in accordance with §§ 300.530-300.534 as having mental retardation, hearing impairments including deafness, speech or language impairments, visual impairments including blindness, serious emotional disturbance, orthopedic impairments, autism, traumatic brain injury, other health impairments, specific learning disabilities, deaf-blindness, or multiple disabilities, who because of those impairments need special education and related services.

(2) The term "children with disabilities" for children ages 3 through 5 may, at a State's discretion, include children—

(i) Who are experiencing developmental delays, as defined by the State and measured by appropriate diagnostic instruments and procedures, in one or more of the following areas: physical development, cognitive development, communication development, social or emotional development, or adaptive development; and

(ii) Who, for that reason, need special education and related services.

(b) The terms used in this definition are defined as follows:

(1) "Autism" means a developmental disability significantly affecting verbal and nonverbal communication and social interaction, generally evident before age 3, that adversely affects a child's educational performance. Other characteristics often associated with autism are engagement in repetitive activities and stereotyped movements, resistance to environmental change or change in daily routines, and unusual responses to sensory experiences. The term does not apply if a child's educational performance is adversely affected primarily because the child has a serious emotional disturbance, as defined in paragraph (b)(9) of this section.

(2) "Deaf-blindness" means concomitant hearing and visual impairments, the combination of which causes such severe communication and other developmental and educational problems that they cannot be accommodated in special education programs solely for children with deafness or children with blindness.

(3) "Deafness" means hearing impairment that is so severe that the child is impaired in processing linguistic information through hearing, with or without amplification, that adversely affects educational performance.

(4) "Hearing impairment" means an impairment in hearing, whether permanent or fluctuating, that adversely affects a child's educational performance but which is not included under the definition of deafness in this section.

(5) "Mental retardation" means significantly subaverage general intellectual functioning existing concurrently with deficits in adaptive behavior and manifested during the developmental period, which adversely affects a child's educational performance.

(6) "Multiple disabilities" means concomitant impairments (such as mental retardation-blindness, mental retardation-orthopedic impairment, etc.), the combination of which causes such severe educational problems that they cannot be accommodated in special education programs solely for one of the impairments. The term does not include deaf-blindness.

(7) "Orthopedic impairment" means a severe orthopedic impairment which adversely affects a child's educational performance. The term includes impairments caused by congenital anomaly (e.g., clubfoot, absence of some member, etc.), impairments caused by disease (e.g. poliomyelitis, bone tuberculosis, etc.), and impairments from other causes (e.g., cerebral palsy, amputations, and fractures or burns, which cause contractures).

(8) "Other health impairment" means having limited strength, vitality or alertness, due to chronic or acute health problems such as a heart condition, tuberculosis, rheumatic fever, nephritis, asthma, sickle cell anemia, hemophilia, epilepsy, lead poisoning, leukemia, or diabetes that adversely affects a child's educational performance.

(9) "Serious emotional disturbance" is defined as follows:

(i) The term means a condition exhibiting one or more of the following characteristics over a long period of time and to a marked degree, which adversely affects educational performance:

(A) An inability to learn which cannot be explained by intellectual, sensory, or health factors;

(B) An inability to build or maintain satisfactory interpersonal relationships with peers and teachers;

(C) Inappropriate types of behavior or feelings under normal circumstances;

(D) A general pervasive mood of unhappiness or depression; or

(E) A tendency to develop physical symptoms or fears associated with personal or school problems.

(ii) The term includes schizophrenia. The term does not include children who are socially maladjusted, unless it is determined that they have a serious emotional disturbance.

(10) "Specific learning disability" means a disorder in one or more of the basic psychological processes involved in understanding or in using language, spoken or written, which may manifest

itself in an imperfect ability to listen, think, speak, read, write, spell, or to do mathematical calculations. The term includes such conditions as perceptual disabilities, brain injury, brain dysfunction, dyslexia, and developmental aphasia. The term does not apply to children who have learning problems which are primarily the result of visual, hearing, or motor handicaps, of mental retardation of emotional disturbance or of environmental, cultural, or economic disadvantage.

(11) "Speech or language impairment" means a communication disorder such as stuttering, impaired articulation, a language impairment, or a voice impairment, that adversely affects a child's educational performance.

(12) "Traumatic brain injury" means an acquired injury to the brain caused by an external physical force, resulting in total or partial functional disability or psychosocial impairment, or both, that adversely affects a child's educational performance. The term applies to open or closed head injuries resulting in impairments in one or more areas, such as cognition; language; memory; attention; reasoning; abstract thinking; judgment; problem-solving; sensory, perceptual and motor abilities; psychosocial behavior; physical functions; information processing; and speech. The term does not apply to brain injuries that are congenital or degenerative, or brain injuries induced by birth trauma.

(13) "Visual impairment including blindness" means an impairment in vision that, even with correction, adversely affects a child's educational performance. The term includes both partial sight and blindness.
(Authority: 20 U.S.C. 1401(a)(1))

Note: If a child manifests characteristics of the disability category "autism" after age 3, that child still could be diagnosed as having "autism" if the criteria in paragraph (b)(1) of this section are satisfied.

§ 300.8 Free appropriate public education.

As used in this part, the term "free appropriate public education" means special education and related services that—

(a) Are provided at public expense, under public supervision and direction, and without charge;

(b) Meet the standards of the SEA, including the requirements of this part;

(c) Include preschool, elementary school, or secondary school education in the State involved; and

(d) Are provided in conformity with an IEP that meets the requirements of §§ 300.340-300.350.
(Authority: 20 U.S.C. 1401(a)(18))

§ 300.9 Include.

As used in this part, the term "include" means that the items named are not all of the possible items that are covered, whether like or unlike the ones named.
(Authority: 20 U.S.C. 1417(b))

§ 300.7 Intermediate educational unit.

As used in this part, the term "intermediate educational unit" means any public authority, other than an LEA, that—

(a) Is under the general supervision of an SEA;

(b) Is established by State law for the purpose of providing free public education on a regional basis; and

(c) Provides special education and related services to children with disabilities within that State.
(Authority: 20 U.S.C. 1401(a)(23))

§ 300.11 Local educational agency.

(a) [Reserved]

(b) For the purposes of this part, the term "local educational agency" also includes intermediate educational units.
(Authority: 20 U.S.C. 1401(a)(8))

§ 300.12 Native language.

As used in this part, the term "native language" has the meaning given that term by section 703(a)(2) of the Bilingual Education Act, which provides as follows:

The term "native language," when used with reference to a person of limited English proficiency, means the language normally used by that individual, or in the case of a child, the language normally used by the parents of the child.
(Authority: 20 U.S.C. 3283(a)(2); 1401(a)(22))

Note. Section 602(a)(22) of the Act states that the term "native language" has the same meaning as the definition from section 703(a)(2) of the Bilingual Education Act. (The term is used in the prior notice and evaluation sections under § 300.505(b)(2) and § 300.532(a)(1).) In using the term, the Act does not prevent the following means of communication:

(1) In all direct contact with a child (including evaluation of the child), communication would be in the language normally used by the child and not that of the parents, if there is a difference between the two.

(2) For individuals with deafness or blindness, or for individuals with no written language, the mode of communication would be that normally used by the individual (such as sign language, braille, or oral communication).

§ 300.13 Parent.

As used in this part, the term "parent" means a parent, a guardian, a person acting as a parent of a child, or a surrogate parent who has been appointed in accordance with § 300.514. The term does not include the State if the child is a ward of the State.

(Authority: 20 U.S.C. 1415)

Note. The term "parent" is defined to include persons acting in the place of a parent, such as a grandmother or stepparent with whom a child lives, as well as persons who are legally responsible for a child's welfare.

§ 300.14 Public agency.

As used in this part, the term "public agency" includes the SEA, LEAs, IEUs, and any other political subdivision of the State which are responsible for providing education to children with disabilities.

(Authority: 20 U.S.C. 1412(2)(B); 1412(6); 1413(a))

§ 300.15 Qualified.

As used in this part, the term "qualified" means that a person has met SEA approved or recognized certification, licensing, registration, or other comparable requirements that apply to the area in which he or she is providing special education or related services.

(Authority: 20 U.S.C. 1417(b))

§ 300.16 Related services.

(a) As used in this part, the term "related services" means transportation and such developmental, corrective, and other supportive services as are required to assist a child with a disability to benefit from special education, and includes speech pathology and audiology, psychological services, physical and occupational therapy, recreation, including therapeutic recreation, early identification and assessment of disabilities in children, counseling services, including rehabilitation counseling, and medical services for diagnostic or evaluation purposes. The term also includes school health services, social work services in schools, and parent counseling and training.

(b) The terms used in this definition are defined as follows:

(1) "Audiology" includes:

(i) Identification of children with hearing loss;

(ii) Determination of the range, nature, and degree of hearing loss, including referral for medical or other professional attention for the habilitation of hearing;

(iii) Provision of habilitative activities, such as language habilitation, auditory training, speech reading (lip-reading), hearing evaluation, and speech conservation;

(iv) Creation and administration of programs for prevention of hearing loss;

(v) Counseling and guidance of pupils, parents, and teachers regarding hearing loss; and

(vi) Determination of the child's need for group and individual amplification, selecting and fitting an appropriate aid, and evaluating the effectiveness of amplification.

(2) "Counseling services" means services provided by qualified social workers, psychologists, guidance counselors, or other qualified personnel.

(3) "Early identification and assessment of disabilities in children" means the implementation of a formal plan for identifying a disability as early as possible in a child's life.

(4) "Medical services" means services provided by a licensed physician to determine a child's medically related disability that results in the child's need for special education and related services.

(5) "Occupational therapy" includes:

(i) Improving, developing or restoring functions impaired or lost through illness, injury, or deprivation;

(ii) Improving ability to perform tasks for independent functioning when functions are impaired or lost; and

(iii) Preventing, through early intervention, initial or further impairment or loss of function.

(6) "Parent counseling and training" means assisting parents in understanding the special needs of their child and providing parents with information about child development.

(7) "Physical therapy" means services provided by a qualified physical therapist.

(8) "Psychological services" includes—

(i) Administering psychological and educational tests and other assessment procedures;

(ii) Interpreting assessment results;

(iii) Obtaining, integrating, and interpreting information about child behavior and conditions relating to learning.

(iv) Consulting with other staff members in planning school programs to meet the special needs of children as indicated by psychological tests, interviews, and behavioral evaluations; and

(v) Planning and managing a program of psychological services, including psychological counseling for children and parents.

(9) "Recreation" includes:

(i) Assessment of leisure function;

(ii) Therapeutic recreation services;

(iii) Recreation programs in school and community agencies; and

(iv) Leisure education.

(10) "Rehabilitation counseling services" means services provided by qualified personnel in individual or group sessions that focus specifically on career development, employment preparation,

achieving independence, and integration in the workplace and community of a student with a disability. The term also includes vocational rehabilitation services provided to students with disabilities by vocational rehabilitation programs funded under the Rehabilitation Act of 1973, as amended.

(11) "School health services" means services provided by a qualified school nurse or other qualified person.

(12) "Social work services in schools" includes—

(i) Preparing a social or developmental history on a child with a disability;

(ii) Group and individual counseling with the child and family;

(iii) Working with those problems in a child's living situation (home, school, and community) that affect the child's adjustment in school; and

(iv) Mobilizing school and community resources to enable the child to learn as effectively as possible in his or her educational program.

(13) "Speech pathology" includes—

(i) Identification of children with speech or language impairments;

(ii) Diagnosis and appraisal of specific speech or language impairments;

(iii) Referral for medical or other professional attention necessary for the habilitation of speech or language impairments;

(iv) Provision of speech and language services for the habilitation or prevention of communicative impairments; and

(v) Counseling and guidance of parents, children, and teachers regarding speech and language impairments.

(13) "Transportation" includes—

(i) Travel to and from school and between schools;

(ii) Travel in and around school buildings; and

(iii) Specialized equipment (such as special or adapted buses, lifts, and ramps), if required to provide special transportation for a child with a disability.

(Authority 20 U.S.C. 1401(a)(17))

Note. With respect to related services, the Senate Report states: The Committee bill provides a definition of related services, making clear that all such related services may not be required for each individual child and that such term includes early identification and assessment of handicapping conditions and the provision of services to minimize the effects of such conditions.

(S.Rep.No. 94-168, p.12 (1975))

The list of related services is not exhaustive and may include other developmental, corrective, or supportive services (such as artistic and cultural programs, and art, music, and dance therapy), if

they are required to assist a child with a disability to benefit from special education.

There are certain kinds of services which might be provided by persons from varying professional backgrounds and with a variety of operational titles, depending upon requirements in individual States. For example, counseling services might be provided by social workers, psychologists, or guidance counselors, and psychological testing might be done by qualified psychological examiners, psychometrists, or psychologists, depending upon State standards.

Each related service defined under this part may include appropriate administrative and supervisory activities that are necessary for program planning, management, and evaluation.

300.17 Special education.

(a) (1) As used in this part, the term "special education" means specially designed instruction, at no cost to the parents, to meet the unique needs of a child with a disability, including—

(i) Instruction conducted in the classroom, in the home, in hospitals and institutions, and in other settings; and

(ii) Instruction in physical education.

(2) The term includes speech pathology, or any other related service, if the service consists of specially designed instruction, at no cost to the parents, to meet the unique needs of a child with a disability, and is considered special education rather than a related service under State standards.

(3) The term also includes vocational education if it consists of specially designed instruction, at no cost to the parents, to meet the unique needs of a child with a disability.

(b) The terms in this definition are defined as follows:

(1) "At no cost" means that all specially designed instruction is provided without charge, but does not preclude incidental fees which are normally charged to nondisabled students or their parents as a part of the regular education program.

(2) "Physical education" is defined as follows:

(i) The term means the development of—

(A) Physical and motor fitness;

(B) Fundamental motor skills and patterns; and

(C) Skills in aquatics, dance, and individual and group games and sports (including intramural and lifetime sports).

(ii) The term includes special physical education, adaptive physical education, movement education, and motor development.

(Authority: 20 U.S.C. 1401(a)(16))

(3) *Vocational education* means organized educational programs which are directly related to

the preparation of individuals for paid or unpaid employment, or for additional preparation for a career requiring other than a baccalaureate or advanced degree.
(Authority: 20 U.S.C. 1401(16))

Note 1: The definition of special education is a particularly important one under these regulations, since a child is not handicapped unless he or she needs special education. (See the definition of children with disabilities in § 300.7.) The definition of related services (§ 300.16) also depends on this definition, since a related service must be necessary for a child to benefit from special education. Therefore, if a child does not need special education, there can be no related services, and the child is not a child with a disability and is therefore not covered under the Act.

Note 2: The above definition of vocational education is taken from the Carl D. Perkins Vocational and Applied Technology Education Act (Pub.L. 98-524, as amended by Pub.L. 101-392). Section 118(a)(3)(A)-(B) of this statute further provides—

Vocational education programs and activities for individuals with handicaps will be provided in the least restrictive environment in accordance with section 612(5)(B) of the Individuals with Disabilities Education Act and will, whenever appropriate, be included as a component of the individualized education program developed under section 614(a)(5) of such Act. Students with handicaps who have individualized education programs developed under section 614(a)(5) of the Individuals with Disabilities Education Act shall, with respect to vocational education programs, be afforded the rights and protections guaranteed such students under sections 612, 614, and 615 of such Act.

§ 300.18 Transition services.

(a) As used in this part, "transition services" means a coordinated set of activities for a student, designed within an outcome-oriented process, that promotes movement from school to post-school activities, including postsecondary education, vocational training, integrated employment (including supported employment), continuing and adult education, adult services, independent living, or community participation.

(b) The coordinated set of activities described in paragraph (a) of this section must—

(1) Be based on the individual student's needs, taking into account the student's preferences and interests; and

(2) Include—

(i) Instruction;

(ii) Community experiences;

(iii) The development of employment and other post-school adult living objectives; and

(iv) If appropriate, acquisition of daily living skills and functional vocational evaluation.
(Authority: 20 U.S.C. 1401(a)(19))

Note: Transition services for students with disabilities may be special education, if they are provided as specially designed instruction, or related services, if they are required to assist a student with a disability to benefit from special education. The list of activities in paragraph (b) is not intended to be exhaustive.

Subpart B—State Plans and Local Educational Agency Applications

State Plans—General

§ 300.110 Condition of assistance.

In order to receive funds under Part B of the Act for any fiscal year, a State must submit a State plan to the Secretary through its SEA, which plan shall be effective for a period of 3 fiscal years.
(Authority: 20 U.S.C. 1231g, 1412, 1413)

§ 300.111 Content of plan.

Each State plan must contain the provisions required in §§ 300.121-300.154.
(Authority: 20 U.S.C. 1412, 1413)

State Plans— Contents

§ 300.121 Right to a free appropriate public education.

(a) Each State plan must include information that shows that the State has in effect a policy that ensures that all children with disabilities have the right to FAPE within the age ranges and timelines under § 300.122.

(b) The information must include a copy of each State statute, court order, State Attorney General opinion, and other State document that shows the source of the policy.

(c) The information must show that the policy—

(1) Applies to all public agencies in the State;

(2) Applies to all children with disabilities;

(3) Implements the priorities established under §§ 300.320- 300.324; and

(4) Establishes timelines for implementing the policy, in accordance with § 300.122.
(Authority: 20 U.S.C. 1412(1), (2)(B), (6); 1413(a)(1))

§ 300.122 Timelines and ages for free appropriate public education.

(a) *General.* Each State plan must include in detail the policies and procedures which the State will undertake or has undertaken in order to ensure that FAPE is available for all children with disabilities aged 3 through 18 within the State not later than September 1, 1978, and for all children with disabilities aged 3 through 21 within the State not later than September 1, 1980.

(b) *Documents relating to timelines.* Each State plan must include a copy of each statute, court order, attorney general decision, and other State documents that demonstrate that the State has established timelines in accordance with paragraph (a) of this section.

(c) *Exception.* The requirement in paragraph (a) of this section does not apply to a State with respect to children with disabilities aged 3, 4, 5, 18, 19, 20, or 21 to the extent that the requirement would be inconsistent with State law or practice, or the order of any court, respecting public education for one or more of those age groups in the State.

(d) *Documents relating to exceptions.* Each State plan must:

(1) Describe in detail the extent that the exception in paragraph (c) of this section applies to the State; and

(2) Include a copy of each State law, court order, and other documents that provide a basis for the exception.

(Authority: 20 U.S.C. 1412(2)(B))

§ 300.123 Full educational opportunity goal.

Each State plan must include in detail the policies and procedures that the State will undertake, or has undertaken, in order to ensure that the State has a goal of providing full educational opportunity to all children with disabilities aged birth through 21.

(Authority: 20 U.S.C. 1412(2)(A))

§ 300.125 Full educational opportunity goal—timetable.

Each State plan must contain a detailed timetable for accomplishing the goal of providing full educational opportunity for all children with disabilities.

(Authority: 20 U.S.C. 1412(2)(A))

§ 300.126 Full educational opportunity goal—facilities, personnel, and services.

Each State plan must include a description of the kind and number of facilities, personnel, and services necessary throughout the State to meet the goal of providing full educational opportunity for all children with disabilities.

(Authority: 20 U.S.C. 1412(2)(A))

§ 300.127 Priorities.

Each State plan must include information that shows that—

(a) The State has established priorities that meet the requirements under §§ 300.320-300.324;

(b) The State priorities meet the timelines under § 300.122; and

(c) The State has made progress in meeting those timelines.

(Authority: 20 U.S.C. 1412(3))

§ 300.128 Identification, location, and evaluation of children with disabilities.

(a) *General requirement.* Each State plan must include in detail the policies and procedures which the State will undertake or has undertaken to ensure that—

(1) All children with disabilities, regardless of the severity of their disability, and who are in need of special education and related services are identified, located, and evaluated; and

(2) A practical method is developed and implemented to determine which children are currently receiving needed special education and related services and which children are not currently receiving needed special education and related services.

(b) *Information.* Each State plan must:

(1) Designate the State agency (if other than the SEA) responsible for coordinating the planning and implementation of the policies and procedures under paragraph (a) of this section.

(2) Name each agency that participates in the planning and implementation and describe the nature and extent of its participation.

(3) Describe the extent that—

(i) The activities described in paragraph (a) of this section have been achieved under the current State plan; and

(ii) The resources named for these activities in that plan have been used.

(4) Describe each type of activity to be carried out during the next school year, including the role of the agency named under paragraph (b)(1) of this section, timelines for completing those activities, resources that will be used, and expected outcomes.

(5) Describe how the policies and procedures under paragraph (a) of this section will be monitored to ensure that the SEA obtains—

(i) The number of children with disabilities within each disability category that have been identified, located, and evaluated; and

(ii) Information adequate to evaluate the effectiveness of those policies and procedures.

(6) Describe the method the State uses to determine which children are currently receiving special education and related services and which children are not receiving special education and related services.

(Authority: 20 U.S.C. 1412(2)(C))

Note 1: The State is responsible for ensuring that all children with disabilities are identified, located, and evaluated, including children in all public and private agencies and institutions in the

State. Collection and use of data are subject to the confidentiality requirements in §§ 300.560-300.576.

Note 2: Under both Parts B and H of the Act, States are responsible for identifying, locating, and evaluating infants and toddlers from birth through 2 years of age who have disabilities or who are suspected of having disabilities. In States where the SEA and the State's lead agency for the Part H program are different and the Part H lead agency will be participating in the child find activities described in paragraph (a) of this section, the nature and extent of the Part H lead agency's participation must, under paragraph (b)(2) of this section, be included in the State plan. With the SEA's agreement, the Part H lead agency's participation may include the actual implementation of child find activities for infants and toddlers. The use of an interagency agreement or other mechanism for providing for the Part H lead agency's participation would not alter or diminish the responsibility of the SEA to ensure compliance with all child find requirements, including the requirements in paragraph (a)(1) of this section that all children with disabilities who are in need of special education and related services are evaluated.

§ 300.129 Confidentiality of personally identifiable information.

(a) Each State plan must include in detail the policies and procedures which the State will undertake, or has undertaken, in order to ensure the protection of the confidentiality of any personally identifiable information collected, used, or maintained under this part.

(b) The Secretary shall use the criteria in §§ 300.560-300.576 of Subpart E to evaluate the policies and procedures of the State under paragraph (a) of the section.

(Authority: 20 U.S.C. 1412(2)(D); 1417(c))

Note: The confidentiality regulations were published in the **FEDERAL REGISTER** in final form on February 27, 1976 (41 FR 8603-8610), and met the requirements of Part B of the Act. Those regulations are incorporated in §§ 300.560-300.576.

§ 300.130 Individualized education programs.

(a) Each State plan must include information that shows that each public agency in the State maintains records of the IEP for each child with disabilities, and each public agency establishes, reviews, and revises each program as provided in §§ 300.340-300.350.

(b) Each State plan must include—

(1) A copy of each State statute, policy, and standard that regulates the manner in which IEPs are developed, implemented, reviewed, and revised; and

(2) The procedures that the SEA follows in monitoring and evaluating those programs.

(Authority: 20 U.S.C. 1412(4) 1413(a)(1))

§ 300.131 Procedural safeguards.

Each State plan must include procedural safeguards that ensure that the requirements of §§ 300.500-300.514 are met.

(Authority: 20 U.S.C. 1412(5)(A))

§ 300.132 Least restrictive environment.

(a) Each State plan must include procedures that ensure that the requirements of §§ 300.550-300.556 are met.

(b) Each State plan must include the following information:

(1) The number of children with disabilities in the State, within each disability category, who are participating in regular education programs, consistent with §§ 300.550-300.556.

(2) The number of children with disabilities who are in separate classes or separate school facilities, or who are otherwise removed from the regular education environment.

(Authority: 20 U.S.C. 1412(5)(B))

§ 300.133 Protection in evaluation procedures.

Each State plan must include procedures which ensure that the requirements in §§ 300.530-300.534 are met.

(Authority: 20 U.S.C. 1412(5)(C))

§ 300.134 Responsibility of State educational agency for all educational programs.

(a) Each State plan must include information that shows that the requirements of § 300.600 are met.

(b) The information under paragraph (a) of this section must include a copy of each State statute, State regulation, signed agreement between respective agency officials, and any other document that shows compliance with that paragraph.

(Authority: 20 U.S.C. 1412(6))

§ 300.135 [Reserved]

§ 300.136 Implementation procedures—State educational agency.

Each State plan must describe the procedures the SEA follows to inform each public agency of its responsibility for insuring effective implementation of procedural safeguards for the children with disabilities served by that public agency.

(Authority: 20 U.S.C. 1412(6))

§ 300.137 Procedures for consultation.

Each State plan must include an assurance that in carrying out the requirements of section 612 of the Act, procedures are established for consultation with individuals involved in or concerned with the education of children with disabilities, including individuals with disabilities and parents of children with disabilities.

(Authority: 20 U.S.C. 1412(7)(A))

§ 300.138 Other Federal programs.

Each State plan must provide that programs and procedures are established to ensure that funds received by the State or any public agency in the State under any other Federal program, including subpart 2 of Part D of chapter 1 of title I of the Elementary and Secondary Education Act of 1965, under which there is specific authority for assistance for the education of children with disabilities, are used by the State, or any public agency in the State, only in a manner consistent with the goal of providing FAPE for all children with disabilities, except that nothing in this section limits the specific requirements of the laws governing those Federal programs.

(Authority: 20 U.S.C. 1413(a)(2))

§ 300.139 Comprehensive system of personnel development.

Each State plan must include the procedures required under §§ 300.380-300.383.

(Authority: 20 U.S.C. 1413(a)(3))

§ 300.140 Private schools.

Each State plan must include policies and procedures that ensure that the requirements of §§ 300.400-300.403 and §§ 300.450-300.452 are met.

(Authority: 20 U.S.C. 1413(a)(4))

§ 300.141 Recovery of funds for misclassified children.

Each State plan must include policies and procedures that ensure that the State seeks to recover any funds provided under Part B of the Act for services to a child who is determined to be erroneously classified as eligible to be counted under section 611 (a) or (d) of the Act.

(Authority: 20 U.S.C. 1413(a)(5))

§§ 300.142-300.143 [Reserved]

§ 300.144 Hearing on application.

Each State plan must include procedures to ensure that the SEA does not take any final action with respect to an application submitted by an LEA before giving the LEA reasonable notice and an opportunity for a hearing under § 76.401(d) of this title.

(Authority: 20 U.S.C. 1413(a)(8))

§ 300.145 Prohibition of commingling.

Each State plan must provide assurance satisfactory to the Secretary that funds provided under Part B of the Act are not commingled with State funds.

(Authority: 20 U.S.C. 1413(a)(9))

Note: This assurance is satisfied by the use of a separate accounting system that includes an audit trail of the expenditure of the Part B Funds. Separate bank accounts are not required. (See 34 CFR 76.702 (Fiscal control and fund accounting procedures).)

§ 300.146 Annual evaluation.

Each State plan must include procedures for evaluation at least annually of the effectiveness of programs in meeting the educational needs of children with disabilities, including evaluation of IEPs.

(Authority: 20 U.S.C. 1413(a)(11))

§ 300.147 Statutory advisory panel.

Each State plan must provide that the requirements of §§ 300.650-300.653 are met.

(Authority: 20 U.S.C. 1413(a)(12))

§ 300.148 Policies and procedures for use of Part B funds.

Each State plan must set forth policies and procedures designed to ensure that funds paid to the State under Part B of the Act are spent in accordance with the provisions of Part B, with particular attention given to sections 611(b), 611(c), 611(d), 612(2), and 612(3) of the Act.

(Authority: 20 U.S.C. 1413(a)(1))

§ 300.149 Description of use of Part B Funds.

(a) State allocation. Each State plan must include the following information about the State's use of funds under § 300.370 and § 300.620:

(1) A list of administrative positions, and a description of duties for each person whose salary is paid in whole or in part with those funds.

(2) For each position, the percentage of salary paid with those funds.

(3) A description of each administrative activity the SEA will carry out during the next school year with those funds.

(4) A description of each direct service and each support service that the SEA will provide during the next period covered by the State plan with those funds, and the activities the State advisory panel will undertake during that period with those funds.

(b) Local educational agency allocation. Each State plan must include—

(1) An estimate of the number and percent of LEAs in the State which will receive an allocation, under this part (other than LEAs which submit a consolidated application);

(2) An estimate of the number of LEAs that will receive an allocation under a consolidated application;

(3) An estimate of the number of consolidated applications and the average number of LEAs per application; and

(4) A description of direct services the SEA will provide under § 300.360.

(Authority: 20 U.S.C. 1412(6))

§ 300.150 State-level nonsupplanting.

Each program plan must provide assurance satisfactory to the Secretary that funds provided under this part will be used so as to supplement and increase the level of Federal (other than funds available under this part), State, and local funds—including funds that are not under the direct control of the SEA or LEAs—expended for special education and related services provided to children with disabilities under this part and in no case to supplant those Federal (other than funds available under this part), State, and local funds unless a waiver is granted in accordance with § 300.589.

(Authority: 20 U.S.C. 1413(a)(9))

Note: This requirement is distinct from the LEA nonsupplanting provision already contained in these regulations at § 300.230. Under this State-level provision, the state must assure that Part B funds distributed to LEAs and IEUs will be used to supplement and not supplant other Federal, State, and local funds (including funds not under the control of educational agencies) that would have been expended for special education and related services provided to children with disabilities in the absence of the Part B funds. The portion of Part B funds that are not distributed to LEAs or IEUs under the statutory formula (20 U.S.C. 1411(d)) are not subject to this nonsupplanting provision. See 20 U.S.C. 1411(c)(3). States may not permit LEAs or IEUs to use Part B funds to satisfy a financial commitment for services that would have been paid for by a health or other agency pursuant to policy or practice but for the fact that these services are now included in the IEPs of children with disabilities.

(H. R. Rep. No. 860, 99th Cong., 21-22 (1986))

§ 300.151 Additional information if the State educational agency provides direct services.

If an SEA provides FAPE for children with disabilities or provides them with direct services, its State plan must include the information required under §§ 300.226, 300.227, 300.231, and 300.235.

(Authority: 20 U.S.C. 1413(b))

§ 300.152 Interagency agreements.

(a) Each State plan must set forth policies and procedures for developing and implementing interagency agreements between—

(1) The SEA; and

(2) All other State and local agencies that provide or pay for services required under this part for children with disabilities.

(b) The policies and procedures referred to in paragraph (a) of this section must—

(1) Describe the role that each of those agencies plays in providing or paying for services required under this part for children with disabilities; and

(2) Provide for the development and implementation of interagency agreements that—

(i) Define the financial responsibility of each agency for providing children with disabilities with FAPE;

(ii) Establish procedures for resolving interagency disputes among agencies that are parties to the agreements; and

(iii) Establish procedures under which LEAs may initiate proceedings in order to secure reimbursement from agencies that are parties to the agreement or otherwise implement the provisions of the agreements.

(Authority: 20 U.S.C. 1413(a)(13))

§ 300.153 Personnel standards.

(a) As used in this part:

(1) "Appropriate professional requirements in the State" means entry-level requirements that—

(i) Are based on the highest requirements in the State applicable to the profession or discipline in which a person is providing special education or related services; and

(ii) Establish suitable qualifications for personnel providing special education and related services under this part to children and youth with disabilities who are served by State, local, and private agencies (see § 300.2);

(2) "Highest requirements in the State applicable to a specific profession or discipline" means the highest entry-level academic degree needed for any State approved or recognized certification, licensing, registration, or other comparable requirements that apply to that profession or discipline;

(3) "Profession or discipline" means a specific occupational category that—

(i) Provides special education and related services to children with disabilities under this part,

(ii) Has been established or designated by the State; and

(iii) Has a required scope of responsibility and degree of supervision.

(4) "State approved or recognized certification, licensing, registration, or other comparable requirements" means the requirements that a State legislature either has enacted or has authorized a State agency to promulgate through rules to estab-

lish the entry-level standards for employment in a specific profession or discipline in that State.

(b)(1) Each State plan must include policies and procedures relating to the establishment and maintenance of standards to ensure that personnel necessary to carry out the purposes of this part are appropriately and adequately prepared and trained.

(2) The policies and procedures required in paragraph (b)(1) of this section must provide for the establishment and maintenance of standards that are consistent with any State approved or recognized certification, licensing, registration, or other comparable requirements that apply to the profession or discipline in which a person is providing special education or related services.

(c) To the extent that a State's standards for a profession or discipline, including standards for temporary or emergency certification, are not based on the highest requirements in the State applicable to a specific profession or discipline, the State plan must include the steps the State is taking and the procedures for notifying public agencies and personnel of those steps and the timelines it has established for the retraining or hiring of personnel to meet appropriate professional requirements in the State.

(d)(1) In meeting the requirements in paragraphs (b) and (c) of this section, a determination must be made about the status of personnel standards in the State. That determination must be based on current information that accurately describes, for each profession or discipline in which personnel are providing special education or related services, whether the applicable standards are consistent with the highest requirements in the state for that profession or discipline.

(2) The information required in paragraph (d)(1) of this section must be on file in the SEA, and available to the public.

(e) In identifying the highest requirements in the State for purposes of this section, the requirements of all State statutes and the rules of all State agencies applicable to serving children and youth with disabilities must be considered.
(Authority: 20 U.S.C. 1413(a)(14))

Note: The regulations require that the State use its own existing highest requirements to determine the standards appropriate to personnel who provide special education and related services under this part. The regulations do not require States to set any specified training standard, such as a master's degree, for employment of personnel who provide services under this part. In some instances, States will be required to show that they are taking steps to retrain or to hire personnel to meet the standards adopted by the SEA that are based on requirements for practice in a specific profession or discipline that were established by other State agencies. States

in this position need not, however, require personnel providing services under this part to apply for and obtain the license, registration, or other comparable credential required by other agencies of individuals in that profession or discipline. The regulations permit each State to determine the specific occupational categories required to provide special education and related services and to revise or expand these categories as needed. The professions or disciplines defined by the State need not be limited to traditional occupational categories.

§ 300.154 Transition of individuals from Part H to Part B

Each State plan must set forth policies and procedures relating to the smooth transition for those individuals participating in the early intervention program under Part H of the Act who will participate in preschool programs assisted under this part, including a method of ensuring that when a child turns age 3 an IEP, or, if consistent with sections 614(a)(5) and 677(d) of the Act, an individualized family service plan, has been developed and implemented by the child's third birthday.
(Authority: 20 U.S.C. 1413(a)(15))

Local Educational Agency Applications— General

§ 300.180 Submission of application.

In order to receive payments under Part B of the Act for any fiscal year an LEA must submit an application to the SEA.
(Authority: 20 U.S.C. 1414(a))

§ 300.181 [Reserved]

§ 300.182 The excess cost requirement.

An LEA may only use funds under part B of the Act for the excess costs of providing special education and related services for children with disabilities.
(Authority: 20 U.S.C. 1414(a)(1), (a)(2)(B)(i))

§ 300.183 Meeting the excess cost requirement

(a) An LEA meets the excess cost requirement if it has on the average spent at least the amount determined under § 300.184 for the education of each of its children with disabilities. This amount may not include capital outlay or debt service.
(Authority: 20 U.S.C. 1402(20); 1414(a)(1))

Note: The excess cost requirement means that the local educational agency must spend a certain minimum amount for the education of its children with disabilities before Part B funds are used. This ensures that children served with part B funds have at least the same average amount spent on them, from sources other than Part B, as do the children in the school district taken as a whole.

The minimum amount that must be spent for the education of children with disabilities is computed under a statutory formula. Section 300.184 implements this formula and gives a step-by-step method to determine the minimum amount. Excess costs are those costs of special education and related services which exceed the minimum amount. Therefore, if an LEA can show that it has (on the average) spent the minimum amount for the education of each of its children with disabilities, it has met the excess cost requirement, and all additional costs are excess costs. Part B funds can then be used to pay for these additional costs, subject to the other requirements of Part B (priorities, etc.). In the Note under 300.184, there is an example of how the minimum amount is computed.

§ 300.184 Excess costs—computation of minimum amount.

The minimum average amount that an LEA must spend under § 300.183 for the education of each of its children with disabilities is computed as follows:

(a) Add all expenditures of the LEA in the preceding school year except capital outlay and debt service—

(1) For elementary school students, if the child with a disability is an elementary school student, or

(2) For secondary school students, if the child with a disability is a secondary school student.

(b) From this amount, subtract the total of the following amounts spent for elementary school students or for secondary school students, as the case may be—

(1) Amounts the agency spent in the preceding school year from funds awarded under part B of the Act and Titles I and VII of the Elementary and Secondary Education Act of 1965; and

(2) Amounts from State and local funds which the agency spent in the preceding school year for—

(i) Programs for children with disabilities;

(ii) Programs to meet the special educational needs of educationally deprived children; and

(iii) Programs of bilingual education for limited English proficient children.

(c) Divide the result under paragraph (b) of this section by the average number of students enrolled in the agency in the preceding school year—

(1) In its elementary schools, if the child with a disability is an elementary school student, or,

(2) In its secondary schools, if the child with a disability is a secondary school student.

(Authority: 20 U.S.C. 1414(a)(1))

Note: The following is an example of how an LEA might compute the average minimum amount it must spend for the education of each of its children with disabilities, under § 300.183. This example follows the formula in § 300.184. Under the statute and regulations, the LEA must make one computation for children with disabilities in its elementary schools and a separate computation for children with disabilities in its secondary schools. The computation for handicapped elementary school students would be done as follows:

a. First, the LEA must determine its total amount of expenditures for elementary school students from all sources— local, State, and Federal (including Part B)—in the preceding school year. Only capital outlay and debt service are excluded.

Example: An LEA spent the following amounts last year for elementary school students (including its elementary school students with disabilities):

(1) From local tax funds......................$2,750,000
(2) From State Funds............................7,000,000
(3) From Federal funds.........................<u>750,000</u>

                                   10,500,000

Of this total, $500,000 was for capital outlay and debt service relating to the education of elementary school students. This must be subtracted from total expenditures:

                           $10,500,000
                           <u>-500,000</u>

Total expenditures for elementary school students (less capital outlay and debt service)..............................=10,000,000

b. Next, the LEA must subtract amounts spent for:

(1) Programs for children with disabilities;

(2) Programs to meet the special educational needs of educationally deprived children; and

(3) Programs of bilingual education for limited English proficient children.

These are funds which the LEA actually spent, not funds received last year but carried over for the current school year.

Example: The LEA spent the following amounts for elementary school students last year:

(1) From funds under Chapter 1 of title I of the Elementary and Secondary Education Act of 1965..........$300,000
(2) From a special State program for educationally deprived children 200,000
(3) From a grant under Part B....................200,000
(4) From State funds for the education of children with disabilities.......................500,000

(5) From a locally-funded program for children with disabilities............................250,000

(6) From a grant for a bilingual education program under Title VII of the Elementary and Secondary Education Act of 1965...............................150,000

Total...1,600,000

(An LEA would also include any other funds it spent from Federal, State, or local sources for the three basic purposes: children with disabilities, educationally deprived children, and bilingual education for limited English proficient children.)

This amount is subtracted from the LEA's total expenditure for elementary school students computed above:

$$\begin{array}{r} \$10,000,000 \\ -1,600,000 \\ \hline 8,400,000 \end{array}$$

c. The LEA next must divide by the average number of students enrolled in the elementary schools of the agency last year (including its students with disabilities).

Example: Last year, an average of 7,000 students were enrolled in the agency's elementary schools. This must be divided into the amount computed under the above paragraph: $8,400,000/ 7,000 students = $1,200/student

This figure is in the minimum amount the LEA must spend (on the average) for the education of each of its students with disabilities. Funds under Part B may be used only for costs over and above this minimum. In this example, if the LEA has 100 elementary school students with disabilities, it must keep records adequate to show that it has spent at least $120,000 for the education of those students, (100 students times $1,200/student), not including capital outlay and debt service.

This $120,000 may come from any funds except funds under Part B, subject to any legal requirements that govern the use of those other funds.

If the LEA has secondary school students with disabilities, it must do the same computation for them. However the amounts used in the computation would be those the local educational agency spent last year for the education of secondary school students, rather than for elementary school students.

§ 300.185 Computation of excess costs— consolidated application.

The minimum average amount under § 300.183 where two or more LEAs submit a consolidated application, is the average of the combined minimum average amounts determined under § 300.184 in those agencies for elementary or secondary school students, as the case may be.
(Authority: 20 U.S.C. 1414(a)(1))

§ 300.186 Excess costs—limitation on use of Part B funds.

(a) The excess cost requirement prevents an LEA from using funds provided under Part B of the Act to pay for all of the costs directly attributable to the education of a child with a disability, subject to paragraph (b) of this section.

(b) The excess cost requirement does not prevent an LEA from using Part B funds to pay for all of the costs directly attributable to the education of a child with a disability in any of the age ranges three, four, five, eighteen, nineteen, twenty, or twenty-one, if no local or State funds are available for nondisabled children in that age range. However, the LEA must comply with the nonsupplanting and other requirements of this part in providing the education and services.
(Authority: 20 U.S.C. 1402(20); 1414(a)(1))

§ 300.190 Consolidated applications.

(a) [Reserved]

(b) *Required applications.* An SEA may require LEAs to submit a consolidated application for payments under Part B of the Act if the SEA determines that an individual application submitted by a local educational agency will be disapproved because:

(1) The agency's entitlement is less than the $7,500 minimum required by section 611(c)(4)(A)(i) of the Act (§ 300.360(a)(1)); or

(2) The agency is unable to establish and maintain programs of sufficient size and scope to effectively meet the educational needs of children with disabilities.

(c) *Size and scope of program.* The SEA shall establish standards and procedures for determinations under paragraph (b)(2) of this section.
(Authority: 20 U.S.C. 1414(c)(1))

§ 300.191 [Reserved]

§ 300.192 State regulation of consolidated applications.

(a) The SEA shall issue regulations with respect to consolidated applications submitted under this part.

(b) The SEA's regulations must—

(1) Be consistent with sections 612(1)-(7) and 613(a) of the Act; and

(2) Provide participating LEAs with joint responsibilities for implementing programs receiving payments under this part.
(Authority: 20 U.S.C. 1414(c)(2)(B))

(c) If an IEU is required under State law to carry out this part, the joint responsibilities given to LEAs under paragraph (b)(2) of this section do not apply to the administration and disbursement of any payments received by the IEU. Those administrative responsibilities must be carried out exclusively by the IEU.

(Authority: 20 U.S.C. 1414(c)(2)(C))

§ 300.193 State educational agency approval; disapproval.

(a)-(b) [Reserved]

(c) In carrying out its functions under this section, each SEA shall consider any decision resulting from a hearing under §§ 300.506-300.513 that is adverse to the LEA involved in the decision.

(Authority: 20 U.S.C. 1414(b)(3))

§ 300.194 Withholding.

(a) If an SEA, after giving reasonable notice and an opportunity for a hearing to an LEA, decides that the LEA in the administration of an application approved by the State educational agency has failed to comply with any requirement in the application, the SEA, after giving notice to the LEA, shall—

(1) Make no further payments to the LEA until the SEA is satisfied that there is no longer any failure to comply with the requirement; or

(2) Consider its decision in its review of any application made by the LEA under § 300.180; or

(3) Both.

(b) [Reserved]

(Authority: 20 U.S.C. 1414(b)(2))

Local Educational Agency Applications— Contents

§ 300.220 Child identification.

Each application must include procedures that ensure that all children residing within the jurisdiction of the LEA who have disabilities, regardless of the severity of their disability, and who are in need of special education and related services are identified, located, and evaluated, including a practical method of determining which children are currently receiving needed special education and related services and which children are not currently receiving needed special education and related services.

(Authority: 20 U.S.C. 1414(a)(1)(A))

Note: The LEA is responsible for ensuring that all children with disabilities within its jurisdiction are identified, located, and evaluated, including children in all public and private agencies and institutions within that jurisdiction. Collection and use of data are subject to the confidentiality requirements in §§ 300.560-300.576.

§ 300.221 Confidentiality of personally identifiable information.

Each application must include policies and procedures that ensure that the criteria in §§ 300.560-300.574 are met.

(Authority: 20 U.S.C. 1414(a)(1)(B))

§ 300.222 Full educational opportunity goal—timetable.

Each application must—(a) Include a goal of providing full educational opportunity to all children with disabilities, aged birth through 21; and

(b) Include a detailed timetable for accomplishing the goal.

(Authority: 20 U.S.C. 1414(a)(1)(C), (D))

§ 300.223 Facilities, personnel, and services.

Each application must provide a description of the kind and number of facilities, personnel, and services necessary to meet the goal in § 300.222.

(Authority: 20 U.S.C. 1414(a)(1)(E))

§ 300.224 Personnel development.

Each application must include procedures for the implementation and use of the comprehensive system of personnel development established by the SEA under § 300.139.

(Authority: 20 U.S.C. 1414(a)(1)(C)(i))

§ 300.225 Priorities.

Each application must include priorities which meet the requirements of §§ 300.320-300.324.

(Authority: 20 U.S.C. 1414(a)(1)(C)(ii))

§ 300.226 Parent involvement.

Each application must include procedures to ensure that, in meeting the goal under § 300.222, the LEA makes provision for participation of and consultation with parents or guardians of children with disabilities.

(Authority: 20 U.S.C. 1414(a)(1)(C)(iii))

§ 300.227 Participation in regular education programs.

(a) Each application must include procedures to ensure that to the maximum extent practicable, and consistent with §§ 300.550-300.553, the LEA provides special services to enable children with disabilities to participate in regular educational programs.

(b) Each application must describe—

(1) The types of alternative placements that are available for children with disabilities, and

(2) The number of children with disabilities within each disability category who are served in each type of placement.

(Authority: 20 U.S.C. 1414(a)(1)(C)(iv))

§ 300.228 [Reserved]

§ 300.229 Excess cost.

Each application must provide assurance satisfactory to the SEA that the LEA uses funds provided under Part B of the Act only for costs which exceed the amount computed under § 300.184 and which are directly attributable to the education of children with disabilities.

(Authority: 20 U.S.C. 1414(a)(2)(B))

§ 300.230 Nonsupplanting.

(a) Each application must provide assurance satisfactory to the SEA that the LEA uses funds provided under Part B of the Act to supplement and, to the extent practicable, increase the level of State and local funds expended for the education of children with disabilities, and in no case to supplant those State and local funds.

(b) To meet the requirement in paragraph (a) of this section, the total amount or average per capita amount of State and local school funds budgeted by the LEA for expenditures in the current fiscal year for the education of children with disabilities must be at least equal to the total amount or average per capita amount of State and local school funds actually expended for the education of children with disabilities in the most recent preceding fiscal year for which the information is available. Allowance may be made for—

(i) Decreases in enrollment of children with disabilities; and

(ii) Unusually large amounts of funds expended for such long-term purposes as the acquisition of equipment and the construction of school facilities.

(Authority: 20 U.S.C. 1414(a)(2)(B))

§ 300.231 Comparable services.

(a) Each application must provide assurance satisfactory to the SEA that the LEA meets the requirements of this section.

(b) An LEA may not use funds under Part B of the Act to provide services to children with disabilities unless the agency uses State and local funds to provide services to those children which, taken as a whole, are at least comparable to services provided to other children with disabilities in that LEA.

(c) Each LEA shall maintain records which show that the LEA meets the requirement in paragraph (b) of this section.

(Authority: 20 U.S.C. 1414(a)(2)(C))

Note: Under the "comparability" requirement, if State and local funds are used to provide certain services, those services must be provided with State and local funds to all children with disabilities in the LEA who need them. Part B funds may then be used to supplement existing services, or to provide addi-

tional services to meet special needs. This, of course, is subject to the other requirements of the Act, including the priorities under §§ 300.320-300.324.

§§ 300.232-300.234 [Reserved]

§ 300.235 Individualized education program.

Each application must include procedures to assure that the LEA complies with §§ 300.340-300.350.

(Authority: 20 U.S.C. 1414(a)(5))

§ 300.236 [Reserved]

§ 300.237 Procedural safeguards.

Each application must provide assurance satisfactory to the SEA that the LEA has procedural safeguards which meet the requirements of §§ 300.500-300.515.

(Authority: 20 U.S.C. 1414(a)(7))

§ 300.238 Use of Part B funds.

Each application must describe how the LEA will use the funds under Part B of the Act during the next school year.

(Authority: 20 U.S.C. 1414(a))

§ 300.239 [Reserved]

§ 300.240 Other requirements.

Each local application must include additional procedures and information which the SEA may require in order to meet the State plan requirements of §§ 300.121-300.153.

(Authority: 20 U.S.C. 1414(a)(6))

Application From Secretary of the Interior

§ 300.260 Submission of application; approval.

(a) In order to receive a grant under this part, the Secretary of the Interior shall submit an application that—

(1) Meets the requirements of section 612(1), 612(2)(C)-(E), 612(4), 612(5), 612(6), and 612(7) of the Act (including monitoring and evaluating activities);

(2) Meets the requirements of section 613(a), (2), (3), (4)(B), (5), (6), (7), (10), (11), (12), (13), (14), and (15), 613(b), and 613(e) of the Act;

(3) Meets the requirements of section 614(a)(1)(A)-(B), (2)(A), (C), (3), (4), (5), and (7) of the Act;

(4) Meets the requirements of this part that implement the sections of the Act listed in paragraphs (a)(1)-(3) of this section.

(5) Includes a description of how the Secretary of the Interior will coordinate the provision of

services under this part with LEAs, tribes, and other private and Federal service providers;

(6) Includes an assurance that there have been public hearings, adequate notice of such hearings, and an opportunity for comment afforded to members of tribes, tribal governing bodies, and affected local school boards before the adoption of the policies, programs, and procedures required under paragraphs (a)(1)-(3) of this section;

(7) Includes an assurance that the Secretary of the Interior will provide such information as the Secretary may require to comply with section 618(b)(1) of the Act, including data on the number of children and youth with disabilities served and the types and amounts of services provided and needed;

(8) Includes an assurance that, by October 1, 1992, the Secretaries of the Interior and Health and Human Services will enter into a memorandum of agreement, to be provided to the Secretary, for the coordination of services, resources, and personnel between their respective Federal, State, and local offices and with SEAs and LEAs and other entities to facilitate the provision of services to Indian children with disabilities residing on or near reservations. That agreement must provide for the apportionment of responsibilities and costs, including, but not limited to, those related to child find, evaluation, diagnosis, remediation or therapeutic measures, and (where appropriate) equipment and medical or personal supplies, or both, as needed for a child to remain in school or a program; and

(9) Includes an assurance that the Department of the Interior will cooperate with the Department of Education in the latter's exercise of monitoring and oversight of this application, and any agreements entered into between the Secretary of the Interior and other entities under the Act and will fulfill its duties under the Act.

(b) Sections 300.581-300.585 apply to grants available to the Secretary of the Interior under this part.

(Authority: 20 U.S.C. 1411(f))

§ 300.261 Public participation.

In the development of the application for the Department of Interior, the Secretary of Interior shall provide for public participation consistent with §§ 300.280-300.284.

(Authority: 20 U.S.C. 1411(f))

§ 300.262 Use of Part B funds.

(a)(1) The Department of the Interior may use five percent of its payment in any fiscal year, or $350,000, whichever is greater, for administrative costs in carrying out the provisions of this part.

(2) The remainder of the payments to the Secretary of the Interior in any fiscal year must be used in accordance with the priorities under §§ 300.320-300.324.

(b) Payments to the Secretary of the Interior under § 300.710 must be used in accordance with that section.

(Authority: 20 U.S.C. 1411(f))

§ 300.263 Applicable regulations

The Secretary of the Interior shall comply with the requirements of §§ 300.301-300.303, §§ 300.305-300.307, and §§ 300.340-300.347, § 300.350, §§ 300.360-300.383, §§ 300.400-300.402, §§ 300.500-300.585, §§ 300.600-300.621, and §§ 300.660-300.662.

(Authority: 20 U.S.C. 1411(f)(2))

Public Participation

§ 300.280 Public hearings before adopting a State plan.

(a) Prior to its adoption of a State plan, the SEA shall—

(a) Make the plan available to the general public;

(b) Hold public hearings; and

(c) Provide an opportunity for comment by the general public on the plan.

(Authority: 20 U.S.C. 1412(7))

§ 300.281 Notice.

(a) The SEA shall provide notice to the general public of the public hearings.

(b) The notice must be in sufficient detail to inform the general public about—

(1) The purpose and scope of the State plan and its relation to Part B of the Act;

(2) The availability of the State plan;

(3) The date, time, and location of each public hearing;

(4) The procedures for submitting written comments about the plan; and

(5) The timetable for developing the final plan and submitting it to the Secretary for approval.

(c) The notice must be published or announced—

(1) In newspapers or other media, or both, with circulation adequate to notify the general public about the hearings; and

(2) Enough in advance of the date of the hearings to afford interested parties throughout the State a reasonable opportunity to participate.

(Authority: 20 U.S.C. 1412(7))

§ 300.282 Opportunity to participate; comment period.

(a) The SEA shall conduct the public hearings at times and places that afford interested parties throughout the State a reasonable opportunity to participate.

(b) The plan must be available for comment for a period of at least 30 days following the date of the notice under § 300.281.

(Authority: 20 U.S.C. 1412(7))

§ 300.283 Review of public comments before adopting plan.

Before adopting its State plan, the SEA shall—

(a) Review and consider all public comments; and

(b) Make any necessary modifications in the plan.

(Authority: 20 U.S.C. 1412(7))

§ 300.284 Publication and availability of approved plan.

After the Secretary approves a State plan, the SEA shall give notice in newspapers or other media, or both, that the plan is approved. The notice must name places throughout the State where the plan is available for access by any interested person.

(Authority: 20 U.S.C. 1412(7))

Subpart C—Services

Free Appropriate Public Education

§ 300.300 Timelines for free appropriate public education.

(a) *General.* Each State shall ensure that FAPE is available to all children with disabilities aged 3 through 18 within the State not later than September 1, 1978, and to all children with disabilities aged 3 through 21 within the State not later than September 1, 1980.

(b) *Age ranges 3-5 and 18-21.* This paragraph provides rules for applying the requirement in paragraph (a) of this section to children with disabilities aged 3, 4, 5, 18, 19, 20, and 21:

(1) If State law or a court order requires the State to provide education for children with disabilities in any disability category in any of these age groups, the State must make FAPE available to all children with disabilities of the same age who have that disability.

(2) If a public agency provides education to nondisabled children in any of these age groups it must make FAPE available to at least a proportionate number of children with disabilities of the same age.

(3) If a public agency provides education to 50 percent or more of its children with disabilities in any disability category in any of these age groups, it must make FAPE available to all its children with disabilities of the same age who have that disability. This provision does not apply to children aged 3

through 5 for any fiscal year for which the State receives a grant under section 619(a)(1) of the Act.

(4) If a public agency provides education to a child with a disability in any of these age groups, it must make FAPE available to that child and provide that child and his or her parents all of the rights under Part B of the Act and this part.

(5) A State is not required to make FAPE available to a child with a disability in one of these age groups if:

(i) State law expressly prohibits, or does not authorize, the expenditure of public funds to provide education to nondisabled children in that age group; or

(ii) The requirement is inconsistent with a court order which governs the provision of free public education to children with disabilities in that State.

(c) *Children aged 3 through 21 on reservations.* With the exception of children identified in § 300.709(a)(1) and (2), the SEA shall be responsible for ensuring that all of the requirements of Part B of the Act are implemented for all children aged 3 through 21 on reservations.

(Authority: 20 U.S.C. 1411(f), 1412(2)(B); S. Rep. No. 94-168 p. 19 (1975))

Note 1: The requirement to make FAPE available applies to all children with disabilities within the State who are in the age ranges required under § 300.300 and who need special education and related services. This includes children with disabilities already in school and children with less severe disabilities, who are not covered under the priorities under § 300.321.

Note 2: In order to be in compliance with §300.300, each State must ensure that the requirement to identify, locate, and evaluate all children with disabilities is fully implemented by public agencies throughout the State. This means that before September 1, 1978, every child who has been referred or is on a waiting list for evaluation (including children in school as well as those not receiving an education) must be evaluated in accordance with §§ 300.530-300.533. If, as a result of the evaluation, it is determined that a child needs special education and related services, an IEP must be developed for the child by September 1, 1978, and all other applicable requirements of this part must be met.

Note 3. The requirement to identify, locate, and evaluate children with disabilities (commonly referred to as the "child find system") was enacted on August 21, 1974, under Pub. L. 93-380. While each State needed time to establish and implement its child find system, the four year period between August 21, 1974, and September 1, 1978, is considered to be sufficient to ensure that the system is fully operational and effective on a State-wide basis.

Under the statute, the age range for the child find requirement (0-21) is greater than the mandated age range for providing FAPE. One reason for the broader age requirement under "child find" is to enable States to be aware of and plan for younger children who will require special education and related services. It also ties in with the full educational opportunity goal requirement, which has the same age range as child find. Moreover, while a State is not required to provide FAPE to children with disabilities below the age ranges mandated under § 300.300, the State may, at its discretion, extend services to those children, subject to the requirements on priorities under §§ 300.320-300.324.

§ 300.301 Free appropriate public education—methods and payments.

(a) Each State may use whatever State, local, Federal, and private sources of support are available in the State to meet the requirement of this part. For example, when it is necessary to place a child with a disability in a residential facility, a State could use joint agreements between the agencies involved for sharing the cost of that placement.

(b) Nothing in this part relieves an insurer or similar third party from an otherwise valid obligation to provide or to pay for services provided to a child with a disability.

(Authority: 20 U.S.C. 1401(18); 1412(2)(B))

§ 300.302 Residential placement.

If placement in a public or private residential program is necessary to provide special education and related services to a child with a disability, the program, including non-medical care and room and board, must be at no cost to the parents of the child.

(Authority: 20 U.S.C. 1412(2)(B); 1413(a)(4)(B))

Note: This requirement applies to placements which are made by public agencies for educational purposes, and includes placements in State-operated schools for children with disabilities, such as a State school for students with deafness or blindness.

§ 300.303 Proper functioning of hearing aids.

Each public agency shall ensure that the hearing aids worn by children with hearing impairments including deafness in school are functioning properly.

(Authority: 20 U.S.C. 1412(2)(B))

Note: The report of the House of Representatives on the 1978 appropriation bill includes the following statement regarding hearing aids:

In its report on the 1976 appropriation bill the Committee expressed concern about the condition of hearing aids worn by children in public schools.

A study done at the Committee's direction by the Bureau of Education for the Handicapped reveals that up to one-third of the hearing aids are malfunctioning. Obviously, the Committee expects the Office of Education will ensure that hearing impaired school children are receiving adequate professional assessment, follow-up and services.

(Authority: House Report No. 95-381, p. 67 (1977)

§ 300.304 Full educational opportunity goal.

(a) Each SEA shall ensure that each public agency establishes and implements a goal of providing full educational opportunity to all children with disabilities in the area served by the public agency.

(b) Subject to the priority requirements of §§ 300.320-300.324, an SEA or LEA may use Part B funds to provide facilities, personnel, and services necessary to meet the full educational opportunity goal.

(Authority: 20 U.S.C. 1412(2)(A); 1414(a)(1)(C))

Note: In meeting the full educational opportunity goal, the Congress also encouraged LEAs to include artistic and cultural activities in programs supported under this part, subject to the priority requirements under §§ 300.320-300.324. This point is addressed in the following statements from the Senate Report on Public Law 94-142:

The use of the arts as a teaching tool for the handicapped has long been recognized as a viable, effective way not only of teaching special skills, but also of reaching youngsters who had otherwise been unteachable. The Committee envisions that programs under this bill could well include an arts component and, indeed, urges that local educational agencies include the arts in programs for the handicapped funded under this Act. Such a program could cover both appreciation of the arts by the handicapped youngsters and the utilization of the arts as a teaching tool per se.

Museum settings have often been another effective tool in the teaching of handicapped children. For example, the Brooklyn Museum has been a leader in developing exhibits utilizing the heightened tactile sensory skill of the blind. Therefore, in light of the national policy concerning the use of museums in federally supported education programs enunciated in the Education Amendments of 1974, the Committee also urges local educational agencies to include museums in programs for the handicapped funded under this Act.

(Authority: Senate Report No. 94-168. p. 13 (1975))

§ 300.305 Program options.

Each public agency shall take steps to ensure that its children with disabilities have available to them the variety of educational programs and services available to nondisabled children in the area served by the agency, including art, music, industrial arts, consumer and homemaking education, and vocational education.

(Authority: 20 U.S.C. 1412(2)(A); 1414(a)(l)(C))

Note: The above list of program options is not exhaustive, and could include any program or activity in which nondisabled students participate.

§ 300.306 Nonacademic services.

(a) Each public agency shall take steps to provide nonacademic and extracurricular services and activities in such manner as is necessary to afford children with disabilities an equal opportunity for participation in those services and activities.

(b) Nonacademic and extracurricular services and activities may include counseling services, athletics, transportation, health services, recreational activities, special interest groups or clubs sponsored by the public agency, referrals to agencies which provide assistance to individuals with disabilities, and employment of students, including both employment by the public agency and assistance in making outside employment available.

(Authority: 20 U.S.C. 1412(2)(A); 1414(a)(1)(C,))

§ 300.307 Physical education.

(a) *General.* Physical education services, specially designed if necessary, must be made available to every child with a disability receiving FAPE.

(b) *Regular physical education.* Each child with a disability must be afforded the opportunity to participate in the regular physical education program available to nondisabled children unless:

(1) The child is enrolled full time in a separate facility; or

(2) The child needs specially designed physical education, as prescribed in the child's IEP.

(c) *Special physical education.* If specially designed physical education is prescribed in a child's IEP, the public agency responsible for the education of that child shall provide the services directly, or make arrangements for it to be provided through other public or private programs.

(d) *Education in separate facilities.* The public agency responsible for the education of a child with a disability who is enrolled in a separate facility shall ensure that the child receives appropriate physical education services in compliance with paragraphs (a) and (c) of this section.

(Authority: 20 U.S.C. 1401(a)(16); 1412(5)(B); 1414(a)(6))

Note: The Report of the House of Representatives on Public Law 94-142 includes the following statement regarding physical education:

Special education as set forth in the Committee bill includes instruction in physical education, which is provided as a matter of course to all non-handicapped children enrolled in public elementary and secondary schools. The Committee is concerned that although these services are available to and required of all children in our school systems, they are often viewed as a luxury for handicapped children.

*   *   *   *   *

The Committee expects the Commissioner of Education to take whatever action is necessary to assure that physical education services are available to all handicapped children, and has specifically included physical education within the definition of special education to make clear that the Committee expects such services, specially designed where necessary, to be provided as an integral part of the educational program of every handicapped child.

(Authority: House Report No. 94-332, p. 9 (1975))

Priorities in the Use of Part B Funds

§ 300.320 Definitions of first priority children and second priority children.

For the purposes of §§ 300.321-300.324, the term:

(a) "First priority children" means children with disabilities who:

(1) Are in an age group for which the State must make FAPE available under § 300.300; and

(2) Are not receiving any education.

(b) "Second priority children" means children with disabilities, within each disability category, with the most severe disabilities who are receiving an inadequate education.

(Authority: 20 U.S.C. 1412(3))

Note 1: After September 1, 1978, there should be no second priority children, since States must ensure, as a condition of receiving Part B funds for fiscal year 1979, that all children with disabilities will have FAPE available by that date.

Note 2: The term "free appropriate public education," as defined in § 300.8, means special education and related services that *** "are provided in conformity with an individualized education program" ***.

New first priority children will continue to be found by the State after September 1, 1978 through on-going efforts to identify, locate, and evaluate all children with disabilities.

§ 300.321 Priorities.

(a) Each SEA and LEA shall use funds provided under Part B of the Act in the following order of priorities:

(1) To provide FAPE to first priority children, including the identification, location, and evaluation of first priority children.

(2) To provide FAPE to second priority children, including the identification, location, and evaluation of second priority children.

(3) To meet the other requirements of this part.

(b) The requirements of paragraph (a) of this section do not apply to funds that the State uses for administration under § 300.620.

(Authority: 20 U.S.C. 1411(b)(1)(B),(b)(2)(B), (c)(1)(B), (c)(2)(A)(ii))

(c) State and local educational agencies may not use funds under Part B of the Act for preservice training.

(Authority: 20 U.S.C. 1413(a)(3); Senate Report No. 94-188, p. 34 (1975))

Note: SEAs as well as LEAs must use Part B funds (except the portion used for State administration) for the priorities. A State may have to set aside a portion of its Part B allotment to be able to serve newly identified first priority children.

After September 1, 1978, Part B funds may be used—

(1) To continue supporting child identification, location, and evaluation activities;

(2) To provide FAPE to newly identified first priority children;

(3) To meet the full educational opportunities goal required under § 300.304. including employing additional personnel and providing inservice training, in order to increase the level, intensity and quality of services provided to individual children with disabilities; and

(4) To meet the other requirements of Part B.

§ 300.322 [Reserved]

§ 300.323 Services to other children.

If an SEA or an LEA is providing FAPE to all of its first priority children, that State or LEA may use funds provided under Part B of the Act—

(a) To provide FAPE to children with disabilities who are not receiving any education and who are in the age groups not covered under § 300.300 in that State; or

(b) To provide FAPE to second priority children; or

(c) Both.

(Authority: 20 U.S.C. 1411 (b)(1)(B), (b)(2)(B), (c)(2)(A)(ii))

§ 300.324 Application of local educational agency to use funds for the second priority.

An LEA may use funds provided under Part B of the Act for second priority children, if it provides assurance satisfactory to the SEA in its application (or an amendment to its application)—

(a) That all first priority children have FAPE available to them;

(b) That the LEA has a system for the identification, location, and evaluation of children with disabilities, as described in its application; and

(c) That whenever a first priority child is identified, located, and evaluated, the LEA makes FAPE available to the child.

(Authority: 20 U.S.C. 1411 (b)(1)(B), (c)(1)(B); 1414(a)(1)(C)(ii))

Individualized Education Programs

§ 300.340 Definition.

(a) As used in this part, the term "individualized education program" means a written statement for a child with a disability that is developed and implemented in accordance with §§ 300.341-300.350.

(b) As used in §§ 300.346 and 300.347, "participating agency" means a State or local agency, other than the public agency responsible for a student's education, that is financially and legally responsible for providing transition services to the student.

(Authority: 20 U.S.C. 1401(a)(20))

§ 300.341 State educational agency responsibility.

(a) *Public agencies.* The SEA shall ensure that each public agency develops and implements an IEP for each of its children with disabilities.

(b) *Private schools and facilities.* The SEA shall ensure that an IEP is developed and implemented for each child with a disability who:

(1) Is placed in or referred to a private school or facility by a public agency; or

(2) Is enrolled in a parochial or other private school and receives special education or related services from a public agency.

(Authority: 20 U.S.C. 1412 (4),(6); 1413(a)(4))

Note: This section applies to all public agencies, including other State agencies (e.g.., departments of mental health and welfare), which provide special education to a child with a disability either directly, by contract or through other arrangements. Thus, if a State welfare agency contracts with a private school or facility to provide special education to a child with a disability, that agency would be responsible for insuring that an IEP is developed for the child.

§ 300.342 When individualized education programs must be in effect.

(a) At the beginning of each school year, each public agency shall have in effect an IEP for every child with a disability who is receiving special education from that agency.

(b) An IEP must—

(1) Be in effect before special education and related services are provided to a child; and

(2) Be implemented as soon as possible following the meetings under § 300.343.

(Authority: 20 U.S.C. 1412 (2)(B), (4), (6); 1414(a)(5); Pub. L. 94-142, Sec. 8(c) (1975))

Note: Under paragraph (b)(2), it is expected that the IEP of a child with a disability will be implemented immediately following the meetings under § 300.343. An exception to this would be (1) when the meetings occur during the summer or a vacation period, or (2) where there are circumstances that require a short delay (e.g., working out transportation arrangements). However, there can be no undue delay in providing special education and related services to the child.

§ 300.343 Meetings.

(a) *General.* Each public agency is responsible for initiating and conducting meetings for the purpose of developing, reviewing, and revising the IEP of a child with a disability (or, if consistent with State policy and at the discretion of the LEA, and with the concurrence of the parents, an individualized family service plan described in section 677(d) of the Act for each child with a disability, aged 3 through 5).

(b) [Reserved]

(c) *Timeline.* A meeting to develop an IEP for a child must be held within 30 calendar days of a determination that the child needs special education and related services.

(d) *Review.* Each public agency shall initiate and conduct meetings to review each child's IEP periodically and, if appropriate, revise its provisions. A meeting must be held for this purpose at least once a year.

(Authority: 20 U.S.C. 1412(2)(B), (4), (6); 1414(a)(5))

Note: The dates on which agencies must have IEPs in effect are specified in § 300.342 (the beginning of each school year). However, except for new children with disabilities (i.e., those evaluated and determined to need special education and related services for the first time), the timing of meetings to develop, review, and revise IEPs is left to the discretion of each agency.

In order to have IEPs in effect by the beginning of the school year, agencies could hold meetings at the end of the school year or during the summer prior to the next school year. Meetings may be held any time throughout the year, as long as IEPs are in effect at the beginning of each school year.

The statute requires agencies to hold a meeting at least once each year in order to review and, if appropriate revise, each child's IEP. The timing of those meetings could be on the anniversary date of the child's last IEP meeting, but this is left to the discretion of the agency.

§ 300.344 Participants in meetings.

(a) *General.* The public agency shall ensure that each meeting includes the following participants:

(1) A representative of the public agency, other than the child's teacher, who is qualified to provide, or supervise the provision of, special education.

(2) The child's teacher.

(3) One or both of the child's parents, subject to § 300.345.

(4) The child, if appropriate.

(5) Other individuals at the discretion of the parent or agency.

(b) *Evaluation personnel.* For a child with a disability who has been evaluated for the first time, the public agency shall ensure—

(1) That a member of the evaluation team participates in the meeting: or

(2) That the representative of the public agency, the child's teacher, or some other person is present at the meeting, who is knowledgeable about the evaluation procedures used with the child and is familiar with the results of the evaluation.

(c) *Transition services participants.* (1) If a purpose of the meeting is the consideration of transition services for a student, the public agency shall invite—

(i) The student; and

(ii) A representative of any other agency that is likely to be responsible for providing or paying for transition services.

(2) If the student does not attend, the public agency shall take other steps to ensure that the student's preferences and interests are considered; and

(3) If an agency invited to send a representative to a meeting does not do so, the public agency shall take other steps to obtain the participation of the other agency in the planning of any transition services.

(Authority: 20 U.S.C. 1401(a)(19), (a)(20); 1412 (2)(B), (4), (6); 1414(a)(5))

Note 1: In deciding which teacher will participate in meetings on a child's IEP, the agency may wish to consider the following possibilities:

(a) For a child with a disability who is receiving special education, the teacher could be the child's special education teacher. If the child's disability is a speech impairment, the teacher could be the speech-language pathologist.

(b) For a child with a disability who is being considered for placement in special education, the teacher could be the child's regular teacher, or a teacher qualified to provide education in the type of program in which the child may be placed, or both.

(c) If the child is not in school or has more than one teacher, the agency may designate which teacher will participate in the meeting.

Either the teacher or the agency representative should be qualified in the area of the child's suspected disability.

For a child whose primary disability is a speech or language impairment, the evaluation personnel participating under paragraph (b)(1) of this section would normally be the speech-language pathologist.

Note 2: Under paragraph (c) of this section, the public agency is required to invite each student to participate in his or her IEP meeting, if a purpose of the meeting is the consideration of transition services for the student. For all students who are 16 years of age or older, one of the purposes of the annual meeting will always be the planning of transition services, since transition services are a required component of the IEP for these students.

For a student younger than age 16, if transition services are initially discussed at a meeting that does not include the student, the public agency is responsible for ensuring that, before a decision about transition services for the student is made, a subsequent IEP meeting is conducted for that purpose, and the student is invited to the meeting.

§ 300.345 Parent participation.

(a) Each public agency shall take steps to ensure that one or both of the parents of the child with a disability are present at each meeting or are afforded the opportunity to participate, including—

(1) Notifying parents of the meeting early enough to ensure that they will have an opportunity to attend; and

(2) Scheduling the meeting at a mutually agreed on time and place.

(b)(1) The notice under paragraph (a)(1) of this section must indicate the purpose, time, and location of the meeting, and who will be in attendance.

(2) If a purpose of the meeting is the consideration of transition services for a student, the notice must also—

(i) Indicate this purpose;

(ii) Indicate that the agency will invite the student; and

(iii) Identify any other agency that will be invited to send a representative.

(c) If neither parent can attend, the public agency shall use other methods to ensure parent participation, including individual or conference telephone calls.

(d) A meeting may be conducted without a parent in attendance if the public agency is unable to convince the parents that they should attend. In this case the public agency must have a record of its attempts to arrange a mutually agreed on time and place such as—

(1) Detailed records of telephone calls made or attempted and the results of those calls;

(2) Copies of correspondence sent to the parents and any responses received; and

(3) Detailed records of visits made to the parent's home or place of employment and the results of those visits.

(e) The public agency shall take whatever action is necessary to ensure that the parent understands the proceedings at a meeting, including arranging for an interpreter for parents who are deaf or whose native language is other than English.

(f) The public agency shall give the parent, on request, a copy of the IEP.

(Authority: 20 U.S.C. 1401(a)(20); 1412 (2)(B), (4), (6); 1414(a)(5))

Note: The notice in paragraph (a) could also inform parents that they may bring other people to the meeting. As indicated in paragraph (c), the procedure used to notify parents (whether oral or written or both) is left to the discretion of the agency, but the agency must keep a record of its efforts to contact parents.

§ 300.346 Content of individualized education program.

(a) *General.* The IEP for each child must include:

(1) A statement of the child's present levels of educational performance;

(2) A statement of annual goals, including short term instructional objectives;

(3) A statement of the specific special education and related services to be provided to the child and the extent to which the child will be able to participate in regular educational programs;

(4) The projected dates for initiation of services and the anticipated duration of the services; and

(5) Appropriate objective criteria and evaluation procedures and schedules for determining, on at least an annual basis, whether the short term instructional objectives are being achieved.

(b) *Transition services.* (1) The IEP for each student, beginning no later than age 16 (and at a younger age, if determined appropriate), must include a statement of the needed transition services as defined in § 300.18, including, if appropriate, a statement of each public agency's and each participating agency's responsibilities or linkages, or both, before the student leaves the school setting.

(2) If the IEP team determines that services are not needed in one or more of the areas specified in § 300.18 (b)(2)(i) through (b)(2)(iii), the IEP must include a statement to that effect and the basis upon which the determination was made.
(Authority: 20 U.S.C. 1401(a)(19), (a)(20); 1412 (2)(B), (4), (6); 1414(a)(5))

Note 1: The legislative history of the transition services provisions of the Act suggests that the statement of needed transition services referred to in paragraph (b) of this section should include a commitment by any participating agency to meet any financial responsibility it may have in the provision of transition services. See House Report No. 101-544, p. 11 (1990).

Note 2: With respect to the provisions of paragraph (b) of this section, it is generally expected that the statement of needed transition services will include the areas listed in § 300.18 (b)(2)(i) through (b)(2)(iii). If the IEP team determines that services are not needed in one of those areas, the public agency must implement the requirements in paragraph (b)(2) of this section. Since it is a part of the IEP, the IEP team must reconsider its determination at least annually.

Note 3: Section 602(a)(20) of the Act provides that IEPs must include a statement of needed transition services for students beginning no later than age 16, but permits transition services to students below age 16 (i.e. "* * * and, when determined appropriate for the individual, beginning at age 14 or younger.") Although the statute does not mandate transition services for all students beginning at age 14 or younger, the provision of these services could have a significantly positive effect on the employment and independent living outcomes for many of these students in the future, especially for students who are likely to drop out before age 16. With respect to the provision of transition services to students below age 16, the Report of the House Committee on Education and Labor on Public Law 101-476 includes the following statement:

Although this language leaves the final determination of when to initiate transition services for students under age 16 to the IEP process, it nevertheless makes clear that Congress expects consideration to be given to the need for transition services for some students by age 14 or younger. The Committee encourages that approach because of their concern that age 16 may be too late for many students, particularly those at risk of dropping out of school and those with the most severe disabilities. Even for those students who stay in school until age 18, many will need more than two years of transitional services. Students with disabilities are

now dropping out of school before age 16, feeling that the education system has little to offer them. Initiating services at a younger age will be critical. (House Report No. 101-544, 10 (1990).)

§ 300.347 Agency responsibilities for transition services.

(a) If a participating agency fails to provide agreed-upon transition services contained in the IEP of a student with a disability, the public agency responsible for the student's education shall, as soon as possible, initiate a meeting for the purpose of identifying alternative strategies to meet the transition objectives and, if necessary, revising the student's IEP.

(b) Nothing in this part relieves any participating agency, including a State vocational rehabilitation agency, of the responsibility to provide or pay for any transition service that the agency would otherwise provide to students with disabilities who meet the eligibility criteria of that agency.
(Authority: 20 U.S.C. 1401(a)(18), (a)(19), (a)(20); 1412(2)(B))

§ 300.348 Private school placements.

(a) *Developing individualized education programs.* (1) Before a public agency places a child with a disability in, or refers a child to, a private school or facility, the agency shall initiate and conduct a meeting to develop an IEP for the child in accordance with § 300.343.

(2) The agency shall ensure that a representative of the private school or facility attends the meeting. If the representative cannot attend, the agency shall use other methods to ensure participation by the private school or facility, including individual or conference telephone calls.

(3) [Reserved]

(b) *Reviewing and revising individualized education programs.* (1) After a child with a disability enters a private school or facility, any meetings to review and revise the child's IEP may be initiated and conducted by the private school or facility at the discretion of the public agency.

(2) If the private school or facility initiates and conducts these meetings, the public agency shall ensure that the parents and an agency representative:

(i) Are involved in any decision about the child's IEP; and

(ii) Agree to any proposed changes in the program before those changes are implemented.

(c) *Responsibility.* Even if a private school or facility implements a child's IEP, responsibility for compliance with this part remains with the public agency and the SEA.
(Authority: 20 U.S.C. 1413(a)(4)(B))

§ 300.349 Children with disabilities in parochial or other private schools.

If a child with a disability is enrolled in a parochial or other private school and receives special education or related services from a public agency, the public agency shall—

(a) Initiate and conduct meetings to develop, review, and revise an IEP for the child, in accordance with § 300.343; and

(b) Ensure that a representative of the parochial or other private school attends each meeting. If the representative cannot attend, the agency shall use other methods to ensure participation by the private school, including individual or conference telephone calls.

(Authority: 20 U.S.C. 1413(a)(4)(A))

§ 300.350 Individualized education program—accountability.

Each public agency must provide special education and related services to a child with a disability in accordance with an IEP. However, Part B of the Act does not require that any agency, teacher, or other person be held accountable if a child does not achieve the growth projected in the annual goals and objectives.

(Authority: 20 U.S.C. 1412(2)(B); 1414(a) (5), (6); Cong. Rec. at H7152 (daily ed., July 21, 1975))

Note: This section is intended to relieve concerns that the IEP constitutes a guarantee by the public agency and the teacher that a child will progress at a specified rate. However, this section does not relieve agencies and teachers from making good faith efforts to assist the child in achieving the objectives and goals listed in the IEP. Further, the section does not limit a parent's right to complain and ask for revisions of the child's program, or to invoke due process procedures, if the parent feels that these efforts are not being made.

Direct Service by the State Educational Agency

§ 300.360 Use of local educational agency allocation for direct services.

(a) An SEA may not distribute funds to an LEA, and shall use those funds to ensure the provision of FAPE to children with disabilities residing in the area served by the LEA, if the LEA, in any fiscal year—

(1) Is entitled to less than $7,500 for that fiscal year (beginning with fiscal year 1979);

(2) Does not submit an application that meets the requirements of §§ 300.220-300.240;

(3) Is unable or unwilling to establish and maintain programs of FAPE;

(4) Is unable or unwilling to be consolidated with other LEAs in order to establish and maintain those programs; or

(5) Has one or more children with disabilities who can best be served by a regional or State center designed to meet the needs of those children.

(b) In meeting the requirements of paragraph (a) of this section, the SEA may provide special education and related services directly, by contract, or through other arrangements.

(c) The excess cost requirements under §§ 300.182-300.186 do not apply to the SEA.

(Authority: 20 U.S.C. 1411(c)(4); 1413(b); 1414(d))

Note: Section 300.360 is a combination of three provisions in the statute (Sections 611(c)(4), 613(b), and 614(d)). This section focuses mainly on the State's administration and use of local entitlements under Part B.

The SEA, as a recipient of Part B funds is responsible for insuring that all public agencies in the State comply with the provisions of the Act, regardless of whether they receive Part B funds. If an LEA elects not to apply for its Part B entitlement, the State would be required to use those funds to ensure that FAPE is made available to children residing in the area served by that local agency. However, if the local entitlement is not sufficient for this purpose, additional State or local funds would have to be expended in order to ensure that FAPE and the other requirements of the Act are met.

Moreover, if the LEA is the recipient of any other Federal funds, it would have to be in compliance with 34 CFR §§ 104.31-104.39 of the regulations implementing section 504 of the Rehabilitation Act of 1973. It should be noted that the term "FAPE" has different meanings under Part B and section 504. For Example, under Part B, "FAPE" is a statutory term that requires special education and related services to be provided in accordance with an IEP. However, under section 504, each recipient must provide an education that includes services that are "designed to meet individual educational needs of handicapped persons as adequately as the needs of nonhandicapped persons are met***" Those regulations state that implementation of an IEP, in accordance with Part B, is one means of meeting the FAPE requirement.

§ 300.361 Nature and location of services.

The SEA may provide special education and related services under § 300.360(a) in the manner and at the location it considers appropriate. However, the manner in which the education and services are provided must be consistent with the requirements of this part (including the LRE provisions in §§ 300.550-300.556).

(Authority: 20 U.S.C. 1414(d))

§ 300.370 Use of State agency allocations.

(a) The State may use the portion of its allocation that it does not use for administration under §§ 300.620-300.621—

(1) For support services and direct services in accordance with the priority requirements under §§ 300.320-300.324; and

(2) For the administrative costs of the State's monitoring activities and complaint investigations, to the extent that these costs exceed the administrative costs for monitoring and complaint investigations incurred during fiscal year 1985.

(b) For the purposes of paragraph (a) of this section—

(1) "Direct services" means services provided to a child with a disability by the State directly, by contract, or through other arrangements; and

(2) "Support services" includes implementing the comprehensive system of personnel development under §§ 300.380-300.383, recruitment and training of hearing officers and surrogate parents, and public information and parent training activities relating to FAPE for children with disabilities.

(Authority: 20 U.S.C. 1411(b)(2), (c)(2))

§ 300.371 State matching.

Beginning with the period July 1, 1978-June 30, 1979, and for each following year, the funds that a State uses for direct and support services under § 300.370 must be matched on a program basis by the State from funds other than Federal funds. This requirement does not apply to funds that the State uses under § 300.360.

(Authority: 20 U.S.C. 1411(c)(2)(B), (c)(4)(B))

Note: The requirement in § 300.371 would be satisfied if the State can document that the amount of State funds expended for each major program area (e.g., the comprehensive system of personnel development) is at least equal to the expenditure of Federal funds in that program area.

§ 300.372 Applicability of nonsupplanting requirement.

Beginning with funds appropriated for Fiscal Year 1979 and for each following Fiscal Year, the requirement in section 613(a)(9) of the Act, which prohibits supplanting with Federal funds, does not apply to funds that the State uses from its allocation under § 300.706(a) of Subpart G for administration, direct services, or support services.

(Authority: 20 U.S.C. 1411(c)(3))

Comprehensive System of Personnel Development

§ 300.380 General.

Each State shall—

(a) Develop and implement a comprehensive system of personnel development that—

(1) Is consistent with the purposes of the Act and with the comprehensive system of personnel development described in 34 CFR § 300.360;

(2) Meets the requirements in §§ 300.381-300.383; and

(3) Is consistent with the provisions on personnel standards in § 300.153; and

(b) Include in its State plan a description of the personnel development system required in paragraph (a)(1) of this section

(Authority: 20 U.S.C. 1413(a)(3), (a)(14))

§ 300.381 Adequate supply of qualified personnel.

Each State plan must include a description of the procedures and activities the State will undertake to ensure an adequate supply of qualified personnel (as the term "qualified" is defined at § 300.15), including special education and related services personnel and leadership personnel, necessary to carry out the purposes of this part. The procedures and activities must include the development, updating, and implementation of a plan that—

(a) Addresses current and projected special education and related services personnel needs, including the need for leadership personnel; and

(b) Coordinates and facilitates efforts among SEA and LEAs, institutions of higher education, and professional associations to recruit, prepare, and retain qualified personnel, including personnel from minority backgrounds, and personnel with disabilities.

(Authority: 20 U.S.C. 1413(a)(3)(A))

§ 300.382 Personnel preparation and continuing education.

Each State plan must include a description of the procedures and activities the State will undertake to ensure that all personnel necessary to carry out this part are appropriately and adequately prepared. The procedures and activities must include—

(a) A system for the continuing education of regular and special education and related services personnel to enable these personnel to meet the needs of children with disabilities under this part;

(b) Procedures for acquiring and disseminating to teachers, administrators, and related services personnel significant knowledge derived from education research and other sources; and

(c) Procedures for adopting, if appropriate, promising practices, materials, and technology, proven effective through research and demonstration.

(Authority: 20 U.S.C. 1413(a)(3)(B))

§ 300.383 Data system on personnel and personnel development.

(a) *General.* The procedures and activities required in §§ 300.381 and 300.382 must include the development and maintenance of a system for determining, on an annual basis, the data required in paragraphs (b) and (c) of this section.

(b) *Data on qualified personnel.* (1) The system required by paragraph (a) of this section must enable each State to determine, on an annual basis—

(i) The number and type of personnel, including leadership personnel, employed in the provision of special education and related services, by profession or discipline;

(ii) The number and type of personnel who are employed with emergency, provisional, or temporary certification in each profession or discipline who do not hold appropriate State certification, licensure, or other credentials comparable to certification or licensure for that profession or discipline; and

(iii) The number and type of personnel, including leadership personnel, in each profession or discipline needed, and a projection of the numbers of those personnel that will be needed in five years, based on projections of individuals to be served, retirements and other departures of personnel from the field, and other relevant factors.

(2) The data on special education and related services personnel required in paragraph (b)(1) of this section must include audiologists, counselors, diagnostic and evaluation personnel, home-hospital teachers, interpreters for students with hearing impairments including deafness, occupational therapists, physical education teachers, physical therapists, psychologists, rehabilitation counselors, social workers, speech-language pathologists, teacher aides, recreation and therapeutic recreation specialists, vocational education teachers, work-study coordinators, and other instructional and noninstructional staff.

(3) The data on leadership personnel required by paragraph (b)(1) of this section must include administrators and supervisors of State or local agencies who are involved in the provision or supervision of services or activities necessary to carry out the purposes of this part.

(c) *Data on personnel development.* The system required in paragraph (a) of this section must enable each State to determine, on an annual basis, the institutions of higher education within the State that are preparing special education and related services personnel, including leadership personnel, by area of specialization, including—

(1) The numbers of students enrolled in programs for the preparation of special education and related services personnel administered by these institutions of higher education; and

(2) The number of students who graduated during the past year with certification or licensure, or with credentials to qualify for certification or licensure, from programs for the preparation of special education and related services personnel administered by institutions of higher education.

(Authority: 20 U.S.C. 1413(a)(3)(A))

§ 300.384-300.387 [Reserved]

Subpart D—Private Schools

Children with Disabilities in Private Schools Placed or Referred by Public Agencies

§ 300.400 Applicability of §§ 300.400-300.402.

Sections 300.401-300.402 apply only to children with disabilities who are or have been placed in or referred to a private school or facility by a public agency as a means of providing special education and related services.

(Authority: 20 U.S.C. 1413(a)(4)(B))

§ 300.401 Responsibility of State educational agency.

Each SEA shall ensure that a child with a disability who is placed in or referred to a private school or facility by a public agency:

(a) Is provided special education and related services:

(1) In conformance with an IEP which meets the requirements under §§ 300.340-300.350;

(2) At no cost to the parents; and

(3) At a school or facility which meets the standards that apply to the SEA and LEAs (including the requirements in this part); and

(b) Has all of the rights of a child with a disability who is served by a public agency.

(Authority: 20 U.S.C. 1413(a)(4)(B))

§ 300.402 Implementation by State educational agency.

In implementing § 300.401, the SEA shall:

(a) Monitor compliance through procedures such as written reports, on-site visits, and parent questionnaires;

(b) Disseminate copies of applicable standards to each private school and facility to which a public agency has referred or placed a child with a disability; and

(c) Provide an opportunity for those private schools and facilities to participate in the development and revision of State standards which apply to them.

(Authority: 20 U.S.C. 1413(a)(4)(B))

§ 300.403 Placement of children by parents.

(a) If a child with a disability has FAPE available and the parents choose to place the child in a private school or facility, the public agency is not required by this part to pay for the child's education at the private school or facility. However, the public agency shall make services available to the child as provided under §§ 300.450-300.452.

(b) Disagreements between a parent and a public agency regarding the availability of a program appropriate for the child, and the question of financial responsibility, are subject to the due process procedures under §§ 300.500-300.515.

(Authority: 20 U.S.C. 1412(2)(B); 1415)

Children with Disabilities in Private Schools not Placed or referred by Public Agencies

§ 300.450 Definition of "private school children with disabilities."

As used in this part, "private school children with disabilities" means children with disabilities enrolled in private schools or facilities other than children with disabilities covered under §§ 300.400-300.402.

(Authority: 20 U.S.C. 1413(a)(4)(A))

§ 300.451 State educational agency responsibility.

The SEA shall ensure that—

(a) To the extent consistent with their number and location in the State, provision is made for the participation of private school children with disabilities in the program assisted or carried out under this part by providing them with special education and related services; and

(b) The requirements in 34 CFR 76.651-76.662 are met.

(Authority: 20 U.S.C. 1413(a)(4)(A))

§ 300.452 Local educational agency responsibility.

Each LEA shall provide special education and related services designed to meet the needs of private school children with disabilities residing in the jurisdiction of the agency.

(Authority: Sec. 1413(a)(4)(A); 1414(a)(6))

Procedures for By-Pass

§ 300.480 By-pass—general.

(a) The Secretary implements a by-pass if an SEA is, and was on December 2, 1983, prohibited by law from providing for the participation of private school children with disabilities in the program assisted or carried out under this part, as required by section 613(a)(4)(A) of the Act and by §§ 300.451-300.452.

(b) The Secretary waives the requirement of section 613(a)(4)(A) of the Act and of §§ 300.451-300.452 if the Secretary implements a by-pass.

(Authority: 20 U.S.C. 1413(d)(1))

§ 300.481 Provisions for services under a by-pass.

(a) Before implementing a by-pass, the Secretary consults with appropriate public and private school officials, including SEA officials, in the affected State to consider matters such as—

(1) The prohibition imposed by State law which results in the need for a by-pass;

(2) The scope and nature of the services required by private school children with disabilities in the State, and the number of children to be served under the by-pass; and

(3) The establishment of policies and procedures to ensure that private school children with disabilities receive services consistent with the requirements of section 613(a)(4)(A) of the Act, §§ 300.451-300.452, and 34 CFR 76.651-76.662.

(b) After determining that a by-pass is required, the Secretary arranges for the provision of services to private school children with disabilities in the State in a manner consistent with the requirements of section 613(a)(4)(A) of the Act and §§ 300.451-300.452 by providing services through one or more agreements with appropriate parties.

(c) For any fiscal year in which a by-pass is implemented, the Secretary determines the maximum amount to be paid to the providers of services by multiplying—

(1) A per child amount which may not exceed the amount per child provided by the Secretary under this part for all children with disabilities in the State for the preceding fiscal year, by

(2) The number of private school children with disabilities (as defined by §§ 300.7(a) and 300.450) in the State, as determined by the Secretary on the basis of the most recent satisfactory data available, which may include an estimate of the number of those children with disabilities.

(d) The Secretary deducts from the State's allocation under this part the amount the Secretary determines is necessary to implement a by-pass and pays that amount to the provider of services. The Secretary may withhold this amount from the State's allocation pending final resolution of any investigation or complaint that could result in a determination that a by-pass must be implemented.

(Authority: 20 U.S.C. 1413(d)(2))

Due Process Procedures

Source: Sections 300.482 through 300.486 appear at 49 FR 48526, Dec. 12, 1984, unless otherwise noted.

§ 300.482 Notice of intent to implement a by-pass

(a) Before taking any final action to implement a by-pass, the Secretary provides the affected SEA with written notice.

(b) In the written notice, the Secretary—

(1) States the reasons for the proposed by-pass in sufficient detail to allow the SEA to respond;

(2) Advises the SEA that it has a specific period of time (at least 45 days) from receipt of the written notice to submit written objections to the proposed by-pass and that it may request in writing the opportunity for a hearing to show cause why a by-pass should not be implemented.

(c) The Secretary sends the notice to the SEA by certified mail with return receipt requested.

(Authority: 20 U.S.C. 1413(d)(3)(A))

§ 300.483 Request to show cause.

An SEA seeking an opportunity to show cause why a by-pass should not be implemented shall submit a written request for a show cause hearing to the Secretary.

(Authority: 20 U.S.C. 1413(d)(3)(A))

§ 300.484 Show cause hearing.

(a) If a show cause hearing is requested, the Secretary—

(1) Notifies the SEA and other appropriate public and private school officials of the time and place for the hearing; and

(2) Designates a person to conduct the show cause hearing. The designee must not have had any responsibility for the matter brought for a hearing.

(b) At the show cause hearing, the designee considers matters such as—

(1) The necessity for implementing a by-pass;

(2) Possible factual errors in the written notice of intent to implement a by-pass; and

(3) The objections raised by public and private school representatives.

(c) The designee may regulate the course of the proceedings and the conduct of parties during the pendency of the proceedings. The designee takes all steps necessary to conduct a fair and impartial proceeding, to avoid delay, and to maintain order.

(d) The designee may interpret applicable statutes and regulations, but may not waive them or rule on their validity.

(e) The designee arranges for the preparation, retention, and, if appropriate, dissemination of the record of the hearing.

(Authority: 20 U.S.C. 1413(d)(3)(A)

§ 300.485 Decision.

(a) The designee who conducts the show cause hearing—

(1) Issues a written decision which includes a statement of findings; and

(2) Submits a copy of the decision to the Secretary and sends a copy to each party by certified mail with return receipt requested.

(b) Each party may submit comments and recommendations on the designee's decision to the Secretary within 15 days of the date the party receives the designee's decision.

(c) The Secretary adopts, reverses, or modifies the designee's decision and notifies the SEA of the Secretary's final action. That notice is sent by certified mail with return receipt requested.

(Authority: 20 U.S.C. 1413(d)(3)(A))

§ 300.486 Judicial review.

If dissatisfied with the Secretary's final action, the SEA may, within 60 days after notice of that action, file a petition for review with the United States court of appeals for the circuit in which the State is located. The procedures for judicial review are described in section 613(d)(3)(B)-(D) of the Act.

(Authority: 20 U.S.C. 1413(d)(3)(B)-(D)))

Subpart E—Procedural Safeguards

Due Process Procedures for Parents and Children

§ 300.500 Definitions of "consent," "evaluation," and "personally identifiable."

(a) As used in this part: "Consent" means that—

(1) The parent has been fully informed of all information relevant to the activity for which consent is sought, in his or her native language, or other mode of communication;

(2) The parent understands and agrees in writing to the carrying out of the activity for which his or her consent is sought, and the consent describes that activity and lists the records (if any) which will be released and to whom; and

(3) The parent understands that the granting of consent is voluntary on the part of the parent and may be revoked at any time.

(b) "Evaluation" means procedures used in accordance with §§ 300.530-300.534 to determine whether a child has a disability and the nature and extent of the special education and related services that the child needs. The term means procedures used selectively with an individual child and does not include basic tests administered to or procedures used with all children in a school, grade, or class.

(c) Personally identifiable means that information includes:

(1) The name of the child, the child's parent, or other family member;

(2) The address of the child;

(3) A personal identifier, such as the child's social security number or student number; or

(4) A list of personal characteristics or other information which would make it possible to identify the child with reasonable certainty.

(Authority: 20 U.S.C. 1415,1417(c))

§ 300.501 General responsibility of public agencies.

Each SEA shall ensure that each public agency establishes and implements procedural safeguards which meet the requirements of §§ 300.500-300.515.

(Authority: 20 U.S.C. 1415(a))

§ 300.502 Opportunity to examine records.

The parents of a child with a disability shall be afforded, in accordance with the procedures in §§ 300.562-300.569 an opportunity to inspect and review all education records with respect to—

(a) The identification, evaluation, and educational placement of the child, and

(b) The provision of FAPE to the child.

(Authority: 20 U.S.C. 1415(b)(1)(A))

§ 300.503 Independent educational evaluation.

(a) *General.* (1) The parents of a child with a disability have the right under this part to obtain an independent educational evaluation of the child, subject to paragraphs (b) through (e) of this section.

(2) Each public agency shall provide to parents, on request, information about where an independent educational evaluation may be obtained.

(3) For the purposes of this part:

(i) "Independent educational evaluation" means an evaluation conducted by a qualified examiner who is not employed by the public agency responsible for the education of the child in question.

(ii) "Public expense" means that the public agency either pays for the full cost of the evaluation or insures that the evaluation is otherwise provided at no cost to the parent, consistent with § 300.301.

(b) *Parent right to evaluation at public expense.* A parent has the right to an independent educational evaluation at public expense if the parent disagrees with an evaluation obtained by the public agency. However, the public agency may initiate a hearing under § 300.506 of this subpart to show that its evaluation is appropriate. If the final decision is that the evaluation is appropriate, the parent still has the right to an independent educational evaluation, but not at public expense.

(c) *Parent initiated evaluations.* If the parent obtains an independent educational evaluation at private expense, the results of the evaluation—

(1) Must be considered by the public agency in any decision made with respect to the provision of FAPE to the child, and

(2) May be presented as evidence at a hearing under this subpart regarding that child.

(d) *Requests for evaluations by hearing officers.* If a hearing officer requests an independent educational evaluation as part of a hearing, the cost of the evaluation must be at public expense.

(e) *Agency criteria.* Whenever an independent evaluation is at public expense, the criteria under which the evaluation is obtained, including the location of the evaluation and the qualifications of the examiner, must be the same as the criteria which the public agency uses when it initiates an evaluation.

(Authority: 20 U.S.C. 1415(b)(1)(A))

§ 300.504 Prior notice; parent consent.

(a) *Notice.* Written notice which meets the requirements under § 300.505 must be given to the parents of a child with a disability a reasonable time before the public agency—

(1) Proposes to initiate or change the identification, evaluation, or educational placement of the child or the provision of FAPE to the child, or

(2) Refuses to initiate or change the identification, evaluation, or educational placement of the child or the provision of FAPE to the child.

(b) *Consent; procedures if a parent refuses consent.* (1) Parental consent must be obtained before—

(i) Conducting a preplacement evaluation; and

(ii) Initial placement of a child with a disability in a program providing special education and related services.

(2) Except for preplacement evaluation and initial placement, consent may not be required as a condition of any benefit to the parent or child.

(2) If State law requires parental consent before a child with a disability is evaluated or initially provided special education and related services, State procedures govern the public agency in overriding a parent's refusal to consent.

(3) If there is no State law requiring consent before a child with a disability is evaluated or initially provided special education and related services, the public agency may use the hearing procedures in §§ 300.506-300.508 to determine if the child may be evaluated or initially provided special education and related services without parental consent.

(c) *Additional State consent requirements.* In addition to the parental consent requirements described in paragraph (b) of this section, a State may require parental consent for other services and activities under this part if it ensures that each public agency in the State establishes and implements effective procedures to ensure that a parent's refusal to consent does not result in a failure to provide the child with FAPE.

(c) *Limitation.* A public agency may not require parental consent as a condition of any benefit to the parent or the child except for the service or activity for which consent is required under paragraphs (b) or (c) of this section.

(Authority: 20 U.S.C. 1415(b)(1)(C), (D); 1412(2), (6))

Note 1: Any changes in a child's special education program, after the initial placement, are not subject to parental consent under Part B, but are subject to the prior notice requirement in paragraph (a) and the IEP requirements of §§ 300.340-300.350.

Note 2: Paragraph (b)(2) of this section means that if State law requires parental consent before evaluation or before special education and related services are initially provided, and the parent refuses (or otherwise withholds) consent, State procedures, such as obtaining a court order authorizing the public agency to conduct the evaluation or provide the education and related services, must be followed.

If, however, there is no legal requirement for consent outside of these regulations, the public agency may use the due process procedures of §§ 300.506-300.508 to obtain a decision to allow the evaluation or services without parental consent. The agency must notify the parent of its actions, and the parent has appeal rights as well as rights at the hearing itself.

Note 3: If a State adopts a consent requirement in addition to those described in paragraph (b) of this section and consent is refused, paragraph (d) of this section requires that the public agency must nevertheless provide the services and activities that are not in dispute. For example, if a State requires parental consent to the provision of all services identified in an IEP and the parent refuses to consent to physical therapy services included in the IEP, the agency is not relieved of its obligation to implement those portions of the IEP to which the parent consents.

If the parent refuses to consent and the public agency determines that the services or activity in dispute is necessary to provide FAPE to the child, paragraph (c) of this section requires that the agency must implement its procedures to override the refusal. This section does not preclude the agency from reconsidering its proposal if it believes that circumstances warrant.

§ 300.505 Content of notice.

(a) The notice under § 300.504 must include—
(1) A full explanation of all of the procedural safeguards available to the parents under § 300.500, §§ 300.502-300.515, and §§ 300.562-300.569;

(2) A description of the action proposed or refused by the agency, an explanation of why the agency proposes or refuses to take the action, and a description of any options the agency considered and the reasons why those options were rejected;

(3) A description of each evaluation procedure, test, record, or report the agency uses as a basis for the proposal or refusal; and

(4) A description of any other factors which are relevant to the agency's proposal or refusal.

(b) The notice must be—
(1) Written in language understandable to the general public, and
(2) Provided in the native language of the parent or other mode of communication used by the parent, unless it is clearly not feasible to do so.

(c) If the native language or other mode of communication of the parent is not a written language, the SEA or LEA shall take steps to ensure—
(1) That the notice is translated orally or by other means to the parent in his or her native language or other mode of communication;
(2) That the parent understands the content of the notice; and
(3) That there is written evidence that the requirements in paragraphs (c)(1) and (2) of this section have been met.

(Authority: 20 U.S.C. 1415(b)(1)(D))

§ 300.506 Impartial due process hearing.

(a) A parent or a public educational agency may initiate a hearing on any of the matters described in § 300.504(a)(1) and (2).

(b) The hearing must be conducted by the SEA or the public agency directly responsible for the education of the child, as determined under State statute, State regulation, or a written policy of the SEA.

(c) The public agency shall inform the parent of any free or low-cost legal and other relevant services available in the area if—
(1) The parent requests the information; or
(2) The parent or the agency initiates a hearing under this section.

(Authority: 20 U.S.C. 1415(b)(2))

Note: Many States have pointed to the success of using mediation as an intervening step prior to conducting a formal due process hearing. Although the process of mediation is not required by the statute or these regulations, an agency may wish to suggest mediation in disputes concerning the identification, evaluation, and educational placement of children with disabilities, and the provision of FAPE to those children. Mediations have been conducted by members of SEAs or LEA personnel who were not previously involved in the particular case. In many cases, mediation leads to solution of differences between parents and agencies without the development of an adversarial relationship and with minimum emotional stress. However, mediation may not be used to deny or delay a parent's rights under this subpart.

§ 300.507 Impartial hearing officer.

(a) A hearing may not be conducted:

(1) By a person who is an employee of a public agency which is involved in the education or care of the child; or

(2) By any person having a personal or professional interest which would conflict with his or her objectivity in the hearing.

(b) A person who otherwise qualifies to conduct a hearing under paragraph (a) of this section is not an employee of the agency solely because he or she is paid by the agency to serve as a hearing officer.

(c) Each public agency shall keep a list of the persons who serve as hearing officers. The list must include a statement of the qualifications of each of those persons.

(Authority: 20 U.S.C. 1414(b)(2))

§ 300.508 Hearing rights.

(a) Any party to a hearing has the right to:

(1) Be accompanied and advised by counsel and by individuals with special knowledge or training with respect to the problems of children with disabilities;

(2) Present evidence and confront, cross-examine, and compel the attendance of witnesses;

(3) Prohibit the introduction of any evidence at the hearing that has not been disclosed to that party at least five days before the hearing;

(4) Obtain a written or electronic verbatim record of the hearing;

(5) Obtain written findings of fact and decisions. The public agency, after deleting any personally identifiable information shall—

(i) Transmit those findings and decisions to the State advisory panel established under § 300.650; and

(ii) Make those findings and decisions available to the public.

(b) Parents involved in hearings must be given the right to—

(1) Have the child who is the subject of the hearing present; and

(2) Open the hearing to the public.

(Authority: 20 U.S.C. 1415(d))

§ 300.509 Hearing decision; appeal.

A decision made in a hearing conducted under this subpart is final, unless a party to the hearing appeals the decision under § 300.510 or § 300.511.

(Authority: 20 U.S.C. 1415(c))

§ 300.510 Administrative appeal; impartial review.

(a) If the hearing is conducted by a public agency other than the SEA, any party aggrieved by the findings and decision in the hearing may appeal to the SEA.

(b) If there is an appeal, the SEA shall conduct an impartial review of the hearing. The official conducting the review shall:

(1) Examine the entire hearing record;

(2) Ensure that the procedures at the hearing were consistent with the requirements of due process;

(3) Seek additional evidence if necessary. If a hearing is held to receive additional evidence, the rights in § 300.508 apply;

(4) Afford the parties an opportunity for oral or written argument, or both, at the discretion of the review official;

(5) Make an independent decision on completion of the review; and

(6) Give a copy of written findings and the decision to the parties.

(c) The SEA, after deleting any personally identifiable information, shall—

(1) Transmit the findings and decisions referred to in paragraph (b)(6) of this section to the State advisory panel established under § 300.650; and

(2) Make those findings and decisions available to the public.

(d) The decision made by the reviewing official is final, unless a party brings a civil action under § 300.511.

(Authority: 20 U.S.C. 1415(c), (d); H. R. Rep. No. 94-664, at p. 49 (1975))

Note 1: The SEA may conduct its review either directly or through another State agency acting on its behalf. However, the SEA remains responsible for the final decision on review.

Note 2. All parties have the right to continue to be represented by counsel at the State administrative review level, whether or not the reviewing official determines that a further hearing is necessary. If the reviewing official decides to hold a hearing to receive additional evidence, the other rights in § 300.508 relating to hearings also apply.

§ 300.511 Civil action.

Any party aggrieved by the findings and decision made in a hearing who does not have the right to appeal under § 300.510 of this subpart, and any party aggrieved by the decision of a reviewing officer under § 300.510 has the right to bring a civil action under section 615(e)(2) of the Act.

(Authority: 20 U.S.C. 1415)

§ 300.512 Timeliness and convenience of hearings and reviews.

(a) The public agency shall ensure that not later than 45 days after the receipt of a request for a hearing—

(1) A final decision is reached in the hearing; and

(2) A copy of the decision is mailed to each of the parties.

(b) The SEA shall ensure that not later than 30 days after the receipt of a request for a review—

(1) A final decision is reached in the review; and

(2) A copy of the decision is mailed to each of the parties.

(c) A hearing or reviewing officer may grant specific extensions of time beyond the periods set out in paragraphs (a) and (b) of this section at the request of either party.

(d) Each hearing and each review involving oral arguments must be conducted at a time and place which is reasonably convenient to the parents and child involved.

(Authority: 20 U.S.C. 1415)

§ 300.513 Child's status during proceedings.

(a) During the pendency of any administrative or judicial proceeding regarding a complaint, unless the public agency and the parents of the child agree otherwise, the child involved in the complaint must remain in his or her present educational placement.

(b) If the complaint involves an application for initial admission to public school, the child, with the consent of the parents, must be placed in the public school program until the completion of all the proceedings.

(Authority: 20 U.S.C. 1415(e)(3))

Note: Section 300.513 does not permit a child's placement to be changed during a complaint proceeding, unless the parents and agency agree otherwise. While the placement may not be changed, this does not preclude the agency from using its normal procedures for dealing with children who are endangering themselves or others.

§ 300.514 Surrogate parents.

(a) *General.* Each public agency shall ensure that the rights of a child are protected when—

(1) No parent (as defined in § 300.13) can be identified;

(2) The public agency, after reasonable efforts, cannot discover the whereabouts of a parent; or

(3) The child is a ward of the State under the laws of that State.

(b) *Duty of public agency.* The duty of a public agency under paragraph (a) of this section includes

the assignment of an individual to act as a surrogate for the parents. This must include a method: (1) for determining whether a child needs a surrogate parent, and (2) for assigning a surrogate parent to the child.

(c) *Criteria for selection of surrogates.* (1) The public agency may select a surrogate parent in any way permitted under State law.

(2) Public agencies shall ensure that a person selected as a surrogate—

(i) Has no interest that conflicts with the interest of the child he or she represents; and

(ii) Has knowledge and skills that ensure adequate representation of the child.

(d) *Non-employee requirement; compensation.* (1) A person assigned as a surrogate may not be an employee of a public agency which is involved in the education or care of the child.

(2) A person who otherwise qualifies to be a surrogate parent under paragraphs (c) and (d)(1) of this section, is not an employee of the agency solely because he or she is paid by the agency to serve as a surrogate parent.

(e) *Responsibilities.* The surrogate parent may represent the child in all matters relating to—

(1) The identification, evaluation, and educational placement of the child; and

(2) The provision of FAPE to the child.

(Authority: 20 U.S.C. 1415(b)(1)(B))

§ 300.515 Attorney's fees.

Each public agency shall inform parents that in any action or proceeding under section 615 of the Act, courts may award parents reasonable attorney's fees under the circumstances described in section 615(e)(4) of the Act.

(Authority: 20 U.S.C. 1415(b)(1)(D); 1415(e)(4))

Protection in Evaluation Procedures

§ 300.530 General.

(a) Each SEA shall ensure that each public agency establishes and implements procedures that meet the requirements of §§ 300.530-300.534.

(b) Testing and evaluation materials and procedures used for the purposes of evaluation and placement of children with disabilities must be selected and administered so as not to be racially or culturally discriminatory.

(Authority: 20 U.S.C. 1412(5)(C))

§ 300.531 Preplacement evaluation.

Before any action is taken with respect to the initial placement of a child with a disability in a special education program, a full and individual evaluation of the child's educational needs must be conducted in accordance with the requirements of § 300.532.

(Authority: 20 U.S.C. 1412(5)(C))

§ 300.532 Evaluation procedures.

State educational agencies and LEAs shall ensure, at a minimum, that:

(a) Tests and other evaluation materials—

(1) Are provided and administered in the child's native language or other mode of communication, unless it is clearly not feasible to do so;

(2) Have been validated for the specific purpose for which they are used; and

(3) Are administered by trained personnel in conformance with the instructions provided by their producer.

(b) Tests and other evaluation materials include those tailored to assess specific areas of educational need and not merely those which are designed to provide a single general intelligence quotient.

(c) Tests are selected and administered so as best to ensure that when a test is administered to a child with impaired sensory, manual, or speaking skills, the test results accurately reflect the child's aptitude or achievement level or whatever other factors the test purports to measure, rather than reflecting the child's impaired sensory, manual, or speaking skills (except where those skills are the factors which the test purports to measure).

(d) No single procedure is used as the sole criterion for determining an appropriate educational program for a child.

(e) The evaluation is made by a multidisciplinary team or group of persons, including at least one teacher or other specialist with knowledge in the area of suspected disability.

(f) The child is assessed in all areas related to the suspected disability, including, where appropriate, health, vision, hearing, social and emotional status, general intelligence, academic performance, communicative status, and motor abilities.

(Authority: 20 U.S.C. 1412(5)(C))

Note: Children who have a speech impairment as their primary disability may not need a complete battery of assessments (e.g., psychological, physical, or adaptive behavior). However, a qualified speech-language pathologist would: (1) evaluate each speech impaired child using procedures that are appropriate for the diagnosis and appraisal of speech and language disorders, and (2) where necessary, make referrals for additional assessments needed to make an appropriate placement decision.

§ 300.533 Placement procedures.

(a) In interpreting evaluation data and in making placement decisions, each public agency shall—

(1) Draw upon information from a variety of sources, including aptitude and achievement tests, teacher recommendations, physical condition, social or cultural background, and adaptive behavior;

(2) Ensure that information obtained from all of these sources is documented and carefully considered;

(3) Ensure that the placement decision is made by a group of persons, including persons knowledgeable about the child, the meaning of the evaluation data, and the placement options; and

(4) Ensure that the placement decision is made in conformity with the least restrictive environment rules in §§ 300.550-300.554.

(b) If a determination is made that a child has a disability and needs special education and related services, an IEP must be developed for the child in accordance with §§ 300.340-300.350.

(Authority: 20 U.S.C. 1412(5)(C); 1414(a)(5))

Note: Paragraph (a)(1) includes a list of examples of sources that may be used by a public agency in making placement decisions. The agency would not have to use all the sources in every instance. The point of the requirement is to ensure that more than one source is used in interpreting evaluation data and in making placement decisions. For example, while all of the named sources would have to be used for a child whose suspected disability is mental retardation, they would not be necessary for certain other children with disabilities, such as a child who has a severe articulation disorder as his primary disability. For such a child, the speech-language pathologist, in complying with the multi-source requirement, might use (1) a standardized test of articulation, and (2) observation of the child's articulation behavior in conversational speech.

§ 300.534 Reevaluation.

Each SEA and LEA shall ensure—

(a) That the IEP of each child with a disability is reviewed in accordance with §§ 300.340-300.350; and

(b) That an evaluation of the child, based on procedures which meet the requirements under § 300.532, is conducted every three years, or more frequently if conditions warrant, or if the child's parent or teacher requests an evaluation.

(Authority: 20 U.S.C. 1412(5)(c))

Additional Procedures for Evaluating Children with Specific Learning Disabilities

§ 300.540 Additional team members.

In evaluating a child suspected of having a specific learning disability, in addition to the requirements of § 300.532, each public agency shall include on the multidisciplinary evaluation team—

(a) (1) The child's regular teacher; or

(2) If the child does not have a regular teacher, a regular classroom teacher qualified to teach a child of his or her age; or

(3) For a child of less than school age, an individual qualified by the SEA to teach a child of his or her age; and

(b) At least one person qualified to conduct individual diagnostic examinations of children, such as a school psychologist, speech-language pathologist, or remedial reading teacher.

(Authority: 20 U.S.C. 1411 note)

§ 300.541 Criteria for determining the existence of a specific learning disability.

(a) A team may determine that a child has a specific learning disability if—

(1) The child does not achieve commensurate with his or her age and ability levels in one or more of the areas listed in paragraph (a)(2) of this section, when provided with learning experiences appropriate for the child's age and ability levels; and

(2) The team finds that a child has a severe discrepancy between achievement and intellectual ability in one or more of the following areas—

(i) Oral expression;

(ii) Listening comprehension;

(iii) Written expression;

(iv) Basic reading skill;

(v) Reading comprehension;

(vi) Mathematics calculation; or

(vii) Mathematics reasoning.

(b) The team may not identify a child as having a specific learning disability if the severe discrepancy between ability and achievement is primarily the result of—

(1) A visual, hearing, or motor impairment;

(2) Mental retardation;

(3) Emotional disturbance;

(4) Environmental, cultural or economic disadvantage.

(Authority: 20 U.S.C. 1411 note)

§ 300.542 Observation.

(a) At least one team member other than the child's regular teacher shall observe the child's academic performance in the regular classroom setting.

(b) In the case of a child of less than school age or out of school, a team member shall observe the child in an environment appropriate for a child of that age.

(Authority: 20 U.S.C. 1411 note)

§ 300.543 Written report.

(a) The team shall prepare a written report of the results of the evaluation.

(b) The report must include a statement of—

(1) Whether the child has a specific learning disability;

(2) The basis for making the determination;

(3) The relevant behavior noted during the observation of the child;

(4) The relationship of that behavior to the child's academic functioning;

(5) The educationally relevant medical findings, if any;

(6) Whether there is a severe discrepancy between achievement and ability which is not correctable without special education and related services; and

(7) The determination of the team concerning the effects of environmental, cultural, or economic disadvantage.

(c) Each team member shall certify in writing whether the report reflects his or her conclusion. If it does not reflect his or her conclusion, the team member must submit a separate statement presenting his or her conclusions.

(Authority: 20 U.S.C. 1411 note)

Least Restrictive Environment

§ 300.550 General

(a) Each SEA shall ensure that each public agency establishes and implements procedures which meet the requirements of §§ 300.550-300.556.

(b) Each public agency shall ensure—

(1) That to the maximum extent appropriate, children with disabilities, including children in public or private institutions or other care facilities, are educated with children who are nondisabled; and

(2) That special classes, separate schooling or other removal of children with disabilities from the regular educational environment occurs only when the nature or severity of the disability is such that education in regular classes with the use of supplementary aids and services cannot be achieved satisfactorily.

(Authority: 20 U.S.C. 1412(5)(B); 1414(a)(1)(C)(iv))

§ 300.551 Continuum of alternative placements.

(a) Each public agency shall ensure that a continuum of alternative placements is available to meet the needs of children with disabilities for special education and related services.

(b) The continuum required under paragraph (a) of this section must—

(1) Include the alternative placements listed in the definition of special education under § 300.17 (instruction in regular classes, special classes, special schools, home instruction, and instruction in hospitals and institutions); and

(2) Make provision for supplementary services (such as resource room or itinerant instruction) to be provided in conjunction with regular class placement.

(Authority: 20 U.S.C. 1412(5)(B))

§ 300.552 Placements.

Each public agency shall ensure that:

(a) The educational placement of each child with a disability—

(1) Is determined at least annually;

(2) Is based on his or her IEP; and

(3) Is as close as possible to the child's home.

(b) The various alternative placements included under § 300.551 are available to the extent necessary to implement the IEP for each child with a disability.

(c) Unless the IEP of a child with a disability requires some other arrangement, the child is educated in the school which he or she would attend if nondisabled.

(d) In selecting the least restrictive environment, consideration is given to any potential harmful effect on the child or on the quality of services which he or she needs.

(Authority: 20 U.S.C. 1412(5)(B))

Note: Section 300.552 includes some of the main factors which must be considered in determining the extent to which a child with a disability can be educated with children who are nondisabled. The overriding rule in this section is that placement decisions must be made on an individual basis. The section also requires each agency to have various alternative placements available in order to ensure that each child with a disability receives an education which is appropriate to his or her individual needs.

The requirements of § 300.552, as well as the other requirements of §§ 300.550-300.556, apply to all preschool children with disabilities who are entitled to receive FAPE. Public agencies that provide preschool programs for nondisabled preschool children must ensure that the requirements of § 300.552(c) are met. Public agencies that do not operate programs for nondisabled preschool children are not required to initiate such programs solely to satisfy the requirements regarding placement in the least restrictive environment embodied in §§ 300.550-300.556. For these public agencies, some alternative methods, for meeting the requirements of §§ 300.550-300.556 include:

(1) Providing opportunities for the participation (even part-time) of preschool children with disabilities in other preschool programs operated by public agencies (such as Head Start);

(2) Placing children with disabilities in private school programs for nondisabled preschool children or private school preschool programs that integrate children with disabilities and nondisabled children; and

(3) Locating classes for preschool children with disabilities in regular elementary schools.

In each case the public agency must ensure that each child's placement is in the LRE in which the unique needs of that child can be met, based upon the child's IEP, and meets all of the other requirements of §§ 300.340-300.350 and §§ 300.550-300.556.

The analysis of the regulations for Section 504 of the Rehabilitation Act of 1973 (34 CFR part 104-Appendix, Paragraph 24) includes several points regarding educational placements of children with disabilities which are pertinent to this section:

1. With respect to determining proper placements, the analysis states: "*** it should be stressed that, where a handicapped child is so disruptive in a regular classroom that the education of other students is significantly impaired, the needs of the handicapped child cannot be met in that environment. Therefore regular placement would not be appropriate to his or her needs ***."

2. With respect to placing a child with a disability in an alternate setting, the analysis states that among the factors to be considered in placing a child is the need to place the child as close to home as possible. Recipients are required to take this factor into account in making placement decisions. The parent's right to challenge the placement of their child extends not only to placement in special classes or separate schools, but also to placement in a distant school, particularly in a residential program. An equally appropriate education program may exist closer to home; and this issue may be raised by the parent under the due process provisions of this subpart.

§ 300.553 Nonacademic settings.

In providing or arranging for the provision of nonacademic and extracurricular services and activities, including meals, recess periods, and the services and activities set forth in § 300.306, each public agency shall ensure that each child with a disability participates with nondisabled children in those services and activities to the maximum extent appropriate to the needs of that child.

(Authority: 20 U.S.C. 1412(5)(B))

Note: Section 300.553 is taken from a new requirement in the final regulations for Section 504 of the Rehabilitation Act of 1973. With respect to this requirement, the analysis of the Section 504 Regulations includes the following statement: "[This paragraph] specifies that children with disabilities must also be provided nonacademic services in as integrated a setting as possible. This requirement is especially important for children whose educational needs necessitate their being solely with other handicapped children during most of each day. To the maximum extent appropriate, children in residential settings are also to be provided opportunities for participation with other children." (34 CFR part 104— Appendix, Paragraph 24.)

§ 300.554 Children in public or private institutions.

Each SEA shall make arrangements with public and private institutions, (such as a memorandum of agreement or special implementation procedures) as may be necessary to ensure that §300.550 is effectively implemented.
(Authority: 20 U.S.C. 1412(5)(B))

Note: Under section 612(5)(B) of the statute, the requirement to educate children with disabilities with nondisabled children also applies to children in public and private institutions or other care facilities. Each SEA must ensure that each applicable agency and institution in the State implements this requirement. Regardless of other reasons for institutional placement, no child in an institution who is capable of education in a regular public school setting may be denied access to an education in that setting.

§ 300.555 Technical assistance and training activities.

Each SEA shall carry out activities to ensure that teachers and administrators in all public agencies—

(a) Are fully informed about their responsibilities for implementing § 300.550; and

(b) Are provided with technical assistance and training necessary to assist them in this effort.
(Authority: 20 U.S.C. 1412(5)(B))

§ 300.556 Monitoring activities.

(a) The SEA shall carry out activities to ensure that § 300.550 is implemented by each public agency.

(b) If there is evidence that a public agency makes placements that are inconsistent with § 300.550 of this subpart, the SEA shall—

(1) Review the public agency's justification for its actions, and

(2) Assist in planning and implementing any necessary corrective action.
(Authority: 20 U.S.C. 1412(5)(B))

Confidentiality of Information

§ 300.560 Definitions.

As used in §§ 300.560-300.576—

Destruction means physical destruction or removal of personal identifiers from information so that the information is no longer personally identifiable.

Education records means the type of records covered under the definition of education records in part 99 of this title (the regulations implementing the Family Educational Rights and Privacy Act of 1974).

Participating agency means any agency or institution which collects, maintains, or uses personally identifiable information, or from which information is obtained under this part.
(Authority: 20 U.S.C. 1412(2)(D); 1417(c))

§ 300.561 Notice to parents.

(a) The SEA shall give notice which is adequate to fully inform parents about the requirements under § 300.128, including—

(1) A description of the extent to which the notice is given in the native languages of the various population groups in the State;

(2) A description of the children on whom personally identifiable information is maintained, the types of information sought, the methods the State intends to use in gathering the information (including the sources from whom information is gathered), and the uses to be made of the information;

(3) A summary of the policies and procedures which participating agencies must follow regarding storage, disclosure to third parties, retention, and destruction of personally identifiable information; and

(4) A description of all of the rights of parents and children regarding this information, including the rights under the Family Educational Rights and Privacy Act of 1974, and implementing regulations in part 99 of this title.

(b) Before any major identification, location, or evaluation activity, the notice must be published or announced in newspapers or other media, or both, with circulation adequate to notify parents throughout the State of the activity.
(Authority: 20 U.S.C. 1412(2)(D); 1417(c))

§ 300.562 Access rights.

(a) Each participating agency shall permit parents to inspect and review any education records relating to their children that are collected, maintained, or used by the agency under this part. The agency shall comply with a request without unnecessary delay and before any meeting regarding an IEP or hearing relating to identification, evaluation, or placement of the child, or to the provision of FAPE to the child, and in no case more than 45 days after the request has been made.

(b) The right to inspect and review education records under this section includes—

(1) The right to a response from the participating agency to reasonable requests for explanations and interpretations of the records;

(2) The right to request that the agency provide copies of the records containing the information if failure to provide those copies would effec-

tively prevent the parent from exercising the right to inspect and review the records; and

(3) The right to have a representative of the parent inspect and review the records.

(c) An agency may presume that the parent has authority to inspect and review records relating to his or her child unless the agency has been advised that the parent does not have the authority under applicable State law governing such matters as guardianship, separation, and divorce.
(Authority: 20 U.S.C. 1412(2)(D); 1417(c))

§ 300.563 Record of access.

Each participating agency shall keep a record of parties obtaining access to education records collected, maintained, or used under this part (except access by parents and authorized employees of the participating agency), including the name of the party, the date access was given, and the purpose for which the party is authorized to use the records.
(Authority: 20 U.S.C. 1412(2)(D); 1417(c))

§ 300.564 Records on more than one child.

If any education record includes information on more than one child, the parents of those children shall have the right to inspect and review only the information relating to their child or to be informed of that specific information.
(Authority: 20 U.S.C. 1412(2)(D); 1417(c))

§ 300.565 List of types and locations of information.

Each participating agency shall provide parents on request a list of the types and locations of education records collected, maintained, or used by the agency.
(Authority: 20 U.S.C. 1412(2)(D); 1417(c))

§ 300.566 Fees.

(a) Each participating education agency may charge a fee for copies of records which are made for parents under this part if the fee does not effectively prevent the parents from exercising their right to inspect and review those records.

(b) A participating agency may not charge a fee to search for or to retrieve information under this part.
(Authority: 20 U.S.C. 1412(2)(D); 1417(c))

§ 300.567 Amendment of records at parent's request.

(a) A parent who believes that information in education records collected, maintained, or used under this part is inaccurate or misleading or violates the privacy or other rights of the child, may request the participating agency which maintains the information to amend the information.

(b) The agency shall decide whether to amend the information in accordance with the request within a reasonable period of time of receipt of the request.

(c) If the agency decides to refuse to amend the information in accordance with the request it shall inform the parent of the refusal, and advise the parent of the right to a hearing under § 300.568.
(Authority: 20 U.S.C. 1412(2)(D); 1417(c))

§ 300.568 Opportunity for a hearing.

The agency shall, on request, provide an opportunity for a hearing to challenge information in education records, to ensure that it is not inaccurate, misleading, or otherwise in violation of the privacy or other rights of the child.
(Authority: 20 U.S.C. 1412(2)(D); 1417(c))

§ 300.569 Result of hearing.

(a) If, as a result of the hearing, the agency decides that the information is inaccurate, misleading, or otherwise in violation of the privacy or other rights of the child, it shall amend the information accordingly and so inform the parent in writing.

(b) If, as a result of the hearing, the agency decides that the information is not inaccurate, misleading, or otherwise in violation of the privacy or other rights of the child, it shall inform the parent of the right to place in the records it maintains on the child a statement commenting on the information or setting forth any reasons for disagreeing with the decision of the agency.

(c) Any explanation placed in the records of the child under this section must:

(1) Be maintained by the agency as part of the records of the child as long as the record or contested portion is maintained by the agency; and

(2) If the records of the child or the contested portion is disclosed by the agency to any party, the explanation must also be disclosed to the party.
(Authority: 20 U.S.C. 1412(2)(D); 1417(c))

§ 300.570 Hearing procedures.

(1) A hearing held under § 300.568 of this subpart must be conducted according to the procedures under § 99.23 of this title.
(Authority: 20 U.S.C. 1412(2)(D); 1417(c))

§ 300.571 Consent.

(a) Parental consent must be obtained before personally identifiable information is—

(1) Disclosed to anyone other than officials of participating agencies collecting or using the information under this part, subject to paragraph (b) of this section; or

(2) Used for any purpose other than meeting a requirement of this part.

(b) An educational agency or institution subject to part 99 of this title may not release information from education records to participating agencies without parental consent unless authorized to do so under part 99 of this title.

(c) The SEA shall include policies and procedures in its State plan which are used in the event that a parent refuses to provide consent under this section.

(Authority: 20 U.S.C. 1412(2)(D); 1417(c))

§ 300.572 Safeguards.

(a) Each participating agency shall protect the confidentiality of personally identifiable information at collection, storage, disclosure, and destruction stages.

(b) One official at each participating agency shall assume responsibility for ensuring the confidentiality of any personally identifiable information.

(c) All persons collecting or using personally identifiable information must receive training or instruction regarding the State's policies and procedures under § 300.129 and part 99 of this title.

(d) Each participating agency shall maintain, for public inspection, a current listing of the names and positions of those employees within the agency who may have access to personally identifiable information.

(Authority: 20 U.S.C. 1412(2)(D); 1417(c))

§ 300.573 Destruction of information.

(a) The public agency shall inform parents when personally identifiable information collected, maintained, or used under this part is no longer needed to provide educational services to the child.

(b) The information must be destroyed at the request of the parents. However, a permanent record of a student's name, address, and phone number, his or her grades, attendance record, classes attended, grade level completed, and year completed may be maintained without time limitation.

(Authority: 20 U.S.C. 1412(2)(D); 1417(c))

Note: Under § 300.573, the personally identifiable information on a child with a disability may be retained permanently unless the parents request that it be destroyed. Destruction of records is the best protection against improper and unauthorized disclosure. However, the records may be needed for other purposes. In informing parents about their rights under this section, the agency should remind them that the records may be needed by the child or the parents for social security benefits or other purposes. If the parents request that the information be destroyed, the agency may retain the information in paragraph (b) of this section.

§ 300.574 Children's rights.

The SEA shall include policies and procedures in its State plan regarding the extent to which children are afforded rights of privacy similar to those afforded to parents, taking into consideration the age of the child and type or severity of disability.

(Authority: 20 U.S.C. 1412(2)(D); 1417(c))

Note: Note that under the regulations for the Family Educational Rights and Privacy Act (45 CFR 99.4(a)), the rights of parents regarding education records are transferred to the student at age 18.

§ 300.575 Enforcement.

The SEA shall describe in its State plan the policies and procedures, including sanctions, which the State uses to ensure that its policies and procedures are followed and that the requirements of the Act and the regulations in this part are met.

(Authority: 20 U.S.C. 1412(2)(D); 1417(c))

§ 300.576 Department.

If the Department or its authorized representatives collect any personally identifiable information regarding children with disabilities which is not subject to 5 U.S.C. 552a (The Privacy Act of 1874), the Secretary shall apply the requirements of 5 U.S.C. section 552a (b) (1)-(2), (4)-(11); (c); (d); (e)(1); (2); (3)(A), (B), and (D), (5)-(10); (h); (m); and (n), and the regulations implementing those provisions in part 5b of this title.

(Authority: 20 U.S.C. 1412(2)(D); 1417(c))

Department Procedures

§ 300.580 [Reserved]

§ 300.681 Disapproval of a State plan.

Before disapproving a State plan, the Secretary gives the SEA written notice and an opportunity for a hearing.

(Authority: 20 U.S.C. 1413(c))

§ 300.582 Content of notice.

(a) In the written notice, the Secretary—

(1) States the basis on which the Secretary proposes to disapprove the State plan;

(2) May describe possible options for resolving the issues;

(3) Advises the SEA that it may request a hearing and that the request for a hearing must be made not later than 30 calendar days after it receives the notice of proposed disapproval; and

(4) Provides information about the procedures followed for a hearing.

(b) The Secretary sends the written notice to the SEA by certified mail with return receipt requested.

(Authority: 20 U.S.C. 1413(c))

§ 300.583 Hearing official or panel.

(a) If the SEA requests a hearing, the Secretary designates one or more individuals, either from the Department or elsewhere, not responsible for or connected with the administration of the program, to conduct a hearing.

(b) If more than one individual is designated, the Secretary designates one of those individuals as the Chief Hearing Official of the Hearing Panel. If one individual is designated, that individual is the Hearing Official.

(Authority: 20 U.S.C. 1413(c))

§ 300.584 Hearing procedures.

(a) As used in §§ 300.581-300.586 the term *party or parties* means the following:

(1) An SEA that requests a hearing regarding the proposed disapproval of its State plan under this part.

(2) The Department of Education official who administers the program of financial assistance under this part.

(3) A person, group or agency with an interest in and having relevant information about the case who has applied for and been granted leave to intervene by the Hearing Official or Panel.

(b) Within 15 calendar days after receiving a request for a hearing, the Secretary designates a Hearing Official or Panel and notifies the parties.

(c) The Hearing Official or Panel may regulate the course of proceedings and the conduct of the parties during the proceedings. The Hearing Official or Panel takes all steps necessary to conduct a fair and impartial proceeding, to avoid delay, and to maintain order, including the following:

(1) The Hearing Official or Panel may hold conferences or other types of appropriate proceedings to clarify, simplify, or define the issues or to consider other matters that may aid in the disposition of the case.

(2) The Hearing Official or Panel may schedule a prehearing conference of the Hearing Official or Panel and parties.

(3) Any party may request the Hearing Official or Panel to schedule a prehearing or other conference. The Hearing Official or Panel decides whether a conference is necessary and notifies all parties.

(4) At a prehearing or other conference, the Hearing Official or Panel and the parties may consider subjects such as—

(i) Narrowing and clarifying issues;

(ii) Assisting the parties in reaching agreements and stipulations;

(iii) Clarifying the positions of the parties;

(iv) Determining whether an evidentiary hearing or oral argument should be held; and

(v) Setting dates for—

(A) The exchange of written documents;

(B) The receipt of comments from the parties on the need for oral argument or evidentiary hearing;

(C) Further proceedings before the Hearing Official or Panel (including an evidentiary hearing or oral argument, if either is scheduled);

(D) Requesting the names of witnesses each party wishes to present at an evidentiary hearing and estimation of time for each presentation; or

(E) Completion of the review and the initial decision of the Hearing Official or Panel.

(5) A prehearing or other conference held under paragraph (b)(4) of this section may be conducted by telephone conference call.

(6) At a prehearing or other conference, the parties shall be prepared to discuss the subjects listed in paragraph (b)(4) of this section.

(7) Following a prehearing or other conference the Hearing Official or Panel may issue a written statement describing the issues raised, the action taken, and the stipulations and agreements reached by the parties.

(d) The Hearing Official or Panel may require parties to state their positions and to provide all or part of the evidence in writing.

(e) The Hearing Official or Panel may require parties to present testimony through affidavits and to conduct cross-examination through interrogatories.

(f) The Hearing Official or Panel may direct the parties to exchange relevant documents or information and lists of witnesses, and to send copies to the Hearing Official or Panel.

(g) The Hearing Official or Panel may receive, rule on, exclude, or limit evidence at any stage of the proceedings.

(h) The Hearing Official or Panel may rule on motions and other issues at any stage of the proceedings.

(i) The Hearing Official or Panel may examine witnesses.

(j) The Hearing Official or Panel may set reasonable time limits for submission of written documents.

(k) The Hearing Official or Panel may refuse to consider documents or other submissions if they are not submitted in a timely manner unless good cause is shown.

(l) The Hearing Official or Panel may interpret applicable statutes and regulations but may not waive them or rule on their validity.

(m)(1) The parties shall present their positions through briefs and the submission of other documents and may request an oral argument or evidentiary hearing. The Hearing Official or Panel shall determine whether an oral argument or an evidentiary hearing is needed to clarify the positions of the parties.

(2) The Hearing Official or Panel gives each party an opportunity to be represented by counsel.

(n) If the Hearing Official or Panel determines that an evidentiary hearing would materially assist the resolution of the matter, the Hearing Official or Panel gives each party, in addition to the opportunity to be represented by counsel—

(1) An opportunity to present witnesses on the party's behalf; and

(2) An opportunity to cross-examine witnesses either orally or with written questions.

(o) The Hearing Official or Panel accepts any evidence that it finds is relevant and material to the proceedings and is not unduly repetitious.

(p)(1) The Hearing Official or Panel—

(i) Arranges for the preparation of a transcript of each hearing;

(ii) Retains the original transcript as part of the record of the hearing; and

(iii) Provides one copy of the transcript to each party.

(2) Additional copies of the transcript are available on request and with payment of the reproduction fee.

(q) Each party shall file with the Hearing Official or Panel all written motions, briefs, and other documents and shall at the same time provide a copy to the other parties to the proceedings.

(Authority: 20 U.S.C. 1413(c))

§ 300.585 Initial decision; final decision.

(a) The Hearing Official or Panel prepares an initial written decision which addresses each of the points in the notice sent by the Secretary to the SEA under § 300.582.

(b) The initial decision of a Panel is made by a majority of Panel members.

(c) The Hearing Official or Panel mails by certified mail with return receipt requested a copy of the initial decision to each party (or to the party's counsel) and to the Secretary, with a notice stating that each party has an opportunity to submit written comments regarding the decision to the Secretary.

(d) Each party may file comments and recommendations on the initial decision with the Hearing Official or Panel within 15 calendar days of the date the party receives the Panel's decision.

(e) The Hearing Official or Panel sends a copy of a party's initial comments and recommendations to the other parties by certified mail with return receipt requested. Each party may file responsive comments and recommendations with the Hearing Official or Panel within seven calendar days of the date the party receives the initial comments and recommendations.

(f) The Hearing Official or Panel forwards the parties' initial and responsive comments on the initial decision to the Secretary who reviews the initial decision and issues a final decision.

(g) The initial decision of the Hearing Official or Panel becomes the final decision of the Secretary unless, within 25 calendar days after the end of the time for receipt of written comments, the Secretary informs the Hearing Official or Panel and the parties to a hearing in writing that the decision is being further reviewed for possible modification.

(h) The Secretary may reject or modify the initial decision of the Hearing Official or Panel if the Secretary finds that it is clearly erroneous.

(i) The Secretary conducts the review based on the initial decision, the written record, the Hearing Official's or Panel's proceedings, and written comments. The Secretary may remand the matter for further proceedings.

(j) The Secretary issues the final decision within 30 calendar days after notifying the Hearing Official or Panel that the initial decision is being further reviewed.

§ 300.586 Judicial review.

If a State is dissatisfied with the Secretary's final action with respect to its State plan, the State may, within 60 calendar days after notice of that action, file a petition for review with the United States court of appeals for the circuit in which the State is located.

(Authority: 20 U.S.C. 1416(b)(1))

§§ 300.587—300.588 [Reserved]

§ 300.589 Waiver of requirement regarding supplementing and supplanting with Part B funds.

(a) Under sections 613(a)(9)(B) and 614(a)(2)(B)(ii) of the Act, SEAs and LEAs must ensure that Federal funds provided under this part are used to supplement and increase the level of Federal, State, and local funds (including funds that are not under the direct control of SEAs or LEAs) expended for special education and related services provided to children with disabilities under this part and in no case to supplant those Federal, State, and local funds. The nonsupplanting requirement applies only to funds allocated to LEAs (See § 300.372).

(b) If the State provides clear and convincing evidence that all children with disabilities have FAPE available to them, the Secretary may waive in part the requirement under sections 613(a)(9)(B) and 614(a)(2)(B)(ii) of the Act if the Secretary concurs with the evidence provided by the State.

(c) If a State wishes to request a waiver, it must inform the secretary in writing. The Secretary then provides the State with a finance and membership report form which provides the basis for the request.

(d) In its request for a waiver, the State shall include the results of a special study made by the State to obtain evidence of the availability of FAPE to all children with disabilities. The special study must include statements by a representative sample of organizations which deal with children with disabilities, and parents and teachers of children with disabilities, relating to the following areas—

(1) The adequacy and comprehensiveness of the State's system for locating, identifying, and evaluating children with disabilities;

(2) The cost to parents, if any, for education for children enrolled in public and private day schools, and in public and private residential schools and institutions; and

(3) The adequacy of the State's due process procedures.

(e) In its request for a waiver, the State shall include finance data relating to the availability of FAPE for all children with disabilities, including—

(1) The total current expenditures for regular education programs and special education programs by function and by source of funds (State, local, and Federal) for the previous school year; and

(2) The full-time equivalent membership of students enrolled in regular programs and in special programs in the previous school year.

(f) The Secretary considers the information which the State provides under paragraphs (d) and (e) of this section, along with any additional information he may request, or obtain through on-site reviews of the State's education programs and records, to determine if all children have FAPE available to them, and if so, the extent of the waiver.

(g) The State may request a hearing with regard to any final action by the Secretary under this section.

(Authority: 20 U.S.C. 1411(c)(3); 1413(a)(9)(B))

Subpart F—State Administration

General

§ 300.600 Responsibility for all educational programs.

(a) The SEA is responsible for ensuring—

(1) That the requirements of this part are carried out; and

(2) That each educational program for children with disabilities administered within the State, including each program administered by any other public agency—

(i) Is under the general supervision of the persons responsible for educational programs for children with disabilities in the SEA; and

(ii) Meets the education standards of the SEA (including the requirements of this part).

(b) The State must comply with paragraph (a) of this section through State statute, State regulation, signed agreement between respective agency officials, or other documents.

(c) This part may not be construed to limit the responsibility of agencies other than educational agencies for providing or paying some or all of the costs of a free appropriate public education to children with disabilities in the State.

(Authority: 20 U.S.C. 1412(6))

Note: The requirement in § 300.600(a) is taken essentially verbatim from section 612(6) of the statute and reflects the desire of the Congress for a central point of responsibility and accountability in the education of children with disabilities within each State. With respect to SEA responsibility, the Senate Report on Pub. L. 94-142 includes the following statements:

This provision is included specifically to assure a single line of responsibility with regard to the education of children with disabilities, and to assure that in the implementation of all provisions of this Act and in carrying out the right to education for children with disabilities, the State educational agency shall be the responsible agency***.

Without this requirement, there is an abdication of responsibility for the education of children with disabilities. Presently, in many States, responsibility is divided, depending upon the age of the handicapped child, sources of funding, and type of services delivered. While the Committee understands that different agencies may, in fact, deliver services, the responsibility must remain in a central agency overseeing the education of handicapped children, so that failure to deliver services or the violation of the rights of handicapped children is squarely the responsibility of one agency. (Senate Report No. 94-168, p. 24 (1975))

In meeting the requirements of this section, there are a number of acceptable options which may be adopted, including the following:

(1) Written agreements are developed between respective State agencies concerning SEA standards and monitoring. These agreements are binding on the local or regional counterparts of each State agency.

(2) The Governor's Office issues an administrative directive establishing the SEA responsibility.

(3) State law, regulation, or policy designates the SEA as responsible for establishing standards for all educational programs for individuals with disabilities, and includes responsibility for monitoring.

(4) State law mandates that the SEA is responsible for all educational programs.

§ 300.601 Relation of Part B to other Federal programs.

This part may not be construed to permit a State to reduce medical and other assistance available to children with disabilities, or to alter a child with a disability's eligibility under Title V (Maternal and Child Health) or Title XIX (Medicaid) of the Social Security Act, to receive services that are also part of FAPE.

(Authority: 20 U.S.C. 1413(e))

Use of Funds

§ 300.620 Federal funds for State administration.

A State may use five percent of the total State allotment in any fiscal year under Part B of the Act, or $450,000, whichever is greater, for administrative costs related to carrying out sections 612 and 613 of the Act. However, this amount cannot be greater than twenty-five percent of the State's total allotment for the fiscal year under Part B of the Act.

(Authority: 20 U.S.C. 1411(b),(c))

§ 300.621 Allowable costs.

(a) The SEA may use funds under § 300.620 for:

(1) Administration of the State plan and for planning at the State level, including planning, or assisting in the planning, of programs or projects for the education of children with disabilities;

(2) Approval, supervision, monitoring, and evaluation of the effectiveness of local programs and projects for the education of children with disabilities;

(3) Technical assistance to local educational agencies with respect to the requirements of this part;

(4) Leadership services for the program supervision and management of special education activities for children with disabilities; and

(5) Other State leadership activities, and consultative services.

(b) The SEA shall use the remainder of its funds under § 300.620 in accordance with § 300.370.

(Authority: 20 U.S.C. 1411(b),(c))

State Advisory Panel

§ 300.650 Establishment.

(a) Each State shall establish, in accordance with the provisions of §§ 300.650-300.653, a State advisory panel on the education of children with disabilities.

(b) The advisory panel must be appointed by the Governor or any other official authorized under State law to make those appointments.

(c) If a State has an existing advisory panel that can perform the functions in § 300.652, the State may modify the existing panel so that it fulfills all of the requirements of §§ 300.650-300.653, instead of establishing a new advisory panel.

(Authority: 20 U.S.C. 1413(a)(12))

§ 300.651 Membership.

(a) The membership of the State advisory panel must be composed of persons involved in or concerned with the education of children with disabilities. The membership must include at least one person representative of each of the following groups:

(1) Individuals with disabilities;

(2) Teachers of children with disabilities;

(3) Parents of children with disabilities;

(4) State and local educational officials;

(5) Special education program administrators;

(b) The State may expand the advisory panel to include additional persons in the groups listed in paragraph (a) of this section and representatives of other groups not listed.

(Authority: 20 U.S.C. 1413(a)(12))

Note: The membership of the State advisory panel, as listed in paragraphs (a)(1)-(5), is required in section 613(a)(12) of the Act. As indicated in paragraph (b), the composition of the panel and the number of members may be expanded at the discretion of the State. In adding to the membership, consideration could be given to having—

(1) An appropriate balance between professional groups and consumers (i.e., parents, advocates, and individuals with disabilities);

(2) Broad representation within the consumer-advocate groups, to ensure that the interests and points of view of various parents, advocates and individuals with disabilities are appropriately represented;

(3) Broad representation within professional groups (e.g., regular education personnel: special educators, including teachers, teacher trainers, and administrators, who can properly represent various dimensions in the education of children with disabilities; and appropriate related services personnel); and

(4) Representatives from other State advisory panels (such as vocational education).

If a State elects to maintain a small advisory panel (e.g., 10-15 members), the panel itself could take steps to ensure that it (1) consults with and receives inputs from various consumer and special interest professional groups, and (2) establishes committees for particular short-term purposes composed of representatives from those input groups.

§ 300.652 Advisory panel functions.

The State advisory panel shall—

(a) Advise the SEA of unmet needs within the State in the education of children with disabilities;

(b) Comment publicly on the State plan and rules or regulations proposed for issuance by the State regarding the education of children with disabilities and the procedures for distribution of funds under this part; and

(c) Assist the State in developing and reporting such information and evaluations as may assist the Secretary in the performance of his responsibilities under section 618 of the Act.

(Authority: 20 U.S.C. 1413(a)(12))

§ 300.653 Advisory panel procedures.

(a) The advisory panel shall meet as often as necessary to conduct its business.

(b) By July 1 of each year, the advisory panel shall submit an annual report of panel activities and suggestions to the SEA. This report must be made available to the public in a manner consistent with other public reporting requirements of this part.

(c) Official minutes must be kept on all panel meetings and shall be made available to the public on request.

(d) All advisory panel meetings and agenda items must be publicly announced prior to the meeting, and meetings must be open to the public.

(e) Interpreters and other necessary services must be provided at panel meetings for panel members or participants. The State may pay for these services from funds under § 300.620.

(f) The advisory panel shall serve without compensation but the State must reimburse the panel for reasonable and necessary expenses for attending meetings and performing duties. The State may use funds under § 300.620 for this purpose.

(Authority: 20 U.S.C. 1413(a)(12))

State Complaint Procedures

§ 300.660 Adoption of State complaint procedures.

Each SEA shall adopt written procedures for:

(a) Resolving any complaint that meets the requirements of § 300.662 by—

(1) Providing for the filing of a complaint with the SEA; and

(2) At the SEA's discretion, providing for the filing of a complaint with a public agency and the right to have the SEA review the public agency's decision on the complaint.

(b) Informing the parents and other interested individuals about the procedures in §§ 300.660-300.662.

(Authority: 20 U.S.C. 2831(a))

§ 300.661 Minimum State complaint procedures.

Each SEA shall include the following in its complaint procedures:

(a) A time limit of 60 calendar days after a complaint is filed under § 300.660(a) to—

(1) Carry out an independent on-site investigation, if the SEA determines that such an investigation is necessary;

(2) Give the complainant the opportunity to submit additional information, either orally or in writing, about the allegations in the complaint;

(3) Review all relevant information and make an independent determination as to whether the public agency is violating a requirement of part B of the Act or of this part; and

(4) Issue a written decision to the complainant that addresses each allegation in the complaint and contains—

(i) Findings of fact and conclusions; and

(ii) The reasons for the SEA's final decision.

(b) An extension of the time limit under paragraph (a) of this section only if exceptional circumstances exist with respect to a particular complaint.

(c) Procedures for effective implementation of the SEA's final decision, if needed, including technical assistance activities, negotiations, and corrective actions to achieve compliance.

(d) The right of the complainant or the public agency to request the Secretary to review the SEA's final decision.

(Authority: 20 U.S.C. 2831(a))

§ 300.662 Filing a complaint.

An organization or individual may file a signed written complaint under the procedures described in §§ 300.600-300.661. The complaint must include—

(a) A statement that a public agency has violated a requirement of part B of the Act or of this part; and

(b) The facts on which the statement is based.

(Authority: 20 U.S.C. 2831(a))

Subpart G—Allocation of Funds; Reports

Allocations

§ 300.700 Special definition of the term State.

For the purposes of § 300.701, § 300.702, and §§300.704-300.708, the term "State" does not include Guam, American Samoa, the Virgin Islands, the Commonwealth of the Northern Mariana Islands, the Federated States of Micronesia, the Republic of the Marshall Islands, or Palau.

(Authority: 20 U.S.C. 1411(a)(2))

§ 300.701 State entitlement; formula

(a) The Secretary calculates the maximum amount of the grant to which a State is entitled under section 611 of the Act in any fiscal year as follows:

(1) If the State is eligible for a grant under section 619 of the Act, the maximum entitlement is equal to the number of children with disabilities aged 3 through 21 in the State who are receiving special education and related services, multiplied by 40 percent of the average per pupil expenditure in public elementary and secondary schools in the United States.

(2) If the State is not eligible for a grant under section 619 of the Act, the maximum entitlement is equal to the number of children with disabilities aged 6 through 21 in the State who are receiving special education and related services, multiplied by 40 percent of the average per pupil expenditure in public elementary and secondary schools in the United States.

(Authority: 20 U.S.C. 1411(a)(1))

(b) [Reserved]

(c) For the purposes of this section, the *average per pupil expenditure in public elementary and secondary schools in the United States*, means the aggregate expenditures during the second fiscal year preceding the fiscal year for which the computation is made (or if satisfactory data for that year are not available at the time of computation, then during the most recent preceding fiscal year for which satisfactory data are available) of all LEAs in the United States (which, for the purpose of this section, means the fifty States and the District of Columbia), plus any direct expenditures by the State for operation of those agencies (without regard to the source of funds from which either of those expenditures are made), divided by the aggregate number of children in average daily attendance to whom those agencies provided free public education during that preceding year.

(Authority: 20 U.S.C. 1411(a)(4))

§ 300.702 Limitations and exclusions.

(a) In determining the amount of a grant under § 300.701:

(1) If a State serves all children with disabilities aged 3 through 5 in the State, the Secretary does not count children with disabilities aged 3 through 17 in the State to the extent that the number of those children is greater than 12 percent of the number of all children aged 3 through 17 in the State;

(2) If a State does not serve all children with disabilities aged 3 through 5 in the State, the Secretary does not count children with disabilities aged 5 through 17 to the extent that the number of those children is greater than 12 percent of the number of all children aged 5 through 17 in the State; and

(3) The Secretary does not count children with disabilities who are counted under Subpart 2 of Part D of Chapter 1 of Title I of the Elementary and Secondary School Education Act of 1965.

(b) For the purposes of paragraph (a) of this section, the number of children aged 3 through 17 and 5 through 17 in any State is determined by the Secretary on the basis of the most recent satisfactory data available.

§ 300.703 Ratable reductions.

(a) *General.* If the sums appropriated for any fiscal year for making payments to States under section 611 of the Act are not sufficient to pay in full the total amounts to which all States are entitled to receive for that fiscal year, the maximum amount which all States are entitled to receive for that fiscal year shall be ratably reduced. In case additional funds become available for making payments for any fiscal year during which the preceding sentence is applicable, those reduced amounts shall be increased on the same basis they were reduced.

(Authority: 20 U.S.C. 1411(g)(1))

(b) *Reporting, dates for Local educational agencies and reallocations.* (1) In any fiscal year in which the State entitlements have been ratably reduced, and in which additional funds have not been made available to pay in full the total of the amounts under paragraph (a) of this section, the SEA shall fix dates before which each LEA shall report to the State the amount of funds available to it under this part which it estimates it will expend.

(2) The amounts available under paragraph (a)(1) of this section, or any amount which would be available to any other LEA agency if it were to submit an application meeting the requirements of this part, which the SEA determines will not be used for the period of its availability, shall be available for allocation to those LEAs, in the manner provided in § 300.707, that the SEA determines will need and be able to use additional funds to carry out approved programs.

(Authority: 20 U.S.C. 1411(g)(2))

§ 300.704 Hold harmless provision.

No State shall receive less than the amount it received under Part B of the Act for fiscal year 1977.

(Authority: 20 U.S.C. 1411(a)(1))

§ 300.705 Allocation for State in which bypass is implemented for private school children with disabilities.

In determining the allocation under §§ 300.700-300.703 of a State in which the Secretary will implement a by-pass for private school children with disabilities under §§ 300.451-300.486, the Secretary includes in the State's child count—

(a) For the first year of a by-pass, the actual or estimated number of private school children with disabilities (as defined in §§ 300.7(a) and 300.450) in the State, as of the preceding December 1; and

(b) For succeeding years of a by-pass, the number of private school children with disabilities who received special education and related services under the by-pass in the preceding year.
(Authority: 20 U.S.C. 1411(a)(1)(A), 1411(a)(3), 1413(d))

§ 300.706 Within-State distribution: Fiscal year 1979 and after.

Of the funds received under § 300.701 by any State for fiscal year 1979, and for each fiscal year after fiscal year 1979—

(a) 25 percent may be used by the State in accordance with § 300.620 and §300.370; and

(b) 75 percent shall be distributed to the LEAs in the State in accordance with § 300.707.
(Authority: 20 U.S.C. 1411(c)(1))

§ 300.707 Local educational agency entitlement; formula.

From the total amount of funds available to all local educational agencies, each local educational agency is entitled to an amount which bears the same ratio to the total amount as the number of children with disabilities aged 3 through 21 in that agency who are receiving special education and related services bears to the aggregate number of children with disabilities aged 3 through 21 receiving special education and related services in all local educational agencies which apply to the SEA for funds under Part B of the Act.
(Authority: 20 U.S.C. 1411(d))

§ 300.708 Reallocation of local educational agency funds.

If an SEA determines that an LEA is adequately providing FAPE to all children with disabilities residing in the area served by the local agency, the SEA may reallocate funds (or portions of those funds which are not required to provide special education and related services) made available to the local agency under § 300.707, to other LEAs within the State which are not adequately providing special education and related services to all children with disabilities residing in the areas served by the other LEAs.
(Authority: 20 U.S.C. 1414(e))

§ 300.709 Payments to Secretary of Interior.

(a) *General.* (1) The Secretary is authorized to make payments to the Secretary of the Interior according to the need for that assistance for the education of children with disabilities on reservations, aged 5 through 21, who are enrolled in

elementary and secondary schools for Indian children operated by or funded by the Secretary of the Interior.

(2) In the case of Indian students aged 3 through 5 who are enrolled in programs affiliated with Bureau of Indian Affairs (BIA) schools that are required by States in which the schools are located to attain or maintain State accreditation and had State accreditation prior to October 7, 1991, the schools may count those children for the purpose of distribution of the funds provided under paragraph (a)(1) of this section to the Secretary of the Interior.

(3) The amount of payment under paragraph (a)(1) of this section for any fiscal year is one percent of the aggregate amounts available to all States under this part for that fiscal year.

(b) *Responsibilities for meeting the requirements of part B.* The Secretary of the Interior shall be responsible for meeting all of the requirements of part B of the Act for the children described in paragraph (a) of this section, in accordance with § 300.260.
(Authority: 20 U.S.C. 1411(f))

§ 300.710 Payments to the Secretary of the Interior for Indian tribes or tribal organizations.

(a) *General.* (1) Beginning with funds appropriated under part B of the Act for fiscal year 1992, the Secretary, subject to this section, makes payments to the Secretary of the Interior to be distributed to tribes or tribal organizations (as defined under section 4 of the Indian Self-Determination and Education Assistance Act) or consortiums of those tribes or tribal organizations to provide for the coordination of assistance for special education and related services for children with disabilities, aged 3 through 5, on reservations served by elementary and secondary schools for Indians children operated or funded by the Department of the Interior.

(2) The amount of the payment under paragraph (b)(1) of this section for any fiscal year is .25 percent of the aggregate amounts available for all States under this part for that fiscal year.

(3) None of the funds allocated under this section may be used by the Secretary of the Interior for administrative purposes, including child count, and the provision of technical assistance.

(b) *Distribution of funds.* The Secretary of the Interior shall distribute the total amount of the .25 percent under paragraph (a) of this section in accordance with section 611(f)(4) of the Act.
(Authority: 20 U.S.C. 1411(f))

§ 300.711 Entitlements to jurisdictions.

(a) The jurisdictions to which this section applies are Guam, American Samoa, the Virgin Islands, the Commonwealth of the Northern Mariana Islands, the Federated States of Micronesia, the

Republic of the Marshall Islands, and Palau, (until the Compact of Free Association with Palau takes effect pursuant to section 101(a) of Pub. L. 99-658).

(b) Each jurisdiction under paragraph (a) of this section is entitled to a grant for the purposes set forth in section 601(c) of the Act. The amount to which those jurisdictions are so entitled for any fiscal year shall not exceed an amount equal to 1 percent of the aggregate of the amounts available to all States under this part for that fiscal year. Funds appropriated for those jurisdictions shall be allocated proportionately among them on the basis of the number of children aged 3 through 21 in each jurisdiction. However, no jurisdiction shall receive less than $150,000, and other allocations shall be ratably reduced if necessary to ensure that each jurisdiction receives at least that amount.

(c) The amount expended for administration by each jurisdiction under this section shall not exceed 5 percent of the amount allotted to the jurisdiction for any fiscal year, or $35,000, whichever is greater.

(Authority: 20 U.S.C. 1411(e))

Reports

§ 300.750 Annual report of children served—report requirement.

(a) The SEA shall report to the Secretary no later than February 1 of each year the number of children with disabilities aged 3 through 21 residing in the State who are receiving special education and related services.

(Authority: 20 U.S.C. 1411(a)(3))

(b) The SEA shall submit the report on forms provided by the Secretary.

(Authority: 20 U.S.C. 1411(a)(3))

Note: It is very important to understand that this report and the requirements that relate to it are solely for allocation purposes. The population of children the State may count for allocation purposes may differ from the population of children to whom the State must make FAPE available. For example, while section 611(a)(5) of the Act limits the number of children who may be counted for allocation purposes to 12 percent of the general school population aged 3 through 17 (in States that serve all children with disabilities aged 3 through 5) or 5 through 17 (in States that do not serve all children with disabilities aged 3 through 5), a State might find that 14 percent (or some other percentage) of its children have disabilities. In that case, the State must make FAPE available to all of those children with disabilities.

§ 300.751 Annual report of children served—information required in the report

(a) In its report, the SEA shall include a table that shows—

(1) The number of children with disabilities receiving special education and related services on December 1 of that school year;

(2) The number of children with disabilities aged 3 through 5 who are receiving FAPE;

(3) The number of those children with disabilities aged 6 through 21 within each disability category, as defined in the definition of "children with disabilities" in § 300.7; and

(4) The number of those children with disabilities aged 3 through 21 for each year of age (3, 4, 5, etc.).

(b). For the purpose of this part, a child's age is the child's actual age on the date of the child count: December 1.

(c) The SEA may not report a child aged 6 through 21 under more than one disability category.

(d) If a child with a disability aged 6 through 21 has more than one disability, the SEA shall report that child in accordance with the following procedure:

(1) A child with deaf-blindness must be reported under the category "deaf-blindness."

(2) A child who has more than one disability (other than a deaf-blind child) must be reported under the category "multiple disabilities."

(Authority: 20 U.S.C. 1411(a)(3); (5)(A)(ii); 1418(b))

§ 300.752 Annual report of children served—certification.

The SEA shall include in its report a certification signed by an authorized official of the agency that the information provided is an accurate and unduplicated count of children with disabilities receiving special education and related services on the dates in question.

(Authority: 20 U.S.C. 1411(a)(3); 1417(b))

§ 300.753 Annual report of children served—criteria for counting children.

(a) The SEA may include in its report children with disabilities who are enrolled in a school or program which is operated or supported by a public agency, and that either—

(1) Provides them with both special education and related services; or

(2) Provides them only with special education if they do not need related services to assist them in benefiting from that special education.

(b) The SEA may not include children with disabilities in its report who:

(1) Are not enrolled in a school or program operated or supported by a public agency;

(2) Are not provided special education that meets State standards;

(3) Are not provided with a related service that they need to assist them in benefiting from special education;

(4) Are counted by a State agency under Subpart 2 of Part D of Chapter 1 of Title I of the Elementary and Secondary Education Act of 1965; or

(5) Are receiving special education funded solely by the Federal Government. However, the State may count children covered under 300.186(b). (Authority: 20 U.S.C. 1411(a)(3); 1417(b))

Note 1: Under paragraph (a), the State may count children with disabilities in a Head Start or other preschool program operated or supported by a public agency if those children are provided special education that meets State standards.

Note 2: Special education, by statutory definition, must be at no cost to parents. As of September 1, 1978, under the FAPE requirement, both special education and related services must be at no cost to parents.

There may be some situations, however, where a child receives special education from a public source at no cost, but whose parents pay for the basic or regular education. This child may be counted. The Department expects that there would only be limited situations where special education would be clearly separate from regular education—generally, where speech services is the only special education required by the child. For example, the child's parents may have enrolled the child in a regular program in a private school, but the child might be receiving speech services in a program funded by the LEA. Allowing these children to be counted will provide incentives (in addition to complying with the legal requirement in section 613(a)(4)(A) of the Act regarding private schools) to public agencies to provide services to children in private schools, since funds are generated in part on the basis of the number of children provided special education and related services. Agencies should understand, however, that if a public agency places or refers a child with a disability to a public or private school for educational purposes, special education includes the entire educational program provided to the child. In that case, parents may not be charged for any part of the child's education.

A State may not count Indian children on or near reservations and children on military facilities if it provides them no special education. If an SEA or LEA is responsible for serving these children, and does provide them special education and related services, they may be counted.

§ 300.754 Annual report of children served—other responsibilities of the State educational agency.

In addition to meeting the other requirements of §§ 300.750-300.753, the SEA shall:

(a) Establish procedures to be used by LEAs and other educational institutions in counting the number of children with disabilities receiving special education and related services;

(b) Set dates by which those agencies and institutions must report to the SEA to ensure that the State complies with § 300.750(a);

(c) Obtain certification from each agency and institution that an unduplicated and accurate count has been made;

(d) Aggregate the data from the count obtained from each agency and institution, and prepare the reports required under §§ 300.750-300.753; and

(e) Ensure that documentation is maintained that enables the State and the Secretary to audit the accuracy of the count.
(Authority: 20 U.S.C. 1411(a)(3); 1417(b))

Note: States should note that the data required in the annual report of children served are not to be transmitted to the Secretary in personally identifiable form. States are encouraged to collect these data in non-personally identifiable form.

AUTHORITY: Sec. 504, Rehabilitation Act of 1973, Pub. L. 93-112, 87 Stat. 394 (29 U.S.C. 794); sec. 111(a), Rehabilitation Act Amendments of 1974, Pub. L 93-516, 88 Stat. 1619 (29 U.S.C. 706); sec. 606, Education of the Handicapped Act (20 U.S.C. 1405), as amended by Pub. L 94-142, 89 Stat. 795.

Subpart A—General Provisions

§ 104.1 Purpose.

The purpose of this part is to effectuate section 504 of the Rehabilitation Act of 1973, which is designed to eliminate discrimination on the basis of handicap in any program or activity receiving Federal financial assistance.

§ 104.2 Application.

This part applies to each recipient of Federal financial assistance from the Department of Education and to each program or activity that receives or benefits from such assistance.

§ 104.3 Definitions.

As used in this part, the term:

(a) "The Act" means the Rehabilitation Act of 1973, Pub. L. 93-112, as amended by the Rehabilitation Act Amendments of 1974, Pub. L. 93-516, 28 U.S.C. 794

(b) "Section 504" means section 504 of the Act.

(c) "Education of the Handicapped Act" means that statute as amended by the Education for all Handicapped Children Act of 1975, Pub. L 94-142, 20 U.S.C. 1401 et seq.

(d) "Department" means the Department of Education.

(e) "Assistant Secretary" means the Assistant Secretary for Civil Rights of the Department of Education.

(f) "Recipient" means any state or its political subdivision, any instrumentality of a state or its political subdivision, any public or private agency, institution, organization, or other entity, or any person to which Federal financial assistance is extended directly or through another recipient, including any successor, assignee, or transferee of a recipient, but excluding the ultimate beneficiary of the assistance.

(g) "Applicant for assistance" means one who submits an application, request, or plan required to be approved by a Department official or by a recipient as a condition to becoming a recipient.

(h) "Federal financial assistance" means any grant, loan, contract (other than a procurement contract or a contract of insurance or guaranty), or any other arrangement by which the Department provides or otherwise makes available assistance in the form of:

(1) Funds;

(2) Services of Federal personnel; or

(3) Real and personal property or any interest in or use of such property, including:

(i) Transfers or leases of such property for less than fair market value or for reduced consideration; and

(ii) Proceeds from a subsequent transfer or lease of such property if the Federal share of its fair market value is not returned to the Federal Government.

(i) "Facility" means all or any portion of buildings, structures, equipment, roads, walks, parking lots, or other real or personal property or interest in such property.

(j) "Handicapped person." (1) "Handicapped persons" means any person who (i) has a physical or mental impairment which substantially limits one or more major life activities, (ii) has a record of such an impairment, or (iii) is regarded as having such an impairment.

(2) As used in paragraph (j)(1) of this section, the phrase:

(i) "Physical or mental impairment" means (A) any physiological disorder or condition, cosmetic disfigurement, or anatomical loss affecting one or more of the following body systems: neurological; musculoskeletal: special sense organs; respiratory, including speech organs; cardiovascular, reproductive, digestive, genito-urinary; hemic and lymphatic; skin; and endocrine; or (B) any mental or psychological disorder, such as mental retardation, organic brain syndrome, emotional or mental illness, and specific learning disabilities.

(ii) "Major life activities" means functions such as caring for one's self, performing manual tasks, walking, seeing, hearing, speaking, breathing, learning, and working.

(iii) "Has a record of such an impairment" means has a history of, or has been misclassified as having, a mental or physical impairment that substantially limits one or more major life activities.

(iv) "Is regarded as having an impairment" means (A) has a physical or mental impairment that does not substantially limit major life activities but that is treated by a recipient as constituting such a limitation; (B) has a physical or mental impairment that substantially limits major life activities only as a result of the attitudes of others toward such impairment; or (C) has none of the impairments defined in paragraph (j)(2)(i) of this section but is treated by a recipient as having such an impairment.

(k) "Qualified handicapped person" means:

(1) With respect to employment, a handicapped person who, with reasonable accommodation, can perform the essential functions of the job in question;

(2) With respect to public preschool elementary, secondary, or adult educational services, a handicapped person (i) of an age during which nonhandicapped persons are provided such services, (ii) of any age during which it is mandatory under state law to provide such services to handicapped persons, or (iii) to whom a state is required to provide a free appropriate public education under section 612 of the Education of the Handicapped Act; and

(3) With respect to postsecondary and vocational education services, a handicapped person who meets the academic and technical standards requisite to admission or participation in the recipient's education program or activity;

(4) With respect to other services, a handicapped person who meets the essential eligibility requirements for the receipt of such services.

(1) "Handicap" means any condition or characteristic that renders a person a handicapped person as defined in paragraph (j) of this section.

§ 104.4 Discrimination prohibited.

(a) *General.* No qualified handicapped person shall, on the basis of handicap, be excluded from participation in, be denied the benefits of, or otherwise be subjected to discrimination under any program or activitiy which receives or benefits from Federal financial assistance.

(b) *Discriminatory actions prohibited.* (1) A recipient, in providing any aid, benefit, or service, may not, directly or through contractual, licensing, or other arrangements, on the basis of handicap:

(i) Deny a qualified handicapped person the opportunity to participate in or benefit from the aid, benefit, or service;

(ii) Afford a qualified handicapped person an opportunity to participate in or benefit from the aid, benefit, or service that is not equal to that afforded others;

(iii) Provide a qualified handicapped person with an aid, benefit, or service that is not as effective as that provided to others;

(iv) Provide different or separate aid, benefits, or services to handicapped persons or to any class of handicapped persons unless such action is necessary to provide qualified handicapped persons with aid, benefits, or services that are as effective as those provided to others;

(v) Aid or perpetuate discrimination against a qualified handicapped person by providing significant assistance to an agency, organization, or person that discriminates on the basis of handicap in providing any aid, benefit, or service to beneficiaries of the recipients program;

(vi) Deny a qualified handicapped person the opportunity to participate as a member of planning or advisory boards; or

(vii) Otherwise limit a qualified handicapped person in the enjoyment of any right, privilege, advantage, or opportunity enjoyed by others receiving an aid, benefit, or service.

(2) For purposes of this part, aids, benefits, and services, to be equally effective, are not required to produce the identical result or level of achievement for handicapped and nonhandicapped persons, but must afford handicapped persons equal opportunity to obtain the same result, to gain the same benefit, or to reach the same level of achievement, in the most integrated setting appropriate to the person's needs.

(3) Despite the existence of separate or different programs or activities provided in accordance with this part, a recipient may not deny a qualified handicapped person the opportunity to participate in such programs or activities that are not separate or different.

(4) A recipient may not, directly or through contractual or other arrangements, utilize criteria or methods of administration (i) that have the effect of subjecting qualified handicapped persons to discrimination on the basis of handicap, (ii) that have the purpose or effect of defeating or substantially impairing accomplishment of the objectives of the recipient's program with respect to handicapped persons, or (iii) that perpetuate the discrimination of another recipient if both recipients are subject to common administrative control or are agencies of the same State.

(5) In determining the site or location of a facility, an applicant for assistance or a recipient may not make selections (i) that have the effect of excluding handicapped persons from, denying them the benefits of, or otherwise subjecting them to discrimination under any program or activity that receives or benefits from Federal financial assistance or (ii) that have the purpose or effect of defeating or substantially impairing the accomplishment of the objectives of the program or activity with respect to handicapped persons.

(6) As used in this section, the aid, benefit, or service provided under a program or activity receiving or benefiting from Federal financial assistance includes any aid, benefit, or service provided in or through a facility that has been constructed, expanded, altered, leased or rented, otherwise acquired, in whole or in part, with Federal financial assistance.

(c) *Programs limited by Federal law.* The exclusion of nonhandicapped persons from the benefits of a program limited by Federal statute or executive order to handicapped persons or the exclusion of a specific class of handicapped persons from a program limited by Federal statute or executive order to a different class of handicapped persons is not prohibited by this part.

§ 104.5 Assurances required.

(a) Assurances. An applicant for Federal financial assistance for a program or activity to which this part applies shall submit an assurance, in a form specified by the Assistant Secretary that the program will be operated in compliance with this part. An applicant may incorporate these assurances by reference in subsequent applications to the Department.

(b) Duration of Obligation; (1) In the case of Federal financial assistance extended in the form of real property or to provide real property or structures on the property, the assurances will obligate the recipient or, in the case of a subsequent transfer, the transferee, for the period during which the real property or structures are for the purpose for which Federal financial assistance is extended or for another purpose involving the provision of similar services or benefits.

(2) In the case of Federal financial assistance extended to provide personal property, the assurance will obligate the recipient for the period during which it retains ownership or possession of the property.

(3) In all other cases the assurance will obligate the recipient for the period during which Federal financial assistance is extended.

(c) Covenants. (1) Where Federal financial assistance is provided in the form of real property or interest in the property from the Department, the instrument effecting or recording this transfer shall contain a covenant running with the land to assure nondiscrimination for the period during which the real property is used for a purpose for which the Federal financial assistance is extended or for another purpose involving the provision of similar services or benefits.

(2) Where no transfer of property is involved but property is purchased or improved with Federal financial assistance, the recipient shall agree to include the covenant described in paragraph (b)(2)

of this section in the instrument effecting or recording any subsequent transfer of the property.

(3) Where Federal financial assistance is provided in the form of real property or interest in the property from the Department, the covenant shall also include a condition coupled with a right to be reserved by the Department to revert title to the property in the event of a breach of the covenant. If a transferee of real property proposes to mortgage or otherwise encumber the real property as security for financing construction of new, or improvement of existing, facilities on the property for the purposes for which the property was transferred, the Assistant Secretary may, upon request of the transferee and if necessary to accomplish such financing and upon such conditions as he or she deems appropriate, agree to forbear the exercise of such right to revert title for so long as the lien of such mortgage or other encumbrance remains effective.

§ 104.6 Remedial action, voluntary action, and self-evaluation

(a) *Remedial action.* (1) If the Assistant Secretary finds that a recipient has discriminated against persons on the basis of handicap in violation of section 504 or this part, the recipient shall take such remedial action as the Assistant Secretary deems necessary to overcome the effects of the discrimination.

(2) Where a recipient is found to have discriminated against persons on the basis of handicap in violation of section 504 or this part and where another recipient exercises control over the recipient that has discriminated, the Assistant Secretary, where appropriate, may require either or both recipients to take remedial action.

(3) The Assistant Secretary may, where necessary to overcome the effects of discrimination in violation of section 504 or this part, require a recipient to take remedial action (i) with respect to handicapped persons who are no longer participants in the recipient's program but who were participants in the program when such discrimination occurred or (ii) with respect to handicapped persons who would have been participants in the program had the discrimination not occurred.

(b) *Voluntary action.* A recipient may take steps, in addition to any action that is required by this part, to overcome the effects of conditions that resulted in limited participation in the recipient's program or activity by qualified handicapped persons.

(c) *Self-evaluation.* (1) A recipient shall, within one year of the effective date of this part:

(i) Evaluate, with the assistance of interested persons, including handicapped persons or organizations representing handicapped persons, its current policies and practices and the effects thereof

that do not or may not meet the requirements of this part;

(ii) Modify, after consultation with interested persons, including handicapped persons or organizations representing handicapped persons, any policies and practices that do not meet the requirements of this part; and

(iii) Take, after consultation with interested persons, including handicapped persons or organizations representing handicapped persons, appropriate remedial steps to eliminate the effects of any discrimination that resulted from adherence to these policies and practices.

(2) A recipient that employs fifteen or more persons shall, for at least three years following completion of the evaluation required under paragraph (c)(1) of this section, maintain on file, make available for public inspection, and provide to the Assistant Secretary upon request: (i) A list of the interested persons consulted (ii) a description of areas examined and any problems identified, and (iii) a description of any modifications made and of any remedial steps taken.

§ 104.7 Designation of responsible employee and adoption of grievance procedures.

(a) *Designation of responsible employee.* A recipient that employs fifteen or more persons shall designate at least one person to coordinate its efforts to comply with this part.

(b) *Adoption of grievance procedures.* A recipient that employs fifteen or more persons shall adopt grievance procedures that incorporate appropriate due process standards and that provide for the prompt and equitable resolution of complaints alleging any action prohibited by this part. Such procedures need not be established with respect to complaints from applicants for employment or from applicants for admission to postsecondary educational institutions.

§ 104.8 Notice.

(a) A recipient that employs fifteen or more persons shall take appropriate initial and continuing steps to notify participants, beneficiaries, applicants, and employees, including those with impaired vision or hearing, and unions or professional organizations holding collective bargaining or professional agreements with the recipient that it does not discriminate on the basis of handicap in violation of section 504 and this part. The notification shall state, where appropriate, that the recipient does not discriminate in admission or access to, or treatment or employment in, its programs and activities. The notification shall also include an identification of the responsible employee designated pursuant to § 104.7(a). A recipient shall make the initial notification required by this paragraph within

90 days of the effective date of this part. Methods of initial and continuing notification may include the posting of notices, publication in newspapers and magazines, placement of notices in recipients' publication, and distribution of memoranda or other written communications.

(b) If a recipient publishes or uses recruitment materials or publications containing general information that it makes available to participants, beneficiaries, applicants, or employees, it shall include in those materials or publications a statement of the policy described in paragraph (a) of this section. A recipient may meet the requirement of this paragraph either by including appropriate inserts in existing materials and publications or by revising and reprinting the materials and publications.

§ 104.9 Administrative requirements for small recipients.

The Assistant Secretary may require any recipient with fewer than fifteen employees, or any class of such recipients, to comply with §§ 104.7 and 104.8, in whole or in part, when the Assistant Secretary finds a violation of this part or finds that such compliance will not significantly impair the ability of the recipient or class of recipients to provide benefits or services.

§ 104.10 Effect of state or local law or other requirements and effect of employment opportunities.

(a) The obligation to comply with this part is not obviated or alleviated by the existence of any state or local law or other requirement that, on the basis of handicap, imposes prohibitions or limits upon the eligibility of qualified handicapped persons to receive services or to practice any occupation or profession.

(b) The obligation to comply with this part is not obviated or alleviated because employment opportunities in any occupation or profession are or may be more limited for handicapped persons than for nonhandicapped persons.

Subpart B—Employment Practices

§ 104.11 Discrimination prohibited.

(a) *General.* (1) No qualified handicapped person shall, on the basis of handicap, be subjected to discrimination in employment under any program or activity to which this part applies.

(2) A recipient that receives assistance under the Education of the Handicapped Act shall take positive steps to employ and advance in employment qualified handicapped persons in programs assisted under that Act.

(3) A recipient shall make all decisions concerning employment under any program or activity

to which this part applies in a manner which ensures that discrimination on the basis of handicap does not occur and may not limit, segregate, or classify applicants or employees in any way that adversely affects their opportunities or status because of handicap.

(4) A recipient may not participate in a contractual or other relationship that has the effect of subjecting qualified handicapped applicants or employees to discrimination prohibited by this subpart. The relationships referred to in this paragraph include relationships with employment and referral agencies, with labor unions, with organizations providing or administering fringe benefits to employees of the recipient, and with organizations providing training and apprenticeship programs

(b) *Specific activities.* The provisions of this subpart apply to:

(1) Recruitment, advertising, and the processing of applications for employment;

(2) Hiring, upgrading, promotion, award of tenure, demotion, transfer, layoff, termination, right of return from layoff and rehiring;

(3) Rates of pay or any other form of compensation and changes in compensation;

(4) Job assignments, job classifications, organizational structures, position descriptions, lines of progression, and seniority lists;

(5) Leaves of absence, sick leave, or any other leave;

(6) Fringe benefits available by virtue of employment, whether or not administered by the recipient;

(7) Selection and financial support for training, including apprenticeship, professional meetings, conferences, and other related activities, and selection for leaves of absence to pursue training;

(8) Employer sponsored activities, including social or recreational programs; and

(9) Any other term, condition, or privilege of employment.

(c) A recipient's obligation to comply with this subpart is not affected by any inconsistent term of any collective bargaining agreement to which it is a party.

§ 104.12 Reasonable accommodation.

(a) A recipient shall make reasonable accommodation to the known physical or mental limitations of an otherwise qualified handicapped applicant or employee unless the recipient can demonstrate that the accommodation would impose an undue hardship on the operation of its program.

(b) Reasonable accommodation may include:

(1) Making facilities used by employees readily accessible to and usable by handicapped persons, and

(2) job restructuring, part-time or modified work schedules, acquisition or modification of equipment or devices, the provision of readers or interpreters, and other similar actions.

(c) In determining pursuant to paragraph (a) of this section whether an accommodation would impose an undue hardship on the operation of a recipient's program, factors to be considered include:

(1) The overall size of the recipient's program with respect to number of employees, number and type of facilities, and size of budget;

(2) The type of the recipient's operation, including the composition and structure of the recipient's workforce; and

(3) The nature and cost of the accommodation needed.

(d) A recipient may not deny any employment opportunity to a qualified handicapped employee or applicant if the basis for the denial is the need to make reasonable accommodation to the physical or mental limitations of the employee or applicant.

§ 104.13 Employment criteria.

(a) A recipient may not make use of any employment test or other selection criterion that screens out or tends to screen out handicapped persons or any class of handicapped persons unless: (1) The test score or other selection criterion, as used by the recipient, is shown to be job-related for the position in question, and (2) alternative job-related tests or criteria that do not screen out or tend to screen out as many handicapped persons are not shown by the Director to be available.

(b) A recipient shall select and administer tests concerning employment so as best to ensure that, when administered to an applicant or employee who has a handicap that impairs sensory, manual, or speaking skills, the test results accurately reflect the applicant's or employee's job skills, aptitude, or whatever other factor the test purports to measure, rather than reflecting the applicant's or employee's impaired sensory, manual, or speaking skills (except where those skills are the factors that the test purports to measure).

§ 104.14 Preemployment inquiries.

(a) Except as provided in paragraphs (b) and (c) of this section, a recipient may not conduct a preemployment medical examination or may not make preemployment inquiry of an applicant as to whether the applicant is a handicapped person or as to the nature or severity of a handicap. A recipient may, however, make preemployment inquiry into an applicant's ability to perform job-related functions.

(b) When a recipient is taking remedial action to correct the effects of past discrimination pursuant to 104.6(a), when a recipient is taking voluntary action to overcome the effects of conditions that resulted in limited participation in its federally assisted program or activity pursuant to 104.6(b), or when a recipient is taking affirmative action pursuant to section 503 of the Act, the recipient may invite applicants for employment to indicate whether and to what extent they are handicapped, *Provided*, That:

(1) The recipient states clearly on any written questionnaire used for this purpose or makes clear orally if no written questionnaire is used that the information requested is intended for use solely in connection with its remedial action obligations or its voluntary or affirmative action efforts; and

(2) The recipient states clearly that the information is being requested on a voluntary basis, that it will be kept confidential as provided in paragraph (d) of this section, that refusal to provide it will not subject the applicant or employee to any adverse treatment, and that it will be used only in accordance with this part.

(c) Nothing in this section shall prohibit a recipient from conditioning an offer of employment on the results of a medical examination conducted prior to the employee's entrance on duty, *Provided*, That: (1) All entering employees are subjected to such an examination regardless of handicap, and (2) the results of such an examination are used only in accordance with the requirements of this part.

(d) Information obtained in accordance with this section as to the medical condition or history of the applicant shall be collected and maintained on separate forms that shall be accorded confidentiality as medical records, except that:

(1) Supervisors and managers may be informed regarding restrictions on the work or duties of handicapped persons and regarding necessary accommodations;

(2) First aid and safety personnel may be informed, where appropriate, if the condition might require emergency treatment; and

(3) Government officials investigating compliance with the Act shall be provided relevant information upon request.

Subpart C—Program accessibility

§ 104.21 Discrimination prohibited.

No qualified handicapped person shall, because a recipient's facilities are inaccessible to or unusable by handicapped persons, be denied the benefits of, be excluded from participation in, or otherwise be subjected to discrimination under any program or activity to which this part applies.

§ 104.22 Existing facilities.

(a) *Program accessibility.* A recipient shall operate each program or activity to which this part applies so that the program or activity, when viewed in its entirety, is readily accessible to handicapped persons. This paragraph does not require a recipient to make each of its existing facilities or every part of a facility accessible to and usable by handicapped persons.

(b) *Methods.* A recipient may comply with the requirements of paragraph (a) of this section through such means as redesign of equipment, reassignment of classes or other services to accessible buildings, assignment of aides to beneficiaries, home visits, delivery of health, welfare, or other social services at alternate accessible sites, alteration of existing facilities and construction of new facilties in conformance with the requirements of § 104.23, or any other methods that result in making its program or activity accessible to handicapped persons. A recipient is not required to make structural changes in existing facilties where other methods are effective in achieving compliance with paragraph (a) of this section. In choosing among available methods for meeting the requirement of paragraph (a) of this section, a recipient shall give priority to those methods that offer programs and activities to handicapped persons in the most integrated setting appropriate.

(c) *Small health, welfare, or other social serice providers.* If a recipient with fewer than fifteen employees that provides health, welfare, or other social services finds, after consultation with a handicapped person seeking its services, that there is no method of complying with paragraph (a) of this section other than making a significant alteration in its existing facilities, the recipient may, as an alternative, refer the handicapped person to other providers of those services that are accessible.

(d) *Time period.* A recipient shall comply with the requirement of paragraph (a) of this section within sixty days of the effective date of this part except that where structural changes in facilities are necessary, such changes shall be made within three years of the effective date of this part, but in any event as expeditiously as possible.

(e) *Transition plan.* In the event that structural changes to facilities are necessary to meet the requirement of paragraph (a) of this section, a recipient shall develop, within six months of the effective date of this part, a transition plan setting forth the steps necessary to complete such changes. The plan shall be developed with the assistance of interested persons, including handicapped persons or organizations representing handicapped persons. A copy of the transition plan shall be made available for public inspection. The plan shall, at a minimum:

(1) Identify physical obstacles in the recipient's facilties that limit the accessibility of its program or activity to handicappped persons;

(2) Describe in detail the methods that will be used to make the facilities accessible;

(3) Specify the schedule for taking the steps necessary to achieve full program accessibility and, if the time period of the transition plan is longer than one year, identify the steps of that will be taken during each year of the transition period; and

(4) Indicate the person responsible for implementation of the plan.

(f) *Notice.* The recipient shall adopt and implement procedures to ensure that interested persons, including persons with Impaired vision or hearing, can obtain information as to the existence and location of services, activities, and facilities that are accessible to and usuable by handicapped persons.

§ 104.23 New construction.

(a) *Design and constrution.* Each facility or part of a facility constructed by, on behalf of, or for the use of a recipient shall be designed and constructed in such manner that the facility or part of the facility is readily accessible to and usable by handicapped persons, if the construction was commenced after the effective date of this part.

(b) *Alteration.* Each facility or part of a facility which is altered by, on behalf of, or for the use of a recipient after the effective date of this part in a manner that affects or could affect the usability of the facility or part of the facility shall, to the maximum extent feasible, be altered in such manner that the altered portion of the facility is readily accessible to and usable by handicapped persons.

(c) *American National Standards Institute accessibility standards.* Design, construction, or alteration of facilities in conformance with the "American National Standard Specifications for Making Buildings and Facilities Accessible to, and Usable by, the Physically Handicapped," published by the American National Standards Institute, Inc. (ANSI A117.1-1961 (R1971)), which is incorporated by reference in this part, shall constitute compliance with paragraphs (a) and (b) of this section. Departures from particular requirements of those standards by the use of other methods shall be permitted when it is clearly evident that equivalent access to the facility or part of the facility is thereby provided. Incorporation by reference provisions approved by the Director of the Federal Register: May 27, 1975. Incorporated documents are on file at the Office of the Federal Register. Copies of the standards are obtainable from American National Standards Institute, Inc., 1430 Broadway, New York, N.Y. 10018.

[45 FR 30936, May 9, 1980: 45 FR 37426, June 3, 1980]

Subpart D—Preschool, Elementary, and Secondary Education

§ 104.31 Application of this subpart

Subpart D applies to preschool, elementary, secondary, and adult education programs and activities that receive or benefit from Federal financial assistance and to recipients that operate, or that receive or benefit from Federal financial assistance for the operation of, such programs or activities.

§ 104.32 Location and notification.

A recipient that operates a public elementary or secondary education program shall annually:

(a) Undertake to identify and locate every qualified handicapped person residing in the recipient's jurisdiction who is not receiving a public education; and

(b) Take appropriate steps to notify handicapped persons and their parents or guardians of the recipient's duty under this subpart.

§ 104.33 Free appropriate public education.

(a) *General.* A recipient that operates a public elementary or secondary education program shall provide a free appropriate public education to each qualified handicapped person who is in the recipient's jurisdiction, regardless of the nature or severity of the person's handicap.

(b) *Appropriate education.* (1) For the purpose of this subpart, the provision of an appropriate education is the provision of regular or special education and related aids and services that (i) are designed to meet individual educational needs of handicapped persons as adequately as the needs of nonhandicapped persons are met and (ii) are based upon adherence to procedures that satisfy the requirements of §§ 104.34, 104.35, and 104.36.

(2) Implementation of an individualized education program developed in accordance with the Education of the Handicapped Act is one means of meeting the standard established in paragraph (b)(1)(i) of this section.

(3) A recipient may place a handicapped person in or refer such person to a program other than the one that it operates as its means of carrying out the requirements of this subpart. If so, the recipient remains responsible for ensuring that the requirements of this subpart are met with respect to any handicapped person so placed or referred.

(c) *Free education*—(1) *General.* For the purpose of this section, the provision of a free education is the provision of educational and related services without cost to the handicapped person or to his or her parents or guardian, except for those fees that are imposed on non-handicapped persons or their parents or guardian. It may consist either of

the provision of free services or, if a recipient places a handicapped person in or refers such person to a program not operated by the recipient as its means of carrying out the requirements of this subpart, of payment for the costs of the program. Funds available from any public or private agency may be used to meet the requirements of this subpart. Nothing in this section shall be construed to relieve an insurer or similar third party from an otherwise valid obligation to provide or pay for services provided to a handicapped person.

(2) *Transportation.* If a recipient places a handicapped person in or refers such person to a program not operated by the recipient as its means of carrying out the requirements of this subpart, the recipient shall ensure that adequate transportation to and from the program is provided at no greater cost than would be incurred by the person or his or her parents or guardian if the person were placed in the program operated by the recipient.

(3) *Residential placement.* If placement in a public or private residential program is necessary to provide a free appropriate public education to a handicapped person because of his or her handicap, the program, including non-medical care and room and board, shall be provided at no cost to the person or his or her parents or guardian.

(4) *Placement of handicapped persons by parents.* If a recipient has made available, in conformance with the requirements of this section and § 104.34, a free appropriate public education to a handicapped person and the person's parents or guardian choose to place the person in a private school, the recipient is not required to pay for the person's education in the private school. Disagreements between a parent or guardian and a recipient regarding whether the recipient has made such a program available or otherwise regarding the question of financial responsibility are subject to the due process procedures of § 104.36.

(d) *Compliance.* A recipient may not exclude any qualified handicapped person from a public elementary or secondary education after the effective date of this part. A recipient that is not, on the effective date of this regulation, in full compliance with the other requirements of the preceding paragraphs of this section shall meet such requirements at the earliest practicable time and in no event later than September 1, 1978.

§ 104.34 Educational setting.

(a) *Academic setting.* A recipient to which this subpart applies shall educate, or shall provide for the education of, each qualified handicapped person in its jurisdiction with persons who are not handicapped to the maximum extent appropriate to the needs of the handicapped person. A recipient shall place a handicapped person in the regular educational environment operated by the recipient unless it is demonstrated by the recipient that the education of the person in the regular environment with the use of supplementary aids and services cannot be achieved satisfactorily. Whenever a recipient places a person in a setting other than the regular educational environment pursuant to this paragraph, it shall take into account the proximity of the alternate setting to the person's home.

(b) *Nonacademic settings.* In providing or arranging for the provision of nonacademic and extracurricular services and activities, including meals, recess periods, and the services and activities set forth in § 104.37(a)(2), a recipient shall ensure that handicapped persons participate with nonhandicapped persons in such activities and services to the maximum extent appropriate to the needs of the handicapped person in question.

(c) *Comparable facilities.* If a recipient, in compliance with paragraph (a) of this section, operates a facility that is identifiable as being for handicapped persons, the recipient shall ensure that the facility and the services and activities provided therein are comparable to the other facilities, services, and activities of the recipient.

§ 104.35 Evaluation and placement.

(a) *Preplacement evaluation.* A recipient that operates a public elementary or secondary education program shall conduct an evaluation in accordance with the requirements of paragraph (b) of this section of any person who, because of handicap, needs or is belived to need special education or related services before taking any action with respect to the initial placement of the person in a regular or special education program and any subsequent significant change in placement.

(b) *Evaluation procedure.* A recipient to which this subpart applies shall establish standards and prceedures for the evaluation and placement of persons who, because of handicap, need or are believed to need special education or related services which ensure that:

(1) Tests and other evaluation materials have been validated for the specific purpose for which they are used and are administered by trained personnel in conformance with the instructions provided by their producer;

(2) Tests and other evaluation materials include those tailored to assess specific areas of educational need and not merely those which are designed to provide a single general intelligence quotient; and

(3) Tests are selected and administered so as best to ensure that, when a test is administered to a student with impaired sensory, manual, or speaking skills, the test results accurately reflect the student's aptitude or achievement level or whatever other factor the test purports to measure, rather than reflects the student's impaired sensory, manual, or speaking skills (except where those skills are the factors that the test purports to measure).

(c) *Placement procedures.* In interpreting evaluation data and in making placement decisions, a recipient shall (1) draw upon information from a variety of sources, including aptitude and achievement tests, teacher recommendations, physical condition, social or cultural background, and adaptive behavior, (2) establish procedures to ensure that information obtained from all such sources is documented and carefully considered, (3) ensure that the placement decision is made by a group of persons, including persons knowledgeable about the child, the meaning of the evaluation data, and the placement options, and (4) ensure that the placement decision is made in conformity with § 104.34.

(d) *Reevaluation.* A recipient to which this section applies shall establish procedures, in accordance with paragraph (b) of this section, for periodic reevaluation of students who have been provided special education and related services. A reevaluation procedure consistent with the Education of the Handicapped Act is one means of meeting this requirement.

§ 104.36 Procedural safeguards.

A recipient that operates a public elementary or secondary education program shall establish and implement, with respect to actions regarding the identification, evaluation, or educational placement of persons who, because of handicap, need or are believed to need special instruction or related services, a system of procedural safeguards that includes notice, an opportunity for the parents or guardian of the person to examine relevant records, an impartial hearing with opportunity for participation by the person's parents or guardian and representation by counsel, and a review procedure. Compliance with the procedural safeguards of section 615 of the Education of the Handicapped Act is one means of meeting this requirement.

§ 104.37 Nonacademic services.

(a) *General.* (1) A recipient to which this subpart applies shall provide non-academic and extracurricular services and activities in such manner as is necessary to afford handicapped students an equal opportunity for participation in such services and activities.

(2) Nonacademic and extracurricular services and activities may include counseling services, physical recreational athletics, transportation, health services, recreational activities, special interest groups or clubs sponsored by the recipients, referrals to agencies which provide assistance to handicapped persons, and employment of students, in-

cluding both employment by the recipient and assistance in making available outside employment.

(b) *Counseling services.* A recipient to which this subpart applies that provides personal, academic, or vocational counseling, guidance, or placement services to its students shall provide these services without discrimination on the basis of handicap. The recipient shall ensure that qualified handicapped students are not counseled toward more restrictive career objectives than are nonhandicapped students with similar interests and abilities.

(c) *Physical education and athletics.* (1) In providing physical education courses and athletics and similar programs and activities to any of its students, a recipient to which this subpart applies may not discriminate on the basis of handicap. A recipient that offers physical education courses or that operates or sponsors interscholastic, club, or intramural athletics shall provide to qualified handicapped students an equal opportunity for participation in these activities.

(2) A recipient may offer to handicapped students physical education and athletic activities that are separate or different from those offered to nonhandicapped students only if separation or differentiation is consistent with the requirements of § 104.34 and only if no qualified handicapped student is denied the opportunity to compete for teams or to participate in courses that are not separate or different.

§ 104.38 Preschool and adult education programs.

A recipient to which this subpart applies that operates a preschool education or day care program or activity or an adult education program or activity may not, on the basis of handicap, exclude qualified handicapped persons from the program or activity and shall take into account the needs of such persons in determining the aid, benefits, or services to be provided under
the program or activity.

§ 104.39 Private education programs.

(a) A recipient that operates a private elementary or secondary education program may not, on the basis of handicap, exclude a qualified handicapped person from such program if the person can, with minor adjustments, be provided an appropriate education, as defined in 104.33(b)(1), within the recipient's program.

(b) A recipient to which this section applies may not charge more for the provision of an appropriate education to handicapped persons than to non-handicapped persons except to the extent that any additional charge is justified by a substantial increase in cost to the recipient.

(c) A recipient to which this section applies that operates special education programs shall operate such programs in accordance with the provisions of §§ 104.35 and 104.36. Each recipient to which this section applies is subject to the provisions of §§ 104.34, 104.37, and 104.38.

Subpart E—Postsecondary Education

§ 104.41 Application of this subpart.

Subpart E applies to postsecondary education programs and activities, including postsecondary vocational education programs and activities, that receive or benefit from Federal financial assistance and to recipients that operate, or that receive or benefit from Federal financial assistance for the operation of, such programs or activities.

§ 104.42 Admissions and recruitment.

(a) *General.* Qualified handicapped persons may not, on the basis of handicap, be denied admission or be subjected to discrimination in admission or recruitment by a recipient to which this subpart applies.

(b) *Admissions.* In administering its admission policies, a recipient to which this subpart applies:

(1) May not apply limitations upon the number or proportion of handicapped persons who may be admitted;

(2) May not make use of any test or criterion for admission that has a disproportionate, adverse effect on handicapped persons or any class of handicapped persons unless (i) the test or criterion, as used by the recipient, has been validated as a predictor of success in the education program or activity in question and (ii) alternate tests or criteria that have a less disproportionate, adverse effect are not shown by the Assistant Secretary to be available.

(3) Shall assure itself that (i) admissions tests are selected and administered so as best to ensure that, when a test is administered to an applicant who has a handicap that impairs sensory, manual, or speaking skills, the test results accurately reflect the applicant's aptitude or achievement level or whatever other factor the test purports to measure, rather than reflecting the applicant's impaired sensory, manual, or speaking skills (except where those skills are the factors that the test purports to measure); (ii) admissions tests that are designed for persons with impaired sensory, manual, or speaking skills are offered as often and in as timely a manner as are other admissions tests; and (iii) admissions tests are administered in facilities that, on the whole, are accessible to handicapped persons; and

(4) Except as provided in paragraph (c) of this section, may not make preadmission inquiry as to

whether an applicant for admission is a handicapped person but, after admission, may make inquiries on a confidential basis as to handicaps that may require accommodation.

(c) *Preadmission inquiry exception.* When a recipient is taking remedial action to correct the effects of past discrimination pursuant to § 104.6(a) or when a recipient is taking voluntary action to overcome the effects of conditions that resulted in limited participation in its federally assisted program or activity pursuant to 104.6(b), the recipient may invite applicants for admission to indicate whether and to what extent they are handicapped, *Provided,* That:

(1) The recipient states clearly on any written questionnaire used for this purpose or makes clear orally if no written questionnaire is used that the information requested is intended for use solely in connection with its remedial action obligations or its voluntary action efforts; and

(2) The recipient states clearly that the information is being requested on a voluntary basis, that it will be kept confidential, that refusal to provide it will not subject the applicant to any adverse treatment, and that it will be used only in accordance with this part.

(d) Validity studies. For the purposes of paragraph (b)(2) of this section, a recipient may base prediction equations on first year grades, but shall conduct periodic validity studies against the criterion of overall success in the education program or activity in question in order to monitor the general validity of the test scores.

§ 104.43 Treatment of students; general.

(a) No qualified handicapped student shall, on the basis of handicap, be excluded from participation in, be denied the benefits of, or otherwise be subjected to discrimination under any academic, research, occupational training, housing, health insurance, counseling, financial aid, physical education, athletics, recreation, transportation, other extracurricular, or other postsecondary education program or activity to which this subpart applies.

(b) A recipient to which this subpart applies that considers participation by students in education programs or activities not operated wholly by the recipient as part of, or equivalent to, an education program or activity operated by the recipient shall assure itself that the other education program or activity, as a whole, provides an equal opportunity for the participation of qualified handicapped persons.

(c) A recipient to which this subpart applies may not, on the basis of handicap, exclude any qualified handicapped student from any course, course of study, or other part of its education program or activity.

(d) A recipient to which this subpart applies shall operate its programs and activities in the most integrated setting appropriate.

§ 104.44 Academic adjustments.

(a) *Academic requirements.* A recipient to which this subpart applies shall make such modifications to its academic requirements as are necessary to ensure that such requirements do not discriminate or have the effect of discriminating, on the basis of handicap, against a qualified handicapped applicant or student. Academic requirements that the recipient can demonstrate are essential to the program of instruction being pursued by such student or to any directly related licensing requirement will not be regarded as discriminatory within the meaning of this section. Modifications may include changes in the length of time permitted for the completion of degree requirements, substitution of specific courses required for completion of degree requirements, and adaptation of the manner in which specific courses are conducted.

(b) Other rules. A recipient to which this subpart applies may not impose upon handicapped students other rules such as the prohibition of tape recorders in classrooms or of dog guides in campus buildings, that have the effect of limiting the participation of handicapped students in the recipient's education program or activity.

(c) *Course examinations.* In its course examinations or other procedures for evaluating students' academic achievement in its program, a recipient to which this subpart applies shall provide such methods for evaluating the achievement of students who have a handicap that impairs sensory, manual, or speaking skills as will best ensure that the results of the evaluation represents the student's achievement in the course, rather than reflecting the student's impaired sensory, manual, or speaking skills (except where such skills are the factors that the test purports to measure).

(d) *Auxiliary aids.* (1) A recipient to which this subpart applies shall take such steps as are necessary to ensure that no handicapped student is denied the benefits of, excluded from participation in, or otherwise subjected to discrimination under the education program or activity operated by the recipient because of the absence of educational auxiliary aids for students with impaired sensory, manual, or speaking skills.

(2) Auxiliary aids may include taped texts, interpreters or other effective methods of making orally delivered materials available to students with hearing impairments, readers in libraries for students with visual impairments, classroom equipment adapted for use by students with manual impairments, and other similar services and actions. Recipients need not provide attendants, indi-

vidually prescribed devices, readers for personal use or study, or other devices or services of a personal nature.

§ 104.45 Housing.

(a) *Housing provided by the recipient.* A recipient that provides housing to its nonhandicapped students shall provide comparable, convenient, and accessible housing to handicapped students at the same cost as to others. At the end of the transition period provided for in Subpart G, such housing shall be available in sufficient quantity and variety so that the scope of handicapped students' choice of living accommodations is, as a whole, comparable to that of nonhandicapped students.

(b) *Other housing.* A recipient that assists any agency, organization, or person in making housing available to any of its students shall take such action as may be necessary to assure itself that such house is, as a whole, made available in a manner that does not result in discrimination on the basis of handicap.

§ 104.46 Financial and employment assistance to students.

(a) *Provision of financial assistance* (1) In providing financial assistance to qualified handicapped persons, a recipient to which this subpart applies may not (i), on the basis of handicap, provide less assistance than is provided to nonhandicapped persons, limit eligibility for assistance, or otherwise discriminate or (ii) assist any entity or person that provides assistance to any of the recipient's students in a manner that discriminates against qualified handicapped persons on the basis of handicap.

(2) A recipient may administer or assist in the administration of scholarships, fellowships, or other forms of financial assistance established under wills, trusts, bequests, or similar legal instruments that require awards to be made on the basis of factors that discriminate or have the effect of discriminating on the basis of handicap only if the overall effect of the award of scholarships, fellowships, and other forms of financial assistance is not discrimmatory on the basis of handicap.

(b) *Assistance in making available outside employment.* A recipient that assists any agency, organization, or person in providing employment opportunities to any of its students shall assure itself that such employment opportunities, as a whole, are made available in a manner that would not violate Subpart B if they were provided by the recipient.

(c) *Employment of students by recipient.* A recipient that employs any of its students may not do so in a manner that violates Subpart B.

§ 104.47 Nonacademic services.

(a) *Physical education and athletics.* (1) In providing physical education courses and athletics and similar programs and activities to any of its students, a recipient to which this subpart applies may not discriminate on the basis of handicap. A recipient that offers physical education courses or that operates or sponsors intercollegiate, club, or intramural athletics shall provide to qualified handicapped students an equal opportunity for participation in these activities.

(2) A recipient may offer to handicapped students physical education and athletic activities that are separate or different only if separation or differentiation is consistent with the requirements of § 104.43(d) and only if no qualified handicapped student is denied the opportunity to compete for teams or to participate in courses that are not separate or different.

(b) *Counseling and placement services.* A recipient to which this subpart applies that provides personal, academic, or vocational counseling, guidance, or placement services to its students shall provide these services without discrimination on the basis of handicap. The recipient shall ensure that qualified handicapped students are not counseled toward more restrictive career objectives than are non-handicapped students with similar interests and abilities. This requirement does not preclude a recipient from providing factual information about licensing and certification requirements that may present obstacles to handicapped persons in their pursuit of particular careers.

(c) *Social organizations.* A recipient that provides significant assistance to fraternities, sororities, or similar organizations shall assure itself that the membership practices of such organizatons do not permit discrimination otherwise prohibited by this subpart.

Subpart F—Health, Welfare, and Social Serivces

§ 104.51 Application of this subpart.

Subpart F applies to health, welfare, and other social service programs and activities that receive or benefit from Federal financial assistance and to recipients that operate, or that receive or benefit from Federal financial assistance for the operation of, such programs or activities.

§ 104.52 Health, welfare, and other social services.

(a) *General.* In providing health welfare, or other social services or benefits, a recipient may not, on the basis of handicap:

(1) Deny a qualified handicapped person these benefits or services;

(2) Afford a qualified handicapped person an opportunity to receive benefits or services that is not equal to that offered nonhandicapped persons;

(3) Provide a qualified handicapped person with benefits or services that are not as effective (as defined in § 104.4(b)) as the benefits or services provided to others;

(4) Provide benefits or services in a manner that limits or has the effect of limiting the participation of qualified handicapped persons; or

(5) Provide different or separate benefits or services to handicapped persons except where necessary to provide qualified handicapped persons with benefits and services that are as effective as those provided to others.

(b) *Notice.* A recipient that provides notice concerning benefits or services or written material concerning waivers of rights or consent to treatment shall take such steps as are necessary to ensure that qualified handicapped persons, including those with impaired sensory or speaking skills, are not denied effective notice because of their handicap.

(c) *Emergency treatment for the hearing impaired.* A recipient hospital that provides health services or benefits shall establish a procedure for effective communication with persons with impaired hearing for the purpose of providing emergency health care.

(d) *Auxiliary aids.* (1) A recipient to which this subpart applies that employs fifteen or more persons shall provide appropriate auxiliary aids to persons with impaired sensory, manual, or speaking skills, where necessary to afford such persons an equal opportunity to benefit from the service in question.

(2) The Assistant Secretary may require recipients with fewer than fifteen employees to provide auxiliary aids where the provision of aids would not significantly impair the ability of the recipient to provide its benefits or services.

(3) For the purpose of this paragraph, auxiliary aids may include brailled and taped material, interpreters, and other aids for persons with impaired hearing or vision.

§ 104.53 Drug and alcohol addicts.

A recipient to which this subpart applies that operates a general hospital or outpatient facility may not discriminate in admission or treatment against a drug or alcohol abuser or alcoholic who is suffering from a medical condition, because of the person's drug or alcohol abuse or alcoholism.

§ 104.54 Education of institutionalized persons.

A recipient to which this subpart applies and that operates or supervises a program or activity for persons who are institutionalized because of handicap shall ensure that each qualified handicapped person, as defined in § 104.3(k)(2), in its program or activity is provided an appropriate education, as defined in 104.33(b). Nothing in this section shall be interpreted as altering in any way the obligations of recipients under Subpart D.

Subpart G—Procedures

§ 104.61 Procedures

The procedural provisions applicable to title VI of the Civil Rights Act of 1964 apply to this part. These procedures are found in §§ 100.6— 100.10 and Part 101 of this title.

APPENDIX C

TABLE OF
SPECIAL EDUCATION CASES
DECIDED BY THE
U.S. SUPREME COURT

Title and Citation (in chronological order)

Southeastern Community College v. Davis, 442 U.S. 397, 99 S.Ct. 2361, 60 L.Ed.2d 980 (1979).

University of Texas v. Camenisch, 451 U.S. 390, 101 S.Ct. 1830, 68 L.Ed.2d 175 (1981).

Pennhurst State School and Hospital v. Halderman, 451 U.S. 1, 101 S.Ct. 1531, 67 L.Ed.2d 694 (1981).
(Pennhurst I)

Pennhurst State School and Hospital v. Halderman, 465 U.S. 89, 104 S.Ct. 900, 79 L.Ed.2d 67 (1984).
(Pennhurst II)

Board of Education v. Rowley, 458 U.S. 176, 102 S.Ct. 3034, 73 L.Ed.2d 690 (1982).

Irving Independent School District v. Tatro, 468 U.S. 883, 104 S.Ct. 3371, 82 L.Ed.2d 664 (1984).

Smith v. Robinson, 468 U.S. 992, 104 S.Ct. 3457, 82 L.Ed.2d 746 (1984).

Honig v. Students of California School for the Blind, 471 U.S. 148, 105 S.Ct. 1820, 85 L.Ed.2d 114 (1985).

Burlington School Committee v. Department of Education of Massachusetts, 471 U.S. 359, 105 S.Ct. 1996, 85 L.Ed.2d 385 (1985).

City of Cleburne, Texas v. Cleburne Living Center, 473 U.S. 432, 105 S.Ct. 3249, 87 L.Ed.2d 313 (1985).

Witters v. Washington Department of Services for the Blind, 474 U.S. 481, 106 S.Ct. 748, 88 L.Ed.2d 846 (1986).

School Board of Nassau County v. Arline, 480 U.S. 273, 107 S.Ct. 1123, 94 L.Ed.2d 307 (1987).

Honig v. Doe, 484 U.S. 305, 108 S.Ct. 592, 98 L.Ed.2d 686 (1988).

Traynor v. Turnage, 485 U.S. 535, 108 S.Ct. 1372, 99 L.Ed.2d 618 (1988).

Dellmuth v. Muth, 491 U.S. 223, 109 S.Ct. 2397, 105 L.Ed.2d 181 (1989).

APPENDIX D

SUBJECT MATTER TABLE
OF RECENT LAW REVIEW ARTICLES

AIDS

AIDS: a university's liability for failure to protect its students. 14 J.C.&
U.L. 529 (1987).

AIDS: an insurable handicap. 9 Hamline J.Pub.L.& Pol'y 117 (1988).

AIDS and right to privacy. 16 S.U.L.Rev. 393 (1989).

AIDS as a handicap? Arline, tuberculosis and AIDS. 19 U.Tol.L.Rev. 859
(1988).

AIDS law: the impact of AIDS on American schools and prisons. 1987
Ann.Surv.Am.L. 117.

AIDS: legal issues in search of a cure. 14 Wm. Mitchell L. Rev. 575 (1988).

Aquila, Frank D. *AIDS and "AFRAIDS" in our schools: whither our
children?* 69 Denv.U.LRev. 315 (1992).

Associates of persons with AIDS: what are their rights? 57 UMKC L.Rev.
559 (1989).

*Asymptomatic infection with the AIDS virus as a handicap under the
Rehabilitation Act of 1973.* 88 Colum.L.Rev. 563 (1988).

Baxley, James F. *Rehabilitating AIDS-based employment discrimination:
HIV infection as a handicap under the Vocational Rehabilitation
Act of 1973.* 19 Seton Hall L.Rev. 23 (1989).

Enforcing the rights to a public education for children afflicted with AIDS.
36 Emory L.J. 603 (1987).

Fear and loathing in the classroom: AIDS and public education. 14 J.Legis.
87 (1987).

Keith, James A. *AIDS in the classroom.* 58 Miss.L.J. 349 (1988).

Lally-Green, M.E. *Is AIDS a handicap under the Rehabilitation Act of 1973
after School Bd. v. Arline and the Civil Rights Restoration Act of
1987?* 19 U.Tol.L.Rev. 603 (1988).

Lawson, Gary. *AIDS, astrology and Arline: towards a causal interpretation
of section 504.* 17 Hofstra L.Rev. 237 (1989).

O'Brien, Rev. Raymond C. *Discrimination: the difference with AIDS.* 6 J.
Contemp.Health L.& Pol'y 93 (1990).

*Opening the schoolhouse door for children with AIDS: the Education for All
Handicapped Children Act.* 13 B.C.Envtl.Aff.L.Rev. 583 (1986).

Protecting children with AIDS against arbitrary exclusion from school. 74
Calif.L.Rev. 1373 (1986).

Public schools and public health: exclusion of children with AIDS. 5 J.L.&
Pol. 605 (1989).

Quick remediation for AIDS victims who cannot afford to wait. Chalk v.
U.S. Dist. Court, 840 F.2d 701, (9th Cir.1989). 26 Hous.L.Rev.
1033 (1989).

Reading, writing, but no biting: isolating school children with AIDS. 37
Clev.St.L.Rev. 337 (1989).

Sullivan, Kathleen M. and Martha A. Field. *AIDS and the coercive power
of the State.* 23 Harv.Civ.Rts.-Civ.Lib.L.Rev. 139 (1988).

The Rehabilitation Act's otherwise qualified requirements and the AIDS virus: protecting the public from AIDS-related health and safety hazards. 30 Ariz.L.Rev. 571 (1988).

Tuberculosis chapters: a model for future AIDS legislation? 32 St. Louis U.L.J. 1145 (1988).

Turnbull, H. Rutherford, III, Alison Paul, and Jan B. Sheldon. *Mandatory AIDS testing for persons with a developmental disability in residential facilities.* 39 U.Kan.L.Rev. 585 (1991).

Wasson, Robert P., Jr. *AIDS discrimination under federal, state and local law after Arline.* 15 Fla.St.U.L.Rev. 221 (1987).

Waters, Robert Craig. *AIDS and the perception of AIDS as handicaps under Florida law.* 17 Fla.St.U.L.Rev. 441 (1990).

Will AIDS fit the mold? School Bd. of Nassau County, Florida v. Arline, 107 S.Ct. 1123 (1987). 41 Ark.L.Rev. 639 (1988).

Without probable cause: the constitutional ramifications of mandatory AIDS testing in the workplace. 57 UMKC L.Rev. 863 (1989).

Attorney's Fees

Attorney fees in special education: sifting through the interpretive maze. 17 Cap.U.L.Rev. 597 (1989).

Civil rights—attorney's fees award—42 U.S.C. § 1988—the United States Supreme Court has held that an award of attorney's fees under 42 U.S.C. § 1988 is not required to be proportionate to the damages awarded a civil rights plaintiff, thus allowing a fee award seven times the amount of compensatory and punitive damages. City of Riverside v. Rivera, 106 S.Ct. 2686 (1986). 26 Duq.L.Rev. 139 (1987).

Education law—the Handicapped Children's Protection Act of 1986: the award of attorney's fees in litigation under the Education of the Handicapped Act. 11 S.Ill.U.L.J. 381 (1987).

Guernsey, Thomas F. *The school pays the piper, but how much? Attorneys' fees in special education cases after the Handicapped Children's Protection Act of 1986.* 23 Wake Forest L.Rev. 237 (1988).

Schreck, Myron. *Attorneys' fees for administrative proceedings under the Education of the Handicapped Act: of Carey, Crest Street and congressional intent.* 60 Temp.L.Q. 599 (1987).

The Supreme Court's interpretation of section 1988 and awards of attorney's fees for work performed in administrative proceedings: a proposal for a result-oriented approach. North Carolina Dep't of Transp. v. Crest Street Comm. Council, Inc., 107 S.Ct. 336 (1986). 62 Wash.L.Rev. 889 (1987).

Classification and Identification

AIDS: does it qualify as a "handicap" under the Rehabilitation Act of 1973? 61 Notre Dame L.Rev. 572 (1986).

Bennett, P.E. *The meaning of "mental illness" under the Michigan Mental Health Code.* 4 Cooley L.Rev. 65 (1986).

Garcia, Sandra Anderson, Eric Drogin, Robert Batey, and Richard E. Spana. *Institutionalized delinquent and maladjusted juveniles: a psycholegal systems analysis.* 68 Neb.L.Rev. 261 (1989).

Gordon, Andrew. Note. *Special education in Massachusetts: reevaluating standards in light of fiscal constraints.* 26 New Eng.L.Rev. 263 (1991).

Herring, May Lou. Note. *Model federal statute for the education of talented and gifted children.* 67 Chi.-Kent L.Rev. 1035 (1991).

Hurley, Brigid. Note. *Accommodating learning disabled students in higher education: schools' legal obligations under § 504 of the Rehabilitation Act.* 32 B.C.L.Rev. 1051 (1991).

Larson, David Allen. *Mental impairments and the Rehabilitation Act of 1973.* 48 La.L.Rev. 841 (1988).

Lynch, Mary A. *Who should hear the voices of children with disabilities: proposed changes in due process in New York's special education system.* 55 Alb.L.Rev. 179 (1991).

Reinstitutionalization of the mentally retarded. 32 Wayne L.Rev. 1105 (1986).

The Education for All Handicapped Children Act: the benefits and burdens of mainstreaming capable handicapped children in a regular classroom. 38 Mercer L.Rev. 903 (1987).

The Rehabilitation Act of 1973; focusing the definition of a handicapped individual. 30 Wm.& Mary L.Rev. 149 (1988).

Thompson, Edward L. *Children in need of mental health treatment; a judge's view of revised public law and new private law proceedings.* 26 Tulsa L.J. 347 (1991).

Discrimination

Administrative res judicata and section 1983: should the rule of preclusion apply to unreviewed state administrative decisions? 10 Nat'l Black L.J. 73 (1987).

An evolutionary step in equal protection analysis. City of Cleburne v. Cleburne Living Center, 105 S.Ct. 3249 (1985). 46 Md.L.Rev. 163 (1986).

Bacharach, Robert E. *Section 1983 and an administrative exhaustion requirement.* 40 Okla.L.Rev. 407 (1987).

A case of handicap discrimination, no transfer required. Coffman v. W. Va. Bd. of Regents, No. 17904, slip op., (W.Va.June 2, 1989). 91 W.Va.L.Rev. 487 (1989).

Citizens with mental retardation and the courts—new barriers for equal protection and due process? Philadelphia Police and Fire Association for Handicapped Children, Inc. v. City of Philadelphia, 699 F.Supp. 1106 (E.D. Pa.1988, rev'd, 874 F.2d 156, 3d Cir.1989). 43 Ark.L.Rev. 423 (1990).

Civil rights litigation I: developments under section 1983 and Title VII. 1986 Ann.Surv.Am.L. 795.

Civil rights litigation II: developments under section 1988. 1986 Ann.Surv.Am.L. 809.

Civil rights: mental disabilities included in Handicapped Discrimination Act's definition of disability. 23 Suffolk U.L.Rev. 421 (1989).

Civil rights—Rehabilitation Act—handicapped individual. School Bd. of Nassau County, Florida v. Arline, 107 S.Ct. 1123 (1987). 26 Duq.L.Rev. 511 (1987).

Coleman, Jennifer A. *42 U.S.C. section 1988: a congressionally-mandated approach to the construction of section 1983.* 19 Ind.L.Rev. 665 (1986).

Constitutional law: although mentally retarded not a quasi-suspect class, denial of special use permit deprived applicants of constitutional right. City of Cleburne v. Cleburne Living Center, 105 S.Ct. 3249 (1985). 25 Washburn L.J. 575 (1986).

Constitutional law—mental health—the mentally handicapped do not constitute a "quasi-suspect" class for purposes of equal protection analysis. City of Cleburne v. Cleburne Living Center, 105 S.Ct. 3249 (1985). 62 N.D.L.Rev. 95 (1986).

Constitutional law—mental retardation is not a quasi-suspect classification. 17 St. Mary's L.J. 1053 (1986).

Contagiousness and the Rehabilitation Act of 1973. School Bd. of Nassau County v. Arline, U.S., 107 S.Ct. 1123 (1987). 14 N.Ky.L.Rev. 435 (1988).

Denial of quasi-suspect status for the mentally retarded and its effect on exclusionary zoning of group homes. City of Cleburne v. Cleburne Living Center, 105 S.Ct. 3249 (1985). 17 U.Tol.L.Rev. 1041 (1986).

Discrimination in the public schools: Dick and Jane have AIDS. 29 Wm.& Mary L.Rev. 881 (1988).

Employment discrimination against the handicapped: analysis of statutory and constitutional protection in Massachusetts. 21 New Eng.L.Rev. 305 (1985-86).

Engel, David M. and Alfred S. Konefsky. *Law students with disabilities: removing barriers in the law school community.* 38 Buffalo L.Rev. 551 (1990).

Equal protection for the mentally retarded? City of Cleburne v. Cleburne Living Center, 105 S.Ct. 3249 (1985). 9 Harv.J.L. & Pub.Pol'y 231 (1986).

Extension within manageable bounds protecting the Handicapped. School Bd. of Nassau County v. Arline, 408 So.2d 706 (Fla.App.1982). 65 Denver U.L.Rev. 319 (1988).

Facial discrimination: extending handicap law to employment discrimination on the basis of physical appearance. 100 Harv.L.Rev. 2035 (1987).

Flaccus, Janet A. *Discrimination legislation for the Handicapped: much ferment and the erosion of coverage.* 55 U.Cin.L.Rev. 81 (1986).

Greene, Kenneth A. *Burdens of proving handicap discrimination using federal employment discrimination law: rational basis or undue burden?* 1989 Det.C.L.Rev. 1053.

Handicap and race discrimination in readmission procedures. Anderson v. Univ. of Wisconsin, 665 F.Supp. 1372 (W.D.Wis.1987). 15 J.C.& U.L. 431 (1989).

Improving handicappers' civil rights in Michigan—preventing discrimination through accommodation. 21 U.Mich.J.L.Ref. 283 (1987/88).

An individualized definition of "handicap" and its application to HIV. 22 U.C.Davis L.Rev. 653 (1989).

Kaufman, Michael J. *Federal and state handicapped discrimination laws: toward an accommodating legal framework.* 18 Loy.U.Chi.L.J. 1119 (1987).

Larson, David D. *What disabilities are protected under the Rehabilitation Act of 1973?* 16 Mem.St.U.L.Rev. 229 (1986).

Maffeo, Patricia A. *Making non-discriminatory fitness-for-duty decisions about persons with disabilities under the Rehabilitation Act and the Americans with Disabilities Act.* 16 Am.J.L.& Med. 279 (1990).

Mims, William C. *The plight of the handicapped infant: The Federal Response.* 15 U.Balt.L.Rev. 449 (1986).

Minow, Martha. *When difference has its home: group homes for the mentally retarded, equal protection and legal treatment of difference.* 22 Harv.C.R. - C.L.L.Rev. 111 (1987).

Perras, Roichard A. and Walter C. Hunter. *Handicap discrimination in employment: the employer defense of future safety risk.* 6 J.L.& Com. 377 (1986).

Protecting children with AIDS against arbitrary exclusion from school. 74 Calif.L.Rev. 1373 (1986).

Rational basis with a bite? City of Cleburne v. Cleburne Living Center, 105 S.Ct. 3249 (1985). 20 U.S.F.L.Rev. 927 (1986).

Real protection against discrimination for society's new outcasts? School Bd. of Nassau County v. Arline, 107 S.Ct. 1123 (1987). 17 Stetson L.Rev. 517 (1988).

Rebell, Michael A. *Structural discrimination and the rights of the disabled.* 74 Geo.L.J. 1435 (1986).

Rehabilitation Act—Department of Health and Human Services may not interfere in medical treatment decision regarding handicapped infants. Bowen v. American Hosp. Ass'n, 106 S.Ct. 2101 (1986). 16 Cum.L.Rev. 607 (1986).

Rothstein, Laura F. *Section 504 of the Rehabilitation Act: emerging issues for colleges and universities.* 13 J.C.& U.L. 229 (1986).

Section 504 of the Rehabilitation Act: a re-examination of the civil rights declaration of the handicapped. 21 Suffolk U.L.Rev. 175 (1987).

Section 504 transportation regulations: molding civil rights legislation to meet the reality of economic constraints. 26 Washburn L.J. 558 (1987).

Shedding tiers for the mentally retarded. City of Cleburne v. Cleburne Living Center, 105 S.Ct. 3249 (1985). 35 DePaul L.Rev. 485 (1986).

Snelling, Phillip H. *Discrimination against children with special health care needs: Title V Crippled Children's Services programs and section 504 of the Rehabilitation Act of 1973.* 18 Loy.U.Chi.L.J. 995 (1987).

Spahr, Diana. Case note. *Constitutional law — dissolution of desegregation decree is proper if school board shows good faith compliance and elimination of vestiges of past de jure discrimination.* [Board of Education v. Dowell, 111 S.Ct. 630 (1991)]. 41 Drake L.Rev. 379 (1992).

Tate, Kathryn W. *The federal employer's duties under the Rehabilitation Act: does reasonable accommodation or affirmative action include reassignment?* 67 Tex.L.Rev. 781 (1989).

Tucker, Bonnie P. *Section 504 of the Rehabilitation Act after ten years of enforcement: the past and the future.* 1989 U.Ill.L.Rev. 845.

United States Commission on Civil Rights—medical discrimination against children with disabilities: an abstract. 6 J.Contemp.Health L.& Pol'y 379 (1990).

What's a handicap anyway? Analyzing handicap claims under the Rehabilitation Act of 1973 and analogous state statutes. 22 Willamette L.Rev. 529 (1986).

Wright, Susan L. Recent development. *The Supreme Court implies a damages remedy for Title IX sex discrimination.* [Franklin v. Gwinnett County Public Schools, 112 S.Ct. 1028 (1992)]. 45 Vand.L.Rev. 1367 (1992).

Education Generally

Broadwell, Cathy A. and John C. Walden. *"Free appropriate public education" after* Rowley: *an analysis of recent court decisions.* 17 J.L.& Educ. 35 (1988).

Cichon, Dennis E. *Educability and education: filling the cracks in service provision responsibility under the Education for All Handicapped Children Act of 1975.* 48 Ohio St.L.J. 1089 (1987).

Constitutional law—no free ride to the schoolhouse gate: equal protection analysis in Kadrmas v. Dickinson Public Schools, 108 S.Ct. 2481 (1988). 20 N.M.L.Rev. 161 (1990).

Culhane, John G. *Reinvigorating educational malpractice claims: a representational focus.* 67 Wash.L.Rev. 349 (1992).

Education and administrative law—education of health-impaired children and administrative due process—state Department of Education possesses statutory authority to promulgate administrative rules governing the admission to school of children afflicted with AIDS provided that department affords all parties appropriate procedural due process under those rules. Bd. of Educ. v. Cooperman, 523 A.2d 655 (1987). 19 Rutgers L.J. 483 (1988).

Engel, David M. *Law, culture, and children with disabilities: education rights and the construction of differences.* 1991 Duke L.J. 166.

Federal bilingual, bicultural education: the failure of entitlement. 59 UMKC L.Rev. 769 (1991).

Fleming, Evelyn R. and Donald C. Fleming. *Involvement of minors in special education decision-making.* 16 J.L.& Educ. 389 (1987).

Guernsey, Thomas F. *When the teachers and parents can't agree, who really decides? Burdens of proof and standards of review under the EAHCA.* 36 Clev.St.L.Rev. 67 (1988).

Herr, Stanley S. *Children without homes: rights to education and to family stability.* 45 U.Miami L.Rev. 337 (1990-1991).

Lawson, Raneta J. *The child seated next to me: the continuing quest for equal educational opportunity.* 16 T.Marshall L.Rev. 35 (1990).

Lynch, Mary A. *Who should hear the voices of children with disabilities: proposed changes in due process in New York's special education system.* 55 Alb.L.Rev. 179 (1991).

Maggs, Gregory E. *Innovation in constitutional law: the right to educate and the tricks of the trade.* 86 Nw.U.L.Rev. 1038 (1992).

Meyen, Edward L. *Symposium Keynote Address: Education reform: the intent and the risks.* 2 Kan.J.L.& Pub.Pol'y 5 (1992).

Moss, Kary L. *Standardized tests as a tool of exclusion: improper use of the SAT in New York.* 4 Berkeley Women's L.J. 230 (1989-90).

Post-secondary education: why can't Johnny read even though his parents are happily married? 29 J.Fam.L. 923 (1990-91).

Rothstein, Laura F. *Students, staff and faculty with disabilities: current issues for colleges and universities.* 17 J.C.& U.L. 471 (1991).

Saideman, Ellen M. *Helping the mute to speak: the availability of augmentative communication devices under Medicaid.* 17 N.Y.U.Rev.L. & Soc.Change 741 (1989-1990).

Stewart, Frank H., Abram S. Gordon and Andrew M. Ostrognai. *Ohio handicap law.* 13 U.Dayton L.Rev. 181 (1988).

The homeless school-age child: can educational rights meet educational needs? 45 U.Miami L.Rev. 537 (1990-1991).

Education of The Handicapped Act/Individuals with Disabilities Education Act

Burden of proof under the Education for All Handicapped children Act. 51 Ohio St.L.J. 759 (1990).

Civil rights—Education of the Handicapped Act. Polk v. Cent. Susquehanna Intermediate Unit 16, 853 F.2d 171 (3d Cir.1988). 62 Temp.L.Rev. 429 (1989).

Daniel, Philip T.K. and Karen Bond Coriell. *Traversing the Sisyphean trails of the Education for All Handicapped Children's Act: an overview.* 18 Ohio N.U.L.Rev. 571 (1992).

Education law—right to a free and appropriate education—the Education for All Handicapped Children Act does not contain an implicit "dangerousness exception." Honig v. Doe, 108 S.Ct. 592 (1988). 20 Rutgers L.J. 561 (1989).

Education law—Wyoming refuses to recognize compensatory education as a remedy under the Education for All Handicapped Children Act of 1975. Natrona County School Dist. No. 1 v. McKnight, 764 P.2d 1039 (Wyo.1988). 24 Land & Water L.Rev. 529 (1989).

Educational law—burden of proof—a school board bears the burden of proving that the education of a handicapped child is "appropriate" under the Education for All Handicapped Children Act of 1975. Lascari v. Bd. of Educ. of Ramapo Indian Hills Regional High School Dist., 116 N.J. 30, 560 A.2d 1180 (1989). 22 Rutgers L.J. 273 (1990).

Exhaustion of administrative remedies: exceptions and predictability. 66 U.Det.L.Rev. 239 (1989).

Goldberg, Steven S. *The failure of legalization in education: alternative dispute resolution and the Education for All Handicapped Children Act of 1975.* 18 J.L.& Educ. 441 (1989).

Guernsey, Thomas F. *The Education for All Handicapped Children Act, 42 U.S.C. § 1983, and § 504 of the Rehabilitation Act of 1973: statutory interaction following the Handicapped Children's Protection Act of 1986.* 68 Neb.L.Rev. 564 (1989).

Huefner, Dixie Snow and Steven F. Huefner. *Publicly financed interpreter services for parochial school students with IDEA-B disabilities.* 21 J.L.& Ed. 223

Hyatt, Sheila K. *The remedies gap: compensation and implementation under the Education for All Handicapped Children Act.* 17 N.Y.U. Rev.L.& Soc.Change 689 (1989-1990).

McMullen, Judith G. *Family support of the disabled: a legislative proposal to create incentives to support disabled family members.* 23 U.Mich.J.L.Rev. 439 (1990).

Mootness and the Education for All Handicapped Children Act: timely decision saves judicial and social costs. Honig v. Doe, 108 S.Ct. 592 (1988). 57 U.Cin.L.Rev. 1101 (1989).

Peel, Drew B. *Comment. Time to learn: borrowing a limitations period for actions under § 1415(e)(2) of the Education for All Handicapped Children Act of 1975.* 1991 U.Chi.Legal Forum 315.

Weber, Mark C. *The transformation of the Education of the Handicapped Act: a study in the interpretation of radical statutes.* 24 U.C. Davis L.Rev. 349 (1990).

What's "appropriate"?: Finding a void for deaf children and their parents in the Education for All Handicapped Children Act. 14 U.Puget Sound L.Rev. 351 (1991).

Eleventh Amendment

Congressional abrogation of state sovereign immunity and the Education for All Handicapped Children Act. Dellmuth v. Muth, 57 U.S.L.W. 4720 (U.S. June 13, 1989). 57 Fordham L.Rev. 877 (1989).

Rudovsky, David. *The qualified immunity doctrine in the Supreme Court: judicial activism and the restriction of constitutional rights.* 138 U.Pa.L.Rev. 23 (1989).

The Eleventh Amendment controversy continues: the availability and scope of relief against state entities under the Education of the Handicapped Act. 22 Ind.L.Rev. 707 (1989).

The Eleventh Amendment pierces the legal shield of EHA protection. Dellmuth v. Muth, 109 S.Ct. 2398 (1989). 23 J.Marshall L.Rev. 487 (1990).

Greenwood, Christopher Dean. Student article. *Congress' new IDEA in special education: permitting a private right of action against state agencies.* 1992 B.Y.U.J.L.& Ed. 49.

Employment

After School Board of Nassau County v. Arline: employees with AIDS and the concerns of the "worried well." School Bd. of Nassau County v. Arline, 107 S.Ct. 1123 (1987). 37 Am.U.L.Rev. 867 (1988).

AIDS and employment discrimination: should AIDS be considered a handicap? 33 Wayne L.Rev. 1095 (1987).

Defining "handicap" for purposes of employment discrimination. 30 Ariz.L.Rev. 633 (1988).

Employment discrimination and AIDS: is AIDS a handicap under section 504 of the Rehabilitation Act? 38 U.Fla.L.Rev. 649 (1986).

Handicap discrimination in the workplace: how to determine if a disability is related to the ability to work. Father Flanagan's Boys' Home v. Goerke, 401 N.W.2d 731 (1987). 21 Creighton L.Rev. 683 (1987-1988).

Handicap provision of Texas employment discrimination statute protects only those individuals whose disabilities severely limit them in performing work-related tasks in general. Chevron v. Redmon, 745 S.W.2d 314 (Tex.1987). 19 Tex.Tech.L.Rev. 1485 (1988).

Handicapped workers: who should bear the burden of proving job qualifications? 38 Me.L.Rev. 135 (1986).

Mandatory AIDS testing—a Fourth Amendment analysis. Glover v. Eastern Nebraska Community Office of Retardation, 867 F.2d 461 (8th Cir., cert. denied, 110 S.Ct. 321 (1989). 23 Creighton L.Rev. 693 (1990).

Protection of AIDS victims from employment discrimination under the Rehabilitation Act. 1987 U.Ill.L.Rev. 355.

Servodidio, G.P. Recent development. *Balancing the interests of the Government and the public employee in the context of political patronage and freedom of speech.* [Kinsey v. Salado Independent School District, 950 F.2d 988, 5th Cir., en banc, cert. denied, 112 S.Ct. 2275 (1992)]. 67 Tul.L.Rev. 550 (1992).

Finance

Browning, Stephen D. Note. *The misguided application of the Sherman Act to colleges and universities in the context of sharing financial aid information.* 33 B.C.L.Rev. 763 (1992).

Inequality in Louisiana public school finance: should educational quality depend on a student's school district residency? 60 Tul.L.Rev. 1269 (1986).

Richardson, Karen. Note. *Education: the constitutionality of Oklahoma's public school financing system: does the state have a duty to provide an adequate education for all schoolchildren?* 44 Okla.L.Rev. 745 (1991).

Stark, Richard J. *Education reform: judicial interpretation of state constitutions' education finance provisions — adequacy vs. equality.* 1991 Ann.Surv.Am.L. 609.

First Amendment

Against a wall of strict separation: Missouri's Church-State doctrine and State provision of special education services to private schools. 53 Mo.L.Rev. 407 (1988).

An educational perspective on the evolution of Lemon. Grand Rapids School District v. Ball, 105 S.Ct. 3216 (1985), and Aguilar v. Felton, 105 S.Ct. 3232 (1985). 1986 B.Y.U.L.Rev. 489.

Bosmajian, Haig. *The judiciary's use of metaphors, metonymies and other tropes to give First Amendment protection to students and teachers.* 15 J.L.& Educ. 439 (1986).

Boswell-Odum, Beth C. Note. *The fighting words doctrine and racial speech on campus.* 33 S.Tex.L.Rev. 261 (1992).

Choper, Jesse H. *The establishment clause and aid to parochial schools—an update.* 75 Calif.L.Rev. 5 (1987).

Danning, Gordon. *Freedom of Speech in public schools: using communication analysis to eliminate the role of educational ideaology.* 19 Hastings Const.L.Q. 123 (1991).

Guernsey, Thomas F. and M. Grey Sweeney. *The Church, the State, and the EHA: educating the handicapped in light of the establishment clause.* 73 Marq.L.Rev. 259 (1989).

Horned, Jeff. *Student free speech rights: "the closing of the schoolhouse gate" and its public policy implications.* 33 S.Tex.L.Rev. 601 (1992).

Kaplin, William A. *"Hate speech" on the college campus: freedom of speech and equality at the crossroads.* 27 Land & Water L.Rev. 243 (1992).

Mitchell, Carolyn M. Comment. *The political correctness doctrine: redefining speech on college campuses.* 13 Whittier L.Rev. 805 (1992).

Salomone, Rosemary C. *Free speech and school governance in the wake of Hazelwood.* 26 Ga.L.Rev. 253 (1992).

Sedler, Robert A. *The unconstitutionality of campus bans on "racist speech:" the view from without and within.* 53 U.Pitt.L.Rev. 631 (1992).

Special education and the non-public school child: a handicap is a nonsectarian condition. 5 L.& Inequality 549 (1988).

Injuries

Henderson, Donald H. *Negligent liability suits emanating from the failure to provide adequate supervision: a critical issue for teachers and school boards.* 16 J.L.& Educ. 435 (1987).

Standard of care, duty & causation in failure to warn actions against mental health professionals. Peck v. Counseling Service of Addison County, Inc., 499 A.2d 422 (Vt.1985). 11 Vt.L.Rev. 343 (1986).

The use of closed-circuit television testing in child sexual abuse cases: a Twentieth Century solution to a Twentieth Century problem. 23 San Diego L.Rev. 919 (1986).

The use of videotaped testimony of victims in cases involving child sexual abuse: a constitutional dilemma. 14 Hofstra L.Rev. 291 (1986).

Placement

Huefner, Dixie Snow. *Special education residential placements under the Education for All Handicapped Children Act.* 18 J.L.& Educ. 441 (1989).

Lane, JoEllen. Note. *The use of the least restrictive environment principle in placement decisions affecting school-age students with disabilities.* 69 U.Det.Mercy L.Rev. 291 (1992).

Retroactive reimbursement: the standard of review for a parent's unilateral placement under the Education for All Handicapped Children Act. 10 Cardozo L.Rev. 2381 (1989).

Schneider, R. Craig. Note. *Multi-factored analysis required for IEP reviews.* [Johnson v. Independent School Dist. No. 4 of Bixby, 921 F.2d 1022 (10th Cir.1990) per curiam, cert. denied, 111 S.Ct. 1685

(1991)]. 18 J.Contemp.L. 177 (1992).

Schools—Education for All Handicapped Children Act of 1975—school officials may not unilaterally change the current educational placement of a student protected under the Act. Honig v. Doe, 108 S.Ct. 592 (1988). 58 Miss.L.J. 387 (1988).

Tweedie, Jack. *Parental rights and accountability in public education: Special education and choice of school.* 7 Yale Law & Policy Rev. 396 (1989).

Weber, Mark C. and Mary Binkelman. *Legal issues in the transition to public school for handicapped infants and children.* 19 J.L.& Educ. 193 (1990).

Related Services

Closen, Michael L., Susan Marie Connor, Howard L. Kaufman and Mark F. Wojcik. *AIDS: testing democracy—irrational responses to the public health crisis and the need for privacy in serologic testing.* 19 J.Marshall L.Rev. 835 (1986).

Donohue, David C. Note. *Restricting related services under the Individuals with Disabilities Education Act.* [Clovis Unified School District v. California Office of Administrative Hearings, 903 F.2d 635 (9th Cir.1990)]. 8 J.Contemp.Health L & Pol'y 407 (1992).

Establishing standards for treating children in mental institutions with psychotropic drugs. 5 Pub.L.F. 215 (1986).

Joint ventures: for profit and nonprofit corporations as partners in providing mental health services. 5 Pub.L.F. 201 (1986).

Law, Social Policy and Contagious Disease: a Symposium on Acquired Immune Deficiency Syndrome (AIDS). 14 Hofstra L.Rev. 1 (1986).

Medical treatment of handicapped infants: who should make the decision? 22 Tul.L.Rev. 259 (1986).

Scott, Elizabeth S. *Sterilization of mentally retarded persons: reproductive rights and family privacy.* 1986 Duke L.J. 806.

Standard of care, duty & causation in failure to warn actions against mental health professionals. Peck v. Counseling Service of Addison County, Inc., 499 A.2d 422 (Vt.1985). 11 Vt.L.Rev. 343 (1986).

Sterilization of the mentally disabled in Pennsylvania: three generations without legislative guidance are enough. 92 Dick.L.Rev. 409 (1988).

The best interest standard in court-authorized sterilization of mentally retarded. In re Debra B., 495 A.2d 781 (Me.1985). 38 Me.L.Rev. 209 (1987).

The Education for All Handicapped Children Act: trends and problems with the "related services" provision. 18 Golden Gate U.L.Rev. 427 (1988).

Student Rights

All aboard: accessible public transportation for disabled persons. 63 N.Y.U.L.Rev. 360 (1988).

An abused child's right to life, liberty and property in the home: constitutional approval of state inaction. DeShaney v. Winnebago County Department of Social Services, 109 S.Ct. 998 (1989). 92 W.Va.L.Rev. 205 (1989).

Administrative law—The Rehabilitation Act does not preclude the Veterans' Administration's denial of educational benefit extensions to primary alcoholics. Traynor v. Turnage, 108 S.Ct. 1372 (1988). 23 Suffolk U.L.Rev. 71 (1989).

Beyond least restrictive alternative: a constitutional right to treatment for mentally disabled persons in the community. 20 Loy.L.A.L.Rev. 1527 (1987).

Fleming, Evelyn R. and Donald C. Fleming. *Involvement of minors in special education decision-making.* 16 J.L.& Educ. 389 (1987).

Griffith, Frederick J., III. New Jersey v. T.L.O. *and its progeny: the Bill of Rights at school.* 5 Cooley L.Rev. 617 (1988).

Involuntary sterilization of mentally retarded minors in Nebraska. 68 Neb.L.Rev. 410 (1989).

Litigation involving Ritalin and the hyperactive child. 1990 Det.C.L.Rev. 125.

Meeting the special educational needs of learning disabled juvenile delinquents. 31 Ariz.L.Rev. 615 (1989).

Perlin, Michael L. *Can mental health professionals predict judicial decision making? Constitutional and tort liability aspects of the right of the institutionalized mentally disabled to refuse treatment: on the cutting edge.* 3 Touro L.Rev. 13 (1986).

Rethinking equality and difference: disability discrimination in public transportation. 97 Yale L.J. 863 (1988).

Ross, Stephen F. *Legislative enforcement of equal protection.* 72 Minn.L.Rev. 311 (1987).

Soifer, Aviam. *Moral ambition, formalism, and the "free world" of DeShaney.* 57 Geo.Wash.L.Rev. 1513 (1989).

State constitutions and statutes as sources of rights for the mentally disabled: the last frontier. 20 Loy.L.A.L.Rev. 1249 (1987).

Sterilization of the mentally disabled in Pennsylvania: three generations without legislative guidance are enough. 92 Dick.L.Rev. 409 (1988).

Symposium: Developmental Disabilities. 39 U.Kan.L.Rev. 519 (1991).

The handicapped in the classroom: the Supreme Court adopts a new standard for the protection of rights in Honig v. Doe, 108 S.Ct. 592 (1988). 24 Willamette L.Rev. 1141 (1988).

Underwood, Julie. *Special education discipline: changing practices after* Honig v. Doe. 17 J.L.& Educ. 375 (1988).

Ziegler, Carol L. and Nancy M. Lederman. *School vouchers: are urban students surrendering rights for choice?* 19 Fordham Urb.L.J. 813 (1992).

Suspension and Expulsion

Congress, Smith v. Robinson, *and the myth of attorney representation in special education hearings: is attorney representation desirable?* 37 Syracuse L.Rev. 1161 (1987).

The legal limits of school discipline for children with handicaps. 69 Or. L.Rev. 117 (1990).

Suspension and expulsion of handicapped children: an overview in light of Doe v. Maher, 793 F.2d 1470 (9th Cir.1986). 14 W.St.U.L.Rev. 341 (1986).

The Americans with Disabilities Act

The Americans with Disabilities Act of 1990: improving judicial determinations of whether an individual is "substantially limited." 75 Minn.L.Rev. 1303 (1991).

The Americans with Disabilities Act of 1990: new legislation creates expansive rights for the disabled and uncertainties for employers. 21 Cumb.L.Rev. 629 (1990-1991).

Arney, D. Todd. Note. *Survey of the Americans with Disabilities Act, Title I: with the final regulation in, are the criticisms out?* 31 Washburn L.J. 522 (1992).

Hill, Wayne A., Jr. Student note. *Americans with Disabilities Act of 1990: significant overlap with § 504 for colleges and universities.* 18 J.C. & U.L. 389 (1992).

Reasonable accommodation under the Americans with disabilities Act: how much must one do before hardship turns undue? 59 U.Cin.L.Rev. 1311 (1991).

Rothstein, Mark A. *Genetic discrimination in employment and the Americans with Disabilities Act.* 29 Hous.L.Rev. 23 (1992).

Stine, Margaret. Comment. *Reasonable accommodation and undue hardship under the Americans with Disabilities Act of 1990.* 37 S.D.L.Rev. 97 (1992).

Yand, James T. *Does your building discriminate against the disabled? Guidelines for bringing existing public accommodations into compliance with the Americans with Disabilities Act.* 4 Hofstra Prop.L.J. 229 (1992).

APPENDIX E

GLOSSARY

Age Discrimination in Employment Act (ADEA) - The ADEA, 29 U.S.C. § 621 *et seq.*, is part of the Fair Labor Standards Act. It prohibits discrimination against persons who are at least forty years old, and applies to employers which have twenty or more employees and which affect interstate commerce.

Americans With Disabilities Act (ADA) - The ADA, 42 U.S.C. § 12101 *et seq.*, went into effect on July 26, 1992. Among other things, it prohibits discrimination against a qualified individual with a disability because of that person's disability with respect to job application procedures, the hiring, advancement or discharge of employees, employee compensation, job training, and other terms, conditions and privileges of employment.

Bona fide - Latin term meaning "good faith." Generally used to note a party's lack of bad intent or fraudulent purpose.

Class Action Suit - Federal Rule of Civil Procedure 23 allows members of a class to sue as representatives on behalf of the whole class provided that the class is so large that joinder of all parties is impractical, there are questions of law or fact common to the class, the claims or defenses of the representatives are typical of the claims or defenses of the class, and the representative parties will adequately protect the interests of the class. In addition, there must be some danger of inconsistent verdicts or adjudications if the class action were prosecuted as separate actions. Most states also allow class actions under the same or similar circumstances.

Collateral Estoppel - Also known as issue preclusion. The idea that once an issue has been litigated, it may not be re-tried. Similar to the doctrine of *Res Judicata* (see below).

Due Process Clause - The clauses of the Fifth and Fourteenth Amendments to the Constitution which guarantee the citizens of the United States "due process of law" (see below). The Fifth Amendment's Due Process Clause applies to the federal government, and the Fourteenth Amendment's Due Process Clause applies to the states.

Due Process of Law - The idea of "fair play" in the government's application of law to its citizens, guaranteed by the Fifth and Fourteenth Amendments. Substantive due process is just plain *fairness*, and procedural due process is accorded when the government utilizes adequate procedural safeguards for the protection of an individual's liberty or property interests.

Education for All Handicapped Children Act (EAHCA) - [see Individuals with Disabilities Education Act (IDEA).]

Education of the Handicapped Act (EHA) - [see Individuals with Disabilities Education Act (IDEA).]

Employee Retirement Income Security Act (ERISA) - Federal legislation which sets uniform standards for employee pension benefit plans and employee welfare benefit plans. It is codified at 29 U.S.C. § 1001 *et seq.*

Enjoin - (see Injunction).

Equal Pay Act - Federal legislation which is part of the Fair Labor Standards Act. It applies to discrimination in wages which is based on gender. For race discrimination, employees paid unequally must utilize Title VII or 42 U.S.C. § 1981. Unlike many labor statutes, there is no minimum number of employees necessary to invoke the act's protection.

Equal Protection Clause - The clause of the Fourteenth Amendment which prohibits a state from denying any person within its jurisdiction equal protection of its laws. Also, the Due Process Clause of the Fifth Amendment which pertains to the federal government. This has been interpreted by the Supreme Court to grant equal protection even though there is no explicit grant in the Constitution.

Establishment Clause - The clause of the First Amendment which prohibits Congress from making "any law respecting an establishment of religion." This clause has been interpreted as creating a "wall of separation" between church and state. The test now used to determine whether government action violates the Establishment Clause, referred to as the *Lemon* test, asks whether the action has a secular purpose, whether its primary effect promotes or inhibits religion, and whether it requires excessive entanglement between church and state.

Ex Post Facto Law - A law which punishes as criminal any action which was not a crime at the time it was performed. Prohibited by Article I, Section 9, of the Constitution.

Exclusionary Rule - Constitutional limitation on the introduction of evidence which states that evidence derived from a constitutional violation must be excluded from trial.

Fair Labor Standards Act (FLSA) - Federal legislation which mandates the payment of minimum wages and overtime compensation to covered employees. The overtime provisions require employers to pay at least time-and-one-half to employees who work more than 40 hours per week.

Federal Labor Relations Authority (FLRA) - The Authority charged with interpreting collective bargaining agreements between federal employers and employees, and with preventing and remedying unfair labor practices by federal employers.

Federal Tort Claims Act - Federal legislation which determines the circumstances under which the United States waives its sovereign immunity (see below) and agrees to be sued in court for money damages. The government retains its immunity in cases of intentional torts committed by its employees or agents, and where the tort is the result of a "discretionary function" of a federal employee or agency. Many states have similar acts.

42 U.S.C. §§ 1981, 1983 - Section 1983 of the federal Civil Rights Act prohibits any person acting under color of state law from depriving any other person of rights protected by the Constitution or by federal laws. A vast majority of lawsuits claiming constitutional violations are brought under § 1983. Section 1981 provides that all persons enjoy the same right to make and enforce contracts as "white citizens." Section 1981 applies to employment contracts. Further, unlike § 1983, § 1981 applies even to private actors. It is not limited to those acting under color of state law. These sections do not apply to the federal government, though the government may be sued directly under the Constitution for any violations.

Free Exercise Clause - The clause of the First Amendment which prohibits Congress from interfering with citizens' rights to the free exercise of their religion. Through the Fourteenth Amendment, it has also been made applicable to the states and their sub-entities. The Supreme Court has held that laws of general applicability which have an incidental effect on persons' free exercise rights are not violative of the Free Exercise Clause.

Handicapped Children's Protection Act (HCPA) - [see also Individuals with Disabilities Education Act (IDEA).] The HCPA, enacted as an amendment to the EHA, provides for the payment of attorney's fees to a prevailing parent or guardian in a lawsuit brought under the EHA (and the IDEA).

Hearing Officer - Also known as an administrative law judge. The hearing officer decides disputes that arise *at the administrative level*, and has the power to administer oaths, take testimony, rule on evidentiary questions, and make determinations of fact.

Immunity (Sovereign Immunity) - Federal, state and local governments are free from liability for torts committed except in cases in which they have consented to be sued (by statute or by court decisions).

Incorporation Doctrine - By its own terms, the Bill of Rights applies only to the federal government. The Incorporation Doctrine states that the Fourteenth Amendment makes the Bill of Rights applicable to the states.

Individuals with Disabilities Education Act (IDEA) - Also known as the Education of the Handicapped Act (EHA), the Education for All Handicapped Children Act (EAHCA), and the Handicapped Children's Protection Act (HCPA). Originally enacted as the EHA, the IDEA is the federal legislation which provides for the free, appropriate education of all children with disabilities.

Individualized Educational Program (IEP) - The IEP is designed to give children with disabilities a free, appropriate education. It is updated annually, with the participation of the child's parents or guardian.

Injunction - An equitable remedy (see Remedies) wherein a court orders a party to do or refrain from doing some particular action.

Issue Preclusion - (see Res Judicata).

Jurisdiction - The power of a court to determine cases and controversies. The Supreme Court's jurisdiction extends to cases arising under the Constitution and under federal law. Federal courts have the power to hear cases where there is diversity of citizenship or where a federal question is involved.

Mainstreaming - Part of what is required for a free, appropriate education is that each child with a disability be educated in the "least restrictive environment." To the extent that disabled children are educated with nondisabled children in regular education classes, those children are being mainstreamed.

Negligence per se - Negligence on its face. Usually, the violation of an ordinance or statute will be treated as negligence per se because no careful person would have been guilty of it.

Overbroad - A government action is overbroad if, in an attempt to alleviate a specific evil, it impermissibly prohibits or chills a protected action. For example, attempting to deal with street litter by prohibiting the distribution of leaflets or handbills.

Per Curiam - Latin phrase meaning "by the court." Used in court reports to note an opinion written by the court rather than by a single judge or justice.

Placement - A special education student's placement must be appropriate (as well as responsive to the particular child's needs). Under the IDEA's "stay-put" provision, school officials may not remove a special education child from his or her "then current placement" over the parents' objections until the completion of administrative or judicial review proceedings.

Preemption Doctrine - Doctrine which states that when federal and state law attempt to regulate the same subject matter, federal law prevents the state law from operating. Based on the Supremacy Clause of Article VI, Clause 2, of the Constitution.

Prior Restraint - Restraining a publication before it is distributed. In general, constitutional law doctrine prohibits government from exercising prior restraint.

Pro Se - A party appearing in court, without the benefit of an attorney, is said to be appearing pro se.

Rehabilitation Act - Section 504 of the Rehabilitation Act prohibits employers who receive federal financial assistance from discriminating against otherwise qualified individuals with handicaps solely because of their handicaps. An otherwise qualified individual is one who can perform the "essential functions" of the job with "reasonable accomodation."

Related Services - As part of the free, appropriate education due to children with disabilities, school districts may have to provide related services such as transportation, physical and occupational therapy, and medical services which are for diagnostic or evaluative purposes relating to education.

Remand - The act of an appellate court in returning a case to the court from which it came for further action.

Remedies - There are two general categories of remedies, or relief: legal remedies, which consist of money damages, and equitable remedies, which consist of a court mandate that a specific action be prohibited or required. For example, a claim for compensatory and punitive damages seeks a legal remedy; a claim for an injunction seeks an equitable remedy. Equitable remedies are generally unavailable unless legal remedies are inadequate to address the harm.

Res Judicata - The judicial notion that a claim or action may not be tried twice or re-litigated, or that all causes of action arising out of the same set of operative facts should be tried at one time. Also known as claim preclusion.

Section 1981 & Section 1983 - (see 42 U.S.C. §§ 1981, 1983).

Sovereign Immunity - The idea that the government cannot be sued without its consent. It stems from the English notion that the "King could do no wrong." This immunity from suit has been abrogated in most states and by the federal government through legislative acts known as "tort claims acts."

Standing - The judicial doctrine which states that in order to maintain a lawsuit a party must have some real interest at stake in the outcome of the trial.

Statute of Limitations - A statute of limitation provides the time period in which a specific cause of action may be brought.

Summary Judgment - Federal Rule of Civil Procedure 56 provides for the summary adjudication of a case if either party can show that there is no genuine issue as to any material fact and that, given the facts agreed upon, the party is entitled to judgment as a matter of law. In general, summary judgment is used to dispose of claims which do not support a legally recognized claim.

Supremacy Clause - Clause in Article VI of the Constitution which states that federal legislation is the supreme law of the land. This clause is used to support the Preemption Doctrine (see above).

Title VII, Civil Rights Act of 1964 (Title VII) - Title VII prohibits discrimination in employment based upon race, color, sex, national origin, or religion. It applies to any employer having fifteen or more employees. Under Title VII, where an employer intentionally discriminates, employees may obtain money damages unless the claim is for race discrimination. For those claims, monetary relief is available under 42 U.S.C. § 1981.

Tort - A tort is a civil wrong, other than breach of contract. Torts include negligence, assault, battery, trespass, defamation, infliction of emotional distress and wrongful death.

U.S. Equal Employment Opportunity Commission (EEOC) - The EEOC is the government entity which is empowered to enforce Title VII (see above) through investigation and/or lawsuits. Private individuals alleging discrimination must pursue administrative remedies within the EEOC before they are allowed to file suit under Title VII.

Vacate - The act of annulling the judgment of a court either by an appellate court or by the court itself. The Supreme Court will generally vacate a lower court's judgment without deciding the case itself, and remand the case to the lower court for further consideration in light of some recent controlling decision.

Void-for-Vagueness Doctrine - A judicial doctrine based on the Fourteenth Amendment's Due Process Clause. In order for a law which regulates speech, or any criminal statute, to pass muster under the doctrine, the law must make clear what actions are prohibited or made criminal. Under the principles of the Due Process Clause, people of average intelligence should not have to guess at the meaning of a law.

Writ of Certiorari - The device used by the Supreme Court to transfer cases from the appellate court's docket to its own. Since the Supreme Court's appellate jurisdiction is largely discretionary, it need only issue such a writ when it desires to rule in the case.

INDEX